Philosophy
Questions & Theories

Senior Authors

Paul G. Paquette
West Ferris Secondary School
North Bay, Ontario

Laura Gini-Newman
Secondary Program Resource Teacher
Peel District School Board

Authors

Peter Flaherty
Runnymede Collegiate Institute
Toronto, Ontario

Michael Horton
Robert F. Hall Catholic Secondary School
Caledon East, Ontario

David Jopling
Department of Philosophy, York University
Toronto, Ontario

Heather Miller
Art Specialist and Consultant
Mackay Miller Education Inc.

Peg Tittle
Nipissing University
North Bay, Ontario

Peter Yan
Robert F. Hall Catholic Secondary School
Caledon East, Ontario

McGraw-Hill Ryerson

Toronto   Montréal   Boston, MA   Burr Ridge, IL   Dubuque, IA   Madison, WI
New York   San Francisco   St. Louis   Bangkok   Beijing   Bogotá   Caracas
Kuala Lumpur   Lisbon   London   Madrid   Mexico City   Milan   New Delhi
Santiago   Seoul   Singapore   Sydney   Taipei

McGraw-Hill Ryerson Limited
A Subsidiary of The McGraw-Hill Companies

COPIES OF THIS BOOK MAY BE OBTAINED BY CONTACTING:

McGraw-Hill Ryerson Ltd.

WEB SITE:
http://www.mcgrawhill.ca

E-MAIL:
orders@mcgrawhill.ca

TOLL-FREE FAX:
1-800-463-5885

TOLL-FREE CALL:
1-800-565-5758

OR BY MAILING YOUR ORDER TO:
McGraw-Hill Ryerson
Order Department
300 Water Street
Whitby, ON L1N 9B6

Please quote the ISBN and title when placing your order.

Philosophy: Questions and Theories

Copyright © 2003, McGraw-Hill Ryerson Limited, a Subsidiary of The McGraw-Hill Companies. All rights reserved. No part of this publication may be reproduced or transmitted in any form or by any means, or stored in a data base or retrieval system without the prior written permission of McGraw-Hill Ryerson Limited, or, in the case of photocopying or other reprographic copying, a licence from CANCOPY (Canadian Copyright Licensing Agency), One Yonge Street, Suite 1900, Toronto, Ontario M5E 1E5.

Any request for photocopying, recording, taping, or information storage and retrieval of any part of this publication shall be directed in writing to CANCOPY.

ISBN: 0-07-091386-2

http://www.mcgrawhill.ca

1 2 3 4 5 6 7 8 9 10 TCP 10 9 8 7 6 5 4 3 2

Printed and bound in Canada

Care has been taken to trace ownership of copyright material contained in this text. The publishers will gladly accept any information that will enable them to rectify any reference or credit in subsequent printings.

National Library of Canada Cataloguing in Publication

Main entry under title:
    Philosophy : questions and theories / authors, Paul Paquette ... [et al.].

Includes index.
For use in grade 12.
ISBN 0-07-091386-2

1. Philosophy. I. Paquette, Paul

B74.P44 2002   100   C2002-901693-2

PUBLISHER: Patty Pappas
EDITORIAL DIRECTOR: Melanie Myers
PROJECT MANAGER: Joseph Gladstone
DEVELOPMENTAL EDITOR: Dyanne Rivers
SUPERVISING EDITOR: Cathy Deak
COPYEDITORS: Krysia Lear, Audrey Dorsch
ADDITIONAL WRITING: Jessica Pegis, Sheila Wawanash, Krysia Lear
PRODUCTION COORDINATOR: Madeleine Harrington
PERMISSIONS EDITORS: Jacqueline Donovan, Paulee Kestin
EDITORIAL ASSISTANT: Erin Parton
INTERIOR DESIGN: Greg Devitt
ELECTRONIC PAGE MAKE-UP: Greg Devitt
ILLUSTRATIONS: ArtPlus Limited
COVER IMAGE: Lawren S. Harris/McMichael Canadian Art Collection
COVER DESIGNER: Sharon Lucas

Reviewers

Anneli Andre-Barrett
The Woodlands Secondary School
Mississauga, Ontario

Jonathan Cowans
Dunbarton High School
Pickering, Ontario

Colleen Chandler
Mother Teresa Catholic Secondary School
Toronto, Ontario

Elva McGaughy
Kingston Collegiate and Vocational Institute
Kingston, Ontario

Constance McLeese
Lisgar Collegiate Institute
Kanata, Ontario

David Neelin
East York Collegiate Institute
Toronto, Ontario

Garfield Gini-Newman
Curriculum Consultant
York Region District School Board

Jim Shearer
Woburn Collegiate Institute
Toronto, Ontario

Larry Trafford
Faculty of Education
York University

Dana Wallace
Westmount Collegiate Institute
Thornhill, Ontario

Jennifer Welchman
Department of Philosophy
University of Alberta
Edmonton, Alberta

Advisers

Jennifer Borda
Appleby College
Oakville, Ontario

Ilan Danjoux
Markham District High School
Markham, Ontario

Stephen Davis
Department of Philosophy
Simon Fraser University
Vancouver, British Columbia

Bruce Fink
Educational Consultant
Ottawa-Carleton District School Board

Nigel Lee
Cameron Heights Collegiate Institute
Kitchener, Ontario

Jack MacFadden
President, OHASSTA
Bradford, Ontario

Darcy Mintz
Cameron Heights Collegiate Institute
Kitchener, Ontario

Rick Olma
White Oaks Secondary School
Oakville, Ontario

Rachel Powell
Dr. Norman Bethune Collegiate Institute
Agincourt, Ontario

Mary Anne Sodonis
Westside Secondary School
Orangeville, Ontario

Paul Sydor
West Elgin Secondary School
West Lorne, Ontario

Jim Terry
Wallaceburg District Secondary School
Wallaceburg, Ontario

Contents

A Tour of Your Textbook X

Introduction: Setting the Stage 2

Chapter 1 Introducing Philosophy 3
The High Cost of Truth 4
What Is Philosophy? 4
The Philosopher's Approach 5
What Philosophers Have Said 6
PHILOSOPHY IN ACTION
    The Allegory of the Cave 8
How Philosophers Have Said It 10
PROFILE
    Thales of Miletus *The First Philosopher* 12
THOUGHT EXPERIMENT
    The Ship of Theseus 14
Why Philosophy Matters 14
Why Study Philosophy? 15
The Areas of Philosophy 17
Connecting the Areas 20
Philosophy's Blind Side: The Marginalized and the Lionized 20
Chapter Review 22

Chapter 2 Introducing Human Nature 24
Being Human 25
Questions That Matter 26
PHILOSOPHY IN ACTION
    The Good Brahman 27
Essentialist Views of Human Nature 33
Challenges to Essentialist Views of Human Nature 37
PROFILE
    Simone de Beauvoir *Pure Transparent Freedom* 41
The Future of the Human Nature Debate 42
Chapter Review 44
CULMINATING ACTIVITY
    Participate in a philosophical discussion at a philosophy café. 46

Unit 1 Logic and the Philosophy of Science 48

Chapter 3 Introducing Logic 49
What Is Logic? 50
The Philosopher's Approach to Logic 50
What Philosophers Have Said 51
PROFILE
    Aristotle *The Mind of the School* 53
How Philosophers Have Said It 54
THOUGHT EXPERIMENT
    Stuck in School Forever 55
Why Logic Matters 56

Reasoning and Critical Thinking 57
PHILOSOPHY IN ACTION
    The Use of Argument 58
The Form of Logical Arguments 60
Validity, Truth, and Soundness 62
Ways of Thinking 63
Chapter Review 64

Chapter 4 Applying Logic 66
Is It Logic or Illogic? 67
Applying Deductive Reasoning 67
Applying Inductive Reasoning 72
PROFILE
    Charles Sanders Peirce *Wasp in a Bottle* 74
Logical Fallacies 75
Logic at Work 80
PHILOSOPHY IN ACTION
    Love Is a Fallacy 81
Chapter Review 86

Chapter 5 Introducing the Philosophy of Science .88
What Is the Philosophy of Science? 89
The Philosopher's Approach to the Philosophy of Science 90
What Philosophers Have Said 90
PROFILE
    Thomas Kuhn *A Revolutionary Theorist* 92
THOUGHT EXPERIMENT
    Thick as a Brick 93
How Philosophers Have Said It 95
Why the Philosophy of Science Matters 96
Challenging the Foundations of Scientific Thought 96
Is Science Objective? 97
Can Scientific Theories Be Proven? 98
PHILOSOPHY IN ACTION
    Imaginary Witness—O.J.'s Blood and the Big Bang, Together at Last 99
Can Science Alone Tell People What the World Is Really Like? 101
Science and Non-Science 103
Are Science and Religion Compatible? 104
Chapter Review 106
CULMINATING ACTIVITY
    Write a philosophical reflection. 108

Unit 2 Metaphysics 110

Chapter 6 Introducing Metaphysics 111
What Is Metaphysics? 112
The Philosopher's Approach to Metaphysics 112
What Philosophers Have Said 113
How Philosophers Have Said It 114
Why Metaphysics Matters 114
Reality and Appearance 114
THOUGHT EXPERIMENT
    Something about Mary 116

The Self 122
PHILOSOPHY IN ACTION
    Meditations on First Philosophy 123
PROFILE
    Jean-Paul Sartre *"Sartre Is France"* 126
Chapter Review 130

Chapter 7 Persons, Minds, and Brains 132
What Is a Person? 133
Personal Identity 136
PHILOSOPHY IN ACTION
    An Essay Concerning Human Understanding 137
THOUGHT EXPERIMENT
    First-Class Travel? 140
Mind and Brain 141
PROFILE
    Ludwig Wittgenstein *A Battle against Bewitchment* 146
Minds, Machines, and Animals 147
Chapter Review 152

Chapter 8 A Meaning for Existence 154
Concepts of a Supreme Being 155
PROFILE
    Baruch Spinoza *Challenging Established Views* 158
The Existence of a Supreme Being 159
Determinism and Freedom 164
THOUGHT EXPERIMENT
    The Conscious Stone 166
The Meaning of Life 168
Chapter Review 172
CULMINATING ACTIVITY
    Write a book or movie review. 174

Unit 3 Epistemology 176

Chapter 9 Introducing Epistemology 177
What Is Epistemology? 178
The Philosopher's Approach to Epistemology 179
What Philosophers Have Said 181
PROFILE
    René Descartes *The First Modern Philosopher* 183
How Philosophers Have Said It 184
Why Epistemology Matters 185
What Is Knowledge? 187
Conditions for Knowledge 188
Kinds of Knowledge 191
Contemporary Thinking about Knowledge 194
Chapter Review 196

Chapter 10 Theories and Methods of Epistemology 198
Does Knowing Begin with Doubt? 199
THOUGHT EXPERIMENT
    The Brain in the Vat 201

The Basis of Knowing 202
Reason as a Basis of Knowing 202
PHILOSOPHY IN ACTION
    Reflections on Language 207
The Senses as a Basis of Knowing .208
Modern Empiricism: The Challenge to Rationalism 209
PROFILE
    Thomas Aquinas *The Dumb Ox* .210
Bridging the Gap between Rationalism and Empiricism 213
Contemporary Epistemology 214
Chapter Review 216

Chapter 11 Knowledge and Truth 218
What Is Truth? 219
A Short History of Truth 220
Knowledge, True Opinion, and True Belief 222
PHILOSOPHY IN ACTION
    Philosophical Themes in The Truman Show 223
Perception and Truth 225
Theories of Truth 229
PROFILE
    Daisetsu Teitaro Suzuki *Interpreting Zen to the West* 233
Does the Truth Matter? 234
Chapter Review 236
CULMINATING ACTIVITY
    Create a concept map poster. 238

Unit 4 Ethics 240

Chapter 12 Introducing Ethics 241
What Is Ethics? 242
The Philosopher's Approach to Ethics 243
What Philosophers Have Said 244
How Philosophers Have Said It 246
Why Ethics Matters 248
Some Metaethical Questions 249
THOUGHT EXPERIMENT
    The Magic Ring 251
PROFILE
    Kongfuzi *The First Great Humanist Philosopher* 253
PHILOSOPHY IN ACTION
    The Land of Certus 255
Chapter Review 260

Chapter 13 Answering Questions That Matter 262
Questions Asked by Ethicists 263
What Is a Good Life? 263
THOUGHT EXPERIMENT
    The Experience Machine 266
What Is a Good Person? 268
What Is the Right Thing to Do? 272
PROFILE
    Harriet Taylor *Thoughts and Speculations Completely in Common* 276
Chapter Review 282

Chapter 14 Ethics in the World 284
A World of Moral Choices 285
Ethics, the Self, and Society 285
Ethics and Science 290
PROFILE
    Peter Singer *The Most Dangerous Man in the World Today* 292
Ethics and the Environment 294
PHILOSOPHY IN ACTION
    Should the West Pay for China's Fridges? 297
Ethics and Computers 300
Ethics and Business 301
Chapter Review 304
CULMINATING ACTIVITY
    Write a feature article for a philosophical magazine. 306

COLOUR INSERT . . . . .I-VIII

Unit 5 Aesthetics 308
Chapter 15 Introducing Aesthetics 309
What Is Aesthetics? 310
The Philosopher's Approach to Aesthetics 311
What Philosophers Have Said 313
PROFILE
    Immanuel Kant *Like a Fine Swiss Watch* 317
How Philosophers Have Said It 319
Why Aesthetics Matters 319
The Value of Art 321
Chapter Review 326

Chapter 16 Theories, Categories, and Types of Art 328
Origins of the Western Tradition 329
Traditional Theories of Art 330
Philosophical Perspectives on Aesthetics 331
PHILOSOPHY IN ACTION
    What Is Art? 332
Categories and Types of Art 336
PROFILE
    Suzi Gablik *Challenging Accepted Ideas* 337
Making Connections 341
Chapter Review 346

Chapter 17 Beauty 348
What Is Beauty? 349
Historical Perspectives on Beauty 349
Contemporary Perspectives on Beauty 350
PHILOSOPHY IN ACTION
    The Critique of Judgment 351
Global Perspectives on Beauty 353
PROFILE
    Jiddu Krishnamurti *Drinking at the Fountain of Eternal Joy and Beauty* 356
Post-Modern Perspectives on Beauty 357
THOUGHT EXPERIMENT
    A Beautiful Life 358

Questions That Matter 358
Art, the Individual, and Society 361
Chapter Review 364
CULMINATING ACTIVITY
    Create an Advertisement. 366

Unit 6 Social and Political Philosophy 368

Chapter 18 Introducing Social and Political Philosophy 369
What Is Social and Political Philosophy? 370
The Philosopher's Approach to Social and Political Philosophy 371
What Philosophers Have Said 371
How Philosophers Have Said It 373
PROFILE
    Martin Luther King Jr. *A Moral Responsibility to Disobey Unjust Laws* 374
Why Social and Political Philosophy Matters 375
Why Do States Exist? 376
The Individual and the State 377
PHILOSOPHY IN ACTION
    The Politics of Recognition 380
Chapter Review 386

Chapter 19 Theories of Social and Political Philosophy .388
The Western Tradition 389
The Eastern Tradition 393
The Social Contract 396
The French Revolution 399
PROFILE
    Mary Wollstonecraft *Advocating a New Social Order* 401
The Struggle between Classes 402
Liberalism versus Marxism: The Great 20th-Century Debate 404
Chapter Review 406

Chapter 20 The Individual, the Law, and Justice 408
The Individual and Society 408
Justice and Law 410
PHILOSOPHY IN ACTION
    Virtual Communities and Virtuous Reality 411
What Is Justice? 415
PROFILE
    Pierre Elliott Trudeau *Translating Philosophy into Action* 420
Contemporary Ideas of Justice 422
THOUGHT EXPERIMENT
    The Veil of Ignorance 424
Chapter Review 426
CULMINATING ACTIVITY
    Challenge the power of "They." 428

TIMELINE 430

Glossary 435
Index 445
Credits 460

A Tour of Your Textbook

Welcome to *Philosophy: Questions and Theories*. This textbook provides an overview of the questions and theories explored over the ages by philosophers from many of the world's traditions. The two chapters of the introductory unit set the stage for the learning that follows. The book then presents a detailed look at six areas of philosophy: logic and the philosophy of science, metaphysics, epistemology, ethics, aesthetics, and social and political philosophy.

Though only three of these areas may be studied in detail, those who wish to gain insights into, and a basic understanding of, areas not studied in class can do so by reading the first chapter of the relevant units. The first chapter of each unit is designed to provide a working understanding of the philosophical area.

To make better use of this textbook and more fully understand its structure, take the tour that follows.

The art on the front cover is a reproduction of a painting by artist Lawren Harris, a member of Canada's famous Group of Seven. It depicts a northern scene dominated by an iceberg. Most of the iceberg remains unseen, floating below the surface of the water. To fully appreciate the awesome power of the iceberg, people must understand its structure. Philosophers approach the big questions of life as if the questions, too, are icebergs — with much of their structure and meaning hidden below the surface. What influences do you think could hide knowledge of the important questions of life?

Lawren S. Harris 1885-1970 • Winter Comes from the Arctic to the Temperate Zone c.1935 • oil on canvas • 74.1 x 91.2 cm • Purchase 1994 • McMichael Canadian Art Collection • 1994.13 • Reprinted by permission of the family of Lawren S. Harris.

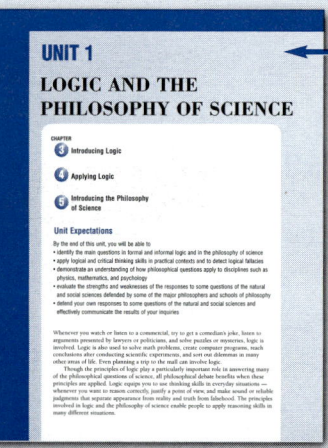

Unit Opener
This page introduces every unit and lists the chapters that make up the unit.

- **Unit Expectations** indicate the overall goals of the unit and the spectrum of ideas you will be studying.
- An **overview** summarizes what the unit is about and how it relates to the course.

Culminating Activity
Concludes every unit. Each culminating activity is designed to help you demonstrate your grasp of the knowledge and skills presented in the unit. At the end of the course, the products of these activities may become part of a philosophical magazine that can be published as a group or class project.

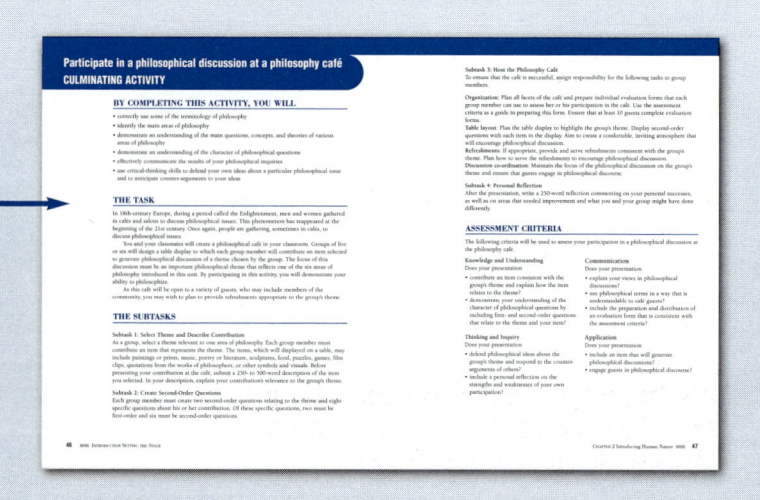

X   MHR

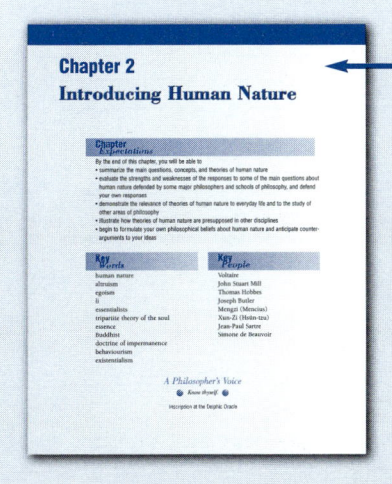

Chapter Opener
This page provides information about the content of the chapter.
- **Chapter Expectations** clearly indicate the specific goals of the chapter.
- **Key Words** lists important terms introduced in the chapter. Knowledge of these terms is necessary to fully understand the concepts and ideas presented.
- **Key People** lists important figures introduced in the chapter.
- **A Philosopher's Voice** is a quotation that relates one philosopher's thought to the focus of the chapter.

Chapter Review
Two pages of review questions and activities that conclude each chapter are designed to help you reinforce your understanding of the material and meet curriculum requirements.

Chapter Summary
A point-form summary reminds you of the ideas developed in the chapter.

Knowledge and Understanding
Activities that help you focus on understanding the essential content of the chapter.

Thinking and Inquiry
Activities that provide you with opportunities to demonstrate critical- and creative-thinking skills, as well as research and inquiry skills.

Communication
Activities that provide you with an opportunity to demonstrate communication skills in a variety of contexts, as well as your ability to use language, symbols, and visuals.

Application
Activities that enable you to apply your ideas and skills, transfer your skills to new contexts, and demonstrate your ability to connect what you have learned in class to other experiences.

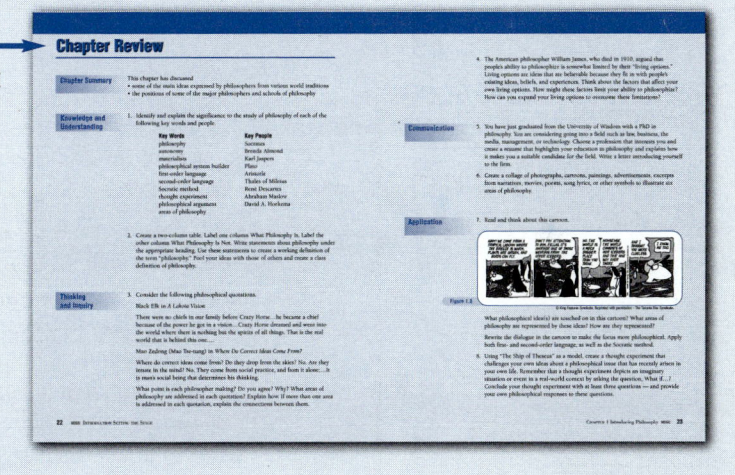

MHR xi

Features

The features of *Philosophy: Questions and Theories* are designed to draw you into the concepts and ideas presented, make the content more relevant, and provide interesting, challenging, and meaningful points of view to help deepen your understanding of the philosophical questions and theories developed in the text.

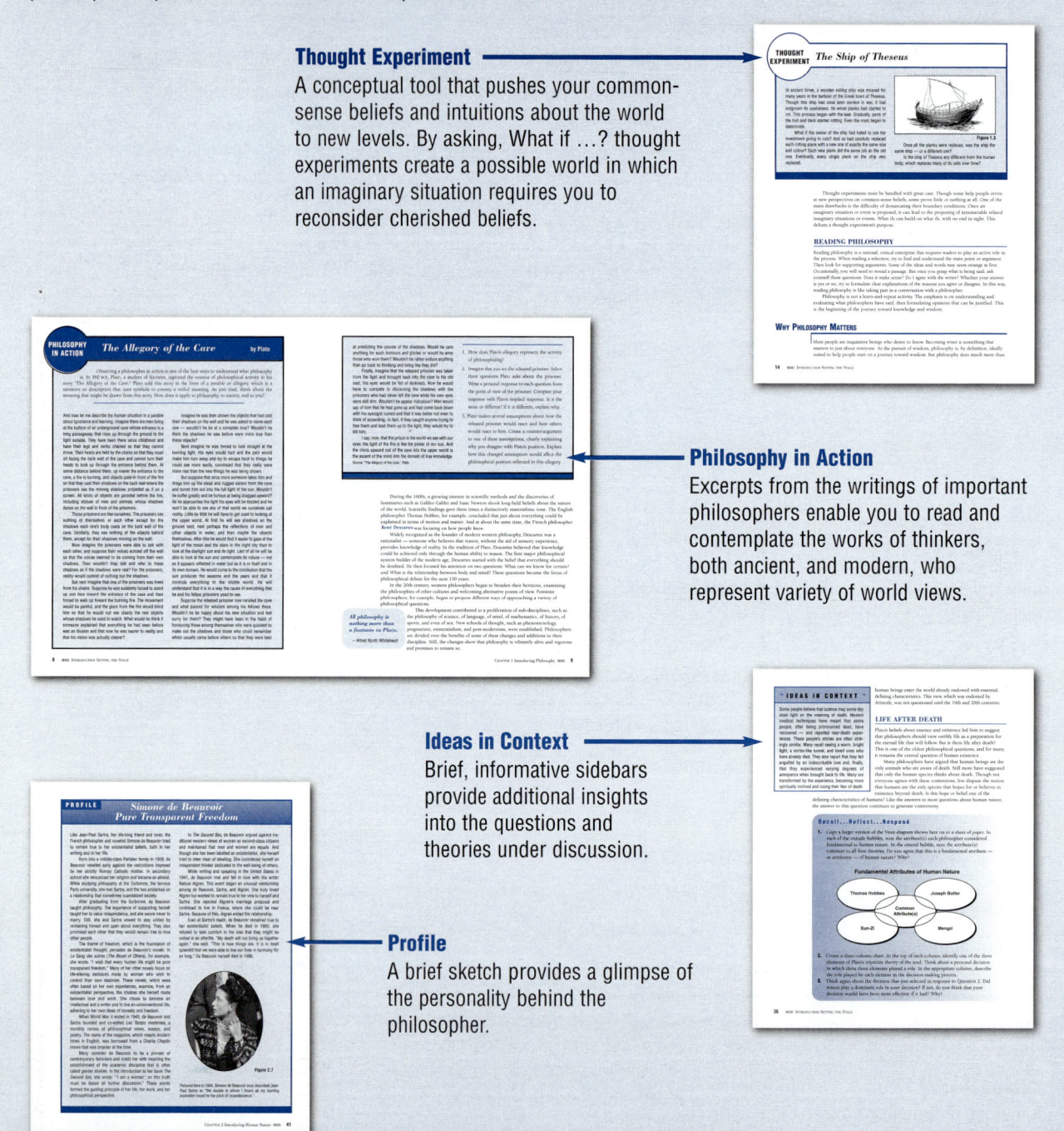

Thought Experiment

A conceptual tool that pushes your common-sense beliefs and intuitions about the world to new levels. By asking, What if …? thought experiments create a possible world in which an imaginary situation requires you to reconsider cherished beliefs.

Philosophy in Action

Excerpts from the writings of important philosophers enable you to read and contemplate the works of thinkers, both ancient, and modern, who represent variety of world views.

Ideas in Context

Brief, informative sidebars provide additional insights into the questions and theories under discussion.

Profile

A brief sketch provides a glimpse of the personality behind the philosopher.

xii   MHR

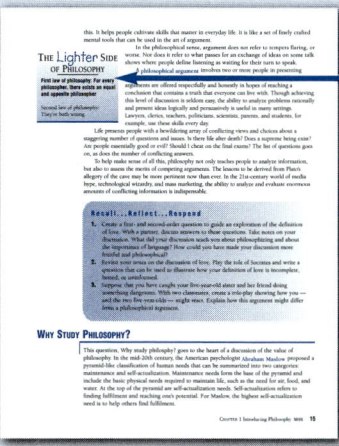

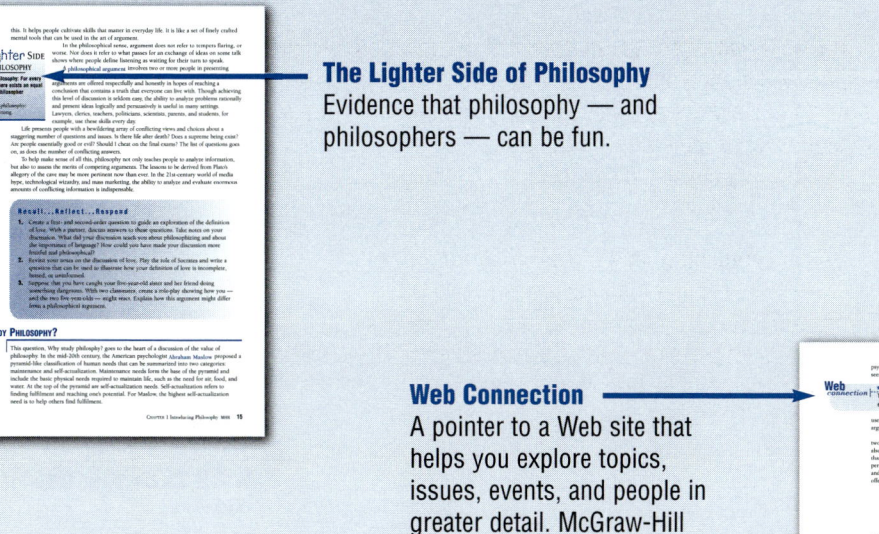

The Lighter Side of Philosophy
Evidence that philosophy — and philosophers — can be fun.

Web Connection
A pointer to a Web site that helps you explore topics, issues, events, and people in greater detail. McGraw-Hill Ryerson monitors and updates these sites on a regular basis.

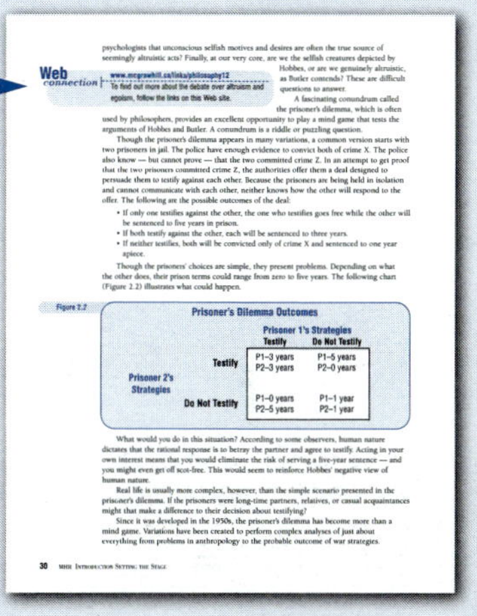

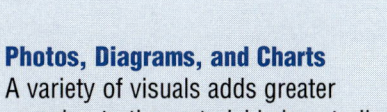

Photos, Diagrams, and Charts
A variety of visuals adds greater meaning to the material being studied. Many captions contain a challenging question meant to encourage you to pause and reflect.

Recall ... Reflect ... Respond
These questions appear three times in every chapter to ensure that you understand the material you have just studied. Taking time to recall, reflect, and respond helps you organize the ideas and content encountered in the preceding pages.

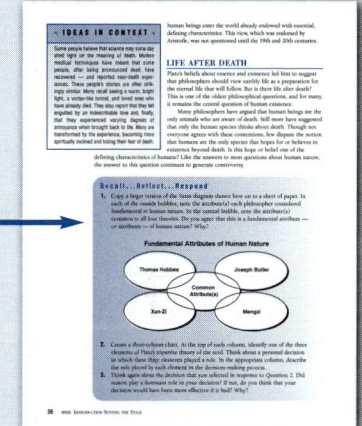

MHR **xiii**

Quotation
Expresses a view, sometimes controversial, on the ideas discussed in the text.

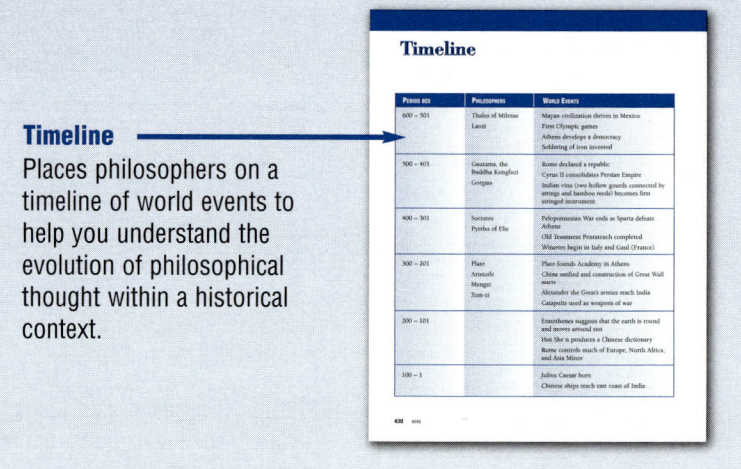

Timeline
Places philosophers on a timeline of world events to help you understand the evolution of philosophical thought within a historical context.

Glossary
A quick reference that defines key words encountered in the text.

Index
An indispensable tool for locating information quickly.

xiv   MHR

Preface

Studying philosophy will plunge you into a lifelong journey toward self- and social awareness. On this journey, you will find yourself wondering about issues dealing with human reasoning, science, reality, knowledge, values, beauty, and social and political practices. As you explore these issues, you will expand your knowledge; develop your ability to think logically, critically, and creatively; communicate your thoughts on philosophical questions and theories; and apply new understandings and wisdom to ideas that have always intrigued humankind.

This textbook is designed to support your exploration of philosophy in a challenging, relevant, and engaging manner. The two chapters of the introductory unit provide an overview that prepares you to explore — with the guidance of your teacher — the key concepts, questions, and skills that are examined in greater detail in the six units that follow. These six units introduce six areas of philosophy and are structured to help you develop the logical-, critical-, and creative-thinking skills needed to evaluate, formulate, and defend responses to the philosophical questions and theories that are the focus of each area.

Though you are expected to study in depth a minimum of three areas of philosophy, those who wish to find out more about areas that have not been selected for detailed study can read the first chapter of each unit. Each of these chapters begins with information designed to provide an overview of the area of philosophy. This overview is organized under five headings.

- What Is …?
- The Philosophers Approach to …
- What Philosophers Have Said
- How Philosophers Have Said It
- Why … Matters

Throughout the book, various features provide opportunities for you to take your philosophical explorations a step farther. These features are described in "A Tour of Your Textbook."

Learning to philosophize requires practice — and this book provides many opportunities to do this. At three points in each chapter, questions encourage you to recall the concepts and ideas introduced, reflect on how these ideas are connected to everyday life, and respond by thinking critically about them. At the end of each chapter, review questions and activities encourage you to demonstrate your knowledge and understanding of philosophical issues, as well as your ability to think critically about them. These questions also encourage you to communicate and apply your understanding in a variety of ways.

Each unit concludes with a culminating activity that enables you to demonstrate how well you have met the curriculum expectations. At the end of the course, the products of these unit-culminating activities may be included in a philosophy magazine that may be a group or class project.

Studying the ideas of philosophers from various traditions will enrich many aspects of your life. It may even help clarify your career goals, whether these involve math, science, art, literature, history and the humanities, or other fields. Philosophy is relevant to all disciplines because it challenges you to think for yourself. It also asks that you work toward developing shared truths that are important to everyone.

As you delve more deeply into the ideas presented in this book, you may notice changes in your thinking, beliefs, and values. You may also notice that you feel more confident about expressing and defending your thoughts, beliefs, and values. Studying philosophy will give you a new perspective on the world. It may even make you a little wiser.

The Authors
June 2002

INTRODUCTION
SETTING THE STAGE

CHAPTER

1 Introducing Philosophy

2 Introducing Human Nature

Unit Expectations

By the end of this introductory unit, you will be able to
- correctly use some of the terminology of philosophy
- identify the main areas of philosophy
- demonstrate an understanding of the main questions, concepts, and theories of various areas of philosophy
- demonstrate an understanding of the character of philosophical questions
- effectively communicate the results of your philosophical inquiries
- use critical-thinking skills to defend your own ideas about a particular philosophical issue and to anticipate counter-arguments to your ideas

People grapple with philosophical questions every day. Embarking on the study of philosophy will lead you to confront language and ideas that may seem strange at first. However, you will find yourself immersed in philosophizing as you expand your knowledge and understanding, develop your thinking and inquiry skills, and hone your ability to communicate and apply your ideas. This process will help you grapple with both personal issues and contemporary social issues and deepen your understanding of human nature and — ultimately — of yourself.

Chapter 1
Introducing Philosophy

Chapter Expectations

By the end of this chapter, you will be able to
- demonstrate an understanding of some of the main ideas expressed by philosophers from various world traditions
- evaluate the positions of some of the major philosophers and schools of philosophy
- use critical- and logical-thinking skills to formulate your own ideas about some of the main questions of philosophy and explain and defend those ideas

Key Words

philosophy
autonomy
materialists
philosophical system builder
first-order language
second-order language
Socratic method
thought experiment
philosophical argument
areas of philosophy

Key People

Socrates
Brenda Almond
Karl Jaspers
Plato
Aristotle
Thales of Miletus
René Descartes
Abraham Maslow
David A. Hoekema

A Philosopher's Voice

To ridicule philosophy is really to philosophize.

Blaise Pascal (1623–1662)

THE HIGH COST OF TRUTH

Figure 1.1

This 18th-century engraving shows the philosopher Socrates awaiting death. As he waits, he is composing a hymn to the Greek god Apollo.

Imagine travelling in ancient Greece. The year is 399 BCE. You have heard amazing stories about the great city of Athens, which you can see in the distance. Inside the city, however, your anticipation fades to disappointment as you gaze around. Signs of destruction are everywhere. Despite the devastation, which is the result of the long war with Sparta, the streets are buzzing with excitement. People are arguing about the trial of a man named **Socrates**, who stands accused of corrupting the young people of the city by preaching false gods.

A glimpse of Socrates makes you wonder what the fuss is about. He is a short, pug-nosed old man with bulging eyes. To hear him speak, however, is to listen to a brilliant thinker. Indeed, this man will eventually be hailed as one of the greatest thinkers in the history of the western world. For now, though, he has been judged, found guilty, and sentenced to die — the result of vague and, by most accounts, unfair charges.

His "crime" has been to wander the streets of Athens asking questions in hopes of discovering the truth. He has been philosophizing.

WHAT IS PHILOSOPHY?

Philosophy is everywhere. Open a newspaper or magazine and you may find one person explaining her philosophy of business and another his philosophy of goal scoring. Friends at school talk about their dating and course-selection philosophies. Talking with friends, you hear expressions like "that's life" and "things happen." Off-the-cuff remarks like these sound philosophical, but they are empty of conviction and reflective thought. They are not philosophical positions. They are more appropriately identified as opinions, theories, or beliefs.

This does not mean that there is not a bit of the philosopher in everyone, however. Humans are philosophical beings. People question and wonder. We are all curious about ourselves and the world around us. Have you ever asked questions like, Who am I? Are humans alone in the universe? How can I know for sure the truth of anything? What is real friendship? Why do bad things happen to people I love? Are right and wrong simply a matter of personal opinion?

Whenever you think about the right or wrong thing to do, you are, to some extent, philosophizing. Whenever you puzzle over a conundrum, such as the meaning of love or friendship, you are philosophizing. If you have ever wondered about how people ought to live, about why evil exists, about the existence and nature of a supreme being, about the possibility of life after death, or even about the meaning of life itself, you have entered — if only briefly — the philosopher's domain. Indeed, the ability to wonder is a distinguishing attribute of philosophers.

Most people feel this sense of wonder. It is important to understand, however, that philosophy is not a magical key that will unlock the secrets of human existence. Nor is it a shortcut to understanding the mysteries of the universe. It will probably not make anyone rich and famous. Still, philosophy does provide an opportunity to evaluate, discuss, and reflect on some intriguing questions and some equally fascinating answers. Philosophy also develops and refines critical-thinking and problem-solving skills.

So, what is philosophy? There is no easy answer to this question. The shortest definition, writes contemporary philosopher Anthony Quinton, is that philosophy is "thinking about thinking." He goes on to say that philosophy is "rationally critical thinking ... about the general nature of the world ..., the justification of belief ..., and the conduct of life ...."

> *All philosophy has its origins in wonder.*
> – Plato

Every dictionary and philosophy textbook will, however, say that the word "philosophy" comes from two Greek words: *philein*, meaning to love, and *sophia*, meaning wisdom. Philosophy, therefore, is the love of wisdom. It is also a passionate commitment to an open-minded search for truth. Still, loving wisdom will not necessarily make anyone wise. Wisdom has little to do with knowing lots of facts, displaying common sense, or even being highly intelligent. It does have much to do with being insightful about human existence and with doing or saying the right thing, at the right place, at the right time, and for the right reasons. Above all, wisdom involves realizing how little humans really know. Coming to this realization is a necessary — and sometimes painful — first step toward achieving wisdom. Taking this step sets the stage for people to philosophize.

THE NATURE AND AIMS OF PHILOSOPHY

Whether philosophy originated in ancient Greece or Asia, and whether even older peoples, such as the ancient Egyptians, were philosophical are contentious issues among some experts. Still, most philosophers accept that western ideas of philosophy originated in Athens in the fifth century BCE. In her book *Exploring Philosophy*, Brenda Almond described what happened when early philosophers plied their trade:

> In this original setting, the activity amounted, in the most general terms, to a willingness to pursue an argument to its conclusion, challenging it at every stage and seeing it as always open to refutation. This stance in itself involves a double commitment: first, commitment to the truth (the point of rejecting arguments which can be shown to be false is to arrive at some which may be reckoned to be true); and secondly, commitment to certain moral virtues implicit in such a method: honesty, openness and impartiality — terms which inescapably lead to some notion of moral right, justice or moral good.

IDEAS IN CONTEXT

Philosophers have often encountered resistance and fierce antagonism. Socrates is the most famous example of a philosopher who died for his profession, but there have been others. Hypatia lived in Alexandria, the capital of Egypt, in the fourth century. Regarded as the greatest philosopher of her day, she was hacked to pieces with sharp shells by angry monks. And Giordano Bruno, an Italian philosopher, scientist, and poet certainly angered the authorities by speaking out. In 1600, he was burned at the stake with a nail through his tongue.

Almond's description clearly demonstrates philosophers' commitment to truth and virtue. Notice, too, that she calls philosophy an activity. In fact, the most distinctive feature of philosophy is that it is something people do. Anyone can read a philosophy book or study philosophical theories, but philosophizing is something people must do for themselves. They must participate in the process.

THE PHILOSOPHER'S APPROACH

> Someone once asked the fourth-century Christian philosopher Augustine of Hippo this question: What is time? Augustine is said to have replied: "If no one asks me, I know; but if any person requires me to tell him, I cannot."

Most people accept the idea of time as an essential part of their daily lives and rarely give it a second thought. This is not the philosopher's way, however. Philosophers like Augustine might ask questions like, Does time really exist? If time exists, what is it?

These are difficult questions. If the answers were simple, then there would be no questions and no philosophical issue.

The philosopher's task is not merely to understand concepts. It is also to try to understand what exists and the nature of that existence. Philosophers want to know the extent to which reliable knowledge can be accumulated. In addition, they want to understand this for themselves and by themselves, without always taking someone else's word for things. The objective of philosophy is autonomy, a term that refers to people's ability to freely make rational decisions for themselves. Philosophy asks people to become autonomous thinkers by thinking for themselves and developing their own philosophical positions based on well-reasoned arguments.

> *This world is not one in which certainty is possible. If you think you've achieved certainty, you are almost certainly mistaken. That is one of the few things you could be certain about.*
>
> – Bertrand Russell

In developing well-reasoned arguments, philosophers ask — and attempt to answer — fundamental questions about life, reality, and just about everything else that gives meaning to human existence. They deal with big questions and small, always emphasizing the discussion of philosophical ideas and concepts and the formulation of logical arguments. Their tools are the rules of logic, critical reflection, clear thinking, and a creative imagination. To philosophize is to be involved in an activity requiring rational and critical thinking. Though opinions can occasionally provide a convenient starting point for discussion, they are not substitutes for well-crafted questions, carefully examined beliefs, or sound arguments.

Many of the objectives and methods of philosophy are similar to those of other disciplines. Philosophers and scientists, for example, have much in common. They share an intense desire to understand everything from how the human mind works to the mysteries of the universe. At the same time, however, they approach these issues differently. Scientists are concerned primarily with the world as it is perceived by the senses — sight, sound, touch, taste, and smell. Scientists might try to explain the workings of the mind by examining how the brain works. They offer hypotheses and theories, then test these by experimenting and observing. Philosophers are interested in much more than observing and explaining the physical processes that so intrigue scientists. Their goal is to understand the *meaning* of these processes.

Though philosophers and scientists are interested in answering questions in different ways, scientists and professionals in many other fields also do philosophy. The fundamental beliefs of professionals such as teachers, lawyers, and journalists often form the philosophy of their field. This philosophy gives meaning to and justifies the existence of a profession. No field of endeavour can exist without a coherent philosophy. This explains the existence of areas of inquiry, such as the philosophy of science, the philosophy of mathematics, the philosophy of law, the philosophy of religion, the philosophy of history, and so on. Philosophy is unique because it is relevant to all these fields.

What Philosophers Have Said

The first recognized western philosophers were Greeks who lived in the sixth and fifth centuries BCE. They were called pre-Socratics because they preceded Socrates. Their primary concern was metaphysics: exploring the nature of reality. They attempted to explain the composition of matter and whether the physical world was in a constant state of change or whether what appeared to be change was nothing but an illusion. Because they concluded that matter is the basis of everything that exists, including human thought, they are often called **materialists**.

People in other parts of the world were asking similar questions at about the same time. The 20th-century German philosopher **Karl Jaspers** called this era, which he considered a turning point in human history, the axial period. Jaspers wrote:

> The most extraordinary events are concentrated in this period. Confucius [Kongfuzi] and Lao-tse [Laozi] were living in China; all the directions of Chinese philosophy came into being, including those of Mo-ti [Mozu], Chuang-tse [Zhaungzi], Lieh-tsu [Liezi], and a host of others; India produced the Upanishads and Buddha, and, like China, ran the whole gamut of philosophical possibilities down to skepticism (the doubting of knowledge), to materialism, sophism (the ability to use rhetoric to make arguments and win debates) and nihilism (the view that life has no meaning); in Iran Zarathustra taught the challenging view of the world as a struggle between good and evil; in Palestine the prophets made their appearance…; Greece witnessed the appearance of Homer, of the philosophers — Parmenides, Heraclitus, and **Plato** — of the tragedians, of Thucydides, and of Archimedes. Everything that is merely intimated by these names developed during these few centuries almost simultaneously in China, India, and the Occident [the West] without any one of these knowing of the others.
>
> What is new about this age, in all three of these worlds, is that man becomes aware of Being as a whole, of himself and his limitations. He experiences the terrible nature of the world and his own impotence. He asks radical questions. Face to face with the void he strives for liberation and redemption. By consciously recognizing his limits he sets himself the highest goals.…
>
> In this age were born the fundamental categories within which we still think today, and the beginnings of the world religions, by which human beings still live, were created. The step into universality was taken in every sense. As a result of this process, hitherto unconsciously accepted ideas, customs, and conditions were subjected to examination, questioned, and liquidated. Everything was swept into the vortex.

In Greece, the combined efforts of three people — Socrates, Plato, and **Aristotle** — set most of the western philosophical agenda for the next 2400 years. Socrates brought the field of ethics into existence. Plato wrote extensively about metaphysics, ethics, and knowledge and developed a distinctive interpretation of human nature. Aristotle was equally prolific in the fields of metaphysics and ethics and founded the discipline of logic. Both Plato and Aristotle were **philosophical system builders**. They originated a complete philosophy that attempted to answer the major philosophical questions.

Web connection
http://www.mcgrawhill.ca/links/philosophy12
To find out more about the similarities and differences in the thought of Kongfuzi and Socrates, follow the links on this Web site.

For 1400 years or more after Aristotle's time, western philosophy focused nearly exclusively on ethics — the proper conduct of one's personal life. This trend was reinforced by the spread of Christianity through Europe during the Middle Ages. The philosophizing that did take place focused largely on discussing the soul, personal immortality, and eternal salvation. Not until the European Renaissance, the period from about 1350 to 1550, was there renewed interest in discussing the kinds of questions that had captivated the ancient Greeks — and not until the early modern age was there a major refocusing of philosophical activity.

PHILOSOPHY IN ACTION

The Allegory of the Cave

by Plato

Observing a philosopher in action is one of the best ways to understand what philosophy is. In 360 BCE, Plato, a student of Socrates, captured the essence of philosophical activity in his story "The Allegory of the Cave." Plato told this story in the form of a parable or allegory, which is a narrative or description that uses symbols to convey a veiled meaning. As you read, think about the meaning that might be drawn from this story. How does it apply to philosophy, to society, and to you?

And now let me describe the human situation in a parable about ignorance and learning. Imagine there are men living at the bottom of an underground cave whose entrance is a long passageway that rises up through the ground to the light outside. They have been there since childhood and have their legs and necks chained so that they cannot move. Their heads are held by the chains so that they must sit facing the back wall of the cave and cannot turn their heads to look up through the entrance behind them. At some distance behind them, up nearer the entrance to the cave, a fire is burning, and objects pass in front of the fire so that they cast their shadows on the back wall where the prisoners see the moving shadows projected as if on a screen. All kinds of objects are paraded before the fire, including statues of men and animals whose shadows dance on the wall in front of the prisoners.

Those prisoners are like ourselves. The prisoners see nothing of themselves or each other except for the shadows each one's body casts on the back wall of the cave. Similarly, they see nothing of the objects behind them, except for their shadows moving on the wall.

Now imagine the prisoners were able to talk with each other, and suppose their voices echoed off the wall so that the voices seemed to be coming from their own shadows. Then wouldn't they talk and refer to these shadows as if the shadows were real? For the prisoners, reality would consist of nothing but the shadows.

But next imagine that one of the prisoners was freed from his chains. Suppose he was suddenly forced to stand up and face toward the entrance of the cave and then forced to walk up toward the burning fire. The movement would be painful, and the glare from the fire would blind him so that he would not see clearly the real objects whose shadows he used to watch. What would he think if someone explained that everything he had seen before was an illusion and that now he was nearer to reality and that his vision was actually clearer?

Imagine he was then shown the objects that had cast their shadows on the wall and he was asked to name each one — wouldn't he be at a complete loss? Wouldn't he think the shadows he saw before were more true than these objects?

Next imagine he was forced to look straight at the burning light. His eyes would hurt and the pain would make him turn away and try to escape back to things he could see more easily, convinced that they really were more real than the new things he was being shown.

But suppose that once more someone takes him and drags him up the steep and rugged ascent from the cave and forces him out into the full light of the sun. Wouldn't he suffer greatly and be furious at being dragged upward? As he approaches the light his eyes will be dazzled and he won't be able to see any of that world we ourselves call reality. Little by little he will have to get used to looking at the upper world. At first he will see shadows on the ground best, next perhaps the reflections of men and other objects in water, and then maybe the objects themselves. After this he would find it easier to gaze at the light of the moon and the stars in the night sky than to look at the daylight sun and its light. Last of all he will be able to look at the sun and contemplate its nature — not as it appears reflected in water but as it is in itself and in its own domain. He would come to the conclusion that the sun produces the seasons and the years and that it controls everything in the visible world. He will understand that it is in a way the cause of everything that he and his fellow prisoners used to see.

Suppose the released prisoner now recalled the cave and what passed for wisdom among his fellows there. Wouldn't he be happy about his new situation and feel sorry for them? They might have been in the habit of honouring those among themselves who were quickest to make out the shadows and those who could remember which usually came before others so that they were best at predicting the course of the shadows. Would he care anything for such honours and glories or would he envy those who won them? Wouldn't he rather endure anything than go back to thinking and living like they did?

Finally, imagine that the released prisoner was taken from the light and brought back into the cave to his old seat. His eyes would be full of darkness. Now he would have to compete in discerning the shadows with the prisoners who had never left the cave while his own eyes were still dim. Wouldn't he appear ridiculous? Men would say of him that he had gone up and had come back down with his eyesight ruined and that it was better not even to think of ascending. In fact, if they caught anyone trying to free them and lead them up to the light, they would try to kill him.

I say, now, that the prison is the world we see with our eyes; the light of the fire is like the power of our sun. And the climb upward out of the cave into the upper world is the ascent of the mind into the domain of true knowledge.

Source: "The Allegory of the Cave." Plato.

1. How does Plato's allegory represent the activity of philosophizing?

2. Imagine that you are the released prisoner. Select three questions Plato asks about the prisoner. Write a personal response to each question from the point of view of the prisoner. Compare your response with Plato's implied response. Is it the same or different? If it is different, explain why.

3. Plato makes several assumptions about how the released prisoner would react and how others would react to him. Create a counter-argument to one of these assumptions, clearly explaining why you disagree with Plato's position. Explain how this changed assumption would affect the philosophical position reflected in this allegory.

During the 1600s, a growing interest in scientific methods and the discoveries of luminaries such as Galileo Galilei and Isaac Newton shook long-held beliefs about the nature of the world. Scientific findings gave these times a distinctively materialistic tone. The English philosopher Thomas Hobbes, for example, concluded that just about everything could be explained in terms of motion and matter. And at about the same time, the French philosopher **René Descartes** was focusing on how people *know*.

Widely recognized as the founder of modern western philosophy, Descartes was a rationalist — someone who believes that reason, without the aid of sensory experience, provides knowledge of reality. In the tradition of Plato, Descartes believed that knowledge could be achieved only through the human ability to reason. The first major philosophical system builder of the modern age, Descartes started with the belief that everything should be doubted. He then focused his attention on two questions: What can we know for certain? and What is the relationship between body and mind? These questions became the focus of philosophical debate for the next 150 years.

In the 20th century, western philosophers began to broaden their horizons, examining the philosophies of other cultures and welcoming alternative points of view. Feminist philosophers, for example, began to propose different ways of approaching a variety of philosophical questions.

> *All philosophy is nothing more than a footnote to Plato.*
> – Alfred North Whitehead

This development contributed to a proliferation of sub-disciplines, such as the philosophy of science, of language, of mind, of mathematics, of history, of sports, and even of sex. New schools of thought, such as phenomenology, pragmatism, existentialism, and post-modernism, were established. Philosophers are divided over the benefits of some of these changes and additions to their discipline. Still, the changes show that philosophy is vibrantly alive and vigorous and promises to remain so.

> **Recall...Reflect...Respond**
>
> 1. Write two statements, one that reflects a philosophical stance and another that reflects an opinion or belief. Explain how the two differ.
> 2. Are you better suited to the study of philosophy or of science? Explain why.
> 3. Create a timeline showing the philosophical themes on which philosophers focused during various historical periods.

How Philosophers Have Said It

In "The Allegory of the Cave," Plato described a group of prisoners chained in a dark cave. One of the prisoners is released from his chains and forced to climb toward a distant light. After spending his entire life in darkness, he finds this very painful. Most readers accept that the prisoner's climb from the darkness to the light symbolizes the search for knowledge.

This search can be difficult, but it is ultimately worthwhile. Plato's story suggests that, like the prisoner who is freed from chains, people can be freed from blindly accepting uninformed opinions. We can enjoy the freedom that comes with arriving at our own views through critical reflection. To do this effectively, however, philosophers must develop certain skills.

LANGUAGE MATTERS

Choosing the correct words for questions and arguments is very important. It can also be difficult. As a result, philosophers pay special attention to language. They are especially concerned with **first-** and **second-order language**. Here are some examples:

First-order language: Is it right or wrong for me to cheat on this test?
Second-order language: What does it mean to say that cheating is right or wrong?

First-order language: His lie caused the mistake.
Second-order language: What does it mean to say that his lie caused the mistake?

As these examples show, second-order language is more general. It is used to clarify first-order language, which refers to specifics. Second-order language is sometimes called higher-order language or even metalanguage. The prefix "meta-" means beyond or of a higher order. Much of philosophy is concerned with second-order language, which helps clarify language use and thinking. This enables philosophers to produce well-reasoned arguments and to arrive at clear, precise conclusions.

DEFINITIONS AND CLARITY

Precision in language is important to philosophers, with good reason. Imprecise language often leads to muddled thinking, confusion, and needless disagreements. Socrates was keenly aware of this. It is the reason he stressed the importance of using precise definitions in philosophical discussions. If you and a friend are discussing the fairness of a pop quiz, for example, the two of you must have similar ideas about the meaning of "fairness" if your discussion is to make sense.

Relying on a dictionary definition might start a discussion, but philosophers prefer to go well beyond this. They seek a deeper, more thorough understanding of the concept being considered. Take freedom. Philosophers who ask, What is freedom? will not find the answer they want in a dictionary. They try to understand the role of freedom in people's lives and thoughts, whether freedom can be misused, and whether it relates to other concepts like equality and justice. The truth they seek cannot be found in a dictionary definition.

> **Web connection**
> http://www.mcgrawhill.ca/links/philosophy12
> To find out more about the definitions of philosophical terms, follow the links on this Web site.

CRITICAL THINKING

The ability to think critically is an essential tool of philosophy. But what is critical thinking? Though definitions vary, most focus on thinking as a process. The American educator Norman J. Unrau, for example, defined it as "reasoned reflection on the meaning of claims about what to believe or what to do." In philosophy, one focus of critical thinking encourages people to re-examine beliefs that they regard as common sense.

THE SOCRATIC METHOD

One highly effective technique that encourages people to challenge common-sense beliefs and develop clear definitions is the Socratic method. This question-and-answer process was named after Socrates, who used it to zero in on knowledge by challenging commonly held assumptions. It works like this:

> Step 1: Socrates asks a question that seems innocent and straightforward (e.g., What is love? What is courage? What is beauty?). The question is often put to a person who has claimed to possess special or expert knowledge of a subject.
> Step 2: The person offers a common-sense definition.
> Step 3: Socrates then offers a counter-example that does not fit the definition given. This example illustrates that the definition is incomplete, biased, or uninformed.
> Step 4: The process continues until a suitable definition is constructed or until the two parties agree that the subject is more complex than originally thought.

Constructing a suitable definition is not easy. The definition must show clearly what all examples of the thing being defined — love, courage, beauty, and so on — have in common. The distinguishing feature of a good definition, then, is that all the examples possess the same common elements. Even if the Socratic method fails to produce a suitable definition, knowing what something is *not* brings people a step closer to knowing what it is.

The Socratic method is also an effective way of responding to those who claim to be right without being able to explain why. Many arguments degenerate to this level. This may be why Socrates described unsupported correct beliefs as true opinions. He regarded these as inferior to knowledge, which involves knowing why something is true and why alternatives are false.

The following selection from Plato's *Euthyphro* illustrates Socrates' method of questioning. In this dialogue, Plato reconstructed the conversation that took place as Socrates challenged the definition of holiness advanced by a young man named Euthyphro.

> *Socrates:* I was not asking you to give me *examples* of holiness, Euthyphro, but to identify the characteristic which makes all holy things holy. There must be some characteristic that all holy things have in common, and one which makes unholy things unholy. Tell me what this characteristic itself is, so that I can tell which actions are holy, and which unholy.

PROFILE

Thales of Miletus
The First Philosopher

Thales of Miletus, who lived from 624 to 546 BCE, is fortunate to have survived long enough to be called the first philosopher. While zealously studying the stars rather than watching where he was going, he is said to have fallen into a well. Fortunately, he was rescued.

Though Thales may have been slightly eccentric, he was highly intelligent, creative, and inventive. He was also shrewd. Aristotle told a story of how this philosopher grew rich by predicting that the next season's olive harvest would be a bumper crop. He then bought all the olive presses available — and so made a fortune when his prediction came to pass.

Thales was born in Miletus, a wealthy port in present-day Turkey. Often called the birthplace of western philosophy, Miletus earned this title because the wealth of some of its citizens, including Thales' family, enabled them to live a life of leisure. This created an environment that encouraged the intellectual activity that would become known as philosophizing.

Thales travelled widely, eventually settling in Greece. While travelling in Egypt, he devised a method for measuring the height of the pyramids. His procedure was as inspiring in its ingenuity as it was beautiful in its simplicity. He waited until the length of his own shadow was the same as his height, then measured the length of each pyramid's shadow. At that precise moment, he reasoned, the length of the shadow of each pyramid would also equal its height. Though this feat of reasoning was impressive, Thales' fame stems from claims that he invented a new way of thinking.

Thales was especially curious about the nature of things and asked this simple but original question: What is everything made of? His observations of many different natural substances led him to believe that they shared striking similarities. In other words, the *many* were related to one another by the *one*. By "the one," Thales meant an underlying substance that was the basis for everything else that existed in nature. Strange as it may seem today, he decided that this substance was water.

He reached this conclusion by relying on the only tool available — observation. His observations told him that water appears in three forms: solid, liquid, and vapour. Rain causes plants to emerge from the ground. Living things need water to survive. Every land mass seems to end where it meets a body of water. Even though Thales' conclusion was incorrect, he deserves full marks for asking the question in the first place — and for trying to answer it. In doing so, he became the first person in recorded history to try to explain natural phenomena using reason rather than superstition and myth.

Though Thales' conclusion about "the one" was false, it displayed some amazingly intuitive and prophetic insights. Especially remarkable was his extraordinary statement that all things can be reduced to one thing. In this, he was correct, as modern physics has demonstrated. All matter is reducible to energy. If this early philosopher had had access to the knowledge and tools available to contemporary scientists, what marvellous discoveries might he have made? No one knows the answer to this question, but many have speculated that his contribution might have been enormous.

Figure 1.2

Much of the information about Thales is based on second-hand accounts by people such as Aristotle, as is this portrait. It was created in the early 1800s, more than 2000 years after the death of this early thinker.

Euthyphro: Well, then holiness is what is loved by the gods and what is not loved by them is unholy.

Socrates: Very good, Euthyphro! Now you have given me the sort of answer I wanted. Let us examine it. A thing or a person that is loved by the gods is holy, and a thing or a person that the gods hate is unholy. And the holy is the opposite of the unholy. Does that summarize what you said?

Euthyphro: It does.

Socrates: But you admit, Euthyphro, that the gods have disagreements. So some things are hated by some gods and loved by other gods.

Euthyphro: True.

Socrates: Then upon your view the same things, Euthyphro, will be both holy and unholy.

Euthyphro: Well, I suppose so.

Socrates: Then, my friend, you have not really answered my question. I did not ask you to tell me which actions were both holy and unholy; yet this is the outcome of your view.

This exchange demonstrates why Athenians on the receiving end of Socrates' penetrating logic and stinging wit might find the experience frustrating and even infuriating. Few doubt that Socrates' relentless questioning was directly connected to the death penalty imposed on him. Fortunately, philosophizing is not as dangerous today.

More to the point, however, is this question: Did Socrates' dialogue with Euthyphro lead to a definition of holiness — or of unholiness? In the end, it did not. This does not mean that the conversation was fruitless. Although little, if anything, was learned about the meaning of holiness and unholiness, Socrates and Euthyphro learned something about what it is *not*. *Euthyphro* provides an excellent lesson in the kind of critical questioning that is characteristic of philosophy.

Web connection
http://wwwmcgrawhill.ca/links/philosophy12
To read more of Euthyphro, follow the links on this Web site.

THOUGHT EXPERIMENTS

Thought experiments are another tool philosophers use to push common-sense beliefs to the breaking point. If people's common-sense beliefs fracture under the strain imposed by a thought experiment, perhaps these beliefs should be re-examined.

Thought experiments, such as the one on the next page, often begin with — or include — the question, What if…? They then depict an imaginary situation or event, something that does not exist, has never existed, and will probably never exist. In other words, thought experiments propose a possible world. Everything in this possible world is the same as in the real world — except for the one imaginary situation or event.

Physicists often use thought experiments to help clarify conceptual puzzles arising from their theories. The 20th-century physicist Albert Einstein, for example, wondered what it would be like to travel at 300 000 kilometres a second on the leading edge of a light beam. What would the traveller see? What would the laws of nature look like? Of course, this experiment was — and is — impossible to carry out. Still, if it had been possible, Einstein said that the traveller would see something that does not exist: a stationary oscillatory field.

THOUGHT EXPERIMENT: *The Ship of Theseus*

In ancient times, a wooden sailing ship was moored for many years in the harbour of the Greek town of Theseus. Though this ship had once seen service in war, it had outgrown its usefulness. Its wood planks had started to rot. This process began with the keel. Gradually, parts of the hull and deck started rotting. Even the mast began to deteriorate.

What if the owner of the ship had hated to see her investment going to ruin? And so had carefully replaced each rotting plank with a new one of exactly the same size and colour? Each new plank did the same job as the old one. Eventually, every single plank on the ship was replaced.

Figure 1.3

Once all the planks were replaced, was the ship the same ship — or a different one?

Is the ship of Theseus any different from the human body, which replaces many of its cells over time?

Thought experiments must be handled with great care. Though some help people arrive at new perspectives on common-sense beliefs, some prove little or nothing at all. One of the main drawbacks is the difficulty of demarcating their boundary conditions. Once an imaginary situation or event is proposed, it can lead to the proposing of innumerable related imaginary situations or events. What ifs can build on what ifs, with no end in sight. This defeats a thought experiment's purpose.

READING PHILOSOPHY

Reading philosophy is a rational, critical enterprise that requires readers to play an active role in the process. When reading a selection, try to find and understand the main point or argument. Then look for supporting arguments. Some of the ideas and words may seem strange at first. Occasionally, you will need to reread a passage. But once you grasp what is being said, ask yourself these questions: Does it make sense? Do I agree with the writer? Whether your answer is yes or no, try to formulate clear explanations of the reasons you agree or disagree. In this way, reading philosophy is like taking part in a conversation with a philosopher.

Philosophy is not a learn-and-repeat activity. The emphasis is on understanding and evaluating what philosophers have said, then formulating opinions that can be justified. This is the beginning of the journey toward knowledge and wisdom.

WHY PHILOSOPHY MATTERS

Most people are inquisitive beings who desire to know. Becoming wiser is something that matters to just about everyone. As the pursuit of wisdom, philosophy is, by definition, ideally suited to help people start on a journey toward wisdom. But philosophy does much more than this. It helps people cultivate skills that matter in everyday life. It is like a set of finely crafted mental tools that can be used in the art of argument.

In the philosophical sense, argument does not refer to tempers flaring, or worse. Nor does it refer to what passes for an exchange of ideas on some talk shows where people define listening as waiting for their turn to speak.

A **philosophical argument** involves two or more people in presenting reasoned ideas for the purpose of discovering the truth. Evidence and arguments are offered respectfully and honestly in hopes of reaching a conclusion that contains a truth that everyone can live with. Though achieving this level of discussion is seldom easy, the ability to analyze problems rationally and present ideas logically and persuasively is useful in many settings. Lawyers, clerics, teachers, politicians, scientists, parents, and students, for example, use these skills every day.

Life presents people with a bewildering array of conflicting views and choices about a staggering number of questions and issues. Is there life after death? Does a supreme being exist? Are people essentially good or evil? Should I cheat on the final exams? The list of questions goes on, as does the number of conflicting answers.

To help make sense of all this, philosophy not only teaches people to analyze information, but also to assess the merits of competing arguments. The lessons to be derived from Plato's allegory of the cave may be more pertinent now than ever. In the 21st-century world of media hype, technological wizardry, and mass marketing, the ability to analyze and evaluate enormous amounts of conflicting information is indispensable.

The Lighter Side of Philosophy

First law of philosophy: For every philosopher, there exists an equal and opposite philosopher

Second law of philosophy: They're both wrong.

Recall...Reflect...Respond

1. Create a first- and second-order question to guide an exploration of the definition of love. With a partner, discuss answers to these questions. Take notes on your discussion. What did your discussion teach you about philosophizing and about the importance of language? How could you have made your discussion more fruitful and philosophical?
2. Revisit your notes on the discussion of love. Play the role of Socrates and write a question that can be used to illustrate how your definition of love is incomplete, biased, or uninformed.
3. Suppose that you have caught your five-year-old sister and her friend doing something dangerous. With two classmates, create a role-play showing how you — and the two five-year-olds — might react. Explain how this argument might differ from a philosophical argument.

WHY STUDY PHILOSOPHY?

This question, Why study philosphy? goes to the heart of a discussion of the value of philosophy. In the mid-20th century, the American psychologist **Abraham Maslow** proposed a pyramid-like classification of human needs that can be summarized into two categories: maintenance and self-actualization. Maintenance needs form the base of the pyramid and include the basic physical needs required to maintain life, such as the need for air, food, and water. At the top of the pyramid are self-actualization needs. Self-actualization refers to finding fulfilment and reaching one's potential. For Maslow, the highest self-actualization need is to help others find fulfilment.

Figure 1.4

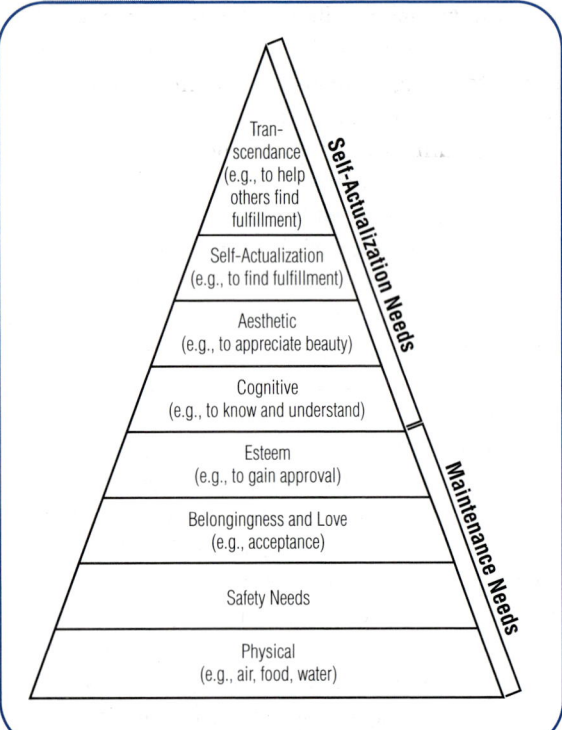

Maslow's hierarchy of needs pyramid, from bottom to top:
- Physical (e.g., air, food, water)
- Safety Needs
- Belongingness and Love (e.g., acceptance)
- Esteem (e.g., to gain approval)
- Cognitive (e.g., to know and understand)
- Aesthetic (e.g., to appreciate beauty)
- Self-Actualization (e.g., to find fulfillment)
- Transcendence (e.g., to help others find fulfillment)

The lower levels are labelled Maintenance Needs; the upper levels are labelled Self-Actualization Needs.

Abraham Maslow believed that once people meet maintenance needs, they seek to satisfy higher-level self-actualization needs.

Think about this highest need in light of Plato's allegory of the cave. After seeing the light of true knowledge, the prisoner returns to the cave to share his newly acquired wisdom with the others. He returns to help others, at great peril to himself. Plato is telling readers that the philosopher, like the prisoner, has an obligation to help others by sharing his knowledge. If Plato and Maslow are correct, philosophy is ideally suited to serve the needs of self-actualized people.

One of the characteristics attributed to self-actualized people is creativity. According to psychologist Carl Rogers, creative people are curious, aesthetically sensitive, intellectually autonomous, flexible in outlook, capable of relating spontaneously to ideas, and willing to examine their own beliefs. These same characteristics and ways of thinking are promoted and cultivated by philosophy.

Philosophy also has a highly practical side. The ability to analyze and assess both sides of an argument is valuable in all areas of life. The critical-thinking and problem-solving skills cultivated by the study of philosophy can be applied to any subject.

David A. Hoekema, an American philosopher, recently pointed out the advantages of studying philosophy in an article titled, "Why Not Study Something Practical, like Philosophy?" Here is a summary of what he found.

- Students majoring in philosophy at university have excellent verbal and analytical skills. They are consistently among the top performers in tests of these skills.
- On the verbal portion of one standardized test, the Graduate Record Examination, philosophy majors outperformed all other humanities majors. Only those studying English came close.
- On the Law School Admissions Test and the Graduate Management Admissions Test, philosophy majors scored substantially higher than students majoring in other humanities fields. Philosophy majors also outperformed those majoring in business and other applied fields, including engineering, and all social-sciences majors, except those studying economics.
- The employment rate for people with PhDs in philosophy is 98.9 percent. This is higher than the average for those with doctorates in the humanities, biology, or the social sciences.
- The median salary of philosophers is only 14 percent lower than that of scientists and engineers, who earn some of the highest incomes in the United States.
- Philosophy is the only field in which the employment rate is the same for men and women.
- Philosophers become lawyers, doctors, administrators, teachers, diplomats, consultants, stockbrokers, bankers, and managers. They are accepted and respected in all professional schools and welcomed into management training programs.

In ancient Greece, the word *sophia*, or wisdom, applied to all areas of knowledge, and for a long time, science and mathematics were considered branches of philosophy. Isaac

Newton, for example, is recognized today as a physicist, but he was known as a natural philosopher in his day. In the 19th century, as philosophy gradually came to be considered a separate discipline from science, its focus became increasingly professional. Many philosophers began producing specialized works that only a relatively small number of people could understand, a trend that continued into the 20th century.

This trend is now changing. Philosophers have begun to reach out to the general public in fascinating ways. Philosophy cafés, where people from all backgrounds and walks of life discuss a variety of philosophical questions, are springing up everywhere. People interested in philosophy are also meeting in Internet discussion groups and chatrooms. And philosophers are writing books with catchy titles like *The Ethics of Star Trek*; *Plato, Not Prozac*; *Aristotle Would Have Liked Oprah*; *Better Living*; and *Sophie's World*. Some have become best-sellers, and all are accessible to the general public. Philosophers are even taking a serious interest in the popular media, be it a stage production of *Macbeth* or a Hollywood science-fiction thriller like *The Matrix*.

In today's world, new and vitally important philosophical questions are being debated as people reflect on developments in genetic engineering, artificial intelligence, and the degradation of the natural environment. Issues like these have the potential to change humanity — and they raise many questions. For example, if machines become as smart as humans, will they request, and be entitled to, equal treatment? If machines become smarter than humans, will they treat people as equals? Or will they become a new superior species?

And as scientists refine their ability to create life and alter the structure of human bodies, what does this mean for the future of the human race? What knowledge do people need in order to consider these developments rationally? Will we possess the wisdom to make the right choices?

These questions — and many more — are important, and philosophy can play an important role in helping to answer them.

Figure 1.5

Canadian philosopher Mark Kingwell is the author of the thought-provoking and entertaining best-seller *Better Living*, which explores the meaning of happiness.

THE AREAS OF PHILOSOPHY

To organize the vast body of thought known as philosophy, philosophers have divided it into various areas of inquiry or **areas of philosophy**. Though philosophers do not always agree on the areas their discipline should be divided into, most would include the following: logic and the philosophy of science, metaphysics, epistemology, ethics, aesthetics, and social and political philosophy.

LOGIC AND THE PHILOSOPHY OF SCIENCE

Logic, which is sometimes called the science of the laws of thought, is the study of formal reasoning. Logicians ask questions like, What is a valid argument? and What is a logical fallacy, or bad argument? An argument is a group of statements designed to justify a conclusion. Logicians explore the procedures of formal reasoning in the form of arguments.

At one time, the job of identifying knowledge and deciding on the truth or falsity of ideas and beliefs rested with authority figures, regardless of their qualifications. Since the 17th century, science has developed more rational and effective ways of explaining the world and acquiring knowledge. In fact, science has been the most important source of new knowledge. Despite this brilliant record, some nagging questions remain: What is science? What differentiates science from non-science? What, exactly, does the term "scientific method" mean and how reliable is this method? What makes a scientific theory true? Is there any kind of knowledge that has nothing to do with science? What distinguishes science from pseudo-science (false science)? These are the kinds of questions raised by philosophers of science.

METAPHYSICS

Can you be certain that what you are reading right now is not a dream or illusion? Do you rely on your senses to tell you what is real? If so, what about the sub-atomic world of particles that cannot be discerned by the senses? Which is the true reality? Could there be many realities? Questions like these are metaphysical. Metaphysics deals with the nature of reality by asking questions like, What is reality? What is real? What is the relationship between mind and matter? What is the self? and What is the meaning of life?

Though human beings may never be able to answer these questions entirely satisfactorily, metaphysical questions are fascinating. They also provide excellent opportunities to reflect and think critically. In addition, metaphysical questions about the existence and nature of a supreme being or beings and people's immortal souls are central to discussions of the meaning of human existence.

Figure 1.6

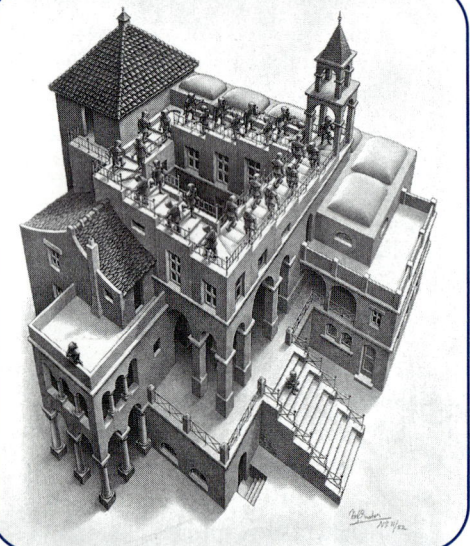

Follow the monks up — or down — the staircase in this picture by M.C. Escher. What does the picture show? What do you think this picture says about the nature of reality?

M.C. Escher's *Ascending and Descending*. © 2002 Cordon Art B.V.–Baarn–Holland. All rights reserved.

EPISTEMOLOGY

At one time or another, just about everyone has uttered this question: "How do you know?" Sometimes, this query is nothing more than the frustrated response of someone who is losing an argument. But if the question is genuine, motivated by a sincere desire to know the reasons for someone else's beliefs, then it may be profoundly epistemological.

The word "epistemology" comes from the Greek word *episteme*, which means knowledge. Epistemology, then, is the study of knowledge or what is worthy of belief by a rational person. The fundamental question asked by epistemologists is, What does it mean to know? From this question flow all sorts of other questions: Can humans know the world as it really is? Are there some things that humans can never know? Are there some things that humans can know with absolute certainty?

Many philosophers believe that epistemology and metaphysics are the pillars that support all other fields of philosophical inquiry. There is sound justification for this belief. After all, if you can answer the questions, What is real? and How do I know? then you will have answered the most basic questions of philosophy.

ETHICS

Do you sometimes find it difficult to decide whether an action is good or bad, right or wrong? When you explore questions of right and wrong, you are doing ethics. Ethicists ask questions like, What are good and evil? What is virtue? Why be morally good? and What obligations do people have toward one another? They answer questions like these by investigating character traits that are good and admirable, as well as traits that are bad and reprehensible. They also study values or moral principles, as well as actions that are good and bad, right and wrong.

The scope of ethics is vast. Ethicists explore the answers to big questions such as, Is euthanasia ever morally permissible? They also explore smaller, specific questions. Suppose that you are walking down the street and encounter a gang of thugs beating someone up. You have not started that karate course you intended to take. Do you rush to the rescue? Under these circumstances, what is the morally right response? What should you do?

AESTHETICS

Aesthetics is the philosophy of art. But what is art? What is the role of art in society? The word "aesthetic" means concerned with beauty, and an aesthete is someone who has a special appreciation of beauty. But what is beauty? Do objective standards of beauty and ugliness exist? These are some of the questions that drive the explorations of philosophers of aesthetics.

Figure 1.7

The artist Pablo Picasso set out to protest the brutality of war in this painting titled *Guernica*. Should art be used to express social and political protest?

Mention the word "art" to a non-expert, and a painting such as the *Mona Lisa* may spring to mind. Most people realize, however, that there is much more to art. Architecture and sculpture are traditionally recognized as art forms. Films, photography, and many forms of music are now considered art. But does the music of the latest chart-topping rapper belong in the same class as the works of classical composers such as Mozart and Beethoven? Are aesthetically inclined chimpanzees — some of whom produce paintings that sell — as worthy of being called artists as Leonardo da Vinci or Pablo Picasso? Should non-traditional forms of expression, such as graffiti or so-called subway art, be defined as art? Are aesthetic experiences inspired by subjective, emotional responses or objective, rational thought? Philosophers of aesthetics grapple with these and many other questions about both the nature of art and the aesthetic experience.

SOCIAL AND POLITICAL PHILOSOPHY

According to Canadian philosopher Joseph Heath, author of *The Efficient Society*, Canada is as close as it gets to Utopia, an imaginary perfect place. Heath's main reason for reaching this conclusion is, as the title of his book suggests, the efficiency of Canadian society.

• IDEAS IN CONTEXT •

At one time, nearly all societies created myths to explain events, such as the origin of the world and other natural phenomena. Misfortune was considered a sign of the gods' displeasure, while success was a sign of being in their good graces. The ancient Greeks believed that their gods looked and acted like humans, though they were immortal and more powerful. Like humans, however, the gods of the ancient Greeks displayed both virtues and vices. Though Socrates, Plato, and Aristotle championed the cause of rational thought over mythical explanations, they nevertheless justified many of their philosophical beliefs by referring to the will of the gods.

In fact, Heath is just one of a long line of philosophers — starting with Plato — who have explored the question of what constitutes the best society.

A variety of other questions arise from this exploration: What are the just limits of state authority? Do people have a right to equal treatment? What are the rights and responsibilities of individual citizens? What is justice? and What is the proper boundary between public policy and private morality? These and many other related questions and issues are the concern of social and political philosophers.

CONNECTING THE AREAS

Though logicians, philosophers of science, metaphysicians, epistemologists, ethicists, aestheticians, and social and political philosophers explore specific questions and theories related to their area of philosophical study, this does not mean that the areas of philosophy are unrelated. On the contrary, philosophical areas are connected in various ways, and philosophers in many areas are often interested in finding answers to similar questions. Their approaches, however, might be different.

Consider this question: Do humans make their own choices or are their choices determined by another force, such as their genes, their environment, or a supreme being? In exploring answers, a metaphysician might seek to understand the reality of being human. What, exactly, is people's real nature? An epistemologist might ask whether anyone can know the answer to this question. And an ethicist might ask whether judging people's actions makes sense if they have no choice in deciding how to act.

Recall...Reflect...Respond

1. Suppose you are writing a letter of reference for a friend who is applying for the job of equity officer in a major law firm. Your friend has a philosophy degree. What skills and characteristics would you highlight in this letter?
2. List three events or activities that you have participated in over the past week. For each, identify the area of philosophy that might have helped you address issues raised by these events. Explain how.
3. Create a second-order question that addresses at least three different areas of philosophy and explain how each area is reflected in this question.

PHILOSOPHY'S BLIND SIDE: THE MARGINALIZED AND THE LIONIZED

Until recently, studies of philosophy in Europe and North America tended to focus on western philosophical traditions. Other points of view, including those of women, were either given short shrift, ignored, or actively discouraged.

Anyone learning without thought is lost; anyone thinking but not learning is in peril.

– Kongfuzi (Confucius)

This lopsided coverage creates a challenge for present-day philosophers. Every society and every culture has a rich philosophical tradition. And within these societies and cultures exists a wealth of sub-traditions that contain a variety of philosophical positions. Furthermore, in many societies, religious and philosophical beliefs merged to form a unified whole. This is especially true of Asia, where religious and philosophical belief systems such as Buddhism, Hinduism, Confucianism, Shintoism, and Taoism arose in ancient times and remain vital today.

Though eastern and western philosophers have contributed greatly to the advancement of knowledge, both traditions contain weaknesses and blind spots. For example, men have dominated both eastern and western philosophy. In the western tradition, there is no female equivalent of Socrates and no black equivalent of Aristotle. Why not?

A simple answer is that, until recently, philosophers did not try any harder than practitioners of other disciplines to incorporate marginalized groups into their ranks. The men who shaped the philosophical tradition assumed that their views applied to everyone regardless of gender, race, or culture. They assumed that their truth was a universal truth.

This is not surprising. Throughout history, few cultures have accepted or even tolerated outsiders, and most languages include derogatory terms to describe foreigners. The ancient Greeks referred to people from other cultures as barbarians. And the Japanese often call westerners "gaijin," a word that may be insulting. This prejudice extended to the philosophies of outsiders.

Though Aristotle, for example, had much to say about justice some 2500 years ago, he accepted slavery as a part of the natural order and dismissed women by describing them as incomplete men.

Can these remarks be excused because they reflect the prevailing wisdom of his era? Some would say yes. Others, however, have pointed out that Plato, Aristotle's teacher, did not share his student's attitude toward women. Plato said that women had the same potential as men if given fair and equal training.

Web connection
http://www.mcgrawhill.ca/links/philosphy12
To find out more about women who have contributed to philosophy, follow the links on this Web site.

Within societies, those who wielded power were reluctant to acknowledge other philosophical traditions or even the thoughts of the powerless. As a result, groups who were marginalized — placed on the margins of society because of their gender, race, culture, religion and so on — had limited opportunities to express their ideas.

The issues raised by marginalized groups were rejected as either irrelevant or a threat to established authority. As well, individuals within the groups themselves had little energy for philosophizing. It is hard to construct a philosophical framework when you are aspiring to, or fighting for, basic equality.

In all societies, those who had the upper hand enjoyed special status when it came to deciding on and dispensing conventional wisdom. In nearly all traditions, this was men — and men determined the philosophical agenda. Until very recently, men decided which questions and theories were worthy of philosophical investigation.

David Hume and Immanuel Kant, two 18th-century philosophers, and Georg W. F. Hegel, one of the most influential philosophers of the 19th century, all made remarks about blacks that today would be found only in white supremacist propaganda. Remarkably, Hume, Kant, and Hegel — all of whom considered themselves meticulous researchers — arrived at their sweeping condemnations without conducting any first-hand observations. They did not have a shred of evidence to support their conclusions.

Do these examples illustrate that prejudice and uninformed opinions are among the worst enemies of truth? Does the fact that such illustrious philosophers could be seduced by prejudice and uninformed opinions underscore the power of these biased attitudes and the threat they represent to both sound judgment and sound philosophy?

As you embark on your journey toward wisdom, think about these questions and formulate your own answers.

Chapter Review

Chapter Summary

This chapter has discussed
- some of the main ideas expressed by philosophers from various world traditions
- the positions of some of the major philosophers and schools of philosophy

Knowledge and Understanding

1. Identify and explain the significance to the study of philosophy of each of the following key words and people.

Key Words	Key People
philosophy	Socrates
autonomy	Brenda Almond
materialists	Karl Jaspers
philosophical system builder	Plato
first-order language	Aristotle
second-order language	Thales of Miletus
Socratic method	René Descartes
thought experiment	Abraham Maslow
philosophical argument	David A. Hoekema
areas of philosophy	

2. Create a two-column table. Label one column What Philosophy Is. Label the other column What Philosophy Is Not. Write statements about philosophy under the appropriate heading. Use these statements to create a working definition of the term "philosophy." Pool your ideas with those of others and create a class definition of philosophy.

Thinking and Inquiry

3. Consider the following philosophical quotations.

   Black Elk in *A Lakota Vision*

   There were no chiefs in our family before Crazy Horse…he became a chief because of the power he got in a vision…Crazy Horse dreamed and went into the world where there is nothing but the spirits of all things. That is the real world that is behind this one….

   Mao Zedong (Mao Tse-tung) in *Where Do Correct Ideas Come From?*

   Where do correct ideas come from? Do they drop from the skies? No. Are they innate in the mind? No. They come from social practice, and from it alone;…It is man's social being that determines his thinking.

   What point is each philosopher making? Do you agree? Why? What areas of philosophy are addressed in each quotation? Explain how. If more than one area is addressed in each quotation, explain the connections between them.

4. The American philosopher William James, who died in 1910, argued that people's ability to philosophize is somewhat limited by their "living options." Living options are ideas that are believable because they fit in with people's existing ideas, beliefs, and experiences. Think about the factors that affect your own living options. How might these factors limit your ability to philosophize? How can you expand your living options to overcome these limitations?

Communication

5. You have just graduated from the University of Wisdom with a PhD in philosophy. You are considering going into a field such as law, business, the media, management, or technology. Choose a profession that interests you and create a résumé that highlights your education in philosophy and explains how it makes you a suitable candidate for the field. Write a letter introducing yourself to the firm.

6. Create a collage of photographs, cartoons, paintings, advertisements, excerpts from narratives, movies, poems, song lyrics, or other symbols to illustrate six areas of philosophy.

Application

7. Read and think about this cartoon.

Figure 1.8

© King Features Syndicate. Reprinted with permission – The Toronto Star Syndicate.

What philosophical idea(s) are touched on in this cartoon? What areas of philosophy are represented by these ideas? How are they represented?

Rewrite the dialogue in the cartoon to make the focus more philosophical. Apply both first- and second-order language, as well as the Socratic method.

8. Using "The Ship of Theseus" as a model, create a thought experiment that challenges your own ideas about a philosophical issue that has recently arisen in your own life. Remember that a thought experiment depicts an imaginary situation or event in a real-world context by asking the question, What if…? Conclude your thought experiment with at least three questions — and provide your own philosophical responses to these questions.

Chapter 2
Introducing Human Nature

Chapter Expectations

By the end of this chapter, you will be able to
- summarize the main questions, concepts, and theories of human nature
- evaluate the strengths and weaknesses of the responses to some of the main questions about human nature defended by some major philosophers and schools of philosophy, and defend your own responses
- demonstrate the relevance of theories of human nature to everyday life and to the study of other areas of philosophy
- illustrate how theories of human nature are presupposed in other disciplines
- begin to formulate your own philosophical beliefs about human nature and anticipate counter-arguments to your ideas

Key Words

human nature
altruism
egoism
li
essentialists
tripartite theory of the soul
essence
Buddhist
doctrine of impermanence
behaviourism
existentialism

Key People

Voltaire
John Stuart Mill
Thomas Hobbes
Joseph Butler
Mengzi (Mencius)
Xun-Zi (Hsün-tzu)
Jean-Paul Sartre
Simone de Beauvoir

A Philosopher's Voice

● *Know thyself.* ●

Inscription at the Delphic Oracle

BEING HUMAN

What does it mean to be human? This vexing question has always fascinated thoughtful people. What makes human beings different from non-human animals? Or machines? Or anything else?

In trying to answer these questions, philosophers, along with psychologists and scientists, have often suggested that human beings are unique in some way. They do not agree, however, on what makes people unique. The 20th-century English philosopher Martin Hollis, for example, said that free will — the ability to make decisions about how to act — is what distinguishes people from non-human animals and machines. Hollis wrote:

> What is man? There have been many attempts to say what makes human beings unique in kind. We are self-conscious, rational, creative, moved by sensibility. We can fall in love, jest, write sonnets, extract square roots, plan for tomorrow. We are capable of faith, hope and charity and, for that matter, of envy, hatred and malice. We know truth from error, right from wrong. The list is long and untidy. Some entries seem only a matter of degree. Animals too can hold beliefs, feel and communicate. Machines can extract square roots and organize a complex plan. With nature not fully understood and computing in its infancy, it is rash to pick out any human attribute, which is not just a matter of degree.
>
> Yet there has been a persistent belief that man is somehow unique in kind. The best favoured candidate is less specific than any of the rough list above. It is free will.... By "free will" I mean the proposition that, when human beings do something, they could (at least sometimes) have done otherwise.

The proper study of mankind is man.

– Alexander Pope

When discussing what being human means and what makes human beings different from anything else, people are talking about **human nature**. "What a piece of work is man!" exclaimed Hamlet in Shakespeare's play. How right he was. For sheer complexity, nothing comes close to human beings. Little wonder, then, that human nature is a challenging subject of study.

Samuel Umen, an American rabbi, summed up this complexity in his book *Images of Man*.

> [Man]...is the strongest being on earth and the weakest....
>
> Two opposite forces meet within him — an impulse for good and an impulse for evil. He is forever in conflict with himself. He sets for himself noble objectives and is driven to ignoble deeds. He longs for peace and makes war. He glorifies freedom and creates systems of enslavement. He prides himself on having a set of Laws from God to keep him on the path of righteousness, but more often than not forsakes it for the enticing promises made to him by the voice of evil. He sanctifies human life and does not hesitate to crush it as if it were a blight. He is compassionate, generous, loving, and forgiving, but also cruel, vengeful, selfish, and vindictive. On the one hand, he claims that his conduct is determined by inexorable laws of nature, by causes beyond his control; and on the other hand, he maintains that he is free to become what he wills, that his destiny is in his own hands. He warns himself that if he should forget the mistakes of his forebears, he will be destined to repeat them; yet, he willfully ignores his warning and is condemned to relive their woeful experiences.
>
> In brief, man is the most paradoxical of paradoxes. He is an anomaly encased in an enigma. He is a bundle of contradictions.

QUESTIONS THAT MATTER

Those who have thought seriously about the issue of human nature have often looked for characteristics, attributes, and modes of thought that have been natural for all people at all times. To focus this search, philosophers have often asked — and debated the answers to — various questions. Here are three of them.

- Do people by nature desire to know?
- Are people by nature altruists or egoists?
- Are people by nature good or evil?

DO PEOPLE BY NATURE DESIRE TO KNOW?

The ancient Greek philosopher Aristotle was acutely aware of the similarities between human beings and animals. At various times, he described humans as "rational animals," "by nature a civilized animal," and "an animal capable of acquiring knowledge."

> *All men by nature desire knowledge.*
> – Aristotle

Aristotle also believed that human beings are different from animals because people do, by nature, desire to know and that human nature drives people to pursue happiness. He anticipated the theories of the 20th-century psychologist, Abraham Maslow, when he remarked that once people have taken care of basic needs, such as the need for food and shelter, they will naturally seek to satisfy their higher, intellectual needs. Like Aristotle, most ancient Greek philosophers believed that happiness and knowledge are mutually supportive and that the pursuit of both is fundamental to human nature.

Starting in the early modern era, however, some philosophers such as the English thinker Jeremy Bentham began to question this assumption. They suggested that seeking physical pleasure rather than intellectual satisfaction is more in keeping with human nature. This idea is repeated every day by people who argue that ignorance is bliss. Which, then, is more in keeping with human nature: to know or not to know?

The 18th-century French writer and philosopher **Voltaire** examined this question in a story titled "The Good Brahman" (see p. 27), but did not arrive at a definitive answer. But **John Stuart Mill**, a 19th-century English philosopher, left no doubt about where he stood on this issue. In *Utilitarianism*, he wrote:

> Now, it is an unquestionable fact, that those who are equally acquainted with and equally capable of appreciating and enjoying both [higher and lower pleasures] do give a most marked preference to the manner of existence which employs their higher faculties. Few human creatures would consent to be changed into any of the lower animals, for a promise of the fullest allowance of a beast's pleasures: no intelligent human being would consent to be a fool, no instructed person would be an ignoramus, no person of feeling and conscience would be so selfish and base, even though they should be persuaded that the fool, the dunce, or the rascal is better satisfied with his lot than they are with theirs.... A being of higher faculties requires more to make him happy, is capable probably of more acute suffering, and certainly accessible to it at more points, than one of an inferior type; but, in spite of these liabilities, he can never really wish to sink into what he feels to be a lower grade of existence....

PHILOSOPHY IN ACTION

The Good Brahman

by Voltaire

This story by the French writer Voltaire, one of the best-known literary figures of the 18th century, highlights the debate over whether acquiring knowledge is something that humans desire by nature. Brahmans are members of the highest Hindu caste, or social class, and are eligible to become priests. The story mentions Brahma, whom Hindus believe is the creator god, and Vishnu. Along with Shiva, Brahma and Vishnu form a triad of gods in the Hindu faith.

I met on my travels an old Brahman, a very wise man, full of wit and very learned; moreover he was rich, and consequently even wiser; for, lacking nothing, he had no need to deceive anyone. His family was very well governed by three beautiful wives who schooled themselves to please him; and when he was not entertaining himself with his wives, he was busy philosophizing.

Near his house, which was beautiful, well decorated, and surrounded by charming gardens, lived an old Indian woman, bigoted, imbecilic, and rather poor.

The Brahman said to me one day: "I wish I had never been born."

I asked him why. He replied:

"I have been studying for forty years, which is forty years wasted; I teach others, and I know nothing; this situation brings into my soul so much humiliation and disgust that life is unbearable to me. I was born, I live in time, and I do not know what time is; I find myself in a point between two eternities, as our sages say, and I have no idea of eternity. I am composed of matter; I think, and I have never been able to find out what produces thought; I do not know whether my understanding is a simple faculty in me like that of walking or of digesting, and whether I think with my head, as I take with my hands. Not only is the principle of my thinking unknown to me, but the principle of my movements is equally hidden from me. I do not know why I exist. However, people every day ask me questions on all these points; I have to answer; I have nothing any good to say; I talk much, and I remain confounded and ashamed of myself after talking.

"It is much worse yet when they ask me whether Brahma was produced by Vishnu or whether they are both eternal. God is my witness that I don't know a thing about it, and it certainly shows in my answers. 'Ah! Reverend Father,' they say to me, 'teach us how it is that evil inundates the whole world.' I am as much at a loss as those who ask me that question; I sometimes tell them that all is for the very best, but those who have been ruined and mutilated at war believe nothing of it, and neither do I; I retreat to my house overwhelmed with my curiosity and my ignorance. I read our ancient books, and they redouble the darkness I am in. I talk to my companions: some answer that we must enjoy life and laugh at men; the others think they know something, and lose themselves in absurd ideas; everything increases the painful feeling I endure. I am sometimes ready to fall into despair, when I think that after all my seeking I know neither where I come from, nor what I am, nor where I shall go, nor what shall become of me."

The state of this good man caused me real pain; no one was either more reasonable or more honest than he. I perceived that the greater the lights of his understanding and the sensibility of his heart, the more unhappy he was.

That same day I saw the old woman who lived in his vicinity: I asked her whether she had ever been distressed not to know how her soul was made. She did not even understand my question: she had never reflected a single moment of her life over a single one of the points that tormented the Brahman; she believed with all her heart in the metamorphoses of Vishnu, and, provided she could sometimes have some water from the Ganges to wash in, she thought herself the happiest of women.

Struck by the happiness of this indigent creature, I returned to my philosopher and said to him:

"Aren't you ashamed to be unhappy at a time when right at your door there is an old automaton who thinks of nothing and who lives happily?"

"You are right," he answered; "I have told myself a hundred times that I would be happy if I was as stupid as my neighbour, and yet I would want no part of such a happiness."

This answer of my Brahman made a greater impression on me than all the rest. I examined myself and saw that indeed I would not have wanted to be happy on condition of being imbecilic.

I put the matter up to some philosophers, and they were of my opinion.

"There is, however," I said, "a stupendous contradiction in this way of thinking."

For after all, what is at issue? Being happy. What matters being witty or being stupid? What is more, those who are content with their being are quite sure of being content; those who reason are not so sure of reasoning well.

"So it is clear," I said, "that we should choose not to have common sense, if ever that common sense contributes to our ill-being."

Everyone was of my opinion, and yet I found no one who wanted to accept the bargain of becoming imbecilic in order to become content. From this I concluded that if we set store by happiness, we set even greater store by reason.

But, upon reflection, it appears that to prefer reason to felicity is to be very mad. Then how can this contradiction be explained? Like all the others. There is much to be said about it.

Source: "The Good Brahman." Voltaire.

---

1. What is the central idea of this story and how does it relate to the attainment of knowledge and happiness?
2. The Brahman says that his unhappiness is the result of his unsuccessful search for answers to some of the main questions of philosophy. List four of these questions and explain how studying particular areas of philosophy might help him.
3. In the last paragraph of the story, Voltaire says, "But upon reflection it appears that to prefer reason to felicity is to be mad." Do you agree with this statement? Why?

ARE PEOPLE BY NATURE ALTRUISTS OR EGOISTS?

Think about a time when you were in a position to perform a good deed, like giving an older person a seat on a bus, giving money to someone in need, or volunteering to help with a school activity. What did you decide to do? People regularly encounter situations like these. Some people choose to help; others choose not to. What motivates those who choose to help? Is it **altruism**, which is unselfish concern for other people? Or is it **egoism**, which means acting in ways that promote our own interests? If people are motivated by the need to make themselves feel good, are their actions egoistic, which means selfish and self-interested, or altruistic and unselfish?

The debate over these questions was crystallized by two English philosophers, **Thomas Hobbes** and **Joseph Butler**, who expressed opposing views of human nature.

In 1651, Hobbes published *Leviathan*, a book that sets out a harshly negative interpretation of humanity. He took the title from the Bible, in which a leviathan is a sea monster who "is a king over all the children of pride." In Hobbes' view, the state was an artificial leviathan that must exert absolute power.

In *Leviathan*, Hobbes said that a human being's life "is solitary, poor, nasty, brutish and short." He also described people as aggressive, greedy, competitive, and anti-social, as well as excessively vain. He believed that everyone acts only to satisfy his or her personal desires. Self-interest is a human being's true nature, said Hobbes.

• IDEAS IN CONTEXT •

The negative view of human nature set out by Thomas Hobbes was greatly influenced by the 17th-century European enthusiasm for science. As a result, Hobbes was intent on giving a scientific account of human nature. His account left no place for goodness, altruism, and the traditional beliefs of Socrates, Plato, and Aristotle, who said that people are by nature capable of being wise, good, virtuous, and altruistic. Hobbes said that the views of the ancient Greeks were hopelessly naive and unrealistic. He maintained that human nature is about appetites, desires, and self-interest.

28 MHR INTRODUCTION SETTING THE STAGE

> *"Selfishness is not living as one wishes to live, it is asking others to live as one wishes to live."*
>
> – Ruth Rendell

Closely related to the idea that people are essentially self-interested was Hobbes' belief that humans are basically anti-social. "Men have no pleasure ... in keeping company," he wrote. When people do get together, he said that their motivation is a desire to dominate others. Co-operation among individuals or groups amounts to nothing but self-interest, he said, and acts of kindness or altruism are only ways for people to soothe their consciences. Even a parent's love for a child is a thinly disguised desire for personal power, he maintained.

Seventy-five years after the appearance of *Leviathan*, Joseph Butler published *Fifteen Sermons Preached at Rolls Chapel*. This book was in many ways a direct rebuttal of Hobbes' harsh view of human nature, which had severely undermined traditional beliefs that emphasized virtue and humanity's capacity for goodness. An Anglican cleric, Butler wanted to rehabilitate these beliefs. He believed that the best way to do this was to show that human nature included positive elements.

Figure 2.1

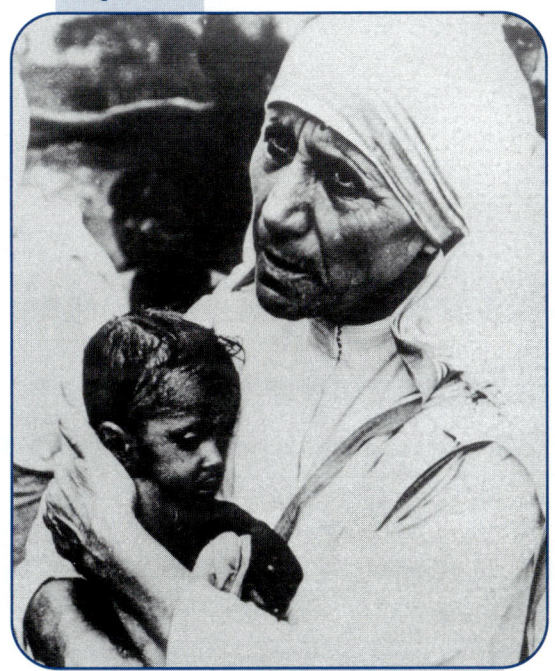

Mother Teresa, a Roman Catholic nun, devoted her life to helping the poor in India. In 1979, her dedication was honoured when she was awarded the Nobel Peace Prize. Was Mother Teresa an altruist or an egoist?

Butler conceded that human nature encompasses a measure of self-interest. It is normal, he argued, for humans to seek their own good. He called this impulse self-love. He also said, however, that human nature includes benevolence, the desire to do something good for someone else. He argued further that self-love and benevolence do not conflict. He believed that human nature consists of various attributes, which are arranged in a hierarchy. At the top of this hierarchy stands conscience, which he said is a distinctively human characteristic. To heed one's conscience is to fully experience one's human nature, said Butler. Conscience is the key to making moral choices — and making moral choices is integral to human nature.

Butler claimed that people do good deeds for no other reason than a desire to do so. Can people take pleasure in doing a good deed without first experiencing a desire to do something good? No, they can't, said Butler, and to claim otherwise is just plain wrong.

In keeping with his theory, Butler insisted that excessive concern about achieving happiness by satisfying personal desires is actually counterproductive because it can lead to unhappiness. To put this theory to the test, ask yourself these questions: Would I want a completely self-interested person for a friend? Would the word "friend" have any real meaning for a completely self-interested person?

Hobbes described human beings as mechanical systems whose actions are determined by whatever desires happen to be strongest at a given moment. Butler countered with this argument:

> A machine is inanimate and passive, but we are agents [people who are capable of thinking about a moral problem, making a decision about how to act, and taking responsibility for this action]. Our constitution is put in our own power. We are charged with it; and therefore are accountable for any disorder or violation of it. Thus nothing can be more contrary to nature than vice [whereas] ... our nature ... is adapted to virtue.

Who was right, Butler or Hobbes? Do you perform good deeds to make yourself feel better, or to make others feel better? Do you accept the contention of many modern psychologists that unconscious selfish motives and desires are often the true source of seemingly altruistic acts? Finally, at our very core, are we the selfish creatures depicted by Hobbes, or are we genuinely altruistic, as Butler contends? These are difficult questions to answer.

> **Web connection**
> www.mcgrawhill.ca/links/philosophy12
> To find out more about the debate over altruism and egoism, follow the links on this Web site.

A fascinating conundrum called the prisoner's dilemma, which is often used by philosophers, provides an excellent opportunity to play a mind game that tests the arguments of Hobbes and Butler. A conundrum is a riddle or puzzling question.

Though the prisoner's dilemma appears in many variations, a common version starts with two prisoners in jail. The police have enough evidence to convict both of crime X. The police also know — but cannot prove — that the two committed crime Z. In an attempt to get proof that the two prisoners committed crime Z, the authorities offer them a deal designed to persuade them to testify against each other. Because the prisoners are being held in isolation and cannot communicate with each other, neither knows how the other will respond to the offer. The following are the possible outcomes of the deal:

- If only one testifies against the other, the one who testifies goes free while the other will be sentenced to five years in prison.
- If both testify against the other, each will be sentenced to three years.
- If neither testifies, both will be convicted only of crime X and sentenced to one year apiece.

Though the prisoners' choices are simple, they present problems. Depending on what the other does, their prison terms could range from zero to five years. The following chart (Figure 2.2) illustrates what could happen.

Figure 2.2

Prisoner's Dilemma Outcomes

	Prisoner 1's Strategies	
Prisoner 2's Strategies	**Testify**	**Do Not Testify**
Testify	P1–3 years P2–3 years	P1–5 years P2–0 years
Do Not Testify	P1–0 years P2–5 years	P1–1 year P2–1 year

What would you do in this situation? According to some observers, human nature dictates that the rational response is to betray the partner and agree to testify. Acting in your own interest means that you would eliminate the risk of serving a five-year sentence — and you might even get off scot-free. This would seem to reinforce Hobbes' negative view of human nature.

Real life is usually more complex, however, than the simple scenario presented in the prisoner's dilemma. If the prisoners were long-time partners, relatives, or casual acquaintances might that make a difference to their decision about testifying?

Since it was developed in the 1950s, the prisoner's dilemma has become more than a mind game. Variations have been created to perform complex analyses of just about everything from problems in anthropology to the probable outcome of war strategies.

Consider, for example, the following everyday scenarios. If a significant number of people cheat on their income taxes, chances are that taxes will go up. If enough people jump the barrier to avoid paying for a subway ride, fares will go up. In these scenarios, the logic of the prisoner's dilemma seems to suggest that placing self-interest ahead of society's interests is ultimately self-defeating.

> **Web connection**
> www.mcgrawhill.ca/links/philosophy12
> To play a variation of the prisoner's dilemma, follow the links on this Web site.

ARE PEOPLE BY NATURE GOOD OR EVIL?

Since the dawn of recorded history, questions about good and evil have preoccupied human beings. What do the terms "good" and "evil" mean? Are human beings fundamentally — or even predominantly — good or evil? Why does evil exist? Why are some people extraordinarily evil while others are models of goodness? Questions like these are also critical to the quest to understand human nature.

Definitions of good and evil are elusive. In the early 20th century, for example, the English philosopher George Edward Moore said that good is a quality beyond definition and maintained that it can be known only by intuition, an experience that is independent of reason.

Despite Moore's claim, philosophers have continued to try to define good and evil. An acceptable working definition might suggest that something is good if it contributes to the happiness and well-being of some or many people without inflicting pain or suffering on anyone. This definition highlights the link between good and evil, showing that they acquire meaning and significance only in relation to each other. Most people would agree, for example, that killing someone for pleasure is monstrously evil and that preventing a murder like this is good. Most people also agree that human beings are able to recognize the difference between good and evil, even if this recognition is intuitive.

A question frequently debated by philosophers is whether some people rationally and consciously choose to do evil. Socrates maintained that the answer is no. Human nature, he said, is such that "to know the good is to do the good." Butler agreed with Socrates, though he also believed that evil results when people violate their nature by carrying out actions that are excessively self-interested.

Other philosophers have disagreed, saying that some people do choose to do evil. As proof, they cite the terrible crimes committed throughout history against both individual people and humanity. This view is sometimes supported by religious arguments. Some Christians, for example, have suggested that humanity has fallen from a state of grace. Their fallen state means that people will choose evil unless religious or legal deterrents compel them to do otherwise or unless they ask God to restore them to a state of grace.

Figure 2.3
Students visit Dachau, site of a World War II Nazi concentration camp. As proof of the existence of evil, some people cite the Holocaust, in which the Nazis killed millions of Jews, people with developmental disabilities, homosexuals, and other people they considered undesirable. Would you agree that this event is evidence of evil? Why?

Whether evil actually exists has also generated a great deal of philosophical debate. One theory suggests that evil is an illusion that does not exist, though this idea has garnered little support. In his book *Dark Nature*, Lyall Watson, a biologist, wrote: "Evil exists and seems to me to have sufficient substance to give it credence as a force in nature … It is part of the ecology and needs to be seen as such … [It] has been here for a very long time, casting its shadow on almost everything we do."

Some societies see evil as a necessary and inevitable complement to good. A complement is something that completes something else. This idea may be best exemplified in the Chinese philosophical concept of yin and yang, which represent negative and positive attributes found in nature and in human beings. Chinese philosophy includes clearly articulated views about the roles of good and evil in human nature. The fourth-century BCE philosopher **Mengzi**, known in the West as Mencius, and the third-century BCE philosopher **Xun-Zi**, known also as Hsün Tzu, were Confucians, followers of Kongfuzi, who is called Confucius in the West. Each proposed a radically different view of human nature.

> *"No man chooses evil because it is evil; he only mistakes it for happiness, the good he seeks."*
> – Mary Wollstonecraft

Mengzi wrote: "Man's nature is naturally good, just as water naturally flows downward. There is no man without this good nature…." To support this claim, Mengzi said that human beings have an innate sense of right and wrong, a natural sympathetic reaction to people in distress or pain, and a natural sense of propriety. In other words, Mengzi believed that the urge to conform to *li*, a word that refers to ritual principles or people's obligations based on their social position, is built into human nature.

Mengzi also believed that evil exists because some people do not cultivate their innate goodness through proper education. He said that when goodness is not nourished, it decays, like anything else that does not receive care and attention. Mengzi would have endorsed the contemporary axiom, Use it or lose it. He made this clear when he wrote:

Figure 2.4

In China, Kongfuzi is often called the first sage, or wise person. Mengzi, pictured here, is known as the second sage.

> If you let people follow their feelings (original nature), they will be able to do good. This is what is meant by saying that human nature is good. If man does evil, it is not the fault of his natural endowment. The feeling of commiseration is found in all men; the feeling of shame and dislike is found in all men; the feeling of respect and reverence is found in all men; and the feeling of right and wrong is found in all men. The feeling of commiseration is what we call humanity; the feeling of shame and dislike is what we called righteousness; the feeling of respect and reverence is what we called propriety (li); and the feeling of right and wrong is what we called wisdom. Humanity, righteousness, propriety and wisdom are not drilled into us from outside. We originally have them with us.

Is this a naive interpretation of human nature? Contemporary critics of Mengzi's theory might argue that education has had 2000 years to work its power on humanity but seems to have failed miserably. Through war and criminal acts, human beings continue to inflict enormous pain and suffering on one another. This casts an enormous shadow of doubt on Mengzi's rosy picture of human nature.

Though Xun-Zi agreed that education is important, his reasons for believing this were different. People are "born with feelings of envy and hate," he wrote. He said that the true purpose of education is to control this dark side of human nature. Xun-Zi argued that Mengzi erred when he failed to distinguish between basic human nature, "which is given by heaven," and conscious activity, which is learned. *Li* is not a product of human nature, he said; rather, it is created by the conscious activity of sages, or wise men, who have learned to control their evil natures. For Xun-Zi, the only difference between sages and criminals was that sages engage in conscious activity. Today, this conscious activity might be called an act of will.

Xun-Zi denied the possibility that a desire to do good can motivate people. "Every man who desires to do good does so precisely because his nature is evil," he wrote. He explained his reasons for arriving at this pessimistic conclusion by saying:

> A man whose accomplishments are meagre longs for greatness; … a poor man longs for wealth; a humble man longs for eminence. Whatever a man lacks in himself he will seek outside. But if a man is already rich, he will not long for wealth, and if he is already eminent, he will not long for greater power. What a man already possesses in himself he will not bother to look for outside. From this we can see that men desire to do good precisely because their nature is evil.

Xun-Zi's argument is based on the idea that those who lack something — wealth, beauty, power, and so on — desire what they do not possess. This sparks jealousy and envy, which lead to evil deeds. Though this argument may apply to some people, does it apply to everyone? Is it possible that some people might prefer to live modestly, trying to achieve happiness rather than wealth and power? And are there not people who, having acquired what they desire, remain unsatisfied and always desire more?

Both Xun-Zi and Hobbes paint a pessimistic, negative picture of human nature, while Mengzi and Butler present an optimistic, positive vision. The argument over whether people are, by nature, good or evil has never been resolved and remains the subject of philosophical debate today.

Recall...Reflect...Respond

1. Create a list of the characteristics of non-human animals and another of the characteristics of humans. Refer to these lists as you write a short, reflective response to this question: Should human and non-human animals have the same rights in society?
2. List three philosophical decisions you have made over the past year. Explain how your view of human nature affected each decision.
3. People are, by nature, honest. Explain whether you agree or disagree with this statement. Use the theories of Thomas Hobbes, Joseph Butler, Mengzi, or Xun-Zi to support your position.

ESSENTIALIST VIEWS OF HUMAN NATURE

The philosophies of Hobbes, Butler, Mengzi, and Xun-Zi focused on the role of desire in motivating people to do either good or evil. Other philosophers have taken a different stand. Sometimes called **essentialists**, they have suggested that reason is the distinguishing feature of human beings. In their view, the conscious ability to think and reason is the essential characteristic of human beings.

Plato was probably the first western thinker to articulate a comprehensive view of human nature. An essentialist, he believed that the ability to reason is the highest and most important distinguishing feature of human beings. This theory was in keeping with his rationalist view, which said that reason, not the senses, provides true knowledge. The following dialogue between Socrates and Glaucon, which appears in *The Republic*, illustrates Plato's belief. Socrates and Glaucon are trying to answer the question, What is the self?

Socrates: Isn't it sometimes true that the thirsty person [who wants to drink] also, for some reason, may want not to drink?

Glaucon: Yes, often.

Socrates: What can we say, then, if not that in his soul there is a part that desires drink and another part that restrains him? This latter part is distinct from desire and usually can control desire.

Glaucon: I agree.

Socrates: And isn't it true in such cases that such control originates in reason while the urge to drink originates in something else?

Glaucon: So it seems.

Socrates: Then we can conclude that there are in us two distinct parts. One is what we call "reason," and the other we call the non-rational "appetites." The latter hungers, thirsts, desires sex, and is subject to other desires.

Glaucon: Yes, that is the logical conclusion.

Socrates: But what about our emotional or spirited element: the part in us that feels anger and indignation?... Anger sometimes opposes our appetites as if it is something distinct from them.... Yet this emotional part of ourselves is [also] distinct from reason.

This dialogue sets out what has become known as Plato's **tripartite (three-part) theory of the soul**. To Plato, the soul was the personality, psyche, mind, or inner self. He believed that the three elements of the soul are

- reason, the highest and most important element
- spirit, which is expressed as emotional states or attributes such as pride, vanity, aggressiveness, and courage
- appetite, the lowest element, which is expressed as desires or needs

> *"False words are not only evil in themselves, but they infect the soul with evil."*
>
> – Plato

Plato said that all three elements are present in everyone and that the kind of person someone is depends on which element dominates. Someone dominated by reason seeks knowledge, truth, and wisdom. A person dominated by spirit might seek power and success, while someone dominated by appetite might seek possessions and wealth.

Plato recognized the potential for these elements to conflict within the soul or self. He believed that reason is the most important element because it enables people to maintain harmony among the elements. Only reason, he said, can show people the best way to live and how to develop properly the elements of

34 MHR INTRODUCTION SETTING THE STAGE

our nature that make us unique. Suppose that you are very thirsty and a frosty glass of water has been placed in front of you. If you suspect that the water is contaminated, you will probably decide not to drink. Reason will prevail over appetite. Or suppose you receive a much lower-than-expected mark on an assignment. You feel frustrated but refrain from expressing this to your teacher because it would be bound to be counterproductive. In this case, reason will prevail over spirit.

Plato's ideas had an enormous impact on subsequent thinkers. Whether philosophers agreed or disagreed with him, his views of human nature set the standard over which people argued for the next 2400 years. Plato's student Aristotle, for example, challenged several of his teacher's basic ideas, yet agreed whole-heartedly that the ability to reason is humanity's supreme, distinctive attribute.

Many Jewish and Christian religious thinkers fall squarely within the essentialist tradition. The fourth-century Christian philosopher Augustine of Hippo, for example, acknowledged the importance of reason, though he believed that the ability to love and serve God took precedence. He said that loving and serving God is humankind's ultimate purpose. Because reason is not a prerequisite for trying to achieve this purpose, everyone can participate in the quest, he said.

The belief that human beings are essentially rational, as Plato suggested, remains strong in western society. Early in the 20th century, for example, Sigmund Freud, who is often called the father of psychology, set out a tripartite theory of personality. He said the human personality consists of the id, the ego, and the superego. The id governs the sexual and aggressive elements of the personality, as well as the instinct for self-preservation; the superego governs the conscience, which puts the brakes on the id; and the ego represents intelligence and perception.

According to some commentators, this was simply Plato's tripartite theory of the soul with a facelift. Others said that Freud's theory was more complex than Plato's and also featured some significant differences. Freud played down the importance of reason, for example. In *From Socrates to Sartre*, philosopher T. Z. Lavine explained how.

> The element of reason which Freud incorporates in the ego is demoted from providing knowledge of the eternal forms to mere scientific understanding without knowledge of the forms. The element of reason which Freud incorporated in the superego is demoted from providing knowledge of the moral forms and the Ideas of the Good to the mere rationalizing of psychological instincts and defence mechanisms.

Whether Freud's ideas were a theoretical refinement of Plato's theories or nothing more than a cosmetic overhaul remains open to debate. What is certain, however, is that Plato's ideas have left their mark on modern theories of human nature, a remarkable accomplishment for someone who lived more than two millennia ago.

ESSENCE AND EXISTENCE

In Plato's view, reasoning takes place in the soul. He was convinced that the soul is distinct from the body, that it existed before birth, and that it continues to exist after the body perishes. This belief raised an important philosophical question: What is the relationship between **essence** and existence?

This relationship is pivotal in discussions of human nature. In a philosophical sense, essence refers to the thing or things that make up the permanent and universal nature of a being or entity. A being's essence is shared by all members of the species. Plato's belief that the human soul existed before birth meant that he also believed that essence precedes existence; in other words,

• IDEAS IN CONTEXT •

Some people believe that science may some day shed light on the meaning of death. Modern medical techniques have meant that some people, after being pronounced dead, have recovered — and reported near-death experiences. These people's stories are often strikingly similar. Many recall seeing a warm, bright light, a vortex-like tunnel, and loved ones who have already died. They also report that they felt engulfed by an indescribable love and, finally, that they experienced varying degrees of annoyance when brought back to life. Many are transformed by the experience, becoming more spiritually inclined and losing their fear of death.

human beings enter the world already endowed with essential, defining characteristics. This view, which was endorsed by Aristotle, was not questioned until the 19th and 20th centuries.

LIFE AFTER DEATH

Plato's beliefs about essence and existence led him to suggest that philosophers should view earthly life as a preparation for the eternal life that will follow. But is there life after death? This is one of the oldest philosophical questions, and for many, it remains the central question of human existence.

Many philosophers have argued that human beings are the only animals who are aware of death. Still more have suggested that only the human species thinks about death. Though not everyone agrees with these contentions, few dispute the notion that humans are the only species that hopes for or believes in existence beyond death. Is this hope or belief one of the defining characteristics of humans? Like the answers to most questions about human nature, the answer to this question continues to generate controversy.

Recall...Reflect...Respond

1. Copy a larger version of the Venn diagram shown here on to a sheet of paper. In each of the outside bubbles, note the attribute(s) each philosopher considered fundamental to human nature. In the central bubble, note the attribute(s) common to all four theories. Do you agree that this is a fundamental attribute — or attributes — of human nature? Why?

Fundamental Attributes of Human Nature

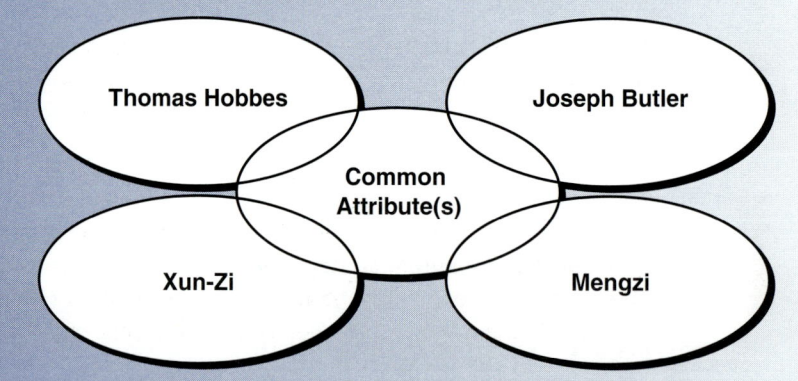

- Thomas Hobbes
- Joseph Butler
- Common Attribute(s)
- Xun-Zi
- Mengzi

2. Create a three-column chart. At the top of each column, identify one of the three elements of Plato's tripartite theory of the soul. Think about a personal decision in which these three elements played a role. In the appropriate column, describe the role played by each element in the decision-making process.
3. Think again about the decision that you selected in response to Question 2. Did reason play a dominant role in your decision? If not, do you think that your decision would have been more effective if it had? Why?

CHALLENGES TO ESSENTIALIST VIEWS OF HUMAN NATURE

Most challenges to traditional essentialist views of human nature crystallized during the 20th century, though their roots can be traced to the 19th century and earlier. Some of the challengers tried to dismantle the entire essentialist edifice; others questioned only specific beliefs.

THE BUDDHIST CHALLENGE

Though Buddhist ideas developed outside the western tradition, Buddhism may represent the most radical challenge to essentialist ideas of human nature, at least from the perspective of western philosophical thought. Founded by Siddhartha Gautama, who was born in India and lived from 563 to 483 BCE, Buddhism maintains that the notion of self is an illusion. The self does not exist. If the self does not exist, arguing about the nature of the self is pointless, an idea that runs contrary to contemporary western notions of personal identity and the importance of individuality.

The doctrine of impermanence, which is the belief that all things, including human beings, are constantly changing and moving, is also central to Buddhist teachings. If human beings are constantly changing, no identifiable characteristic can endure over time. Buddhists maintain that clinging to the illusion of self causes only pain and suffering. People suffer because they are searching for something that does not exist. The futility of their search leads to insecurity and anxiety. Buddhists believe that the very notion of self creates destructive thoughts that promote egoism, selfish desire, and negative feelings toward others.

In the Buddhist view, even the idea of happiness is permeated with anxiety. When they are happy, most people ask themselves questions like, Will this happiness last? How long will it last? How can I hold on to it? This anxiety makes lasting happiness impossible.

Is it fundamental to human nature to worry constantly about happiness? Is lasting peace and joy impossible to achieve? Do you agree that the idea of self is the source of all human suffering? Though founded in Asia, Buddhism has become increasingly influential in the West, where many embraced its ideas in the last half of the 20th century.

Web connection
www.mcgrawhill.ca/links/philosophy12
To find out more about Buddhist ideas of human nature, follow the links on this Web site.

THE SCIENTIFIC CHALLENGE

Science has certainly created a better world and contributed enormously to people's knowledge of the universe and human beings. When it comes to human nature, however, the world of science is as beset by controversy as the world of philosophy.

Some scientists and social scientists have tried to challenge essentialism by reducing human nature to the basic elements of matter and mechanical processes. This approach is not new. Hobbes was one of the earliest advocates of the idea that humans are much like machines.

Though some of today's scientists offer more complex explanations than Hobbes, their conclusions are often similar to his. They analyze human beings, then present them as a sophisticated piece of biochemical and biomechanical machinery. Thinking and reasoning are considered to be nothing more than the result of electro-chemical actions in the brain.

This materialistic view of human nature denies that thinking and reasoning are proof of a mind at work. It says, as philosopher Gilbert Ryle maintained, that there is no "ghost in the machine."

If these scientists are correct, it means that people are little different from non-human animals. We are just somewhat higher up the evolutionary chain, perhaps because we are more adept at using our brains.

In *Dark Nature: A Natural History of Evil*, contemporary biologist Lyall Watson wrote that the answer to questions about human nature is simple: it is dark and it is evil.

> It would be foolish to ignore the possibility that evil is not peculiar to human nature. There seems to be a lot of it about right now, and maybe it is not confined to our particular ecology at all. It could even be universal. And if it is, then it becomes necessary to see evil as a force of nature, as a biological reality.... I believe it will help to know that evil is commonplace and widespread, perhaps not even confined to our species.... The sad fact is that we are born selfish. So, of course, are all other living things.

In support of his argument, Watson pointed out that other species, such as chimpanzees, are capable of elaborate deceptions and intrigue, as well as planned acts of physical violence that would be called murder in human society. But does proof that chimpanzees are capable of aggressive, brutish behaviour support the theory that humans are essentially evil and selfish?

Some scientists say no, as does American science reporter Natalie Angier. After the September 11, 2001, terrorist attack on the United States, Angier's *New York Times* column explained the reason for the tens of thousands of acts of generosity that took place after the tragedy.

Figure 2.5

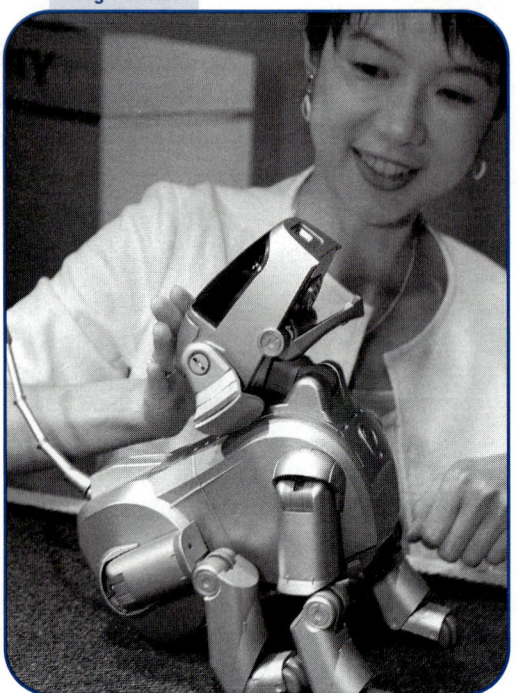

This dog robot, created in Japan, is said to contain sensors and programs that enable it to move and behave just like a living dog. Do you think that a robot can ever be the same as a living creature?

> Altruism and heroism. If not for these radiant badges of our humanity, there would be no us, and we know it.... And while biologists in no way claim to have discovered the key to human nobility, they do have their own spin on the subject. The altruistic impulse, they say, is a non-denominational gift, the birthright and defining characteristic of the human species.

Though Angier's sweeping generalization about biologists may not be entirely accurate, many biologists do support the notion mentioned in her column. Angier also wrote that most biologists concur with anthropologist Barbara Smuts, who has concluded that biologists are beginning to recognize that the best way to compete is often to co-operate. This conclusion echoes the lessons about co-operation outlined in the prisoner's dilemma.

Finally, Angier cited several sources that challenge Watson's dark vision of animal nature. One of these is primatologist Richard Wrangham, who has studied red colobus monkeys. Wrangham found that when set upon by chimpanzees, which are much bigger and stronger, the male monkeys confront their attackers. Though the monkeys often die in the ensuing struggle, their tactic enables mothers and offspring to escape.

Web connection
www.mcgrawhill.ca/links/philosophy12
To find out more about Richard Wrangham's reserach, follow the links on this Web site.

Is the monkeys' action a genetic imperative at work or a sign of altruism in nature? The answer is open to debate. Still, Angier said that some biologists are beginning to think that co-operation and generosity may be the motive.

Just as biologists disagree about human nature, so do psychologists. Freud, for example, argued that human beings have innate drives focused on sex and aggression. He said that relief can be achieved only by the selfish satisfaction of desires.

The 20th-century American psychologist Carl Rogers presented a more optimistic view. Rogers argued that the impulse to goodness is basic to human nature. He said that people are growth-oriented and progressive when conditions are favourable. They become aggressive and harmful only when alienated from their basic nature.

Rogers himself acknowledged that this theory seems to express conflicting views of human nature: people choose the good when free to do so but may also find themselves in the grip of alienating forces that control their behaviour.

B.F. Skinner, another 20th-century American psychologist, took a neutral view of human nature. Skinner believed that people's behaviour is completely controlled by their environment, a theory that is called **behaviourism**. As a result, behaviourists like Skinner limit their study of human behaviour to what can be observed and make no judgments about whether behaviour is good or bad.

Behaviourists' methods ignore people's states of mind or consciousness, as well as their motives. As a result, behaviourists attribute no actions to human nature. Instead, they view humans as organic machines, which are programmed by their environment to act in certain ways. This means that humans are not free.

Though scientists and social scientists have reached no agreement about human nature, their investigations have refocused the philosophical debate over the issue. In addition to asking, What is human nature? philosophers now also ask, Is there such a thing as human nature?

Figure 2.6

Rescue workers search the rubble of New York's World Trade Center. The selfless efforts of these workers and others in the days and weeks after the terrorist attacks of September 11, 2001, have been cited as proof that people are, by nature, altruistic. Do you agree? Why?

THE FEMINIST CHALLENGE

Feminist philosophers have argued, with considerable justification, that sexist assumptions pervade traditional western philosophy. In particular, they have questioned the essentialists' emphasis on reason as the defining characteristic of human nature.

Plato maintained that reason must take precedence over desires and emotions. In his view, however, men and women are equal in their ability to reason and were equally capable of becoming leaders of society. Aristotle did not agree with his teacher. In his view, men's superior reasoning ability meant that they should naturally rule over women.

Aristotle's views on the reasoning ability of men and women became entrenched in western thought. Many influential philosophers, such as Augustine of Hippo, Immmanuel Kant, and Georg W.F. Hegel, accepted this belief and argued that women are inferior to men.

In addition to challenging traditional western ideas about the abilities of women, many feminist philosophers have also challenged the essentialist

Women are capable of education, but they are not made for activities which demand a universal faculty such as the more advanced sciences, philosophy and certain forms of artistic production....

— G.W.F. Hegel

assumption that reason, which is traditionally associated with men, is superior to emotions. In the feminist view, this assumption symbolizes more than two millennia of subjugation and injustice.

Does the feminist challenge to essentialism warrant a serious rethinking of traditional notions about reason and emotion? There may be no easy answer to this question. Still, it is an important question that must be addressed — and this is just what contemporary philosophers are doing.

Web connection
www.mcgrawhill.ca/links/philosophy12
To find out more about the feminist challenge to essentialism, follow the links on this Web site.

THE EXISTENTIALIST CHALLENGE

Rooted in the 19th century, existentialism is a philosophical movement that became prominent in the 20th century and remains an important force at the beginning of the 21st.

Existentialists concern themselves with human existence: the problems humans face and the place of humans in the universe. The roots of existentialism are found in the thought of the 19th-century Danish philosopher Søren Kierkegaard, though it is most closely associated with a school that emerged in the mid-20th century. Consisting of several branches, including Christian and atheistic existentialism, the movement has generated a broad range of views.

The issues of despair, depression, anxiety, meaninglessness, and nothingness recur in existentialist writing. Kierkegaard's works are filled with anxiety and despair. He wrote, for example: "I stick my finger into existence — it smells of nothing. Where am I? What is this thing called the world? Who is it who has lured me into the thing, and now leaves me here? Who am I? How did I come into the world? Why was I not consulted?"

In Kierkegaard's world, happiness and self-fulfillment are out of the question. Life simply is not conducive to pleasure and happiness. Resisting existential *angst*, a German word for anxiety, is futile. *Angst* is a permanent, universal feature of modern humanity.

Kierkegaard rejected traditional values and social conventions. He was even skeptical of the meaningfulness of truth and reason, the foundation of classical rationalism. His ideas stood in direct opposition to the essentialist belief that rationality is the distinguishing attribute of humanity. Because of Kierkegaard's bleak vision, existentialists are often described as pessimistic and gloomy.

> "Man will do nothing unless he has first understood that he must count on no one but himself; that he is alone, abandoned on earth in the midst of his infinite responsibilities; without help, with no other aim than the one he sets himself, with no other destiny than the one he forges for himself on this earth."
>
> — Jean-Paul Sartre

The French philosopher Jean-Paul Sartre, an influential 20th-century existentialist, did not agree that existentialism emphasized the darker side of human life. He suggested that those who accused the movement of being too gloomy were frightened by existentialism's emphasis on freedom and choice.

Like Simone de Beauvoir, Albert Camus, and many other existentialists, Sartre was an atheist, someone who does not believe in a supreme being. As a result, his views directly contradicted those of Plato and the many philosophers who followed in the footsteps of this ancient Greek.

Sartre's view of human nature can be summed up in this three-word sentence: Existence precedes essence. In *Existentialism and Human Emotions*, he explained what this sentence meant.

It means that, first of all, man exists, turns up, appears on the scene, and, only afterwards, defines himself. If man, as the existentialist conceives him, is indefinable,

PROFILE

Simone de Beauvoir
Pure Transparent Freedom

Like Jean-Paul Sartre, her life-long friend and lover, the French philosopher and novelist Simone de Beauvoir tried to remain true to her existentialist beliefs, both in her writing and in her life.

Born into a middle-class Parisian family in 1908, de Beauvoir rebelled early against the restrictions imposed by her strictly Roman Catholic mother. In secondary school she renounced her religion and became an atheist. While studying philosophy at the Sorbonne, the famous Paris university, she met Sartre, and the two embarked on a relationship that sometimes scandalized society.

After graduating from the Sorbonne, de Beauvoir taught philosophy. The experience of supporting herself taught her to value independence, and she swore never to marry. Still, she and Sartre vowed to stay united by remaining honest and open about everything. They also promised each other that they would remain free to love other people.

The theme of freedom, which is the foundation of existentialist thought, pervades de Beauvoir's novels. In *Le Sang des autres* (*The Blood of Others*), for example, she wrote: "I wish that every human life might be pure transparent freedom." Many of her other novels focus on life-altering decisions made by women who wish to control their own destinies. These novels, which were often based on her own experiences, examine, from an existentialist perspective, the choices she herself made between love and work. She chose to become an intellectual and a writer and to live an unconventional life, adhering to her own ideas of honesty and freedom.

When World War II ended in 1945, de Beauvoir and Sartre founded and co-edited *Les Temps modernes*, a monthly review of philosophical views, essays, and poetry. The name of the magazine, which means modern times in English, was borrowed from a Charlie Chaplin movie that was popular at the time.

Many consider de Beauvoir to be a pioneer of contemporary feminism and credit her with inspiring the establishment of the academic discipline that is often called gender studies. In the introduction to her book *The Second Sex*, she wrote: "'I am a woman'; on this truth must be based all further discussion." These words formed the guiding principle of her life, her work, and her philosophical perspective.

In *The Second Sex*, de Beauvoir argued against traditional western views of women as second-class citizens and maintained that men and women are equals. And though she has been labelled an existentialist, she herself tried to steer clear of labelling. She considered herself an independent thinker dedicated to the well-being of others.

While writing and speaking in the United States in 1947, de Beauvoir met and fell in love with the writer Nelson Algren. This event began an unusual relationship among de Beauvoir, Sartre, and Algren. She truly loved Algren but wanted to remain true to her vow to herself and Sartre. She rejected Algren's marriage proposal and continued to live in France, where she could be near Sartre. Because of this, Algren ended the relationship.

Even at Sartre's death, de Beauvoir remained true to her existentialist beliefs. When he died in 1980, she refused to take comfort in the idea that they might be united in an afterlife. "My death will not bring us together again," she said. "This is how things are. It is in itself splendid that we were able to live our lives in harmony for so long." De Beauvoir herself died in 1986.

Figure 2.7

Pictured here in 1940, Simone de Beauvoir once described Jean-Paul Sartre as "the double in whom I found all my burning aspiration raised to the pitch of incandescence."

it is because at first he is nothing. Only afterward will he be something, and he himself will have made what he will be. Thus, there is no human nature, since there is no God to conceive it. Not only is man what he conceives himself to be, but he is also only what he wills himself to be after this thrust toward existence.

Sartre also wrote: "Man is nothing else but what he makes of himself. Such is the first principle of existentialism." In Sartre's view, people create their selves every moment of every day according to the choices they make. People's existence precedes their essence. By contrast, the essence of things that lack consciousness, such as desks, tables, insects and paper cutters, is determined before they come into existence.

If human beings are what they make themselves, said Sartre, it follows that they are free to make choices and that they — and they alone — are responsible for their choices. Making choices is inevitable. Even someone who decides not to choose between two alternatives is still making a choice: choosing not to choose.

Web connection
www.mcgrawhill.ca/links/philosophy12
To find out more about existentialism, follow the links on this Web site.

Sartre also maintained that if existence precedes essence, people cannot use human nature to excuse evil deeds and poor choices. In his view, there is no human nature. People are free and alone — alone because God does not exist. As a result, people have no one to blame but themselves. In this respect, Sartre concluded, every person is "condemned to be free."

Recall...Reflect...Respond

1. Create a three-column table titled "Challenges to Essentialism." In the first column, list the challenges that maintain that human nature is essentially good. In the second, list the challenges that maintain that it is essentially evil, and in the last, list the challenges that maintain that it is neutral.

Challenges to Essentialism		
Essentially Good	Essentially Evil	Neutral

2. Which aspects of existentialism might you consider integrating into your own personal views about human nature? Why? Which would you not consider? Why?

3. In *Star Trek: The Next Generation*, one of the characters is a complex robot named Data. Data wants to become more human and is, at times, required to defend his existence by proving his humanness. Explain to Data how he might do this using each of the challenges to essentialism.

THE FUTURE OF THE HUMAN NATURE DEBATE

With an equally deep sense of conviction and certainty, some thinkers have declared human nature to be essentially good and altruistic; others have judged it to be predominantly evil and selfish. Still others have denied the very idea of human nature, arguing that people are free to create themselves.

Disagreements about the nature of human beings cut across disciplines and occur within disciplines. Philosophers disagree among themselves about human nature, as do scientists and social scientists. On occasion, some philosophers agree with the ideas of some scientists and social scientists about human nature. On other occasions, they disagree.

The bewildering variety of views of human nature has led some philosophers to question whether it is wise to even attempt to construct a meaningful theory of what it means to be human. Francisco Miró Quesada, a contemporary Peruvian philosopher, for example, argued that no single theory can encompass the complexity of human reality.

Miró Quesada said that attempts to come up with theories explaining human behaviour, which is inherently unpredictable, have led to bizarre consequences. He pointed out that some theories have been used to justify murder, torture, and other actions that are morally wrong.

Despite Miró Quesada's call for an end to theorizing, thinkers continue to speculate about human nature. In *The Brighter Side of Human Nature*, for example, writer Alfie Kohn pointed to one of the enigmas of human nature.

He wrote:

> Think, for example, of the expression, "I'm only human." The emphasis is on the middle word: it is what we fail to do or be that seems to us most noteworthy. The phrase "human nature," meanwhile, is reserved ... for what is nasty and negative in our repertoire. We invoke it to explain selfishness rather than service, competition rather than co-operation, egocentricity rather than empathy. On any given day we may witness innumerable gestures of caring, ranging from small acts of kindness to enormous sacrifices, but never do we shrug and say, "Well, what did you expect? It's just human nature to be generous."

Kohn's point is that our understanding of the world around us — what we say, think, and do — is inevitably linked to our ideas about what human beings are like. The urge to live a meaningful life appears to be linked to a basic human need to ask questions like, What is a human being? and What am I?

In the final analysis, the impulse to figure out what human beings are about may just be ... human nature.

> *"No human being can really understand another, and no one can arrange another's happiness."*
> – Graham Greene

Chapter Review

Chapter Summary

This chapter has discussed
- the main questions, concepts, and theories of human nature
- the responses to some of the main questions about human nature defended by some major philosophers and schools of philosophy
- the relevance of philosophical theories of human nature to everyday life and to the study of other areas of philosophy
- how theories of human nature are presupposed in other disciplines

Knowledge and Understanding

1. Identify and explain the significance to the study of philosophy of the following philosophers and epistemological concepts:

Key Words	Key People
human nature	Voltaire
altruism	John Stuart Mill
egoism	Thomas Hobbes
li	Joseph Butler
essentialists	Mengzi (Mencius)
tripartite theory of the soul	Xun-Zi (Hsün-tzu)
essence	Jean-Paul Sartre
Buddhist	Simone de Beauvoir
doctrine of impermanence	
behaviourism	
existentialism	

2. List three key philosophical questions relating to human nature. Then list three more questions that arise from each.

Thinking and Inquiry

3. John Stuart Mill wrote: "It is better to be a human being dissatisfied, than a pig satisfied, better to be Socrates dissatisfied, than a fool satisfied. And if the fool or pig are of a different opinion, it is because they only know their own side of the question. The other party to the comparison knows both sides."

   Write a brief description of your beliefs about human nature. Use Mill's statement to support your position or address it as a counter-argument to your position.

4. Theories of human nature often provide the foundation for social and political structures. How might Thomas Hobbes and Joseph Butler have responded to each of the following questions? Write a description of a social or political structure that might be the result of each response.

   a) Do people have a right to equal treatment in society?
   b) Should individual citizens be free to do what they want?
   c) What rights and responsibilities should individual citizens possess?
   d) What are the just limits of state authority?

Communication

5. You are surveying public opinion to find out whether people's reactions to the feminist challenge to essentialism warrants a rethinking of traditional western views of reason and emotion. Write six philosophical questions related to this issue and use these questions in your survey. Conduct your survey on six people: three females and three males. Summarize your findings in a report.

6. Create a mind map to illustrate theories that challenge essentialist views of human nature. Place essentialism and its definition at the centre. Surround this with the names — and descriptions — of theories that challenge essentialism. Draw a line between essentialism and each of these theories. On each line, note how the theory challenges the essentialist view. From each theory, draw a line outward. On this line, note the key philosophical questions answered by the theory and identify the area of philosophy addressed by each question. Your finished visual will summarize the theories challenging essentialism and show how ideas about human nature are embedded in many areas of philosophy.

Application

7. Examine this cartoon. What aspect of human nature is Calvin focusing on? Which theory of human nature does his philosophizing reflect? How does Calvin feel about his conclusion? If Calvin were an essentialist, how might his view be reflected differently?

Figure 2.8

CALVIN AND HOBBES © Watterson. Reprinted with permission of UNIVERSAL PRESS SYNDICATE. All rights reserved.

8. Imagine that scientists have brought Plato back to life. You have been granted permission to conduct the first interview with this ancient philosopher. Prepare five questions that you would like to ask him and makes notes of the answers that he would be likely to give. Then imagine that you have been asked to describe the experience of interviewing Plato on a TV talk show. With a partner playing the show's host, create a role-play of this interview.

Participate in a philosophical discussion at a philosophy café.
CULMINATING ACTIVITY

EXPECTATIONS

By completing this activity, you will
- correctly use some of the terminology of philosophy
- identify the main areas of philosophy
- demonstrate an understanding of the main questions, concepts, and theories of various areas of philosophy
- demonstrate an understanding of the character of philosophical questions
- effectively communicate the results of your philosophical inquiries
- use critical-thinking skills to defend your own ideas about a particular philosophical issue and to anticipate counter-arguments to your ideas

THE TASK

In 18th-century Europe, during a period called the Enlightenment, men and women gathered in cafés and salons to discuss philosophical issues. This phenomenon has reappeared at the beginning of the 21st century. Once again, people are gathering, sometimes in cafés, to discuss philosophical issues.

You and your classmates will create a philosophical café in your classroom. Groups of five or six will design a table display to which each group member will contribute an item selected to generate philosophical discussion of a theme chosen by the group. The focus of this discussion must be an important philosophical theme that reflects one of the six areas of philosophy introduced in this unit. By participating in this activity, you will demonstrate your ability to philosophize.

As this café will be open to a variety of guests, who may include members of the community, you may wish to plan to provide refreshments appropriate to the group's theme.

THE SUBTASKS

Subtask 1: Select Theme and Describe Contribution
As a group, select a theme relevant to one area of philosophy. Each group member must contribute an item that represents the theme. The items, which will displayed on a table, may include paintings or prints, music, poetry or literature, sculptures, food, puzzles, games, film clips, quotations from the works of philosophers, or other symbols and visuals. Before presenting your contribution at the café, submit a 250- to 500-word description of the item you selected. In your description, explain your contribution's relevance to the group's theme.

Subtask 2: Create Second-Order Questions
Each group member must create two second-order questions relating to the theme and eight specific questions about his or her contribution. Of these specific questions, two must be first-order and six must be second-order questions.

Subtask 3: Host the Philosophy Café
To ensure that the café is successful, assign responsibility for the following tasks to group members.

Organization: Plan all facets of the café and prepare individual evaluation forms that each group member can use to assess her or his participation in the café. Use the assessment criteria as a guide in preparing this form. Ensure that at least 10 guests complete evaluation forms.
Table layout: Plan the table display to highlight the group's theme. Display second-order questions with each item in the display. Aim to create a comfortable, inviting atmosphere that will encourage philosophical discussion.
Refreshments: If appropriate, provide and serve refreshments consistent with the group's theme. Plan how to serve the refreshments to encourage philosophical discussion.
Discussion co-ordination: Maintain the focus of the philosophical discussion on the group's theme and ensure that guests engage in philosophical discourse.

Subtask 4: Personal Reflection
After the presentation, write a 250-word reflection commenting on your personal successes, as well as on areas that needed improvement and what you and your group might have done differently.

ASSESSMENT CRITERIA

The following criteria will be used to assess your participation in a philosophical discussion at the philosophy café.

Knowledge and Understanding
Does your presentation

- contribute an item consistent with the group's theme and explain how the item relates to the theme?
- demonstrate your understanding of the character of philosophical questions by including first- and second-order questions that relate to the theme and your item?

Thinking and Inquiry
Does your presentation

- defend philosophical ideas about the group's theme and respond to the counter-arguments of others?
- include a personal reflection on the strengths and weaknesses of your own participation?

Communication
Does your presentation

- explain your views in philosophical discussions?
- use philosophical terms in a way that is understandable to café guests?
- include the preparation and distribution of an evaluation form that is consistent with the assessment criteria?

Application
Does your presentation

- include an item that will generate philosophical discussions?
- engage guests in philosophical discourse?

UNIT 1
LOGIC AND THE PHILOSOPHY OF SCIENCE

CHAPTER

3 Introducing Logic

4 Applying Logic

5 Introducing the Philosophy of Science

Unit Expectations

By the end of this unit, you will be able to
- identify the main questions in formal and informal logic and in the philosophy of science
- apply logical- and critical-thinking skills in practical contexts and detect logical fallacies
- demonstrate an understanding of how philosophical questions apply to disciplines such as physics, mathematics, and psychology
- evaluate the strengths and weaknesses of the responses to some questions of the natural and social sciences defended by some of the major philosophers and schools of philosophy
- defend your own responses to some questions of the natural and social sciences and effectively communicate the results of your inquiries

Whenever you watch or listen to a commercial, try to get a comedian's joke, listen to arguments presented by lawyers and politicians, and solve puzzles or mysteries, logic is involved. Logic is also used to solve math problems, create computer programs, reach conclusions after conducting scientific experiments, and sort out dilemmas in many other areas of life. Even planning a trip to the mall can involve logic.

Though the principles of logic play a particularly important role in answering many of the philosophical questions of science, all philosophical debate benefits when these principles are applied. Logic equips you to use thinking skills in everyday situations — whenever you want to reason correctly, justify a point of view, and make sound or reliable judgments that separate appearance from reality and truth from falsehood. The principles involved in logic and the philosophy of science enable people to apply reasoning skills in many different situations.

Chapter 3
Introducing Logic

Chapter Expectations

By the end of this chapter, you will be able to
- demonstrate an understanding of the main questions in logic
- correctly use the terminology of logic
- distinguish valid from invalid arguments and sound from unsound arguments
- explain the relevance of logic to mathematics, computer science, and artificial intelligence
- classify philosophical arguments
- apply logical- and critical-thinking skills to evaluate or defend positions in philosophical writings
- describe how the ideas of philosophers have influenced subsequent philosophers

Key Words

logic
deduction
induction
three laws of thought
argument
premise
conclusion
logical consistency
logical contradiction
syllogism
validity
sound

Key People

Robert Pirsig
Aristotle
Peter Abelard
George Boole
Gottlob Frege
Kurt Gödel
Jerry Seinfeld
Michael Mazzarese

A Philosopher's Voice

Histories make men wise; poets, witty; the mathematics, subtile; natural philosophy, deep; moral, grave; logic and rhetoric, able to contend.

Francis Bacon (1561–1626)

What Is Logic?

You are not being logical! You have probably heard people make accusations like this countless times. But what do they mean? Suppose Tom and Sasha are arguing about the merits of Romeo cellular phones. Sasha says the phones are awkward to hold, the casing is fragile, and the service is expensive and gimmicky. These drawbacks make Romeo phones a bad buy, she says. Tom maintains that none of this matters. Romeo phones have more ring tones than other brands. Because he likes this feature, he plans to buy a Romeo. Sasha angrily ends the discussion by shouting, "You're not being logical!"

Though Tom and Sasha arrived at different conclusions about Romeo cellphones, both tried to apply the laws of **logic** to their dispute. The word "logic" comes from the Greek word *logos*, which means speech or reason (or reasoned speech). In Greek, the phrase *logike tekhne* means the art or craft of speech. As a result, logic is the area of philosophy that studies correct reasoning and sound judgment.

Logicians — those who study logic — are chiefly concerned with well-constructed arguments. Applying methods of correct reasoning helps people separate appearance from reality and truth from falsehood. Logic can be used to expose faulty arguments by examining assumptions about what is true and the process of reaching conclusions.

As for whether Tom really was being illogical, a logician would want to know more before agreeing with Sasha's assessment. Perhaps the debate between Tom and Sasha was more about stating opinions than facts. Logic is not concerned with the quality or nature of people's views — whether they are liberal or conservative, generous or stingy, serious or frivolous. It is concerned only with whether statements can be justified.

The Philosopher's Approach to Logic

Logic involves two forms of reasoning: **deduction** and **induction**. Each form has its own characteristics, and both forms are used every day.

Deduction, or deductive logic, is based on deductive reasoning, the process of drawing a specific conclusion from a general statement or premise. Deduction goes from the big picture to the little picture.

Induction, or inductive logic, by contrast, is based on inductive reasoning, the process of observing particular things and making generalizations — drawing general conclusions — about them. Induction goes from the little picture to the big picture.

Figure 3.1

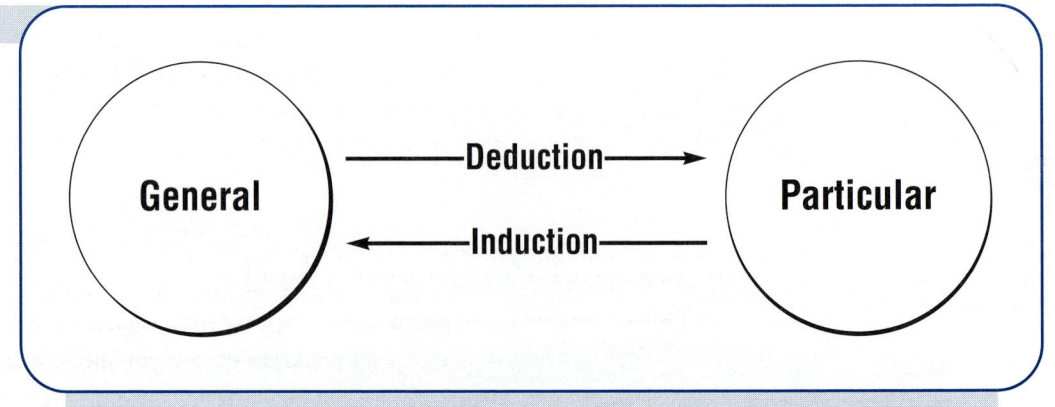

Deduction moves from the general to the particular. Induction moves from the particular to the general.

To see how induction works, try placing your school courses in the following categories. Some courses may fit into more than one category.

- courses that deal with language
- courses that deal with historical figures
- courses that involve numerical calculations
- courses that do not fall into any of these categories

Think about the reasoning process you used to classify your courses. You probably thought about the particular characteristics of each course, then made a generalization about it. Perhaps you placed math, physics, and geography in the category of courses involving numerical calculations. You might have asked yourself, Okay, what happens in geography? Well, there are calculations of distance, longitude, and latitude. So, yes, geography can be classified as a course that involves numerical calculations! By thinking about the particulars involved in geography, you inferred or concluded that this course belongs in a particular category.

Robert Pirsig explained the inductive process in his best-selling book *Zen and the Art of Motorcycle Maintenance*. Pirsig used the operation of a motorcycle to illustrate his explanation.

> Inductive inferences start with observations of the machine and arrive at general conclusions. For example, if the cycle goes over a bump and the engine misfires, and then goes over another bump and the engine misfires, and then goes over another bump and the engine misfires, and then goes over a long smooth stretch of road and there is no misfiring, and then goes over a fourth bump and the engine misfires again, one can logically conclude that the misfiring is caused by the bumps. That is induction: reasoning from particular experiences to general truths.

Deduction goes in the opposite direction. It deals with reasoning that tries to reach a specific conclusion from a general statement. Its rules determine whether a conclusion is justified. Does one statement lead to another? This question is important, because deductive logic involves certainty, whereas inductive logic is about drawing the most reasonable conclusion based on the evidence. Think about your courses again. Make a general statement about one of them, such as, "English is a compulsory course for every Grade 12 student."

What can you conclude from this statement? If English is compulsory in Grade 12, can you say, "I'm in Grade 12, so I must take English"? Yes. Can you also conclude that you get high marks in English? No. Deductive logic does not allow you to reach this conclusion, even though it may be true. Deduction involves drawing a conclusion based only on the information contained in a statement or set of statements — and nothing else.

In *Zen and the Art of Motorcycle Maintenance*, Pirsig also described the deductive process.

> Deductive inferences ... start with general knowledge and predict a specific observation. For example, if, from reading the hierarchy of facts about the [motorcycle], the mechanic knows the horn of the cycle is powered exclusively by electricity from the battery, then he can logically infer that if the battery is dead, the horn will not work. That is deduction.

WHAT PHILOSOPHERS HAVE SAID

The Greek philosopher Aristotle, who lived from 384 to 322 BCE, first articulated the principles and techniques of formal logic. Contemporary logicians still use the tools he developed.

Aristotle's founding work on logic is the *Organon,* which is made up of six treatises: Categories, On Interpretation, Prior Analytics, Posterior Analytics, Topics, and On Sophistical Refutations. The title of this work — an organon is an instrument or tool — reflects Aristotle's concept of logic. Departing from the custom of the day, he believed that logic is not a separate discipline; rather, it is a tool that can be used in every branch of knowledge.

One of Aristotle's most important contributions to logic was the **three laws of thought**.

- *The law of non-contradiction* says that something cannot be said both to be and not to be at the same time and in the same respect. For example, if the statement "Tom exists" is true, it cannot also be false. Tom cannot exist and not exist at the same time.
- *The law of the excluded middle* says that something must either be or not be. For example, the statement "Sasha exists" must be either true or false. There is no third, or middle, possibility. Either Sasha exists, or she does not exist.
- *The law of identity* says that something is what it is. For example, Tom is Tom, and Sasha is Sasha. To say "Tom is Sasha" is untrue.

> ### • IDEAS IN CONTEXT •
>
> Aristotle believed that his three laws of thought were universal and could not be questioned. More than 2000 years after his death, however, quantum theory — the study of matter at the atomic and subatomic level — challenged this assertion. Physicists now believe that every object in the universe changes about 1043 times a second. In other words, no object in the universe is ever constant. It is always changing. This has led some philosophers to conclude that quantum reality refutes Aristotle's laws. Think about it. By the time you say, "Tom is Tom," Tom has already changed!

Though contemporary logicians have developed more complex systems of logic in which true and false are not the only possibilities, mathematicians still use Aristotle's laws as their primary tools.

Aristotle also developed the rules for deductive reasoning. He showed how correct forms of reasoning lead from true premises, or opening statements, to valid conclusions. Both science and philosophy have benefited from this contribution.

When universities were founded in Europe during the Middle Ages, logic — and especially deductive logic — was an important part of the curriculum. In keeping with Aristotle's view of logic as a tool, it was the first of the seven liberal arts to be studied, before grammar, rhetoric, geometry, arithmetic, astronomy, and music. In the 12th century, a French monk and philosopher, **Peter Abelard,** combined Aristotle's ideas about logic with some of the tenets of Roman Catholic religious doctrine. The result was the Scholastic movement, an attempt to merge reason and faith.

> *By doubting we come to inquiry, and by inquiry we perceive truth.*
>
> – Peter Abelard

In his book *Sic et Non (Yes and No)*, Abelard compiled contradictory viewpoints on 158 philosophical and theological questions. His method of examining arguments to root out their logical strengths and weaknesses was to become an important feature of western education. In medieval Europe, however, Church leaders were not pleased with this approach.

In the 17th century, the focus began to shift to inductive reasoning. The English philosopher and statesman Francis Bacon, for example, emphasized inductive reasoning as a tool of science, laying the foundation of the scientific method.

In the 19th and 20th centuries, mathematicians began to use logic heavily in their discipline. The 19th-century English mathematician **George Boole,** for example, took logic in the direction of algebra. He showed that statements in a chain of deductive reasoning can be represented by numbers and algebraic equations. Known as Boolean logic or symbolic logic, Boole's system was a form of algebra in which all values are reduced to either true or false. This system is now used in many computer applications.

PROFILE

Aristotle
The Mind of the School

From birth, Aristotle was well connected to the people who wielded power in ancient Greece. Born in 384 BCE in Stagira, a northern colony that bordered Macedonia, he lived a life of privilege in a prosperous family. His father, Nichomachus, was a court physician and friend of King Amyntas II of Macedonia, and Aristotle formed a close friendship with Philip, Amyntas's son.

Nichomachus probably educated his son, introducing him to the medical ideas and practices of the time. This may have sparked Aristotle's life-long fascination with observing natural phenomena. As a boy, he insisted on systematically breaking down, analyzing, dissecting, and classifying natural phenomena — and ideas.

Despite his privileged upbringing, Aristotle was not immune to tragedy. When he was 17, both his parents died, and he was sent to Athens to finish his education. There he enrolled in Plato's Academy.

In 367 BCE, Athens was the intellectual centre of the western world, and Plato was the leading philosopher. Plato quickly recognized the genius of his new student and nicknamed him the mind of the school. Despite their respect for each other, though, teacher and student could not have been more different. Plato was an introvert. He dealt in abstraction and advised withdrawing from the world to live a life of contemplation. Aristotle, by contrast, was obsessed with exploring the physical world and all of human experience. He dealt in observation, evidence, and proof.

Although they grew apart, Aristotle revered Plato. He stayed at the Academy until Plato died in 347 BCE. Aristotle then spent five years travelling in present-day Turkey and the nearby islands. During his travels, he acted as a political adviser to various rulers and also established academies. Mostly, he continued studying. He observed fish and birds and dissected specimens. His colleagues considered his methods distasteful. They viewed themselves as thinkers who were above such dirty work.

By 342 BCE, Aristotle's childhood friend Philip had inherited the throne of Macedonia. When King Philip asked Aristotle to tutor his impetuous 13-year-old son Alexander, Aristotle returned to Stagira. Alexander was no ordinary student, however. Within a few years, armies under his command had conquered much of the ancient western world, including Greece — and he had become known as Alexander the Great.

When Philip died in 335 BCE, Aristotle returned to Athens to establish his own school, the Lyceum. For the next 12 years, with Alexander's support, the philosopher taught and wrote treatises. Then, in 323 BCE, Alexander died suddenly. His death rocked Aristotle. For the first time in his life, the philosopher's connections to power and influence worked against him. Resentful of Macedonian rule, Athenian leaders charged the philosopher with impiety.

Aristotle fled for his life. Some said that he did this to save Athenians from sinning twice against philosophy. This was a reference to the city's execution of Socrates 76 years earlier. Aristotle died the next year at the age of 62.

The range of Aristotle's writing is enormous. It explored areas such as astronomy, biology, psychology, physics, metaphysics, ethics, politics, rhetoric, literature, art, and, of course, logic. Much of his work has been lost, however. Still, the writings that did survive shaped the ideas of the western philosophers and scientists who followed.

Like Plato, Aristotle never stopped thinking about thinking. His empirical method of observation and description was almost entirely new. Surprisingly easy to read, his writings are critical and careful and always mixed with a strong dose of common sense. Without the mind of the school, western philosophy as it is known today would have evolved quite differently.

Figure 3.2

This bust of Aristotle was created long after his death and is probably a fanciful representation of his appearance. Some of Aristotle's contemporaries reported that he had small eyes and spindleshanks — long, thin legs. These reports, however, may have been inspired by malice.

Another 19th-century mathematician **Gottlob Frege** continued the trend toward merging logic and math. Frege, who was German, developed a system showing that all of mathematics can be reduced to logical laws. And in the 20th century, the English mathematician and philosopher Bertrand Russell wrote that the whole foundation of math can be deduced from a few logical principles.

The work of philosophers like Frege and Russell was later overturned by **Kurt Gödel**, an Austrian-born American mathematician who showed that some mathematical statements cannot be proved even if the correct rules and principles are applied. In other words, some mathematical propositions operate as "true" within the system, but they cannot be proven. Gödel's discovery, which is considered one of the most important breakthroughs of the 20th century, showed that mathematics is not a "finished" discipline, as many once believed. Some people say that Gödel's theory of incompleteness proves that computers will never be able to master all mathematics because computers operate according to closed logical systems. According to Gödel, mathematics defies closed systems like these.

Recall...Reflect...Respond

1. What are the two main branches of logic and how do they differ?
2. Write a one-paragraph reflection on the value of logic in your personal life.
3. Use concrete examples from your own life to illustrate the differences between Aristotle's three laws of thought.

HOW PHILOSOPHERS HAVE SAID IT

Would you trust your car to a mechanic who called one of his tools a thingamajig? Your body to a surgeon who asked for a whatchamacallit? Every discipline has its own lexicon of technical terms, and logic is no exception.

Figure 3.3

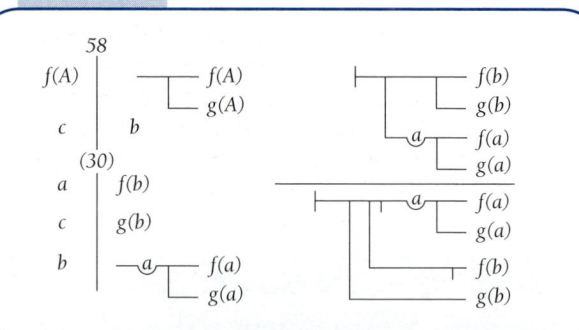

Gottlob Frege's symbolic logic looked like this. These particular symbols show how Frege might develop a logical argument like, If this ostrich is a bird and it cannot fly, then it follows that some birds cannot fly.

When logicians refer to an **argument**, for example, they are not talking about raised voices and flaring tempers. An argument is a series of statements consisting of a **premise** or premises and a **conclusion**, which should follow from the premises. A premise is a factual statement, or proposition, such as, All humans are mortal. Premises provide a reason for believing the conclusion.

In logic, an argument may be a response to a question, but it never opens with a question (e.g., Are you a mortal?) or a command (e.g., Go to your room). This is because questions and commands do not state facts. They are not even statements. Statements can be true or false. Questions and commands are neither.

Logical consistency follows from Aristotle's three laws of thought and refers to statements that do not contradict each other. Take these two statements:

My mother is 45 years old.
My mother is married.

54 MHR UNIT 1 LOGIC AND THE PHILOSOPHY OF SCIENCE

THOUGHT EXPERIMENT

Stuck in School Forever

The bell rings to signal the end of the school day. In your classroom, books slam shut as the teacher quickly reminds everyone of the homework assignment. Looking forward to hanging with your friends for a while, you gather your books and prepare to leave the room. But have you ever considered that getting to the door of your classroom might be impossible?

Think about what's involved. Before you get to the door, you must get to a point halfway there. And before you reach that halfway point, you must reach a point halfway to that, then a point halfway to that point … and so on. What seemed like a simple trip to the door actually involves passing an infinite number of halfway points.

Reaching each halfway point will take a specific amount of time. And because there are an infinite number of halfway points, passing through all of them to reach the door will take an infinite amount of time. You don't have an infinite amount of time, so you will never get out of your classroom. You will be stuck where you are forever.

Figure 3.4

If getting out of your classroom is impossible, how will you meet your friends?

The ancient Greek philosopher Zeno of Elea devised a similar thought experiment, called the paradox of bisection, to show that the laws of motion involve a logical contradiction. In his view, things that involve logical contradictions cannot exist. Because this thought experiment shows that motion involves a logical contradiction, he said that motion cannot exist. Still, Zeno did not deny that people do seem to move from place to place.

But if motion is impossible, how can people move about? Philosophers such as David Hume, Immanuel Kant, and Georg W.F. Hegel tried unsuccessfully to explain away this paradox. In fact, it was not explained till the 20th century when philosophers, mathematicians, and scientists developed a different model of space and time to show that Zeno's apparent logical contradiction was based on false assumptions. To do this, they used different concepts of space, time, and motion, as well as different mathematical concepts of line, number, measure, and sum of a series.

These statements are logically consistent because they do not contradict each other. A **logical contradiction** or inconsistency exists when statements cannot co-exist. The following two statements, for example, contradict each other — and violate Aristotle's law of non-contradiction.

My mother is 45 years old.
My mother is 25 years old.

A **syllogism** is one the basic forms of argument introduced by Aristotle. The basic syllogism contains two premises and a conclusion.

One famous syllogism is

Premise: All humans are mortals.
Premise: I am a human.
Conclusion: I am a mortal.

The aim of argument, or of discussion, should not be victory, but progress.

— Joseph Joubert

In this argument, the first two statements are premises. The first is a major premise. The second is a minor premise. The third is the conclusion. The word "all" in the first sentence is called a quantifier. Examples of other quantifiers are "some," "none," and "every."

When assessing arguments, logicians distinguish between validity and truth. Validity refers to the correctness of the reasoning. Truth refers to the truth of the content of the statements. Logicians are more concerned with an argument's validity than with the truth of its statements.

Take the following example:

Premise: All humans are immortal.
Premise: I am a human.
Conclusion: Therefore, I am immortal.

Though the major premise is untrue, this argument is still valid because the conclusion follows logically from the premises. The reasoning is correct.

Deductive arguments like these syllogisms are always either valid or invalid. The same test cannot be applied to inductive arguments, which are usually known as either strong (reliable) or weak.

Why Logic Matters

In school and in life, logic is an invaluable tool. Every day, people figure out how to accomplish tasks, evaluate what other people say, assess what they see and hear in the media, and justify their decisions and actions to others.

Logic can help everyone do these things better, and maybe even faster. In school, using logic can help you solve problems in many subjects. It enables you to distinguish fact from opinion, and to remain skeptical of information that is not well presented or argued. With logic on your side, you are far less likely to behave in a way that serves someone else's interests and not your own. Has your application for a job ever been rejected because your would-be employer believed that all teenagers are irresponsible? Armed with logic, you might have been able to counteract this perception. Similarly, when you argue with your parents, using logic might help you achieve more favourable results.

Logic helps you assess the day's headlines and determine what is true, what is probably true, and what must be false. Which political policies are likely to help the environment? Will humanity benefit from stem-cell research? Or from genetically modified foods? Are professional athletes overpaid? Is pollution the inevitable price to be paid for progress and global trade? As a thinking tool, logic enables you to size up arguments, develop your own views, and approach issues responsibly.

Thinking logically also helps people understand how one thing really does lead to another. Understanding this principle can encourage you to move from the known to the unknown, whether in math, physics, computer science, philosophy, or daily living.

Since the 19th century, philosophers and others have carefully examined the foundations of logical and mathematical systems, opening up exciting new vistas. The computer revolution of the 20th century might never have happened without the advances proposed by Boole. His system of logic, which is sometimes called Boolean algebra, enabled computer developers to automate logic and use it to make computers run.

Since Boole's time, logic has all but become a branch of computer science. Today, however, some computer logic is "fuzzy." At one time, computer operations were based on values that were strictly binary, true or false, off or on, 1 or 0. Now, computing can be based on degrees of truth, or somewhere between 1 and 0. The degree of imprecision in fuzzy logic is especially useful in artificial intelligence studies. It also means that computerized appliances and control systems, which are used in subways, factories, and household electronics, can be programmed to "think" more like humans, or at least to anticipate what humans might want or need next. In other words, these computers assess and compute based on a variety of values that include percentages, context, and educated calculations.

> **IDEAS IN CONTEXT**
>
> Boole's system of logic not only helped in the design of computer circuitry, but also forms the basis of database searches. Many Internet search engines are based on Boolean logic, using words called "operators." The words "and," "or," and "not" are the three main operators. Using a search engine that allows the use of these words makes searches more specific and findings more relevant.

This development is likely to lead to advanced methods of searching and working with data on the Internet. Think about what happens when you enter a word that has many meanings into a search engine. If the word is "iron," for example, the computer has no way of knowing whether you are after a person's last name, a vitamin supplement, a laundry appliance, golf clubs, a geological study, or a cartoon superhero. This means that your search results are likely to display hits for all these uses of the word.

> **Web connection**
>
> www.mcgrawhill.ca/links/philosophy12
>
> To find out more about fuzzy logic, follow the links on this Web site.

In an attempt to make Internet searches more intuitive, computer scientists are developing something called the Semantic Web. In this instance, the word "semantic" refers to something that can be processed by a machine. The Semantic Web will enable computers to process and "understand" data that they now merely display. For the Semantic Web to function, computers must have access to structured collections of information that they can use to conduct automated reasoning. This new research is well under way.

> **Recall...Reflect...Respond**
>
> 1. List the philosophers of logic whose ideas influenced the development of our understanding of mathematics and computer science.
> 2. What is the best music video? Write an argument that you might use to support your answer to this question. Compare your argument with that of a partner. Which argument is stronger? Explain why.
> 3. How does fuzzy logic mimic the way humans think?

REASONING AND CRITICAL THINKING

Why did the chicken cross the road? Just about everyone knows the answer to this old joke: To get to the other side. Making a joke is a lot like making an inference. To get a joke is to connect the joke's opening line and its punch line. To make an inference is to draw a conclusion from a statement or set of statements. Making inferences is an important element of reasoning.

PHILOSOPHY IN ACTION

The Use of Argument

by Tom Morris

Tom Morris is an American philosopher and author of many best-selling philosophical works, including *If Aristotle Ran General Motors*. After teaching philosophy at Notre Dame University for 15 years, he founded the Morris Institute for Human Values. This think tank applies philosophical thought to contemporary business and life issues.

In this excerpt from *Philosophy for Dummies*, Morris talks about logic and how it applies to everyday life.

When I was in graduate school in the late '70s, I often started my day by watching a talk show on television. Even in those early days of audience participation and debate-oriented talk shows, I was amazed at what people seemed to think constituted a reasonable exchange of differing ideas. The squared jaws, red faces, and bulging veins that accompanied such rejoinders as "Oh *yeah*?" "Who *says*?" and "That's just *your* opinion!" seemed impervious to the call of real argument. This was, of course, long before chair-throwing, kicking, spitting, and hair pulling began to serve as the vehicles of televised argument. And I'm not just referring metaphorically to the syndicated talk shows of political pundits here. As a culture, North Americans these days seem to misunderstand what argument at its best really is.

In philosophy, an argument is a reasoned presentation of ideas, where you marshal evidence in favour of the truth of a conclusion. Arguments, in their essence, aren't something that you direct at people as you would a gun that you're aiming at a target. You don't primarily argue *with* someone or *at* someone; you present an argument for a conclusion, which you often intend as a means to persuade someone else, but sometimes employ just as a means of discovering for yourself where the truth lies.

So, in philosophy, arguments aren't the sorts of things that you win or lose. They're not like games or athletic contests of the mind. Even if you engage in an argument with another person in the colloquial sense over a substantive issue — and you truly want to convince your interlocutor of the persuasiveness of your viewpoint — you'd better be able to construct a good argument in the philosophical sense as well. And studying some philosophy helps you know how to do so better than you may already.

In every walk of life, we need to be able to give a reasoned presentation of our beliefs in such a way as to persuade other people. Lawyers aren't the only ones who must worry about convincing others to accept a particular point of view. Persuasive argument is an important part of every management job, is a requirement in the arsenal of every challenged parent, and is as important to preachers and teachers as to practising scientists. A good argument helps us to intellectually "see" where the truth lies.

In my first year at college, I discovered an important truth about the limitations of argument. For some reason, hair had always been an issue in my family — head hair *and* facial hair. Until I went away to college, my parents had insisted that I shave daily and keep the hair on my head cut fairly short. Off on my own, I let my hair get long and began to grow a Fu Manchu moustache. This bit of rebellion occurred during the early '70s, when a good deal of "the '60s" actually took place. Bell-bottomed pants, ridiculous shirts, and long hair ruled. I shudder now to think what I looked like, but I was exercising my new-found freedom and experimenting with my appearance. A few months later, I saw my mother for the first time since the inception of my new, hirsute look. She offered me a hundred dollars on the spot to shave off my moustache and refused to go to any public place with me until I did. I wish I hadn't taken a stand on principle. Two weeks later, my 'stache itched me half to death, and I shaved with no reward. But that day, mother was adamant and trying any strategy she could. She even went to far as to say to me, point blank, "Something's psychologically *wrong* with anyone who has a beard or moustache!"

I was in my first philosophy course at the time, and was learning how to argue a point, so I wasn't about to let this one pass. I suddenly remembered what philosophers call "argument by counter-example" — that is, you can refute any general claim of the form *All As are Bs* by producing one example of a B that is not an A. Employing the standard "But, *Mother* ..." opening of any frustrated adolescent bent on proving a point, I started enumerating aloud all the great personages of history I could think of who had moustaches or beards and yet who were, by any fair estimation, paragons of psychological health and worldly success. Working my way from ancient Greece through the American Civil War, and not forgetting Southern paradigms such as Robert E. Lee, I was taken up short and momentarily struck mute by a sudden realization.

"Mother," I said with all the conviction I could muster, suddenly certain that I had unassailable proof of my own conviction that facial hair and sound psychological health can go quite well together, "Dad has always had a moustache!"

"You see what I'm saying?" she instantly replied.

An old country-music lyric says, "One man's ceiling is another man's floor." Sometimes traffic can flow both ways in the analysis or assessment of an argument. What I'd thought was the most decisive possible refutation by counter-example of a general claim that I knew to be false was taken by my dialogue partner as a particularly clear confirmation of her own emphatic view to the contrary.

Of course, people can sometimes reasonably differ on the obviousness of a piece of evidence cited in an argument, or they can blind themselves to the truth and can even refuse to listen to rational argument at all. The best intellectual reasoning can fail completely to overrule strongly opposed passions.

In the right context, the ability to argue cogently can prove of great importance for seeing where truth lies and for convincing others to join us in its pursuit. Good argument isn't always guaranteed to produce the good result you may desire, but good argument is better than bad argument any day of the week. And argument, along with imagination and emotion, can provide part of a total case for enlisting the whole person in believing or acting on an important truth. Rational argument is one of the most distinctive of genuinely human abilities and one strongly cultivated by philosophy.

Source: From *Philosophy for Dummies* ® by Tom Morris, Ph. D. Copyright © 1999 Wiley Publishing, Inc. All rights reserved. Reproduction here by permission of the publisher.

The Dangers of Argument: A Short Survival Guide

How can you actually use argument well and even make progress in an argument with another person?...

First is the pragmatic advice, such as, "In arguing, answer your opponent's earnest with a jest and his jest with an earnest." — Leontinus Gorgias (as quoted in Aristotle's *Rhetoric*). In other words, keep the person with whom you're arguing off balance.

The psychological advice warns us most often about the limits of argumentation in dealing with another person and the truth at the same time. Sir Thomas Browne, for example, warned, "In all disputes, so much as there is of passion, so much there is of nothing to the purpose." Debate, you often hear, typically generates more heat than light. Know that likelihood going in. Passion clouds reason. And in the context of an interpersonal argument or debate, people are willing to do anything to save face.

Finally, some modest philosophical advice of a practical bent: Protagoras did affirm that every question has two sides. And Henry Fielding added in the 18th century that "Much can be said on both sides." Whenever you see sincere, intelligent people supporting a cause or arguing a point of view, you can expect ... to find more than sheer foolishness in that position or cause. By extrapolation, I think I can say that, in all the history of philosophy, with all the competing schools of thought and opposed points of view, you're never going to come across large numbers of sincere, intelligent, and relatively well-informed people who are just completely wrong in every way. So always try to remain open-minded and look for the truth that any opposing view may capture.

And, of course, life consists of much more than argument. Socrates once remarked, "You are fond of argument, and now you fancy that I am a bag of arguments." You don't want to avoid argument, and yet neither do you want to constantly seek it out as the only thing in life worth your time.

1. List three characteristics of the popular idea of argument and three characteristics of philosophical argument. How are these characteristics influenced by the purpose of and audience for these arguments?
2. Which kind of argument provides greater social value? Why?
3. Morris says that the purpose of argument is not necessarily to win. With a partner, talk about this point of view, drawing examples from your own life.

Here are a few other possible punch lines for the classic chicken joke:

Plato: For the greater good.
Karl Marx: Because it was a historical inevitability.
Aristotle: It follows from the nature of chickens to cross roads.
Stone Cold Steve Austin: Must have seen me comin'.
Albert Einstein: Whether the chicken crossed the road or the road crossed the chicken depends on your frame of reference.

Note the expression "it follows from" and words such as "because," "must have," and "depends" in these answers. In a joke, terms like these link the opening line and the punch line. In a logical argument, these words are called inference indicators. They show that the first statement is connected to the concluding statement.

Words or expressions that usually signal the premise of an argument are

as	for	can be inferred from
as shown by	for the reason that	is implied by
as indicated by	assuming that	given that
given that	on the assumption that	since

Words or expressions that often introduce a conclusion are

therefore	then	we may infer that
so	as a result	this implies that
hence	it follows that	this leads one to believe that
consequently	in conclusion	this demonstrates that
thus	accordingly	this shows that

The Form of Logical Arguments

Logic is concerned with the form of an argument and whether this form and the reasoning used to formulate statements and arrive at a conclusion are correct. Reasoning involves the ability to understand connections, use inference indicators, and make inferences. Arguments that do these things correctly are bound to be well constructed.

A logical argument can be as short as two statements, in which the first statement provides the reason, or grounds, for the second statement. Take this sentence:

I was born 18 years ago. Therefore [inference indicator], I am 18 years old.

The word "syllogism" comes from a Greek word meaning "propositions considered together." The syllogism is another short argument form. It is made up of a premise or premises and a conclusion. Premises are the factual statements that lead to the conclusion, the thing you want to prove. The premises must lead to the conclusion in a formally correct way.

Premise: All humans are mortals.
Premise: I am a human.
Conclusion: Therefore, I am a mortal.

This syllogism is a deductive argument that moves from the general to the specific. Its two premises lead to a conclusion. Its form is correct — and the argument is therefore valid — because the conclusion is inferred from the premises.

In logic, the word "inference" has a much more specific meaning than it does in everyday speech. For example, if Tom says, "I think that Romeo cellphones are too expensive," Sasha may be influenced to think that they are expensive because Tom says so and he tends to be price-conscious. This kind of inference is not considered an inference in logic, however.

Figure 3.5

Frank and Ernest © NEA. Reprinted by permission.

In logic, as in everyday life, syntax, or word order, is crucial.

In a logical deductive argument, the parts must be connected so that the inference or conclusion follows directly from the premise (or premises). The premises guarantee the conclusion because the argument is formally correct.

Inductive arguments do not rely on form in the same way as deductive arguments. The following example shows why.

Observation of evidence: Every butterfly I see has two wings.
Observation of evidence: I have never seen a butterfly without two wings.
Conclusion: Butterflies have two wings.

Figure 3.6

Comedian Jerry Seinfeld maintains that all comedy is "a kind of bogus proof." What do you think he means by this?

The conclusion of this argument cannot be proven beyond a doubt. All the butterflies you have seen may have two wings, and you may never have seen a butterfly without two wings. Still, this does not mean that one-winged or even three- or four-winged butterflies do not exist. You may simply never have seen them.

Over time, the work of logicians has become increasingly abstract because they are trying to escape the illogical nuances of language. The process of deductive logic has become deeply connected to the language and symbols used to express the movement from one statement to the next. In fact, logicians and mathematicians have created their own language of abstract symbols to prevent everyday language from adding its own kinds of confusion.

Comedian **Jerry Seinfeld** has found a unique use for the illogical nuances of language. They are one of the foundations of his comedy sketches.

"You set up a fallacious [incorrect] premise and then prove it with rigorous logic," Seinfeld told *Scope* magazine. "It just makes people laugh." Many of Seinfeld's routines rely on this technique, as the following classic sketch shows:

Let's get one thing straight about dry cleaning right now. It doesn't exist. There's no such thing as dry cleaning. There's no way of cleaning with dry, washing with dry, or doing anything with dry. Dry itself is nothing. You can't use it. You can't do anything with it. It's not there. Dry is nothing. Are you listening to me? We walk into these places with big signs out front, "Dry Cleaning," and somehow never question how they were able to put this absurd concept over on us.

CHAPTER 3 Introducing Logic MHR **61**

If I gave you a filthy shirt and said, "I want this immaculate. And no liquids!" What are you going to do? Shake it? Tap it? Blow on it? Give me a break. You almost can't get something dirty with dry, let alone cleaning it.

Validity, Truth, and Soundness

Syllogisms or deductive arguments are valid when their form is correct so that the conclusion, as Aristotle said, "follows of necessity from" the premises. This does not mean, however, that the conclusion is true. Although an argument may be valid, its conclusion may be based on one or more false premises. Take this example:

All mice chase cats.
Socrates is a mouse.
Therefore, Socrates chases cats.

The form of this argument is correct, so the conclusion is valid. The major premise is not true, however. Mice do not chase cats. The minor premise is also untrue. Socrates is a philosopher. This means that the argument is based on faulty premises. As a result, the conclusion may be valid, but it is not true.

In a deductive argument, the truth of the premises guarantees the truth of the conclusion. If the conclusion of a valid argument is false, then at least one premise must also be false.

An argument is said to be **sound** if its form is valid and its premises are true. This is the most desirable situation. Sound arguments, in which the form is correct and the premises and conclusion are true, are the most effective.

In logic, soundness doesn't apply to inductive reasoning. Inductive reasoning is either reliable or unreliable.

Deductive arguments are only one form of argument, however. Most people's general knowledge of the world is acquired through inductive reasoning. This kind of reasoning is considered reliable if the evidence makes the conclusion likely or probable. Proof is not required.

The strength or reliability of this kind of argument depends on a number of factors. In a scientific study, it could depend on how many people submit evidence and whether these people represent the general population. In a criminal investigation, it could depend on whether all possible origins of the evidence are considered and evaluated. Blood spatters, for example, can result from self-injury or homicide, and expert investigators must often determine which scenario is more likely. When inductive reasoning is involved, much depends on whether the evidence truly leads to a conclusion or is merely coincidence. Furthermore, while deductive validity is an all-or-nothing affair, inductive reliability is often a matter of degree.

Historically, deductive logic has been concerned with the truth-value of statements and the process of reaching conclusions. Depending on the society in which logic is practised, this process has yielded widely varying results. Ancient and medieval philosophers, for example, used logic to prove the existence of an "unmoved mover" or supreme being. Today, the results of logic are more evident in scientific and technological applications, such as increasingly sophisticated logic boards in computers.

At the same time, forms of inductive logic have never been so omnipresent or so often misunderstood and abused. Every day, people make political and

> *There are two sides to every question.*
> – Protagoras

marketing decisions on the basis of surveys, focus groups, and opinion polls that may be based on faulty procedures and insufficient or unrepresentative samples. Hasty generalizations abound and examples of faulty logic are everywhere. To see examples, just turn to the letters-to-the-editor page of your community newspaper or tune in to a television or radio talk show.

> **Recall...Reflect...Respond**
> 1. Describe the differences in the way scientists and mathematicians use logic to solve problems.
> 2. List five examples of the illogical nuances of language that Jerry Seinfeld might use to inspire a comedy sketch (e.g., drive on a parkway, giant shrimps).
> 3. Suppose you are trying to solve a murder mystery. Which form of logic are you more likely to apply? Why? Are there circumstances in which you might use the other form of logic to help identify the murderer? Explain.

WAYS OF THINKING

In the western tradition of logic, Aristotle's three laws of thought are considered to be the foundation of all thought and discourse, or talk. The influence of this ancient philosopher is everywhere. Or is it? In an article titled "Where Do Leaders Come from?" author **Michael Mazzarese** emphasizes that the western approach tends to leave out other traditions, such as Chinese and Hindu philosophy. Interestingly, Mazzarese is not even a philosopher. He's an executive coach who helps companies cultivate excellent leaders in the workplace. Yet even in this arena, says Mazzarese, a western-only focus can overlook important perspectives:

> Today's leaders cannot be paralyzed by ambiguity. They must learn how to keep their balance while moving ahead with limited resources and, at times, with insufficient data. This presents a challenge for those of us schooled in a system of logic based on ideas of Plato, Aquinas, Kant and Wittgenstein. Western logic is neat and tidy. Everything has a place and must be in its place. Eastern thought has a different outlook. It is not bound by the assumptions of western dichotomy: good-evil; male-female; high quality-low cost; etc. It is steeped in the traditions of Buddha, Lao-tse [Laozi], and Shinto.
>
> For example, the symbols for male and female in the West are two separate symbols representing two separate structures. A dichotomy. In the East they use one symbol, the yin/yang. Two opposites within one structure. Not cohabiting but co-existing. One and different at the same time. Drives you crazy, right? But that's the point. The West demands one or the other. The East lives with one and the other. While western thought keeps us busy trying to fit things into our dichotomous paradigms, eastern thought will have our leaders busy implementing ideas and getting them out to the customer, fine-tuning along the way. That's an important lesson.

In other words, there are different ways to approach life in Mazzarese's view. Still, the idea that no assumption should be left unexamined — logic's great legacy — will serve you well at school, at home, with your friends, and in your career.

Chapter Review

Chapter Summary

This chapter has discussed
- the main questions in logic
- the terminology of logic
- valid and invalid arguments and sound and unsound arguments
- the relevance of logic to mathematics, computer science, and artificial intelligence
- philosophical arguments
- how the ideas of philosophers have influenced subsequent philosophers

Knowledge and Understanding

1. Identify and explain the significance to the study of logic of each of the following key words and people.

Key Words	Key People
logic	Robert Pirsig
deduction	Aristotle
induction	Peter Abelard
three laws of thought	George Boole
argument	Kurt Gödel
premise	Jerry Seinfeld
conclusion	Michael Mazzarese
logical consistency	
logical contradiction	
syllogism	
validity	
sound	

2. Create a list of the main questions of logic that are implicitly addressed by the study of logic.

Thinking and Inquiry

3. Aristotle's three laws of thought form the basis of all logical claims, but these laws cannot themselves be logically proven. Still, Aristotle argued that they can be demonstrated.

   The starting point for all such proofs is that our opponent shall say something which is significant both for himself and for another; for this is necessary, if he really is to say anything. For, if he means nothing, such a man will not be capable of reasoning, either with himself or with another. But if anyone says something that is significant, demonstration will be possible; for we shall already have something definite. The person responsible for the proof, however, is not he who demonstrates but he who listens; for while disowning reason he listens to reason. And again he who admits this has admitted that something is true apart from demonstration.

According to Aristotle, how can the three laws of thought be demonstrated? How does this demonstration illustrate that words and language cannot make sense without these three laws of thought?

4. Developments in artificial intelligence may soon allow implants to be placed in the brain to make humans supremely logical. If this were possible now, would placing an implant in your brain make you more — or less — human? Write a personal reflection that explains and defends your opinion. Support your opinion by applying at least one of the two forms of logic.

Communication

5. With a group, create a role play of a courtroom trial. Assign roles to the crown attorney, defence attorney, defendant, and witnesses. After each group presents its role play to the class, discuss the validity and soundness or strength of the logic applied in the questions and answers.

6. Locate a series of logic puzzles in a book or on the Internet. Choose one that requires the use of inductive reasoning to arrive at a solution. Write a series of questions to help guide people to the answer.

Application

7. The following cartoon frames are numbered 1 through 8, but this sequence does not represent the logical order of events portrayed in the pictures. On a sheet of paper, place the numbers in a sequence that represents a more logical order. Write a series of arguments to support the order you selected.

Used with permission of Sterling Publishing Co., NY, NY, from *Critical Thinking Puzzles* by Michael A. DiSpezio, © 1996 by Michael A. DiSpezio, illustrated by Myron Miller

Figure 3.7

8. Create a concept map to illustrate the evolution of western logic. On the map, show how the ideas of one philosopher influenced the ideas of subsequent philosophers. Include questions that may have guided the progress of ideas and visuals that show how various philosophers responded to these questions.

Chapter 4
Applying Logic

Chapter Expectations

By the end of this chapter, you will be able to
- demonstrate an understanding of the main questions in logic
- correctly use the terminology of logic
- classify philosophical arguments
- distinguish valid from invalid arguments, sound from unsound arguments, and reliable from unreliable arguments
- apply logical- and critical-thinking skills to evaluate or defend positions in philosophical writings
- apply logical- and critical-thinking skills to problems that arise in jobs and occupations

Key Words

categorical syllogisms
disjunctive syllogisms
hypothetical syllogisms
abductive reasoning
fallacies
formal fallacy
informal fallacy
media literacy

Key People

Charles Sanders Peirce

A Philosopher's Voice

One ought, every day at least, to hear a little song, read a good poem, see a fine picture, and, if it were possible, to speak a few reasonable words.

Johann Wolfgang von Goethe (1749–1832)

Is It Logic or Illogic?

The character in this cartoon (Figure 4.1) is using deductive reasoning in the form of a syllogism to reach a conclusion. But are his premises true? Is the form of the argument valid? Is it sound? Does his conclusion make sense? Or is something terribly wrong with his reasoning?

As this cartoon demonstrates, applying logic is sometimes more easily said than done. Although everyone values logic, people are sometimes illogical without even being aware of it.

Figure 4.1

Sometimes, people are illogical on purpose. They want to fool others into agreeing with them. Other times, emotion takes over and gets in the way of logical argument. Illogic can also arise from using — and misusing — the English language, which is a flexible, though complex, communication tool. More often, though, illogic, which is really a lack of logic, is the result of sloppy thinking.

Applying Deductive Reasoning

Logicians are interested in the rules and procedures of correct reasoning. In the case of deductive reasoning, the goal is to produce what logicians call a sound argument. A deductive argument is sound if the reasoning is valid (i.e., the form is correct) and the premises are true. Traditional syllogisms are the most common form of deductive argument.

SYLLOGISMS

Syllogisms are often grouped into three categories: categorical, disjunctive, and hypothetical. Each category takes its name from the kind of propositions or statements the syllogism contains. Categorical syllogisms contain categorical propositions; disjunctive syllogisms contain disjunctive propositions; and hypothetical syllogisms contain hypothetical propositions.

Syllogisms need not be expressed in words. Letters and numbers can also be used (e.g., All A are B).

Categorical Syllogisms

Aristotle was the first to use **categorical syllogisms**, which state whether things belong — or do not belong — in categories. In categorical syllogisms, the major premise, minor premise, and conclusion express propositions that categorize things. All categorical syllogisms include

- a middle term that appears in the major and minor premises
- a predicate term that appears in the major premise and the conclusion
- a subject term that appears in the minor premise and the conclusion

This example illustrates a commonly quoted categorical syllogism:

middle term —— **All humans are mortals.** —— predicate term

subject term —— **Socrates is a human.** —— middle term

subject term —— **Therefore, Socrates is a mortal.** —— predicate term

Like all good deductive arguments, this syllogism proceeds from a general premise to a specific conclusion. This argument is both valid and sound because its form is correct and its premises are true. Expressed in letters, the form of the Socrates syllogism would look like this.

All A are B.
C is an A.
Therefore, C is a B.

Compare the Socrates syllogism with this example.

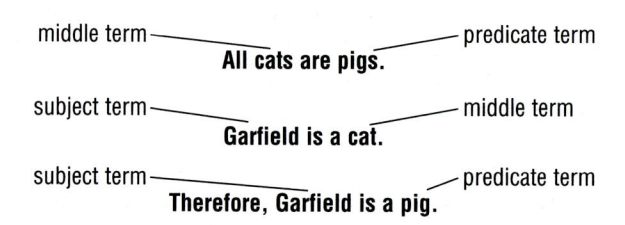

middle term —— **All cats are pigs.** —— predicate term

subject term —— **Garfield is a cat.** —— middle term

subject term —— **Therefore, Garfield is a pig.** —— predicate term

This syllogism is also valid because it is expressed in the same correct form as the Socrates syllogism. Expressed in letters, the form looks like this.

All A are B.
C is an A.
Therefore, C is a B.

Something is wrong with this argument, however. Its major premise is false. If one or both premises of a syllogism are false, the argument cannot be sound, even though it may be valid. Validity is governed by the form of the argument, while soundness is governed by both the form and the truth of the premises.

Another characteristic of categorical syllogisms is that their propositions can be universal or particular. A universal proposition refers to all things included — or not included — in a category. Here are examples.

All students are people. (All A are B.)
No dogs are cats. (No A are B.)

When only one or some members of a category are included — or not included — in the propositions of a categorical syllogism, the proposition is particular. Here are two examples.

Garfield is a cat. (A is a B.)
Some gymnasts are girls. (Some A are B.)

Web connection

www.mcgrawhill.ca/links/philosophy12
To read more about categorical syllogisms, follow the links on this Web site.

Testing the Validity of Categorical Syllogisms

How do you know whether a categorical syllogism is valid or invalid? Sometimes it is hard to tell. Still, logicians have developed a number of rules to govern validity. For example, two negative propositions can never result in a positive conclusion. A negative proposition says that something does not belong in a class of things. As a result, the conclusion cannot go on to say that something does belong in a class. Here is an example:

No cats are fashion designers. (No A are B.)
No dogs are cats. (No C are A.)
Therefore, dogs are fashion designers. (Therefore, C are B.)

This syllogism is invalid, not to mention ridiculous. Both premises express negative propositions, yet the conclusion expresses a positive.

Another rule states that when one of the premises expresses a negative, the conclusion must also be negative. This rule is ironclad. Here is an example:

No cars are toys. (No A are B.)
Toys are things you play with. (B are C.)
Therefore, cars are things you play with. (Therefore, A are C.)

Though the idea of playing with cars may be appealing, this syllogism is invalid because it draws a positive conclusion when one of the premises expresses a negative proposition.

Another important rule is that no conclusion can be drawn from two particular propositions. Here is an example:

John is a student. (A is a B.)
Some students are members of the school swim team. (Some B are C.)
Therefore, John is a member of the school swim team. (Therefore, A is a C.)

In this syllogism, both premises express particular propositions. As a result, no conclusion can be drawn from them.

Categorical syllogisms can also be shown on Venn diagrams, which can be used to test the validity of syllogisms. Take this example:

All teachers are educators. (All A are B.)
Nadine is a teacher. (C is an A.)
Therefore, Nadine is an educator. (Therefore, C is a B.)

On a Venn diagram, this syllogism would look like this:

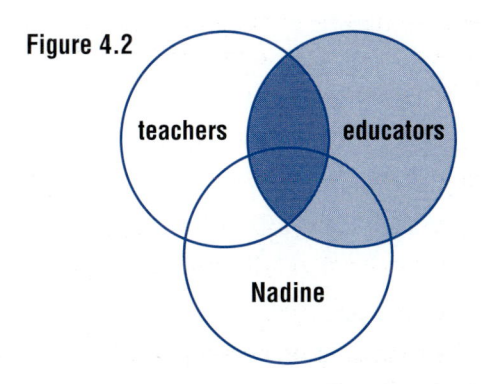

Figure 4.2

All teachers are educators. The two circles intersect.

Figure 4.3

Nadine is a teacher. Nadine's circle and the teachers' circle interesct.

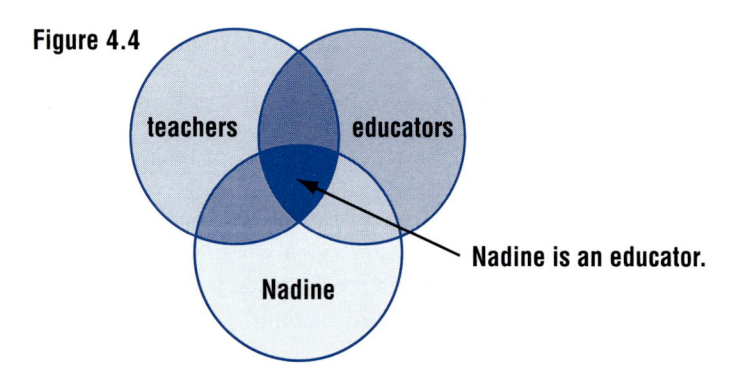

Figure 4.4

Nadine is an educator.

Therefore Nadine is an educator. The Venn Diagram shows that this syllogism is valid because Nadine's circle intersects with both the teachers' and educators' circles.

Once the premises have been entered in the circles, the conclusion can be "read." If it cannot, the syllogism is invalid.

DISJUNCTIVE SYLLOGISMS

Disjunctive syllogisms open with either-or statements. In logic, the word "disjunctive" means involving a choice. A disjunctive syllogism, therefore, expresses a choice. It states that either one thing is true or the other thing is true — and leaves open the possibility that both may be true. This is because, in logic, the word "or" means "either or both." When logicians do not want to mean both, they specifically say "either, but not both." Here is an example of a disjunctive syllogism:

Either Tom or Sasha (or both) is a baseball fan. (Either A or B is a C.)
Tom is not a baseball fan. (A is not a C.)
Therefore, Sasha is a baseball fan. (Therefore, B is a C.)

In this example, the major premise states that one of two things is the case: either Tom is a baseball fan or Sasha is a baseball fan. The use of the word "or" includes the idea "or both." In the example, the words "or both" are placed in parentheses as a reminder of this. This reminder is not usually included in disjunctive syllogisms, however. The idea that "or" means "or both" is understood.

The minor premise of this syllogism denies one of the alternatives; in this case, that Tom is a baseball fan. The conclusion then accepts the other alternative. If Tom is not a baseball fan, then Sasha must be a baseball fan.

This is the valid form of this argument. It is important to be cautious, however, because it is easy to create invalid disjunctive syllogisms. Here is an example:

Either Tom or Sasha is a baseball fan. (Either A or B is a C.)
Sasha is a baseball fan. (B is a C.)
Therefore, Tom is not a baseball fan. (Therefore, A is not a C.)

This conclusion is invalid because the word "or" in the first statement includes the idea "or both." Just because Sasha is a baseball fan, it does not follow that Tom is *not* a baseball fan. Both could be fans, as the major premise stated.

Only one rule governs disjunctive syllogisms: to be valid, the premises must contain a denial of one alternative, and the conclusion must affirm the other.

HYPOTHETICAL SYLLOGISMS

Hypothetical syllogisms are also a popular form of argument. In logic, a hypothesis is a proposition suggested as a basis for reasoning. It is not necessarily true. Hypothetical syllogisms are often easy to spot because they usually contain if-then statements. At least one of the premises must express a hypothesis, which begins with the word "if." Think of this kind of argument as tracing a chain of actions and reactions. Here is an example.

If you water the garden, the tomato plants will grow. (If A, then B.)
If the plants grow, then you will have some tomatoes to eat. (If B, then C.)
Therefore, if you water the garden, then you will have some tomatoes to eat. (Therefore, if A, then C.)

Here is a slightly different form of the same syllogism.

If you water the garden, the tomato plants will grow. (If A, then B.)
You water the garden. (A.)
Therefore, the tomato plants will grow. (Therefore, B.)

Hypothetical syllogisms are considered valid if the if-then chain is built correctly. Both these syllogisms are valid because their form is correct, but their soundness is open to question. Even if you water the garden, many other factors may interfere with the growth of the tomatoes. They may not get enough sun, for example, or they may be infested with pests.

What happens if the hypothetical propositions do not express a true cause-and-effect relationship? Consider this argument:

If you buy that shirt, you will get a date. (If A, then B.)
If you get a date, you will be married in one year. (If B, then C.)
Therefore, if you buy that shirt, you will be married within one year. (Therefore, if A, then C.)

You probably already know that buying a great shirt will not guarantee you a date and that getting a date will not catapult you into marriage within a year. Even though the truth of the individual cause-and-effect propositions contained in this syllogism is suspect, the argument is valid. Whether it is sound is another matter entirely.

Figure 4.5

Farcus by David Waisglass / Gordon Coulthart

"So, I say if it's not worth doing well, it's not worth doing at all."

The right hypothesis can lead to a course of action — or not.

Applying Inductive Reasoning

Deductive reasoning is about validity. Inductive forms of reasoning, however, deal with probabilities. As a result, inductive reasoning is said to be reliable or unreliable, rather than valid or invalid. Inductive reasoning moves from the particular to the general. It involves drawing a conclusion or making a generalization based on specific evidence. The more reliable the evidence, the more reliable the reasoning.

Suppose that a dog breeder said that all the breeds of dogs she had ever seen had noses, and that she had seen quite a few breeds in her day. If she concluded that all dogs have noses, her argument would be considered reliable. If a young child, by contrast, encountered a friendly dog and decided that all dogs are therefore friendly, his conclusion would be considered unreliable.

What is the difference between these two situations? The dog breeder had seen many dogs and never encountered one without a nose. The child, however, saw only one dog and drew a conclusion based on limited evidence. Determining whether the evidence represents a wide enough sample to reach a reliable conclusion is an important factor in determining the reliability of inductive arguments.

Argument by analogy is a slightly different form of induction. An analogy proposes a similarity between two distinct things because other similarities have been observed. Suppose, for example, that you tried to play a CD yesterday and it skipped badly because it was scratched. You have another CD with a scratch. Before playing it, you conclude that it, too, will skip.

The key to making useful analogies is to consider only relevant information. Suppose your Ramasutra CD skips because is scratched. You have another Ramasutra CD and conclude that it will not play properly either — because it is a Ramasutra CD. Bad analogy. Can you spot why?

Asking two questions can help sort out whether an analogy is reliable.

Figure 4.6

In this still from an old Sherlock Holmes movie, actor Clive Brooks plays the great detective using his reasoning powers as he examines a gun.

- Is the information relevant (i.e., does it apply to the matter being discussed)?
- Is enough information provided to establish its relevance?

Inductive reasoning is most important in the field of criminal law. Arthur Conan Doyle's fictional detective Sherlock Holmes, for example, is often credited with marvellous powers of deduction. Despite what his fans might say, however, the technique Holmes uses is not deduction. It is induction, as the following scene from a story titled "The Red-Headed League" shows.

The scene takes place after Holmes' assistant, Dr. Watson, has described a client, Jabez Wilson, to his boss. According to Watson, Wilson is in every way "an average commonplace British tradesman, obese, pompous, and slow." Though Watson does note that Wilson wears "a square pierced bit of metal dangling down as an ornament," Holmes' assistant suggests that their client is otherwise unremarkable, except for "his blazing red head, and the expression of extreme chagrin and discontent upon his features."

Then Watson describes what happens when Holmes — the master — takes over.

[Holmes said,] "Beyond the obvious facts that he has at some time done manual labour, that he takes snuff, that he is a Freemason, that he has been in China, and that he has done a considerable amount of writing lately, I can deduce nothing else."

72 MHR Unit 1 Logic and the Philosophy of Science

Mr. Jabez Wilson started up in his chair, with his forefinger upon the paper, but his eyes upon my companion.

"How, in the name of good-fortune, did you know all that, Mr. Holmes?" he asked. "How did you know, for example, that I did manual labour? It's as true as gospel, for I began as a ship's carpenter."

"Your hands, my dear sir. Your right hand is quite a size larger than your left. You have worked with it, and the muscles are more developed."

"Well, the snuff, then, and the Freemasonry?"

"I won't insult your intelligence by telling you how I read that, especially as, rather against the strict rules of your order, you use an arc-and-compass breastpin."

"Ah, of course, I forgot that. But the writing?"

"What else can be indicated by that right cuff so very shiny for five inches, and the left one with the smooth patch near the elbow where you rest it upon the desk?"

"Well, but China?"

"The fish that you have tattooed immediately above your right wrist could only have been done in China. I have made a small study of tattoo marks and have even contributed to the literature of the subject. That trick of staining the fishes' scales a delicate pink is quite peculiar to China. When, in addition, I see a Chinese coin hanging from your watch-chain, the matter becomes even more simple."

Mr. Jabez Wilson laughed heavily. "Well, I never!" said he. "I thought at first that you had done something clever, but I see that there was nothing in it, after all."

In this situation, Holmes actually moves from the particular to the general. He makes general observations based on specific evidence, showing himself to be a master of induction rather than deduction.

> **Recall...Reflect...Respond**
>
> 1. In chart form, summarize the rules governing valid deductive syllogisms.
> 2. Create an argument by analogy about the effectiveness of the computers located in your school's resource centre.
> 3. Reread the excerpt in which Sherlock Holmes explains how he knows certain things about his client, Jabez Wilson. Would you have considered Holmes's conclusions reliable if Wilson had not confirmed their accuracy? Why?

ABDUCTIVE REASONING

Abductive reasoning, a term coined by the 19th-century American philosopher **Charles Sanders Peirce**, is a kind of inductive reasoning. Similar to an educated guess, abductive reasoning is based on the best explanation for what has been observed. While inductive reasoning leads to a generalization or a general rule based on several pieces of evidence, abductive reasoning is used to explain a specific case. In fact, it can be argued that Holmes' brand of inductive reasoning was, in fact, abductive reasoning.

Suppose you overhear two students talking outside the principal's office on the first day of school. You recognize neither of them but notice that they are dressed up and

PROFILE
Charles Sanders Peirce
Wasp in a Bottle

A remarkable American scientist, mathematician, and logician, Charles Sanders Peirce (pronounced "purse") had a versatile, analytical mind — and a messy life. He made enemies as well as friends and occasionally treated his friends so badly that they became enemies, too.

Peirce was born in 1839 in Cambridge, Massachusetts. His father, Benjamin, taught mathematics at Harvard University and schooled his son by assigning him mathematical problems, then checking his solutions. As a result, Peirce acquired a lifelong habit of thinking through problems entirely on his own.

Peirce entered Harvard when he was just 16 years old and graduated when he was 20. Then his father helped him land a job with the United States Coast and Geodetic Survey, which Benjamin had helped found. In 1879, Benjamin again used to his influence to help Peirce get a second job teaching logic at Johns Hopkins University. Some members of the Johns Hopkins faculty resented this use of parental influence. When Peirce's father died, their resentment boiled over.

One of Peirce's resentful colleagues was Simon Newcomb, an influential mathematician and astronomer. Newcomb told the school's president about Peirce's adulterous relationship with a woman who was not yet his second wife. In the prudish 1880s, a relationship like this was considered scandalous — and Peirce was fired. Still, Newcomb was not satisfied. He and a group of friends made sure Peirce did not get assignments to teach or give public lectures. Newcomb even managed to have Peirce's work at the Geodetic Survey terminated in 1891.

Though both Peirce and his second wife had inherited enough money to live comfortably, a series of reckless business decisions left them struggling. A stock market crash in 1893 finished them off financially. By 1895, Peirce was mostly down and out in New York, though he still belonged to an elitist retreat called the Century Club. One patron recalls meeting him there:

> He is a mathematician, that sort of a man of failed life so far as professional recognition goes, but of acknowledged extraordinary ability, and is positively the most agreeable person in the city ... like Socrates in his willingness to discuss anything and in his delight in posing things and expressing things.

Soon after this encounter, the Century Club cancelled Peirce's membership. He had fallen behind in paying his dues, and members accused him of drunkenness, petty thefts, and forgery.

Peirce worked hard all his life, writing constantly and producing essays. Though he did manage to make a little money from publishing a few articles, most of his writing remained unpublished during his lifetime. All the while, he also worked on a pet project, which he described as fashioning "a philosophy like that of Aristotle, that is to say, to outline a theory so comprehensive that, for a long time to come, the entire work of human reason ... shall appear as the filling up of its details."

Peirce's physical ailments, which included manic depression and a painful form of neuralgia, a disease of the nerves, prevented him from succeeding in a conventional way. He once compared himself to "a wasp in a bottle," buzzing furiously in a glass cage formed by his own self-conception and other people's reaction to it.

When Peirce died in 1914, his writings were in disarray, and few people were interested in them. This situation has changed, however, as philosophers have come to realize their value. Since 1975, scholars have been compiling and publishing Peirce's works in chronological order so that his contribution to philosophy can be truly appreciated. The results so far are astounding. Long after his death, Peirce has come to be considered one of the most accomplished logicians of modern times.

Figure 4.7
Charles Sanders Peirce helped found a significant school of thought called American pragmatism.

IDEAS IN CONTEXT

Like Aristotle, Charles Sanders Peirce was interested in science. He wanted to know how things worked. One of Peirce's early papers was titled "How to Make Our Ideas Clear." Peirce believed that when an idea is clear, its meaning can be seen in its practical effects. He was actually proposing a logic of effects, rather than a logic of causes. Peirce was most concerned with the *usefulness* of an idea. Along with his fellow American philosophers John Dewey and William James, he is credited with founding a school of epistemology called pragmatism. Pragmatists say that the meaning of an idea is identical to its effects.

appear a little anxious. You conclude that this is typical new-student behaviour. To arrive at this general conclusion about the students' behaviour, you used inductive reasoning.

Imagine the same scenario again. This time, you conclude that the students are new to the school. To arrive at this conclusion about the specific students, you used abductive reasoning, which involves making a best guess or giving a best explanation. Whether you are right depends on whether there are other explanations for the same event. Perhaps there are, and you don't know about them. Perhaps you thought of other explanations and discarded them. Scientists use a similar process when trying to explain a new or surprising event. Abduction involves not only coming up with an explanation, but also testing it.

LOGICAL FALLACIES

How can people assess arguments in everyday life when speakers interrupt each other, talk too quickly, or simply walk away in a huff? Doing so is certainly more challenging than deciding whether a syllogism is valid or invalid. Still, bad arguments tend to display predictable logical **fallacies**, which are flaws or faults, that help people assess the soundness of arguments.

All fallacies try to persuade without providing legitimate grounds for accepting the conclusion. People may commit fallacies accidentally or use them deliberately to manipulate others. People who can identify the most common patterns of incorrect reasoning are less likely to use fallacious reasoning themselves — or to be fooled by someone else's fallacious reasoning.

Logical fallacies can be formal or informal. Both are arguments that sound persuasive but fail to provide logical support for their conclusions. A **formal fallacy** is a structural error in deductive logic. This error in form makes a syllogism invalid. An **informal fallacy** is a kind of argument that persuades by means other than reason. An informal fallacy might appeal to emotion, for example.

Figure 4.8

"VERY CREATIVE. VERY IMAGINATIVE. LOGIC... THAT'S WHAT'S MISSING."

What comment is cartoonist Sidney Harris making about the relative imortance of creativity, imagination, and logic?

FORMAL FALLACIES

Syllogisms that are invalid — incorrect in form — are fallacious. Though some examples of fallacious syllogisms were provided earlier, they are not the only kinds. Formal fallacies come in many forms. One occurs when a new premise that has no connection to the first is introduced. Consider this example of a fallacious disjunctive syllogism.

> I'll either study tonight or watch TV.
> I have a test in the morning.
> Therefore, I will watch *Law and Order* and crack the books right after that.

> *If most of us are ashamed of shabby clothes and shoddy furniture, let us be more ashamed of shabby ideas and shoddy philosophy.*
>
> – Albert Einstein

The conclusion of this syllogism may very well describe what is likely to happen — if you do not fall asleep and do neither. Still, this argument is invalid because the second premise does not deny one of the alternatives expressed in the first. Instead, it introduces a completely new premise. In fact, this fallacy is sometimes called the little premise from nowhere.

Here is a fallacious hypothetical syllogism. Can you spot the fallacy?

If it rained last night, then the street will be wet in the morning.
The street is wet this morning.
Therefore, it must have rained last night.

At first glance, this argument sounds persuasive. Compare its form with either form of a valid hypothetical syllogism, however, and the error in reasoning shows up.

Form of Example (Invalid)	Valid Form
If A, then B	If A, then B
B	A
Therefore, A	Therefore, B

The fact that the streets are wet this morning does not necessarily mean that it rained last night. Perhaps a water main broke or a street-cleaning truck washed the street.

INFORMAL FALLACIES

People commit fallacies all the time, sometimes with good reason. Now and then everyone makes a hasty generalization. This kind of incorrect reasoning can occur when someone wants to make a point but does not want to take the time — or perhaps spend the money — to prove it. In the field of criminal law, for example, evidence is sometimes not as strong as first assumed and the result is a plea bargain.

Other informal fallacies are easier to spot. Many of these were identified by early logicians who assigned them Latin names at a time when Latin was the language of scholars. Many of these Latin names have persisted.

Informal fallacies tend to fall into three groups: fallacies of relevance, fallacies of presumption, and fallacies of ambiguity.

Fallacies of Relevance

Fallacies of relevance fail to provide support for their conclusions.

Appeal to Force (*argumentum ad baculum*)
In an appeal to force, someone in a position of power makes threatening statements to force a conclusion.

> I'm the teacher here, and I say that Kim Campbell was Canada's greatest prime minister. Therefore, Kim Campbell is Canada's greatest prime minister.

Though this argument may be an effective way of forcing someone to agree — or pretend to agree — it offers no grounds for believing that the conclusion is true.

Appeal to Pity (*argumentum ad misericordiam*)
An appeal to pity tries to force a conclusion by evoking sympathy. It does this by focusing on the distressing condition of the speaker or another group.

> Hey, I'm just a teenager whose only method of transportation is a skateboard. If you give me this ticket, officer, my parents will take away my skateboard, and then I won't be able to attend school. Wouldn't that make you feel bad?

This argument is fallacious because the teenager's circumstances are irrelevant to the issue of whether he committed a violation.

Appeal to Emotion (*argumentum ad populum*)

An appeal to emotion relies on emotionally charged language to arouse strong feelings and force a conclusion.

> As all clear-thinking residents of our fine province have already realized, Candidate X's plan for financing public housing is nothing but the bloody-fanged wolf of free-market capitalism cleverly disguised in the harmless sheep's clothing of concern for children. I urge you to reject this plan — and this candidate.

In this example, the fallacy arises because no reason for rejecting Candidate X's plan is stated.

Irrelevant Conclusion (*ignoratio elenchi*)

A fallacy of irrelevant conclusion tries to establish the truth of a proposition by offering an argument that supports a different conclusion.

> Kids need a lot of attention, and working parents don't have as much time to provide this attention as stay-at-home parents, so mothers should not work outside the home.

The premises of this argument might support a conclusion about working parents in general, but they do not lead to a conclusion about mothers only. Though clearly fallacious, arguments like this serve to distract attention from the issue.

Appeal to Authority (*argumentum ad verecundiam*)

In an appeal to authority, the opinion of someone famous or accomplished in a particular area is offered as a guarantee of the truth of a conclusion. Along with attacks on the person and appeals to ignorance, this fallacy involves the mistaken assumption that there is a connection between the truth of a proposition and some feature of the person who asserts or denies it.

> On DUDE Radio, I heard Jennifer Lopez say that spiders are insects. So spiders must be insects.

As a pattern of reasoning, the assumption made in this argument is clearly mistaken. No proposition must be true because an individual — no matter how talented or successful — believes it. Even experts can be mistaken. People may accept this kind of testimony as evidence, but never as proof.

Attack on the Person (*argumentum ad hominem*)

The flip side of an appeal to authority is an *ad hominem* argument, which attacks the person who makes the argument. In Latin, *ad hominem* means "concerning the man." The aim of this fallacy is to force rejection of a conclusion by mounting a personal attack on the person who holds the opinion.

> So you think that a 12-month school year would be a good thing? Well, you're a terrible student and your locker's a complete mess. So your opinions aren't worth considering.

A form of this fallacy is sometimes called poisoning the well. This comes from the expression, "You're poisoning the well before anyone can drink from it." In any of their varieties, *ad hominem* arguments are fallacious because they attack the person rather than the argument. In logic, personal characteristics are irrelevant.

Appeal to Ignorance (*argumentum ad ignoratiam*)
An appeal to ignorance tries to argue that something is true because it has not been proven false, or conversely, that something must be false because it has not been proven true.

> No one has proven that there is no intelligent life on the moons of Jupiter, right? So you have to admit that intelligent life exists on the moons of Jupiter.

A lack of evidence to support or refute a proposition does not guarantee that the opposite is true.

FALLACIES OF PRESUMPTION

Like fallacies of relevance, fallacies of presumption fail to support their conclusions. Fallacies of presumption do this, however, by stating a further proposition that is uncertain or implausible. They often contain unwarranted assumptions.

Accident
A fallacy of accident begins with a statement that is true as a general rule. It then errs by applying this principle to a specific case that is unusual in some way.

> Hey, you know the rule — always tidy your room. Don't talk to me about the fire in the corner. Just get that room cleaned up.

This fallacy arises because the general rule has not permitted any exceptions.

Converse Accident
The reverse of a fallacy of accident, a fallacy of converse accident begins with a specific case that is unusual in some way, then errs by deriving a general rule from this case.

> Felix Potvin likes cats, and he sure is an excellent goalie. I guess this means that people who like cats make excellent goalies.

Clearly, a single instance is not enough to establish the truth of the general principle expressed in this argument. Because this conclusion could easily be false even though the premise is true, the argument is unreliable.

False Cause (*post hoc ergo propter hoc*)
A fallacy of false cause infers the presence of a causal connection simply because events seem to be related in time or place. This fallacy is sometimes referred to as the *post hoc*, a shortened version of the Latin phrase *post hoc ergo propter hoc*, which means "after this, therefore because of this."

> I watched a movie on Thursday night, and woke up with a sore throat on Friday. I'm not going to watch movies anymore because they give me a sore throat.

Figure 4.9

"DOESN'T IT SEEM STRANGE THAT THE CLEANERS WOULD SHRINK ALL OF YOUR PANTS?"

Which fallacy of presumption has this man committed?

Begging the Question (*petitio principii*)
The fallacy called begging the question is sometimes hard to spot because it bases the conclusion of an argument on a premise or premises that need to be proven as much as the conclusion.

> Capital punishment is necessary. People who kill others in car crashes should be executed.

In this example, the conclusion is based on a premise that needs to be debated every bit as much as the conclusion. The premise takes for granted that capital punishment is necessary. This may be untrue.

People often misuse the phrase "begging the question" to mean evading the question, raising the question, or refraining from answering the question. In logic, these meanings are incorrect. Begging the question means to base a conclusion on an unproven assumption.

Complex Question
A fallacy of complex question presupposes the truth of a conclusion by including it in the statement of the premise or premises of the argument.

> Have you stopped watching so much television? You haven't stopped? Well then, you're still watching way too much television.

In this example, the conclusion — that you're watching too much television — simply restates the premise. To accept the truth of the conclusion, you must accept the truth of the premise.

FALLACIES OF AMBIGUITY
Several patterns of incorrect reasoning arise from the imprecise use of language. A word, phrase, or sentence is ambiguous when it has two or more distinct meanings. These shifting meanings can result in a number of fallacies. So can confusing grammar.

Figure 4.10

How has cartoonist Mike Baldwin used the ambiguity of language to comment on a social condition?

Equivocation
Fallacies of equivocation use an ambiguous word or phrase in two or more different ways within the same argument.

> Really exciting novels are rare, and rare books are expensive. So really exciting novels must be expensive.

In this example, the word "rare" is used in two different ways in the premises of the argument. As a result, the link established in the conclusion is false. Sometimes used very subtly, and even unintentionally, this fallacy can undermine deductive arguments that are otherwise valid.

Amphiboly
Fallacies of amphiboly occur when the construction of a sentence creates ambiguity.

> Most stores carry jeans for people with 32 waists.

How many waists do you have? In this example, the premise can be interpreted in different ways, creating the possibility of a fallacious inference. This kind of ambiguity becomes an issue when people try to base an argument on the statement.

Composition

Fallacies of composition involve drawing a conclusion about a whole or a group based on the features of its parts.

> You like gelatin, marshmallows, and pickles, so I know you're going to love the gelatin-marshmallow-and-pickle salad that's on the lunch menu in the cafeteria.

Even when something positive can be said of each individual part, it does not follow that the same can be said of the whole, as this example shows.

Division

Fallacies of division are the inverse of fallacies of composition. Fallacies of division involve drawing a conclusion about a part based on the properties of the whole.

> Zuhair's parents live in a fancy condominium complex, so their apartment must be fancy.

In this example, the attribute "fancy" cannot be inferred about individual units in the condominium complex.

Web connection
www.mcgrawhill.ca/links/philosophy12
To find out more about logical fallacies, follow the links on this Web site.

Recall...Reflect...Respond

1. Think of an example of abductive reasoning. On a mind map, brainstorm other possible explanations for the conclusion that was reached. Given these alternative explanations, evaluate the reliability of your initial conclusion.
2. Write two examples of formal fallacies and two of informal fallacies. Create a Venn diagram that shows how all four examples fail to provide logical support for their conclusions.
3. Think of an example of an informal fallacy that you have witnessed, experienced, or committed yourself. Present this fallacy to the class and explain what conclusion you think it was intended to force.

LOGIC AT WORK

Real-life arguments are rarely as straightforward as tidy syllogisms. To keep arguments lively, people often spice them up with real-life examples and rhetorical devices that lend emotional impact. Clever rhetoric can mask a bad argument, however. Have you ever felt persuaded by an advertisement or a political speech, yet remained suspicious that the reasoning might be faulty? It is sometimes hard to spot a bad argument as words flow. Still, recasting arguments in syllogistic form can help expose illogic.

PHILOSOPHY IN ACTION

Love Is a Fallacy

by Max Shulman

Max Shulman, the author of this story, was a humorist and screenwriter who often focused on philosophical issues. One of his literary creations was Dobie Gillis, a teenaged character who observed life with wry philosophical humour. Dobie Gillis became the hero of a 1950s film and, later, a popular TV situation comedy.

Shulman published the story excerpted here in 1951. The narrator is a first-year law student who wants to date a young woman who is already going out with his friend Petey Bellows. As the story unfolds, logic and fallacies play an unusual role.

"I've got to have a raccoon coat," Petey said passionately. "I've got to!"

"Petey, why? Look at it rationally. Raccoon coats are unsanitary. They shed. They smell bad. They weigh too much. They're unsightly. They —"

"You don't understand," he interrupted impatiently. "It's the thing to do. Don't you want to be in the swim?"

"No," I said truthfully.

"Well, I do." He declared. "I'd give anything for a raccoon coat. Anything!"

My brain, that precision instrument, slipped into high gear. "Anything?" I asked, looking at him narrowly.

"Anything," he affirmed in ringing tones.

I stroked my chin thoughtfully. It so happened that I knew where to get my hands on a raccoon coat. My father had had one in his undergraduate days; it lay now in a trunk in the attic back home. It also happened that Petey had something I wanted. He didn't have it exactly, but at least he had first right on it. I refer to his girl, Polly Espy.

The narrator slyly questions Petey to find out how serious he is about Polly. When Petey confides that they are not going steady, the narrator heads home for the weekend and returns to school with his father's raccoon coat. He then meets Petey.

I threw open the suitcase and revealed a huge, hairy, gamy object that my father had worn in his Stutz Bearcat in 1925.

"Holy Toledo!" said Petey reverently. He plunged his hands into the raccoon coat and then his face. "Holy Toledo!" he repeated fifteen or twenty times.

"Would you like it?"

"Oh yes!" he cried, clutching the greasy pelt to him. Then a canny look came into his eyes. "What do you want for it?"

"Your girl," I said, mincing no words.

"Polly?" he said in a horrified whisper. "You want Polly?"

"That's right."

The narrator persuades a reluctant Petey to accept the deal, then makes a date with Polly. On the date, he determines that Polly is charming but needs some lessons in thinking. He decides to begin by teaching her logic. On their next date, he starts explaining fallacies.

"First let us examine the fallacy called *dicto simpliciter* [sweeping generalization, which is related to the fallacy of irrelevant conclusion]."

"By all means," she urged, batting her eyelashes eagerly.

"*Dicto simpliciter* means an argument based on an unqualified generalization. For example: Exercise is good. Therefore everybody should exercise."

"I agree," said Polly earnestly. "I mean exercise is wonderful. I mean it builds the body and everything."

"Polly," I said gently, "the argument is a fallacy. Exercise is good is an unqualified generalization. For instance, if you have heart disease, exercise is bad, not good. Many people are ordered by their doctors not to exercise. You must qualify the generalization. You must say exercise is usually good, or exercise is good for most people. Otherwise, you have committed a *dicto simpliciter*. Do you see?"

The narrator then moves on to explain hasty generalizations.

"Listen carefully: You can't speak French. I can't speak French. Petey Bellows can't speak French. I must therefore conclude that nobody at the University of Minnesota can speak French."

"Really?" said Polly, amazed. "Nobody?"

I hid my exasperation. "Polly, it's a fallacy. The generalization is reached too hastily. There are too few instances to support such a conclusion."

Then he launches into an explanation of the post hoc *or false cause fallacy.*

"Listen to this. Let's not take Bill on our picnic. Every time we take him with us, it rains."

"I know somebody just like that," she exclaimed. "A girl back home — Eula Becker, her name is. It never fails. Every single time we take her on a picnic —"

"Polly," I said sharply. "It's a fallacy. Eula Becker doesn't cause the rain. She has no connection with the rain. You are guilty of *post hoc* if you blame Eula Becker."

On their next date, the narrator explains the appeal to pity or ad misericordiam *fallacy.*

"Listen closely," I said. "A man applies for a job. When the boss asks him what his qualifications are, he replies that he has a wife and six children at home, the wife is disabled, the children have nothing to eat, no clothes to wear, no shoes on their feet, there are no beds in the house, no coal in the cellar, and winter is coming."

A tear rolled down each of Polly's pink cheeks. "Oh, this is awful, awful," she sobbed.

"Yes, it's awful, I agreed, "but it's no argument. The man never answered the boss's question about his qualifications. Instead he appealed to the boss's sympathy. He committed the fallacy of *ad misericordiam*. Do you understand?"

"Have you got a handkerchief?" she blubbered.

The narrator then tosses one last fallacy Polly's way. Can she detect it?

"Two men are having a debate. The first one gets up and says, 'My opponent is a notorious liar. You can't believe a word that he is going to say' ... Now, Polly, think. Think hard. What's wrong?"

I watched her closely, as she knit her creamy brow in concentration. Suddenly a glimmer of intelligence — the first I had seen — came into her eyes. "It's not fair," she said with indignation. "It's not a bit fair. What chance has the second man got if the first man calls him a liar before he even begins talking?"

"Right!" I cried exultantly. "One hundred percent right. It's not fair. The first man has poisoned the well before anybody could drink from it."

Within a few days, Polly masters logical fallacies. Delighted, the narrator decides that he will ask her to go steady. On their next date, he broaches the subject.

"My dear," I said, favouring her with a smile, "we have now spent five evenings together. We have gotten along splendidly. It is clear that we are well matched."

"Hasty generalization," she repeated. "How can you say that we are well matched on the basis of only five dates?"

I chuckled with amusement. The dear child had learned her lessons well. "My dear," I said, patting her hand in a tolerant manner, "five dates is plenty. After all, you don't have to eat a whole cake to know that it's good."

"False analogy," said Polly promptly. "I'm not a cake. I'm a girl."

I chuckled with somewhat less amusement. The dear child had learned her lessons perhaps too well. I decided to change tactics. Obviously the best approach was a simple, strong, direct declaration of love. I paused for a moment while my massive brain chose the proper words. Then I began:

"Polly, I love you. You are the whole world to me, and the moon and the stars and the constellations of outer space. Please, my darling, say that you will go steady with me, for if you will not, life will be meaningless. I will languish. I will refuse my meals. I will wander the face of the earth, a shambling, hollow-eyed hulk."

There, I thought, folding my arms. That ought to do it.

"*Ad misericordiam*," said Polly....

"Polly," I croaked, "you mustn't take all these things so literally. I mean this is just classroom stuff. You know that the things you learn in school don't have anything to do with life."

"*Dicto simpliciter*," she said, wagging her finger at me playfully.

That did it. I leaped to my feet, bellowing like a bull. "Will you or will you not go steady with me?"

"I will not," she replied.

"Why not?" I demanded.

"Because this afternoon I promised Petey Bellows I would go steady with him."

I reeled back, overcome with the infamy of it. After he promised, after he made a deal, after he shook my hand! "The rat!" I shrieked, kicking up great chunks of turf. "You can't go with him, Polly. He's a liar. He's a cheat. He's a rat."

"Poisoning the well," said Polly, "and stop shouting. I think shouting must be a fallacy too."

With an immense effort of will, I modulated my voice. "All right," I said. "You're a logician. Let's look at this thing logically. How could you choose Petey Bellows over me? Look at me — a brilliant student, a tremendous intellectual, a man with an assured future. Look at Petey — a knothead, a jitterbug, a guy who'll never know where his next meal is coming from. Can you give me one logical reason why you should go steady with Petey Bellows?"

"I certainly can," declared Polly. "He's got a raccoon coat."

Source: "Love Is a Fallacy." Max Shulman.

1. Use the terminology of logic to explain what is wrong with the narrator's logic in his final attempt to win Polly over.
2. Rewrite Polly's closing response to the narrator in the form of a valid disjunctive syllogism.
3. Test this disjunctive syllogism by representing it with letters or showing it on a Venn diagram. Is it valid?

RECASTING ARGUMENTS

Some — though certainly not all — arguments can be tested by recasting them as syllogisms. The key to doing this successfully is to find and restate the premises and conclusion of the argument. Take this argument:

> Let's play Scrabble. No? Why not? Board games are loads of fun, so I know that you'll love Scrabble.

It is often easiest to identify the conclusion first. In many cases, this is signalled by inference indicators such as "therefore," "thus," "as a result," "it follows that," and "so." Place this statement in the final position. In the example, the conclusion is

> Therefore, Scrabble is an enjoyable activity.

Then look for the premises, which are sometimes indicated by words such as "because," "since," "as," or "otherwise." You may only need to rearrange the propositions to make the argument a syllogism. In the example, the premises might be

All board games are enjoyable activities.
Scrabble is a board game.

Reassemble the premises and conclusion, and the argument looks like this:

All board games are enjoyable activities. (All A are B.)
Scrabble is a board game. (C is an A.)
Therefore, Scrabble is an enjoyable activity. (Therefore, C is a B.)

In this form, this argument is valid but not necessarily sound.

Words that indicate quantity (e.g., "a few," "a number of," and "several") can be restated as "some." And if the elements of an argument have been scrambled, each must be restored to

> *There is nothing more wholesome for us than to find problems that quite transcend our powers.*
>
> – Charles Sanders Peirce

its proper position. "Bankers? Friendly people," for example, can be recast as "All bankers are friendly people." In every case, the goal is to fairly represent what is being asserted in the form of a proposition

One way to verify an argument is to think of another argument in the same form that can act as a counter-example. If the counter-example is not valid or true, then the original argument is not valid or sound. Consider this argument, for example:

> Some students are not social climbers.
> All exam-takers are students.
> Therefore, exam-takers are not social climbers.

Now take apart this syllogism and assign a letter to each part of the propositions.

> Some A are not B.
> All C are A.
> Therefore, C are not B.

Then substitute another example for the letters.

> Some animals are not mammals.
> All dogs are animals.
> Therefore, dogs are not mammals.

Now it is easier to see that the two propositions are true, but the conclusion is invalid.

Recall...Reflect...Respond

1. Draw a flowchart that indicates the steps involved in verifying an argument.
2. Suppose you had an argument with someone you know. List factors that would help you decide whether this person's arguments were valid, sound, or reliable. Explain.
3. How might the list of factors generated in your response to the previous question help you improve communication in your relationship with this person in Question 2? Explain.

ASSESSING INFORMATION

Today, more than at any other time, people are saturated with information. As a result, there has never been a greater need for people to apply the principles of logic to **media literacy**, which refers to the ability to communicate in various media as well as the ability to understand and evaluate the messages of contemporary mass media.

In addition to reducing arguments to syllogisms and spotting formal and informal fallacies, people can do other things to enhance their media literacy — and to separate appearance from reality and information from persuasion.

Web connection
www.mcgrawhill.ca/links/philosophy12
To learn more about media literacy, follow the links on this Web site.

Here are some questions to ask about information you read, see, and hear in the media:

- Who paid for the message? Why?
- Who owns the medium in which the message was presented? Why is this message there?

- Who produced it? Is there a motive or agenda?
- What does the message say? How does it say it?
- What format does the producer use? What are the advantages of this format?
- What methods and techniques does the producer use to make the message believable? Do people speak for a point of view or a product? Who do these people represent? Are other views represented as well?
- Who is being targeted? What age group? What ethnic group? What socio-economic group? What text or images make you think this?
- Are values being expressed? Why? What are they?
- What kind of lifestyle is presented? Why? Is there a subtext (hidden message) that you should be aware of?
- Who makes money or benefits from this message?
- What stories are not being told in this piece?
- In what ways is this a healthy or unhealthy example of using the media?
- What can you do with the information you have obtained?

Because the findings of polls and surveys, for example, may be biased, identifying who commissioned and paid for a survey is important. This will help you decide whether bias might be a problem. It is also important to analyze other information presented in surveys. Sometimes the questions used do not offer genuine alternatives to people who are responding. Imprecise findings also can result from sample sizes that inadvertently exclude people because they are too small or insufficiently varied.

Here are some questions to ask about survey results.

- Organization: Who determined who was sampled and what was learned?
- Design of questions: Do they lead respondents to answer in a particular way?
- Sampling: Is it representative enough to give a clear reading?
- Data collection: Is it well planned, careful, and clear?
- Data processing: Is it careful and accurate?
- Analysis: Is it impartial? Did it produce consistent results? Are the results useful?

Figure 4.11

Harry S. Truman displays a newspaper that incorrectly reported his defeat by Thomas Dewey (no relation to the philosopher John Dewey) in the 1948 U.S. presidential election. The newspaper took a chance and based its headline on a poll that predicted a Dewey victory. This poll is a famous example of a poorly conceived survey.

Chapter Review

Chapter Summary

This chapter has discussed
- some of the main questions in logic
- some of the terminology of logic
- the nature of philosophical arguments
- valid and invalid arguments, sound and unsound arguments, and reliable and unreliable arguments

Knowledge and Understanding

1. Identify and explain the significance to the study of logic of each of the following key words and people.

   Key Words
   categorical syllogism
   disjunctive syllogism
   hypothetical syllogism
   abductive reasoning
   fallacies
   formal fallacy
   informal fallacy
   media literacy

   Key People
   Charles Sanders Peirce

2. On a chart, summarize the three forms of syllogism, including their distinguishing features, the rules that govern their validity, and the form each must take to satisfy the rules.

Thinking and Inquiry

3. On a three-bubble Venn diagram like the one shown here, summarize the characteristics of the three groups of informal fallacies and show how all three contain elements common to all logical fallacies.

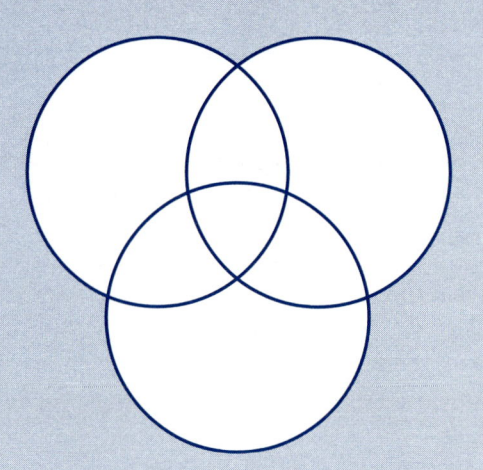

4. Logic is an essential tool of mathematics, as the following anecdote shows.

   Imagine Romeo riding a horse toward a castle. A ladder leans against the side of the castle. It leads to the room where Juliet lives. The bottom rung of the ladder is more than two metres above the ground. The ladder is not broken. It is in good condition. Someone who gets to each step of the ladder can climb to the next. Can an able-bodied person, Romeo, use the ladder to reach Juliet? The answer is yes, provided Romeo can get to the first or bottom rung of the ladder. It is not otherwise.

   What principles of logic must be applied to reach the conclusion given in this anecdote? Is this conclusion valid? Sound? Reliable? What important lesson does this anecdote teach mathematicians about using logic in the quest for mathematical solutions?

Communication

5. Form a group and discuss the relevance of logic to other areas of study. Choose one group member to record the points raised during the discussion. Ensure that all group members have an opportunity to contribute and that everyone applies the principles of logic. When the discussion is finished, the recorder should summarize the results and present them to the class.

6. The school principal has asked your class to create posters showing tips to help all students distinguish between good (valid, sound, and reliable) arguments and bad (invalid, unsound, and unreliable) arguments. The purpose of the posters is to raise awareness of good and bad arguments and to increase students' understanding of the benefits of this awareness. Working individually or in groups, design and create a poster that meets the principal's criteria.

Application

7. As games developers for Marker Brothers Games Ltd., your team is creating a board game called Fallacy. Working with a partner or in a group, create a game that requires players to show their understanding of logical arguments and fallacies. Fashion a game board, equipment, and written instructions for playing the game. Test your game by asking members of another team to play it.

8. Advertisers often use focus groups made up of members of the public to test reaction to TV commercials before they are broadcast. Select and record a current television commercial. Create questions that you might ask participants in a focus group assembled to assess reaction to the commercial. How would you answer each question? How would you improve the commercial to ensure that it is emotionally appealing, yet does not camouflage bad arguments?

Chapter 5
Introducing the Philosophy of Science

Chapter Expectations

By the end of this chapter, you will be able to
- demonstrate an understanding of some of the main questions of the philosophy of science
- evaluate the strengths and weaknesses of some of the major philosophies of science, making reference to classical texts
- formulate and defend your own responses to some of the major questions of the philosophy of science
- explain how philosophical theories have influenced the development of the natural and social sciences

Key Words

paradigm shift
causality
post-modernism
feminist
falsificationism
anarchistic epistemology
instrumentalism
logical positivism
pseudo-science
naturalism
phenomenology
NOMA principle

Key People

Nicolaus Copernicus
Francis Bacon
Shirley Tilghman
Thomas Kuhn
Isaac Newton
Charles Darwin
Albert Einstein
David Hume
David Deutsch
Karl Popper
Willard Van Orman Quine
Paul Feyerabend

A Philosopher's Voice

The whole of science is nothing more than a refinement of everyday thinking.

Albert Einstein (1879–1955)

WHAT IS THE PHILOSOPHY OF SCIENCE?

For most of recorded history, the quest for scientific knowledge was considered part of the philosophical search for wisdom. In 16th- and 17th-century Europe, for example, **Nicolaus Copernicus**, Galileo Galilei, **Francis Bacon**, and others who contributed to the changes in thinking that became known as the scientific revolution did so as philosophers, not as scientists.

One of the changes sparked by the scientific revolution was the creation of a distinction between philosophy and science. People started to think of them as separate disciplines.

In fact, the word "scientist" is less than 200 years old. It first appeared in written English in 1834. Though some English universities continued to offer science courses under the name natural philosophy as late as the 1890s, philosophy and science were by then usually considered separate disciplines in Europe and North America. Now, more than a hundred years later, their origin in a single discipline is sometimes forgotten.

Still, many philosophers and scientists continue to link the two disciplines. Canadian molecular biologist **Shirley Tilghman**, for example, spent years conducting genetic research. Like many scientists, Tilghman is also a philosopher. Her membership in the American Philosophical Society signals her interest in exploring philosophical questions related to her field of research.

When questions asked by philosophers and scientists converge and overlap, they are called the philosophy of science. Philosophers of science examine issues raised by scientific research and methods and also assess the implications for humanity of scientific theories and discoveries. They ask questions like, Is science objective? Can scientific theories be proven? Can science alone tell people what the world is really like? What is the difference between science and non-science? Are the social sciences possible? Is astrology science? and Are science and religion compatible? Questions like these provide a framework for exploring the role of science in the world.

Figure 5.1

Halley's Comet becomes visible to earth about once every 75 years. At one time, people believed that the appearance of comets signalled that strife was coming. Philosophers like Isaac Newton and Edmond Halley, after whom the comet is named, relegated these beliefs to the realm of superstition.

NATURE AND AIMS OF THE PHILOSOPHY OF SCIENCE

Both philosophers and scientists seek knowledge of the world and of human beings. They approach this quest in different ways, however. Many scientists focus on explaining how. In general, scientists ask first-order questions like, How do genes work? Philosophers ask second-order questions like, Is genetic research morally right? Scientists develop theories based on experiments and the study of observable phenomena, while philosophers reach conclusions through a process of questioning, discussion, and debate.

Consider recent discoveries that have helped astronomers broaden their knowledge of the universe. Despite these discoveries, most astronomers are reluctant to offer answers to questions about why the universe was created and whether people are on earth for a reason.

IDEAS IN CONTEXT

The interests of scientists and philosophers of science often converge. In *A Brief History of Time*, for example, physicist Stephen Hawking deals with black holes and the big-bang theory. At the end of his best-seller, Hawking speculates that science may be on the verge of discovering a "theory of everything" to explain all the physical forces operating in the universe. If this happens, he believes that humans may be able to explain why the universe came into existence. Some of Hawking's fellow scientists share his optimism, though others are skeptical. They point out that the complexity of the universe may be forever beyond human understanding.

This is because astronomers, like other scientists, seek physical proof — and no physical evidence proves or disproves the answers to these questions.

Questions like these are the bread and butter of philosophers of science, however. Still, they acknowledge that their answers are likely to be tentative and speculative — and may have more in common with the views of philosophers of religion than those of scientists.

The word "science" comes from the Latin *scientia*, which means knowledge. Like philosophy, contemporary science has become a discipline of specialties. Its branches are the physical sciences (physics, chemistry, and astronomy), the life sciences (biology, zoology, botany, and physiology), and the social sciences (anthropology, economics, sociology, psychology, and political science). Some people define the physical and life sciences as hard sciences and the social sciences as soft sciences. And in some circles, there is debate over whether the soft sciences even qualify as a branch of science.

THE PHILOSOPHER'S APPROACH TO THE PHILOSOPHY OF SCIENCE

Logic forms the basis of scientific thinking, and the logical techniques of inductive and deductive reasoning are the basic tools of scientific inquiry. At the same time, philosophers of science ask many of the same questions as philosophers in other areas. Their questions might be metaphysical (e.g., What is the relationship between mind and matter?). They might also be ethical (e.g., Is this action morally right?), epistemological (e.g., What can humans know?), aesthetic (e.g., Can judgments about beauty be objective?), or social and political (e.g., What role should the state play in scientific research?).

WHAT PHILOSOPHERS HAVE SAID

In the western tradition, the preSocratic philosophers — so called because they predated Socrates — were the first to try to explain the nature of the universe. These ancient Greek thinkers posed questions about the nature of matter, energy, animate and inanimate objects, and the human mind. They set out to find explanations that were more reason-based than the religious, superstitious, or mythological beliefs that prevailed at the time. More than 2500 years later, philosophers and scientists continue to be fascinated by the same questions.

Atomism was one theory developed by some preSocratics. This theory, which was remarkably similar to contemporary theories of matter, said that the physical world is made up of bits of matter so small that they are invisible to the naked eye.

Despite the work of the preSocratics, the fourth-century BCE philosopher Aristotle is considered the first true philosopher of science. Like the preSocratics, Aristotle was interested in nature and in explaining the origins, function, and purpose of natural phenomena. He and the students of his school in Athens collected specimens of plants, animals, minerals, and other objects. They carefully observed these objects, recorded the data, and classified their findings.

Web connection
www.mcgrawhill.ca/links/philosophy12
To find out more about preSocratic philosophers, follow the links on this Web site.

Figure 5.2

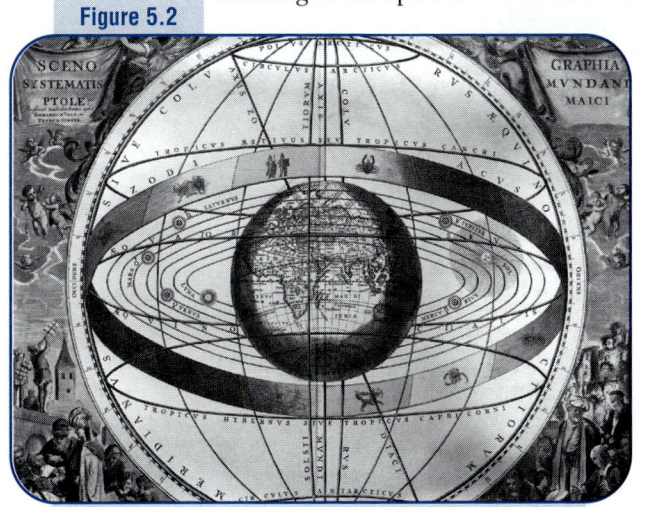

This map from a 17th-century Dutch atlas shows the earth at the centre of the universe. How would a map of the universe created today be different?

Aristotle's systematic approach to observing, recording, and classifying data dominated thinking in Europe and the Middle East for more than a millennium after his death. Christian thinkers like the 13th-century Italian philosopher Thomas Aquinas incorporated Aristotle's theories into their religious teachings.

One of these theories stated that the earth is the centre of the universe, a belief that was later supported by the second-century CE Egyptian philosopher Claudius Ptolemy. Ptolemy's geocentric, or earth-centred, theory said that the sun, moon, and stars revolve around the earth in perfect spherical orbits. The placement of the earth at the centre of the universe accorded with Christian teachings about God's creation of the universe according to a purposeful design — and the central importance of humanity in this design. As a result, the geocentric theory became part of the official doctrine of the Roman Catholic Church, which came to dominate Europe in the Middle Ages.

The geocentric theory of the universe dominated Europe for more than a thousand years after Ptolemy. Because few people dared challenge official views during this time, scientific investigation came almost to a standstill.

The spirit of scientific inquiry was kept alive by 12th-century Muslim philosophers, who preserved and built on the writings of Plato, Aristotle, Ptolemy, and other ancient thinkers. In *The Making of Humanity*, Robert Briffault described the debt owed by western thinkers to their medieval Muslim counterparts: "What we call science arose in Europe as a result of a new spirit of enquiry, of new methods of experiment, observation, measurement, of the development of mathematics, in a form unknown to the Greeks. That spirit and those methods were introduced into the European world by the Arabs."

Finally, in 16th- and 17th-century Europe, a number of scientific breakthroughs shattered previous assumptions about the world. These breakthroughs sparked a **paradigm shift**, a phrase coined by the 20th-century American physicist and historian and philosopher of science **Thomas Kuhn** who lived from 1922 to 1996. The term "paradigm" describes a way of thinking about the world. A paradigm underlies the theories and methods used by scientists during a particular period. A paradigm shift occurs when one way of thinking about the world is discredited and replaced with a completely different view.

The breakthrough that sparked the paradigm shift that began in the mid-1500s was Copernicus's challenge to the geocentric view of the universe. Copernicus's theory was heliocentric, or sun-centred. It placed the sun, not the earth, at the centre of the universe. This radical theory, which shook the foundations of western knowledge, was supported by other discoveries, such as those of Galileo Galilei and Johannes Kepler.

The discoveries of Copernicus and the thinkers who followed in his footsteps challenged views that had been sanctioned by both Church and political leaders. As a result, these scientific trailblazers were viewed as a threat to the established order and often met with hostility. Some, such as Galileo, were even persecuted.

IDEAS IN CONTEXT

The impact of Thomas Kuhn's notion of paradigm shifts extended well beyond the domain of the philosophy of science. The expression "paradigm shift" became a catch-phrase that is now applied to any major change in the outlook, perspective, or attitudes of society. It has been used, for example, to describe the change that occurred in the 1960s, when western values with respect to politics, sex, religion, culture, and other aspects of life underwent dramatic changes.

PROFILE
Thomas Kuhn
A Revolutionary Theorist

When the American physicist Thomas Kuhn published *The Structure of Scientific Revolutions* in 1962, it touched off a debate over how scientists conduct research and how scientific theories are developed and transformed. This debate continues today.

Born in Cincinatti, Ohio, in 1922, Kuhn was educated as a theoretical physicist, but his studies led him to develop a deep interest in the history and philosophy of science. As he thought about the history of science, he decided that its history is not the steady accumulation of knowledge. Rather, he said that scientific history is marked by "a series of peaceful interludes punctuated by intellectually violent revolutions."

Kuhn called these revolutions paradigm shifts because they change people's way of thinking about the world. He argued that the victory of one scientific paradigm, such as the heliocentric theory of the universe or the theory of natural selection, over another does not represent the triumph of "good" science over "bad" or even of "better" ideas over "worse." Rather, he said that paradigms replace each other as a result of protracted intellectual struggle. "Novelty emerges only with difficulty, manifested by resistance, against a background provided by expectation."

These paradigm shifts sweep away old paradigms and utterly transform the way scientists think about their fields of inquiry. For this reason, Kuhn said that comparing an old paradigm and a new one is not only impossible, but also pointless. The two paradigms are so different that they are incomparable.

Kuhn believed that most scientists conduct their research within the confines of a paradigm, even if they are not aware of doing so. Their discoveries and advances may add to and improve the existing paradigm, but they do not challenge its fundamentals. Kuhn called this method of scientific investigation normal science.

When scientists like Copernicus appear on the scene and formulate new theories that strike at the heart of an existing paradigm, said Kuhn, the scientific community enters a revolutionary period. As a result of the dramatic paradigm shift that follows, scientists are never again able to understand the world in the previous way. They approach their investigations with new eyes.

Who challenges old paradigms? In Kuhn's view, it is nearly always scientists who are either very young or very new to the field. He wrote: "These are the men who, being little committed by prior practice to the traditional rules of normal science, are particularly likely to see that those rules no longer define a playable game and to conceive another set that can replace them."

At first glance, Kuhn's own experience seems to contradict his assertion about the role of young scientists in sparking paradigm shifts. *The Structure of Scientific Revolutions* was published when he was 40. A closer look reveals, however, that he actually wrote the manuscript when he was a young graduate student at Harvard University. Kuhn died in 1996.

Figure 5.3

Since it was published, Thomas Kuhn's *The Structure of Scientific Revolutions* has sold more than a million copies in 16 languages and is required reading for courses in education, history, and psychology — as well as in the history and philosophy of science.

In 1620, the English philosopher Francis Bacon published a book that laid the foundation of what has become known as the scientific method. Titled *The New Organon*, the book introduced a systematic method of formulating hypotheses or theories based on evidence provided by the senses. Bacon stipulated that these theories must then be tested against even more evidence provided by the senses. The purpose of this process is to arrive at a general truth.

Web connection
www/mcgrawhill.ca/links/philosophy12
To find out more about Galileo, follow the links on this Web site.

Because of his emphasis on evidence provided by the senses, Bacon is considered an empiricist. An empiricist is someone who believes that knowledge comes from experiences provided by the senses: hearing, seeing, smelling, tasting, and touching.

In 1687, the English philosopher Isaac Newton took Bacon's thinking about the scientific method several steps farther. His *Mathematical Principles of Natural Philosophy* used calculus, a new form of abstract mathematics that he had invented, to prove that the physical laws of motion are universal.

Because he relied on reason to support his theories, Newton is considered a rationalist. Rationalists believe not only that reason enables people to know things that the senses do not reveal, but also that it is the primary source of knowledge. Newton's reliance on abstract mathematical principles broke new ground in people's thinking about natural phenomena and blazed the way for the philosophers and scientists who followed.

THOUGHT EXPERIMENT: *Thick as a Brick*

Suppose you have travelled to the historic city of Pisa, Italy. There, you climb the famous leaning tower and throw a brick off the top. As the brick falls, it splits in two. Though the two pieces are not the same size, each is lighter than the original. What will happen? Will the two pieces slow down and fall at a speed that relates to their size? Will the larger piece reach the ground before the smaller one? Or will the two pieces continue to fall side by side at the original rate, reaching the ground at the same time?

This thought experiment was created by Galileo Galiei, who was born in 1564 near Pisa. He had already tested his theory, so he knew the answer to the questions. He and his students had dropped two balls of differing weights off the tower and found that both reached the ground at the same time.

They had conducted this experiment to test Aristotle's theory that said that heavier objects fall faster than light ones. Aristotle had never tested his theory because he didn't believe in experiment. In his view, the theory was logical — and that was that. As result, for more than 1800 years, people assumed that if you dropped a 50-gram ball and a 500-gram ball from the same height, the heavier ball would reach the ground first.

If Galileo thought that people would accept that his experiment disproved Aristotle's theory, he was sadly mistaken. Few were ready to give up a belief that not only had been passed down through generations, but was also endorsed by religious and political leaders.

Figure 5.4

CHAPTER 5 Introducing the Philosophy of Science MHR 93

Like many thinkers who contributed to the scientific revolution in Europe, Newton believed firmly in the Christian God. His theories helped reconcile scientific theory and religious belief. The Christian God could still be viewed as the creator who set the universe in motion according to a purposeful design.

Figure 5.5

By the 18th century, scientific ideas and instruments had become the rage among wealthy Europeans. This painting pokes fun at some of these people, who appear to lack even a basic understanding of how to use a telescope and magnifying glass.

The idea that a divinely created purposeful design governs the universe was challenged in the mid-19th century by the work of scientists such as **Charles Darwin**. In *On the Origin of Species by Means of Natural Selection*, published in 1859, Darwin suggested that the world is the result of a struggle for survival rather than a carefully planned creation of God. Darwin's theory of natural selection says that in the competition for scarce resources, the weak die and the strongest and best adapted to the environment survive to pass on their genes. Because Darwin's theory altered people's view of the world, this paradigm shift is often called the Darwinian revolution.

Darwin's work was not the only challenge to western notions of the world as a well-ordered place that exists to fulfil a higher purpose. In the 20th century, **Albert Einstein**'s theory of relativity had a profound impact on the way people understand themselves and their origins. As the 20th century unfolded, catastrophic events, such as world wars and acts of genocide, and an increasing reliance on technology further eroded many people's faith in God. This faith was often replaced with an equally fervent faith in science.

As science continues to provide people with greater knowledge of the world they live in, philosophers of science have become even more concerned about the effects of scientific discoveries on human society. The 20th-century Japanese philosopher Keiji Nishitani, for example, wondered whether science is pushing the world toward nihilism. The word "nihilism" comes from the Latin nihil, which means nothing.

If science tells people that they are nothing but masses of particles functioning according to laws beyond human control, asked Nishitani, does this confirm the nihilist view that life has no value or meaning? He concluded that the answer is no, saying that people must not think of themselves as science does. Rather, he said, people must create their own meaning.

Nishitani's thinking shows how the role of philosophers has changed over the millennia. At first, philosopher-scientists were concerned with expanding human knowledge by describing and explaining natural phenomena. They then moved on to focus on the methods of arriving at scientific knowledge. Then, as philosophy and science became separate disciplines, philosophers of science began to ask questions about how scientific discoveries transform the way people think and live.

Recall...Reflect...Respond

1. How is the philosophy of science different from science?
2. Choose a scientific paradigm shift and explain how it changed the way people viewed the world.
3. Describe how you resolved a recent dilemma. Does your method of resolving the dilemma suggest that you are by nature a philosopher or a scientist? Explain why.

How Philosophers Have Said It

Philosophers of science and scientists often use the same terms. Whereas scientists use these terms matter of factly, philosophers of science often look beyond the commonly accepted meanings of terms to question the beliefs and assumptions that underlie them.

Take causality, or cause and effect, a concept that is central to scientific inquiry — and everyday life. When a connection between two events is observed, people conclude that the first event causes the second. Suppose you observe a child kicking a ball. You see the child's foot hit the ball, then notice the ball moving away from the child's foot. You conclude that the kick was the cause and the movement of the ball was the effect.

The 18th-century Scottish philosopher David Hume challenged this conclusion. Hume maintained that even if you saw the child kick the ball millions of times, it would be wrong to conclude that there is a cause-and-effect relationship between the kick and the ball's movement. He said that it is impossible to predict with certainty that the next time the child kicks the ball, the effect will be the same.

Hume's challenging of the causality paradigm called into question inductive reasoning, a critical element of the scientific method. Scientists and philosophers of science continue to grapple with this problem today. If observations do not conclusively demonstrate a causal link between events, they ask, how can observation provide proof of anything?

Another term scientists and philosophers of science use every day is "theory," yet this word has a variety of meanings. Sometimes, it means an unproven idea, a hunch, or a hypothesis. A theory may also be a series of accepted statements that explain natural phenomena in a way that is widely accepted as fact.

Darwin's theory of natural selection, for example, explains how human beings and other life forms have developed and changed over time. On the basis of the evidence available for study, most scientists and philosophers of science regard this theory as "proven."

In some cases, disagreement exists over whether an idea constitutes a theory. David Deutsch, a contemporary English physicist and philosopher of science, has proposed the existence of other universes parallel to our own. As a result of his study of subatomic particles, which are invisible to the naked eye, Deutsch suggests that people actually exist in a multiverse, several universes at once. In some circles, Deutsch's theory is considered unjustified conjecture; in others, it is considered a viable theory that has yet to be proven or disproven.

Figure 5.6

Like many in the 18th century, David Hume was an avid billiards player. He used the collision of billiard balls to illustrate his theory that causality cannot be proven.

Web connection
www.mcgrawhill.ca/links/philosophy12
To find out more about David Deutsch's theory of parallel universes, follow the links on this Web site.

Many contemporary philosophers of science take the view that theories are best understood as tentative answers to scientific questions. These answers enable scientists to draw broad conclusions from the specific phenomena they are studying.

For a scientific theory to be accepted as law, it must

- be formulated in a meaningful way
- refer to facts that prove its validity
- be based on claims that justify its truth
- adequately explain the phenomenon it concerns

Philosophers of science do not necessarily accept laws in the same way as scientists. Philosophers ask whether scientific laws define connections between natural phenomena or merely describe events that have been observed to operate in a regular, predictable manner. Are so-called laws of nature universally valid? they ask. Or are they nothing more than haphazard connections between events? And do scientists err when they propose theories and laws on the basis of observing these events? Investigating answers to epistemological questions like these is an important part of the work of philosophers of science.

Why the Philosophy of Science Matters

At the dawn of the 21st century, scientific discoveries continue to spark tremendous change in nearly every aspect of people's lives. The nuclear age would not have been possible without the 20th-century breakthroughs in physics made by Albert Einstein and other scientists. The science of genetics has reached a point where cloning humans and creating artificial life forms are serious possibilities. Developments in computer science and neurology have led to speculation that it may not be long before a nearly human form of artificial intelligence is created. Biologists and other scientists warn that technological development and industrial growth are causing severe environmental damage that may have catastrophic effects on the planet's ecosystem. And astronomers continue to probe the origins, composition, and scope of the universe.

These scientific developments have had profound economic, social, political, and cultural consequences. They have changed the way people think about — and live in — the world. What is the meaning of these developments? To what uses have these developments been put, and how can they be used to benefit — rather than harm — society? These are the questions asked by philosophers of science.

Challenging the Foundations of Scientific Thought

Scientists and the public like to think of scientific research as objective, uninfluenced by emotion or personal values. They also like to think that scientific theories and laws are proven and that science can explain what the world is really like. Just as Hume questioned the notion of causality, however, some 20th-century philosophers called into question these fundamental assumptions of science.

Their questioning led to what some observers call the science wars, a debate over the kinds of answers science can provide. This debate continues today.

Is Science Objective?

Challenges to the notion of scientific objectivity have come from various sources, many of whom suggest that science is theory-laden. By this, they mean that scientific research is not value-free, but is always coloured by the paradigm and theories scientists have in mind as they begin to investigate. Critics claim that these notions influence the entire research process, including the choice of focus for an investigation, the data that are gathered, and the conclusions that are reached.

Though the objectivity of scientific explanations and theories has been questioned, many important scientists and philosophers of science continue to view the scientific method as the most reliable way of understanding human beings' place in the world. "Science offers the best answers to the meaning of life," wrote the British biologist Richard Dawkins. "Science offers the privilege of understanding before you die why you were ever born in the first place."

THE POST-MODERNIST RESPONSE

Post-modernism has been defined in a variety of ways. It is a catch-all term that was coined in the 20th century and often used to identify a cultural and philosophical trend that has pervaded many aspects of contemporary western society and the arts. Its adherents question the meaning of terms like "truth," "knowledge," "reality," "objectivity," "rationality," and "progress." These terms have formed the basis of ideas in western culture since the scientific revolution.

Among the ideas challenged by post-modernists is scientists' claims that their research is objective and value-free. Social constructionism, a school of thought championed by Kuhn, is often considered a form of post-modernism. In Kuhn's view, science is a social construct, a body of knowledge that is constructed and deeply influenced by the economics, society, politics, and culture of the dominant race, class, and gender of a society.

Post-modernists are also radical skeptics. Skeptics doubt all assumptions until they are proven, and some even challenge the idea that knowledge is possible. Post-modernists not only challenge the validity of scientific methods of discovery, but also dispute the notion that objective facts exist. They say that even the language used to express facts is laden with cultural attitudes that influence the way people understand facts.

To many, accepting the post-modernist view starts society down the path toward skepticism and even nihilism. If all scientific findings are to be considered tainted by sexism, racism, male bias, and class prejudice, they argue, any hope that science can help people understand the world is eliminated.

The Lighter Side of Philosophy

How many Kuhnian social constructionists does it take to change a light bulb?

You're still thinking of a light bulb in the old way, in terms of incremental change. We don't need a light bulb with more attributes. A paradigm shift is happening. We need ubiquitous luminescence.

THE FEMINIST RESPONSE

Until recently, science — like most other fields of intellectual inquiry — was dominated by men. Women were actively discouraged from pursuing a career or even an interest in science. Most scientific research was conducted by men and guided by men's assumptions, methods, and values.

IDEAS IN CONTEXT

To launch her career in molecular biology, Canadian scientist Shirley Tilghman was forced to challenge stereotypes. When she was a 16-year-old straight-A student in the early 1960s, her high school guidance counsellor advised her to become an executive secretary. At the time, many people still thought that a career in science was inappropriate for women.

Tilghman ignored this advice and studied science at university. She went on to work on the team that helped clone the first mammalian gene and become the founding director of Princeton University's Institute for Genomics. In 2001, she was appointed president of the university.

Take breast cancer research. For a long time, scientists did little or no research into its causes and cures. Some feminist thinkers suggest that this was because breast cancer strikes mainly women and was not, therefore, considered an important or prestigious area of research for male scientists.

In the 20th century, various feminist thinkers began to challenge previously held assumptions in many areas, including science. Some charged that science embodies a male understanding of the world and ignores women's ways of knowing. As an example, they point to humanity's relationship with nature. Since the time of the scientific revolution, the underlying assumption has been that nature is a force that humans must master and dominate.

Feminist ecologists say that this view has been responsible for much of the environmental damage inflicted on the earth. They believe that people must develop what biologist Barbara McLintock calls "a feeling for the organism." This is a sense of respect for and a more nurturing relationship with the natural environment.

THE SCIENTIFIC REALIST RESPONSE

Scientific realists approach the idea of scientific objectivity from a different perspective. They maintain that the objects of scientific study and theorizing exist independently of the minds of the scientists themselves. For this reason, realists say that theories can claim to be objectively true. They base this belief on two claims. The first is the metaphysical claim that material reality exists separately from people's mental concept of it. The second is the related epistemological claim that human beings can know what exists and can find out the truth about the laws and theories that explain it.

CAN SCIENTIFIC THEORIES BE PROVEN?

The belief that scientific theories provide definitive answers to questions about the nature of the world is common among scientists and the public at large. Some philosophers of science, however, dispute this notion. The debate over what can be proven by scientific theories has taken many twists and turns. Three of these are represented by the views of the 20th-century philosophers Karl Popper, Willard Van Orman Quine, and David Deutsch.

KARL POPPER'S RESPONSE

Karl Popper, a German philosopher of science, said that the quest to disprove theories is at the heart of the scientific method. This argument challenged the traditional view that science involves a search for proof. Instead, Popper advanced a theory called falsificationism.

Science never gives up searching for truth, since it never claims to have achieved it.
— John Polanyi

Falsificationism is the idea that science is a process of making conjectures, or guesses, and refutations. Popper said that scientists then set out to prove their guesses false. In Popper's view, scientific theories cannot be proved; they can only resist falsification. Theories that do resist falsification, however, can be tentatively accepted.

WILLARD VAN ORMAN QUINE'S RESPONSE

Quine, an American philosopher of science, took a different approach to the issue of proving scientific theories. He said that no theory can ever be refuted because alternative or auxiliary hypotheses can always be advanced to support it.

DAVID DEUTSCH'S RESPONSE

Many philosophers and scientists chart a middle course between these opposing points of view. In *The Fabric of Reality*, for example, Deutsch wrote:

> Science is a process not of deriving predictions from observations, but of finding explanations. We seek explanations when we encounter a problem with existing ones. We then embark on a problem-solving process. New explanatory theories begin as unjustified conjectures, which are criticized and compared according to the criteria inherent in the problem. Those that fail to survive this criticism are abandoned. The survivors become the new prevailing theories, some of which are themselves problematic and so lead us to seek even better explanations. The whole process resembles biological evolution.

Recall...Reflect...Respond

1. With a partner, list three widely held health-related theories that rely on causality for proof (e.g., smoking causes cancer).
   a) Choose one of these theories and debate its validity with your partner. One of you should argue from the point of view of someone who agrees with David Hume; the other should argue from the point of view of someone who does not.
   b) With your partner, choose another theory and brainstorm a list of values that may have influenced the objectivity of the research that supports the theory. Explain the possible effect of each item on your list.
   c) With your partner, debate the validity of the third theory. One of you should argue from Karl Popper's point of view; the other from Willard Van Orman Quine's point of view.

CAN SCIENCE ALONE TELL PEOPLE WHAT THE WORLD IS REALLY LIKE?

Until fairly recently, most scientists were confident that the scientific method could provide human beings with reliable information about what the world is really like. During the 20th century, however, developments like Einstein's theory of relativity, quantum mechanics, evolutionary theory, artificial intelligence, and a new skeptical epistemology have contributed to what some philosophers of science speculate is an emerging paradigm shift.

This emerging paradigm says that scientific explanations of the world are merely interpretations of observable or theoretical phenomena. Rather than representing true reality, these interpretations may represent nothing more than the mindset of the members of the scientific community that embraces them.

PHILOSOPHY IN ACTION

Imaginary Witness —
O.J.'s Blood and the Big Bang, Together at Last

by George Johnson

In 1994, two people — Nicole Brown Simpson and Ronald Goldman — were murdered in Los Angeles, California. Investigators charged O.J. Simpson, a former professional football star who was Brown Simpson's estranged husband, with the crime. Simpson's jury trial, which was broadcast live on national and international television, transfixed viewers and made headlines for months. A key element of the testimony at the trial was difficult-to-understand DNA evidence. Simpson was eventually acquitted, though he was later found liable for the deaths at a civil trial.

This piece by journalist George Johnson, who writes extensively about science, appeared in the *New York Times* as the trial was unfolding. In it, Johnson imagines what might have happened if philosophers Karl Popper and Willard Van Orman Quine had been called to testify about the validity of the DNA evidence. Johnson's article shows how doubt can be raised by scientific evidence.

For the squirming jurors held captive in Judge Lance A. Ito's Los Angeles courtroom, the last couple of weeks of DNA testimony must seem like the worst possible visitation of a well-known recurrent nightmare: It's the last week of the semester and suddenly you remember the science class you forgot you signed up for and never thought to attend. Too late to drop it now. In a vast, silent hall, you stare at the final exam with its sickening thicket of meaningless symbols and equations. Your head swimming with the nausea of incomprehension, you run for the exit, but the security guards stop you at the door.

You're being asked to comprehend the incomprehensible, and to compound the horror, you learn it is not your grade point average at stake, but whether a man will be convicted of murder.

With its charts of copulating nucleotides and numbing presentations about introns, exons and the differences between the polymerase chain reaction and restriction fragment length polymorphism, the O. J. Simpson trial has taken on the tedious, didactic flavour of every bad science class you were forced to sit through. But as unwanted as this crash course in molecular genetics might be, perhaps the jurors are being exposed subliminally to a deeper, more disquieting lesson — one about the very nature of knowledge, scientific, legal and otherwise.

Throughout the ordeal, courtroom commentators have agonized over whether jurors without advanced degrees, much less college diplomas, can grasp the molecular intricacies well enough to make a reasoned determination of Mr. Simpson's fate. But perhaps the confused expressions on the jurors' faces betrays a more profound incomprehension — a realization that even in science, truth is always tentative. Even in science, the facts are inevitably open to interpretation.

The Next Expert

If the trial were truly to plumb the depths of the scientific issues at play in Judge Ito's courtroom, the testimony of DNA experts would have to be followed by testimony from some of the philosophers, living and dead, who have contemplated these issues. And so, as if the trial were not already long enough, imagine that the defence has called to the stand a surprise witness, the renowned philosopher of science Sir Karl Popper, who died last year.

"You may think," he declares, "that the prosecution has proved beyond a shadow of a doubt that the DNA in the blood on the gate at the crime scene is Mr. Simpson's, or that the DNA in the bloody sock and glove is a mixture of O.J.'s and the unfortunate victims'. But I say the prosecution is being naive about the scientific method.

"A scientist begins," Dr. Popper reminds the jury, "by formulating a hypothesis — the idea, say, that the moon circles the earth, the stars are powered by hydrogen fusion, the blood on the sidewalk is Mr. Simpson's. Then the scientist designs an experiment to test what has been supposed.

"However," Dr. Popper says, raising his voice just enough to strip the glaze from the jurors' eyes, "a hypothesis can only be negated, never proved."

The prosecution groans. Sir Karl is trying to snow the jury with the old Problem of Induction.

"There is a story we philosophers tell," Dr. Popper continues. "No matter how many white swans you see, you are not entitled to conclude that all swans are white. A black one may be lurking around the corner."

One of the lawyers from the defence team raises his brow and asks Dr. Popper pointedly: "Are you saying that these blood samples on which the prosecution's case hinges are like the white swans?"

"That's correct," Sir Karl says.

"And no matter how many labs match blood samples to Mr. Simpson or to the victims, one can never know if a fourth lab or a hundredth will come back with a negative result?"

"All it takes is one black swan," Dr. Popper says. "And since there can always be one more test, the prosecution can never 'prove' its point. That's the nature of scientific induction. No hypothesis can be verified, it can only resist falsification."

At this point, the prosecution, having anticipated Dr. Popper's philosophical dodge, calls its own expert witness, the philosopher of science W.V.O. Quine.

"Don't be so sure about the devastating effect of that hypothetical black swan," Dr. Quine warns the jury. "Popper may tell you that the prosecution's case is always on the verge of being proved wrong. But there is something he is leaving out: The Problem of the Auxiliary Hypothesis."

He pauses for effect.

"Even if you do see a black swan," he says, "that doesn't necessarily mean that your hypothesis about swan whiteness has been refuted. Perhaps this black swan is really white, but a disease of some sort blackened its feathers. Perhaps it fell into a coal bin. Perhaps through a momentary neurological defect — a misfiring neuron — your visual system incorrectly registered the colour. And even if a hundred people say they saw the black swan, it's possible that an errant electromagnetic field somehow distorted their brain waves."

The prosecutor, sensing that the testimony is veering toward the abstruse, steers Dr. Quine to the point. "So you're saying that even if the defence conjured up that imaginary negative blood test, this would not necessarily overturn the prosecution's hypothesis about the blood on the sock."

"That's right," Dr. Quine says. "A negative experimental result cannot be said to overturn a specific hypothesis, whether it's about swans or bloodstains. You can always explain away the outcome with an auxiliary hypothesis."

"You mean somebody might have botched the test?" the prosecutor says.

"Well, yes," Dr. Quine replies. "But I'm talking about something far more subtle than contamination or clumsiness. Every experiment is embedded in a vast network of assumptions, beliefs, theories."

"Does that mean," the prosecutor asks, "that if the result is negative, the fault could lie anywhere within this sprawling spider web of knowledge?" He looks aghast. "So, Popper just told us that a hypothesis can never be proven true, and now you're saying that a hypothesis can never be proven false!"

The jury's hush is broken by Judge Ito. "What next?" he barks. "Will we call a deconstructionist to the stand to argue about post-modern justice?" Then he orders the jury to wipe from their minds all this philosophical obfuscation. "Scientists and philosophers might be troubled by these objections," he says. "But in a trial, we must tolerate a lower standard of evidence: 'proof' beyond a reasonable doubt."

What No One Saw

Sir Karl and Dr. Quine exchange knowing glances, as if to say, "If only it were so simple."

Like the murders of Nicole Brown Simpson and Ronald L. Goldman, so many of the universe's pivotal events have no eyewitnesses — the big bang, the beginning of life on earth and its subsequent unfolding: Not one of these events had an eyewitness. In trying to understand them, we rely on circumstantial evidence that is always open to debate and interpretation. And like a scientific hypothesis, a conviction can always be overturned.

But there is one gnawing difference. No one can know first-hand what actually happened when the universe violently burst into life. Presumably there is one person who knows whether O. J. Simpson committed the murder. And that is O. J. Simpson.

Science in the late 20th century may be able to peer into a man's DNA and match it to a spot of blood on a sidewalk. Will science in the late 21st century be able to peer into his neurons and read the memories imprinted there? Can it conceivably wipe away all the epistemological troubles and prove beyond a doubt, reasonable or otherwise, that someone committed a crime?

Probably not. The neural data, like the DNA tests, would also be subject to interpretation. They too are records, not events. If anything is certain it is that in the search for truth we are always one step removed.

Source: "Imaginary Witness — O.J.'s Blood and the Big Bang, Together at Last." *New York Times*, May 21, 1995. George Johnson. Copyright © 1995 by the *New York Times*. Reprinted by permission.

---

1. How does Popper's argument become futile in light of the legal standard of evidence: proof beyond a reasonable doubt?
2. What is the weakness of Popper's theory according to Quine?
3. Which philosopher's position on the relationship between theory and observation do you believe possesses greater social value? Why?

THE ANARCHISTIC EPISTEMOLOGIST RESPONSE

The 20th-century Austrian philosopher **Paul Feyerabend** challenged the notion that the scientific method provides the key to understanding the world. Feyerabend argued that it is impossible for scientists to predict what knowledge they will obtain in the future. For this reason, he maintained that the scientific method should not be the only method of inquiry human beings use to make sense of their surroundings.

Feyerabend's approach became known as **anarchistic epistemology** because it denied the existence of a body of rules that can be used to decide what counts as knowledge. Like Kuhn, Feyerabend believed that the history of science is a history of differing viewpoints. From this, he concluded that future scientists may develop paradigms that explain the universe in very different ways.

Feyerabend also criticized what he viewed as the undue influence of the scientific establishment on political leaders. He considered this to be a modern version of the power that the medieval Christian Church used to suppress ideas that challenged its supremacy. As a result, he advocated the separation of the state from science. "The time is overdue for adding the separation of state from science to the now customary separation of state and church," he wrote in his 1975 book *Against Method*. "Science is only one of the many instruments man has invented to cope with his surroundings. It is not the only one, it is not infallible, and it has become too powerful, too pushy, and too dangerous to be left on its own."

Figure 5.7

When space expeditions transmitted views like this of Earth, the images gave human beings a new perspective on their planet and its place in the universe. How might this have changed the way we view ourselves?

THE INSTRUMENTALIST RESPONSE

Instrumentalism is a school of thought that says that scientific theories are not true descriptions of reality, but merely useful instruments — or tools — that enable scientists to impose a sense of order on random, even chaotic, natural phenomena. Instrumentalists point out that many of these phenomena, such as subatomic particles, cannot be observed with even the most powerful microscopes. As a result, their existence can only be inferred.

Though instrumentalists do not necessarily challenge the validity of these inferences, they do maintain that they should be viewed only as ways of thinking about reality. This means that scientific theories need not be supported by solid empirical evidence based on observations and experiments.

In this sense, instrumentalists agree with Feyerabend and other skeptics who suggest that because past scientific theories have been proven false, current beliefs are likely to be challenged in the future.

Scientists always have the conceit that we have discovered the ultimate truth and pity the people in the past for their ignorance. We forget that people in the future will be looking back and pitying us.

— Edward Harrison

THE LOGICAL POSITIVIST RESPONSE

The 19th-century French thinker Auguste Comte first proposed **logical positivism** as a way of applying the scientific method to the study of society. Comte believed that human thought had developed through a series of stages to the point where knowledge is derived from the systematic collection of observable facts.

In the 20th century, a group of Austrian and German philosophers of science — called the Vienna Circle — picked up on Comte's ideas. Their goal was to eliminate speculative, metaphysical notions from scientific thinking and research. This group exerted an important influence on philosophy in the English-speaking world. Their approach became known as logical positivism.

For a scientific statement to be valid, logical positivists believe that it must either be true by definition (e.g., 2 + 2 = 4) or subject to verification by evidence presented by the senses (e.g., It is raining). In this sense, they believe that science can tell people what the world is really like. At the same time, however, they maintain that most scientific, religious, aesthetic, and ethical claims are meaningless because they cannot meet this standard of verification.

Suppose that someone said, "Science is reliable." A logical positivist would argue that this statement cannot be verified and is, therefore, meaningless. Those who challenge the logical positivist view point to a fundamental contradiction in their thought, however. By their own standards of proof, an assertion that says, "This statement is meaningless" is in itself meaningless.

SCIENCE AND NON-SCIENCE

Few people today dispute the idea that the so-called hard sciences qualify as science. At the same time, there is debate over whether other areas of study can claim the status of science. One of these is the soft sciences, such psychology and sociology. Another is an area that is sometimes called **pseudo-science** or false science. Astrology and the study of extra-sensory perception, or ESP, and unidentified flying objects, or UFOs, are often placed in this category.

ARE SOCIAL SCIENCES POSSIBLE?

Some thinkers do not consider the soft or social sciences — sociology, anthropology, psychology, political science, and economics — to be sciences at all because they focus on human behaviour. For this reason, they are not considered scientific in the same way as so-called hard sciences such as physics, chemistry, and biology.

Those who take this position sometimes argue that human beings are not the same as Hume's billiard balls. The observer and the observed are members of the same species, and human behaviour is far more complex and unpredictable than most of the phenomena that "hard" scientists study.

Others disagree. Comte, for example, believed that scientific methods can be applied to social phenomena. As a result, he is known as the founder of sociology, the study of human society. Comte's view was bolstered in the 20th century by the rise of a school of thought called **naturalism**. Naturalists such as Quine argue that everything, including human behaviour, belongs in nature and can therefore be studied in the same way as natural phenomena. Quine refused to accept any distinction between knowledge derived from the senses and other kinds of knowledge. As a result, he viewed philosophy, the hard sciences, and the soft sciences as a single collaborative project whose purpose is to understand the world.

The ideas of Edmund Husserl, an early 20th-century German philosopher, also contributed to the blurring of the boundaries between the hard and soft sciences. Husserl founded a school of thought called **phenomenology**. Phenomenologists believe that things in the real world and people's consciousness of things in the real world are the same thing. This thing is "being." In Husserl's view, being is not a separate reality. It is human consciousness.

When combined with the idea that there is no distinction between kinds of knowledge, phenomenological ideas gave a tremendous boost to those who believe that science is made up of both the hard and soft sciences.

IS ASTROLOGY SCIENCE?

Astrology, which was at one time linked with astronomy, is an example of a discipline that is now considered a non- or pseudo-science. Why is astrology considered a pseudo-science? Paul Thagard, a philosopher of science who has studied astrology, argues that a pseudo-science is a theory that purports to be scientific, but is less progressive or explanatory than alternative theories. As a result, pseudo-sciences like astrology face serious problems. Among these problems, Thagard says, is that their advocates make little or no attempt to develop or improve theories in response to criticisms and are selective in choosing evidence to confirm a theory's validity. This is the case with astrology, he says.

Until the 16th century, people believed that the earth was the centre of the universe. They also believed that the heavenly bodies that revolved around the earth exerted a celestial influence on human affairs, the weather, and nature. This view suggested that free will is an illusion and that people's fates are beyond their control.

Web connection
www.mcgrawhill.ca/links/philosophy12
To find out more about the history of astrology, follow the links on this Web site.

Medieval astrologers cast horoscopes that claimed to chart people's life cycles. It was not uncommon for European monarchs to summon a court astrologer during crises to cast a chart that would be used to help make decisions. As the heliocentric theory of the universe gained acceptance, however, the foundations of astrology were undermined. Still, astrology continues to attract millions of adherents. Galileo, Kepler, and Newton took it seriously, and 20th-century leaders like Adolf Hitler, Canadian prime minister Mackenzie King, and American president Ronald Reagan consulted the stars.

Recall...Reflect...Respond

1. Some countries, such as Canada, have imposed rules to govern genetic research. Is this the right thing to do? Support your position from the point of view of an anarchistic epistemologist, an instrumentalist, or a logical positivist.
2. Can the study of human behaviour be considered a science? Choose an example of human behaviour and explain how the scientific method can — or cannot — be applied to it.
3. Read your horoscope in today's newspaper or look it up on the Internet. Does its accuracy — or inaccuracy — prove that astrology is — or is not — a science? Why?

ARE SCIENCE AND RELIGION COMPATIBLE?

Since ancient times, the relationship between philosopher-scientists and religious leaders has often been troubled. In the view of many, scientific findings cast doubt on deeply held religious beliefs, such as the existence of God, the existence of the human soul, life after death, miracles, and other matters of faith that lie at the heart of many of the world's religions. The preSocratic philosophers, for example, wanted to find scientific, rather than mythical or religious, explanations for natural phenomena. Averroës, one of the medieval Muslim philosophers who were responsible for preserving the works of the ancient Greeks, said that theologians — those who study the existence of a supreme being — are unfit to interpret divine law correctly. In the 16th and 17th centuries, leaders of the European Roman Catholic Church persecuted thinkers such as Galileo. And in the 19th century, Darwin's theory of natural selection was disputed in some religious circles. This theory still encounters resistance from some religious groups who oppose its teaching in schools.

> *Science without religion is lame; religion without science is blind.*
>
> – Albert Einstein

Some writers have called this continuing tension between science and religion a war. In 1894, for example, Andrew Dickson White published a two-volume book titled *History of the Warfare of Science and Theology*. According to science writer and paleontologist Stephen Jay Gould, however, it may be time to call a truce in this war. Gould maintains that science and religion are not irreconcilable.

To show why, he developed the non-overlapping magisteria or **NOMA principle**. Magisteria, a word that comes from Latin, are areas of authority and teaching. According to Gould, science has one magisterium and religion has another. Science is, or should be, the study of what is. It should explain natural phenomena. Religion — and philosophy — should speculate on what should be and offer moral guidance to people searching for a sense of meaning in their lives.

In Gould's view, religion and philosophy lie outside the realm of science. Though scientists can try to explain how the universe came into being, what it is composed of, and what may happen to it in the future, they can offer no definitive answers to questions that explore why humans exist. In addition, science cannot set down rules governing how people should treat one another or what kind of society would promote human well-being and happiness.

The difference between science and philosophy was underlined by Noam Chomsky, an American philosopher and linguist. Chomsky wrote, "As soon as questions of will or decision or reason or choice of action arise, human science is at a loss."

The anthropic principle — *anthropos* is Greek for human being — shows how the views of scientists and religious thinkers may be reconciling. This principle, which is gaining acceptance among astronomers, says that certain constants operate in the universe. These constants, such as gravity or the mass of atomic particles, are so finely tuned that the slightest variation would have resulted in an entirely different universe — or no universe at all. Some thinkers say that this principle demonstrates that a form of intelligent purpose, a supreme being, was behind the creation of the universe. The British particle physicist John Polkinghorne, who is also an ordained Anglican priest, supports this view. He wrote: "God created a world that cannot make itself. It is not the puppet theatre of a cosmic tyrant."

Web connection
www.mcgrawhill.ca/links/philosophy12
To read more about the science wars, follow the links on this Web site.

The Gaia hypothesis, which is sometimes called scientific hylozoism, is another theory that is helping to reconcile science and religion. Gaia was the Greek goddess of the earth, and the word hylozoism derives from the Greek words *hyle*, which means matter, and *zoe*, which means life. Adherents of hylozoism believe that all matter is alive, either in and of itself or in combination with the *anima mundi*, a Latin phrase that means the soul of the world. This perspective accords with the values of environmentalists who believe that human beings must preserve the earth's ecosystem. Destruction of the ecosystem will result in the obliteration of most, if not all, life forms, including human beings.

As scientists become more reflective about the nature of their enterprise and religious thinkers come to appreciate the benefits of a scientific understanding of the world, the possibility of sharing ideas is becoming a reality. The anthropic principle and scientific hylozoism are just two examples of areas in which science and religion converge.

Chapter Review

Chapter Summary

This chapter has discussed
- some of the main questions of the philosophy of science
- the strengths and weaknesses of some of the major philosophies of science, making reference to classical texts
- how philosophical theories have influenced the development of the natural and social sciences

Knowledge and Understanding

1. Identify and explain the significance to the philosophy of science of each of the following key words and people.

Key Words	Key People
paradigm shift	Nicolaus Copernicus
causality	Francis Bacon
post-modernism	Shirley Tilghman
feminism	Thomas Kuhn
falsificationism	Isaac Newton
anarchistic epistemology	Charles Darwin
instrumentalism	Albert Einstein
logical positivism	David Hume
pseudo-science	David Deutsch
naturalism	Karl Popper
phenomenology	Willard Van Orman Quine
NOMA principle	Paul Feyerabend

2. On a chart, fill in a heading for each area of philosophy, omitting the philosophy of science. Under each heading, write a question that might be asked by philosophers of science about the area. Write a paragraph summarizing how the philosophy of science and other areas of philosophy overlap.

Thinking and Inquiry

3. In this excerpt from the novel *Jurassic Park* by American author Michael Crichton, a mathematician attacks the misuse of science. Which philosopher or philosophy of science is best represented by the mathematician's words? Write a paragraph to support your answer.

   > We are witnessing the end of the scientific era. Science, like other outmoded systems, is destroying itself. As it gains in power, it proves itself incapable of handling the power. Because things are going very fast now. Fifty years ago, everyone was gaga over the atomic bomb. That was power. No one could imagine anything more. Yet, a bare decade after the bomb, we began to have genetic power. And genetic power is far more

potent than atomic power. And it will be in everyone's hands. It will be in kits for backyard gardeners. Experiments for school children. Cheap labs for terrorists and dictators. And that will force everyone to ask the same question: What should I do with my power? — which is the very question science says it cannot answer.

4. The 1997 film *Contact* depicted the conflict between science and religion by highlighting the differing opinions of Ellie Arroway, a scientist, and Palmer Joss, a religious scholar. Both are trying to deal with the significance to humanity of the possible existence of life in other parts of the universe.

    You have been asked to write the screenplay for a sequel to *Contact*. Through a dialogue between Arroway and Joss, you plan to depict their differences over this question: Can science alone tell us what the world is really like? Portray this dialogue in a one-page scene.

Communication

5. You have been asked to write an article for *Why?* a philosophy magazine. The article, titled "The Ghost of Darwin" will argue that Darwin's theory of natural selection continues to influence the social sciences. Write the article, focusing on one of the social sciences.

6. Create a poster illustrating a paradigm shift that has occurred in science. Use illustrations, symbols, and text to show how the ideas of some philosophers influenced the ideas of others.

Application

7. This painting by the surrealist artist Salvador Dali is titled *The Persistence of Memory* (see also p. I).

    Figure 5.8

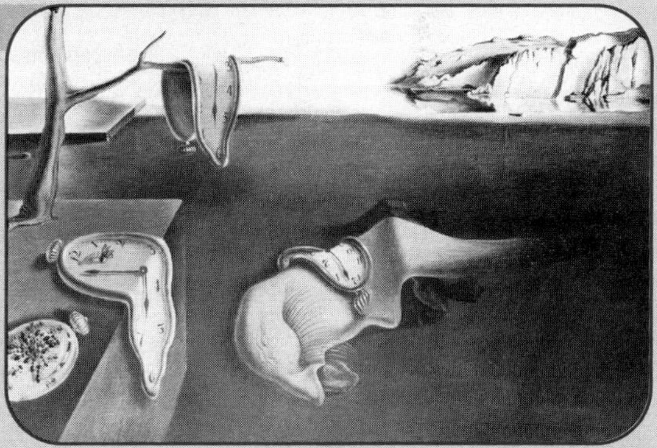

    What do you think Dali was trying to say about natural phenomena? What was he trying to say about time? Find evidence in the painting to support your responses. Does this painting support theories that say that science is a social construct? Why?

8. You are the host of a radio debate on this question: Should scientists continue trying to create artificial intelligence? The panelists will be an Aristotelian philosopher, a Newtonian philosopher, and a Darwinian philosopher. Prepare three questions, one for each panelist. To prepare yourself to guide the debate, summarize how each is likely to answer your question.

Write a philosophical reflection.
CULMINATING ACTIVITY

EXPECTATIONS

By completing this activity, you will
- identify the main questions in formal and informal logic and in the philosophy of science
- apply logical and critical thinking skills in practical contexts and to detect logical fallacies
- demonstrate an understanding of how philosophical questions apply to disciplines such as science, mathematics, and psychology
- evaluate the strengths and weaknesses of the responses to some questions of the natural and social sciences defended by some of the major philosophers and schools of philosophy
- defend your own responses to some questions of the natural and social sciences and effectively communicate the results of your inquiries

THE TASK

Thomas Kuhn's theory of paradigm shifts suggests that scientific theories that are widely accepted today may be abandoned in the future. This makes it important to examine all scientific theories and issues according to the principles of logic.

This culminating activity requires you to assess your own ideas and views and to detect logical fallacies in your own thinking. To do this, you will select a film or novel that focuses on one or more of the important issues of the philosophy of science. After developing questions to help you evaluate thinking — your own and that of philosophers — on the issues, you will write a personal response to the questions raised. To ensure that the arguments you present are sound and reliable, you will assess the logical strengths of your response by applying the principles of correct reasoning.

At the end of this course, your reflection may be combined with the products of other unit-culminating activities to create a philosophy magazine.

THE SUBTASKS

Subtask 1: Graphic Organizer
Select a movie or novel that addresses one or more of the main questions of the philosophy of science. After reviewing the film or novel, create a graphic organizer that outlines these questions and the way they are addressed as the plot develops. In addition, summarize the responses to the same questions that might be given by at least two major philosophers or schools of philosophy. Choose philosophers or schools that represent differing views.

Subtask 2: Plot Summary
Referring to your graphic organizer, write a plot summary of the film or novel you selected. Outline the key events, showing clearly how these are raised or addressed in the philosophical questions identified on the organizer.

Subtask 3: Guiding Questions
Write 10 questions to help guide your personal response to the philosophical issues raised by the film or novel you selected. Be sure to include a balance of first- and second-order questions.

Subtask 4: First Draft
Write a personal philosophical reflection, adhering to the structure of the reflective writing form. As a guide, use the questions you formulated, as well as the assessment criteria. In your reflection, evaluate the responses of two philosophers or schools of philosophy to the questions you have identified.

Subtask 5: Analysis of Your Argument
Prepare a chart outlining your main arguments, the kind of reasoning applied when making each argument, the fallacies you may have committed, and suggestions for correcting the fallacies. Ensure that your reflection also meets the assessment criteria. You may wish to ask an editor and other reviewers — your teacher, peers, parents, or others — to comment as well. Attach the guiding questions and this analysis to the first draft of your reflection.

Subtask 6: Final Draft
Rewrite your reflection so that it presents valid, sound, and reliable responses to the questions and issues.

ASSESSMENT CRITERIA

The following criteria will be used to assess your reflection.

Knowledge and Understanding
Does your reflection

- identify the main questions in the philosophy of science raised by in the film or novel?
- identify the kinds of reasoning used in your arguments?

Thinking and Inquiry
Does your reflection

- include the differing responses of at least two philosophers or schools of philosophy?
- include an evaluation of these differing responses in your own responses to the questions?

Communication
Does your reflection

- communicate arguments with clarity and logical consistency?
- apply the features of the reflective writing form?

Application
Does your reflection

- include guiding questions that apply first- and second-order language and clearly connect to the main questions in the philosophy of science?
- include an analysis of your application of logic in your first draft?

UNIT 2
METAPHYSICS

CHAPTER

6 Introducing Metaphysics

7 Persons, Minds, and Brains

8 A Meaning for Existence

Unit Expectations

By the end of this unit, you will be able to
- summarize the main questions, concepts, and theories of metaphysics
- evaluate the strengths and weaknesses of the responses to some of the main questions of metaphysics defended by some major philosophers and schools of philosophy, and defend your own responses
- demonstrate the relevance of metaphysical questions and theories to everyday life
- illustrate how metaphysical theories are presupposed in other subjects

What is reality? What is a personal identity? Does a supreme being exist? Are human actions determined or free? What is the meaning of life? These are some of the central questions of metaphysics — and of day-to-day existence. Deciding whether a supreme being exists and whether life holds meaning affects people's values. Knowing who we are and whether we control the path of our life defines how we deal with various moral decisions, such as making promises and taking responsibility for our actions. Knowing what is real enables us to direct our actions to the world as it is, rather than pursue actions that are shaped by illusions, distortions, or misinformation. In other words, studying metaphysics enables people to respond to questions that affect human existence.

Chapter 6
Introducing Metaphysics

Chapter Expectations

By the end of this chapter, you will be able to
- demonstrate an understanding of some of the main questions in metaphysics
- evaluate the positions of some of the major philosophers and schools of philosophy on some of the main metaphysical questions
- formulate your own clear and cogent responses to some of the fundamental questions of metaphysics and defend your responses in philosophical exchanges with others
- explain with reference to some classic texts how various metaphysical theories that answer various questions make a difference in people's attitudes toward practical issues
- classify philosophical conclusions
- apply logical- and critical-thinking skills to evaluate and defend positions in philosophical writings

Key Words

metaphysics
idealist
realist
materialism
monists
dualists
ontology
determinism
substance
essence
form

Key People

George Berkeley
Plato
Thomas Hobbes
Baruch Spinoza
René Descartes
Laozi (Lao-tzu)
Martin Heidegger
Jean-Paul Sartre
Stuart Hampshire
Richard Rorty

A Philosopher's Voice

The great majority of mankind are satisfied with appearances, as though they were realities, and are often more influenced by the things that seem than by those that are.

Niccolò Machiavelli (1469–1527)

WHAT IS METAPHYSICS?

Metaphysics is the study of the basic structures of reality: being and nothingness, time and eternity, freedom and determinism, mind and body, thinghood and personhood, space and time, and a supreme being and nature. The 20th-century American philosopher Wilfrid Sellars said that metaphysics is the study of how things, in the most general sense of the term "things," hang together, in the most general sense of this term.

Many philosophers have called metaphysics "first philosophy" because it examines questions that lie at the heart of many other areas of philosophy. Take this epistemological question: What can I know? Before even trying to answer this question, metaphysicians would say that people should determine what the knowing I — the self — really is. Or take this central question of social and political philosophy: Do people have rights? Before trying to answer this question, metaphysicians would say that it is necessary to determine what a person is. Similarly, before trying to answer the ethical question, Why be moral? metaphysicians would say that people should first determine whether they are even free to choose to be moral. In other words, metaphysical questions must be answered before many other philosophical questions can be considered.

IDEAS IN CONTEXT

The term "metaphysics" has an odd beginning. Contrary to popular belief, it means neither beyond the physical, super-physical, nor supernatural. The term originated by accident when scholars were interpreting the works of Aristotle centuries after his death. They found that titles were missing from some of the essays about the problem of being. In the edition the scholars were reading, the essays with the missing titles followed Aristotle's writings on physics. As a result, they came to be called *ta meta ta physika biblia* in Greek, the language the scholars were reading in. This phrase means "the books that come after the physics." This was later abbreviated to *The Metaphysics*.

THE PHILOSOPHER'S APPROACH TO METAPHYSICS

Like philosophers in every other area of philosophy, metaphysicians begin by asking questions. One of the most basic questions is also one of the simplest — and most difficult: What, ultimately, is reality? This question leads to many others: What are the basic constituents — the basic building blocks — of reality? How many basic building blocks are there? One or many? What are the basic building blocks made of? Are they material or mental, or are they made of something that is neither material nor mental? Once these questions have been raised, a number of related questions follow: What is matter? What is mind? What is it to exist? What is "being"? Why is there something and not nothing?

Many metaphysical questions have a direct bearing on people's lives. These include questions like, What is a person? What is the self? What is the relation of my mind to my body? Am I free or is my life determined by other forces? What is the meaning of life? What is eternity, and do I have a place in it? Does a supreme being exist? If a supreme being does not exist, can my life have a meaning?

Some people have suggested that scientists are the best qualified to answer questions about reality. According to contemporary theories of quantum physics, reality is composed of subatomic particles: atoms, electrons, protons, quarks, and so on. The chair on which you are now sitting, and which seems so real

Figure 6.1

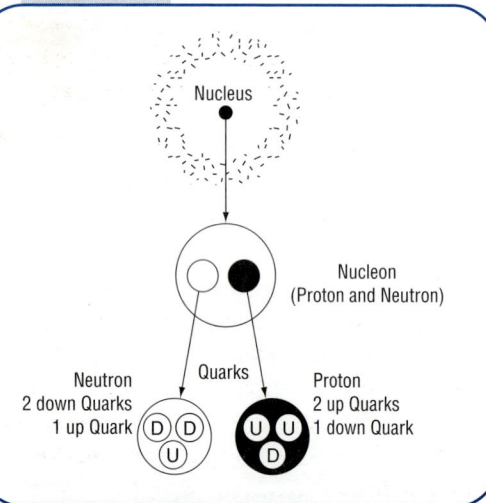

The nucleus of this hydrogen atom is made up of protons and neutrons. Protons and neutrons are thought to be composed of three quarks, though no one has proved the existence of quarks. Does this affect scientists' ability to describe reality?

and solid to you, is really a cloud of subatomic particles that are held together by a buzzing electromagnetic force field. It is much less rigid than you think it is. For that matter, you, too, are really a cloud of swarming subatomic particles. You might not experience yourself this way, but this is how scientists would describe you.

Though theories of quantum physics may explain what matter is, do they explain what reality is? If metaphysical questions about the nature of reality could be answered by scientists, there would be little need for metaphysicians. In fact, metaphysicians argue that the answers to these questions do not lie in science. Observing that scientific theories come and go, they point out that theories devised in the early 1900s are now regarded as out of date. A hundred years from now, today's theories may meet the same fate.

Metaphysicians believe that trying to answer metaphysical questions by citing empirical data — data gathered through the five senses — is an inherently unsatisfying approach. As a result, they try to supply answers that are general and durable enough that they will not become outdated. A great deal of metaphysical reasoning, in other words, proceeds in an a priori manner through reasoning rather than sense experience. Philosophical thought ranges farther than scientific thought, which depends on empirical thought.

WHAT PHILOSOPHERS HAVE SAID

Philosophers are not the only ones who have tried to answer questions about the nature of reality. One non-philosophical theory is called common-sense realism. Common-sense realists believe that what people perceive under ordinary conditions is reality. A common-sense realist would assert that the world consists of objects — redwood trees, sewer grates, skateboards, human beings, and so on — that can be perceived by the senses. Added to this list might be less obvious things, such as minds and souls. Many philosophers take issue with common-sense realism on the grounds that common sense is more often driven by ignorance or laziness than by the ideal of seeking the truth.

Philosophers from various traditions have offered a variety of theories, including idealism, realism, materialism, monism, and dualism, to explain reality. The 18th-century Irish philosopher George Berkeley, for example, was an idealist and a Church of England (Anglican) bishop. Berkeley denied the existence of material things, saying that reality ultimately consists of ideas and the minds that house them. He maintained that what people "common-sensically" view as material objects are really bundles of ideas that God placed in humans.

Platonic realism, a theory named for the ancient Greek philosopher Plato, offers a different answer. Platonic realists say that reality consists ultimately of ideal forms, or ideas, that are timeless, unchanging, immaterial, and more perfect than the world of changeable things that people encounter every day through sense perception.

Materialism, which is also known as physicalism, was first proposed by the ancient Greek PreSocratic philosophers. It says that everything is physical or that reality consists of matter. Materialists define matter as particles in motion and forces such as gravity. Materialists say that even something as elusive as consciousness is simply a material phenomenon, a by-product of activity in the human brain. The 17th-century English philosopher Thomas Hobbes defended this view, as do the contemporary Canadian philosophers Patricia and Paul Churchland.

Monists say that reality consists of one all-encompassing thing and that all particular things are manifestations or expressions of this one thing. The one thing may be material or it may be mental. According to the 17th-century Jewish-Dutch philosopher Baruch Spinoza, it may also be divine.

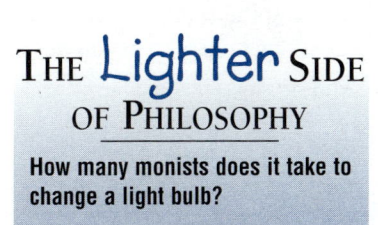

THE Lighter SIDE OF PHILOSOPHY

How many monists does it take to change a light bulb?

Silly question. There is only ONE monist.

In contrast to monists, **dualists** say that reality consists of two fundamentally different kinds of things: mind and matter. Though these two things have nothing in common, they are considered capable of interacting. The 17th-century French philosopher **René Descartes** advocated this view.

How Philosophers Have Said It

Like geologists, ornithologists, and auto mechanics, metaphysicians use a technical vocabulary to express their ideas. The common-sense terms used in daily life are too ambiguous and vague to be of use to metaphysicians. Though metaphysicians often develop their own vocabulary and definitions, most can agree on the meaning of certain terms that are used over and over.

Ontology, for example, is the area of metaphysics that deals with the nature of being and reality. **Determinism** is the theory that every event, including one's own choices and actions, is determined by a chain of causes extending back in time.

Metaphysicians also talk about **substance**. By this, they mean something that has an independent existence. Substance is the basic element of which things are made and may be either mental or material. In addition, metaphysicians use the term **essence**. The essence of a thing is its fundamental nature, its unchanging blueprint, the thing that makes it what it is.

Why Metaphysics Matters

Next time you bite into your favourite spinach and squid pizza, you are unlikely to be troubled by metaphysical questions. You will probably not ask yourself, Is this thing real? Nevertheless, metaphysical questions do arise in everyday life, often in ways that are quite significant.

Consider this question: Does a supreme being exist? Answering this question matters to millions of people. Many believe that if a supreme being exists, then their lives have a purpose, their values have an objective grounding, and death does not bring about their complete annihilation. For them, knowing that a supreme being exists is a source of comfort.

Many people also believe that if a supreme being does not exist, then — as the Russian novelist Fyodor Dostoyevsky suggested — everything is permissible. If everything is permissible, there would be no absolutes and it would be up to everyone to invent his or her own meaning for life. Some people find this view terrifying and a source of despair; others find it liberating.

Consider, too, this question: What is a person? This matters in medicine, law, and medical ethics, especially in debates about abortion and euthanasia. When does a human being become a person and thereby start to enjoy the rights of persons? Is it at the moment of conception, at the moment of birth, at some time in between, or at a certain point after birth? And when does a human being stop being a person and stop enjoying the rights of persons? Is it at the moment of brain death? Or at the cessation of conscious awareness? The answers to these questions affect everyone.

Reality and Appearance

Imagine this scenario. It is dark where you live, but your eyes are so accustomed to darkness that you do not notice it. You like it where you are. Something exciting is always happening in front of you. Figures move back and forth, make sounds, chatter, and exchange things. You have a front-row seat on a bustling scene. The people beside you are also absorbed in watching. You enjoy trading stories about and explanations of what the figures are doing and speculating on what will happen next.

Of course, you do not have much room to move. Because of the chains around you, you cannot get up or turn around. But this does not matter. You are comfortable. Food is delivered; you are warm and dry; and there is that wonderful show in front of you. You are content, even though you notice that your leg and arm muscles are becoming weak because you are not using them. This does not bother you because you do not want get up anyway. The chains are barely noticeable.

As you watch the figures and talk to your companions about them, one day blends into another. Days pass into months, months pass into years, and years pass into decades. Before you know it, you are old. Looking back on your life, you conclude that you have lived well.

Now imagine this scenario. It is dark where you live, but your eyes are so accustomed to darkness that you do not notice it. You like it where you are. Something exciting is always happening in front of you. Figures move back and forth, make sounds, chatter, and exchange things. You have a front-row seat on a bustling scene. The people beside you are also absorbed in watching. You enjoy trading stories about and explanations of what the figures are doing and speculating on what will happen next.

But something is bothering you. You keep noticing the chains on your legs and neck. Why are they there? Why are you not allowed to move? What is behind you? You ask your companions these questions, and they tell you to relax and stop thinking so much. They are content to watch and offer stories and explanations. This is not enough for you, however. You sense that the stories do not explain anything and come to believe that they are inventions created to make things seem okay.

One day, driven by curiosity, you bend the chains just enough so that you can get up on your knees and turn around. At first, a bright light blinds you. It takes several days to figure out what you are looking at. You have never seen things like this before. A fire is blazing at the back of an enormous cavern. Between you and the fire, people are moving across a platform. You can see their faces and hear them speak. After several days of study, you realize that what you have been watching for so many years were the *shadows* of these people! These shadows had been projected on to the wall in front of you. You had taken shadows for real things. All the stories and explanations you and your companions had devised were completely wrong.

This realization overwhelms you with excitement. In a burst of energy, you break free of the chains. You look down at your companions and feel sorry for them. They do not know that the show consists of mere shadows. They do not have the faintest idea that something more real is happening behind them. They look up at you fearfully and implore you to replace the chains. Laughing at their timidity, you strike out toward the fire.

> *Behold! human beings living in an underground den ... Like ourselves ... they see only their own shadows, or the shadows of one another, which the fire throws on the opposite wall of the cave.*
>
> – Plato

Once you reach the fire, you study it carefully and soon realize that this is not the end of your journey. Behind the fire, you spy a narrow opening leading out of the cavern. Peering into it, you see a long cave, sloping upwards. At the end of the cave is a tiny speck of intense white light, far brighter than the light from the fire. You are drawn to it as if to a beacon. You start climbing.

Many days later, you reach the entrance of the cave. As you stumble out, you are blinded by the intense light. When you can finally focus, you see things that you had never imagined in your wildest dreams. Before you is a strange array of objects: flowers, clouds, trees, animals, and insects. The colours are dazzling. You notice that all these objects cast shadows, but the light that makes these shadows is not like the light of the fire. It is infinitely stronger. It is somewhere above you, but you cannot look at it now.

After many weeks, you turn your eyes skyward and look at the source of the light. This is the sun, casting the most beautiful and pure light you have ever seen. You realize that you are at the end of your journey.

Still, you think about your old friends and realize that they are sleepwalking through life like zombies. They are confusing shadows with reality. Though you are tempted to bask in the sunlight, you decide that it is your duty to return to the cave to liberate them. Nobody should have to live like that, you tell yourself.

The journey back into the cave is harrowing, but knowing that your friends will welcome your news makes it easier. When you arrive, you can barely see anything. Your friends see you and are puzzled. "Where have you been?" they ask. "Come and join us. Put the chains on and watch the wonderful show."

Declining their invitation, you tell them about your discoveries: the platform with the figures, the fire casting the shadows, the cave, the sunlit world, and the sun. They look at you silently. You then gently inform them that they are mistaking shadows for real objects. They are in bondage. Their world is not the real world but a world of appearances.

Strangely, your words make no sense to them. They think you have gone mad. "Are you blind? This is obviously the real world," they say. "Just look around. Use your eyes. Use your common sense. How can you not see the beautiful moving figures, the sights and the sounds? Everyone here agrees that this is real."

THOUGHT EXPERIMENT — Something about Mary

Meet Mary. She is the world's greatest colour scientist, living in a time far in the future when the science of human vision is complete. She spends her days performing interesting experiments on brains and eyeballs. Mary knows everything about the workings of the human brain and, in particular, about the eye, the optic nerve, and the visual cortex. She can provide an accurate and comprehensive description of the workings of the eye and brain when they are busily engaged in perceiving light and colour. She can talk about the rods and cones in the eyeball, the electrical impulses that flow along the optic nerve, and so on.

But there's something about Mary. She herself is unable to distinguish colours. She has never actually seen any colours. She lives in a black, white, and grey world. To her, tomatoes and strawberries are tasty but grey.

Figure 6.2

If Mary knows everything there is to know about how the brain works when it perceives colours, does she know what it's like to see colours like red?

The contemporary philosopher Frank Jackson, who devised this thought experiment, says that the answer to this question is no. Jackson says that neuroscience can tell people nothing about the specific subjective character — the qualitative feel — of perceptual experiences. Phenomenal properties, such as seeing red, are not captured by objective descriptions of the brain activities that make the perception of those properties possible. As a result, these properties cannot be identified with those activities.

What do you think? If Mary gains the ability to distinguish colour one day, perhaps thanks to an operation, will she realize that she had been missing something important? Will she realize that her conception of the colour experiences of others was not complete?

You realize that you do not know how to talk to people who have no conception of reality. Your former companions cannot grasp the difference between object and shadow, reality and appearance. You consider returning to the sunlit world. Though you believe that they are wasting their lives, you reason that it might be better to respect their ignorance-is-bliss attitude.

If both these scenarios are familiar, it is because they are variations of Plato's "Allegory of the Cave," which appeared in Chapter 1. This allegory raises one of the central debates of metaphysics: how to distinguish between reality and appearance. The prisoners symbolize most ordinary people. Just as the prisoners consider the shadows to be real, so most people consider everything that they see, hear, touch, taste, and smell to be real. They feel no need to question appearances. They are comfortable with their sensory-based understanding of the world and are unaware of the other dimensions of reality. Their lives are unreflective and untroubled.

Figure 6.3

This representation of Plato's allegory of the cave was painted in the 16th century. Which figures represent the characters in Plato's story?

The philosopher who leaves the cave is unsatisfied by the explanations that other people give and the debates about what the figures are doing. This philosopher thinks that there must be something more, something on the other side of the world of appearances.

The world of flickering shadows is the world of common-sense perception and belief. This world changes constantly. It is the subject of unending debate and confusion, and it is full of ambiguity. Unlike this world of appearances, the real world lit by the sun is clear, visible, and steady. Where appearances are transient, imperfect, and insubstantial, reality is permanent, unchanging, and perfect.

The story about the cave also illustrates how philosophers' attempts to identify the ultimate structures of reality often conflict with common-sense beliefs. Philosophers' explanations of reality often spark uncomprehending reactions and sometimes even political repression.

Recall...Reflect...Respond

1. Metaphysics is often described as one of the pillars of philosophy. Referring to some of the main questions of metaphysics, explain why this might be so.
2. Some people think that scientists are better qualified than metaphysicians to answer questions about reality. Do you agree? Explain why.
3. Consider the two scenarios suggested by Plato's "Allegory of the Cave." Which scenario best represents your approach to everyday life? Citing examples from your own life, explain why.

PLATO'S IDEAL WORLD

Take a pencil and draw a freehand circle with a diameter of 12 cm. Beside it, draw another freehand circle with the same diameter. Are the two circles the same? From a distance, they might look pretty close, but the first circle is not *perfectly* circular. Perhaps it is a little flat on one side and a little too rounded on the other. The line is lighter is some spots than in others. Your second circle is also not perfectly circular. And neither circle is exactly 12 cm in diameter.

Now take a compass and draw two more circles, each with a radius of 6 cm. When you compare them, what do you see? Are they the same? Though they may be more similar to each other than the freehand circles, even these are not identical. Upon close inspection, you see small differences. Again, neither circle is perfect.

Perhaps a computer-generated circle will be perfect. Type the co-ordinates in a draw program and a perfect circle seems to appear on the monitor. But is it really perfect? You get out your magnifying glass and see that the line of the circle is made up of thousands of tiny dots, or pixels. Though each dot looks the same from a distance, irregularities appear when they are viewed under the magnifying glass. What is more, the dots do not form a perfectly continuous and perfectly curving line.

You are now really going in circles. Circles are everywhere, but each is flawed in some way. Moreover, because each circle occupies space and exists at a particular time, each can be erased or changed. In five hundred million years, nothing will remain of the circles in your notebook.

Notice, also, that when you talk about circles in general, you do not have in mind the particular circles you just drew. You do not say, "This particular *circle-like* figure, at this particular time and place, with this slightly flattened side ..." When you do geometry, you talk about *the* circle.

> *And the true order of going, or being led by another, to the things of love, is to begin from the beauties of earth and mount upwards for the sake of that other beauty, using these steps only, and from one going on to two to all fair forms to fair practices, and from fair practices to fair notions, until from fair notions he arrives at the notion of absolute beauty, and at last knows what the essence of beauty is.*
>
> — Plato

Here is the question: Is there any perfect circle — or are there just many imperfect circles pretending to be perfect? Is the very idea of a perfect circle a fiction? If so, what makes all particular circles similar? What glue holds together the class of all particular circles?

Plato had an answer to these questions. He said that there must be a perfect circle, which all particular circles copy. Unlike the circles you have drawn, the perfect circle is unchangeable. You cannot erase it. It exists independently of you, and it continues to exist even if you are not thinking about it. Indeed, it is not even located in time or space. It cannot be pointed to or photographed, like ordinary objects located in space and time. Nor can it be said to have existed at a certain time. It has no history. If it existed in space and time, it would be subject to change and would not, therefore, be perfect. What is true of the perfect circle is always true of it.

Though this perfect circle does not exist in time and space and is not visible, Plato said that it is still a *thing*. It is not a fiction or an image. It is thing of a very special kind, however. It is an *ideal* thing, rather than a material thing. It has the same kind of existence as ideas. Though the perfect circle is an ideal thing, said Plato, it is also *more real* than particular circles. He maintained that its existence as an unchanging, non-physical, non-temporal, and non-spatial object is the purest form of existence possible.

Plato regarded the perfect circle as the ultimate model for all circles. In his view, any circle drawn by people not only copies the perfect circle, but also partakes of it. In other words, the circles you drew participated in the perfect circle and drew some of their reality from it. The perfect circle gave its form to the circles you drew. Though countless circles, some large and some small, exist in the physical world, there is only one perfect and ideal circle. It is neither large nor small.

THE FORMS

Because the perfect circle gives form to particular circles, Plato called it a form. By "form," he meant the essence of any particular circle. Without this essence, particular circles could not exist. According to Plato, every geometric figure people can draw, from circles to squares to triangles, has a corresponding form.

Plato took his arguments much farther than this, however. He claimed that there is a form for every particular item that exists in the world perceived by people, whether the particular items are tables, salamanders, tulips, or groundhogs. Behind the external world of imperfect and ever-changing particulars is the world of forms, a world of unchanging perfection. The world of forms, however, cannot be known by the senses. It is known only through pure thought.

Plato also claimed that there is an ideal form for human beings. The world, he observed, is populated with many different human beings: big and small, tall and short, young and old. Despite their vast differences, all are recognizable as human beings. People do not confuse human beings with wombats; nor does anyone entertain paralyzing doubts about where the class of human beings ends and the class of wombats begins. What makes people human beings is that each copies and partakes of the perfect and timeless form of the human being.

Plato extended this way of thinking to morality and aesthetics. Just as there is an ideal form of the human being, he said, there is also an ideal form of justice, an ideal form of courage, and an ideal form of beauty. All particular acts of justice and courage and all particular beautiful objects copy and partake of their respective ideal forms.

IDEAS IN CONTEXT

In his philosophy, Plato was very concerned with the form of justice. This concern was shaped by the death of Socrates, his revered teacher. Plato believed that the death sentence handed to Socrates was evidence that democracy in Athens was on the verge of collapse. As a result, he began thinking — and writing — about his own theory of justice. He envisioned a society in which justice reigned supreme. He believed that justice is a "human virtue" that makes people self-consistent and good and promotes a well-ordered society.

In Plato's view, however, not all forms are equal in metaphysical stature. Some forms are more specific than others, and some are more inclusive. The form of horse, for example, falls under the broader form of animal — and because animals are beings, the form of animal falls under the broader form of being. According to Plato, the highest form, the form that encompasses all others, is the form of the good. It is beyond — and superior to — the form of being.

Plato likened the role played by the form of the good to the role played by the sun, the same sun that enlightens the philosopher who escapes from the cave. Just as the sun is the source of all light, life, and vision, so the good is the source of all reality, intelligibility, and truth. But though the form of the good lies behind all values and all existence, it is not itself an entity or thing. Nor can it be perceived by means of the senses. It can be reached only by pure thought.

Plato's "Allegory of the Cave" is thus a story about an encounter with the form of the good. The journey undertaken by the prisoner who leaves the cave represents the mind's journey from the world of transient and imperfect objects, which are accessible only to sense perception, to the world of ideal and perfect forms, which are accessible only to pure reason. The ultimate destination of the journey is the form of the good, located at the pinnacle of all forms.

Though Aristotle agreed with his teacher Plato that people must look behind the changing surface of things to see their deep and universal structures, he saw no need to propose the existence of a transcendent world of unchanging and timeless forms that can be apprehended only by pure reason. He said that deep universal structures are embedded in particular things of this world. Real circularity is found within particular circles, and real beauty is found within particular beautiful objects.

Web connection
www.mcgrawhill.ca/links/philosophy12
To find out more about Plato and his theory of forms, follow the links on this Web site.

TAOISM: REALITY AND THE TAO

Not everyone agrees with Plato's view that the ultimate nature of reality is accessible to human beings through reason. Some philosophers, particularly mystics, believe that reason is incapable of apprehending ultimate reality. They believe that reason chops up the oneness of reality into separate bits and pieces, like a gigantic metaphysical cookie cutter that forces people to think in terms of particular things instead of wholes. Mystics believe that the ultimate nature of reality can be grasped only by a special kind of intuition that transcends reason.

One such mystic was the Chinese sage **Laozi**, also known as Lao-tzu, who lived in the sixth century BCE. Laozi's book, *Tao-te Ching* (*Classic of the Way of Power*), is the first expression of the philosophy of Taoism. The Tao, which is sometimes translated as "the one" or "the way," is the fundamental principle of the universe as a whole. Taoists believe that all things come from the Tao, which sustains all things in being. Though the Tao existed before the universe began, it is not identical with the universe and it is not like anything within the universe. In other words, it is not a particular thing or a locatable event, although it makes things and events possible. Nor is it like a person or a god.

> *The way that can be spoken of*
> *Is not the constant way;*
> *The name that can be named*
> *Is not the constant name.*
>
> – Laozi

The Tao is often described in negative terms: it is not this and it is not that. If you were to ask Laozi for a precise *positive* description of the Tao, he would tell you that it cannot be named or described using words. Indeed, even the word "Tao" is just a word, a physical sign, which no one should mistake for the reality that it picks out. When Laozi used words to compose *Tao-te Ching*, he wanted his readers to be aware that his words were imperfect tools. The Taoist sage is someone who understands the limits of language and who sometimes resorts to silence rather than more words.

Laozi observed that all things in nature are in a state of constant flux or change: day turns to night, summer turns to winter, the strong become weak, the weak become strong. No state is permanent. Behind this flux, however, is a deep pattern: the endless cycle of development and decline. It is the Tao that is responsible for this cycle. Everything develops, reaches full strength, and then declines. The cycle is inevitable.

Taoists believe that the oneness of the Tao is expressed in nature in a twofold manner, in yin and yang. Yin is the passive element of nature, and yang the active element. Corresponding to yin are being, receiving, night, rest, earth, and decline. Corresponding to yang are doing, giving, day, activity, heaven, and development. In the Taoist view, yin and yang are in constant interplay. Like dance partners, they are distinct yet inseparable. Each is the expression of the other, and neither is permanent or dominant.

Knowing that nothing is permanent and that yin always yields to yang and vice versa, the Taoist sage waits. He or she does not try to force nature. Striving to be at one with the Tao, the sage lives a life of simplicity and tranquility and avoids getting caught up in the desires of the senses, particularly artificial desires. These desires can interfere with the apprehension of the Tao. The sage's goal is to be nature's companion, following the way of the Tao.

Figure 6.4

This ancient Chinese yin-yang symbol was developed to portray the ebb and flow of nature. How does it do this?

THE QUESTION OF BEING

What is "being"? What does it mean to be? Is "being" a thing, a substance, a process, or a kind of super-thing? What is the relation of "being" to particular things that exist? These are some of the most basic ontological questions. Plato believed that "being" is an ideal and timeless form, second in power only to the form of the good. All particular things that exist partake of this form.

Aristotle, by contrast, said that "being" is the substance to which all properties can be ascribed, though it is not itself a property. Laozi thought that the Tao, that which is behind the existence of everything, cannot be described at all. It is not a being like the particular entities in the universe.

In 1927, the German philosopher **Martin Heidegger** published *Being and Time*, a book that influenced the development of existential philosophy. Heidegger argued that western metaphysics had been on the wrong track since the time of Plato because it had misconceived the question of Being. Most philosophers, he argued, had made the mistake of thinking of "Being" as a kind of thing or entity, such as a form or a special kind of substance.

Heidegger also argued that Descartes had sent philosophy spinning off in the wrong direction by drawing an unreconcilable distinction between the subject (the mind) and the object (the world) and by asserting that epistemology is "first philosophy." As a result, said Heidegger, the question of Being had been displaced so thoroughly that it had been either completely forgotten or trivialized. He said that people had lost their sense of wonder at the fact of Being. Heidegger regarded ontology as first philosophy and maintained that the first question of philosophy is, What is the meaning of Being? This conflicted with Descartes's assertion that the first question is, How do we know?

Heidegger argued that there is an ontological difference between "Being" and beings. He identified particular things or entities, such as shoes, trees, comets, dogs, and human beings, as beings. By contrast, he said, "Being" is that in virtue of which these particular beings exist. But "Being" is not itself a being. It is not a particular entity. Nor is it the most general or all-inclusive of all beings, a kind of super-being. Indeed, he said that it is not a thing at all: it is, in some respects, no thing.

Figure 6.5

The German philosopher Martin Heidegger's ideas about "being" influenced the existentialists who came to prominence later in the 20th century.

If "Being" is not a being of some sort, then what is it? Heidegger argued that the way to understand "Being" is in terms of time, but not the kind of time portrayed by clock time. The time he meant was lived time. Heidegger suggested that people think of "Being" as a verb — rather than as a noun. He said that "Being" is the most fundamental of verbs. There can be no more basic verb and no more basic temporal process. Understood this way, "Being" stands to particular beings as a kind of background, from which particular things stand out. But the background is not to be confused with the various beings in the foreground.

One way to understand Heidegger's meaning is to compare "Being" with something else, such as light. Objects are made visible by means of light, but light itself is not seen and is not itself an object. If light is seen at all, it is seen only by means of the objects it illuminates. In the same way, "Being" is not itself a being, but it is by means of "Being" that particular beings stand out and become intelligible.

Heidegger argued that human beings have a unique relationship with "Being." Human beings are not things. Instead of being defined by definite factual properties, human beings are defined by future-oriented possibilities of "Being." He said that the essence of a human being "lies in the fact that in each case it has its being to be, and has it as its own." In other words, "Being," when it is understood as a transitive verb, is an issue for every human being.

Your "Being" is always in question. It does not come ready-made. You — and you alone — must come to terms with your own Being. This means that you alone must take a stand on whether to be or not to be. And you alone must decide whether to be yourself or not yourself.

These decisions cannot be avoided. No one else can take over the task of working out the question of Being for you. Heidegger claimed that many people try to evade these difficult questions. They pretend that an issue is already settled or distract themselves with day-to-day concerns or hide behind social roles or drift along with the crowd, letting the crowd's values determine their own. Existentialist philosophers call this inauthenticity, which is a kind of forgetting of "Being." This happens when people forget that they must take hold of their existence in a lucid and authentic manner. To existentialists, the term "authentic" refers to the idea of being true to oneself when making choices.

> ### Recall...Reflect...Respond
> 1. Think about Plato's theory of forms. Does it affect your beliefs about memory and how it is formed? Explain why.
> 2. How do the theories of Plato and Laozi differ in their responses to the question, What are the constituents of reality? Explain.
> 3. Does Martin Heidegger's theory of being help reconcile the differences between the theories of reality advanced by Plato and Laozi? Explain why.

THE SELF

Everyone has a self. And all of us think that we are acquainted with our self to some degree. Some people believe that they know their own self better than anyone else knows it. Most people love to talk about it, and some people even try to explore it. When they do, what are they exploring? What is the self? What is it made of? How do people get to know it? How many selves do people have?

VARIETIES OF THE SELF

Philosophers have proposed various theories in answer to questions about the self. The most prominent are the substance theory, the bundle theory, the narrative theory, and the project theory.

Proposed by Descartes, the substance theory maintains that the self is a determinate and unitary thing — a substance — that persists over time. The self is not a material substance, however. It is mental. According to Descartes, the self controls the body and the brain in the same way as a captain controls a ship. The substantial self is a unity that cannot be divided and is not subject to decomposition or change.

As the subject of experience, the self supports changing experiences, but does not itself change. It is the thing that has or owns these experiences. Descartes argued that people enjoy a privileged access to their selves, which they know better than they know anything outside them.

The bundle theory of the self was proposed by the 18th-century Scottish philosopher David Hume, as well as by Buddhist philosophers. This theory holds that the self is a bundle or a collection of bits and pieces of experience. Hume argued that when he engaged in introspective thought, or thought about himself, as Descartes had, he found no thing-like self waiting to be discovered. All he encountered were fleeting ideas, sensory impressions, fragmentary memories, passing desires, and other bits and pieces. He found neither unity in

PHILOSOPHY IN ACTION

Meditations on First Philosophy

by René Descartes

The full title of *Meditations on First Philosophy*, which René Descartes published in 1641, was *Meditations on First Philosophy in Which Is Proved the Existence of God and the Immortality of the Soul*. For Descartes, this book was the first of several in which he planned to tear down the edifice of human knowledge and rebuild it from the bottom up.

Descartes was aware, however, that the Italian astronomer Galileo Galilei had been persecuted and imprisoned just eight years earlier for challenging conventional scientific ideas. Descartes knew that he was treading on dangerous ground — and he did not wish to suffer Galileo's fate. As a result, he decided to gain the support of Roman Catholic Church officials by starting his explorations with metaphysical arguments that they could accept.

Meditation Two
Concerning the Nature of the Human Mind

… I suppose that everything I see is false. I believe that none of what my deceitful memory represents ever existed. I have no senses whatever. Body, shape, extension, movement, and place are all chimeras [a fantastic or grotesque fancy or product of the imagination]. What then will be true? Perhaps just the single fact that nothing is certain.

But how do I know there is not something else, over and above all those things that I have just reviewed, concerning which there is not even the slightest occasion for doubt? Is there not some God … who instills these very thoughts in me? But why would I think that, since I myself could be the author of these thoughts? Am I not then at least something? But I have already denied that I have any senses and any body. Still I hesitate; for what follows from this? Am I so tied to a body and to the senses that I cannot exist without them? But I have persuaded myself that there is absolutely nothing in the world: no sky, no earth, no minds, no bodies. Is it then the case that I too do not exist? But doubtless I did exist, if I persuaded myself of something. But there is some deceiver or other who is supremely powerful and supremely sly and who is always deliberately deceiving me. Then too there is no doubt that I exist, if he is deceiving me. And let him do his best at deception, he will never bring it about that I am nothing so long as I shall think that I am something. Thus, after everything has been most carefully weighed, it must finally be established that this pronouncement "I am, I exist" is necessarily true every time I utter it or conceive it in my mind.

But I do not yet understand sufficiently what I am — I, who now necessarily exist. And so from this point on, I must be careful lest I unwittingly mistake something else for myself, and thus err in that very item of knowledge that I claim to be the most certain and evident of all. Thus, I will meditate once more on what I once believed myself to be, prior to embarking upon these thoughts....

What then did I use to think I was? A man, of course. But what is a man? Might I not say a rational animal? No, because then I would have to inquire what "animal" and "rational" mean. And thus from one question I would slide into many more difficult ones.... Now it occurred to me first that I had a face, hands, arms, and this entire mechanism of bodily members.... It next occurred to me that I took in food, that I walked about, and that I sensed and thought various things; these actions I used to attribute to the soul. But as to what this soul might be, I either did not think about it or else I imagined it a rarefied I-know-not-what, like a wind, or a fire, or ether, which had been infused into my coarser parts. But as to body I was not in any doubt.... [B]y "body," I understand all that is capable of being bounded by some shape, of being enclosed in a place, and of filling up a space in such a way as to exclude any other body from it; of being perceived by touch, sight, hearing, taste, or smell; of being moved in several ways....

But now what am I, when I suppose that there is some supremely powerful and, if I may be permitted to say so, malicious deceiver who deliberately tries to fool me in any way he can? Can I not affirm that I possess at least a small measure of all those things which I have already said belong to the nature of the body? I focus my attention on them, I think about them, I review them again, but nothing comes to mind. I am tired of repeating this to no purpose. But what about those things I ascribed to the soul? What about being nourished or moving about? Since I now do not have a body, these are surely nothing but fictions. What about sensing? Surely this too does not take place without a body; and I seemed to have sensed in my dreams many things that I later realized I did not sense. What about thinking? Here I make my discovery: thought exists; it alone cannot be separated from me. I am; I exist — this is certain. But for how long? For as long as I am thinking; for perhaps it could also come to pass that if I were to cease all thinking I would then utterly cease to exist. At this time I admit nothing that is not necessarily true. I am therefore precisely nothing but a thinking thing; that is, a mind, or intellect, or understanding, or reason — words of whose meanings I was previously ignorant. Yet I am a true thing and am truly existing; but what kind of thing? I have said it already: a thinking thing.

What else am I? I will set my imagination in motion. I am not that concatenation [series of linked events or things] of members we call the human body. Neither am I even some subtle air infused into these members, nor a wind, nor a fire, nor a vapour, nor a breath, nor anything I devise for myself. For I have supposed these things to be nothing....

But what then am I? A thing that thinks. What is that? A thing that doubts, understands, affirms, denies, wills, refuses, and that also imagines and senses....

But what am I to say about this mind, that is, about myself? For as yet I admit nothing else to be in me over and above the mind. What, I ask, am I who seems to perceive this wax [external physical objects] so distinctly? Do I not know myself not only much more truly and with greater certainty, but also much more distinctly and evidently? For if I judge that the wax exists from the fact that I see it, certainly from this same fact that I see the wax it follows much more evidently that I myself exist. For it could happen that what I see is not truly wax. It could happen that I have no eyes with which to see anything. But it is utterly impossible that, while I see or think I see (I do not now distinguish these two), I who think am not something.... For since I now know that even bodies are not, properly speaking, perceived by the senses or by the faculty of imagination, but by the intellect alone ... I manifestly know that nothing can be perceived more easily and more evidently than my own mind.

Meditation Six
Concerning the Existence of Material Things, and the Real Distinction between Mind and Body

... Now my first observation here is that there is a great difference between a mind and a body in that a body, by its very nature, is always divisible. On the other hand, the mind is utterly indivisible. For when I consider the mind, that is, myself insofar as I am only a thinking thing, I cannot distinguish any parts within me; rather, I understand myself to be manifestly one complete thing. Although the entire mind seems to be united to the entire body, nevertheless, were a foot or an arm or any other bodily part to be amputated, I know that nothing has been taken away from the mind on that account. Nor can the faculties of willing, sensing, understanding, and so on be called parts of the mind, since it is one and the same mind that wills, senses, and understands. On the other hand, there is no corporeal or extended thing I can think of that I may not in my thought easily divide into parts; and in this way I understand that it is divisible. This consideration alone would suffice to teach me that the mind is wholly diverse from the body....

Source: From René Descartes, *Meditations on First Philosophy* (published together with *Discourse on Method*), translated by Donald Cress, Hackett Publishing, 1993, pp. 63-66, 69, 100-101. Reprinted by permission of Hackett Publishing Company, Inc. All rights reserved.

1. Describe the thought process Descartes followed to reach the conclusion that he is a thing that thinks.
2. What key assumption enables Descartes to arrive at this conclusion? Do you believe this assumption is valid? Why?
3. An important philosophical question asks whether persons remain the same over time. How does Descartes's theory of self respond to this question? Explain.

these perceptions nor a thread that gave them continuity. As a result, he concluded that the self is nothing but a loosely knit collection — a bundle — of perceptions.

The narrative theory, which was proposed by the 20th-century French philosopher Paul Ricoeur and others, maintains that the self is defined by narrative structure and unity. People make sense of their experiences by narrating them. This narrative situates them in a story that traces their development and links them to the stories of others. In your story, for example, you are the central character, as well as the central author or co-author. Whatever unity the self possesses is a function of the unity of the narrative under which it is identified. A fragmented narrative is thus a fragmented self. Unlike the stories told in books, the narrative self has no neat and tidy ending. As long as life goes on, new narratives can always be discovered in situations past and present. New stories can be told, and old stories can be retold or dropped.

The project theory of the self was proposed by the 20th-century French existentialist philosopher Jean-Paul Sartre. This theory maintains that the self needs to be thought of in temporal terms, more as an event in time than as a thing. The self is neither a static thing, nor a bundle, nor a point-like ego at the centre of experience. Rather, it is a dynamic and future-oriented project. Like the project of building a bridge, said Sartre, the self is always under active construction. It is never finished.

The self is not given to people ready-made or with instructions for constructing it. Sartre said that the project, which defines each person, is more or less coherent. The feelings, desires, and thoughts that someone displays in her everyday behaviour are expressions of a single fundamental project.

In keeping with the holistic idea that the whole is contained in the part, Sartre claimed that there is a thematic organization and an inherent meaning in this totality. A particular case of jealousy, for instance, carries an enormous amount of information about someone's project. According to Sartre, the case of jealousy "signifies for the one who knows how to interpret it, the total relation to the world by which the subject constitutes himself as a self."

Web connection
www.mcgrawhill.ca/links/philosophy12
To read more about the self, follow the links on this Web site.

SELF-DECEPTION AND SELF-KNOWLEDGE

Inscribed above the entrance to the temple of the oracle at Delphi in ancient Greece were these words: *gnothi seauton*, or know thyself. The wisdom of this saying has echoed through the millennia. Self-knowledge is considered one of the goods of human life.

But what does knowing yourself mean? Is there any objectivity in this endeavour? How is self-knowledge possible? Are there limits on what a person can know of her- or himself? Before trying to answer these questions, consider how starkly self-deception stands in relation to self-knowledge.

SELF-DECEPTION

How often have you heard it said that someone is not being honest with himself or that someone else is fooling herself? Accusations like these mean that the people in question have somehow convinced themselves of something that they know to be untrue. Consider the imaginary case of an athlete who has terminal cancer, but who refuses to acknowledge her condition. As she grows weaker, she continues to believe that she is physically fit, and she continues to reject what she would normally accept as strong medical evidence. She continues to train and compete. When she loses, she resorts to lame rationalizations. At the same time as she pretends not to notice the

*In sooth, I know not why I am so sad:
It wearies me; you say it wearies you;
But how I caught it, found it, or came by it,
What stuff 'tis made of, whereof it is born,
I am to learn;
And such a want-wit sadness makes of me,
That I have much ado to know myself.*

– William Shakespeare

PROFILE

Jean-Paul Sartre
"Sartre Is France"

As a boy, Jean-Paul Sartre was small in stature, cross-eyed, and precociously intelligent. Born in Paris, France, in 1905, he tried to fit in with the other children in his neighbourhood and at school. When his efforts at friendship were rejected, the lonely child retreated into the world of books. He filled the hours by writing, creating his own fanciful world on paper and nurturing dreams of becoming a famous writer.

In 1929, while Sartre was a student at the École Normale Supérieure in Paris, he met Simone de Beauvoir, one of the first women to attend the prestigious school, which had previously admitted only men. The two fell in love, attended classes together, shared ideas, read each other's work, went skiing, and travelled.

This relationship would last their entire lives, though they never married or even lived together. Marriage, they declared, is a repressive bourgeois institution. Still, the two always managed to live in the same apartment building, usually on different floors.

When World War II broke out, Sartre was drafted to serve at the front. Captured by the Germans, he was imprisoned in Stalag XII D, a prisoner-of-war camp. This experience shaped his thinking about freedom. He realized that human beings are free, even when they are in chains, and began to develop his existential philosophy.

In the meantime, the Germans had captured Paris and much of France. Returning to occupied Paris after a year of imprisonment, Sartre began writing for an underground Resistance paper. During this period, he also wrote his famous philosophical treatise *Being and Nothingness*, as well as several controversial plays, including *No Exit*.

Much of Sartre's writing was done in the bohemian cafés of Paris's Left Bank. One of his favourites was the Café des Deux Magots, which still exists. Sartre frequently drew on scenes of café life — a role-playing waiter, a woman on a date, a missed rendezvous — to illustrate his philosophical ideas.

After the war, existential philosophy came into vogue in Paris, and Sartre became its most famous advocate. He and de Beauvoir found themselves at the centre of an influential literary and philosophical community that included the philosophers Maurice Merleau-Ponty and Albert Camus, the psychoanalyst Jacques Lacan, the artist Jean Cocteau, the writer Jean Genet, and others.

Sartre and de Beauvoir began to travel the world, speaking at political rallies, giving lectures and interviews, and meeting famous people such as Fidel Castro, Che Guevara, Nikita Kruschev, the president of the Soviet Union, Josip Broz Tito, the president of Yugoslavia, and the Hollywood filmmaker John Huston, for whom Sartre wrote a screenplay about Sigmund Freud. The philosopher's childhood dream of fame had come true.

When Sartre was named winner of the Nobel Prize for literature in 1964, he declined to accept the prestigious honour, claiming that the award was nothing but a popularity contest run by the capitalist publishing industry. And because he was an avowed atheist, the Roman Catholic Church banned all his works.

Unlike many ivory-tower intellectuals, Sartre remained an "engaged" philosopher. He was politically active, defended unpopular causes in the name of freedom, and never shied away from controversy. In the late 1950s and early 1960s, for example, he publicly denounced France's colonial rule of Algeria and campaigned for the withdrawal of French troops from this African colony.

Because of this, some people called him a traitor and demanded that he be arrested. Resisting these demands, the French president Charles de Gaulle said, "Sartre is France. One cannot arrest France."

Sartre continued to support various socialist causes, student protests, and the peace movement until his death in 1980. When he died, more than a million people joined the funeral procession through the streets of Paris.

Figure 6.6
Drafted to serve in the French army during World War II, Jean-Paul Sartre was an awkward soldier. This photograph captures his discomfort.

worsening symptoms, she devotes more time to things she never bothered to do before, such as writing a will, keeping a diary, contacting long-lost friends, and spending time with her family. But she denies the significance of these activities. She is self-deceived. She somehow knows that she has terminal cancer, and at the same time she somehow does not know. She leaves a trail of signs that indicate that she is somehow aware that what she is affirming and acting upon is false.

What is the explanation for this strange phenomenon? How can one and the same person be both the deceiver and the deceived?

On the surface, deceiving oneself seems to be a variation of deceiving another person. The self deceives itself in the same way as it might deceive another person. Just as you lie to another person, for example, so you lie to yourself. But this explanation is only partly satisfactory. Deceiving another person involves two people: the deceiver and the deceived.

Self-deception is different because the deceiver and the deceived are the same person. If you are the deceiver, you must be aware of the truth of the thing you are deceiving yourself about. If you are also the deceived, you must also be unaware of this truth. But how is this possible?

First, self-deception is not deliberate. The deceiver does not make a conscious decision to deceive him- or herself. A carefully planned decision to deceive yourself would be as self-defeating as telling yourself a joke. Still, though self-deception is not deliberate, it is also not an accident, like slipping on ice.

Self-deception involves forming an intention to do something. It is a form of goal-directed behaviour, which accomplishes a purpose that benefits the deceiver. In the case of the self-deceiving athlete mentioned earlier, for example, the goal may be to avoid considering her own fear of death. For reasons like this, self-deception is behaviour that seems to be directed toward a specific goal. At the same time, it is not deliberate or consciously planned.

> *When you want to believe in something you also have to believe in everything that's necessary for believing in it.*
> – Ugo Beth

Attempts to maintain a state of self-deception with any degree of psychological consistency result in division of the self. The athlete in denial, for example, cannot be at one with herself. She cannot pursue a course of action that flows naturally and spontaneously from her beliefs. She is unable to act decisively upon her belief that she is healthy. Why? Because her belief that she is healthy lacks the kind of solid evidence that characterizes her other beliefs about the world.

To accommodate her belief that she is healthy, the athlete must arbitrarily relax the standards of evidence that she uses in everyday contexts. This is rarely successful. Finding herself holding beliefs that are not adequately supported by the evidence, she either ignores the scantiness of the evidence or covers up its implications with rationalizations. At the same time, she remains vaguely aware of the weakness of her rationalizations. She cannot completely erase her awareness of the weakness of the evidence for her belief that she is healthy. And she cannot conveniently forget that she has relaxed her standards of evidence.

Recall...Reflect...Respond

1. Which theory of the self matches most closely your thinking about this subject? Choose a partner who has selected a different theory. Defend your thinking to each other.
2. Reconsider the case of the athlete who has terminal cancer. Besides self-deception, are there other possible explanations for her behaviour? If so, what are they? Are any of these explanations consistent with the meaning of self-deception? Explain why.
3. Have you ever deceived yourself? How did you come to realize that you had practised self-deception?

SELF-KNOWLEDGE

Self-knowledge is often held up as an ideal to which everyone should aspire. People who are knowledgeable about their selves have explored answers to the question, Who am I? In doing so, they have gone beyond offering superficial answers, such as, I am the child of so-and-so, or I weigh 60 kg, or I was born in 1982. People with self-knowledge know with some clarity the direction that their lives are taking, the values that matter to them, the motives that move them to action, and the goals they hold dear.

Self-knowledge is more than a matter of having opinions, hunches, or feelings about these important issues, however. Sometimes people who *feel* strongly that they know themselves get it wrong. They are deluded or caught up in what other people think about them, or they have made hasty judgments.

Because the way people *appear* to themselves is not always the way they actually *are*, self-knowledge involves reflective self-inquiry and self-evaluation. It also involves more than simply relying on what other people think. Only one person can work out the answer to the question, Who am I? You. This question cannot be answered by anyone else.

> *I know that I exist; the question is, What is this "I" that I know?*
>
> – René Descartes

But what, exactly, is involved in answering this question? The contemporary American-based English philosopher **Stuart Hampshire** argues that self-knowledge involves acquiring knowledge about the causes of your desires, beliefs, emotions, and character traits. This knowledge can include learning about unconscious desires and childhood conditioning.

Hampshire agrees with thinkers such as Sigmund Freud and Baruch Spinoza, who maintained that many of these causes are hidden from people's conscious awareness. Think about a time when you have reacted to something but did not know why you reacted, or when you had certain feelings about someone but did not know why you had these feelings.

According to Hampshire, working out an adequate answer to the question, Who am I? requires people to engage in a process of rational, reflective detachment from the first-person point of view. In other words, you must step back from your day-to-day immersion in the world — and in your self — and take a more objective point of view. Seeing your self from the outside will allow you to observe aspects of your self — and the causal history of your self — that often go unnoticed. In Hampshire's view, reflective detachment ensures a degree of objectivity in self-inquiry. Without it, he says, subjective bias interferes with the inquiry.

Like Spinoza, Hampshire connects self-knowledge with freedom of mind. He says that the more people reflect upon the causes that make them who they are, the more this reflection changes them. Reflective self-inquiry, in other words, has the power to modify the very self that is the object of reflection and to make it different from the way it would have been if it had not been targeted for reflection.

As people learn more about the causal mechanisms that explain their desires, beliefs, and character traits, says Hampshire, they are placed in a position to anticipate these mechanisms — and to either modify or reinforce them. As a result, an increase in self-knowledge leads to an increase in the range of self-determination.

The contemporary American philosopher **Richard Rorty** proposes a very different view of self-knowledge. The self, he argues, is a text made up of dense thematic layers, woven and rewoven over time into a highly distinctive pattern. No single strand runs

Figure 6.7

Stanley was deeply disappointed when, high in the Tibetan mountains, he finally found his true self.

How did Stanley's true self differ from his idea of himself? What might Richard Rorty have said to ease Stanley's disappointment?

throughout, nor is the pattern always the same. According to Rorty, the self is dynamic and ever-changing. The weaving never stops.

If the self is a text, then people can come to know it as they know all texts: through creative reading. In Rorty's view, working out an answer to the question, Who am I? is like trying to answer the question, What is the meaning of this text? In neither case can people expect to arrive at a final answer.

Just as deciphering the meaning of a text like the Bible changes from one generation of readers to the next, so trying to interpret what the self is changes from one period of a person's life to the next. The inquiry must inevitably remain incomplete. Because it is a text, it is a continuing story.

Because of this, Rorty is skeptical of the idea that people can find one particular answer to the question, Who am I? He argues that people stop believing that the goal of self-knowledge is to get at the so-called facts about the self — because no such facts exist. Rather than thinking that there is one final answer to the question of who they are, says Rorty, people must recognize that they have at their disposal only an endless supply of free-floating and ultimately contingent *discourses* — ways of talking and ways of weaving together texts — about who they are.

Just as there can be no final self-knowledge, so there can also be no progress, says Rorty. There is only change and drift, one reweaving of the text followed by another.

This does not mean, however, that anything goes when people try to answer questions about who they are. Reflective self-inquiry is shaped by practical and social constraints and by historical circumstance. Some texts are better at coping with circumstances than others, but none enjoys elevated status. According to Rorty, self-knowledge is simply a matter of finding newer — but not more objective, or better justified, or more existentially authentic — ways of describing the self in response to the uncertainties of life.

Web connection
www.mcgrawhill.ca/links/philosophy12
To find out more about Richard Rorty's view of the self, follow the links on this Web site.

Chapter Review

Chapter Summary

This chapter has discussed
- some of the main questions in metaphysics
- the positions of some of the major philosophers and schools of philosophy on some of the main metaphysical questions
- how various metaphysical theories about the answers to various questions make a difference in people's attitudes to practical issues

Knowledge and Understanding

1. Identify and explain the significance to the study of metaphysics of each of the following key words and key people.

Key Words	Key People
metaphysics	George Berkeley
idealist	Plato
realism	Thomas Hobbes
materialism	Baruch Spinoza
monists	René Descartes
dualists	Laozi (Lao-tzu)
ontology	Martin Heidegger
determinism	Jean-Paul Sartre
substance	Stuart Hampshire
essence	Richard Rorty
form	

Thinking and Inquiry

2. Create a chart with the headings shown here. Summarize the main metaphysical theories that respond to the questions, What is reality? What is being? and What is self? In the last column, classify each theory according to whether it states empirical fact or recommends ways people ought to act.

Metaphysical Question	Theory	Philosophers	Classification of Conclusions

3. In *A Treatise of Human Nature*, David Hume offered this description of memory:

> When any impression has been present with the mind, it again makes its appearance there as an idea [in] two different ways: either when in its new appearance it retains a considerable degree of its first vivacity, and is somewhat intermediate betwixt an impression and an idea: or when it entirely loses that vivacity, and is a perfect idea. The faculty, by which we repeat our impressions in the first manner, is called the MEMORY, and the other the IMAGINATION.… The ideas of memory are much more lively and strong than those of the imagination, and … the former faculty paints its objects in more distinct colours, than any which are employ'd by the latter. When we remember any past event, the idea of it

flows in upon the mind in a forcible manner; whereas in the imagination the perception is faint … and cannot without difficulty be preserv'd by the mind steddy and uniform for any considerable time.

How does Hume distinguish between memory and imagination? How do you tell the difference between memory and imagination?

4. Mystics claim that logic and reason are imperfect tools that cannot explain the ultimate nature of reality. Write a philosophical reflection about the importance of logic and reason in responding to the metaphysical question, What are the ultimate constituents of reality? Defend your ideas in a philosophical exchange with one of your classmates.

Communication

5. Films such *A.I.: Artificial Intelligence* and *Bicentennial Man* have explored the metaphysical question, What is a person? by examining whether a machine can be considered human and can therefore claim the rights awarded humans. Create a plot outline for a new science fiction movie that focuses on the question, What is the self?

6. Create a diagram to show the differences in the way physical scientists and metaphysicians respond to questions of reality. Use images and words that illustrate the main questions of reality and the responses provided by scientists and metaphysicians.

Application

7. Examine this portion of a pointillist picture by Melissa Schatzmann (Figure 6.8). Tell a partner what you see. What does your partner see? Is it the same as what you see? Is the object of this picture real? To you? To your partner? How does each of you define real?

Figure 6.8

Compare what you see in this picture with Figure 6.9 on p. I. Read the caption under the picture. Interpret this artwork in light of at least one theory of reality. What does this experience with art tell you about reality?

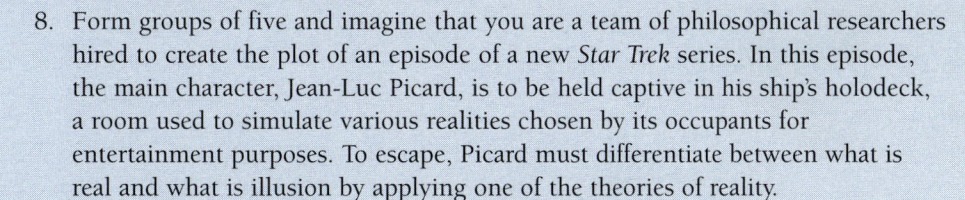

8. Form groups of five and imagine that you are a team of philosophical researchers hired to create the plot of an episode of a new *Star Trek* series. In this episode, the main character, Jean-Luc Picard, is to be held captive in his ship's holodeck, a room used to simulate various realities chosen by its occupants for entertainment purposes. To escape, Picard must differentiate between what is real and what is illusion by applying one of the theories of reality.

Each team member must choose one theory of reality and participate in a debate about its suitability for use by Picard. Prepare for the debate by listing the strengths and weaknesses of each theory, including the one you chose. Hold the debate and decide which theory best meets Picard's needs.

Chapter 7
Persons, Minds, and Brains

Chapter Expectations

By the end of this chapter, you will be able to
- demonstrate an understanding of some of the main questions in metaphysics
- evaluate the positions of some of the major philosophers and schools of philosophy on some of the main metaphysical questions
- formulate your own clear and cogent responses to some of the fundamental questions of metaphysics and defend your responses in philosophical exchanges with others
- explain with reference to some classic texts how various metaphysical theories about various questions make a difference in people's attitudes toward practical issues such as making promises, memory, and taking responsibility for past events
- apply logical and critical-thinking skills to evaluate and defend positions in philosophical writings
- clearly explain your own views in philosophical discussions in class and in exchanges with peers
- compare the problems, principles, methods, and conclusions of various philosophers
- describe ways in which the ideas of philosophers have influenced subsequent philosophers
- clearly explain your views and display philosophical reasoning skills in written papers, using accepted forms of documentation as required

Key Words
personhood
personal identity
survival
mind-brain problem
identity theorists
eliminative materialism
functionalism
Turing test
strong artificial intelligence
intentionality
Chinese room

Key People
John Locke
Daniel Dennett
Mary Ann Warren
Annette Baier
Derek Parfit
Patricia and Paul Churchland
Thomas Nagel
Alan Turing
John Searle
Steven Pinker

A Philosopher's Voice

This above all: to thine own self be true,
And it must follow, as the night the day,
Thou canst not then be false to any man.

William Shakespeare (1564–1616)

What Is a Person?

Imagine this scenario. It is late at night, and you are asleep. A black limousine comes to a quiet stop in front of your house. Two hooded figures emerge and stealthily unlock your front door. Once inside your house, they grab Descartes, your pet orangutan, bundle her into the limo, and zoom off.

Descartes is transported to a secret laboratory where she becomes the subject of a painful experiment that tests the effects of a noxious drug on the central nervous system. The drug leaves her blind and disabled. Rather than keep her alive, the experimenters give her a lethal injection. A year later, police raid the lab and charge the owners with a variety of offences, among them drug trafficking and the illegal manufacture of narcotics. The charges resulting from the treatment of Descartes — theft, cruelty to animals, and destruction of property — are minor and carry light sentences.

Now imagine this scenario. It is late at night, and you are asleep. A black limousine comes to a quiet stop in front of your house. Three hooded figures emerge and stealthily unlock your front door. Once inside your house, they grab you, bundle you into the limo, and zoom off.

You are taken to a secret laboratory where you become the subject of a painful experiment that tests the effects of a noxious drug on the central nervous system. You are left blind and disabled. Rather than keep you alive, the experimenters give you a lethal injection. A year later, police raid the lab and charge the owners with a variety of offences, among them drug trafficking and the illegal manufacture of narcotics. But the charges resulting from their treatment of you — kidnapping and murder — are the most serious and carry life sentences.

How are these two scenarios different? Some people might say that one involves killing an animal and the other murdering a person — two very different actions. Others might say that there are no differences. In both cases, the victim of the crime was a feeling, conscious, self-aware entity.

Like you, Descartes is clever, communicative, and emotional. According to the law, however, Descartes is not a person. She is an animal and a piece of property. As a result, she is not protected by the rights that protect people. She can be bought and sold legally. Killing her is cruel, but it is not murder. Only persons can be murdered.

Figure 7.1

In Canada, an orangutan like this one, pictured nibbling on a radish, cannot claim the rights that protect people. Is the law right? If not, how would you change it?

THE CONCEPT OF PERSON

The concept of **personhood** — or what it means to be a person — is an essential component of most legal and moral systems. To be considered a person is to be considered the holder of certain rights and privileges, most fundamentally the right to life.

The distinction between person and thing is fundamental in everyday conversations and in legal and moral systems. But how are persons distinguished from things? Does a clear line separate one from the other? How can we tell where personhood ends and thinghood begins? These questions have important practical consequences. To regard a particular entity as a person is to regard it as a member of the community of persons; in other words, as part of the moral community. To decide that a particular entity is not a person is to exclude it from the moral community.

But who — or what — should be included in the community of persons? Does this community include animals? Machines? How broad should the definition be? Who decides who gains admittance to the community?

On the one hand, the problem with a broad concept of person is that it risks overpopulating the world with persons. If non-human entities such as orangutans are identified as persons, then what is to prevent the inclusion of other animals, reptiles, insects, and even plants and minerals? On the other hand, the problem with a narrow concept of person is that it risks depopulating the world of persons by excluding entities — even some human beings — who might otherwise be considered persons.

The 18th-century English philosopher John Locke defined a person as "a thinking intelligent being, that has reason and reflection, and can consider itself as itself, the same thinking thing, in different times and places; which it does only by that consciousness which is inseparable from thinking." For Locke, the basic ingredients of personhood include rationality, thought, consciousness, self-consciousness, and self-identity.

In Locke's view, the mere fact that an entity has a human body, or human biology, is not sufficient to make it a person. Locke's definition was both far-sighted and controversial. It was far-sighted because it allowed for the possibility that other non-human creatures might have the requisite cognitive, or reasoning, properties to be worthy of the title "person." It was controversial because it did not claim that all persons are human beings, nor did it claim that all human beings are persons.

Daniel Dennett, a contemporary American philosopher of cognitive science, tried to improve on Locke's concept by identifying six basic conditions of personhood. They are

- rationality
- conscious mental states and intentionality
- being the subject of a special stance or attitude of regard by other persons
- reciprocating this person-regarding stance
- the capacity for verbal communication
- self-consciousness

Like Locke's definition of person, Dennett's concept is broad enough to allow non-human creatures, such as dolphins and apes, into the community of persons. At the same time, however, his definition might exclude certain human beings.

Though most of Dennett's conditions are primarily mental in nature, two — being the subject of a special stance or attitude of regard by other persons and reciprocating this person-regarding stance — are social. In Dennett's view, people do not begin to treat a living creature as a person only after the objective fact of its personhood has been established. Rather, a creature's treatment as person makes it a person. In other words, the very fact that a creature is recognized as a person by other persons helps to make it a person.

> **IDEAS IN CONTEXT**
>
> A quick look at history shows that the criteria governing who is admitted into the community of persons have changed over the years. In ancient Greece, for example, only land-owning men were considered to be persons. Children, slaves, and women were not. With changes in the concept of person have come new forms of inclusion or exclusion, and with them new forms of tolerance and new forms of discrimination.

> *The spirit is the true self, not that physical figure which can be pointed out by your finger.*
>
> – Cicero

134 MHR Unit 2 Metaphysics

The contemporary American moral philosopher **Mary Ann Warren** has discussed the concept of person from the point of view of the debate over abortion. The question she tackles is puzzling: Just when does personhood begin? Is a one-month-old fetus a person? Is an eight-month-old fetus a person? Does personhood begin at the moment of conception, or of birth, or later? Warren assumes that once society has a coherent concept of person, people will be in a position to know whether abortion is morally right or wrong. If a fetus is considered a person, then abortion would be wrong because it would have the same right to life as all other persons.

Like Locke and Dennett, Warren identified several essential conditions of personhood. These conditions, which are primarily cognitive, include the following:

- consciousness of objects and events and the ability to feel pain
- reasoning and problem-solving abililty
- the ability to carry out self-motivated activities
- the ability to communicate messages of an indefinite variety of types
- the presence of self-concepts and self-awareness

Warren qualified her position by claiming that a creature need not satisfy all these conditions to be considered a person. Meeting the first two or three might be enough, she said.

Some people might argue that the criteria set out by Locke, Dennett, and Warren are too restrictive because they might exclude infants, people who are developmentally challenged, and those who have suffered brain damage. Yet these people are certainly considered persons. And eight-day-old infant, for example, may not be able to use language, but people would normally consider him or her a person. Similarly, someone suffering from late-stage Alzheimer's disease may have lost the ability to reason, but this would not make her or him any less a person.

In response to challenges like these, Locke, Dennett, and Warren might soften their position by counting as persons those creatures who display the *potential* for rationality, language use, consciousness, and so on. Doing this would substitute one set of problems for another, however. How would potentiality for consciousness or language use be established?

Annette Baier, a contemporary American ethicist, is critical of theories that present personhood as a test that some entities pass and others fail. Baier says that "person tests" too often reflect the narrow values of those who design them. The tests also tend to set up conditions, such as consciousness and rationality, that assign greater importance to individual cognitive powers and personal memory than to interpersonal dynamics and social role. The underlying assumption is that persons are moral atoms, disconnected from others.

In addition, says Baier, the emphasis of the tests on the cognitive conditions of personhood seems to imply that people can float free of their own history, dependency, mortality, and biology. Baier proposes a naturalist view of persons as embodied, interpersonally responsive, and dependent creatures. In *Moral Prejudices: Essays on Ethics*, she wrote: "Persons are born to earlier persons, and learn the arts of personhood from other persons. These arts include the self-consciousness which follows from mutual recognition, along with the sort of representation that speech makes possible…. The first persons we recognize as such are those who greet us, call to us, answer our calls. Our personhood is responsive…."

Web connection
www.mcgrawhill.ca/links/philosophy12
To find out more about moral personhood, follow the links on this Web site.

Personal Identity

How is it that people can go through so much change and yet remain the same persons? Think about your own life. Over time, you change. You shed old habits and develop new ones. Your social circle changes. Your beliefs and attitudes change. You go through a continuing cycle of loss, growth, integration, and disintegration. While all these changes are occurring, your body is aging. Cells are constantly dying and being replaced. Does anything remain the same in the midst of this flux? Are you the same person from one time to another?

Despite the many changes that occur, most people regard themselves as the same person over time. You do not, for example, regard the self that was you last year as numerically separate from the self that is you today. Your past self is not separate from your today's self in the same way as your self is distinct from the self of your best friend. You and your best friend add up to two people, but you and your self of the past add up to one person.

What is more, you do not refer to your past self in the third-person as "he" or "she," as if it were a stranger. You use the first-person singular "I." Nor do you disown your younger self's actions, as if they belonged to another person. Though there may be qualitative differences between who you were last year (e.g., shy and gullible) and who you are now (e.g., extroverted and savvy), you are still the same you. It seems that you are numerically the same, though qualitatively different.

What makes you the same person over time? Is it something in your physical makeup, such as your genetic code or your neurobiology? Or is it something psychological, such as your memories, plans, or projects? Or is it something spiritual, such as a non-material soul that resists decay even as your body ages?

Questions like these involve the problem of **personal identity**, a debate that has vexed philosophers for many years and has led to the invention of some ingenious thought experiments.

John Locke was one of the first philosophers to address the problem. If his definition of a person as a thinking, intelligent, and reflective being is accurate, then how is this being the same from one time to another? What is the metaphysical glue that holds this being together over time? Locke believed that neither the body nor the brain looms large in the answers to these questions. Because bodies come and go, change and decay, he viewed the body as a kind of housing for personhood. He also believed that spiritual substance — or the immaterial soul — is unimportant.

For Locke, the most important component of personal identity is "continuing consciousness." By this, he meant the ability to remember, to relive, to take responsibility for past actions, and to think of events and actions in relation to the self. In Locke's view, you remain the same person as long as your consciousness can place you in the past, thereby enabling you to relive the past with some of the same feelings that you had at the time. If there is a break in the continuity of your consciousness, such as a gap caused by amnesia, Locke maintained that you are no longer the same person. If there are two or more distinct consciousnesses that cannot communicate with each other, then there are two or more persons.

To see what Locke means, imagine that you are a sleepwalker. You wander about the house and have no recollection of your antics the next morning. How would you feel if the police arrested you one morning on charges of vandalism? As evidence, they produce a videotape showing you spray-painting graffiti on your neighbour's mini-van. You do not remember doing this. You look at the video with horror. There you are, but it is not you. It is as if your body were possessed by a stranger. You feel no sense of ownership over the actions of the vandal on the videotape and no sense of responsibility or shame. Why should you take responsibility for something you did not do?

> *A biography is considered complete if it merely accounts for six or seven selves, whereas a person may well have as many thousand.*
>
> – Virginia Woolf

PHILOSOPHY IN ACTION

An Essay Concerning Human Understanding

by John Locke

An English philosopher who lived from 1632 to 1704, John Locke believed that people have an intuitive knowledge of their own existence. In these excerpts from *An Essay Concerning Human Understanding*, which was published in 1690, he explores issues of personhood and personal identity.

9. *Personal identity.* ... We must consider what person stands for; which, I think, is a thinking intelligent being, that has reason and reflection, and can consider itself as itself, the same thinking thing, in different times and places; which it does only by that consciousness which is inseparable from thinking, and, as it seems to me, essential to it: it being impossible for any one to perceive without perceiving that he does perceive. When we see, hear, taste, feel, meditate, or will anything, we know that we do so. Thus it is always as to our present sensations and perceptions: and by this everyone is to himself that which he calls self: it not being considered, in this case, whether the same self be continued in the same or divers substances. For, since consciousness always accompanies thinking, and it is that that makes everyone to be what he calls self, and thereby distinguishes himself from all other thinking things, in this alone consists personal identity....

10. *Consciousness makes personal identity.* ... For, it being the same consciousness that makes a man be himself to himself, personal identity depends on that only, whether it be annexed solely to one individual substance, or can be continued in a succession of several substances. For as far as any intelligent being can repeat the idea of any past action with the same consciousness it had of it at first, and with the same consciousness it has of any present action; so far it is the same personal self. For it is by the consciousness it has of its present thoughts and actions, that it is self to itself now, and so will be the same self, as far as the same consciousness can extend to actions past or to come....

15. ... For should the soul of a prince, carrying with it the consciousness of the prince's past life, enter and inform the body of a cobbler, as soon as deserted by his own soul, every one sees he would be the same person with the prince, accountable only for the prince's actions:...

18. *Persons, not substances the objects of reward and punishment.* In this personal identity is founded all the right and justice of reward and punishment; happiness and misery being that for which everyone is concerned for himself, and not mattering what becomes of any substance, not joined to, or affected with that consciousness....

19. ... To punish Socrates waking for what the sleeping Socrates thought, and waking Socrates was never conscious of, would be no more of right than to punish one twin for what his brother-twin did, whereof he knew nothing, because their outsides were so like, that they could not be distinguished....

20. ... But yet possibly it will still be objected, suppose I wholly lose the memory of some parts of my life, beyond a possibility of retrieving them, so that perhaps I shall never be conscious of them again; yet am I not the same person that did those actions, had those thoughts that I once was conscious of, though I have now forgot them? To which I answer, that we must here take notice what the word I is applied to; which, in this case, is the man only. And the same man being presumed to be the same person, I is easily here supposed to stand also for the same person. But if it be possible for the same man to have distinct incommunicable consciousness at different times, it is past doubt the same man would at different times make different persons; which, we see, is the sense of mankind in the solemnest declaration of their opinions, human laws not punishing the mad man for the sober man's actions, nor the sober man for what the mad man did, thereby making them two persons: which is somewhat explained by our way of speaking in English when we say such an one is "not himself," or is "beside himself."

23. *Consciousness alone unites remote existences into one person.* Nothing but consciousness can unite remote existences into the same person; the identity of substance will not do it....

Could we suppose two distinct incommunicable consciousnesses acting the same body, the one constantly by day, the other by night; and, on the other side, the same consciousness, acting by intervals, two distinct bodies: I ask, in the first case, whether the day- and the night-man would not be two as distinct persons as Socrates and Plato? And whether, in the second case, there would not be one person in two distinct bodies, as much as one man is the same in two distinct clothings?

26. *"Person" as a forensic term* [a term applied to things used in courts of law]. Person, as I take it, is the name for this self. Wherever a man finds what he calls himself, there, I think, another may say is the same person. It is a forensic term, appropriating actions and their merit; and so belongs only to intelligent agents, capable of a law, and happiness, and misery. This personality extends itself beyond present existence to what is past, only by consciousness, whereby it becomes concerned and accountable, owns and imputes to itself past actions, just upon the same ground and for the same reason as it does the present. All which is founded in a concern for happiness, the unavoidable concomitant of consciousness; that which is conscious of pleasure and pain desiring that that self that is conscious should be happy. And therefore whatever past actions it cannot reconcile or appropriate to that present self by consciousness, it can be no more concerned in than if they had never been done:… For, supposing a man punished now for what he had done in another life,… what difference is there between that punishment and being created miserable? And therefore, conformable to this, the apostle tells us that, at that great day, when everyone shall "receive according to his doings, the secrets of all hearts shall be laid open." The sentence shall be justified by the consciousness all persons shall have, that they themselves, in what bodies soever they appear, or what substances soever that consciousness adheres to, are the same that committed those actions, and deserve that punishment for them.

Source: From *An Essay Concerning Human Understanding.* John Locke.

1. According to Locke, what is personal identity and how does it relate to his concept of self?

2. Locke uses examples of problems or situations to arrive at a definition of personal identity. What do these examples suggest about the relationship between Locke's concept of personal identity and people's memory of or responsibility for past events?

3. Given Locke's views on personal identity, how would he react to a drunk driver's disclaiming responsibility for a collision because she or he could not recollect its happening? Do you agree with Locke? Why?

If you believe that the vandal is not you, your reaction is Lockean. You are committed to the idea that two persons — you and someone else — have occupied your body at different times. You believe that you are defined mainly by your consciousness, not by your physical body. Where your conscious awareness ends, your person also ends.

Locke's thinking raised many questions about personal identity. Will the person who bears my name five years from now be the same person as I am today? Is the person who bore my name 16 years ago the same person as I am today?

The contemporary British philosopher Derek Parfit said that questions like these do not always have definitive answers — and may be less important than many philosophers think. Parfit argued that what really matters is people's survival, or their continued existence, over time, not their identity over time. Parfit said that survival is a much less metaphysically demanding concept than identity because identity is an all-or-nothing proposition. The debate over identity raises questions about whether you are you or whether you are someone else. Survival, by contrast, is a matter of degree. It involves a greater or lesser part of you at one time overlapping with a greater or lesser part of you at another time.

But what are the parts that overlap? In Parfit's view, they are simply psychological links, such as memories, plans, and intentions. For survival, it is not necessary for all of a person's memories, plans, and intentions to overlap. The memories, plans, and intentions that make up people's lives, he claimed, are not as deeply integrated as many assume.

Parfit argued that the idea of survival applies in the real world. Over a lifetime, people can expect only parts of their current selves to survive. Though each person has a single life, earlier and later selves occupy different stages of it. By the time you turn 85, for example, much of your 16-year-old self may have faded away. Parfit said that people are connected psychologically to other stages of their life by overlapping links of memory and intention rather than some sort of metaphysical glue. These memory and intention links are like those of a chain-link fence. Each link is connected to another, but no single thread runs through the entire fence to hold it together.

Parfit's views on personal identity have unusual moral implications. If your current self fades over time, for example, you may not deserve the penalty you received 15 years ago when you were caught spray-painting that mini-van. The self who committed that act may have faded away almost completely. Similarly, a promise that you made to a friend five years ago may no longer apply with the force of a promise made today. The promise was made not by you but by a past self — and it was made to the past self of your friend. Though Parfit's view seems to weaken some moral relationships, it strengthens others. If you start smoking now, for example, then a decision made by your current self may harm your future self.

Web connection
www.mcgrawhill.ca/links/philosophy12
To read more about Derek Parfit, follow the links on this Web site.

Parfit also maintained that the question of whether you are the same person as before cannot always be answered definitively. Think of a business that employs 50 people and closes its doors after operating for 10 years. Twenty years later, it reopens, hiring some old employees and some new. Is it the same business? Parfit claimed that this is an empty question because no one can provide a definitive yes-or-no answer.

In his view, the same principle applies to persons. Imagine that you faced this question: Am I about to die or am I going to continue living? According to Parfit, this question may not always have a simple yes or no answer.

What would happen, though, if you had been cloned, then discovered that you were going to die? Parfit argued that you would not need to fear dying. With a clone, your prospects of survival are very good. Someone who is just like you will take over the living of your life, and that is all that matters.

Recall...Reflect...Respond

1. List the characteristics and qualities that philosophers have used to describe what a person is. Then list the characteristics and qualities that philosophers have used to describe what a person is not. Consult these two lists to write a one-sentence definition of personhood.
2. Brainstorm with a group to create a list of people, creatures, and things that would qualify as persons according to your definition. Then create a similar list of people, creatures, and things that would not qualify as persons. Is your definition broad or narrow? Explain why. After thinking about the lists, would you consider revising your definition? Why?
3. Suppose someone said, "I can't take responsibility for what I did last year. That person's actions are as alien to me as the actions of a complete stranger." How would you react? Would this statement make sense to philosophers whose theories address the questions, What is the self? and What is personal identity? Explain why.

THOUGHT EXPERIMENT

First-Class Travel?

What if a machine could transport you from one place to another faster than the speed of light? You step into the machine, hook up some electrodes, press a button, lose consciousness for a split second — and next thing you know, you are sitting in a similar machine on the other side of the planet, being greeted by a guy saying, "G'day mate." In less than a second, the teletransporter has whisked you from Canada to your favourite sheep farm in Wagga Wagga, New South Wales, Australia.

You look at your body, and everything seems to be the same. Even that bothersome bit of spinach that was stuck between your front teeth is still there.

Here's what happened. The machine scanned every molecule in your brain and body. As it did, it destroyed your brain and body. All that remained was a little puddle of thick, smelly goo. The information recorded by the machine was transmitted to a satellite high above Pago Pago in the South Pacific, then to a machine in Wagga Wagga. The Australian machine created a replica you out of new matter. For the split second while you were unconscious, you existed not as a normal embodied person, but as an informational blueprint.

The replica who stepped out of the machine in Wagga Wagga looks just like you, remembers everything you remember, thinks the same thoughts as you, reacts the same way as you, and has the same desires and plans. Physically and psychologically, the two of you are exactly the same. If the replica turned up at your school, everyone would think that it was you.

Is stepping into the teletransporter a way of travelling — or a way of dying? Would you choose to travel this way if you knew that your current brain and body would be destroyed and that what appeared at your destination would be an exact replica of you. This replica would be psychologically and experientially — but not bodily — continuous with you.

Figure 7.2

Derek Parfit designed the teletransporter thought experiment to address this question: What makes a person one and the same person at two different times?

Materialists would say that what is necessary to remain the same over time is the continued existence of the body and brain. Obviously, they would not step into the machine because they would regard what happens as a way of dying. After all, once the teletransporter scans all the information, it destroys your body. Poof! Vaporized! There is a drastic break in bodily continuity.

Those who defend the psychological view respond that what is necessary for being the same over time is some kind of psychological and experiential continuity, such as direct memories of your past, flowing intention–act sequences, continuous desires and beliefs, and overlapping chains of experiences. For them, stepping into the machine is a great way of travelling. The gap in bodily continuity and the destruction of your original body and brain do not matter. What more, they would ask, could you possibly want? It doesn't matter that the cause of your psychological continuity and connectedness is — for a split second — a machine rather than a body. Your psychology and experiences — the things that matter to your survival — have been preserved.

So, would you step into the teletransporter if you wanted to visit Wagga Wagga? Or if you were late for school?

Mind and Brain

Inside your head, just millimetres behind the bridge of your nose, is a squishy 1.4 kg lump of meat: your brain. It is made up of a hundred billion nerve cells. Neuroscience has shown that when you think a particular thought — such as, The dog ate my homework — waves of electrical activity shoot through a portion of this brain tissue.

But what is the connection between the thought and the physical event in the tissue inside your head? How can mere electrical activity mean anything, as your thoughts mean something? How can a physical event be *about* something, as a thought is? How can tiny electrical impulses that you neither see nor experience represent those interesting portions of the world occupied by dogs and math homework and disbelieving math teachers? Is your thought about homework nothing but electrical activity in your brain? If so, then what about bigger things like your personality, your consciousness, your sense of self, and your feelings of love? Are these no more than electrical waves in squishy tissue?

This is the **mind-brain problem** — and philosophers differ enormously in the ways they try to solve it.

THE MATERIALIST'S SOLUTION

Materialists maintain that everything that exists, including a person's thoughts, consciousness, and personality, is made of matter. Nothing non-material exists in reality.

But what is matter? In ancient Greece, matter was thought to be composed of tiny, solid atoms that bump into one another and accumulate to form larger bodies. Today, theories of matter are much more complex and involve atoms, electrons, and quarks in a shifting force field of energy.

Most contemporary materialist theories are based on four principles.

There exists no kind of spiritual substance or entity of a different nature from that of which matter is composed.
— Hugh Elliot

- Science is the objective study of reality.
- Reality is objective.
- Every fact in reality can be known.
- The only things that exist are physical in nature.

THE IDENTITY THEORIST'S SOLUTION

Identity theorists say that all mental states are identical to brain states. Take a thought like, The hippo in my swimming pool smells bad. According to identity theorists, your thinking this thought — your mental state — is nothing but a physical event in your brain. This means that every mental state you find yourself in during the day is identical to a specific brain state. A one-to-one correlation exists between the two. Though neuroscientists have not yet established all the identities between mental states and brain states, they are slowly closing in on a complete account.

What do people mean when they say that a mental state is identical to a brain state, especially as the two seem to be so different? Compare a mental state to light or sound. A mental state is a brain state in the same way as light is electromagnetic waves, or sound is compression waves racing through the air. At one time, the identities between the way things appear (as light or sound) and what they really are (electromagnetic waves or compression waves) were unknown. Now that science understands these identities, people can refer to these phenomena either way. As research in neuroscience progresses, the same thing will happen with mental states and brain states. For every mental-state term people use to describe the thoughts in their brains, there will be a corresponding brain-state term that refers to the same thing.

Critics of identity theory argue that mental states are simply too different from brain states to be considered the same thing. They point out that when people examine their own mental and emotional processes, they encounter thoughts and feelings, not the electrochemical impulses that these feelings are identical with.

A related objection is that brain states do not mean anything, whereas mental states do. When you think about the hippo in your pool, your thought is *about* something. As a result, it is meaningful, and it is either true or false. But electrical activity in your brain is no more meaningful — and no more true or false — than the electrical current that buzzes in the wires in your house. It is not *about* something in the same way as a thought is about something. It simply is what it is.

THE ELIMINATIVIST MATERIALIST'S SOLUTION

Eliminativist materialism, a theory proposed by two Canadian philosophers, Patricia and Paul Churchland, is the view that common-sense psychology is a radically false theory of human behaviour and will eventually be eliminated and replaced by one based on neuroscience. The Churchlands believe that the everyday psychological terms people use to describe themselves and others — terms such as "belief," "desire," "guilt," and "envy" — do not explain what really drives human behaviour.

Eliminativists illustrate this by pointing to parallels in the history of science. In medieval Europe, for example, people believed that those who were mentally ill were possessed by demons. Today, scientific psychology has shown that the causes of mental illness often lie in brain disorders. The possession explanation is false and has been all but eliminated.

Eliminativists maintain that the same fate awaits common-sense psychology. They say that when neuroscience is complete, people will use brain-state terms to identify what are now called desires, beliefs, and attitudes. Instead of saying, "I am in pain," someone might say something like, "C-fibres are firing in section L2 of my cortex." This will eliminate people's entire mentalist self-conception.

Critics point out that eliminativism exaggerates the inability of common-sense psychology to explain people's mental states, while overlooking its successes. They say that if the terms of common-sense psychology were really so inadequate, then all communication would have ceased long ago. Critics also say that if eliminativists are right, it follows that no human being has ever been conscious and no mental-state term has ever referred to anything at all.

THE FUNCTIONALIST'S SOLUTION

Functionalism, another version of materialism, says that mental states can be realized, or made real, in various ways. One way is through the brain tissue inside your cranium. Another way is through silicon chips. With the right hardware and software, functionalists say that computers can understand things and have a variety of mental states.

Take calculators, for example. Though all calculators do arithmetic, not all calculators are made of the same materials or designed the same way. When you punch 2 + 2 into your mother's 1976 calculator, and your friend does the same thing with his brand new calculator, different processes happen in the two machines. Still, both come up with the same result: 4.

Their hardware may be different, but their output is the same. Mental states work in a similar way. Different brains can produce the same thoughts. As a result, functionalists often repeat this motto: Minds are to brains as software is to hardware.

Functionalists argue that several important features define mental states:

- their causal relations with other mental states
- their causal relations with bodily behaviour (output)
- their causal relations with the environment (input)

This is the input-output definition of mental states. Suppose that hippo in your swimming pool steps on your foot. You would be in a lot of pain. What a functionalist means by pain is simply the combined effect of the environmental input (hippo foot causing bodily damage), internal states (distress, shock), and output behaviour (grimacing and grabbing your crushed foot). Any state that satisfies these conditions is a pain state.

Functionalist *Star Trek* fans like to remind people that they should not fall prey to species chauvinism, the view that only human brains can support thought and consciousness. They remind us that Data, a *Star Trek* character, has a mind, even though his insides look like a spaghetti junction of wires and silicon chips, rather than a 1.4 kg lump of meat. Appealing to our sense of cosmic generosity, functionalists claim that there are more ways than one for nature to produce a thinking, perceiving creature.

THE DUALIST'S SOLUTION

Though there are a number of different kinds of dualism, all dualists agree that consciousness cannot be reduced to matter. As a result, dualists maintain that no science can fully explain consciousness.

SUBSTANCE DUALISM

Substance dualists such as Descartes maintain that reality is composed of two fundamentally different things: mental substances and material substances. They believe that, as a non-material entity or substance, the human mind exists independently of the body. They also believe that the mind interacts with the body, sending messages to and receiving messages from it. They don't explain, however, just how this mysterious interaction actually works.

Substance dualists say that the essential characteristic of minds is that they are thinking, while the essential characteristic of material things is that they are extended. By "extended," they mean that, unlike minds, material substances take up space and can be identified in terms of their length, breadth, and height. When you think something like, A fat worm is writhing happily in the gravy sauce, this thought takes up no space. Substance dualists also maintain that minds are different from material substances because they cannot be divided. It makes no sense to talk about half a mind in the same way as you might talk about half a writhing worm.

Descartes described minds as the subjects or owners of various mental states that come and go with great rapidity over the course of a day. This multiplicity

Figure 7.3

"THE COMPUTER IS CLAIMING ITS INTELLIGENCE IS REAL, AND OURS IS ARTIFICIAL."

How does this cartoon poke fun at the mind-brain debate?

of mental states does not affect the essential unity of the owner, however. No matter how many thoughts you have and no matter how many different directions these thoughts pull you in, Descartes maintained, your mind remains a unity.

THE SUBJECTIVIST'S SOLUTION

What is consciousness? What is it made of? What is its function? Can there be a science of consciousness? On the face of it, consciousness seems to be indefinable. It is not like an object, with definite measurable properties, and it cannot be observed from the outside. In fact, subjectivists like the contemporary American philosopher Thomas Nagel argue that consciousness is unique because it constitutes a fully independent dimension of reality. He said that science will never explain it.

Nagel argued that conscious and non-conscious things are fundamentally different. Saying that an organism is conscious means that there is something that it is like to *be* that organism. Saying that a thing is non-conscious, however, means that there is nothing that it is like to *be* that thing.

If this idea seems difficult to follow, consider that people often ask what something, such as bungee jumping, is like to *do*. What is it like to jump from a 90-metre tower with a bungee cord tied to your ankles? One possible answer is that it is like flying. Comparisons like this may fail to get across exactly what bungee jumping is like, but we still assume that there is *something* that it is like.

Just as you can ask what something is like to *do*, you can also ask what something is like to *be*. There is something that it is like to *be* a bat, a hippo, and you, for example. But it is not like anything to be a brick, a bell, or a blue suede shoe. Bricks, bells, and blue suede shoes have no subjectivity.

In other words, conscious things have a point of view, but non-conscious things do not. Subjectivity is tied to having a point of view. Consider bats. Though bats have experiences, their cognitive, neurological, and perceptual makeup is radically different from that of human beings. As a result, their experiences are very different from ours. Besides being furry and having rat-like facial features, bats are as blind as, well, bats. When they fly, they use echolocation to prevent their running into things. Can a human being know what it is like to be a bat? Can people draw conclusions about the inner life of a bat by thinking about their own inner life?

Twinkle, twinkle, little bat,
How I wonder what you're at,
Up above the world you fly,
Like a tea-tray in the sky.

— Lewis Carroll

Nagel argued that it is pointless for people to try to imagine themselves as winged, blind, sonar-producing, and insect-gobbling creatures. He said that the human imagination is not up to this task because it is unavoidably anthropocentric, or centred on human experience. Even if you could imagine what it is like to be blind, you would be imagining a human form of blindness. In other words, even if you subtracted the sense of sight from your five senses, your experience would still be a human experience. And even if you could master the skill of echolocation, it would still be you — a human — experiencing echolocation, not you — a bat — experiencing it. The best you could do is *imagine* what it is like to *behave* like a bat, but this is different from *knowing* what it is like for a bat to *be* a bat.

Scientists can provide objective information about bats, but this does reveal anything about the specific subjective character of bat experience. Scientists cannot tell us what it is like to *be* a bat. What scientists describe from the outside also has an inside — and it is this inside that is beyond human ability to conceive. There is something that it is like to be a bat, and whatever it is, it is accessible only in terms that can be understood by bats, from their point of view. In other words, some facts about reality are accessible only from certain points of view. Though objective facts can be understood from many points of view, subjective facts cannot.

Critics charge that Nagel's view sets the bar for experiential understanding too high. If you must be a bat to understand what it is like for a bat to *be* a bat, then this suggests that only you can understand what it is like to *be* you. No one else could acquire an exact replica of your unique experiential fingerprint, because no one experiences things exactly as you do. Nagel's critics say that the implications of this view are too drastic because they suggest that people are experientially insulated not only from other species, but also from other human beings. They may even suggest that people are experientially insulated from their past selves. Do you know what it is like to be your one-year-old self, when you were a drooling toddler struggling with the basics of toilet training?

THE MONIST'S SOLUTION

Monists believe that reality is ultimately composed of one thing or one type of thing. They disagree, however, on just what this thing is. One kind of monism is panpsychism, which says that reality is composed entirely of minds. Another is materialism, which says that reality is composed entirely of matter. The 17th-century Jewish-Dutch philosopher Baruch Spinoza was one of the most famous monists — and one of the severest critics of substance dualism.

Whereas Descartes proposed that reality consists of two radically different kinds of things — mental substances and material substances — Spinoza said that reality consists of only one thing. He identified this one, infinite, all-inclusive substance as "God or Nature" and said that this single substance expresses itself in infinite ways and in an infinite number of dimensions.

Mind and body, which Spinoza called thought and extension, are aspects of the one substance, which itself is neither exclusively mental nor exclusively material. As a result, he said, mental-state terms and body- or brain-state terms refer to the same thing in different — but equally valid — ways. He maintained that one way cannot be reduced to the other, nor can one be explained in terms of the other. "Whether we conceive Nature under the attribute of Extension or under the attribute of Thought or under any other attribute, we find one and the same order, or one and the same connection of causes — that is, the same things following one another," he wrote.

Recall...Reflect...Respond

1. How do materialists, identity theorists, eliminative materialists, functionalists, dualists, subjectivists, and monists respond to the question, What is the relationship between mind and matter?
2. List some of the criticisms of various versions of materialism and explain whether — and how — other mind-brain theories respond to these criticisms.
3. Imagine what it would be like to describe your emotions and behaviour using only brain-state terms. Would this affect your views on personal identity? Would it alter your concept of self? Why?

PROFILE
Ludwig Wittgenstein
A Battle against Bewitchment

Born in 1889, Ludwig Wittgenstein grew up in an atmosphere of privilege. His father was one of the wealthiest industrialists in Austria, and Wittgenstein's seven sisters and brothers were accomplished artists and musicians. The Wittgensteins regularly socialized with famous artists, composers, and writers at their sumptuous home in Vienna, the Austrian capital.

As a young man, Wittgenstein studied mathematics and physics and earned a degree in engineering in Berlin. He travelled to England to study aeronautical engineering at the University of Manchester, where he designed airplane propellers. During this time, he became interested in the foundations of mathematics and moved to Cambridge University to study with the British philosopher and mathematician Bertrand Russell.

Wittgenstein wrote much of his first major work, the *Tractatus Logico-Philosophicus*, while he serving in the Austrian army in the trenches of Europe during World War I. He finished the book in an Italian prisoner of war camp. Published in 1921, three years after the end of the war, the *Tractatus* set out a system of a priori metaphysics that tried to explain the relationship between language and the world.

After the war, Wittgenstein gave away the fortune he had inherited and worked as a teacher in a primary school in a small Austrian farming village. Feeling that he was unsuccessful as a teacher, he moved on to work as a gardener's assistant in a monastery, then as an architect on his sister's house in Vienna.

In 1929, Wittgenstein returned to Cambridge University, submitted the *Tractatus* as his doctoral thesis and passed the exam with flying colours. He was soon appointed to the chair in philosophy at Cambridge. But he was no ordinary academic. He wore old, rough clothes and a worn leather jacket rather than the academic gowns traditionally worn by professors. He detested academic snobbishness and disliked professional philosophy, which he felt promoted cleverness rather than depth. He even tried to convince his own graduate students to give up their dreams of pursuing careers in philosophy.

Wittgenstein's lectures were so intense that afterwards he would go to the movies and try to unwind by watching hour after hour of Westerns. His students were so captivated by his forceful personality that they imitated his style of dress and speech.

During World War II, Wittgenstein worked in England as a hospital orderly and as an assistant in a medical lab. Fed up with academic philosophy, he resigned from the chair at Cambridge in 1947 and moved to a desolate cottage on the west coast of Ireland, where he wrote his final works.

Though the *Tractatus* had a tremendous influence on thinking about metaphysics, Wittgenstein came to regard metaphysics as nonsense and philosophy as an intellectual disease from which philosophers should seek a cure. "Philosophy is a battle against the bewitchment of our intelligence by means of language," he wrote.

Wittgenstein eventually rejected everything he had written in the *Tractatus*, likening the book to an exquisitely constructed watch whose only flaw was that it failed to keep time. Metaphysics, he argued, is no more than the "shadow of grammar." It is a false explanation. Believing that metaphysicians had been duped by language, Wittgenstein devised a kind of therapy to cure philosophers of the idea that philosophy's task is to inquire into the essence of things.

In his book *Philosophical Investigations*, he wrote: "The real discovery is the one that makes me capable of stopping doing philosophy when I want to. — The one that gives philosophy peace, so that it is no longer tormented by questions which bring itself in question." Wittgenstein died in 1951.

Figure 7.4

Photographed in 1920 when he qualified as a teacher, Ludwig Wittgenstein is wearing the leather jacket that would become his trademark.

Minds, Machines, and Animals

Can machines think? Can Deep Blue, the IBM computer that has beaten a human grand chess master at chess, think? Can Data, a *Star Trek* character, think? These are challenging questions. Before tackling their answers, however, metaphysicians are likely to step back and ask some even more fundamental questions. Could it be that the question of whether machines can think is poorly formed? Could it be that this question contains hidden assumptions about the nature of thinking? Is there a less biased and less ambiguous question?

THE TURING TEST

To cast light on the question of whether machines can think, the English computer scientist and philosopher **Alan Turing** invented what he called the imitation game. This game is played by three people: a man, a woman, and a judge of either sex. The man pretends to be a woman, the woman must try to prove that she is the woman, and the judge must discover which of the contestants is the woman.

Here is one way the imitation game might unfold. Contestant A is Romeo Romanceburger, contestant B is Juliet Jello, and contestant C, the interrogator, is Bill Rattlespear, a starving, out-of-work writer. Romeo and Juliet know each other well. When not playing extras on the hit TV show *Estuarywatch*, they spend a great deal of time on the beach, whispering sweet nothings into each other's ears.

When the game begins, the two lovebirds are separated and placed in two separate rooms. Each room has an e-mail connection to Bill Rattlespear, who has never met the two contestants and does not know which has been assigned to each room. By peppering Romeo and Juliet with questions and examining their e-mailed responses, he must figure out which is Juliet.

Because Juliet must prove that she is a woman, she tries to help Rattlespear as much as possible. She sends honest answers to each of his questions. When he asks, for example, what colour her hair is, she types, "It's platinum blonde."

Romeo must try to fool Rattlespear into concluding that he is Juliet. When he receives questions, he sends back the detailed answers that he thinks Juliet would give. To emphasize his point, he also types things like, "Don't listen to him. I am the real woman here."

As it turns out, Romeo is a convincing liar, and Bill is easily fooled. Romeo wins the game and is reunited with his sweetheart. Bill walks away from the game, still starving and out of work, though he now has some ideas for a play that he is thinking of calling *Romanceburger and Jello*.

Though this version of Turing's game might entertain TV viewers if it were turned into a game show, it would leave most philosophers yawning. But what if television executives, always on the lookout for new ideas, developed a daring variation of the imitation game to attract an audience of deep thinkers? It might be called *Imitation Game, Version 2.0*. In one room would be the latest supercomputer, and in the other a human being. In this version of the game, the computer would try its hardest to convince the interrogator that it is the human being, while the human being does the same.

Turing devised the imitation game because he believed that the question, Can machines think? was ambiguous and biased. He saw little point in arguing about the ultimate nature of mind. A more interesting question, in his view, was this: Could a machine fool the interrogator into thinking that it is a person?

In 1950, Turing predicted that computers in the year 2000 would be so sophisticated that the average interrogator would have no more than a 70 percent chance of making the right identification after five minutes of questioning. His prediction has come true.

Turing believed that if a computer can converse in a way that would fool a human being, then it has shown that it can think. It has passed the **Turing test**. The fact that the machine cannot run a race or walk the dog does not matter. Nor does it matter that the computer does not have a brain. What counts is whether it can behave intelligently.

Many philosophers criticized Turing's conclusions. Some point out that the test shows only that a computer can simulate thinking, saying that a simulation is not the same as the real thing. They add that the test shows only that a human performance can easily be mimicked — by people or computers — as long as they have been given formal rules to follow under well-defined circumstances. But formal rules, such as "If X, then Y" or chains of 1s and 0s, are empty of meaning. Critics say that a computer is nothing but a tool that can be used to manipulate formal symbols and engage in syntactical operations. Neither function requires knowledge of the real world.

STRONG ARTIFICIAL INTELLIGENCE

Consider HAL, the supercomputer in the Stanley Kubrick film *2001: A Space Odyssey*. It — or he — can talk to you, answer your questions, offer advice, fly a spaceship, and beat you at chess. It even seems to have feelings. Would you be willing to say that it can think? That it is conscious? That it is a person?

Figure 7.5

In the movie *2001: A Space Odyssey*, the supercomputer HAL tries to kill one of the astronauts. Does this mean that HAL can think??

Defenders of the **strong artificial intelligence** thesis would say yes. They hold the functionalist view that mental states can be realized in different ways and believe that a computer could be programmed to think. The brain tissue inside your cranium is one material in which thoughts can be actualized or made real. Silicon chips are another way. With the right hardware and software, computers can understand things and have a variety of mental states.

According to strong AI theory, human beings are also com-puters because they process, store, encode, decode, and manipulate information in orderly ways. This suggests that if humans are computing machines, they can — at least in principle — be duplicated by other machines not built from tissue. And the parts that do the thinking can — at least in principle — be replaced. Parts of human brain could be rebuilt using synthetic materials. The ultimate goal of strong AI theorists is to build a person.

Critics of strong AI theory point out that machines have no originality. They simply do what they are programmed to do. The output of the machine is the direct result of the inputs, the program, and the physical structure of the machine. They say that human beings are, by contrast, genuinely creative. In response, proponents of strong AI claim that human creativity is a natural process that neuroscientists will one day be able to explain.

Another criticism of strong AI theory holds that similarities between the human brain and computing machinery are overstated. These critics say that the two have little in common. As a result, machines cannot serve as biologically realistic models of brains.

THE CHINESE ROOM

One objection to the Turing test and strong artificial intelligence theory is that computers cannot make meaning. They do not generate meaning, understand meaning, or live in a world of meanings. The symbols that computers manipulate are not meaningful to the computers themselves. These symbols are meaningful only to the human beings who interpret them.

This means that computers lack what philosophers call **intentionality**. When philosophers refer to intentionality, they mean that states of mind are about or represent things. What computers do is not about anything or directed toward anything. Mental states, by contrast, are intentional.

They are about something. When you have a desire, for example, it is a desire for something. When you feel sad, you are sad about something.

The American philosopher **John Searle** devised a thought experiment called the **Chinese room** to show that computers lack intentionality. Imagine a room with two small openings, one at the front and one at the back. You are inside the room. You speak English. You do not speak Chinese. In front of you is a book of rules, written in English. It tells you how to match Chinese symbols. Whenever you get a particular Chinese symbol, the book tells you how to match it with another Chinese symbol. The book does not, however, tell you what the symbols mean.

Now imagine there are people outside the room. They slide pieces of paper with Chinese symbols on them through the opening. You go to your book, match the symbols, write the new symbol on another piece of paper, and pass it through the other opening.

You become proficient at doing this. The combinations of symbols you put together in response to the incoming pieces of paper are quite complex. They begin to resemble the combinations that native Chinese speakers might put together. The people outside the room are amazed. They submitted questions to the room, and answers came out the other side. The room, they conclude, must be intelligent because it understands Chinese.

This is a false conclusion. You, the keeper of the room, do not understand Chinese, and the symbols are meaningless to you. You have simply manipulated empty symbols.

The analogy is obvious. The Chinese room is a computer, the book of rules is the program, the incoming papers are input, and the outgoing papers are output. Though computers may be programmed to mimic human performance, they have neither understanding nor intentionality. They are rule-following devices, not minds. They do not understand the real world or generate meanings, and they do not have any intention of achieving specific effects on the world through their responses.

Real understanding involves more than manipulating empty symbols. According to Searle, human biochemistry, evolutionary history, anatomy, and neurophysiology are essential to the mind.

Recall...Reflect...Respond

1. Does the Turing test prove that machines can think and can, therefore, be considered people? Defend your response.
2. Does John Searle's Chinese room thought experiment prove that machines cannot think and cannot, therefore, be considered people? Defend your response.
3. Create a short, imaginary dialogue in which Alan Turing and John Searle debate the question of whether machines can think.

INTELLIGENCE IN NON-HUMAN ANIMALS

Does your pet rat Sock-Rat-Tease have a mind? Is it conscious? Does it experience pain or pleasure? Do the ants that you crunch underfoot on your way to school have minds? Are they conscious?

René Descartes is famous for arguing that only human beings possess minds. Non-human animals, he said, are biological machines, without consciousness, thought, or feeling. As a result, Descartes viewed them in the same light as clocks and steam engines, saying that their cries of pain are no different from the chimes of a clock. He identified these cries as mechanical reflexes, not expressions of the experience of pain.

If there is no difference between machines and animals, Descartes argued, it is possible, at least in principle, to build a machine that is behaviourally indistinguishable from an animal. In this situation, Descartes maintained that it would be impossible to distinguish between your pet rat and a robot rat. He said that the same is not true of humans. No humanoid robot could be built to behave so convincingly that people would have no way of telling whether it had a mind of its own.

Descartes offered two reasons for this. First, he argued that machines — and by implication, non-human animals — can never be genuine language users. Language is unique to humans. Only people enjoy linguistic creativity, and only people can generate countless meaningful sentences and respond to an indefinite range of utterances.

Animals and machines, by contrast, can only mimic language, said Descartes. A machine like a computer might be programmed to spew out specific words when it receives certain input, but it could never assemble the words in different ways to respond to all the possible situations it might encounter. No matter how large its memory for words, it will never be different from the battery-operated talking dolls that children play with.

> *Man is the only animal that laughs and weeps; for he is the only animal that is struck with the difference between what things are, and what they ought to be.*
>
> – William Hazlitt

Descartes also argued that machines and animals have extremely restricted problem-solving abilities. A machine's output and an animal's behaviour are geared to respond only to a limited range of environmental input. Neither can acquire the ability to deal with the infinite variety of situations that humans encounter in life. Human beings, by contrast, are all-purpose problem solvers, he said. We are creative, flexible, and adaptive when faced with new situations.

Descartes's theory of non-human animals as machines has been challenged by some intriguing counter-examples. Consider Kanzi, a bonobo ape who lives at the Georgia State University Language Research Centre in Atlanta. Though apes do not have vocal chords and cannot therefore formulate spoken words, Kanzi has learned to communicate with a symbol board. On the board are geometric symbols standing for words like "cup," "banana," "tree," and so on.

Kanzi was not explicitly taught how to use the symbol board. He learned language the same way human children do: by observing others and by trial and error. Kanzi can now produce about 250 symbol-words and understand thousands more words. He can answer simple questions, obey simple commands and requests, and inform others of his desires. He spontaneously puts together "sentences" of three or four symbols. Sue Savage-Rumbaugh, who runs the research program involving Kanzi, also claims that he understands grammatical concepts such as word order.

Does Kanzi offer compelling proof that animals have minds? It may not be quite as simple as this. First, some important questions must be answered.

- Do animals have consciousness? Do they feel pain, hear sounds, and taste things?
- Do animals have intentionality? Do they have ideas or beliefs about things?
- Do animals have thought processes? Do they make plans or solve problems?
- Do animals have language?

Few people today would agree with Descartes's contention that animals are non-conscious machines. Some theorists, however, claim that though animals are conscious, they cannot think and cannot entertain intentional states. Others claim that though animals are conscious and may entertain ideas, they do not have language.

Figure 7.6

Kanzi is a bonobo ape like this. Does the researchers' work with Kanzi prove that non-human animals have minds?

Steven Pinker, a Canadian linguist and professor at the Massachusetts Institute of Technology, argues that people should not confuse a communication system such as that used by some apes with a language. Pinker says that language is bi-directional. In conversations, humans take turns speaking, but the communication displayed by apes lacks this dimension. Pinker also says that language is grammatically structured, whereas animal communication systems lack this structure. Kanzi's so-called sentences are short chains of symbols with no internal structure and no inflection for verb tenses or agreement. They are more like word jumbles than structured sentences.

Finally, Pinker claims that Kanzi's object signs are overly general. When Kanzi uses the sign for "toothbrush," he might be referring to almost any aspect of the situation with which the toothbrush is typically associated: "toothbrush," "toothpaste," "brushing teeth," and so on.

Pinker claims that trying to teach animals to use human language as a way of showing that they have biological worth is a misguided idea. Their failure to acquire human language is not a shortcoming. Pinker maintains that it simply shows that non-human animals cannot be fitted by force into the human mould. "A human would surely do no better if trained to hoot and shriek like a chimp, a symmetrical project that makes about as much scientific sense," he wrote.

Web connection
www.mcgrawhill.ca/links/philosophy12
To find out more about Kanzi, follow the links on this Web site.

Chapter Review

Chapter Summary

This chapter has discussed
- some of the main questions in metaphysics
- the positions of some of the major philosophers and schools of philosophy on some of the main metaphysical questions
- how various metaphysical theories about various questions make a difference in people's attitudes toward practical issues such as making promises, memory, and taking responsibility for past events
- the problems, principles, methods, and conclusions of various philosophers

Knowledge and Understanding

1. Identify and explain the significance to the study of metaphysics of each of the following key words and people.

Key Words	Key People
personhood	John Locke
personal identity	Daniel Dennett
survival	Mary Ann Warren
mind-brain problem	Annette Baier
identity theorists	Derek Parfit
eliminative materialism	Patricia and Paul Churchland
functionalism	Thomas Nagel
Turing test	Alan Turing
strong artificial intelligence	John Searle
intentionality	Steven Pinker
Chinese room	

2. Identify two important metaphysical questions addressed in this chapter and create a graphic organizer that summarizes the positions of the main philosophers or schools of philosophy on these two questions.

Thinking and Inquiry

3. Compare René Descartes's view of the self with the views suggested in the following excerpts. Which position do you support? Explain your position and why you disagree with each of the others.

   David Hume in *Personal Identity*

   > If any impression gives rise to the idea of self, that impression must continue invariably the same, through the whole course of our lives.... But there is no impression constant and variable. Pain and pleasure, grief and joy, passions and sensations succeed each other, and never all exist at the same time. It cannot therefore be from any of these impressions, or from any other, that the idea of self is derived; and consequently there is no idea.

   "No Self" from *Questions of King Milinda* (a Buddhist scripture)

   > [King Milinda asked the sage Nâgasena,] "Is it the outward form then (Rûpa) that is Nâgasena, or the sensations (Vedanâ), or the ideas (Saññâ), or the confections (the constituent elements of character, Samkhârâ), or the consciousness (Viññâna), that is Nâgasena?"

And to each of these also [Nâgasena] answered no.
"Then is it all these Skandhas combined that are Nâgasena?...
Is there anything outside of the five Skandhas that is Nâgasena?"
And still he answered no.

4. Do you believe that machines and animals should be granted the same rights as human beings? If so, why? If not, what rights — if any — should they be granted? Why?

Communication

5. Create a timeline showing how philosophical definitions of person have changed over time. Extend the timeline into the future, speculating on how definitions of person will continue to change.

6. Write a 500-word formal position paper that responds to this question: Has the definition of person become broader or narrower over time? To help formulate your response, draw on information on the timeline created earlier.

Application

7. The following cartoon (Figure 7.7) also appeared in Chapter 2 and shows that philosophical issues may be approached from a variety of perspectives. What characteristic of humans is Calvin wondering about? How might he respond to the question, Can machines and animals be persons? Reflect on your answers to these questions and draw an additional frame for the cartoon. In the frame, show Calvin's possible response to the question, What is a person?

Figure 7.7

CALVIN AND HOBBES © Watterson. Reprinted with permission of UNIVERSAL PRESS SYNDICATE. All rights reserved.

8. Choose an important metaphysical question and examine how two philosophers have responded to it. Create an imaginary dialogue between the two philosophers. Your goal is to show the similarities and differences in their approach, methods, and conclusions.

Chapter 8
A Meaning for Existence

Chapter Expectations

By the end of this chapter, you will be able to
- demonstrate an understanding of some of the main questions in metaphysics
- evaluate the positions of some of the major philosophers and schools of philosophy on some of the main metaphysical questions
- formulate your own clear and cogent responses to some of the fundamental questions of metaphysics and defend your responses in writing and in philosophical exchanges with others
- explain with reference to some classic texts how metaphysical theories about various questions make a difference in people's attitudes to practical issues
- demonstrate an understanding of the influence that metaphysical ideas about topics such as causality, space and time, and the infinite have on other disciplines
- compare the problems, principles, methods, and conclusions of various philosophers

Key Words

theism
deism
polytheists
pantheists
ontological argument
cosmological argument
argument from design
atheists
free will
hard determinists
soft determinists
nihilists

Key People

Anselm of Canterbury
David Hume
Blaise Pascal
Karl Marx
Friedrich Nietzsche
Gottfried Wilhelm Leibniz
Sigmund Freud
Albert Camus
Arthur Schopenhauer
Leo Tolstoy

A Philosopher's Voice

We had the sky, up there, all speckled with stars, and we used to lay on our backs and look up at them, and discuss about whether they was made, or only just happened.

— Huck Finn in *The Adventures of Huckleberry Finn*

Concepts of a Supreme Being

In Mark Twain's book *The Adventures of Huckleberry Finn*, Huck and his friend Jim floated lazily down the Mississippi River on a raft. The two had plenty of time to philosophize, especially at night, when they lay on their backs and watched the stars as they appeared to slowly arc across the sky. They wondered whether the stars were made — or whether they just happened.

Perhaps you have done the same thing on a clear summer night. Have you stretched out on your back and looked up at the stars, wondering where they came from, where they are going, who or what made them, what place you occupy in the universe, whether other creatures like you are out there somewhere, and whether your life has a purpose in the larger scheme of things?

Looking up at the stars, you might have decided that the universe is an accident, a fluke that might not have happened at all or that might have turned out completely differently. Or you might have decided that some intelligence — a grand architect — not only designed and created it, but also runs it. You might have felt intensely alone, overwhelmed by the immensity of the dark empty spaces. Or you might have felt that you were not alone, that a presence was everywhere. Or you might have simply fallen asleep and had a nice dream about lying under the stars on a clear summer night.

The question raised by Huck Finn and Jim is essentially a question about the existence of a supreme being. Did something, or someone, make the stars, the galaxies, and the entire universe, or did these things come about by chance?

Suppose for a moment that a creator of the universe exists. Is this creator a supreme being? If so, then what is this supreme being like? What is he, she, or it made of? And how is this supreme being related to the universe that she, he, or it created? Is this supreme being more powerful and more perfect than all the power and perfection contained in the universe? Could the universe have been made by a being who is less than all-powerful?

Figure 8.1

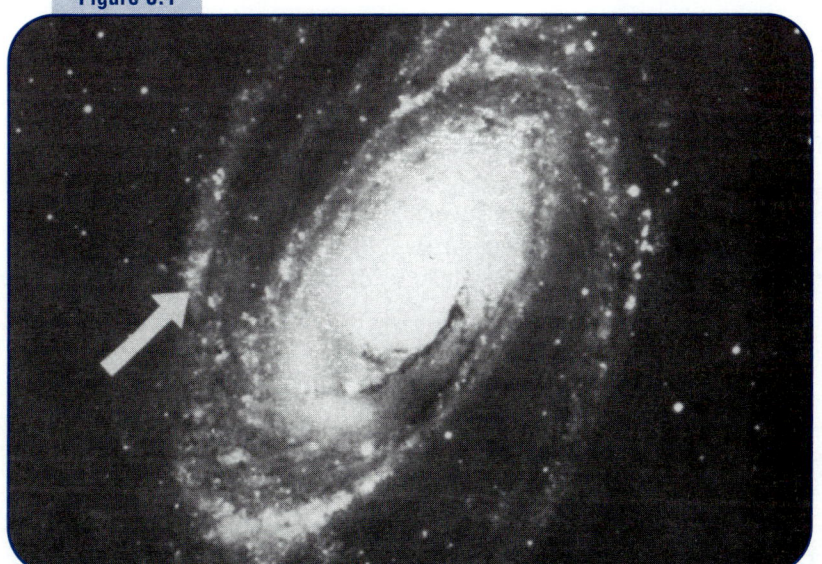

The arrow in this picture points to the sun, one of several hundred billion stars in the Milky Way.

These are metaphysical questions. They lead naturally to a number of epistemological questions. How do people *know* that the universe was created by some agent, and that this agent is a supreme being named God or Allah or Yahweh or Vishnu or something else? Is the mere presence of the starry night sky proof that a supreme being exists? Is the supreme being's signature somehow written throughout nature, like a trademark? Can we perceive this supreme being, as we perceive things around us? If not, is there some other way to know that a supreme being exists? Can the existence of a supreme being be proven using rational arguments that do not rely on sense experience?

Some people are not troubled by these questions because they take the existence of a supreme being on faith. They say they know that this being exists because they feel her, his, or its presence in their hearts. Others simply accept what they read in religious texts or what their religious teachers have told them about the existence of this being. Still others believe that miracles support the existence of a supreme being. And some others maintain that their prayers have been answered, and only a supreme being could have done this.

At the same time, many people believe — with equal conviction — that it is obvious that no supreme being exists. These people believe that humans are alone in the universe. Some see no signs of a supreme being's existence, or they see a world of suffering and death and conclude that a supreme being could not have possibly created this.

Most philosophers take neither of these positions. For them, faith alone is not enough to show that a supreme being exists, nor are the words of religious authorities or religious texts, nor are feelings of a cosmic presence. Similarly, feelings of cosmic aloneness are not enough to show that a supreme being does *not* exist.

> *Faith must trample under foot all reason, sense, and understanding.*
> – Martin Luther

How, then, do philosophers approach questions about a supreme being? Generally, they maintain that answers to these questions can be supported by reason and argument. Though they disagree about the answers to these questions and about the methods of argument, they do agree that rational arguments can be made to either support or deny the existence of a supreme being.

Philosophers also disagree about the meaning of the concept of a supreme being. Some say that a supreme being is the supremely perfect and supremely powerful being who created the universe. Others go farther, saying that this being is a supremely perfect personal being. Still others go even farther, saying that that the supreme being is eternal, omnipotent, omniscient, and perfectly good, just, and loving.

Some philosophers maintain that there are many gods, while others say that there is only one. Finally, some philosophers believe that all these concepts of a supreme being are fiction. The disagreement among philosophers is similar to the disagreement among other people.

THEISM

The Greek word *theos* means god. Many English words that describe theories of a god or gods and the study of a god or gods, such as **theism** and theology, are based on this Greek word.

> *If God did not exist, it would be necessary to invent him.*
> – Voltaire

When theists look up at a star-speckled night sky, they see the work of a perfect, all-powerful, all-loving, personal supreme being who is worthy of worship. Theists believe that this being was fully present in the creation of the universe and can intervene in it at any moment by way of miracles and revelations. This, theists argue, is a sign of this being's interest in the well-being of its creation.

DEISM

The word **deism** comes from *deus*, the Latin word for god. When deists look up at a night sky, they see a divine celestial machine running on automatic pilot. They believe that a supreme being created this infinitely harmonious machinery but remains an absentee boss. In other words, the supreme being does not intervene in the course of history as a divine corrective force that performs miracles or hands down revelations. If this supreme being needed to intervene, it would imply that a mistake in the original creation required a kind of omnipotent cosmic repair person.

POLYTHEISM

The English prefix poly- comes from a Greek word that means many. As a result, it is not surprising that when **polytheists** look up at the night sky, they see the work of many powerful gods, each with a particular role to fulfill in the governance of the universe. One god may look after justice, another fertility, another seasons, and so on. Nature, like a huge corporation, is infinitely complex and many faceted, so each of the gods who rule over it must be like a specialist caretaker who tends a small plot in the cosmic landscape.

MONOTHEISM

When monotheists look up at the stars, they see the work of one supreme, perfect, and all-powerful maker. Despite their differences, many of the world's monotheistic religions, such as Christianity, Islam, and Judaism, maintain that the supreme being is a person. By this, they do not mean that she, he, or it is human or has a human form; rather, they mean that this being is characterized by a mind, a will, and an ability to communicate, as well as by certain emotions, such as love and compassion.

PANTHEISM

The Greek word *pan* means all, so when **pantheists** look up at the stars, they see a supreme being everywhere. This being extends over the same space, time, and limits as nature. As a result, pantheists believe in a divinized nature and a naturalized divinity. Everything in the universe contains the spirit of this being. This divinity is not, however, a personal supreme being or a supreme being with human characteristics. It is impersonal.

PANENTHEISM

When panentheists look up at the night sky, everything they see is in a supreme being. The 17th-century Dutch-Jewish philosopher Baruch Spinoza was a panentheist. When he looked up at the night sky, in an attempt to understand the universe *sub specie aeternitatis* (under the aspect of eternity) rather than *sub specie durationis* (under the aspect of time), he saw a universe that is pervaded by God.

For Spinoza, this supreme being was all that there was. It is the totality of all being. There was nothing outside God and nothing that was beyond God's reality. Everything that existed, from the largest galaxies in the universe to the smallest neutrinos, from microscopic organisms to human beings and whales, and from space and time to minds and their thoughts, was part of God.

> *I believe in Spinoza's God, who reveals Himself in the orderly harmony of what exists, not in a God who concerns himself with fates and actions of human beings.*
>
> – Albert Einstein

Though Spinoza believed that God is omnipotent, or all-powerful, omniscient, or all-knowing, and self-causing, he rejected the idea that this being is a kind of person. He argued that thinking about this divinity in terms of human properties distorts God's reality. By this, he did not mean that people cannot think about God at all; rather, he meant that people must be cautious when attributing properties to God. He said that the characteristics that someone attributes to the supreme being often say more about who the person is than about what the supreme being is. In *The Ethics*, Spinoza wrote that the mind of God and the human mind have as much in common as the constellation of stars known as the Dog constellation and a dog that barks. In other words, they agree in name only.

PROFILE

Baruch Spinoza
Challenging Established Views

Baruch Spinoza was born in Amsterdam, the capital of the Netherlands, in 1632, when this city was at the height of its golden age. Home to Rembrandt and René Descartes, Amsterdam was a wealthy, powerful, and vibrant city. Spinoza's parents were Sephardic Jews from Portugal. They had fled the persecution of the Roman Catholic Inquisition and found in Amsterdam a haven where they could practise their religion freely.

Their son was a brilliant student who by his mid-teens had discovered philosophy. Spinoza's thinking became increasingly independent and radical. He started to call into question the orthodox religious conceptions that he had been taught in school. He found contradictions in Jewish holy books and began to doubt claims about miracles and the authority of the prophets.

Jewish religious authorities found his views intolerable. At first, they tried to change his views using traditional theological arguments. Then they threatened him with excommunication. He refused to change his views. Finally, his teachers and rabbis were fed up. On July 27, 1656, when he was 24 years old, Spinoza was excommunicated from the Jewish faith, in which he had been raised.

The ban pronounced upon him by the Rabbis was merciless:

> By the decree of the Angels and the word of the Saints we ban, cut off, curse and anathematize Baruch de Espinoza ... with all the curses written in the Torah: Cursed be he by day and cursed by night, cursed in his lying down and cursed in his waking up, cursed in his going forth and cursed in his coming in; and may the L[ord] not want his pardon, and may the L[ord]'s wrath and zeal burn upon him.... We warn that none may contact him orally or in writing, nor do him any favour, nor stay under the same roof with him, nor read any paper he made or wrote.

As a result, Spinoza moved away from Amsterdam to the small town of Rhynsburg, where he made a living as a lens grinder, a high-tech profession at the time. He lived frugally, had few possessions but many friends, never travelled far, never married, wrote philosophy, and corresponded with the leading free thinkers and scientists of the day. He avoided the limelight, adhering to his family motto, which was *Caute* — Caution.

Still, news of his work spread, and the German philosopher Gottfried Wilhelm Leibniz visited him to discuss philosophy. At one point, Spinoza was offered the chair of philosophy at the University of Heidelberg, an honour he graciously declined on the grounds that it would compromise his philosophical freedom. He said that he could not teach philosophy without becoming "a disturber of the peace." Across Europe, he had the reputation of being a dangerous, subversive thinker.

During his life, Spinoza published only two works of philosophy. His masterpiece, *The Ethics,* was published only after his death in 1677. This book describes an ethics of joy.

> It is the part of a wise man to refresh and invigorate himself in moderation with good food and drink, as also with perfumes, with the beauty of blossoming plants, with dress, music, sporting activities, theatres and the like, in which every man can indulge without harm to another. For the human body is composed of many parts of various kinds which are continually in need of fresh and varied nourishment so that the entire body may be equally capable of all the functions that follow from its own nature, and consequently that the mind may be equally capable of simultaneously understanding many things.

Spinoza died at the age of 45, from a congenital lung disease that was complicated by the glass dust he had inhaled for years while grinding lenses. Friends who visited him during his final days described the serenity and strength with which he met his end. "A free man," wrote Spinoza, "thinks of nothing less than of death, and his wisdom is not a meditation upon death but upon life."

Figure 8.2

This portrait of Baruch Spinoza was painted in 1670. Spinoza was one of the main advocates of 17th-century rationalism.

Spinoza disagreed with the traditional distinction between creator and creation, or God and nature. Many people believe that God created nature in a profoundly mysterious act of creation. They say that God is not a part of the creation, or inside it, like a builder who moves into the house that he or she has built. Nature is material, changeable, and defined by physical properties. God, however, is none of these. They maintain that although God created time and set in motion a series of events that make up the total history of the universe, God is not part of these events. God is not of time, and God is not identical with nature.

> *Whatever is, is in God, and nothing can be or be conceived without God.*
>
> – Baruch Spinoza

Spinoza disagreed. First, he could not see how an immaterial, non-temporal, or spiritual, being could interact with a material, temporal, or non-spiritual, world. He said that two things with such different properties could not possibly influence each other, so there could be no causal interaction between them. Second, he argued that if nature were somehow separate from God — if it were a separate being or substance — it would limit God's infinity. If God is infinite, he said, nothing can limit God. In other words, nothing can be outside God or have an existence separate from God.

Ideas like these drew the attention of Jewish religious authorities, who eventually barred Spinoza from practising the Jewish faith and ordered other Jews to shun him. Jews were not to speak or write to him, or read his works.

Web connection
www.mcgrawhill.ca/links/philosophy12
To find out more about Baruch Spinoza, follow the links on this Web site.

Recall...Reflect...Respond

1. Do you believe that the existence of a supreme being can be proved — or disproved — by reason and argument? Or is this a subjective judgment based on personal feelings? Explain.
2. Do you think that concepts of a supreme being and concepts of nature are different? Why?
3. How well does Baruch Spinoza's concept of a supreme being deal with the weaknesses implicit in other philosophical arguments about the existence of a supreme being? Explain fully.

THE EXISTENCE OF A SUPREME BEING

Philosophers who believe that the stars were created by a supreme being face questions like, How can you prove that they were made? How can you prove that there is a maker? and How can you prove that a supreme being exists? In the western tradition, the best-known philosophical arguments in favour of the existence of a supreme being are the ontological argument, the cosmological argument, and the argument from design.

THE ONTOLOGICAL ARGUMENT

The **ontological argument** was first developed by the Christian theologian, **Anselm of Canterbury**, who lived from 1033 to 1109. Anselm's argument is a priori. It does not rely on evidence presented by the senses; rather, it works only with concepts and reasoning. His ontological argument begins by defining God as a supremely perfect being. At this point in his reasoning, what Anselm proposed was a definition only. He said nothing about whether anything in reality corresponds to the definition. As a definition, his proposal is no different from definitions of other real or imaginary things, such as tooth fairies and hobgoblins.

Anselm argued that if God is supremely perfect, it follows that God is also all-powerful, all-knowing, and self-causing, and that God must also have all other perfections. One of the perfections included in the definition must be the perfection of existence. If God does not possess existence, then God would be missing one all-important feature that is possessed by all existing things — and would be less than perfect. Because this would contradict the definition of God as supremely perfect, God must exist.

Some critics have argued that a definition like this simply tells people that they have a concept of God, just as they have concepts of iguanas and unicorns. Anselm disagreed. He said that God is the one thing that exists both as a concept in the human mind and as a reality outside the mind. Everything else, by contrast, can easily be conceived as not existing. For example, you might easily conceive of a world in which your favourite food does not exist. But if you accept Anselm's definition of God, you cannot do this with God. The moment you try to think of God as a mere concept in your mind, the definition forces you to acknowledge that God must exist outside your mind as well. What forces you? The logic governing your use of concepts.

Web connection
www.mcgrawhill.ca/links/philosophy12
To find out more about Anselm of Canterbury, follow the links on this Web site.

THE COSMOLOGICAL ARGUMENT

In *The Adventures of Huckleberry Finn*, Huck and Jim's discussions focused on whether the stars were made or "only just happened." Along the way, they might have discussed whether what caused the stars to exist was itself caused, and if so, what caused it, and if this thing was caused, what caused it — and so on back through time. But does this cause-and-effect series stretch back in time forever? Is it an endless chain? Or does it stop somewhere, in some thing or some agent that is not itself caused and is not itself part of the series?

Questions like these raise the issue of whether the universe has a start button. If it does, where did the start button come from? Is there a definite point at which everything started? If there is a starting point, was there something before it?

The **cosmological argument** begins with the simple observation that it is impossible for any natural thing in the world to be the sole source of its own existence. In other words, it is impossible for anything to create itself. Everything comes from something else. But at some point in the cause-and-effect series, say cosmologists, there must be a cause that is not itself caused. The function of this cause is to bestow existence on all other things.

Consider your own existence. You came into being as a result of your parents, who came into being as a result of their parents, who came into being as a result of their parents, and so on. None of your ancestors created her- or himself. But the chain of causes cannot be endless. It must begin somewhere, with an originating family member who was not caused by any preceding member. Cosmologists say that this beginning point is a supreme being.

Critics have noted that even if this argument is valid, it does not prove the existence of a transcendent supreme being. The most it shows is that the chain of cause and effect that makes up the history of the universe has a beginning.

However, that beginning is not necessarily an all-powerful, all-knowing being. A scientific materialist might argue, for example, that this beginning point is something material, like the big bang.

> *The celestial order and the beauty of the universe compel me to admit that there is some excellent and eternal Being, who deserves the respect and homage of men.*
>
> – Cicero

This scientific argument has also been challenged. Critics ask, Did the big bang cause itself or was it caused by something else? In other words, did the big bang come from nothing or from something? If it came from something, was that something a supreme being?

THE ARGUMENT FROM DESIGN

After watching the orderly movement of the constellations in the sky, Huck and Jim might have concluded that some form of intelligence created, and maintains, the beautiful display. If they did, their conclusions would be similar to those of philosophers who argue that the orderliness of the universe suggests that an all-powerful agent is responsible for creating this order. This position is called the **argument from design**, or the teleological argument.

Figure 8.3

In the *Creation of Adam*, painted on the ceiling of the Sistine Chapel, the Italian Renaissance painter Michelangelo portrayed the hand of God (right) touching Adam's hand.

Supporters of this argument say that the order that characterizes the universe could not have come from nowhere or from nothing, nor could it have emerged spontaneously at some distant point in the past. They claim that the universe is as orderly as a perfectly harmonious machine, or the workings of an infinitely large clock, which a clockmaker must have designed and set in motion.

Many philosophers have challenged this view. Some have pointed out that even if some sort of cosmic order does exist, it does not follow that this order was created by an all-powerful and benevolent, supreme being. It might just as well have been created by an evil demon, a very powerful computer, or some other very powerful intelligence.

Others have challenged the premise of cosmic order, maintaining that the apparent orderliness of the universe is deceiving. They say that cosmology and astronomy are showing that the universe, far from being neat and tidy, is really a dark, messy, and mysterious cauldron of quasars, collapsing galaxies, dark matter and dark energy, black holes, big bangs, and big crunches.

The 18th-century Scottish philosopher **David Hume**, for example, rejected the comparison between nature and human-made machines. Hume argued that the infinitely diverse world of nature does not fit the model of human-made machines because there are simply too many differences between nature and machines. And even if there is order in nature, it is unjustifiably anthropocentric to suppose that it is the result of a form of intelligence that resembles human intelligence.

PASCAL'S WAGER

The 17th-century French mathematician and philosopher **Blaise Pascal** proposed a very different proof of the existence of a supreme being. Pascal argued that metaphysical proofs of the existence of God were so remote from everyday experience and so complicated in logical structure that they were destined to have little success in convincing people to believe in God. He said that these proofs were signs of unabashed human pride, and they failed to recognize the role of emotions and the need for personal redemption.

Pascal suggested that people view the question of God's existence as they would a bet. Suppose that you did this. As with any bet, you would have two choices: God does exist or God does not exist. This bet could be the most significant of your life, however, and before placing it, you decide to analyze the possible outcomes of your choice. Four outcomes are possible.

1. If you choose to believe in God and it turns out that God exists, then you have bet, and won big. Because Pascal was speaking from the Christian perspective, he suggested that the reward would likely be eternal life. In betting terms, the gains of betting on God's existence are infinite.
2. If you choose not to believe in God, and it turns out that God does exist, then you have lost big and risk eternal suffering in hell. In betting terms, the losses associated with betting that God does not exist are infinite.
3. If you choose to believe that God exists and you live accordingly, and yet it turns out that God does not exist, then your losses are minimal. All that you have given up are a few selfish pleasures and vices.
4. If you choose to live as if there is no God, and it turns out that God does not exist, then you have won the bet. Big deal! Your gain is the relatively insignificant one of being right. And of course, you would realize this only after you are dead (if realization is possible in that state).

Pascal said that from a gambler's point of view, people are better off living and acting as if there is a God. It's a safe bet: the losses are relatively small and the benefits are relatively great, at least when weighed against the alternatives.

Web connection
www.mcgrawhill.ca/links/philosophy12
To find out more about Blaise Pascal, follow the links on this Web site.

ATHEISM

Karl Marx, a 19th-century German-English sociologist, historian, and economist, wrote that religion is the opiate of the masses. A character in a book by **Friedrich Nietzsche**, a 19th-century German philosopher, said that God is dead — and we have killed him. And the 20th-century French novelist, playwright, and philosopher Jean-Paul Sartre wrote that the concept of God is a contradiction in terms, like the concept of a square circle.

Marx, Nietzsche, and Sartre were **atheists**. They rejected the idea of the existence of an omniscient and omnipotent supreme being whose task it is to create and sustain the world, to create humans in his, her, or its image, and to give to human existence a purpose for living.

To support this position, atheists propose a variety of arguments. One argument says that human history is a saga of calamity, evil, war, poverty, death, and suffering. Atheists who take this position say that it is inconceivable that a supremely perfect and benevolent being could create such an imperfect world. And if human beings were really created in the image of a loving divinity, it is inconceivable that they could be so cruel to one another.

Some theists have challenged this argument, saying that it is based on a false premise. Some say that humans have rejected God and in using their free will to do so, are responsible for the problems of evil.

Others claim that the perception of evil in the world is perceiver-relative; that is, it depends entirely on the perspective of the perceiver. From people's

> *Most intellectual people do not believe in God, but they fear him just the same.*
>
> – Wilhelm Reich

limited human perspective, evil seems to be real. But if human beings could see the history of the universe from God's perspective, they would see that everything is working out for the good, according to a divine plan. Theists who take this position say that the finite human perspective prevents people's understanding of this plan in its entirety, and maintain that faith is required where understanding fails.

The 18th-century German philosopher Gottfried Wilhelm Leibniz proposed an analogy to explain the theistic position. Imagine, said Leibniz, that you are standing before a massive painting that is 100 kilometres wide and 100 kilometres high. It towers above you, beyond the clouds, and extends far beyond the horizon to your left and right. You can see only a few hundred metres of the painting, and what you can see seems to be a jumbled mess. There appears to be no order to it. But if you were able to step back several kilometres to an elevated vantage point from which you could view the entire painting at once, you would see the most beautifully ordered, detailed, and harmonious artwork ever created. Your complaints about its messiness would vanish instantly. What is more, said Leibniz, you would realize that your complaints are just like complaints about evil and suffering in the world. They are a function of an extremely limited perspective.

Some critics say that the perceiver-relativity argument is an inadequate response to the atheist's criticism because any state of affairs in the universe is compatible with it. Imagine that the state of the universe is a thousand times worse than it is now — that there is a thousand times more evil, suffering, and pain. An atheist would once again raise the question of how God could have created such an imperfect universe. The theist would once again claim that the perception of suffering and evil is perceiver-relative. But the same reply could be made if the universe is a million times worse than it is now, and again when it is a billion times worse, and so on. Similarly, if the state of the universe became a thousand times better, the same explanation would hold. Critics of the theistic position say that explanations that cover every conceivable state of affairs, and that systematically evade all possible falsification, are not real explanations. If there is no possible way to show that these explanations are false, say critics, they do not make much sense.

Some atheists approach the question of the existence of a supreme being from a psychological point of view. They argue that the concept of a supreme being is a soothing fiction, not unlike the fictions created to entertain children, such as Santa Claus or the tooth fairy. They say that believing in a supreme being fulfills people's deep-seated psychological need for security, order, and meaning in a world that is overwhelmingly hostile and incomprehensible.

Sigmund Freud, who founded psychoanalysis in the late 19th century, claimed that God is an invention that satisfies a deep-seated, human emotional craving for authority. "There is no question that religion derives from the need for help and the anxiety of the child and mankind in its early infancy," Freud wrote. He said that the helplessness adults experience in the world, like that experienced by infants, is converted into a fantasy in which a sovereign father figure beneficently bestows security in exchange for complete submission. He maintained that religion is the childhood of the human mind, and that psychological maturity requires people to overcome this.

> ### • IDEAS IN CONTEXT •
>
> The atheism of Karl Marx and Friedrich Nietzsche was inextricably linked to their radical critique of 19th-century society. They regarded conventional religion and conventional morality as the two greatest swindles ever perpetrated on humankind. These institutions, they argued, prevent people from taking control of their own lives, and distract them from living in the here-and-now by giving them false hopes of a glorious afterlife, or false fears of eternal damnation. God, wrote Nietzsche, is the weakness of the will to live.

> *I think if God wanted to leave a sign that he created the universe and he existed in it, he would have created some incredibly beautiful universe with exceptionally good moral human beings, rather than this chaos where we have to struggle to survive.*
>
> – Nick Smith

A similar argument has been made from a neurobiological perspective. Those who adopt this point of view say that belief in a supreme being can be explained as a function of the chemistry of human brains. They say that what people interpret as religious experiences, such as talking to God or feeling that they are in the presence of God, represents nothing but changes in the activity of certain parts of their brains. The causes of this activity are entirely this-worldly. Though people may feel that they are talking to a supreme being, there is in fact no divinity on the other side of their experience. To support this claim, some neuroscientists have conducted experiments that show that certain kinds of artificial neuro-electrical stimulation on the brain can trigger religious experiences in experimental subjects.

Finally, a number of atheists have used the discoveries of modern science as a basis for rejecting the idea of the existence of a supreme being. They claim that the concept of a supreme being is a useless and unverifiable hypothesis and say that everything in nature can be explained adequately using the tools of modern science. As a result, they say that there is no need to suggest that a supreme being is the creator of nature.

These atheists also say that scientific investigation fails to reveal any credible evidence for the existence of a supreme being. They add that scientific discoveries have already challenged ideas once cherished by major religions, especially the idea that human beings occupy a privileged place at the top of the great chain of being.

Recall...Reflect...Respond

1. Do you think that there is order in the structure of the universe? Could this order be there even if we do not see it? Is the mere fact of the existence of the universe — the idea that there is something rather than nothing at all — a sign of the existence of order? Explain your response.
2. Think about Pascal's wager. How much would you be willing to bet that a supreme being does — or does not — exist? Would you be willing to bet your life? Why?
3. Are people's experiences of a supreme being a function of their brain states and nothing else? Explain your response.

DETERMINISM AND FREEDOM

Imagine that it's the bottom of the ninth inning of the final game of the World Series. Your team is losing 12-9. You are at bat, with the bases loaded, two out, and a full count. If you hit a grand slam, your team will win by one run. The fans will go wild, and you will be a hero. If you strike out or fly out, you will be the goat. What will determine the outcome?

The pitcher is nervous. He knows that he could be the goat as easily as you. His windup starts a domino-like chain of microscopic events that unfold at lightning speed. As his arm goes back, his grip on the ball increases by 2.5 grams per square centimetre. In addition, the sweat on his hands causes his right index finger to slip 0.039 centimetres to the right, which he unconsciously corrects by moving his thumb 0.0198 centimetres to the left. One of the muscles in his lower back tightens slightly more than usual, which makes his follow-through 0.158 centimetres shorter than normal.

He releases the ball, and at a point exactly 0.9985 metres from his hand, a micro-gust of wind deflects it upward by 0.0001016 centimetres. At 4.35 metres from his hand, a pocket of warmer air, caused by the heat generated by the fans in the stadium, makes the ball rise by 0.0001651 centimetres.

At 5.7 metres from his hand, the speed of the pitch is decreasing, and a tiny indentation — caused by a slight imperfection in the manufacturing process — starts to have an effect on the ball. The ball begins to wobble, ever so slightly, which reduces its velocity by a tiny fraction more. A tenth of a centimetre from the point of impact with the bat, the ball meets a pocket of micro-turbulence caused by the movement of the bat. This slows it another tiny fraction.

As you were expecting, the pitch is a fastball, high and inside. You swing — and connect. The ball rockets far beyond the outfield bleachers. You have just hit the longest home run in World Series history. The fans go berserk. You touch home plate, and your teammates hoist you on their shoulders. You are the toast of the town.

Baseball is a game of cause and effect. Millions of causes go into the outcome of a single pitch: the shape of the ball, the pitcher's muscles, the air temperature, local wind patterns, and so on. The list is endless. Also endless is the list of millisecond-to-millisecond changes that take place in the batter's body, including the brain and optic nerve as they track the oncoming projectile.

Analysis, like this one of a pitch, reveals the deeply textured causal fabric of the world. Every event is caused by previous events, which are themselves caused by previous events, and so on. In addition to conducting a minute causal analysis of the pitch in that World Series game, you could also conduct a causal analysis of what happened just before the pitch was released, or just before the windup, and so on. This causal analysis could conceivably be extended back to the beginning of the game, or even farther to the morning of the game, and so on. In principle, there is no limit to how far back the causal analysis could extend.

Determinists believe that every physical event that occurs in the universe is caused by previous events that unfold according to causal laws. Unlike those who believe in **free will** — the idea that the will is uncaused — they say that there are no uncaused events in the universe. There are no breaks or gaps in the densely woven fabric of the universe.

Figure 8.4

Joe Carter runs the bases after hitting the grand slam home run that won the World Series for the Toronto Blue Jays in 1993.

HARD DETERMINISM

Fastball pitches are physical events in which cause and effect seem easy to identify. But what about mental events, like emotions, desires, and beliefs? What about consciousness and personality? Are these part of the causal fabric of nature? Are they causally determined or are they the result of chance or people's free will? These questions raise other important questions: Are human actions determined by past events in the same way as baseball pitches? If so, is there any room left for freedom? Is it possible for people's actions, thoughts, and desires to be part of a causal chain of events, yet still be free? Or is there something about human beings — perhaps their will — that remains independent of the series of causes and effects?

Hard determinists say that *all* thoughts, actions, and desires are caused by previous events, which are themselves caused by previous events, and so on back in time. If you wake up in a bad mood, for example, a hard determinist would say that there is a cause for it in the immediate or not-so-immediate past. You may not, however, be aware of this cause.

THOUGHT EXPERIMENT

The Conscious Stone

Picture a smooth, round stone that is thrown by a small boy into a pond. The stone arcs upward for the first 10 metres, then starts to fall toward the water. Imagine that in the middle of its downward trajectory, the stone suddenly becomes conscious of itself and its surroundings. It starts to have thoughts, desires, and feelings. It feels the rush of air and its downward momentum. It also sees the clouds in the sky above and the surface of the pond below. Conscious of its movement, the stone declares, "I am moving toward the pond of my own free will. I have decided to fall at precisely the rate at which I am now falling. Below me is my target, which I have chosen. I am the cause of my motion."

Obviously, the stone is mistaken. It is falling because of the force of gravity and the momentum imparted by the boy, not of its own volition. Its motion is determined entirely by forces external to it.

This, wrote Baruch Spinoza, who was a determinist, is the *image* of our freedom. We think ourselves free only to the extent that we are ignorant of the infinitely complex and hidden range of causes that determine us to take action. According to Spinoza, free will is an illusion. Our every action, experience, thought, and emotion is determined by previous causes, which form a chain extending infinitely backward in time. Spinoza wrote:

> This, then, is that human freedom which all men boast of possession, and which consists solely in this, that men are conscious of their desire and unaware of the causes by which they are determined. In the same way a baby thinks that it freely desires milk, an angry child revenge, and a coward flight. Again, a drunken man believes that it is from free decision that he says what he later, when sober, would wish to have concealed. So, too, the delirious, the loquacious, and many others of this kind believe that they act from free decision, and are not carried away by impulse.

Think about what you are doing right now. Is your reading of this thought experiment an act of free will or is it caused by something else? If it is caused by something else, what was this something? And what are the causes of the causes?

Figure 8.5

(Speech bubble: "I'M GLAD I CHOSE TO FALL INTO THE POND.")

Hard determinists believe that free will is an illusion. They say, for example, that willing yourself to do X rather than Y is just as causally determined as any other thing in the universe. Your psychological and behavioural makeup — even your personality — is formed *for* you, not *by* you.

What formed it? Forces and conditions that were active long before you developed the ability to understand things, make rational choices, or exercise your will. These forces include your early childhood conditioning, your psychological development, your education, your genetic endowment, your neurophysiological development, your social conditioning, and your exposure to external events.

The theory of hard determinism has important implications for ideas about blame and punishment. If you did not choose your psychological and behavioural makeup, and if the little control you now exert over this makeup is determined by forces beyond your control, how can you be held responsible for your actions? Hard determinism seems to suggest that people are prisoners of their character, past, and biology.

Though hard determinists suggest that people are carried along like minuscule pieces of flotsam on the tide of unfolding events, is this how people actually experience themselves? Some philosophers argue that the answer is no. They say that people believe that when they act, they are doing so freely.

Confronted by the need to make a decision, for example, people usually feel that they have a choice between two or more alternatives. They do not experience themselves as being pushed or pulled by external forces, nor do they feel that their choice is predictable. Looking back after having made the choice, they believe that they also could have done something else.

For most people, the feeling of being free is not merely a matter of subjective experience. Most legal and moral systems regard all people, with the exception of infants and those with diminished cognitive faculties, as agents who are capable of exhibiting self-control and self-direction. In other words, legal and moral systems consider people responsible for their actions.

THEORIES OF FREEDOM

Philosophers have advocated various theories of freedom. The theory of agent causation, for example, holds that people are free because they are the originating sources of action, rather than mere reactors to, or conduits for, external forces.

Supporters of this theory say that, as agents, people use their reasoning ability to decide on courses of action, and these actions are not causally determined. In performing an action, for example, you make certain events happen. Nothing and no one causes you to make those events happen. Critics of this view have argued that it seems to make the self into a kind of god, with tremendous powers of self-creation.

The theory of free will holds that the will is perfectly insulated from all external causes. No matter how powerful the external influence, supporters of this theory say that the will remains unperturbed. Though the body and brain are physical entities that are subject to the deterministic laws of nature, the will remains outside these laws. It is not part of the brain, although it can interact with the brain and send messages telling it to perform an action.

According to this theory, even prisoners in chains enjoy freedom of will. The fact that they are unable to act does not make their will any less free. Though they cannot act freely, they can still will freely. Some critics have pointed out that a free or uncaused will is an unconstrained will. Because it is not constrained by anything, its actions will be jerky and capricious, more like random explosions than meaningful actions. In response to this criticism, some philosophers have argued that a truly free will is a will that is governed by reason.

> *Freedom is nothing else but a change to be better.*
> – Albert Camus

Existentialists support the view that human beings are radically free. Sartre, for example, argued that it is entirely up to human beings to define themselves because no a priori blueprints, no moral absolutes, no divine commandments, and no innately given values exist to guide people's decisions about how to be. Human beings are alone and abandoned in the universe, say existentialists. The price of being radically free is a disturbing sense of the groundlessness of all values, ideals, and projects. This sense of groundlessness can lead to moments of existential *angst*, or anxiety.

Sartre said that people are "condemned" to be free. This freedom is a burden that they must bear at all times and in all situations. He said that people did not give themselves this freedom, nor can they erase it, though they often deny it and pretend that it does not exist.

SOFT DETERMINISM

Soft determinists say that freedom and determinism are compatible. They do not necessarily agree, however, on how the two are compatible.

Some soft determinists say that, instead of thinking of freedom as the opposite of causality, or as something that requires suspending the laws of cause and effect, it might be thought of as self-determination. They say that people are free if they are self-determined rather than externally determined — if the causes of their actions lie mainly inside themselves rather than outside themselves.

This view does not eliminate the idea of causality. Instead, it relocates it inside people, making it part of the self's action upon itself and the world. It says that the more self-determining people are, the more free they are. Viewed in this light, freedom is an achievement rather than a given.

Other soft determinists say that, instead of thinking of freedom as something that goes against causality, it could be reconceived as simply doing what one wants to do. If you are a prisoner in chains, for example, then you are not free because you cannot do what you want to do. But if you are under no external compulsion, then you are free. You can do what you want to do, though your desires are still causally determined, like everything else in nature.

Critics have pointed out that this view of freedom fails to distinguish between doing those things you want to do and doing those things you *really* want to do. What you *really* desire may become evident to you only after a great deal of reflection. Introducing this distinction, however, raises the thorny issue of real versus illusory desires.

Web connection
www.mcgrawhill.ca/links/philosophy12
To read more about free will and determinism, follow the links on this Web site.

THE MEANING OF LIFE

What is the meaning of life? For some, this is the fundamental philosophical question, beside which all other questions pale. The 20th-century Algerian-French novelist and philosopher Albert Camus, for example, wrote that "judging whether life is or is not worth living amounts to answering the fundamental question of philosophy."

Despite its fundamental nature, the question, What is the meaning of life? continues to puzzle. It is a metaphysical question that also has profound practical and ethical consequences. Having an answer — or not having an answer or having a confused or incoherent answer — can shape a person's entire outlook on life.

Many people, both philosophers and non-philosophers, have struggled to find answers to this question. The fact that some answers are less believable or practical than others suggests that people should not take everything they hear at face

Figure 8.6
© 2002 Tribune Media Services, Inc. All Rights Reserved. Reprinted with permission.

Why do you suppose Skyler is hoping for a multiple-choice question?

168   MHR UNIT 2 METAPHYSICS

value. A little philosophical caution is in order. The mere fact that someone *claims* to know the answer to this question does not mean that she or he has the answer.

Suppose, for example, that you are an investigative reporter assigned to write an article on how two dozen people answer the question, What is the meaning of life? You decide that your approach will be philosophically ruthless. Some people you interview say that they believe that the meaning of life is found in acquiring money. "Why?" you ask. They respond that money equals security, or that it buys happiness or freedom. "Why?" you ask. They don't know. Other people believe the answer lies in being powerful or famous. "Why?" you ask again. They don't really know. One or two suggest that it's better than being a nobody. "Why?" you ask. Again, they don't know.

Others you interview believe the answer is to be found in the pursuit of sensual pleasures, like sex and food, or intellectual pleasures, like reading poetry or making scientific discoveries. "Why?" you ask. "Just because," one interviewee says. "Because pleasure is good," says another. "Why?" you ask. No answer is forthcoming. You conclude your story with the observation that conventional beliefs about the meaning of life all too often go unexamined: people take them for granted, or they are afraid to subject them to further questioning, or they can't be bothered to think of alternatives.

> *The unexamined life is not worth living.*
> – Socrates

This is precisely the point at which philosophers step in. Philosophers, said Nietzsche, are the physicians of civilization. They prod and probe its guiding ideas and unexamined assumptions; they disturb peoples' consciences; they diagnose what ails them; and they occasionally offer prognoses.

Philosophers have pointed out that the question about the meaning of life really takes three different forms. First, you might ask, What is the meaning or purpose of there being a universe at all? More starkly phrased, this question means, Why is there something rather than nothing at all? Second, you might ask, Why do human beings exist at all? or Do human beings as a species exist for some purpose or as part of some larger plan? Is there a point to our being here on this small planet at this particular time in the history of the universe — or is it a fluke? Third, you might ask, What is the meaning of *my* life? This is the most common form of the question. Is there any meaning to my life that will remain after my death? Five hundred years from now — or five hundred million years from now — will it matter that I existed? If there is some meaning in my existing, is it something that I discover or something that I invent? Or is it all for nothing?

THE NIHILIST APPROACH TO THE MEANING OF LIFE

Nihilists argue that life is meaningless. Life is absurd, they say. Because nothing matters, they maintain, all human striving is pointless. Not only will the greatest works of art, the greatest scientific achievements, and the noblest actions mean nothing if the universe is collapsing upon itself in 500 billion years, but these things also mean nothing now. That they *seem* to matter is nothing but an illusion. **Arthur Schopenhauer**, a 19th-century German philosopher, wrote: "We can regard our life as a uselessly disturbing episode in the blissful repose of nothingness.… Human existence must be a kind of error."

The Lighter Side of Philosophy

How many nihilists does it take to change a light bulb?

Well, actually, changing the light bulb really doesn't matter

Some philosophers have suggested that if nothing matters, then, strictly speaking, it does not matter that nothing matters. It is therefore pointless for nihilists to even try to defend their point of view. But though defending nihilism may not seem rational, this approach to life nevertheless expresses an attitude of utter despair that befalls some people. Near the end of Albert Camus's existentialist novel *The Stranger*, the hero, who is about to be executed for a murder that he has pointlessly committed, rejects the pleas of the priest who was sent to offer absolution: "Nothing, nothing matters," the hero shouts, overwhelmed by the emptiness of all values and the absurdity of all striving.

THE THEISTIC APPROACH TO THE MEANING OF LIFE

Theists say that human life is meaningful because a supremely loving, transcendent, and omnipotent being has given people the gift of existing and this gives life a purpose. In some respects, say theists, the meaning of your life does not depend upon you. The meaning is out there, as part of God's plan, and you must discover it. Without the existence of God, they say, your life would have no meaning.

Theists differ on the role of reason in the search for the meaning of life. Some, like Pascal and the 19th-century Russian writer and philosopher **Leo Tolstoy**, maintained that human reason is inherently weak and limited in its ability to guide people in the right direction. Only faith will lead people to God and reveal the meaning of life. Other theists uphold the role of reason in the search for the meaning of life. Descartes, for instance, believed that human reason plays a central role in guiding people, even if it cannot fully reveal the nature of God.

Tolstoy's autobiography, *My Confession*, vividly illustrates one person's search for the meaning of life. When the author was in his 50s, he experienced a crisis that brought him to the brink of suicide. Rich and famous by then, he suddenly began to doubt the point of living. At first, his doubts were merely annoying, and he dismissed them. But they began to haunt him, and he was eventually paralyzed by them. "I felt that what I was standing on had given way, that I had no foundation to stand on, that that which I lived by no longer existed, and that I had nothing to live by," he wrote.

> **Web connection**
> www.mcgrawhill.ca/links/philosophy12
> To find out more about Leo Tolstoy, follow the links on this Web site.

In search of an answer, Tolstoy turned to scientists, theologians, and intellectuals. In his view, none helped. Scientists, who suggested that he was no more than a random collection of atoms in a vast cosmic soup, had little of personal value to say about the meaning of life. Theologians offered only mysterious answers that defied rational understanding. Intellectuals had nothing but sophisticated opinions.

In the end, Tolstoy found his answer by observing the lives of simple peasants, whose religious faith supported them through good times and bad. He believed that the peasants never questioned whether God existed, accepted their problems without vexation or perplexity, and never once felt that it was all for nothing.

> ### Recall...Reflect...Respond
> 1. If you had the power to give either determinism or free will to someone you love, which would you choose? Why?
> 2. Is nihilism a philosophically defensible position? Could you live your life as a nihilist? Explain why.
> 3. If you were a physicist or astronomer, would your research be influenced by metaphysical ideas about the existence of a supreme being? Explain your response.

THE NON-THEISTIC APPROACH TO THE MEANING OF LIFE

The non-theistic answer holds that the meaning of life is found in the practices of this world, rather than through an other-worldly orientation. Though life has no objective meaning, non-theists believe that it has meaning in a subjective sense. In other words, they say, meaning is something that people make up as they go along, rather than something they discover. Jean-Paul Sartre argued that though life has no objective or God-given meaning, it could have a subjective meaning.

Sartre's argument began with an analogy. Human artifacts like computers and cookie cutters start off life as ideas, he said. Once, there were no cookie cutters. Pastry chefs cut cookies by hand. At some point, the idea of a cookie cutter popped into the head of one of these chefs. By toying with the idea, the chef came up with a blueprint that specified the design and function of cookie cutters. Once the blueprint was ready, the production of cookie cutters could proceed, making the lives of chefs everywhere a little easier. The concept preceded the object.

No such blueprints exist for human beings. There is, Sartre claimed, no God or cosmic designer who first devises the concept of human being, then creates them according to the concept. Human beings are thrown randomly into the world, with no pre-given essence or God-given function to make their lives meaningful. People simply exist and define themselves afterwards. Nothing dictates in advance what people are going to be or what they will make of themselves.

The atheistic existentialist view, Sartre claims, assigns greater dignity to human beings than to non-human entities. Human beings exist in a way that is different from all other things. Unlike cauliflowers and lobsters, he said, people are self-conscious and self-defining. And if people are free to define themselves, they are also entirely responsible for what they make of themselves. They have no one to blame but themselves.

For Sartre, then, the meaning of life is invented, not discovered. People are like painters. Faced with a blank canvas, it is entirely up to us to choose what colours to paint with, what style to use, what perspective to adopt, and what subject matter to paint. And like artists, we must take sole responsibility for the finished product. Just as the artist who blames her work on a bad paintbrush is fooling herself, so any individual who blames his life situation on others is fooling himself about his freedom.

Figure 8.7

"WHILE WE'RE WORKING ON THE SECRET OF LIFE, DR. HELMHOLZ, THERE, IS TRYING TO UNRAVEL ITS MEANING."

What comment is cartoonist Sidney Harris making about the difference in the way scientists and philosophers approach questions about life?

Chapter Review

Chapter Summary

This chapter has discussed
- some of the main questions in metaphysics
- the positions of some of the major philosophers and schools of philosophy on some of the main metaphysical questions
- the influence of some metaphysical ideas about topics such as causality, space and time, and the infinite on other disciplines, such as physics and astronomy

Knowledge and Understanding

1. Identify and explain the significance to the study of metaphysics of each of the following key words and people.

Key Words	Key People
theism	Anselm of Canterbury
deism	David Hume
polytheists	Blaise Pascal
pantheists	Karl Marx
ontological argument	Friedrich Nietzsche
cosmological argument	Gottfried Wilhelm Leibniz
argument from design	Sigmund Freud
atheists	Albert Camus
free will	Arthur Schopenhauer
hard determinists	Leo Tolstoy
soft determinists	
nihilists	

2. Create a graphic organizer that summarizes the three main metaphysical questions dealt with in this chapter and the positions of the main philosophers and schools of philosophy on these questions.

Thinking and Inquiry

3. In *A Brief History of Time*, physicist Stephen Hawking wrote

   > When we combine quantum mechanics with general relativity, there seems to be a new possibility that did not arise before: that space and time together might form a finite, four-dimensional space without singularities or boundaries, like the surface of the earth but with more dimensions. It seems that this idea could explain many of the observed features of the universe, such as large-scale uniformity and also the smaller-scale departures from homogeneity, like galaxies, stars, and even human beings. But if the universe is completely self-contained, with no singularities or boundaries, and completely described by a unified theory, that has profound implications for the role of God as Creator.... Even if there is only one possible unified theory, it is just a set of rules and equations. What is it that breathes fire into the equations and makes the universe for them to describe?

   Explain how Hawking's view of the metaphysical ideas of causality and space and time, as well as the existence of a supreme being, accord with your own ideas.

4. In the film *Contact*, astronomer Ellie Arroway and religious scholar Palmer Joss search for answers to two metaphysical questions: What is the meaning of life? and Does God exist? When others doubt her story of travelling to the centre of the universe, Arroway says,

> Is it possible that it didn't happen? Yes. As a scientist I must concede that I … had an experience. I can't prove it or explain it … I was given something wonderful, something that changed me forever, a vision of the universe … that tells us we belong to something that is greater than ourselves, that we are not … alone. I wish I could share that. I wish that everyone, if even for one moment, can feel that awe and humility, and a hope.

Considering Arroway's words and various philosophical responses to her questions, write a personal reflection about whether the approaches of science and religion can ever be reconciled when answering these questions.

Communication

5. This chapter presents many analogies to support ideas. Create a list of criteria that make up a good analogy. Write your own analogy to support your personal philosophical position on an important metaphysical question.

6. Are human actions governed by free will? Create a children's picture story that applies a philosophical response to this question in a lesson about a child taking responsibility for his or her actions.

Application

7. Which opposing views of the meaning of life is Calvin struggling with in this cartoon (Figure 8.8)? Sketch another frame that reflects your own response to the question, What is the meaning of life?

Figure 8.8

CALVIN AND HOBBES © Watterson. Reprinted with permission of UNIVERSAL PRESS SYNDICATE. All rights reserved.

8. Imagine that you are discussing the meaning of life with three great thinkers. Create the conversation that might take place and present it in the form of a role-play.

Write a book or movie review.
CULMINATING ACTIVITY

EXPECTATIONS

By completing this activity, you will

- demonstrate an understanding of the main questions, concepts, and theories of metaphysics
- evaluate the strengths and weaknesses of responses to some of the main questions of metaphysics defended by some major philosophers and schools of philosophy and defend your own responses
- demonstrate the relevance of metaphysical questions and theories to everyday life
- illustrate how metaphysical theories are presupposed in other subjects
- correctly use metaphysical terms
- demonstrate an understanding of the unique character of metaphysical questions
- effectively use a variety of print and electronic sources and telecommunications tools in research
- effectively communicate the results of your inquiries

THE TASK

Metaphysical questions permeate every aspect of human existence. Perhaps this is why so many books and movies focus on answering questions such as, What is reality? What is the meaning of life? and Does a supreme being exist?

Books and movies that deal with metaphysical questions challenge people to clarify their responses to the questions raised. Preparing a review of a book or movie that presents metaphysical issues is one way of doing this.

This culminating activity requires you to select and review a book or movie that deals with an issue of metaphysical importance. In doing so, you will draw on your understanding of metaphysical questions, concepts, and theories to evaluate how effectively the book or movie handles them.

At the end of this course, this review may be combined with the products of other unit-culminating activities to create a philosophy magazine.

THE SUBTASKS

Subtask 1: Select a Book or Movie
Conduct research to create a list of three books or movies that interest you and deal with metaphysical questions. When conducting this research, use a variety of print and electronic sources and telecommunications tools. Summarize the plot and theme of each book or movie and assess its metaphysical relevance. Choose the one that you believe possesses the greatest metaphysical significance to be the focus of your review.

Subtask 2: Respond to the Metaphysical Questions
To demonstrate your understanding of the nature of metaphysical questions, create a list of the metaphysical questions raised in the book or movie you selected. Summarize how your selection responds to these questions and compare these responses to the responses of various philosophers and schools of metaphysical thought. Summarize your findings on a graphic organizer.

Subtask 3: Determine Your Selection's Metaphysical Relevance
Analyze the metaphysical relevance of the book or movie by deciding whether the content and presentation of the metaphysical issues it presents are of universal significance or are limited to a particular audience.

Subtask 4: Identify the Role of Metaphysics in the Theme
What role does metaphysics play in the development of the theme presented in the book or movie you selected? Write a point-form response to this question.

Subtask 5: Write the Book or Movie Review
Read several book and movie reviews to become familiar with their form, content, and language conventions. Drawing on the analysis you conducted earlier, write a review that identifies and evaluates the treatment of the metaphysical themes raised in the book or movie you selected.

ASSESSMENT CRITERIA

The following criteria will be used to assess your book or movie review.

Knowledge and Understanding
Does your review

- identify the main questions of metaphysics raised in the book or movie?
- summarize how the book or movie's content responds to these questions?

Thinking and Inquiry
Does your review

- compare the responses to key metaphysical questions presented in the movie or book to the responses provided by various philosophers and schools of metaphysical thought?
- analyze the scope of the metaphysical relevance of the selected movie or book?

Communication
Does your review

- use metaphysical terms?
- include with it a graphic organizer that presents the information set out in Subtask 2?
- use the appropriate form and language conventions?

Application
Does your review

- demonstrate your understanding, analysis, and evaluation of the main questions, concepts, and theories of metaphysics?
- defend your responses to the metaphysical questions raised in the book or movie?

UNIT 3
EPISTEMOLOGY

CHAPTER

9 Introducing Epistemology

10 Theories and Methods of Epistemology

11 Knowledge and Truth

Unit Expectations

By the end of this unit, you will be able to
- identify the main questions, concepts, and theories of epistemology
- evaluate the strengths and weaknesses of responses by some major philosophers and schools of philosophy to some of the main questions of epistemology, and defend your own responses
- demonstrate the relevance of philosophical theories of epistemology to concrete problems in everyday life
- explain how various epistemological theories apply to subject areas such as psychology

How do people know? What is knowledge and how is it acquired? Is knowledge simply what people believe to be true? Is knowledge acquired whenever someone states an opinion about something? When — and how — do opinions and beliefs become knowledge? What is truth?

These are epistemological questions, and philosophers' answers to these questions are as varied as the questions themselves. Investigating what we know and how we know it is fundamental to the philosophical quest for wisdom. This quest is a personal journey that will shape how you define yourself, your relationships with others, and the world around you, as well as how you will choose to live your life.

Chapter 9
Introducing Epistemology

Chapter Expectations

By the end of this chapter, you will be able to
- identify and demonstrate your understanding of some of the main questions, concepts, and theories of epistemology
- evaluate the strengths and weaknesses of some of the responses of philosophers to some of the main questions, concepts, and theories of epistemology
- formulate your own ideas about some of the main questions of epistemology
- formulate your own ideas about how theories of knowledge apply in various situations

Key Words

epistemology
rationalists
empiricists
a priori knowledge
a posteriori knowledge
justified true belief
direct knowledge
indirect knowledge
knowledge by acquaintance
knowledge by description
competence knowledge
propositional knowledge

Key People

Kongfuzi (Confucius)
Plato
Aristotle
René Descartes
Immanuel Kant
Socrates
Bertrand Russell
Edmund Gettier

A Philosopher's Voice

It is not enough to have a good mind. The main thing is to use it well.

René Descartes (1596–1650)

What Is Epistemology?

Examine this photograph (Figure 9.1) of a building in Carcassonne, France. What do you see? How many windows do you see? How many people do you see?

Figure 9.1

Look again at the photograph. Would it surprise you to learn that only the two windows on the top right are real? Or that the picture includes no real people? The four other windows and the people are a *trompe l'oeil* — a French expression that means "deceive the eye." The person who crafted this clever deceit did so by painting additional windows and people on a blank wall. Does this explanation change your knowledge of what is pictured in the photograph?

Trompe l'oeil are not the only examples of situations that make people wonder whether the world perceived through their senses and comprehended by their minds is what it appears to be. Have you ever smiled and waved at someone you know, only to come to the embarrassing realization that the person is a complete stranger? Or looked up at the night sky and noticed that the size of the moon seems to have changed? The senses can be deceived — and people's minds often become unknowing accomplices in the deception.

Drawing incorrect conclusions based on sensory experience is nothing new. Six hundred years ago, for example, it was common knowledge that the earth was flat and that the sun revolved around the earth. Now people think they know better or that they cannot be as easily fooled, though modern technology actually makes it much easier to deceive people. Photographs, for example, can be doctored to make a person look angelic or downright vicious, stunningly beautiful or pathetically ugly.

On a grander scale, consider the commonly accepted and celebrated fact that the Americans landed astronauts on the moon in 1969. More than 30 years later, the landing was called into question. A small, vocal, and well-informed group has claimed that the whole episode was an expensive hoax perpetrated for political and military reasons. The "evidence" became the subject of a one-hour television documentary. Though the documentary ended on an inconclusive note, the controversy raised an important philosophical question: What constitutes sufficient and proper justification for claiming to know something?

Questions about knowledge — what it is and how it can be acquired, as well as when someone can claim to have it — have a long history. In the fourth century BCE, the Chinese philosopher Zhuangzi wondered how a person can even know what is and is not real:

> Once upon a time, I, Zhuangzi, dreamt I was a butterfly, fluttering hither and thither.... I was conscious only of following my fancies as a butterfly, and was unconscious of my individuality as a man. Suddenly, I waked, and there I lay, myself again. Now I do not know whether I was then a man dreaming I was a butterfly, or whether I am now a butterfly dreaming I am a man.

Zhuangzi's story illustrates that questions about knowledge have long captivated the human imagination.

The preceding examples illustrate that evidence presented to the senses and analyzed by the powers of reason are not necessarily reliable. People cannot always be certain of what they know or how they know things — and this is what epistemology is about.

The term "epistemology" comes from the Greek word *episteme*, which means "knowledge." The English suffix "-ology," which means "the study or theory of," is also borrowed from a Greek word. In Greek, *logos* means "reason" and is the source of both the English suffix "-ology" and the English word "logic." The most straightforward definition of epistemology, then, is the study of knowledge. Epistemologists — those who study epistemology — try to answer questions like, What is knowledge? and What does it mean to know?

NATURE AND AIMS OF EPISTEMOLOGY

Everyone has an epistemological mindset. Every day, people ask epistemological questions like, How do you know that? Are you sure that is true? Is that a fact? and Is that your opinion? Questions like these are epistemological because they explore the nature of knowledge. They ask how someone has come to know something; they inquire into the scope and limits of knowledge; or they try to discover the degree of certainty attached to particular knowledge.

Figure 9.2

Which of these two views of the same stick is accurate? Is the stick straight or is it bent? How do you *know*?

Suppose someone asks you to describe a stick. You might say, "That stick is straight, about 2.5 cm in diameter and about 30 cm long." Now think about what might happen if the stick is placed in a pail of water. The stick would appear to bend. But is it really bent? If asked this question, you might draw on your knowledge of science to answer, "No, the stick is straight. It just appears to be bent because of the refraction of light through the water." Epistemologists might respond to your statement by asking questions like, "How do you know that the stick is straight?" "How do you know that the stick does not bend once it is placed in the water?" and "Why do you accept your perception that the stick is straight over your perception that the stick is bent?"

When they ask questions like these, epistemologists are exploring the nature, scope, limits, and origin of human knowledge. As a result, every field of philosophy involves epistemological questions, and epistemology touches on every field of philosophy. This is why epistemology is often called one of the pillars of philosophy.

THE PHILOSOPHER'S APPROACH TO EPISTEMOLOGY

In their exploration of human knowledge, epistemologists ask questions like, What is knowledge? Under what conditions can we claim to have knowledge? Can people know the world as it really is? Are there some things that people can know with absolute certainty? and Are there some things that humans can never know? How can we claim to know anything — and why? Questions like these probe the foundation of knowledge, the relation between knowledge and truth, and the roles played by reason and the senses — sight, hearing, touch, smell, and taste — in acquiring knowledge.

The answers to these questions are of great importance because they constitute a theory of knowledge, or an epistemology. A person's epistemology affects how she or he perceives the world. It determines our conception of reality.

By asking questions about knowledge, epistemologists approach issues differently from, for example, scientists. A scientist investigating the qualities of the stick mentioned earlier might say that it is straight because she has observed it and her observations can be confirmed by others who have performed independent experiments. In compiling her observations, the scientist used her sense of sight to conclude that the stick is straight. Two words sum up the scientist's approach: experimentation and observation. An epistemologist, however, might question the evidence presented by the scientist's senses. He might challenge not only the scientist's claim to know that the stick is straight but also, if he takes an extreme position, the scientist's claim to know that the stick even exists.

Both science and philosophy are disciplines in which there is a long tradition of disagreement. Just as scientists do not always agree about the best way of acquiring scientific knowledge and determining what constitutes reliable knowledge, epistemologists often disagree about the best way of acquiring various kinds of knowledge. Four hundred years ago, scientists said that the earth was the centre of the universe. Then along came the astronomer Copernicus with the bad news: science was wrong, and a long-cherished belief was abandoned.

Because both science and epistemology deal with the nature of reality, findings in science can have a strong impact on what constitutes reality. At the beginning of the 20th century, Albert Einstein rocked the world of conventional physics with his theories of relativity; yet he balked at the uncertainty suggested by quantum mechanics, saying, "God does not play dice with the universe." In saying this, he meant that a predictable, orderly system of cause and effect is at work in nature and the universe. In the 1930s, however, another scientist, Werner Heisenberg, seemed to demonstrate that this was not so. His work challenged the idea of an orderly system of cause and effect. This development shook many scientists' traditional faith in a materialistic interpretation of the universe.

Knowledge is the knowing that we cannot know.

– Ralph Waldo Emerson

Though many still favour a materialistic approach, many others think that the odds favour an idealistic interpretation. They believe that the ultimate reality of the universe will be found to be immaterial. This debate causes philosophers to wonder whether humans will ever know the way the universe really is. If humanity ever obtains conclusive knowledge about this cosmic subject, will reason or the senses provide the necessary clues and confirming evidence? These are important epistemological questions.

Recall...Reflect...Respond

1. List the epistemological questions introduced so far.
2. Divide these questions into groups dealing with the following epistemological ideas: the senses, reason, and certainty.
3. Think about a recent conversation you have had with friends, family, or teachers. Do any of the questions apply to what you discussed? How? Complete the following chart to show how this conversation helped you formulate your own ideas about some of the main questions of epistemology.

What was your conversation about?	What epistemological questions did it address?	What was your position on the question?

WHAT PHILOSOPHERS HAVE SAID

Philosophers have always grappled with questions of the nature, scope, limits, and origin of knowledge. They have always tried to come to grips with the question of what people know — and how they know it. As early as 2500 years ago, the Chinese philosopher **Kongfuzi**, better known in the West as Confucius, said about knowledge: "To realize that you know something when you do, and to realize that you do not when you do not — this then is knowledge." He is also thought to have said, "Real knowledge is to know the extent of one's ignorance." The implications of these two statements are clear: wise people do not pretend or claim to know more than they actually do.

On the subject of knowledge, Kongfuzi was a no-nonsense, down-to-earth philosopher who emphasized the concrete and the practical. And in what may be the shortest autobiography ever written, he leaves no doubt that acquiring knowledge is a life-long process:

> At 15 my heart and mind were set upon learning; at 30 I took my stance; at 40 I was no longer of two minds; at 50 I realized the order prevailing in the world; at 60 my ear was attuned; at 70 I could give my heart and mind free rein without overstepping the mark.

Kongfuzi meant that it was only toward the end of his life that he was able to speak with the authority and wisdom of someone who knows what he is talking about. His words warn people to be careful about assuming that they know more than they do.

Half a world away and more than a century after Kongfuzi lived, the ancient Greek philosopher **Plato** compared people's minds to an aviary, which is an enclosure of birds:

> Let us now suppose that in the mind of each man there is an aviary of all sorts of birds — some flocking together apart from the rest, others in small groups, others solitary, flying anywhere and everywhere.... We may suppose that the birds are all kinds of knowledge, and that when we were children, this receptacle was empty; whenever a man has gotten and detained in the enclosure a kind of knowledge, he may be said to have learned or discovered the thing which is the subject of the knowledge: and this is to know.

Plato's ideas about knowledge, however, were even more complicated than this. He believed that the things people perceive through the senses are subject to change because these things disintegrate, dissolve, and wear down. As a result, he argued that knowledge acquired through the senses is unreliable because people can never generate more than opinions about objects belonging to the sensory world. Only the power of reason — undistracted by the senses and bodily needs — can reveal genuine, true knowledge. And reason, he claimed, is the tool that provides understanding of the eternal, unchanging, and unseen world of ideas, which he called "forms."

Plato said that these forms are innate because they exist in every human mind from birth — and he believed that learning simply involves remembering them. The experiences of the senses help people do this. According to Plato, the human mind includes from birth the innate idea of a horse, a chair, a table, and so on. For every object that exists in the material world of the senses, a corresponding idea exists in the human mind. He believed that this world of forms represents a non-material reality that is superior to humans' earthly existence.

Plato's theory of innate ideas laid the groundwork for the debate over the nature, scope, limits, and origin of knowledge that would occupy western philosophers for the next 2000 years. When western philosophers wrote about knowledge in later centuries, they lined up behind Plato — or behind **Aristotle**, Plato's most famous student. Aristotle did not agree completely with his teacher's theories. Though Aristotle accepted that the abstract knowledge of the world of forms is superior, he also maintained that all knowledge comes from experience. To Aristotle, "experience" meant evidence acquired through the senses. Still, he also believed in the importance of reason, so much so that he said that reason is the characteristic that distinguishes human beings. He did not, however, accept Plato's notion of innate ideas, believing instead that reason came into play only after people experienced things through their senses.

Though Plato and Aristotle, as well as the philosophers who followed them, certainly considered theories of knowledge, epistemology was never the chief focus of their philosophical investigations This changed in the 17th century when the French scientist, mathematician, and philosopher **René Descartes** revolutionized philosophy — at least in western circles — by placing epistemology centre stage. As a result of Descartes's work, the pivotal philosophical question became, What can I know for certain?

In developing his theories, he used a method that is commonly called Descartes's method. Seeking to construct a new foundation for all knowledge, he cast aside all previous beliefs about knowledge, philosophical and otherwise. In his quest to know, he decided to accept nothing as true that he did not clearly recognize to be so. He would trust neither his senses nor his reason and would accept only what he could know with absolute certainty. Using this method of systematic doubt, he was confident that he could know one thing for certain. He expressed this certainty in his famous argument "*Cogito ergo sum*," a Latin sentence that means "I think, therefore I am."

Descartes thought carefully about the problem of certainty before formulating the cogito argument. In fact, he devised a number of counter-arguments that called all knowledge into question, including his knowledge of his own existence! In his dream argument, for example, he maintained that dreaming experiences are indistinguishable from waking experiences. A more famous argument of his, sometimes called a thought experiment, was even more extreme. This argument, known as the evil-genius argument, suggested the possibility that all sensory experiences, as well as all ideas and thoughts about reality, are planted in people's minds by an all-powerful evil genius.

Descartes's hypothetical scenario raised the possibility that reality, as people perceive it, is an illusion. How would anyone know? Could people be, as suggested in various 20th-century works of science fiction, wired up brains in jars, made to think and experience what they believe to be reality? Descartes reasoned, however, that even if an evil genius is at work, something must exist to experience the illusion — and he concluded that, at the very least, he existed as a thinking being. This "thing that thinks," as he referred to himself, was conscious. It could think about the fact that it was thinking and be aware that this was happening. This he could not doubt. This line of reasoning led him to his famous cogito argument, which became the cornerstone of his philosophy.

Descartes maintained that the human mind could come to know things independently of physical reality — and that people come to this knowledge by using the power of their own reason. His theories focused new attention on the debate over the nature of knowledge and set the stage for the emergence in the 19th century of epistemology as a separate branch of western philosophy.

Descartes's ideas and methods did not go unchallenged, however. By the time he died in 1650, a rival school of epistemology had appeared. John Locke, an English philosopher,

Figure 9.3

Descartes's famous argument — "I think, therefore I am — is one of the most satirized philosophical theories. This cartoon shows Popeye, a character who is famous for saying "I yam what I yam," studying Descartes.

PROFILE
René Descartes
The First Modern Philosopher

René Descartes hated to get up in the morning — and he had the best of excuses. Born in 1596 in La Haye (now Descartes), France, he was a puny child whose mother died when he was a year old. His maternal grandmother, who took over his care, coddled her sickly grandson and tried to build his strength by encouraging him to linger in bed every day.

As a member of the minor nobility, Descartes's father was a prosperous landowner who could afford to send his son away from home to be educated at a Jesuit college. Even at school, the priests allowed their frail student to spend most of the morning in bed. As a result, rising late became a life-long habit.

In fact, Descartes's habit of lingering in bed till at least 11 a.m. may have contributed to his interest in science and philosophy, which were considered one subject at the time. Descartes once wrote to a friend that he used his lying-in time to meditate and think. More and more, this thinking led him to question traditional learning, which he came to believe was based on shaky foundations.

When he was 18, Descartes earned a law degree and later studied mathematics and military architecture in the Netherlands. When his formal education ended, he set out to travel around Europe, saying that he was studying the book of the world. Throughout this time, his doubts about traditional learning grew stronger. As a result, the young man came up with a grandiose scheme to formulate an entirely new system of science.

As a first step in this process, he wrote *Rules for the Direction of the Mind*, which set out procedures for arriving at reasoned answers to questions. He went on to write and publish many other works, including *Discourse on Method*. He wrote this book in French rather than Latin, the language used by most scholars of his era, because he wanted everyone, including women, to be able to read his work and learn to use his methods.

Descartes's writing caught the attention of other thinkers, some of whom published works challenging his ideas. Descartes wrote detailed replies in response to these challenges. These debates among the great thinkers of Europe attracted widespread attention and made the French philosopher something of a celebrity.

Among those attracted by Descartes's fame was Queen Christina of Sweden, who invited him to instruct her in the latest scientific methods. Descartes accepted the invitation in the fall of 1649, arriving in Stockholm just as winter was about to set in. Unlike Descartes, the 22-year-old queen was an early riser, who decreed that her instruction must take place at 5 a.m. Already suffering from the cold — Descartes commented that in winter men's thoughts freeze like water — the 53-year-old philosopher found the early-morning sessions torture. After a session on Feb. 1, 1650, he came down with pneumonia, a deadly disease in an era when medical treatment was rudimentary. Eleven days later, he died.

Descartes's emphasis on reason changed forever the way people thought about questions of science and philosophy. For 150 years after his death, nearly all the important works of philosophy were influenced by questions he had raised — and contemporary philosophers still refer to his ideas. As a result, he is often called the first modern philosopher.

Figure 9.4

René Descartes's ideas about science were all the rage in 17th-century Europe. This drawing shows the philosopher giving an early-morning lesson to Queen Christina of Sweden.

spearheaded the attack on Descartes's theory that reason is the primary source of knowledge. Whereas Descartes had championed reason in a manner similar to Plato, Locke borrowed heavily from Aristotle. According to Aristotle, the mind is a *tabula rasa* at birth. *Tabula rasa* is a Latin phrase that means blank slate. Taking his cue from Aristotle, Locke argued that the human mind is blank, or empty, until sensory experience puts something into it. In other words, ideas are the byproducts of sensory experience.

The hotly contested debate between these two opposing schools of thought occupied philosophers well into the 18th century. At that time, Immanuel Kant, a German philosopher, tried to bridge the gap. He accepted some — and rejected other — elements of both schools.

Descartes had reasoned that he was a "thing that thinks" — a conscious being, but that was as far as he went. For Descartes consciousness was as inexplicable as it was real, and he simply accepted it as one of life's mysteries.

Kant, however, made consciousness, the way humans process ideas, a central feature of his philosophy. Think about yourself and a friend. Your ideas are your own, and your friend's ideas are his. His ideas do not suddenly pop into your mind — and vice-versa. Based on this simple fact, Kant proposed a concept summed up by the phrase "unity of consciousness." He said that a person's consciousness — thoughts, beliefs, hopes, fears and so on — are unified in her mind and no one else's.

Kant's theory suggested that knowledge, whether it is the product of reason or the result of sense perception, is bound together — or unified — by the human mind. Kant said that the process of uniting — or synthesizing — innate ideas and sense perception into a single consciousness is a mental activity that must take place before anything can be known. Kant also developed theories to explain how intuition and cause-and-effect work in human consciousness. In the end, Kant's ideas failed to completely bridge the gap between the rival theories. Nevertheless, his ideas shook the world of epistemology to its very foundation.

Web connection
www.mcgrawhill.ca/links/philosophy12
To find out more about Immanuel Kant, follow the links on this Web site.

In the 20th century, new schools of epistemological thought began to emerge. Some epistemologists insisted that only knowledge arrived at through logic, mathematics, or science is reliable. Others suggested that the only true knowledge is that upon which most people agree. Still others argued that attempts to define knowledge are always influenced by the personal and cultural background of the philosopher creating the definition. In the 21st century, the philosophical debate over the nature, scope, limits and origin of knowledge continues to rage as strongly as it did in ancient times.

How Philosophers Have Said It

Just as philosophers have argued about the nature, scope, limits, and origin of knowledge, they have also disagreed over the precise meaning of many of the terms used in epistemological debates. As a result, various philosophers have interpreted these terms differently. This is not unusual. All disciplines face similar problems. The more abstract the concepts being discussed, the greater the chances that disagreements will occur. Despite this, some terms are used repeatedly. They can be defined in a way that is acceptable to most philosophers.

Where does knowledge come from? This is the basic question of epistemology, and it is also the question that has divided western philosophers for 2500 years. Philosophers who believe that knowledge comes from exercising the human ability to reason — the ability to move from thought to thought and to draw conclusions — are called rationalists. The English words "reason," "rational," and "rationalists" come from the same Latin word *ratio*, which means reason. Rationalists believe that reason not only enables people to know things

The Lighter Side of Philosophy

How many epistemologists does it take to change a light bulb?

Three. One to change it and two to stand around arguing about whether knowledge of the light bulb is a product of the senses or reason.

that the senses do not reveal, but also that it is the primary source of knowledge. Plato and Descartes, for example, were rationalists.

Philosophers who maintain that knowledge comes from experience — evidence presented by the senses — are called **empiricists**. Aristotle and Locke, for example, were empiricists. The philosophical terms "empirical" and "empiricists" are not related to the word "empire." They come from the Greek word *empeiria*, which means experience.

Few philosophers, however, believe that knowledge comes only from reason or only from experience. Even those who are labelled rationalists or empiricists usually acknowledge that knowledge is acquired by combining reason and experience, though they may disagree on just how much of each is involved in the process.

Western epistemologists have developed a specialized vocabulary to talk about knowledge. One of these terms is a priori, a phrase that means "from before" in Latin. When talking about **a priori knowledge**, epistemologists mean knowledge that is gained before sense experience. In other words, a priori knowledge does not depend on evidence provided by the senses, but is derived strictly from our mental ability to reason. Rationalists such as Plato and Descartes were especially inclined to emphasize the importance of a priori knowledge. Plato's theory of innate ideas, for example, was a kind of a priori knowledge, though it was not called this in ancient Greece. A priori knowledge is true and indubitable, which means that it cannot be doubted.

Rationalists argue that mathematical ideas are a priori. When Einstein, for example, experienced the flash of inspiration that led to the development of the theory of relativity, he was using pure reason to arrive at a fundamental truth about the reality of the universe. The same can be said of human knowledge of the origins of the universe, black holes, dark matter, and other phenomena. Rationalists say that mathematical formulas and the power of reason — not sensory experiences — are the tools scientists used to discover these cosmic truths.

Epistemologists call knowledge that depends on evidence presented by the senses or experience a posteriori, a term that means "from after" or "from a later time" in Latin. When talking about **a posteriori knowledge**, epistemologists mean knowledge that is gained after sense experience. In other words, a posteriori knowledge depends on evidence provided by the senses. Empiricists such as John Locke and David Hume emphasized and favoured a posteriori knowledge.

Suppose that you know that all swans are white. Then you see a black swan. This experience changes your knowledge of swans. You now know that most — but clearly not all — swans are white. Your knowledge of swans is said to be a posteriori because it has been altered by evidence presented by your sense of sight.

Figure 9.5

Five Senses / Extreme Empiricists ————————— Reason / Extreme Rationalists

If beliefs about the origin of knowledge were pictured on a continuum like this, most epistemologists would fall somewhere toward the middle. Where would you place yourself on the continuum?

Why Epistemology Matters

For a number of reasons, knowledge is an excellent concept for philosophical analysis. It's an immensely practical subject of discussion because just about every plan people make and action they take is based on knowledge of some sort. Everyone uses the noun "knowledge" and the verb "to know."

Consider the repercussions of the inadequate knowledge expressed by the following statements:

- I didn't think I was that close.
- I didn't know the pool was that shallow.
- I didn't know the roof was going to cave in.

Being as clear as possible about what constitutes knowledge can pay dividends.

Just about everyone is an epistemologist in everyday life. At work, at school, at home, and in social situations, people engage in epistemological debates of some description. They may never use the terms developed by epistemologists to describe epistemological exercises, but this does not mean that people are not doing what epistemologists do — inquiring into the nature, scope, limits, and origin of knowledge.

When your mother says, "Hurry up, or you'll be late for school," she is using her knowledge of time to predict an outcome. When you respond, "No, I won't. I have lots of time," you are using your knowledge of time to question your mother's prediction and make your own. Without calling your disagreement an epistemological debate, you and your mother have engaged in exactly that.

Every day we compile "facts," form opinions and beliefs, and explain why we favour one belief or opinion over another. When we do this, we are "doing" epistemology.

Non-philosophers find some epistemological debates, such as the one between rationalists and empiricists, strange and sometimes even pointless. They often take the position that what you see is what you get, a view that is sometimes called common-sense realism. They tend to accept unquestioningly that the senses provide an accurate picture of reality. For common-sense realists, all crows are black and all birds can fly. End of discussion. Assumptions like these are, at best, unsatisfactory and, at worst, mistaken. Common-sense realism is not the philosopher's way, nor is it the way of anyone genuinely wishing to know the truth of things.

Recall...Reflect...Respond

1. Create a graphic organizer like the following to summarize the differences between rationalists and empiricists.

School of Epistemology	Philosophers Contributing to School	Main Epistemological Questions Addressed by Each Philosopher	Philosopher's Major Contributions to Study of Epistemology
Rationalism			
Empiricism			

2. Classify each of the following knowledge claims as a priori knowledge or a posteriori knowledge. Once you have done this, consider what the statements in each group have in common. Use these common characteristics to create your own definition of a priori knowledge and a posteriori knowledge.

> All babies know how to swim.
> Walking is second nature to me.
> That's a rose-scented perfume.
> Nikita learned to play that song by watching her piano teacher play it.
> The grocery list is gone so Dad must have gone shopping for groceries.
> I don't think that we should worry about being lost anymore because I can see light at the end of the tunnel.

3. Various schools of epistemological thought have been introduced in this chapter. Which one most closely matches your own view? Provide evidence of your position in the form of a response to one of the main epistemological questions raised in this chapter.

WHAT IS KNOWLEDGE?

Attempts to define knowledge have concerned philosophers for thousands of years. Siddhartha Gautama, also called the Buddha, who founded Buddhism in northeastern India in the sixth century BCE, may have been the first to develop a definition. He said that knowledge is belief produced by a reliable means of knowledge. But finding a reliable means was no easy task. The Buddha rejected most commonly accepted sources of knowledge, such as authority and reason. Instead, he said that knowledge involves changing your life rather than simply tucking information away in your head. Since that time, philosophers from many traditions have struggled with the same issue, yet a definition of knowledge remains as elusive today as it did in ancient times.

OPINIONS, BELIEFS, AND KNOWLEDGE

Can people know anything with absolute certainty? If so, how? These are important questions for epistemologists, who distinguish among opinions, beliefs, and knowledge.

Like most people, epistemologists consider opinions to be the least reliable statements. To illustrate why, take the example of two friends who decide to taste a new brand of cola. One of the two takes a sip and says, "This is great." The other says, "This tastes like ditchwater." Based on a sensory experience, each has expressed an opinion of the new cola. Because their sensory experiences are not the same, however, their opinions are not the same. A third friend would consider neither of their statements true or false.

In a similar way, a teacher who asks you to write an essay outlining your opinion of rationalism or empiricism cannot classify your response as true or false because opinion statements are not matters of truth or falsity. Still, one opinion is not necessarily as good as another. People often express opinions without adequate information. A student who is always late for the first class of the school day, for example, may provoke this observation by another student: "If Nancy can't get up early enough to get to school on time, she must be lazy." Someone else who knows Nancy better might point out that she volunteers in a pre-school children's breakfast program, which prevents her from getting to class on time. As a result, the second student would defend Nancy on the grounds that the accusations against her are unwarranted. The opinion of one of these students is informed; the opinion of the other is not. There is a difference in the quality of the two opinions, and epistemologists — like most people — consider an informed opinion to be worth more than an uninformed opinion.

Statements that express beliefs are considered somewhat more reliable than statements that express opinions because belief statements can be classified as true or false. When someone says, "I believe that my car is parked on Main Street," chances are good that the car is parked exactly where he says it is — unless he is suffering from memory loss or his car has been towed away because it was parked illegally. In either case, his belief about where the car is parked can be checked and verified as true or proven false.

Figure 9.6

This pyramid illustrates the relative reliability of opinion, belief, and knowledge statements. At the bottom, indicating that they are least reliable, are opinion statements. Belief statements appear above opinion statements because they are considered more reliable. At the top of the pyramid are knowledge statements, which are considered the most reliable.

When the words "I know that ..." start a sentence in everyday speech, they imply that the claim that follows is more reliable than a statement of opinion or even a statement of belief. For example, saying "I know that triangles have three sides" implies a greater degree of reliability than saying "In my opinion, triangles have three sides" or "I believe that triangles have three sides."

CONDITIONS FOR KNOWLEDGE

Why do people think that claims to know are more reliable than claims to hold an opinion or a belief? What conditions are necessary for a claim to qualify as knowledge? Questions like these are inextricably linked to the issue of defining knowledge.

TRUE BELIEF

In the western philosophical tradition, epistemologists from Plato onward have argued that at least two conditions must be fulfilled before anyone can claim to have knowledge. These conditions are truth and belief. Take the statement "I know that rocks are hard," for example. According to those who define knowledge as true belief, you can state that you know that rocks are hard if

- the statement that rocks are hard is true
- you believe that rocks are hard

As a result, knowledge is sometimes defined as true belief, though this definition has always been questioned. In his dialogue *Theaetetus*, Plato himself challenged this definition by creating a conversation between his own teacher, Socrates, and a student named Theaetetus. In fact, Socrates was long dead by the time Plato wrote his work, but Theaetetus was based on one of Plato's students. This student went on to become a well-known mathematician.

In the following excerpt from *Theaetetus*, Plato based his argument against accepting true belief as a definition of knowledge by citing what happens in a courtroom when jury members are persuaded to accept as true evidence presented by lawyers.

Theaetetus: ... True belief is knowledge. At any rate, true belief is incorrigible [cannot be corrected] and always has fine and beneficial consequences ...

Socrates: ... There's a whole area of expertise which proves that true belief isn't knowledge.

Theaetetus: What do you mean? Which area of expertise?

Socrates: The one practised by those paragons of wisdom, who are called orators and lawyers. I'm sure you appreciate that these people do not teach, but use their expertise to persuade and make others believe whatever they want them to believe. Or do you think that there are teachers skilful enough to be able, in the short time allotted, satisfactorily to teach the truth about events, when the people they are teaching weren't there in person at the robbery or whatever crime it was?

Theaetetus: No, I don't think that at all. I think they can only persuade.

Socrates: And to persuade people is to make them believe something, in your opinion?

Theaetetus: Yes, certainly.

Socrates: Now, when a jury has been persuaded, fairly, of things which no one but an eyewitness could possibly know, then, in reaching a decision based on hearsay, they do so without knowledge, but get hold of true belief, given that their verdict is fair because what they have been made to believe is correct.

Theaetetus: Absolutely.

Socrates: But if true belief and knowledge were identical, my friend, then even the best juryman in the world would never form a correct belief, but fail to have knowledge; so it looks as though they are different.

Plato was not the only philosopher to challenge the definition of knowledge as true belief. In the 20th century, for example, the British philosopher **Bertrand Russell** put forth a similar argument. Russell wrote that knowledge cannot be true belief because it might be based on a false belief:

> At first sight, we might imagine that knowledge could be defined as "true belief." When what we believe is true, it might be supposed that we have achieved knowledge of what we believe. But this would not accord with the way in which the word is commonly used. To take a very trivial instance: if a man believes that the late prime minister's last name began with a B, he believes what is true, since the late prime minister was Sir Henry Campbell Bannerman. But if he believes that Mr. Balfour was the late prime minister, he will still believe that the late prime minister's last name began with a B, yet this belief, though true, would not be thought to constitute knowledge.... Thus it is clear that a true belief is not knowledge when it is deduced from a false belief.

Another example can also be used to illustrate Russell's argument. Suppose you visit a friend's house where you are offered a choice of flavoured drinks. You choose your favourite: raspberry. The drink tastes so good that you decide that it must have been made from fresh raspberries. And because the drink was made from fresh raspberries, you also conclude that it has provided your required daily intake of Vitamin C.

Your friend's mother points out that the drink was not, in fact, made from fresh raspberries. It was a mixture of water and chemically manufactured raspberry powder. Because Vitamin C was added, however, you did receive the right amount of this vitamin. Though your conclusion was true, it was based on an initial belief that was false. In Russell's view, this means that your conclusion is not knowledge.

Web connection
www.mcgrawhill.ca/links/philosophy12
To find out more about Bertrand Russell, follow the links on this Web site.

JUSTIFIED TRUE BELIEF

Like ancient philosophers, contemporary epistemologists continue to try to define knowledge. If, as Plato showed in *Theaetetus*, truth and belief are not the only conditions necessary for knowledge, what else is required? Though this question was not answered in *Theaetetus*, Plato is often credited with suggesting that the missing element is justification. As a result, western philosophers accepted **justified true belief** as a definition of knowledge for a long time.

According to this definition, three conditions are necessary to claim knowledge. Those who accept that knowledge is justified true belief say that you can make a knowledge claim like "I know that rocks are hard" if

- the statement that rocks are hard is true
- you believe that rocks are hard
- you are justified in believing that rocks are hard

The analysis of knowledge as justified true belief prevailed until 1963. That is when an American philosopher, Edmund Gettier, rocked the world of epistemology by challenging this definition. Gettier published two cases suggesting that someone can have a justified true belief that is false. If a justified true belief can be false, Gettier argued, then knowledge cannot be defined as justified true belief.

Since Gettier's cases were published, other philosophers have presented similar challenges. Like Gettier's cases, these arguments usually cite instances when a justified true belief can be shown to be false.

Suppose that Farrah, a student in your class, tells you that she was given a new yellow convertible for her birthday. She says that she drives the car and has the ownership certificate to prove that it is hers. What is more, you have seen a new yellow convertible parked in the school's student parking area. As a result, you accept Farrah's claim.

Web connection
www.mcgrawhill.ca/links/philosophy12
To find out more about Gettier's cases, follow the links on this Web site.

Talking to another student after school, you say, "Someone in my class owns a new yellow convertible."

Your statement is a knowledge claim because it meets the three conditions for knowledge: the statement is true; you believe it is true; and you are justified in believing it is true.

Suppose, though, that Farrah does not own the new yellow convertible — but someone else in the class does. Your knowledge claim still meets the three conditions necessary for knowledge. It is still true (someone in your class *does* own a new yellow convertible); you still believe it is true; and you are still justified in believing it is true. There is no knowledge, however, because the justification for making the claim is false.

To counter Gettier's cases and other similar arguments, some contemporary philosophers have suggested that knowledge can still be defined as justified true belief if a fourth condition is added to the three that were traditionally thought necessary for knowledge. This fourth condition stipulates that the justification for believing something cannot depend on a false statement.

Philosophers who accept that four conditions are necessary for knowledge agree that you can make a knowledge claim like "I know that rocks are hard" if

Figure 9.7

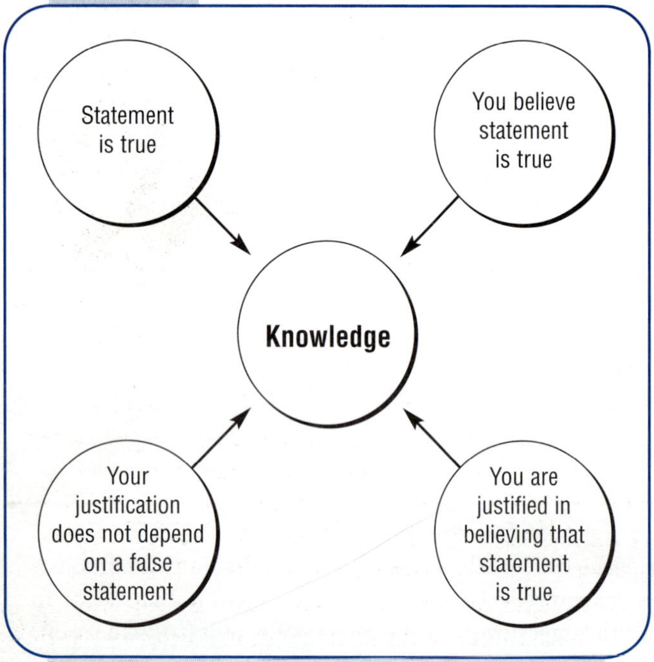

Statement is true → Knowledge
You believe statement is true → Knowledge
Your justification does not depend on a false statement → Knowledge
You are justified in believing that statement is true → Knowledge

Some philosophers support the idea that a claim to *know* can be made if these four conditions are met. What do you think?

190 MHR UNIT 3 EPISTEMOLOGY

> *Do not believe hastily.*
> — Ovid

- The statement that rocks are hard is true.
- You believe that rocks are hard.
- You are justified in believing that rocks are hard.
- Your justification for believing that rocks are hard does not depend on a false statement.

As a result of the debate sparked by Gettier, the focus of the debate over a definition of knowledge shifted. Rather than concentrating on what constitutes knowledge, epistemological debate began to zero in on justification — and what, if anything, constitutes adequate justification.

KINDS OF KNOWLEDGE

People make many knowledge claims every day. Expressions like, I know (something or someone), I know that …, I know where …, I know why …, and I know whether …. often introduce these claims, suggesting that they involve different kinds of knowledge. In exploring the nature, scope, limits, and origin of knowledge, epistemologists have developed various ways of distinguishing among the various kinds of knowledge. Though these philosophers — and others — may have used different terms to distinguish between various kinds of knowledge and may have presented their arguments in different ways, all were seeking to discover how people know what they know.

DIRECT AND INDIRECT KNOWLEDGE

Direct knowledge and indirect knowledge play an important role in people's lives, and epistemologists from many traditions believe that it is important to distinguish between the two.

Direct knowledge, which is also called simple knowledge or perceptual knowledge, is acquired through experience — by perceiving something through the senses. It is knowledge of things as they are. It involves immediate experience that does not depend on anything else. For example, at this moment, you are having the direct experience of reading these words.

Indirect knowledge, which is also called complex knowledge or inferential knowledge, is acquired by using the power of reason to connect pieces of direct knowledge. In this sense, indirect knowledge is a posteriori. It is a result of experience.

Though direct knowledge does not rely on indirect knowledge, indirect knowledge *does* rely on direct knowledge. Most of the knowledge acquired by humans is indirect because it is not based on knowledge acquired directly through the senses; rather, it is acquired by connecting pieces of direct knowledge.

Imagine, for example, that you are looking at a chair. Your knowledge of it at this moment is direct because you are experiencing the chair through your sense of sight. Some epistemologists would argue that the chair and your perception of it are identical.

Imagine that you then sit on the chair — and can no longer see its legs. Despite this, you are confident that the legs exist and will hold you up. This knowledge is indirect. To reach this conclusion, you relied on your ability to connect various pieces of direct knowledge that you had previously gained through direct experience. You concluded that the chair would hold you up because of your direct knowledge of the chair, of the chair's legs, and of the fact that the chair held you up without collapsing.

Most philosophers acknowledge that indirect knowledge is not always reliable. If you sat in the chair and it collapsed, the indirect knowledge you used to infer — or conclude — that the legs are strong enough to hold you would have been unreliable.

KNOWLEDGE BY ACQUAINTANCE AND KNOWLEDGE BY DESCRIPTION

In one way or another, philosophers from many traditions have distinguished between direct and indirect knowledge. Gautama, for example, called direct knowledge "perception" and said, "Perception is knowledge resulting from sense-object contact." Aristotle said much the same thing.

He wrote "Actual [direct] knowledge is identical with its object." Aristotle and others who came later said that knowledge that is acquired directly cannot be judged true or false. It would be pointless, for example, to ask if it is true or false that you are now reading the words on this page. As a result, direct knowledge is different from indirect knowledge, which does require justification because it can be judged true or false.

> *We do have perceptual access to the real world and those arguments that say we don't are bad arguments.*
>
> – John Searle

A similar argument was put forward in the 20th century by Russell, who used the terms **knowledge by acquaintance** and **knowledge by description** to distinguish between direct and indirect knowledge. Russell argued that direct knowledge, or knowledge by acquaintance, involves only the senses. As a result, he said, knowledge by acquaintance is the same thing as sense perception.

If you were in your house and heard barking in the backyard, your knowledge of this sound at the moment it was being made would be direct because you would be perceiving it through your sense of hearing. Then, as a result of this direct knowledge, you might infer that your dog is creating the sound. But because you cannot see your dog, your knowledge that your dog is causing the ruckus is indirect knowledge, or knowledge by description.

Russell maintained that all knowledge by description depends on knowledge by acquaintance. In the case of your dog, the connection between your indirect knowledge that your dog is barking and your direct knowledge of the sound made by your dog is clear.

What happens, though, when your history teacher tells you that John A. Macdonald was the first prime minister of Canada? How can you call this information knowledge if you have no direct knowledge of John A. Macdonald or of Canada in 1867?

Russell would argue that the fact of John A. Macdonald's prime ministership qualifies as knowledge by description, even though it is not based on your own direct knowledge. He would say that this information can be tracked back through history to eyewitness accounts in 1867 newspapers. These eyewitness accounts constitute someone else's knowledge by acquaintance, and Russell argued that knowledge by description can be based on your own knowledge by acquaintance — or someone else's.

Like Aristotle, Russell argued that knowledge by acquaintance needs no justification because it is self-explanatory or self-evident. As a result, it cannot be judged true or false.

COMPETENCE AND PROPOSITIONAL KNOWLEDGE

Twentieth-century epistemologists have also grappled with the difference between the kinds of knowledge suggested by the phrases "know that" and "know how." You may, for example, know *how* to swim. Your swimming know-how does not mean that you can explain this knowledge to a friend in a way that will enable her to develop the same skill. This kind of knowledge, or know-how, is often called **competence knowledge**, or knowledge-as-ability. It is the kind of knowledge that is acquired more readily by seeing something demonstrated rather than by hearing about it.

At the same time, you may know that Canadian swimmer Alex Baumann won two gold medals at the 1984 Summer Olympics. Knowing that Baumann was a champion swimmer does not involve the skill of swimming; rather, it involves possessing a specific piece of information, which can be conveyed in words. This kind of knowledge is often called **propositional knowledge**.

The term "propositional" comes from the word "proposition." Some epistemologists use the words "statement" and "proposition" as synonyms. Others distinguish between the meaning of the two terms. To see why and how, consider the following sentences:

What's your name?
Close the door!
Gosh!
Ali is two metres tall.

The first three sentences have no truth value because they cannot be judged true or false. The last sentence, however, can be either true or false. In epistemological terms, sentences that contain truth value are called statements.

Epistemologists who distinguish between statements and propositions say that a statement is the form — the language, words, and grammar — used to express a proposition, which is the idea. For example, the English sentences, It is snowing and Snow is falling, as well as the French sentence, *Il neige*, are statements. In different forms, all three statements express the same proposition or idea.

Figure 9.8

Foundationalists
Experience
a posteriori
Knowledge
a priori
Innate Ideas
Anti-foundationalists

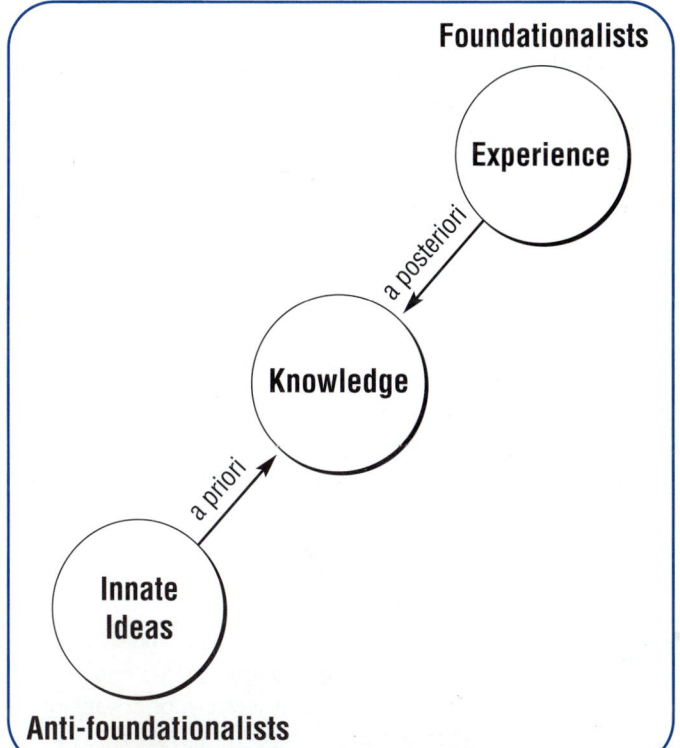

This diagram illustrates the different approaches to knowledge taken by foundationalists and anti-foundationalists.

FOUNDATIONALISM AND ANTI-FOUNDATIONALISM

Philosophers like Aristotle, Descartes, and Russell are sometimes called foundationalists because they maintain that all knowledge rests on a foundation of direct knowledge. This a posteriori knowledge consists of basic things that humans perceive directly through experience.

Anti-foundationalists disagree with this interpretation. Like Plato, they maintain that knowledge is innate. This a priori knowledge is independent of experience.

The debate between foundationalists and anti-foundationalists highlights the issue of justification and relates to the issue of knowledge as justified belief. Foundationalists say that direct knowledge is self-explanatory or self-evident. As a result, foundationalists maintain that direct knowledge needs no justification.

Anti-foundationalists take a different approach. They argue that justification does not need to rest on a foundation of any kind. They say that knowledge is adequate if it can be justified by other things people know.

> **Recall...Reflect...Respond**
>
> 1. Explain how direct knowledge and indirect knowledge are related to knowledge by acquaintance and knowledge by description. Give an example of each.
> 2. The definition of knowledge has gone through an evolution. Draw a timeline to illustrate how the definition of knowledge has developed over time. Include a present-day example of a knowledge claim or argument to illustrate the various stages in this evolutionary process.
> 3. One of the main goals of epistemology is to define human knowledge. Consider philosophers' thinking about the kinds of knowledge introduced in this chapter. List the common characteristics of the various kinds of knowledge. Create a series of questions that you could ask a friend to enable him or her to arrive at a definition of human knowledge containing these common characteristics.

Contemporary Thinking about Knowledge

For most of recorded western history, the search to define knowledge was guided by the assumption that knowledge is rational, objective, and universal. In other words, most philosophers assumed that a definition of knowledge must be grounded in reason, must be unaffected by feelings or opinions, and must be acceptable to everyone. This quest reached its peak in the 17th century when Descartes emphasized the role of reason. Even after Descartes, philosophers continued to work within a framework that tried to analyze knowledge in terms that were rational, objective, and universal.

In the 19th and 20th centuries, some philosophers began to question these assumptions. They suggested that knowledge is not rational, objective, or universal; rather, they said, it is subjective and personal. It is influenced by people's individual perspectives on the world, and these perspectives are dictated by factors such as people's personal, social, economic, and cultural background. As a result, they said that knowledge depends on who we are — and who we are dictates how we know the world.

Those who maintain that knowledge is subjective and personal are sometimes called subjectivists. Subjectivists would argue, for example, that Descartes's theories were not based on pure reason at all. They would say that his assumptions were coloured by his personal, social, economic, and cultural background. Some factors that may have influenced Descartes's view of the world include

- the death of his mother when he was very young
- his father's social standing as a member of the minor French nobility
- his family's economic status as prosperous landowners
- his education by Jesuit priests, who taught rigorous thinking and the use of logic
- his membership in a 17th-century European culture

The idea that knowledge may be subjective rather than rational, objective, and universal has raised questions about the focus of western epistemology. These questions have sparked interest in finding out more about groups and schools of thought that western philosophers have often ignored or dismissed.

Women have always participated in philosophical debates, yet their contributions are rarely mentioned in surveys of the history of philosophy. Take this chapter, for example. So far, all the philosophers mentioned have been men. Is this coincidence? Is it because only men have been great thinkers? Is it because social attitudes often played down the importance of

IDEAS IN CONTEXT

Pythagoras, a Greek philosopher who predated Plato, may be most famous for the Pythagorean theorem, but this is not his only claim to fame. He is also known as the first feminist philosopher. In the sixth century BCE, men dominated Greek society. Women had few rights and were rarely educated. Yet Pythagoras welcomed them at his school and encouraged them to investigate scientific and philosophical questions. His own theories were often influenced by women. Among Pythagoras's best-known students were his wife, Theano, and his daughters, as well as Themistoclea, who is often identified as the first woman philosopher.

women's contribution to the debates of the day or discouraged women from participating at all? Or are there other reasons?

When answering these questions, philosophers have taken a variety of approaches. Some have focused on combing the historical record to discover women whose contributions have been minimized. Others have wondered whether women and men view the world in different ways. Still others have focused on arguing that traditional western epistemology is sexist because it associates reason with men and emotion with women — and accepts without question that reason is superior to emotion. Those who engage in exploring whether women's way of knowing the world is different from men's are often called feminist epistemologists.

Feminist epistemologists do not necessarily discount the importance of reason in developing a theory of knowledge. Some do argue, however, that concrete experience, common sense, emotion, and intuition play a more central role in women's ideas about knowledge than in men's. As a result, they say that women and men have different ideas about what constitutes sufficient and proper justification for making knowledge claims, and they maintain that it is important to strike a balance between the two points of view.

The difference between objective and subjective claims to knowledge can be illustrated by the case of a woman who claims to have been physically abused. A police officer and a therapist would respond differently to this claim.

Web connection
www.mcgrawhill.ca/links/philosophy12
To find out more about early Greek women philosophers, follow the links on this Web site.

Because a police officer's job is to investigate the claim of abuse, she must examine the facts to make a decision about laying charges that can be proven in court. Her interest would be legal. As a result, her questions would focus on what happened. Who abused you? Where did the abuse take place? How did it happen? Were there witnesses? A police officer might photograph the victim's injuries and gather other physical evidence pointing to the guilt of the abuser. Though the police officer might be sensitive to the woman's feelings, feelings would not play an important role in the investigation.

A therapist would take a different approach. Because he is not an investigator, he would have little interest in what really happened or in gathering objective evidence proving the identity of the abuser or even that the abuse took place. His job is to help the woman cope with her feelings about what happened so that she can function effectively. As a result, his questions would focus on her feelings, not on the facts of the case. Did she feel powerless? Did she feel fear? Did she feel that she was somehow responsible for the abuse?

The police officer's interest is objective: gathering evidence to build a legal case proving that abuse has occurred. Her knowledge of the case is grounded in reason. The therapist's interest is subjective: dealing with the woman's feelings, regardless of whether abuse can be proven in court. His knowledge is grounded in emotion. Some philosophers have suggested that the police officer's objective point of view represents a masculine perspective, while the therapist's subjective view represents a feminine perspective. Other philosophers have taken issue with this interpretation, arguing that these differences are not rooted in gender.

The introduction of the idea of subjectivity to the debate about knowledge has also prompted contemporary philosophers to explore how similar debates have unfolded in other cultures. Some philosophers are now specializing in fields such as African, eastern, and Aboriginal epistemology. Their work has highlighted the importance of examining ideas from all cultures.

Chapter Review

Chapter Summary

This chapter has discussed
- some of the main questions, concepts, and theories of epistemology
- the strengths and weaknesses of some of the responses of philosophers to some of the main questions, concepts, and theories of epistemology
- how epistemologists have tried to define knowledge

Knowledge and Understanding

1. Identify and explain the significance to the study of epistemology of the following key words and key people.

Key Words	Key People
rationalists	Kongfuzi
empiricists	Plato
a priori knowledge	Aristotle
a posteriori knowledge	René Descartes
justified true belief	Immanuel Kant
direct knowledge	Socrates
indirect knowledge	Bertrand Russell
knowledge by acquaintance	Edmund Gettier
knowledge by description	
competence knowledge	
propositional knowledge	

2. On a two-circle Venn diagram, group the philosophers introduced in this chapter according to whether they are rationalists or empiricists. After completing the diagram, select one philosopher and explain his or her influence on the development of rationalism or empiricism.

Thinking and Inquiry

3. In *Phaedo*, Plato said: "It seems that so long as we are alive, we shall continue closest to knowledge if we avoid as much as we can all contact and association with the body, except when they are absolutely necessary, and instead of allowing ourselves to become infected with its nature, purify ourselves from it until God himself gives us deliverance." In this excerpt, Plato is responding to the philosophical question, Can humans know the world as it really is? Evaluate the strengths and weaknesses of his statement.

4. Can anyone possess knowledge that is universal? Does knowledge depend on culture, race, sex, or social, moral, or political considerations? Consider the knowledge you possess. Respond to these questions in the form of a personal philosophical reflection. Be sure to defend your ideas logically and critically.

Communication

5. Because you wish to become a therapist dealing in cases of physical, emotional, and psychological abuse, you plan to study psychology at university. With your entrance application, you are required to include a formal report on the kinds of knowledge that are most reliable. Write the report that you would include with your application. Be sure to use the proper format for report writing.

6. You have recently been hired to help a university philosophy department create a marketing poster that promotes the study of epistemology. Create a poster that includes visuals, symbols, and quotations to illustrate what epistemology is all about. Be sure to include a slogan or title that captures the essence of the study of epistemology.

Application

7. Read the following excerpt from Jeffrey Hopkins' book, *Cultivating Compassion*. Hopkins is a professor of Tibetan Buddhist studies at the University of Virginia.

   > Because we [in the West] are so reliant on the medium of sight, we see persons in categories such as black, white, yellow, and red. In Tibetan monastic education, one of the first things that young monastics are asked in the debating courtyards is: "Is a white horse white?" The proper answer is, "No, the colour of a white horse is white." A horse, like a human, is a being, and beings are not colours. Colours are material. Persons are not material. Persons are designated in dependence upon mind and body, but they are neither mind nor body, nor a collective of mind and body.

   How does Hopkins' account of Tibetan teachings challenge western epistemological theories?

8. Playing the role of either a rationalist or an empiricist, prepare five questions that you would ask René Descartes about the differences between his theory of rationalism and that of Plato. Then assume the role of Descartes and respond to the questions.

Chapter 10
Theories and Methods of Epistemology

Chapter Expectations

By the end of this chapter, you will be able to
- demonstrate an understanding of some of the main questions of epistemology
- evaluate the strengths and weaknesses of the responses of some of the major philosophers and major schools of epistemology to some of the main epistemological questions
- formulate your own ideas about some of the main questions of epistemology and explain and defend these ideas in philosophical exchanges with others
- describe instances in which philosophical problems of knowledge that occur in everyday contexts can be clarified and analyzed using philosophical theories of epistemology
- compare the problems, principles, methods, and conclusions of various philosophers
- describe how the ideas of philosophers have influenced subsequent philosophers

Key Words

skepticism
deductive reasoning
linguistics
inductive reasoning
causality
anti-foundationalism
pragmatism
deconstructionism
edifying

Key People

Thomas Nagel
Pyrrho of Elis
Nagarjuna
Noam Chomsky
Thomas Aquinas
John Locke
David Hume
Jacques Derrida
Richard Rorty

A Philosopher's Voice

Knowledge is the conformity of the object and the intellect.

Averroës (c.1126–1198)

DOES KNOWING BEGIN WITH DOUBT?

Epistemology is about understanding how things can be known — and whether they can be known at all. Because of this, doubt plays an important role in many theories of epistemology.

In his book *What Does It All Mean?* the contemporary American philosopher **Thomas Nagel** showed how doubt can challenge people's understanding of what is real. Suppose, for example, that you and a friend are seated in a restaurant eating chocolate ice cream, something you both enjoy. How do you know that your friend is experiencing the same taste as you? Here are two ways you might find out.

- You could taste your friend's ice cream. This way, you will know that it tastes the same as yours. But will you really know this? Or will tasting your friend's ice cream prove only that it tastes the same to *you* as your ice cream?
- You could blindfold yourselves and ask a third person to present you both with various flavours of ice cream, including chocolate. If the two of you correctly identify the chocolate ice cream, you will know that you are both tasting the same thing. But again, will you really know this? Or will this experiment merely prove that each of your taste experiences correlates to what each of you identify as chocolate? What is chocolate to you could be potato dumpling to your friend.

Nagel took questions like these a step farther. Why even assume that your friend tastes food? he asked. Perhaps your friend's taste sensation is something that you have never even experienced or imagined. Perhaps your friend "hears" tastes, the way you hear music. How do you know whether your friend is having a taste experience at all? If you continue asking questions like these, you might eventually conclude that nothing is real except your own direct experience of the world, said Nagel. "Maybe your relatives, your neighbours, your cat and your dog have no inner experiences whatever," he wrote. "If they don't, there is no way you could even find out."

SKEPTICISM

Philosophers like Nagel ask questions like these because it is in their nature to be skeptical — to have a questioning attitude. Skeptics doubt all assumptions until they are proven, and some even challenge the idea that knowledge is possible.

Traditionally, philosophers have used **skepticism** as a tool, not as a philosophical position. As a tool, skepticism leads philosophers to question assumptions. In the ice cream example, a skeptical attitude led Nagel to question the assumption that two people taste chocolate ice cream in the same way. The more extreme version of skepticism, which denies that knowledge is even possible, has never been fully accepted in mainstream philosophy. This is because philosophers do try to offer answers, whereas extreme skeptics offer none.

What is more, the extreme version of skepticism — doubting everything — leads to a paradox, or contradiction. If you say that you doubt everything, then you must also doubt your own statement that you doubt everything.

Skepticism flourished in various places in the ancient world: Greece, Egypt, China, and India. **Pyrrho of Elis** was one of the earliest Greek skeptics. Born in about 360 BCE, he taught that nothing can be known. He doubted all knowledge that is derived from the senses and maintained that reason is no help in discovering knowledge because it is based on unreliable knowledge derived from the senses.

> *I know nothing except the fact of my ignorance.*
>
> — Socrates

Furthermore, said Pyrrho, every proposition that seems to be supported by evidence has an opposite proposition that seems to be supported by equally good evidence. You might say, for example, that the sky is blue. Someone else might look at the sky and say the opposite: that it is not blue, but black or grey or, at sunset, red. Pyrrho used this theory of opposites to support his contention that people cannot claim to have knowledge of anything.

At about the same time, similar ideas were advanced by Zhuangzi in China and by Philo in Egypt. Several hundred years later, the Buddhist monk **Nagarjuna**, who was born in 150 CE, drew on skepticism to support the Buddhist idea that denying the desires of the self leads to nirvana or enlightenment. Nothing, including the self, has an independent reality of its own, said Nagarjuna. He maintained that this realization is an important step on the path toward enlightenment.

> **Web connection**
> www.mcgrawhill.ca/links/philosophy12
> To find out more about Nagarjuna, follow the links on this Web site.

During the first century CE, the Greek philosopher Aenesidemus made an important contribution to skepticism. Building on Pyrrho's idea that every proposition has an opposite, Aenesidemus showed that one person can experience both the proposition and its opposite. The same person, for example, can experience the sky as blue during the day and not blue at night. Because people cannot claim to have knowledge, Aenesidemus advised against making judgments at all.

To show that claims to knowledge are unreliable, Aenesidemus proposed 10 arguments, sometimes called modes of doubt.

1. People's feelings and perceptions differ.
2. Physical and mental differences among people make things appear different.
3. Different senses give people different impressions of things.
4. People's perceptions depend on their physical and intellectual condition when something is perceived.
5. Things appear different at different distances and in different positions.
6. People do not perceive things directly. Everything is perceived through a medium (e.g., people see things through air).
7. Variations in the quantity, colour, motion, and temperature of things make them appear different.
8. People perceive familiar and unfamiliar things in different ways.
9. What people call knowledge is based only on the relation of things to other things or to themselves. Knowledge does not tell people what a thing is in itself.
10. People's opinions and customs are different in different countries.

Though skepticism is not considered a school of philosophical thought, it has contributed greatly to philosophical debate. René Descartes was just one of many philosophers who used skepticism as a tool. Today, a skeptical attitude helps people evaluate information. The contemporary British philosopher Roger Scruton noted that skepticism can help people identify "beliefs which are basic to our world view, and whose truth we do not question." By identifying and challenging the grounds for these beliefs, skepticism shows that the beliefs may not be justified.

The next time you tell a friend that you know something, ask yourself why and how you know it. Do you really know it, or is it based on a cherished belief that you have never questioned? You might be surprised at your answer.

THOUGHT EXPERIMENT

The Brain in the Vat

As you were sleeping last night, a team of brilliant — but evil — neuroscientists crept into your room, injected a powerful sedative into your arm, and carried you off to an isolated, top-secret laboratory in Houston, Texas. There, after strapping you to an operating table, surgeons carefully sawed a big hole in the top of your head and removed your brain. After disposing of your body, they transferred your brain to a vat of nutrients and carefully connected up every dangling nerve ending to an electrode. Each electrode was then plugged into a huge computer.

The computer was programmed by a team of psychologists who, unknown to you, had studied you closely for several years. They have extensive knowledge of your behaviour, psychology, neurobiology, and bodily dimensions, as well as your likes and dislikes and your memories and moods. The program they have written enables the computer to send signals to your brain. These signals are exact replicas of the sensory impulses that used to travel back and forth to your brain whenever you saw, smelled, touched, heard, or tasted something with your senses.

After what seems like a long and restful sleep, you wake up. You open your eyes to your bedroom, with its poster-covered walls, magazine-littered floor, and clothes strewn everywhere. You smell burnt toast coming from the kitchen, hear the smoke alarm go off, and figure that one of your annoying siblings has turned the toaster dial way up on the mistaken assumption that this makes it work faster. Moron, you think to yourself. You get dressed, go to school, and meet your friends. Everything's normal, right?

Wrong. You are a brain in a vat. In Texas. Everything seems normal, but it isn't. It's all fake. You don't have arms, legs, hands, hair, or a face. Your body is a lifeless, de-brained hulk in another room of the lab. All your doors of perception — your ears, eyes, nose, tongue, and skin — are permanently shut down. Yet, everything is fake, it's a completely convincing fake. The computer's input to your brain is so true to life that your brain's experiences are nearly indistinguishable from your normal experiences.

So, how do you know that you are not, right now, a brain in a vat in Texas? How can you prove that your life did not take a turn for the worse late last night?

This brain-in-the-vat thought experiment was created by Harvard University philosopher Hilary Putnam. Just as Descartes created his evil-genius argument, Putnam invented this experiment to refute radical skepticism. As a brain in a vat, he wrote, you would not be connected to the real world in the way you think you are. None of the words you use would actually refer to things in the real world; they would only *seem* to refer. And none of your thoughts would actually represent things in the real world; they would only *seem* to represent. They would not be causally connected with the world in the right way.

Think about what might happen if the programmers decide to introduce you to some local Texas cuisine by programming the computer to give you the experience of tasting red hot chili peppers for the first time. You line up in your high school cafeteria, order some fries, drown them in a gallon of red hot pepper sauce, and shovel them into your mouth. After the paramedics have revived you, all you can say is, "Hey man, those red hot chili peppers are red hot." But you are a brain in a vat. You were not really in your high school cafeteria. There are no paramedics. You don't have a mouth or a tongue, even though you think you do. The entire episode was stimulated by the electrodes connected to the part of your brain that deals with taste sensations. Putnam's point is that you cannot know that the chili peppers are red hot because you do not know from experience that this is true.

Putnam does not believe that people are brains in vats. Happily, most people do not believe this. But how do you prove it? Whether you are a brain in a vat or a normal

Figure 10.1

embodied person (a brain in a body), Putnam argued that the statement "I am a brain in a vat" would always be false.

If you were to say as a normal embodied person, "I am a brain in a vat," you would be wrong, or at least seriously deluded. But if you really were a brain in a vat and you said, "I am a brain in a vat, and proud of it," your statement would be false because the words you utter are not real words. They are nothing but vat words, a jumble of computer-generated electrical impulses. Your words would not refer to actual objects in the real world, such as brains and vats. They would not refer to what they seem to refer to.

Try putting this another way. If I am a brain in a vat, then I cannot think that I am a brain in a vat or refer to myself as one; but I can think that I am a brain in a vat; therefore, I am not a brain in a vat.

THE BASIS OF KNOWING

Plato, Aristotle, Descartes, and Immanuel Kant were some of the philosophers who helped shape western approaches to epistemology. Until relatively recently, western epistemologists could be divided into two main groups: the rationalists, who date back to Plato, and the empiricists, whose ideas are rooted in Aristotle's thought. For two millennia, the views of rationalists and empiricists were considered irreconcilable. In the 18th century, however, Immanuel Kant tried to bridge the gap between them. In the centuries after Kant, new schools of philosophy began to emerge and question the epistemological traditions of western philosophy.

REASON AS A BASIS OF KNOWING

Theories of knowing are called rationalistic when they claim that true knowledge can be acquired by reason alone. Rationalists argue that sensory experience is not a reliable source of knowledge because the sensory world can deceive. Have you ever failed to recognize someone you know well, for example? Perhaps that person had grown a beard, put on weight, or changed hairstyles. If challenged, you might maintain that you know Hakim or Janice or Paul. But if you relied on your senses alone, how could you make this claim? After all, you failed to recognize a friend!

Rationalists believe that there is a much more reliable source of knowledge than the senses. This is rational thought, or reason.

PLATO

Plato believed in the existence of two worlds: the visible, imperfect world of the senses, sometimes called the material world, and the invisible, perfect world of forms or innate ideas. This belief laid the groundwork for the rationalist approach. Plato observed that the visible, material world of the senses changes constantly. The water in a lake may be warm today, for example, but cold tomorrow. In Plato's view, this meant that the material world can never be known. As a result, he concluded that it is less real than the invisible world of forms.

The world of forms is the truest reality, said Plato. This world can be known because it is innate: it already exists within the human mind. No one has seen the perfect rock

Figure 10.2

World of Senses	World of Forms
Visible	Invisible
Material	Immaterial
Changing	Unchanging
Particular	Universal
Accessible through the senses	Accessible through reason

In Plato's view, five qualities distinguish the world of the senses from the world of forms.

concert, for example, but some people claim to know what a perfect rock concert is. Plato might argue that a form for the perfect rock concert exists in people's minds, and that this form is used to judge all other performances. Plato believed that humans perceive everything in the world according to its form, which is innate in the mind. Everyone's mind holds a form for material objects, such as chairs and trees, as well as for concepts, such as justice and beauty. Plato did not believe that the form is part of the thing. The form is separate, he said. It exists in a perfect, invisible universe known only to the mind.

Plato wrote 25 dialogues in which he featured his teacher Socrates as a main character. In *Meno*, Plato portrays Socrates in conversation with a young boy, a slave with no experience of mathematics. Plato's goal is to show that the boy already possesses the knowledge necessary to solve the problem but has forgotten it. Socrates' task is to draw forward the boy's forgotten knowledge. Here is the problem Socrates posed.

Square A has four 2.54 cm sides. Square B is double the area of Square A. How long is each side of Square B?

At first, the boy incorrectly guesses that the sides are 5.08 cm long. However, through careful questioning, Socrates leads him to see that this would result in a square with an area four times greater than the area of the first square. By continuing to question and criticize, Socrates finally guides the boy to the correct answer: each side of Square B is the length of the diagonal of Square A.

In relaying this anecdote to a companion, Socrates underscored the idea that the boy had never studied geometry. Therefore, he concluded, the boy's knowledge must be a kind of recollection.

Socrates: But if he always possessed this knowledge he would always have known; or if he has acquired the knowledge he could not have acquired it in this life, unless he has been taught geometry; for he may be made to do the same with all geometry and every other branch of knowledge. Now, has any one ever taught him all this? You must know about him, if, as you say he was born and bred in your house.

Meno: And I am certain that no one ever did teach him.

Socrates: And yet he has the knowledge?

Meno: The fact, Socrates, is undeniable.

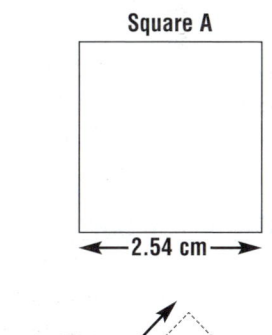

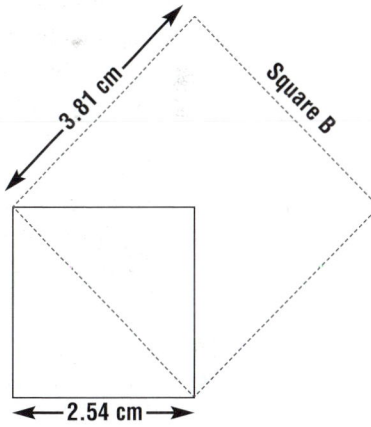

In Plato's view, people embark on an intellectual journey that involves moving from dreaming and imagining, to believing, to thinking, and finally, to true knowing. As suggested in his "Allegory of the Cave," this journey involves finding true knowledge by climbing upward by stages that involve increasingly reliable varieties of knowing. At each stage of the journey, people must question their assumptions. Only centuries after Plato lived was this questioning identified as skepticism.

The first stage of knowing is dreaming and imagining. Plato said that things that are dreamed or imagined are merely images or copies of things and therefore cannot be known.

The next stage involves objects or patterns that can be clearly perceived. Though these provide more reliable information, Plato said that this information still amounts only to beliefs. Instead of saying "That is my car," for example, Plato would encourage you to say, "I believe that that is my car." Of course, you could still act on your belief and drive away in your car!

Plato believed that people move to the next stage of knowing only when they start using their reason to formulate principles or make assumptions. When they do this, they begin to move away from the visible world of sense perception toward the invisible world of forms. A mathematical example illustrates how people cross from one world to the other. Suppose you are looking at a rectangle. When you are asked to calculate its area, you stop focusing on the shape of the rectangle and what it looks like. Instead, you summon up the principle that its area is equal to its length times its width. By knowing this principle, you can support your conclusion about the area of the rectangle.

> **IDEAS IN CONTEXT**
>
> Culture plays a role in determining whether new assumptions are formulated and accepted. In Plato's time, for example, Athens was a class-conscious society where equality was not even contemplated. As a result, Plato not only accepted social divisions, but also promoted them. In his view, workers were to work, and the social elite was to rule. Plato recommended a kind of communal living for people in the elite, however, because he thought that people with money and power should not become too interested in the physical world or physical pleasures. Plato was actually something of an ascetic, a person who abstains from all forms of pleasure. He valued contemplation more highly than recreation.

Every day, people make — and use — assumptions. All cultures, disciplines, faith groups, political parties, and civic organizations hold assumptions about how the world works. These assumptions inevitably lead to certain conclusions. Until the early 20th century in Canada, for example, many people assumed that women were intellectually inferior to men and therefore belonged at home, raising children. These assumptions about the nature of women led to several conclusions.

- Women should not vote.
- Women should not be allowed to enter certain professions.
- Women should not be allowed to hold appointed or elected office.

Then something happened. Women began challenging the underlying assumption that they were intellectually inferior. This sparked people to reconsider this assumption and change their conclusions about what women should — and should not — be allowed to do. By the late 1920s, laws and policies barring Canadian women from voting, entering various professions, and holding office had disappeared. Rather than accepting the old assumptions, women had created new assumptions, which led to a new understanding of women's place in society.

Plato advocated reasoning upward through the stages of knowing to find these new assumptions, which he said are real and can be known. He argued against "thinking down" through the stages to old conclusions. History is full of examples of new assumptions. Nicolaus Copernicus's theory of the solar system, Albert Einstein's theory of relativity, Mohandas Gandhi's revolution based on non-violence, and Bishop Desmond Tutu's advocacy of forgiving oppressors are examples of what happens when thinkers do not accept existing scientific, cultural, and moral assumptions. Plato would say that these people reasoned their way upward to arrive at true knowledge of the forms, the final stage of his intellectual journey.

This diagram illustrates Plato's idea of the stages of people's journey upward to true knowledge.

Plato's Intellectual Journey		
World	**What Is Known**	**Kind of Knowing**
World of the invisible	Forms, universal concepts	Knowing
World of the invisible	Assumptions, relations, concepts	Thinking
World of the visible	Objects perceived by senses	Believing
World of the visible	Images	Imagining and Dreaming

Recall...Reflect...Respond

1. How did Pyrrho of Elis use the idea of opposites to support his theory of skepticism, and how did subsequent philosophers build on this idea?
2. Think about a conversation that led you to discover something you thought you would never understand. Or about a conversation that failed to guide you to an understanding of something. Does this personal experience support or refute Plato's theory of knowledge? Explain how.
3. Plato's theory of knowledge says that using assumptions moves people away from the visible world of the senses and leads to knowing. What assumptions of extreme skeptics led them to conclude that knowledge is not possible? How might Plato argue that this theory does not lead to true knowledge?

RENÉ DESCARTES

Like Plato, the 17th-century French philosopher René Descartes doubted that the senses are an avenue to knowledge and used skepticism as a tool in his quest to discover the difference between believing and knowing. He believed that human experience offers no grounds for believing anything, including that one's own body is real. He used his dream and evil-genius arguments to support this theory. Though Descartes maintained that all claims to knowledge must be open to challenge, he was actually trying to establish a kind of knowledge that could not be challenged.

In the process of doubting everything, Descartes realized that he could not doubt two facts. First, he could not doubt that he was doubting. Second, because he was doubting, there had to be a doubter. He used a form of systematic, orderly thinking called **deductive reasoning** to establish this truth. The term "deductive reasoning" is used because every statement must be deduced, or derived, from a previous statement that is assumed to be true.

Deductive reasoning involves moving from one statement, or premise, to the next in order to arrive at a certainty, something that can be known beyond doubt. Descartes said that all knowledge can be acquired this way. As the diagram on the following page shows, Descartes used deductive reasoning to arrive at his most famous statement of certainty: I think, therefore I am.

IDEAS IN CONTEXT

Descartes's questioning attitude was in some ways a product of his time. Born in 1596, he came of age in the 17th century at a time when ideas that people had accepted for centuries were being challenged. The Protestant followers of Martin Luther were questioning Roman Catholic doctrines. Nicolaus Copernicus had revolutionized the way people thought about the universe by proposing that the earth and planets revolved around the sun. And Galileo Galilei was using the newly invented telescope to introduce scientific ideas that changed the way people thought about the physical world around them.

Descartes's Deductive reasoning			
Statement	I doubt everything.	TRUE
Statement	Doubting everything means that there must be doubting.	TRUE
Statement	If there is doubting, there must be a doubter.	TRUE
Certainty	I doubt, therefore I must exist (I think, therefore I am.)	TRUE

Descartes's beliefs were similar to Plato's in many ways. Both believed that ideas are innate and that people can use their natural ability to reason to discover these ideas. In addition, both started by questioning knowledge acquired through sense perception.

Plato never doubted the existence of the external world, however. Though he believed that the external world changes and that people's perceptions of it are subject to error, he did not deny that the physical world exists. In this respect, Descartes's views differed from those of Plato. Descartes denied the existence of the physical world.

The two also differed in an even more important way. Plato focused on the content of the thought rather than the thinking. Like most ancient Greek philosophers — with the exception of the skeptics — his approach assumed that the external world exists and that the philosopher's role is to try to understand it.

Descartes took the opposite view. He focused on the thinker and the thinking process rather than the content of the thought. He shifted the emphasis of understanding knowledge from content to process. This was his great contribution to western epistemology.

The difference in focus is illustrated by the answers the two philosophers might give to this often-repeated philosophical question: If a tree falls in the forest and no one is around, does it make a noise?

Plato would have answered yes. For him, the external world exists. It does not matter whether anyone is around to perceive it. Descartes, however, would have said no. Because no one is around to hear the tree fall, there is no noise. The external world does not exist outside people's minds.

NOAM CHOMSKY: A CONTEMPORARY RATIONALIST?

The theories of Plato and Descartes, which emphasize reason, are considered the cornerstones of rationalism, which continues to flourish today. The contemporary American philosopher and social critic Noam Chomsky, for example, maintains that the theory of innate ideas helps explain certain mysteries in the field of linguistics, which is the study of the structure of human language.

Language learning is an incredibly complex task, yet Chomsky observed that four-year-olds are capable of producing and recognizing a wide range of sentences that they have not heard before. How do children, regardless of culture, heritage, and geographical location, master language in such a short time?

Chomsky theorizes that children are able to do this because the knowledge of language is hard-wired in humans. In particular, people have an innate ability to comprehend what he calls the deep structure of language. Deep structure is the foundation of language. Very young children show their understanding of deep structure by communicating in ways that can be understood by others. A child who says, "Me go night-night," is an example. Similarly, children can infer meaning from sentences that they have never composed themselves, such as "It's time for you to go to sleep now."

Chomsky refers to the structures of a specific language as surface structure. These include the rules of spelling, phonics, style, grammar, and usage. These, he says, must be learned. An adult who has learned the surface structure of English, for example, would say, "I'm going to bed," not, "Me go night-night." This suggests that a child who says "Me go night-night" is not copying adults. In fact, this kind of misapplied grammar is unique to children.

PHILOSOPHY IN ACTION

Reflections on Language
by Noam Chomsky

In this excerpt from his book *Reflections on Language,* Noam Chomsky explains why he studies language and how the study of language relates to the study of knowledge.

In the excerpt, he claims that children have "relatively slight exposure" to language during their growing years. By this, Chomsky does not mean to imply that children do not hear language; rather, he suggests that they do not hear much formal language. This is because the language they hear is spoken language. When people speak, they often do so in sentence fragments, interrupt themselves and others, and change the subject.

Why study language? There are many possible answers, and by focusing on some I do not, of course, mean to disparage others or question their legitimacy. One may, for example, simply be fascinated by the elements of language in themselves and want to discover their order and arrangement, their origin in history or in the individual, or the ways in which they are used in thought, in science or in art, or in normal social interchange.

One reason for studying language — and for me personally the most compelling reason — is that it is tempting to regard language, in the traditional phrase, as "a mirror of mind." I do not mean by this simply that the concepts expressed and distinctions developed in normal language use give us insight into patterns of thought and the world of "common sense" constructed by the human mind. More intriguing, to me at least, is the possibility that by studying language we may discover abstract principles that govern its structure and use, principles that are universal by biological necessity and not mere historical accident, that derive from mental characteristics of the species.

A human language is a system of remarkable complexity. To come to know a human language would be an extraordinary achievement for a creature not specifically designed to accomplish this task. A normal child acquires this knowledge on relatively slight exposure and without specific training. He can then quite effortlessly make use of an intricate structure of specific rules and guiding principles to convey his thoughts and feelings to others, arousing in them novel ideas and subtle perceptions and judgments. For the conscious mind, not specially designed for the purpose, it remains a distant goal to reconstruct what the child has done intuitively and with minimal effort. Thus language is a mirror of mind in a deep and significant sense. It is a product of human intelligence, created anew in each individual by operations that lie far beyond the reach of will or consciousness.

By studying the properties of natural languages, their structure, organization, and use, we may hope to gain some understanding of the specific characteristics of human intelligence. We may hope to learn something about human nature; something significant, if it is true that human cognitive capacity is the truly distinctive and most remarkable characteristic of the species. Furthermore, it is not unreasonable to suppose that the study of this particular human achievement, the ability to speak and understand a human language, may serve as a suggestive model for inquiry into other domains of human competence and action that are not quite so amenable to direct investigation.

Source: From *Reflections on Language.* Noam Chomsky.

---

1. How does this excerpt demonstrate that Noam Chomsky is a rationalist?
2. Select one idea or statement that supports Plato's theory of knowledge and one that supports Descartes's theory. Explain how each does so.
3. Which theory of knowledge — Plato's or Descartes's — does Chomsky seem to support? Provide evidence of the analysis you conducted to reach this conclusion.

The Senses as a Basis of Knowing

A school of philosophers known as empiricists challenged the rationalists' emphasis on innate ideas, reasoning, and the unreliability of sensory experience as a source of knowledge. Empiricists believe that the mind is a blank slate at birth, though it is ready to understand. People acquire knowledge only as the mind experiences the world through the senses.

Like rationalism, empiricism is a concept usually identified with western philosophical traditions. Philosophers from other traditions advanced similar ideas, however. In first-century China, for example, Wang Chong said that everything people know about the world comes from experiencing it. And in seventh-century India, the Buddhist philosopher Dharmakirti believed that all knowledge comes from sense perception.

ARISTOTLE

The western empiricist tradition originated in the thought of Plato's student Aristotle, who challenged his teacher's theory of knowledge. Much more interested in the physical world than Plato, Aristotle believed that this is made up of matter, which can be sensed, and the immaterial essence of matter, which cannot. Unlike Plato, Aristotle believed that a thing's immaterial essence is bound up with its matter. It is not separate from it. Though Plato located his forms in another world, Aristotle placed the essence of things in themselves.

Take a rock, for example. Plato believed that it exists in two separate worlds: the world of the senses and the world of ideas or forms. Aristotle believed that both matter and essence are present in the rock.

Though he believed that sense perceptions are important, Aristotle also believed in the importance of reason. He focused on **inductive reasoning**, however. Inductive reasoning involves observing particular things, then using the particular observations to make a generalization. A generalization is a general notion inferred from particular observations. Unlike deductive reasoning, which moves from the general to the particular, inductive reasoning moves from the particular to the general.

When you were a child, for example, you probably learned to distinguish cats from dogs by observing the characteristics of each. At first, you might have observed that both cats and dogs have fur, four legs, and a tail. But you probably also observed differences. Dogs are usually bigger than cats, their eyes and faces are different, and they move differently. They also make different noises. Dogs bark and cats meow. Once you have observed the particular characteristics of each, you might make a generalization about the differences between cats and dogs.

Plato believed that the world of objects perceived by the senses is a poor copy of the abstract world of forms. Aristotle, by contrast, believed that the abstract world is based on the world of objects perceived by the senses. He did not

Figure 10.3

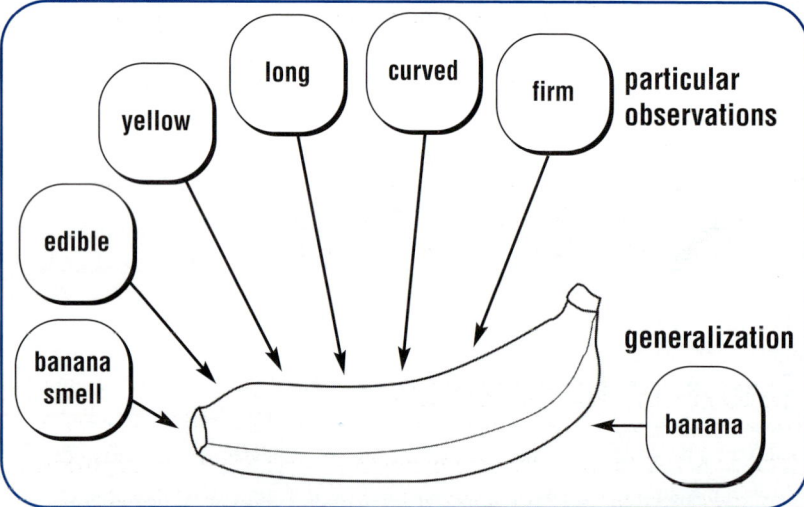

People use inductive reasoning every day to make generalizations and draw conclusions. How might you use inductive reasoning today?

believe that people are born with innate ideas that they recollect to identify, for example, a man, woman, dog, or cat. He believed that people experience individual qualities, then reason inductively to form an abstract idea of these things.

Sense experience and inductive reasoning are the foundations of Aristotle's theory of knowledge. In his view, sense perception without reasoning cannot uncover the essence of things.

THOMAS AQUINAS

Over the centuries that the Romans dominated most of Europe and during the early Middle Ages, Aristotle's ideas were nearly forgotten. They were kept alive largely through the efforts of Muslim scholars and philosophers such as Avicenna and Averroës, who wrote commentaries on them. These commentaries came to the attention of **Thomas Aquinas**, a 13th-century Dominican monk who refocused the attention of European philosophers on the teachings of Aristotle.

Like Aristotle, Aquinas rejected Plato's idea that a world of forms exists separately from the physical world. Aquinas insisted that both matter and essence are bound up in physical objects. He viewed human beings, for example, as the union of soul and body, or matter and form.

Though Aquinas believed that knowledge begins with sense perception, he also said that knowledge can grow beyond the sensory world when reason is applied to sensory experience. Like Aristotle, he believed in using inductive reasoning to arrive at generalizations or universals. Unlike Aristotle, however, Aquinas was operating within a distinctly Christian framework, and he believed that the world is orderly and intelligible, or able to be understood, because it reflects the nature of God.

At the time, Aquinas's endorsement of the material world was fairly radical. It meant, for example, that he stood firmly behind scientific inquiry in an era when few people dared challenge the fixed ideas about the world that were sanctioned by the Roman Catholic Church, which dominated Europe. Aquinas's belief in the material world laid the groundwork for the empiricist movement that would develop several hundred years later.

Recall...Reflect...Respond

1. Both Plato and René Descartes used skepticism to develop their theories of knowledge. For which philosopher was it a more important tool? Explain why you think so.
2. Write two statements that show the difference between the surface structure and the deep structure of language.
3. With a partner, list the things you know about your classroom (e.g., location, structure, appearance, atmosphere, etc.). Describe how you obtained each item of knowledge. Is your acquisition of knowledge about your classroom more consistent with the rationalist or empiricist view? Explain why.

MODERN EMPIRICISM: THE CHALLENGE TO RATIONALISM

Though Aristotle and Aquinas laid the foundations for empiricist epistemology, their theories were later challenged by the rationalist interpretation of Descartes. For several decades, Descartes's view of knowledge prevailed — until it was questioned by **John Locke, David Hume**, and other philosophers who are credited with founding modern empiricism.

PROFILE

Thomas Aquinas
The Dumb Ox

By the time he was 20 years old, Thomas Aquinas had decided to join the Dominican Order of monks. The decision outraged his wealthy Italian family. His mother Theodora, Countess of Teano, did not object to her son's taking religious vows, but her hope was that he would become the abbot, or leader, of a monastery.

In the 13th century, monasteries were centres of wealth, and becoming an abbot was often a ticket to personal riches. This was Theodora's ambition for her son. The Dominican Order had formed in reaction to this worldly focus. Dominicans took vows of poverty and devoted themselves to teaching and preaching.

Aquinas's mother was so alarmed by her son's decision that she ordered his brothers, who were soldiers, to kidnap him. Family members kept him captive in a fortress for nearly two years while they tried to persuade him to change his mind. When nothing worked, he was set free and immediately joined the Dominicans.

According to the custom of the time, Aquinas had begun his education when he was five years old. He was sent to study with the Benedictine monks at Monte Cassino, a monastery near Rome. A serious child, he asked difficult questions, learned quickly, and displayed a prodigious memory. Many years later, a colleague said that Aquinas remembered everything he had read, so that his mind was like a huge library.

Aquinas's talents were certainly noticed by his teachers. In 1236, when he was only 11, they decided that he should not be left in obscurity and advised his delighted family that he was intellectually ready to attend the University of Naples.

At Naples, Aquinas studied the standard subjects: logic and rhetoric, the natural sciences, music, math, geometry, and astronomy. Because he was heavyset and quiet, his fellow students nicknamed him the dumb ox. While in Naples, Aquinas formed his determination to join the Dominicans.

After leaving his family's prison, Aquinas travelled to Paris and later to Cologne in present-day Germany. While in Cologne, he was raised to the priesthood. By 1250, he had returned to teach at the University of Paris, and there he received a degree in theology.

As a Dominican, Aquinas devoted his life to teaching, preaching, writing, and praying. He was a student of Aristotle and also admired the Muslim scholars Avicenna and Averroës, who had renewed interest in the works of the ancient Greeks. A prolific writer, he composed more than 60 works, though not all were written in his own hand. He was given assistants, and he would often dictate to several scribes at the same time.

Aquinas's most famous work is the *Summa Theologica*, in which he used the methods of Plato and Aristotle — reason and abstraction — to explain the Christian faith. At about the same time, the pope appointed him archbishop of Naples. Certain that his calling was write the *Summa*, Aquinas knew that he would be unable to write and carry out the duties of an archbishop. He begged to be excused from the appointment. When the pope agreed, Aquinas turned his attention to writing his masterwork. Though Aquinas himself viewed the *Summa* as nothing more than a manual of Christian doctrine compiled for the use of his students, others hailed it as a reasoned summary of Christian theology and philosophy.

In the largely Roman Catholic Europe of the 13th century, Aquinas was constantly in demand as a teacher and adviser. Though he died in 1274, his influence lives on. On the Internet today, there is even a Thomistic humour page and an Aquinas Café.

Figure 10.4

After his death, Thomas Aquinas was declared a saint by the Roman Catholic Church. In this illustration, created long after his death, his status as a saint is indicated by the halo around his head.

JOHN LOCKE

By the time the English philosopher John Locke was born in 1632, René Descartes was already making his name as a rationalist thinker. Rejecting Descartes's rationalism, which drew heavily on Plato's theories, Locke sought out the ideas of Plato's student Aristotle. In the process, Locke launched a school of thought that is often called the British empiricist movement.

Like Aristotle, Locke believed that the mind is a blank slate at birth and that the senses play an important role in acquiring knowledge and thus writing on that slate. He set out his rejection of the theory of innate ideas in *An Essay Concerning Human Understanding*:

> Let us then suppose the mind to be … white paper, void of all characters, without any ideas: — How comes it to be furnished? Whence comes it by that vast store which the busy and boundless fancy of man has painted on it with almost endless variety? Whence has it all the materials of reason and knowledge? To this I answer, in one word, from experience. In that all our knowledge is founded.

Locke said that people taste, smell, touch, see, and hear the external world. He used the term "sensation" to describe this experience of the world. This sensation produces an impression in the mind. The mind mulls over these impressions, a process he called reflection. Reflection produces an idea.

Web connection
www.mcgrawhill.ca/links/philosophy12
To read more of Locke's *Essay Concerning Human Understanding*, follow the links on this Web site.

If you accidentally place your hand on a hot stove burner, for example, you experience a sensation. This sensation forms an impression in your mind. Your mind reflects upon this impression and produces an idea. In this case, the idea might be called "Hot!"

Locke also believed that ideas are either simple or complex. A simple idea, such as "hot," is created by a simple sensation, such as the heat of a stove burner. A complex idea, however, is created by combining simple sensations and impressions. Imagine that you are examining a tomato in your kitchen. This tomato would provide several simple sensations, including colour (red), texture (firm), taste (sweetish), and shape (round). Combining and reflecting on these simple sensations would create a complex idea. In this case, the idea would be "tomato."

If all knowledge arises from sense experience, how did Locke explain non-material ideas such as a supreme being or infinity? For Locke, the answer was simple. These ideas may be created by the imagination, but they originate in simple sensations. For example, if you claimed to have seen a unicorn, Locke would say that you produced this complex idea by combining several simple impressions: horn of a narwhale, body of a horse, tail of a lion, beard of a goat, and legs of a deer. Each characteristic of the unicorn can be traced to a simple sensation.

Locke was aware of the skeptics' arguments that people sense things in different ways and that the accuracy of sensations can be questioned. As a result, he suggested that all matter has both primary and secondary qualities. Primary qualities are characteristics that are objective, such as height and weight. These characteristics convey facts. They exist in the thing itself,

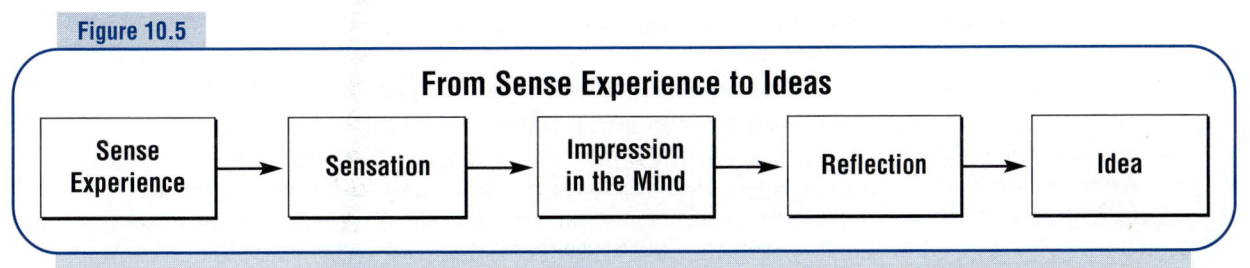

Figure 10.5

From Sense Experience to Ideas

Sense Experience → Sensation → Impression in the Mind → Reflection → Idea

This diagram shows how Locke's theory of knowledge links sense experiences to ideas. Do you think that Locke's ideas make sense?

can be determined with certainty, and do not rely on subjective judgments. If you weigh 75 kilograms, for example, no one can reasonably say that you weigh 25 kilograms. Or if a ball is round, no one can reasonably say that it is a triangle.

Secondary qualities, by contrast, do rely on subjective, or personal, judgments. They can be described as the effect things have on individual people. Colour, taste, and sound are secondary qualities. If you bite into a lemon, for example, and say that it's sour, you are describing your idea of sourness. A friend might do the same thing and describe the lemon's taste as tangy or refreshing. Locke would deny that you and your friend are contradicting each other because secondary qualities are subjective: they depend on the perceiver. Knowledge that comes from secondary qualities does not provide objective facts about things.

DAVID HUME

Born in 1711, a few years after Locke died, the Scottish philosopher David Hume shared his predecessor's interest in creating a theory of knowledge that was practical, straightforward, and clear. Neither Locke nor Hume placed any faith in the theory of innate ideas. This theory is the basis of rationalist thought. If knowledge could not be located in the everyday world of the senses, they disregarded it. Their goal was to demonstrate that ideas are a product of sense perception.

Though Hume adopted Locke's theory of impressions and ideas, he refined it somewhat. Locke believed that impressions come from the senses and that ideas come from reflecting on impressions. Hume proposed that impressions are livelier than ideas. For example, when you put your hand on a hot stove, the impression of hot is livelier than the idea of hot that you have when you relate the story several months later. At the same time, Hume realized that there might be exceptions to this theory, such as nightmares. He acknowledged that a nightmare about an event that happened years earlier can seem even livelier than the event itself!

Hume's most intriguing contribution to the theory of knowledge, however, was his challenge of the idea of **causality**. Causality refers to the cause-and-effect relationship between events. Imagine what would happen if you pushed your sandwich off the edge of the cafeteria table.

> Cause: You push your sandwich off the edge of the cafeteria table.
> Effect: Your sandwich drops to the floor.

Most thinkers agree that causality enables humans to reason beyond their sense impressions and explain the way the world works. You are hungry, so you eat; you water the plants, so they grow; and you want to stay fit, so you exercise.

Hume disputed this notion of causal connections. Because causality is not one of the sensations experienced by the senses, he questioned its existence. Though he believed that people embrace the idea of causality only because it helps them make sense of the world, he maintained that no one can prove that causality exists.

Hume used the example of billiard balls to support this claim. When Billiard Ball A rolls and strikes Billiard Ball B, Ball B starts to roll. This leads people to conclude that Ball A caused Ball B to move. Hume questioned this conclusion. He would not accept as proof the fact that Ball B always moves when it is struck by Ball A. Just because something always happened in the past does not mean that it will always happen in the future, he said.

Hume said that when people experience two events that are connected in space and time, they assume a causal connection between the two. This connection is realized after the second event — the effect — occurs. And when people see certain events linked over and over again, they begin to expect Event B to follow Event A. Hume dismissed this expectation as custom or habit and

> *I assert that nothing ever comes to pass without a cause.*
>
> – Jonathan Edwards

denied that it proved the existence of a causal connection between the two events. Any causal connection, he said, is a figment of the human imagination.

Hume's denial of the concept of causality showed his deep skepticism of anything that cannot be perceived by the senses. Not since the ancients had a philosopher been so enthusiastically doubtful of theories that explain why things happen or how people know they happen. His argument also challenged scientific knowledge, much of which is based on observing cause-and-effect relationships. If Hume was correct, this scientific knowledge was unjustified.

BRIDGING THE GAP BETWEEN RATIONALISM AND EMPIRICISM

As a student, the 18th-century German philosopher Immanuel Kant had been schooled in Descartes's theories of reason and logic. When Kant came across Hume's skeptical philosophy, he described the experience as like waking up from a "dogmatic slumber." After reading Hume, he began to see empiricism in a new light — and he set out to show that both reason and the senses can be sources of knowledge.

Kant divided knowledge into two categories: a posteriori and a priori. He thought that a posteriori knowledge comes from sense experience. The sky is blue, the stove is hot, and William is tall are statements that express a posteriori knowledge.

At the same time, he believed in the existence of a priori knowledge, knowledge that is independent of the senses. The source of a priori knowledge is the human mind, which organizes and unifies a posteriori knowledge according to certain innate concepts.

> There can be in us ... no connection or unifying of one bit of knowledge with another, unless there is a unified consciousness which precedes all the data of perception.
> – Immanuel Kant

Kant classified these concepts into 12 categories, the most important of which is causality. In Kant's view, the mind is programmed to impose causality on events experienced by the senses. Though people are not able to see causality because it is a relationship between objects rather than the objects themselves, he maintained that causality exists in the world because the human mind puts it in the world.

This view means that the external world may be quite different from the way people perceive it, something that Kant acknowledged. He said that people can never know what this external world is really like.

Until Kant proposed this theory, rationalists had emphasized the importance of reason as a source of knowledge and assigned sense experience a lesser role. Empiricists, by contrast, had emphasized the importance of sense experience. They either assigned reason a lesser role or dismissed it completely. Kant's theory tried to bridge the gap between the two schools of thought by emphasizing the importance of both the senses and reason.

Kant's theory freed philosophers to move beyond their pigeonholes. No longer were they defined as either rationalists or empiricists. This broadened the scope of epistemological study and enabled philosophers to propose new theories of knowledge.

Recall...Reflect...Respond

1. Are there some things that humans can never know? This is one of the main questions of epistemology. How does Hume's theory of knowledge answer this question?
2. Describe a personal experience in which you arrived at an understanding of an idea. Explain how Locke would have described the process you went through. Do you think his explanation described your experience accurately? Explain why.
3. Create a list of characteristics of traditional views of epistemology. For each characteristic, name an epistemological theory that supports the characteristic.

CONTEMPORARY EPISTEMOLOGY

Until the 19th century, traditional western epistemologists had assumed that there is a world to be understood, if only people could figure out a way of doing this. In the late 1800s, however, some philosophers began to question this approach. Their approach is sometimes called **anti-foundationalism** because it freed them from the idea that all knowledge must rest on a foundation of reality.

PRAGMATISM

One version of anti-foundationalism is **pragmatism**, a movement that developed in the United States as a reaction against traditional epistemology. The term "pragmatism" means valuing the practical and the useful. Pragmatists argue that people should believe only things that are useful to them. The leading pragmatists were John Dewey, who lived from 1859 to1952, William James, who lived from 1842 to 1910, and Charles Peirce, who lived from 1839 to1914.

Like skepticism, pragmatism is more a philosophical position or approach than a school of thought. Traditional epistemologists begin their investigations by trying to identify principles. They look for reality, which they believe to be a single thing. This approach is called monism, a term that comes from the Greek word *monos*, which means single or alone.

> *We only think when we are confronted with a problem.*
> – John Dewey

Pragmatists sidestep the debate about the nature of knowing. They believe that reality is not a single thing. This approach is called pluralism. Whereas traditional thinkers accept only their own philosophy of being and knowing, pragmatists are willing to accept different philosophies. They ask, What practical difference does it make if there are forms or essences, fixed principles, or many principles? They believe that truth changes as people change and that human conduct is a more important issue.

Pragmatists believe that the meaning of an idea is identical to its effects. So, for example, if believing in a supreme being results in peace and harmony in the world and this effect is valued by most people, then this effect is the definition of a supreme being. In his book *Philosophy in the Twentieth Century*, James explained it this way:

> To attain perfect clearness in our thoughts of an object ... we need only consider what conceivable effects of a practical kind the object may involve. What sensations we are to expect from it, and what reactions we must prepare. Our conceptions of these effects whether immediate or remote, is then for us the whole of our conception of that object.

Though pragmatism has never been considered a major school of epistemology, it is considered a useful tool for supporting the way people think about the needs, goals, and values of human beings. The pragmatists' claims that there is no fixed reality and that the truth can be modified helped pave the way for some of philosophical movements of the 20th century.

DECONSTRUCTIONISM

Deconstructionism is another form of anti-foundationalism. Founded in the late 1960s by the Algerian-born French philosopher **Jacques Derrida**, deconstructionism, like pragmatism, challenged traditional western ways of thinking.

Through a process called deconstruction, which means taking apart, Derrida tried to show that the meaning expressed by language is not stable. In his view, the meaning intended by a writer is never the same as the meaning assumed by a reader. Even a writer who uses a particular word to convey a certain meaning on one occasion may use the same word to convey a different meaning at a different time.

Suppose you said, "I see a dog." The word "dog" can mean many different things. The person to whom you are speaking might suppose that you mean a canine. The same person might also suppose that you mean a despicable man or youth, or a sausage, or something worthless, or something that represents any of the other meanings of the word "dog." Even if both you and your listener assume that you mean a canine, the word may still conjure up many different images. Included in these images may be completely different perceptions of dogs. One of you may perceive dogs as friendly creatures, for example, while the other perceives them as animals to be feared.

For these reasons, deconstructionists maintain that language cannot be trusted. There is no such thing as the pure transfer of a writer's meaning to a reader because language always gets in the way of thought. As a result, say deconstructionists, there can be no certainty.

> **THE Lighter SIDE OF PHILOSOPHY**
>
> **How many deconstructionists does it take to change a light bulb?**
>
> On the contrary, Ottawa is the capital of Canada.

Web connection
www.mcgrawhill.ca/links/philosophy12
To find out how to use deconstructionism to impress your friends, follow the links on this Web site.

EDIFYING

The contemporary American philosopher **Richard Rorty** is an anti-foundationalist who is interested in both pragmatism and deconstructionism. He says that there is no objective world and no inner essence that can be known.

Traditional philosophers attempted to build monistic systems to explain reality. Rorty advocates replacing traditional ideas of system building with what he calls **edifying**. For Rorty, edifying means redefining the world over and over again in order to make it work better. In his book *Philosophy and the Mirror of Nature*, he wrote:

> Edifying philosophers want to keep space open for the sense of wonder which poets can sometimes cause — wonder that there is something new under the sun. Something which is not an accurate representation of what was already there, something which … cannot be explained and can barely be described.

Rorty also claims that people use language and create meaning according to their place in history and society. Scientists, for example, may use one kind of language, while animal-rights activists may use another. Both groups use language to justify their actions, though one group may speak of what is "verifiable" while the other may speak of what is "ethical." Once people believe that the language they are using is the only correct one, says Rorty, they become like system builders. He implores people to remain open to new meanings of language and attitudes and to be tolerant of many different ways of understanding the world.

Clearly, modern epistemology is moving in directions that would have been unimaginable to Plato, Aristotle, Descartes, or even Kant. One interesting aspect of contemporary epistemology is its resistance to definitions and fixed principles. But if epistemologists deny the existence of knowledge and truth, can epistemology continue to exist as a discipline? Or is the possibility of many understandings just part of the natural evolution of thinking?

Chapter Review

Chapter Summary

This chapter has discussed
- some of the main questions of epistemology
- the responses of some of the major philosophers and major schools of epistemology to some of the main epistemological questions
- instances in which philosophical problems of knowledge that occur in everyday contexts can be clarified and analyzed using philosophical theories of epistemology
- the problems, principles, methods, and conclusions of various philosophers
- how the ideas of philosophers have influenced subsequent philosophers

Knowledge and Understanding

1. Identify and explain the significance to the study of epistemology of each of the following key words and people.

Key Words	Key People
skepticism	Thomas Nagel
deductive reasoning	Pyrrho of Elis
linguistics	Nagarjuna
inductive reasoning	Noam Chomsky
causality	Thomas Aquinas
anti-foundationalism	John Locke
pragmatism	David Hume
deconstructionism	Jacques Derrida
edifying	Richard Rorty

2. Choose one school of epistemological thought and create a flow chart that illustrates how the ideas of epistemologists influenced one another. Begin by identifying one philosopher and describing this philosopher's main ideas. Show how this philosopher's ideas were revised by later philosophers.

Thinking and Inquiry

3. In his book *Zen Knowledge*, the Japanese Buddhist Daisetz T. Suzuki, who lived from 1870 to 1966, wrote:

   > We can divide knowledge into two categories: intuitive knowledge which is *prajna* whereas discursive knowledge is *vijnana*. To distinguish further: *prajna* grasps reality in its oneness, in its totality; *vijnana* analyzes it into subject and object. Here is a flower; we can take this flower as representing the universe itself. We talk about the petals, pollen, stamen and stalk; that is physical analysis. Or we can analyze it chemically into so much hydrogen, oxygen, etc. Chemists analyze a flower, enumerate all its elements and say that the aggregate of all those elements makes up the flower. But they have not exhausted the flower; they have simply analyzed it. That is the *vijnana* way of understanding a flower. The *prajna* way is to understand it just as it is without analysis or chopping in into pieces. It is to grasp it in its oneness, in its totality, in its suchness (*sono mame*) in Japanese.…The moment grasped by *prajna*-intuition is satori.… To get satori, all things which crowd into our daily life consciousness must be

wiped off clean.... To realize satori is very difficult, as the Buddha found.... [When you realize satori,] then you understand all things and are at peace with the world as well as with yourself.

Create a chart comparing *prajna* and *vijnana* with theories of knowledge advanced by three other schools of epistemological thought.

4. In Canada, eyewitnesses to crimes are expected to tell the truth in court about what they saw. A defence lawyer then challenges the truth of the testimony by cross-examining the witness. From the point of view of one of the epistemologists mentioned in this chapter, write a report supporting or challenging the assumption that this is a good way of arriving at knowledge of what really happened.

Communication

5. Suppose that you are trying to help a friend figure out how people arrive at knowledge. Write the dialogue that might occur between the two of you. Incorporate the thinking of epistemologists whose theories you support.

6. Imagine that film director Steven Spielberg has asked you to create a map for a new Indiana Jones film. The map will guide Jones, who is travelling through India (or another country of your choice) in a quest for the treasure of true knowledge. As befits an adventurer, Jones must encounter challenges along the way. On your map, draw symbols at four spots where Jones will meet these challenges. For each symbol, write two epistemological questions that Jones must answer before continuing his quest.

Application

7. Read this poem, titled "Song of the Earthdream," by Nunya Ageya, an Aboriginal American

> Here,
> under this grass,
> I will soon release my mind
> to travel where it must,
> when, soaring,
> I revisit the Earth-mother.
>
> Here,
> under these roots,
> I will go when my heart walks
> the path of sacred smoke,
> when, wondering,
> I revisit the Earth-mother.
>
> Here,
> under this earth,
> I will learn the Earthdream song
>
> I dance to all my life,
> when, singing,
> I revisit the Earth-mother
>
> Here,
> under these stones,
> I will find the centre of
> the circle my soul walks,
> when, living,
> I revisit the Earth-mother.

What does the poet experience through her senses? In her mind? What knowledge does she bring to her experience? What knowledge does she seek? After reflecting on your answers to these questions, identify the epistemological question that is the theme of this poem.

8. From the perspective of a mathematician or scientist, write a series of questions that refute David Hume's denial of causality. You may wish to consult your math or science teacher.

Chapter 11
Knowledge and Truth

Chapter Expectations

By the end of this chapter, you will be able to
- demonstrate an understanding of the main philosophical questions of epistemology
- evaluate the strengths and weaknesses of the responses of some of the major philosophers and major schools of epistemology to some of the main epistemological questions
- formulate your own ideas about some of the main questions of epistemology and explain and defend these ideas in philosophical exchanges with others
- describe instances in which philosophical problems of knowledge occur in everyday contexts and can be clarified and analyzed using philosophical theories of epistemology
- compare the problems, principles, methods, and conclusions of various philosophers
- describe how the ideas of philosophers have influenced subsequent philosophers

Key Words

truth
common-sense realism
representative theory of perception
subjective idealism
solipsism
phenomenalism
correspondence theory
coherence theory
pragmatic theory
instrumentalism

Key People

Linda Martín Alcoff
Felipe Fernández-Armesto
Daisetsu Teitaro Suzuki
John McGuire
George Berkeley
Roderick M. Chisholm
A.C. Ewing
Georg W.F. Hegel
Charles Peirce
William James
John Dewey
Richard Rorty

A Philosopher's Voice

The man who tells you truth does not exist is asking you not to believe him. So don't.

– Roger Scruton (1944–)

WHAT IS TRUTH?

When Pontius Pilate, the Roman governor who ordered the crucifixion of Jesus Christ, asked, "What is truth?" it is unlikely that he fully appreciated the complexity of his question. Pilate did not wait for an answer, and it is possible that he cared little about the response. For him, the question amounted to nothing more than a way of sidestepping the dilemma he faced.

In everyday discussions, most people accept what are regarded as common-sense, or generally accepted, notions of **truth**. If asked to define truth, for example, you might start by saying that it is the opposite of a lie, then add that a lie is the opposite of truth. A moment's reflection will tell you, however, that this definition is circular and, therefore, not very helpful. If asked to be more precise by explaining how you decide what is true and false, you might say that truth is something that you just know or feel. In other words, many people believe that they grasp truth intuitively.

> *Humanly speaking, let us define truth, while waiting for a better definition, as a statement of facts as they are.*
>
> – Voltaire

Only when you try to define or explain truth to someone else do you realize how difficult the concept really is. This realization would place you in good company. In the western tradition, philosophers since the time of the ancient Greeks have debated the nature of truth. They have discussed issues such as whether it is relative or absolute, whether it is necessarily a positive element in human affairs — and whether there is even such a thing as truth and, if there is, whether it is a subject worth discussing.

In *Epistemology: The Big Questions*, contemporary philosopher **Linda Martín Alcoff** acknowledged the difficulty of pinning down a definition of truth when she wrote,

> Truth is one of the most complex and confusing topics in epistemology. Definitions and concepts of truth are often conflated with accounts of the criteria of truth, and the object of the debate, or what counts as truth itself, proves to be an enigmatic creature.
>
> It may seem odd, but for most epistemologists today truth is a non-issue. In the first place, although truth is a part of most definitions of knowledge, it is usually considered to belong within the provenance of metaphysics rather than epistemology, within the question of what there is rather than how we know. But second, it is often thought not to have even metaphysical interest.

Whether truth is an epistemological or metaphysical issue is debatable, as philosophical issues usually are. But the claim that truth is a non-issue is also highly questionable. Two recently published books, **Felipe Fernández-Armesto**'s *Truth: A History and a Guide for the Perplexed* and Jeremy Campbell's *The Liar's Tale*, indicate continued interest in the subject. What is more, truth is often discussed in philosophy magazines, and a recent issue of *O, The Oprah Magazine* included a splashy feature on truth. The evidence — and evidence is one of the commonly recognized components of truth — indicates that truth continues to interest people. It also seems in no imminent danger of becoming extinct as an issue of philosophical debate, whether this debate is epistemological, metaphysical, or otherwise.

Web connection
www.mcgrawhill.ca/links/philosophy12
To read more about truth, follow the links on this Web site.

Many philosophers also believe that the question of defining truth demands an answer, no matter how tentative it might be. Definitions of truth and the criteria used to distinguish truth from falsehood affect people's philosophical beliefs. More important, the way we conceive of truth shapes our view of ourselves, our relationships, and the world around us, as well as the manner in which we live our lives.

Because philosophy means the love of wisdom, acquiring knowledge is a central feature of philosophical investigation. But knowledge, which is traditionally defined as "justified true belief," is a complex and elusive goal. Of the three concepts — justification, truth, and belief — truth is the most difficult to define.

Through the ages, philosophy, art, religion, and science have, to varying degrees, claimed to possess and dispense truth. Tributes to truth abound in the western tradition. In Plato's world of forms, for example, truth is second only to the good.

"To know the good is to do the good" is a famous statement that Plato attributed to his teacher Socrates. In writing this, Plato was no doubt expressing his own view as well. For him, truth was necessary to know and to do the good. He had an unshakable belief in the existence of unequivocal, objective, and absolute truths, which he believed were an important, positive good in human affairs.

Some philosophers have argued that Plato valued truth too highly, and they have tried to minimize its importance. They have claimed that truth does not deserve its lofty status because it is a pipe dream, or illusion, one that is sometimes negative and dangerous.

In light of divergent beliefs like these, it is not surprising that a universally acceptable definition of truth remains elusive. Perhaps one of the key reasons for this is that so much is at stake.

Many western philosophers have exalted the search for truth as the noblest of activities, maintaining that it is synonymous with philosophy itself. Others, starting with some of Plato's contemporaries, have said that seeking truth is not a praiseworthy pursuit. Some have even argued that lies should be valued as much as, if not more than, truth. Today, many people believe that truth, like reality, is ever changing and cannot be pinned down. They have given up on truth, declaring it either irrelevant or dead.

The debate over the nature of truth is largely a phenomenon of western philosophy, which focuses strongly on opposites, or dualities: good and bad, right and wrong, truth and falsehood. In contrast, some eastern philosophical traditions are more focused on the oneness of reality. Truth is not considered separately.

> *Absolute truth is indestructible. Being indestructible, it is eternal. Being eternal, it is self-existent. Being self existent, it is infinite. Being infinite, it is vast and deep. Being vast and deep, it is transcendental and intelligent.*
>
> – Kongfuzi

The Japanese Zen Buddhist philosopher Daisetsu Teitaro Suzuki, who lived from 1870 to 1966, pointed out, for example, that knowledge is divided into two parts: *prajña*, or intuitive knowledge, and *vijñāna*, or knowledge based on reason. The western mind, said Suzuki, focuses on *vijñāna*, whereas Zen is more concerned with *prajña*.

As a result, what began in the western philosophical tradition as a noble quest for rock-solid truths has dissolved into a quicksand of uncertainty. Those who continue to hold a common-sense view of truth may wonder how people got themselves in such a mess. One of the key reasons, according to contemporary Canadian philosopher John McGuire, is the "confusion that ... exists in our society over the distinction between reality and fiction."

A Short History of Truth

Humankind's preoccupation with truth is probably as old as the species. In his book titled *Truth: A History and a Guide for the Perplexed*, Fernández-Armesto identified four truth-finding techniques that dominated four successive stages of inquiry into truth. Although only one technique dominated during each period, all four have always been present in varying degrees. They are:

Stage 1: The truth you feel. During early recorded history, truth was registered emotionally or by non-sensory and non-rational kinds of perception.

Stage 2: The truth you are told. This kind of truth succeeded, or supplemented, the truth you feel. It refers to truths people are told by members of what Fernández-Armesto called "a truth world," which is made up of various human, oracular, divine, or scriptural authorities. In this category, he also included the notions of poetic truths, revelation, and truth detected by consensus, as well as concepts of innate truth.

Stage 3: The truth of reason. This kind of truth succeeded the truth you are told. It refers to truth that people discover rationally by thinking for themselves and using their ability to reason.

Stage 4: The truth you perceive through your senses. This kind of truth succeeded the truth of reason. It refers to truth that is discovered empirically.

In western philosophy, the first sustained debate over the nature of truth began in the time of Plato and the Sophists, a group of itinerant teachers in ancient Greece. The views expressed by Protagoras, perhaps the most famous Sophist, were of special concern to Plato. He found Protagoras' claim that "man is the measure of all things" especially abhorrent.

Protagoras' relativist, skeptical view suggests that one person's opinion is as good as another's, and that what is true for a friend could be false for you. At the time, this was a new and radical concept of knowledge in general and of truth in particular. It suggested that virtues and values such as truth are merely human creations and that there is nothing objective, natural, or absolute about them. As a result, they are subject to change according to the needs, desires, and whims of a particular society.

Because he believed that truth is fixed, permanent, and independent of individual subjective opinion, Plato said that the Sophists' ideas posed a threat that must be vigorously opposed. In one of his dialogues, *Theaetetus*, he delivered a blistering attack on the Sophist position. If Protagoras is right in claiming that man is the measure of all things, he said, then one person's wisdom, knowledge, or truth is as good as any other's. And that conclusion, for Plato, was sheer stupidity.

Web connection
www.mcgrawhill.ca/links/philosophy12
To read more of *Theaetetus,* follow the links on this Web site.

To see what Plato meant, imagine that you have been wheeled into an operating room and are about to undergo delicate brain surgery. Would you prefer a trained brain surgeon or the local butcher to carry out the operation? The surgeon's knowledge of the human brain may not be absolute or infallible, but Plato would insist that it is closer to the truth.

The debate that started with Plato and the Sophists raises some important philosophical questions: Does truth have an absolute, fixed nature that endures for all times in all places? Or is truth subjective, prone to change according to time, place, societal inclinations, and individual preferences? Also at issue is whether knowledge and truth are obtained through the senses or through reason. These key questions were raised more than 2500 years ago and are still being debated today.

Plato, the rationalist champion, said that knowledge and truth are acquired through reason. His student Aristotle acknowledged the importance of reason but placed greater emphasis on the senses as the source of truth and knowledge. As a result, Aristotle is considered one of the earliest champions of empiricism.

After the time of Plato and Aristotle, the conflicting claims to knowledge made by the proponents of rationalism and empiricism were not seriously debated again until the early modern age. From the 16th to the 18th century, the battle was waged between the continental rationalists (René Descartes, Baruch Spinoza, and Gottfried Wilhelm Leibniz) on the one side, and the British empiricists (John Locke, **George Berkeley**, and David Hume) on the other.

Among these giants of philosophy, Descartes is probably the most significant. Making a determined attempt to arrive at certain truths, Descartes began his philosophical investigations by doubting everything. After considerable reflection, he arrived at what he called the one indisputable truth: I think, therefore I am. From this one truth, he felt confident that he could pursue other unassailable truths.

Descartes's optimism was premature, however. In fact, some philosophers contend that Descartes's method of doubt — called "Cartesian doubt" from *Cartesius*, the Latin form of Descartes's name — is at least partly responsible for the relativism and skepticism of the 20th century, a trend that shows few signs of abating at the beginning of the 21st century.

Just as Descartes's ideas of rationalism as a source of truth have been criticized, so have the ideas of the 18th-century empiricists. Fernández-Armesto, for example, summarized their efforts with this remark: "[They] found it hard to produce arguments for the existence of anything except themselves."

KNOWLEDGE, TRUE OPINION, AND TRUE BELIEF

In *Meno*, one of Plato's dialogues, Socrates draws this conclusion: "That there is a difference between right opinion and knowledge is not at all a conjecture with me but something I would particularly assert that I know. There are not many things of which I would say that, but this one, at any rate, I will include among those that I know."

Socrates' point is that someone who possesses knowledge also possesses true opinion. Conversely, he said, it is possible to have a true opinion without necessarily having knowledge.

But is this merely playing with words? Not at all, say many philosophers. Suppose you recognize a friend entering the school ahead of you. You conclude that you are justified in believing that your friend is now in the school. You rush to catch up, but as you draw closer, you realize that you were mistaken. The person you are trying to catch up to has the same general features as your friend, but is not your friend. And a moment later, you see your friend walking down the hall from the opposite direction. Because, as you now discover, your friend was in the school at the time you drew your conclusion, the opinion you formed earlier was certainly true.

But was this opinion knowledge? No. A case of mistaken identity that coincidentally leads to a true opinion does not qualify as a claim to knowledge. You might, for example, guess today that an elephant will trudge into your classroom tomorrow. If this really happens, you can classify your guess as a true opinion, but it is not something that you *know*.

In *Theaetetus*, Plato asked, "What is the distinction between knowledge and true, or right, opinion?" He then attempted to incorporate the many kinds of knowledge under one definition. Most philosophers argue that he did not succeed. Taking a closer look at the problems stemming from Plato's question does, however, help to clarify notions of knowledge in general and truth in particular.

Plato's question tries to isolate the element that, when added to true opinion, constitutes knowledge. Philosophers have come up with no easy or definitive answer to this question. In *Theory of Knowledge*, **Roderick M. Chisholm** summarizes a typical philosophical response: "It is often said that *adequate evidence* is that which, when added to true opinion, yields knowledge."

For most people, adequate evidence is necessary for judging something to be true. But the idea of adequate evidence also raises philosophical problems.

> *If you do not tell the truth about yourself you cannot tell it about other people.*
>
> –Virginia Woolf

PHILOSOPHY IN ACTION
Philosophical Themes in The Truman Show
by John Michael McGuire

This review of the film *The Truman Show* first appeared in the magazine *Philosophy Now*. In it, Canadian philosopher John Michael McGuire explored the sophisticated philosophical issues that underlie this movie. McGuire is now an assistant professor at Hanyang University in South Korea.

Let's begin with a brief description of the plot. The story is about a man named Truman Burbank (played by Jim Carrey), who is born and raised inside an extremely large television studio that has been designed to resemble the real world. Indeed, the studio is so large and designed so well that Truman grows up unaware of the fact that he is inside a studio. He simply believes that his little community, known as Sea Haven, is a part of the real world just like any other. The illusion is not merely temporary, but rather extends throughout Truman's life, from his birth until the time we meet him at the age of 29.

This, perhaps, is enough of the plot to appreciate the first point of philosophical significance to the movie, which is its treatment of the problem of skepticism. Like so many other philosophical issues, the problem of skepticism can be traced back as far as the ancient Greeks. Nevertheless, it was Descartes who placed this problem at the very heart of modern philosophy when he used it as a foil in his attempt to provide a firm foundation for scientific knowledge, which was only beginning to flourish in his day. In his *Meditations*, Descartes invoked the idea of an evil genius — an omnipotent but malignant being whose sole purpose is to deceive us in all our perceptual experiences and beliefs — to challenge the idea that we have certain knowledge of the world around us. Given the logical possibility that such a creature exists, how can we be certain that our beliefs about the world are not radically mistaken? How, Descartes asked, can we be certain that we are all not utterly deceived?

The Truman Show presents a similar skeptical problem, but in the most convincing of ways. [The character] Christof [the director of the show] is clearly the evil genius that Descartes posited, but whereas Descartes's malignant demon is a creature of pure fantasy, the character of Christof and the conspiracy that he orchestrates seem dangerously real. Indeed, it is worth asking the question of what would prevent such a conspiracy from actually occurring. Of course, there never has been a TV show such as *The Truman Show*, but that is not the question. The question is whether there *could* be such show.

There is a clear trend in western, and especially U.S., popular culture away from "acting" and towards "real life." ... In this cultural context it is not difficult to imagine a show like *The Truman Show* taking place, not only because of the enormous public demand for "real entertainment," but also because of the confusion that already exists in our society over the distinction between reality and fiction. If, for example, I ever turned on the TV to find a show like *The Truman Show*, I simply would not know whether or not it was real, just as I don't know whether or not the people that present their confessionals on *The Jerry Springer Show* are actors who are paid to make fools of themselves. The same can be said for *The People's Court* and about a dozen other TV shows I can think of. In each case, I simply follow along, partly believing, partly doubting. I used to believe that the stories on *60 Minutes* were true, until I read that even they pay actors to provide material for their "documentaries." Now, like many other people, I simply don't know what to believe on TV or in the movies.

So the first point of philosophical significance in *The Truman Show* is that it presents an intriguing example of how a person could be radically mistaken in his beliefs about the world. I am not suggesting that any of us currently are experiencing, or ever will experience, the sort of deception that Truman did. But even if we never will experience such deception, it is worth asking the question of how we *know* this to be true. How can you be certain that you are not the unwitting star of a television drama that the rest of the world watches for their amusement? More generally, in virtue of what can you be certain that the people around you are not conspiring to deceive you about who you are? These are, perhaps, purely philosophical questions, but they are also good questions insofar as they lead us to reflect upon our concepts of knowledge, certainty, and belief.

What, if anything, is the point of this movie? Enough has been said so far to show that a central theme is surely the struggle to overcome ignorance and illusion in the quest for truth. While none of us are very likely to experience the sort of massive conspiracy orchestrated against Truman, all of us, to one extent or another, are in a state of ignorance and illusion. People around us lead us to believe things about themselves and ourselves that simply aren't true. Companies, who want our money, seduce us with lies about their products. Politicians, who want our votes, make promises they don't intend to keep. It was Shakespeare who said, "All the world's a stage," and though he was speaking metaphorically, there is an important truth in his remark. Our lives are filled with lies and illusions, and it behooves us to overcome these in the quest for truth, just as Truman did.

If this were all there were to *The Truman Show* it would still be a good story, but I interpret the movie as delivering, or at least encouraging us to reflect upon, a much more specific and more important message. Of all the sources of deception and illusion in our contemporary lives, none is more potent and pervasive than the popular media in general and television in particular. In this century, in the western world at least, television has been more important than any other technology in shaping our views about the world. It is the medium through which the majority of people receive the majority of their beliefs. And yet the medium is clearly deceptive, not just superficially, but fundamentally, perhaps not in and of itself, but at least in the socio-political context in which it exists. The fact that the TV is, and has been for some time, the most effective vehicle for advertising and marketing, is a fact that must not be, but so often is, ignored. The TV is much more than a communications device; it is a means by which broadcasting companies sell viewers to their advertisers.... [It] is not surprising to find that truth is not an important concept in the world of TV.

What Truman Burbank leaves behind at the end of *The Truman Show* is not only a grand illusion — a conspiracy that usurped his autonomy — it is, more specifically, the world of television. It is, quite literally, a TV studio that Truman exits, and in doing so he puts an end to a TV show that has captivated the viewing public for 29 years. This is the point that must not go unnoticed, the ultimate point of the story. If we really do care about truth, autonomy, and freedom of thought, then we must, like Truman Burbank, walk away from the world of television.

One of the most striking images in *The Truman Show* is of the people, the viewing public, who are so "captivated" by *The Truman Show* that they are, one could say, "glued" to their TV sets. A thought that came to my mind upon seeing this was of Plato's allegory of the cave.

Plato's story depicts a group of prisoners chained in a dark cave, constrained by their chains to stare at a wall in front of them. Behind them is a fire that casts shadows on the wall in front of them, these shadows being the prisoners' only source of knowledge of the world. The knowledge of reality that can be gleaned in this way is obviously limited and vastly inferior to the sort of knowledge that one could get by breaking free of one's chains and exiting the cave to glimpse the real world in the full light of day.

Part of the reason why Plato presented this allegory, of course, was to reinforce his idea that there are in fact two worlds: the real world and the world of illusion. And it is the philosopher, Plato believed, who turns his gaze from the deformed images that populate the world of illusion to contemplate the pure ideas of the real world. Plato also believed that it was the role of education to effect this conversion, from illusion to truth. Substituting the TV for Plato's world of illusion, we can say that Truman Burbank is a paradigmatic philosopher and teacher, one that even Plato would applaud. And until we follow Truman in freeing our minds by renouncing television, we the members of the TV nation are like the prisoners in Plato's cave.

A final thought. That the leading role in this highly philosophical movie is played by Jim Carrey may at first seem odd. For Carrey's previous roles, such as in *Dumb and Dumber* or *The Cable Guy*, are so ridiculous that he makes Jerry Lewis look like a philosopher. However, on second thought, Carrey was an excellent choice for this role precisely because his previous roles have been so ridiculous. For *The Truman Show* is ultimately about a transition that takes place in the main character's life, a transition from ignorance to wisdom, and this is a transition that Carrey seems to make not only as an actor in *The Truman Show*, but also as a person, in doing *The Truman Show*. Imagine that: Jim Carrey, the philosopher king!

Source: "Films." John McGuire. In *Philosophy Now*. June-July 2001.

---

1. What important epistemological question does John McGuire tackle in this film review?
2. Think about a time when you struggled in search of truth. How was your experience similar to or different from Truman's quest?
3. On the basis of the opinions expressed in this piece, would you classify McGuire as a rationalist or an empiricist? Why?

Who, for example, decides what constitutes adequate evidence and what criteria are used to make this decision? Suppose someone says, "The truth of the matter is that school X is the best in the province." Students, parents, and teachers from other schools would probably challenge this statement, and understandably so. How could anyone even begin to gather evidence to substantiate the truth of a claim like this? What criteria would be used, and how would the importance of each piece of evidence be determined?

Suppose, too, that a friend of yours plays the stock market. Before making a move, he checks all relevant information, including the opinions of the experts. When making a decision about whether to buy, sell, or hold, however, he does so on the basis of the number of barks from his faithful dog, Nostradamus. Your friend has a true belief and adequate evidence, but at the same time it is incorrect to believe that he "knows." Chisholm would say that it is possible for your friend to have adequate evidence, and therefore, to know, but without knowing that he knows.

Recall...Reflect...Respond

1. Summarize four responses to the epistemological question, What is truth?
2. Suppose a friend told you that tomorrow's classes are cancelled so that school staff can attend a meeting to discuss closing the school completely because asbestos has been discovered in classrooms. How would you determine the truth of your friend's statement? How might a skeptic assess the effectiveness of the process you used?
3. How do Plato and René Descartes respond to this question: What counts as a justification in claiming to know something? Which response do you find most helpful in working out your own answer to the same question? Why?

PERCEPTION AND TRUTH

Perception must be involved in any serious discussion of the concept of truth. The way we perceive things — and what we accept as true — relates to the way we grasp, or interpret, the world and the objects in it. In other words, perception is a psychological process of awareness that occurs when the senses are stimulated. What people see and hear, for example, seems so obvious and natural that they seldom give these processes a second thought.

Philosophers do, however. They examine the relationship, or connection, between the knower and the thing that is known — and often disagree over the character of the relationship. The dispute focuses on how people perceive reality, a process that determines how, and the extent to which, they grasp and define truth.

PLATO AND PERCEPTION

In the western tradition, debate over the relationship between truth and perception began with Socrates and Plato. At one point in *Theaetetus*, Theaetetus concludes that knowledge can be defined as perception. As Socrates sees it, however, Theaetetus has simply reiterated, in a disguised form, Protagoras' claim that truth is whatever it appears to be to each person.

Protagoras' point has some merit. Consider this scenario, for example. Shortly after entering the classroom, Chung claims that he is cold, while Judy says that she is warm. Disputing either claim would be foolish. Chung and Judy perceive (or feel) the temperature of the classroom differently. This may be the result of a variety of factors, such as the clothing they are wearing, their health, and so on. As a result, each is expressing a claim about what is true for him or her personally. Plato would likely concede this point. He might even acknowledge that perception can be a useful tool or a good starting point on the road to truth and knowledge. He would argue, however, that it is not the same as truth or knowledge.

Plato's views about the inadequacy of perception, which he associated with the senses, led to his theory of forms. In fact, his theory of forms distinguishes clearly between knowledge and perception. Closely associated with this distinction are two arguments that are central to Plato's overall philosophy. The first is that knowledge must be objective, real, and independent of the person acquiring the knowledge. The second is that something more than the senses is required if knowledge is to be acquired and truth is to be found. In Plato's view, this "something more" is reason.

Plato's rationalism — his faith in reason as the source of knowledge — led him to reject the views of the Sophists as irrational. In Plato's view, accepting Protagoras' claim that one truth is as good as another would lead to absurd conclusions. For example, he asked how Protagoras could justify calling himself a teacher if everyone could make similar claims to possess truth, knowledge, and wisdom.

For that matter, how could anyone justify accepting the title of teacher, either at the time of Plato or now? If Protagoras was correct, it would mean that anyone could claim to be as knowledgeable as anyone else in math, music, sports, and so on. Claiming this, however, would not make it true. For Plato, then — and probably for most people — there must be more to truth and knowledge than perception.

COMMON-SENSE REALISM

In attempts to clarify the relationship between truth and perception, contemporary philosophers have proposed several theories. **Common-sense realism**, which is also known as naïve realism, comes closest to representing the everyday uncritical and unreflective notion of perception that many people are comfortable with.

Figure 11.1

René Magritte, *Ceci n'est pas une pipe*, 1929.
© Estate of René Magritte/SODRAC (Montréal) 2002

Ceci n'est pas une pipe.

"*Ceci n'est pas une pipe*" means "This is not a pipe." In this painting, artist René Magritte set out to challenge common sense notions of reality and truth. How did he do this?

According to common-sense realists, what you see is what you get. In other words, people perceive or experience objects and the world exactly as they are. What the senses detect — what is grasped mentally — and the object being perceived are one and the same.

Most critics of common-sense realism say that it fails to account for things like hallucinations, dreams, mirages, and optical illusions. None of these phenomena corresponds to reality, but all qualify as perceptions. In addition, critics say that people's sensory perceptions cannot detect various natural phenomena. The movement of the earth is a classic example.

REPRESENTATIVE THEORY OF PERCEPTION

The English philosopher John Locke is usually acknowledged as the originator of the **representative theory of perception**, which is also known as epistemological dualism. In Locke's view, objects exist as distinct and separate entities from human beings. But objects also exist in the human mind as psychological entities.

Locke said that external objects trigger the perception process by stimulating the human sense organs — and the sensations generated by the sense organs stimulate the mind to create an *idea* of the object. Still, said Locke, the idea in the mind is merely a representation of the object. The object and the idea are separate and distinct. Locke's explanation of this phenomenon has been compared to what happens when a camera photographs an object. Just as a photograph of a car, for example, is not the same as the car itself, so ideas of objects created in the human mind are not the same as the objects themselves. Like photographs, these ideas are representations.

Objections to representative theory are similar to those directed at common-sense realism. Critics say that the "pictures" registered by the senses are unreliable indicators of truth. Think about times when you have mistaken a faraway object for something else, for example. Or how mistakes in perception often lead to conflicts in eyewitness accounts of the same event. Those who challenge the representative theory of perception say that both circumstances demonstrate that the "pictures" people perceive are unreliable sources of truth.

SUBJECTIVE IDEALISM

Subjective idealism, a theory credited to the 18th-century British philosopher **George Berkeley**, maintains that ideas created by sensations are all that people can know for sure. In other words, what is perceived as real or true consists only of ideas in the mind. As a result, said Berkeley, there is no basis for concluding that external objects actually exist outside the human mind.

Carried to its ultimate and extreme conclusion, subjective idealism leads to a position called **solipsism**. A solipsist believes that only he or she exists to perceive things, whether these things are objects or people. If you were a solipsist, you would believe that objects and people exist only if you think about them. The moment you stop thinking about them, they no longer exist. This would be like saying to your friends or family, "I'm the only one who is real. You and all other objects are figments of my imagination."

> ### THE *Lighter* SIDE OF PHILOSOPHY
>
> Say, did you hear about the guy who went to the solipsist convention?
>
> He was the only one who showed up.

Not surprisingly, subjective idealism has few followers. Most people — philosophers and non-philosophers alike — go about their daily business assuming that a real world made up of objects exists. Indeed, in the view of critics of subjective idealism, to do anything else would be foolish. Some objects that exist in the real world are downright dangerous, and dismissing them as mere ideas in the mind could be a fatal mistake.

Subjective idealism also encounters the burden-of-proof objection regarding truth. If there is no outside world of real objects, how can people know that any two minds perceive the same thing? What one person perceives as a mouse, another might perceive as an elephant. And how can anyone be sure that his or her mind is not the only one that exists?

Finally, if "to be is to be perceived," as Berkeley claimed, how does anyone know that the mind — which does the perceiving — exists?

> **Web connection**
> www.mcgrawhill.ca/links/philosophy12
> To find out more about George Berkeley, follow the links on this Web site.

PHENOMENALISM

In an attempt to clarify ideas about perception and truth, Immanuel Kant developed a theory called **phenomenalism**. According to Kant, human beings are incapable of perceiving objects in the world as they really are. He said that the best that people can do is to know objects as they *appear*. Kant used the term "phenomena" to refer to things as they appear to the senses and "noumena" to refer to things that are thought or known by pure reason. Kant's noumena are similar to Plato's forms.

Kant argued that the human mind has a certain structure, or form. This form is dictated by specific innate categories — time, space, and causation — within the mind. These categories, he said, are a priori. They exist in the mind before sense experience. Anything that people experience, therefore, is perceived first as a phenomenon in time and space. The human mind's ability to reason prompts it to perceive all events in the context of cause and effect. In other words, time, space, and causation are attributes of the mind rather than characteristics of the physical world.

Figure 11.2

common-sense realism — representative theory of perception — phenomenalism — subjective idealism

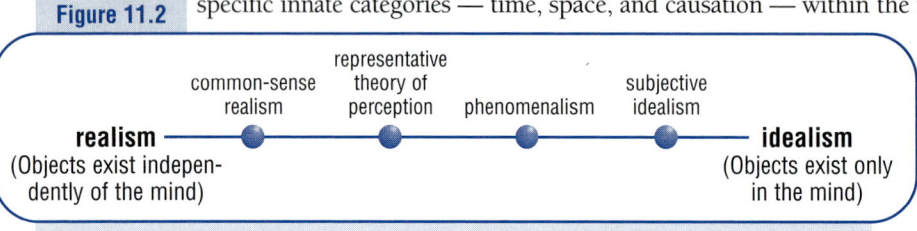

realism (Objects exist independently of the mind) ⟷ **idealism** (Objects exist only in the mind)

Realism and idealism would fall at opposite ends of a perception continuum. The representative theory of perception falls in the middle, and other theories take their place on either side of this. On this continuum, where would you place your own ideas about perception?

Kant's theory said that rationalists were partly right and partly wrong when they insisted that knowledge and truth can be discovered exclusively through reason, and that the same was true of empiricists who insisted that knowledge and truth can be discovered through the senses. Kant's approach was an attempt to reconcile the two schools of thought.

Kant insisted that both the senses and reason play a role in arriving at truths about the world. He also distinguished between the "object in itself" (as it is in reality) and the way it appears. He said that the process whereby the senses pick up raw data, which the mind interprets through the categories of time, space, and causation, ensure that people can never possess certain knowledge of the world in general or of the specific things within it.

Kant's theory means that people can never know the world as it really is — and this makes it impossible for human beings to acquire certain knowledge because all knowledge is suspect. It also means that people can, at best, acquire only partial truths and certainly cannot acquire the kinds of objective truths that Plato sought.

• IDEAS IN CONTEXT •

When he suggested in the 18th century that time and space exist in the mind rather than in the real world, Immanuel Kant was ahead of his time. In the 20th century, for example, the physicist Albert Einstein declared that time is an illusion. He said that there is no distinction between past, present, and future. Julian Barbour, a theoretical physicist and author of *The End of Time*, also recently concluded that time does not exist. And according to Don Page, a cosmologist at the University of Alberta, when scientists do come up with an accurate and true theory of what the universe is really like, neither time nor space will be part of the equation.

Recall...Reflect...Respond

1. Explain how the psychological process of perception leads to varying interpretations of what people can know to be true.
2. Choose one theory of perception and truth and draw from your personal experience to provide one example that supports it and another that refutes it.
3. Choose one of the main questions of epistemology and explain which theory of truth and perception responds to it best.

THEORIES OF TRUTH

In response to philosophers who doubt the possibility of discovering truth, the 20th-century French philosopher and writer Jacques Maritain wrote: "The sole philosophy open to those who doubt the possibility of truth is absolute silence — even mental." In fact, many philosophers have persevered in the quest to find an all-inclusive theory of truth. Three of the most widely accepted are correspondence theory, coherence theory, and pragmatic theory.

THE CORRESPONDENCE THEORY OF TRUTH

The correspondence theory of truth is the oldest, best known, and most widely used conception of truth. Supporters of this theory maintain that there is a relationship — or correspondence — between people's internal beliefs and the realities of the external world. In other words, truth involves an agreement between thought on the one hand and reality on the other.

In some respects, correspondence theory represents a common-sense approach to truth because it claims that a belief is true if it agrees with a fact or coincides with something about the physical world. This common-sense view coincides with people's everyday procedures for determining truth. Suppose you believe that your classroom contains a chalkboard. This belief is true if it corresponds to the facts about the room. If you believe that a pink, 250-kilogram mouse is lurking in the back corner of the classroom, however, your classmates would probably be justified in dismissing your belief as false.

The correspondence theory also applies to mental or emotional states and experiences. If Shandra believes that she likes Marcus, for example, then her belief is true if she does indeed like Marcus. If you believe that you have a headache, then your belief is true if you do, in fact, have a headache. It is unlikely that anyone would try to contradict either Shandra or you.

Of all the theories of truth, the correspondence theory offers the most direct link between an objective reality and statements about that reality. In this context, "objective" means independent of a mind perceiving that reality.

Bertrand Russell, a supporter of correspondence theory, said that something is true if it corresponds to something real, a fact that is independent of the perceiver. In *The Problems of Philosophy*, he stressed that both truth and falsehood are properties of people's beliefs. A theory of truth, he said, must "admit of its opposite, falsehood." He maintained that the theories of truth proposed by many philosophers ignore or gloss over falsehood. He considered this a mistake.

Russell said that neither truth nor falsehood can exist without beliefs. To understand what he meant, imagine a world without thoughts, a world that consists only of matter. Without thoughts, beliefs could not exist, and if beliefs did not exist, truth and falsehood could not exist. As a result, Russell concluded that truth and falsehood are properties of beliefs.

Critics of correspondence theory claim that it oversimplifies the concept of truth and covers only a narrow range of possible truth situations. Suppose, for example, that you are driving with two friends and see a black animal dart across the highway. You are certain that the animal was a bear. The first friend says that you need glasses. The animal was not a bear; it was a large, black dog. If both you and your friend persist in your beliefs, how is the truth to be determined?

> ### IDEAS IN CONTEXT
>
> Scientific realism, a theory supported by Albert Einstein, is similar to correspondence theory. Einstein believed that a basic underlying reality or truth exists in the universe and can be known. This belief led him to reject ideas proposed by 20th-century scientists who were exploring theories of quantum physics. As a result, Einstein devoted the final 20 years of his life to finding a unified field theory that would support his realist belief in a single, underlying, objective truth that can be discovered about the universe.

The second friend is a correspondence theorist who was looking at something else and did not see the animal herself. She might point out that one of you is probably correct and therefore holds a view that corresponds to the facts. Alternatively, she might suggest that you could both be wrong. Perhaps the animal in question is the panther that recently escaped from the zoo. Whichever course she follows, she will maintain that there is an objective reality or fact concerning the true nature of the animal that crossed the road. The critic's reply, of course, is that even if all three of you acknowledge that an objective truth exists, none of you is in a position to determine what it is.

Even critics who concede that correspondence theory might be useful for determining truth in areas involving facts insist that other areas of human experience and belief cannot be said to correspond to facts. Although many people have firm beliefs about the existence of a supreme being and an eternal soul, for example, correspondence theory is of little use in establishing the truth of either. Similarly, even if most people believe in evolution as a truth that has been confirmed by scientific investigation, correspondence theory cannot be used to confirm its truth because it is not an object or a thing that people can perceive.

> *There are two kinds of truth: those of reasoning and those of fact. The truths of reasoning are necessary and their opposite is impossible; the truths of fact are contingent and their opposite is possible.*
>
> – Gottfried Wilhelm Leibniz

In *The Fundamental Questions of Philosophy*, the 20th-century philosopher **A.C. Ewing** voiced another objection to correspondence theory.

> I have used the terms "belief" or "judgment" for what is true or false. Now this may be understood as referring either to your mental state of believing or to what is believed. But our state of believing is plainly not true; a psychological state cannot be sensibly called true or false. The theory therefore applies, if at all, only to "belief" or "judgment" in the sense of what is believed or "judged." ("Judgment" is used by philosophers as a term to cover both knowledge and belief.) The technical term in philosophy for what we judge or believe is "proposition," and, strictly speaking, it is only propositions which can be true.

THE COHERENCE THEORY OF TRUTH

As a result of the objections to correspondence theory, some philosophers decided to look for an entirely different theory of truth. One of these was the German philosopher **Georg W.F. Hegel**, who lived from 1770 to 1831. Hegel was one of the chief architects of the **coherence theory**, which emerged in the 19th century. According to this theory, a belief is considered true not because of a correspondence between someone's internal belief and a fact in the real world, but because the belief coheres, or is consistent, with an existing belief or body of knowledge.

> *Truth, like light, blinds. Falsehood, on the contrary, is a beautiful twilight that enhances every object.*
>
> —Albert Camus

Whereas correspondence theory emphasizes agreement with fact, coherence theory emphasizes the consistency of ideas in relation to one another. Rather than focusing on the relationship between a belief or judgment and a fact, coherence theory focuses on the relationship among beliefs or judgments.

Suppose, for example, that you walk into your room and discover that the furniture and all your belongings have been moved around. Of course, you want to know what happened. Suppose further that you are a coherence theorist. If someone suggests that ghosts are responsible, you will accept or reject this explanation based on whether it coheres with the rest of your beliefs about supernatural beings, life after death, and so on. You might also suspect that one of your siblings is responsible, perhaps as a way of getting back at you for a trick you played on him in the past. Or, without being fully conscious of it, you might also make mental calculations that combine elements of both theories.

In Ewing's view, coherence theory "avoid[s] the difficulty as to how we could know that judgments corresponded to something which was not itself a judgment." In addition, coherence theory allows for degrees of truth, which some philosophers find appealing. It also allows for the possibility that a belief that is now accepted as truth or knowledge might be rejected as false in the future.

Figure 11.3

Georg W.F. Hegel was an idealist who disagreed with Immanuel Kant's phenomenalist theory of perception. How does Hegel's idealism correspond with his coherence theory of truth?

The history of science is full of examples of theories or beliefs that were abandoned in favour of others that cohered more closely to the scientific knowledge of the time. One of the best known is the earth-centred theory of the solar system, which was abandoned in the mid-1500s when the sun-centred theory came into favour. The sun-centred theory was adopted not because it had been verified by facts, but because it was simpler and cohered better with other scientific beliefs.

Critics of coherence theory point out that it cannot guarantee truth. They say that a set of beliefs could cohere perfectly with one another but still be false. The fate of the earth-centred theory of the universe, which prevailed in Europe for more than a thousand years, illustrates this point.

Though some critics acknowledge that coherence theory may be useful when dealing with complex scientific theories, such as quantum theory, where observable facts are difficult to confirm, they also point out that the worth of a theory is determined by its ability to predict observable facts. If facts cannot be confirmed, some have suggested that people might as well revert to mythological explanations of the world rather than struggle with complex theories.

Critics have also said that coherence theory requires the testing of the consistency of new ideas or beliefs with other ideas and beliefs that are considered true. In *Introduction to Philosophy*, William James Earle explained that this can present a problem. He wrote: "No one (with the possible exception of an all-knowing deity) is in possession of all true statements.... Our actual practice is to check candidate truths for consistency ... with our beliefs."

Finally, some have objected to coherence theory's acceptance of degrees of truth. Ewing, for example, wrote:

> A judgment is, strictly speaking, either true or false, and cannot be more or less true, and it surely is obvious that "2 + 2 = 4" and "Washington is the capital of the United States" are absolutely true. It might be replied that the advocates of the coherence theory were not using "truth" in the ordinary sense of the term, but we are looking for a definition of the word in the ordinary sense, not in some exotic sense.... To say A is consistent with B is to say that A and B may both be true; to say that A follows necessarily from B is to say that, if B is true, A must be true. So it seems that anyone who defines truth in terms of coherence is defining truth in terms of itself, thus committing a vicious circle. Finally, it is surely obvious that judgments are true not because of their relation to other judgments, but because of their relation to something objective which is not itself a judgment. This brings us back to the correspondence theory of truth.

Ewing means that coherence theory seems, in the end, to rely on correspondence. Though a new judgment or idea may cohere with previous judgments, what do the previous judgments cohere with? Somewhere down the line, there must be one or more judgments that do not cohere with anything. These initial judgments or ideas can be said to be true only if they refer to facts; in other words, the foundation of coherence theory is correspondence theory.

Coherence theorists challenge this argument, saying that only coherence theory can verify judgments about so-called facts. Suppose, for example, that you say that the tables in your school cafeteria are rectangular. How would you confirm the truth of this judgment? Probably by going to the cafeteria and looking at the tables. Your perception of the tables would confirm that your initial judgment was correct. According to the 20th-century American coherence theorist Brand Blanshard, this process of confirming your initial judgment represents coherence, not correspondence.

PRAGMATIC THEORY

Perhaps because the arguments of both correspondence and coherence theorists seem to end up going round in a vicious circle, some philosophers attempted to develop other approaches that would sidestep the objections and counter-objections that characterized the debate over these two theories. One of these was the **pragmatic theory** of truth.

This theory, which holds that the terms "true" and "false" relate directly to the use*ful*ness and use*less*ness of beliefs, propositions, or statements, is usually associated with the American philosophers **Charles Peirce**, who lived from 1839 to 1914, **William James**, who lived from 1842 to 1910, and **John Dewey**, who lived from 1859 to 1952. Though pragmatists do not always agree about the details of the theory, they believe that if something works, is useful, or is successful, then it is true. According to pragmatic theory, then, truth must be discussed in terms of consequences.

Pragmatists object to traditional ideas that truths are fixed and absolute. They prefer to think that human beings create their own truths. James, for example, wrote: "Truth is made, just as health, wealth, and strength are made, in the course of experience." For a belief to be considered true, he said, it must have some sort of "cash-value."

In James' view, debates over whether a judgment corresponds to a fact or whether a theory coheres with other theories are irrelevant. He said that if an idea or judgment makes a positive, practical difference in people's lives, then it is true. If it does not, it is false.

Though the pragmatists of the first half of the 20th century thought it worthwhile to define truth, those of the early 21st century tend to dismiss even this effort as a waste of time. The American pragmatist **Richard Rorty** insists that today's pragmatists do not even offer a theory of truth. He maintains that there is no way people can know when they have reached the truth or whether they are even close to the truth.

Stephen Stich, another contemporary American philosopher, takes pragmatism a step farther. He contends that truth does not matter, adding that people should not care whether their beliefs are true or false. Rather, he says, people should be concerned about whether their beliefs help them achieve more substantial goals, such as happiness and well-being. In some respects, Stich's position is similar to the beliefs of the ancient Greek Sophists.

Pragmatism is a widely accepted philosophy that has even found a niche in science, where it is often called **instrumentalism** because theories are regarded as instruments or tools. For the scientific pragmatist, the truthfulness of a theory depends mainly on its ability to predict useful results.

Despite its widespread acceptance, pragmatism has been severely criticized. Some have suggested that a belief can be true but not work and, conversely, that a belief can be false but work quite well. People who do not like to exercise, for example, might benefit if they believed that they would die at a young age. Or a student might believe that the way to get

PROFILE

Daisetsu Teitaro Suzuki
Interpreting Zen to the West

The Buddhist scholar and philosopher Daisetsu Teitaro Suzuki, usually known simply as D.T. Suzuki, is often credited with bringing knowledge of Zen, a Japanese school of Buddhism, to the West.

Born in Kanazawa, Japan, in 1870, Suzuki attended Tokyo University. While there, he began training in Zen, and under the guidance of Zen master Shaku Sôen, he experienced *satori*, which means "sudden enlightenment" in Japanese. This experience was to affect his life profoundly.

After graduating, Suzuki moved to the United States. For the next 13 years, he worked for a publisher and pursued his interest in Zen on his own time. During this period, he translated several Zen works into English and published his own book, *Outline of Mahayana Buddhism*.

Suzuki left the United States in 1907 and travelled through Europe before making his way back to Japan, where he became a university teacher. In 1921, he founded the Eastern Buddhist Society and began publishing *The Eastern Buddhist*, a magazine devoted to Buddhist thought. At the same time, he continued translating and writing works in English. His goal was to make Zen better known to western society.

In one of his works, titled *Zen Buddhism and Its Influence on Japanese Culture*, Suzuki explained Zen's emphasis on simplicity and self-effacement. He also discussed Zen's influence on activities such as Samurai philosophy and swordsmanship, and tea ceremonies. All Suzuki's writings displayed his ability to convey Zen's seemingly inexpressible essence to English-speaking audiences.

According to Suzuki, knowledge consists of two parts: *prajña*, or intuitive knowledge; and *vijñâna*, or knowledge derived from reason. "*Prajña* grasps reality in its oneness, in its totality; *vijñâna* analyzes it into subject and object," he wrote. To illustrate this point, he compared knowledge to a flower. The western way, he said, is to analyze the flower's physical and chemical properties. But this analysis does not lead to true knowledge of the flower. "The *prajña* way is to understand it just as it is without analysis or chopping it into pieces. It is to grasp it in its oneness, in its suchness."

Suzuki contended that analytical knowledge consists of dividing reality into small segments. Doing so, he said, kills reality. Though westerners think that they arrive at understanding and truth by analyzing things, this belief is false. "We fail to see that the result of dissection is not reality itself, and when we take this analysis as a basis of our understanding, it is inevitable that we go astray, far away from the truth. Because in this way we shall never reach the final solution of the problem of reality," he wrote.

In other words, said Suzuki, the western goal of fully understanding something as simple as a flower cannot be achieved through analysis. Once a flower is cut up into dozens of pieces, it is no longer a flower.

What westerners must realize, he said, is that the flower, like the universe, is one. Reality is oneness. This is the reality that *prajña* grasps. It is a process whereby people become one with the flower, and only in so doing do they truly understand. "The moment grasped by *prajña*-intuition is *satori*," he wrote.

Suzuki eventually spent a great deal of time teaching and lecturing in Japan, the United States, and other countries. When he died in 1966, he was mourned as the chief interpreter of Zen Buddhism to the West. At various times, western thinkers such as Carl Jung, Aldous Huxley, and Martin Heidegger, one of the best-known philosophers of the 20th century, acknowledged the influence of Suzuki's ideas on their thought.

Figure 11.4

D.T. Suzuki was a tireless teacher and lecturer who continued working until his death at the age of 96.

ahead is to cheat on tests. As long as he gets away with this, pragmatism seems to suggest that his belief is true. If he suddenly gets caught and expelled from school, however, does his belief about cheating suddenly become false?

Pragmatism contends that a true belief or true judgment is one that has been accepted by a society or community. Various societies and communities have different acceptance standards and criteria, however. What happens when two communities take opposing views on an issue? Are both views true? Does it really make sense to grant a community a licence to decide truth? If a society believes that genocide works because the consequences benefit the majority, is this belief true?

Questions like these have sparked critics to charge that pragmatism ignores serious ethical issues. They say that if people rely on positive consequences and community acceptance as criteria for judging truth, they are saying, as the Sophists did, that might is right. Critics also contend that equating truth with usefulness is bad epistemology and fraught with peril. They maintain that people must pursue the truth with honesty even if its consequences prove detrimental to their well-being.

George Orwell's novel *1984* attacks pragmatism by examining what might happen if defining truth is left to human beings. This book highlights the need to ask ourselves what we should believe, what we should doubt, and what we should reject.

The story takes place in Oceania, a fictitious totalitarian regime ruled by Big Brother, who is always watching people. A ruling Party mired in sophistry and skepticism obliterates the distinctions between truths and lies. The Party's three slogans are War Is Peace, Freedom Is Slavery, and Ignorance Is Strength.

In Oceania, the Ministry of Truth governs the news, entertainment, and education; the Ministry of Peace is concerned with war; the Ministry of Love handles law and order; and the Ministry of Plenty is in charge of economic matters. Criteria for determining truth, in the usual sense of the word, do not exist. What *is* true is what the Party *proclaims* to be true. Thus, the lie becomes truth, or vice-versa, according to the Party's wishes.

Recall...Reflect...Respond

1. Why has the relationship between correspondence and coherence theories of truth been called a vicious circle?
2. If you are a supporter of the pragmatic theory of truth, how might you deal with a friend who has lied to you about a matter of great personal value?
3. Think about the way truth is portrayed in George Orwell's novel *1984*. Respond to this portrayal as a supporter of the correspondence, coherence, or pragmatic theory of truth.

DOES THE TRUTH MATTER?

In *Truth: A History and a Guide for the Perplexed*, Fernández-Armesto claims that truth has fallen on hard times. He gives this assessment of the situation:

> The retreat from truth is one of the great dramatic, untold stories of history. We ought to make an attempt to trace its course because it may help to explain one of the great puzzles of the modern world. For professional academics in the affected

disciplines, to have grown indifferent to truth is an extraordinary reversal of traditional obligations; it is like physicians renouncing the obligation to sustain life or theologians losing interest in God.... The trashing of truth began as an academic vice, but the debris is now scattered all over society. It is spread through classroom programs, worthy in themselves, designed to equip students with psychological proprieties, like self-satisfaction and a sense of identity, or with social virtues such as tolerance and mutual respect. Like many admirable aims, these can have evil consequences. In a society of concessions to rival viewpoints, in which citizens hesitate to demand what is true and what is false, it becomes impossible to defend the traditional distinctions between what is right and what is wrong, which are relativized in turn. Unless it is true, what status is left for a statement like "X is wrong" where X is, say, adultery, infanticide, euthanasia, drug dealing, Nazism, pedophilia, sadism.... It becomes like everything else in western society today, a matter of opinion, and we are left with no moral basis for encoding some opinions rather than others, except the tyranny of the majority.

In fact, Fernández-Armesto's complaint is nothing new. In ancient Athens, Plato challenged the Sophist view that truth is relative. And in the 16th century, the French philosopher Michel Eyquem de Montaigne asked, "What kind of truth is this which is true on one side of a mountain and false on the other?"

Still, Fernández-Armesto raises important issues. If the answers to all questions are subjective and relative, the truth does not matter because no right or wrong answer exists. But even relativists cannot escape the fact that they believe that they have the better answer; otherwise, they must concede that what they say is pointless. Most philosophers point out that in real life some answers are better than others. Anything less is either a pale imitation of philosophy or not philosophy at all.

> *Truth does not change because it is, or it is not, believed by a majority of the people.*
>
> — Giordano Bruno

Despite the claims of some contemporary philosophers, issues of truth and falsehood continue to generate lively discussion and debate. The last decade or so has seen a flurry of both scholarly and popular books and articles on the subject. A *Time* magazine cover story in October 1992, for example, was titled "Lying: Everybody's Doin' It, Honest." In 1998, Geoff Pevere of the *Toronto Star* wrote an article titled "It's True: Society Is Built on Lies." And truth made the cover of the January 2002 issue of *O, The Oprah Magazine*. Articles like these are just the tip of the iceberg. Even philosophers like Richard Rorty, who recommends giving up the search for truth because it is an unattainable ideal, must, in the end, grapple with the concept, if only to speak negatively about it.

Based on evidence like this, it seems unlikely that philosophers — or non-philosophers — have abandoned the quest for truth.

Chapter Review

Chapter Summary

This chapter has discussed
- some of the main philosophical questions of epistemology
- the strengths and weaknesses of the responses of some of the major philosophers and major schools of epistemology to some of the main epistemological questions
- instances in which philosophical problems of knowledge occur in everyday contexts
- the problems, principles, methods, and conclusions of various philosophers
- how the ideas of philosophers have influenced subsequent philosophers

Knowledge and Understanding

1. Identify and explain the significance to the study of epistemology of each of the following key words and people.

Key Words	Key People
truth	Linda Martín Alcoff
common-sense realism	Felipe Fernández-Armesto
representative theory of perception	Daisetsu Teitaro Suzuki
subjective idealism	John McGuire
solipsism	George Berkeley
phenomenalism	Roderick M. Chisholm
correspondence theory	A.C. Ewing
coherence theory	Georg W.F. Hegel
pragmatic theory	Charles Peirce
instrumentalism	William James
	John Dewey
	Richard Rorty

2. Create a mind map that shows which theories of truth respond to three of the main questions of epistemology, and summarize how each does so.

Thinking and Inquiry

3. In *The Seven Spiritual Laws for Parents*, author Deepak Chopra applies eastern philosophy when he gives the following advice to parents.

   > We lie in order to remain safe, to avert danger of punishment. Fear of punishment implies inner tension, and even if a lie does protect us from perceived danger, it rarely if ever relieves this inner tension. Only the truth can do that. When a young child is taught that telling the truth will result in a good feeling, she has taken the first step toward the realizing that truth has a spiritual quality. It isn't necessary to use punishment.

   Explain Chopra's advice in your own words. If you were a parent, would you take this advice? Why?

4. Psychologists and psychiatrists frequently deal with people who must come to terms with their perceptions of truth, whether in the form of a painful memory of the past or the painful realization of the truth of their present circumstances. In the form of a personal reflection, consider the various theories of truth and decide which approach might help someone heal the pain associated with these truths.

Communication

5. Some contemporary philosophers such as Richard Rorty have suggested that the search for truth is futile. Write a 500-word essay explaining your thoughts on this issue. Support your position by citing the ideas of various philosophers, showing how their ideas have influenced subsequent philosophers.

6. Write a poem that describes what it is like to *be* the truth. You might start with the words, "I am …"

Application

7. Examine this photograph (Figure 11.5) of a sculptor's depiction of *Archaeoraptor liaoningensis*.

Figure 11.5

This picture of a reconstructed bird-like dinosaur originally appeared in *National Geographic*. The sculpture was created using as evidence a skeleton that had been discovered in China. After publishing the article, the magazine's editors discovered that the skeleton was a hoax. Which epistemological school of thought does this incident support? Why? Does this incident change the way you would respond to the question, What is truth? Explain why.

8. Write the dialogue that might have occurred between two philosophers whose ideas about truth clash. Include statements that set out each philosopher's theory, statements that show the criticisms of their theories, and statements that you believe could be used to counter the criticisms.

Create a concept map poster.
CULMINATING ACTIVITY

EXPECTATIONS

By completing this activity, you will
- identify the main questions, concepts, and theories of epistemology
- evaluate the strengths and weaknesses of responses to some of the main questions of epistemology defended by some major philosophers and schools of philosophy, and defend your own responses
- demonstrate the relevance of philosophical theories of epistemology to concrete problems in everyday life
- explain how various epistemological theories apply to subject areas such as psychology
- demonstrate an understanding of the unique character of philosophical questions
- effectively use a variety of print and electronic sources and telecommunications tools in research
- effectively communicate the results of your inquiries

THE TASK

The study of knowledge requires an understanding of the relationships among the main questions, concepts, and theories of epistemology. You will work in a group to create a concept map poster. This will enable you to demonstrate this understanding and help you prepare to formulate and defend your own ideas about epistemological issues. Displaying your concept map in poster form will enable your group to share this understanding with others in your school or community.

At the end of this course, this poster may be included as a special insert in a philosophy magazine.

THE SUBTASKS

Subtask 1: Annotated Bibliography

Form a group of about five. Each group member should select one philosopher as a focus of investigation. Begin your research by identifying at least 10 print and electronic sources that will be useful in obtaining the information needed to answer the following guiding questions. List the sources you have identified in the form of an annotated bibliography.
1. Which main questions, concepts, and theories of epistemology are dealt with by the philosopher you selected?
2. How does this philosopher approach the questions, concepts, and theories you identified?
3. How are this philosopher's theories relevant to the problems of knowledge in everyday life?
4. Do this philosopher's theories apply to other subject areas, such as psychology? If so, how?

Subtask 2: Note-Taking Graphic Organizer

Summarize your research findings on a graphic organizer.

Subtask 3: Individual Concept Map
Using the questions in Subtask 1 as a guide, organize your ideas on cards or adhesive notes that can be used to help you sort and classify ideas as you search for relationships. Transfer these ideas to a piece of paper, then draw lines to link them. Place words on these lines to illustrate your thinking about the relationships shown.

Subtask 4: Personal Reflection
Study your concept map. Identify the strengths and weaknesses of the responses of the philosopher you selected to one important epistemological question. Ask yourself what is missing from the philosopher's responses, which responses appealed to you, and what counter-arguments you might propose. Write a 300- to 500-word personal reflection that formulates and defends your own responses to the epistemological question you selected.

Subtask 4: Group Concept Map
Explain to the group the ideas and relationships illustrated on your concept map and listen carefully as other group members do the same. Analyze everyone's concept map to discover links that show how the thoughts and theories of the philosophers are similar to or different from each other. Work with the group to create a poster-sized concept map that shows the relationships among the thoughts and ideas of all the philosophers selected. Use interesting visuals to enhance the appearance of your group's poster.

ASSESSMENT CRITERIA

The following criteria will be used to assess your concept map poster.

Knowledge and Understanding
Does your poster

- include with it an annotated bibliography that identifies and evaluates a variety of print and electronic research sources?
- include with it a graphic organizer that identifies the main epistemological questions, concepts, and theories addressed by the philosopher you selected?

Thinking and Inquiry
Does your poster

- include with it an individual concept map that shows how the philosopher you selected responds to an important epistemological question?
- include with it a personal reflection that formulates and defends your own ideas about this important epistemological question?
- identify the relationships among the epistemological questions, concepts, and theories dealt with by the philosophers selected by your group?

Communication
Does your poster

- illustrate in an appropriate and visually appealing format the relationships among the epistemological questions, concepts, and theories dealt with by the philosophers selected?
- include with it a personal reflection that applies the conventions of a personal reflection?

Application
Does your poster

- show that you have transferred to it the results of your research and your responses to the guiding questions?
- make connections among the concepts, ideas, theories, approaches, and conclusions shown on individual concept maps?
- include with it a reflection that draws on the ideas and thoughts of various philosophers to formulate and defend your own ideas about an important epistemological question?

UNIT 4
ETHICS

CHAPTER

12 Introducing Ethics

13 Answering Questions That Matter

14 Ethics in the World

Unit Expectations

By the end of this unit, you will be able to
- demonstrate an understanding of the main questions, concepts, and theories of ethics
- evaluate the strengths and weaknesses of responses to ethical questions and moral problems defended by some major philosophers and schools of philosophy, and defend your own responses
- describe how problems in ethics and the theories that address them may be illustrated in stories
- illustrate the relevance of philosophical theories of ethics to concrete moral problems in everyday life
- demonstrate an understanding of how philosophical theories of ethics are implicit in other subjects

What should I do? People ask this question of themselves and others every day. This question lies at the heart of all decisions that call for applying values and classifying actions as good or bad, right or wrong. But what do good and bad — and right and wrong — mean? What is morality and does it matter? Are moral choices possible, and if so, how meaningful are they if they represent nothing more than our personal values? For more than two millennia, philosophers and others have tried to answer these questions.

Linked to these questions are others such as, What is a good life? and What is a good person? All these questions show that there is wide variation in the way philosophers of ethics approach moral issues. Still, considering the questions, concepts, and theories of ethics put forward by various philosophers helps people develop their own answers to the moral questions that humankind has always grappled with.

Chapter 12
Introducing Ethics

Chapter Expectations

By the end of this chapter, you will be able to
- identify some of the main questions asked by ethicists
- evaluate the responses of some major philosophers and some major schools of ethics to some of the main ethical questions
- use critical and logical thinking to defend your ideas about ethical issues
- demonstrate how moral problems and dilemmas that occur in everyday contexts can be analyzed using a variety of philosophical theories
- demonstrate how problems in ethics and the theories that address them may be illustrated in stories

Key Words

ethics
morals
theories of action
theories of character
theories of value
virtue
humanism
moral agent
nihilism
ethical absolutists
ethical universalists
ethical relativists

Key People

Moses
Gautama (the Buddha)
Kongfuzi (Confucius)
Plato
Aristotle
Averroës
Virginia Held
Kwame Gyekye
Gorgias
Paul Kurtz
Nancy Midgley
Mohandas Gandhi

A Philosopher's Voice

Moral philosophy is nothing but a tangle of troubles.

George Kateb (1931–)

WHAT IS ETHICS?

Beggars like the man in this photograph (Figure 12.1) are a common sight on the streets of many of Canada's cities. If you were the pedestrian whose feet can be seen, how would you respond? If you had a loonie in your pocket, would you drop it into the beggar's tin?

Figure 12.1

As you walked past this beggar, you might ask yourself, What should I do? Should I ignore this man or help him? What is the right thing to do? Why?

When people ask questions like these, they are "doing" **ethics**. When making decisions about how to act, some people use what they call the gut test: if it feels right, do it. Others follow their conscience. But what really makes their gut respond the way it does? And what, exactly, is their conscience? Is it a collection of moral habits taught by parents or learned from friends? Is it something people are born with? Can someone's gut feeling or conscience be wrong? Some people use the law as their guide. Is this an appropriate guide? Can the law be wrong? Are there issues that are not covered by the law? These are the kinds of questions that ethicists — people who study ethics — grapple with.

Ethics comes to English from the Greek word *ethos*, which means character. Ethicists investigate character traits that are good and admirable, as well as traits that are bad and reprehensible. This leads them to study actions that are good and bad, right and wrong, and to ask how people should act. If philosophy is the study of wisdom, then ethics is the study of practical wisdom about personal behaviour — of exercising good judgment about actions. Making these judgments involves reflecting on the answers various people have given to ethical questions.

The term "ethics" is often used synonymously with "**morals**" or "morality," words that come from the Latin word *mores*, which means character, custom, or habit. Ethics and morality are so closely linked that ethics is often called moral philosophy and ethicists are often called moral philosophers. Still, some philosophers distinguish between morals or morality and ethics. They define "morals" or "morality" as customary beliefs about how people should be and act. They define "ethics" as the study of theories about these beliefs.

NATURE AND AIMS OF ETHICS

The study of ethics can be divided into three main categories: normative theories, metaethics, and applied ethics.

Ethicists often classify normative theories or the theories of morals and morality into three categories: **theories of action**, **theories of character**, and **theories of value**.

Theories of action deal with questions about how people should act — and why. Consider the difference between these two questions:

- *Do* students copy essays from the Internet and present them as their own?
- *Should* students copy essays from the Internet and present them as their own?

The first question, which asks whether students actually copy essays, is of no concern to ethicists because it *describes*, rather than *prescribes*, behaviour. The second question, which asks what students should do, *is* the concern of ethicists because it prescribes behaviour.

Theories of character deal with questions about character traits that are good and bad. These theories are sometimes called virtue theories or virtue ethics because they examine **virtues**: character traits, such as courage and wisdom, that are considered morally good.

Theories of value deal with questions about people's values. Values are assessments of worth. Questions about values might include, What is goodness? Badness? Justice? Injustice? Do these words objectively describe people or acts or are they simply names for subjective responses to people or acts? If they are simply names, are they unique to each person or are they determined by culture? Do people share certain values?

Metaethical questions can be asked about issues in all three areas. The term "metaethics" combines the prefix "meta-," which means beyond or of a higher order, with the word "ethics." Metaethics involves examining the meaning of the terms used when exploring ethical questions, as well as the methods used to carry out this exploration. Metaethicists also explore how — and in what sense — ethical judgments can be justified. Take the question, What should I do? Before attempting to answer this question, a metaethicist might examine the question itself by asking, "What is the meaning of 'should'?"

Applying theories of action, character, or value to ethical dilemmas is often called applied ethics. Ethical dilemmas arise in just about any field of human endeavour: business, sports, medicine, the environment, computers, and so on. As a result, ethicists work in all these areas.

Ethicists ask — and try to answer — general questions like, "What kind of life should a person lead?" "What is a good life?" "What are good and evil?" "What is virtue?" "Why be moral?" and "What obligations do people have to one another?" Exploring the answers to questions like these leads them to consider specific questions like, "What should I do in this situation?" or "What is the right thing to do in this case?"

> *Morality is not properly the doctrine of how we may make ourselves happy, but how we may make ourselves worthy of happiness.*
>
> – Immanuel Kant

THE PHILOSOPHER'S APPROACH TO ETHICS

When ethicists or moral philosophers discuss the kinds of lives people should lead, explore what people ought to do, and suggest character traits and values that are desirable and those that are not, they are prescribing behaviour. As a result, their approach is often called prescriptive or normative. The word "prescriptive" comes from "prescribe," while the word "normative" comes from "norm," which means a standard used to judge human behaviour. Saying thank you to acknowledge an act of kindness, for example, is a norm in many societies and cultures.

An ethicist's prescriptive or normative approach to issues is different from the descriptive approach of social scientists, such as psychologists or sociologists. If you kept your loonie firmly in your pocket as you walked by the beggar mentioned earlier, social scientists might describe your behaviour — without making a judgment about whether it is right or wrong.

Ethicist would take a different approach. They might pronounce your behaviour selfish — and they would also make a judgment about whether being selfish is right or wrong, good or bad. To an extent, this judgment would be an opinion. Like most philosophers, however, ethicists argue that some opinions are better than others. Opinions that are supported by sound arguments are worth more than opinions that are not. The ethicist's goal is to distinguish well-supported opinions about ethical issues from not-so-well-supported opinions and sound ethical judgments from not-so-sound judgments.

> **Recall...Reflect...Respond**
>
> 1. List six general questions that ethicists try to answer. Choose three and, for each, write a related question that deals with a specific ethical issue. Specify whether the related questions deal with theories of action, theories of character, or theories of value.
> 2. When faced with a moral choice, from where or whom do you seek guidance? List resources that you consult. Which of these resources do you consider most reliable? Explain why.
> 3. A friend found a $100 bill on the floor of a convenience store near your school. Write a brief paragraph reporting on the incident from a psychologist's point of view. Then do the same from an ethicist's point of view. Ensure that your paragraphs show how the approach of the psychologist and ethicist differ.

WHAT PHILOSOPHERS HAVE SAID

Philosophers from various traditions have always struggled to answer ethical questions like, What should I do? What is the good life? Why be moral? and What obligations do people have to one another? In many societies, finding the answers to these questions was the job of priests, prophets, and elders. Even today, people often look to religious leaders or elders for guidance about how to act.

One of the earliest recorded moral codes is found in accounts of a Hebrew prophet named **Moses**, who lived in Egypt about 1200 BCE. According to Jewish and Christian tradition, a supreme being called Yahweh, or God, gave Moses two stone tablets. Inscribed on the tablets were the Ten Commandments. These are rules of behaviour that still form the foundation of both the Jewish and Christian moral codes. The Ten Commandments forbid killing, stealing, lying, committing adultery, coveting neighbours' possessions, and worshipping other gods. They also command people to honour their parents.

In the sixth century BCE, similar ideas about behaviour were developed by **Gautama**, an Indian philosopher who is also known as the Buddha.

At about the same time as Gautama was developing his ideas, **Kongfuzi** (Confucius), a Chinese philosopher, was developing one of the earliest humanist codes of behaviour. **Humanism** emphasizes the human or secular (non-religious) realm over the religious or spiritual realm, and focuses on the role of free will or choice in making moral decisions. Kongfuzi's version of humanism stressed concern for others. "What you do not like when done to yourself, do not do to others," he said. This maxim, which is sometimes called the Golden Rule of Confucianism, was echoed hundreds of years later in the Golden Rule of Christian teaching: "Do unto others as you would have them do unto you."

The philosophers of ancient Greece, where the western philosophical tradition took root, lived in a society that worshipped many gods. Like their counterparts in other parts of the world, these philosophers explored the relationship between ethics and religion. One of the most controversial questions they asked was this: Is something right because it is favoured by the gods, or do the gods favour it because it is right? The answer to this question has been debated ever since.

The Greeks also set the stage for debate on another ethics question: What character traits make someone a good person? **Plato** and his student, **Aristotle**, came up with a list that included justice, courage, generosity, and modesty. Aristotle took the discussion a step farther than his teacher by developing an idea that he called the Golden Mean. He said that virtue — or moral excellence — is the mean, which is a middle path between two extremes of behaviour. Generosity, for example, is a mean between stinginess and wastefulness.

In about 30 CE, Jesus Christ, a Jew and founder of Christianity, added another important idea to ethical thinking. He said that people were to forgive one another rather than seek revenge. He also emphasized the importance of love in human relations. As Christianity spread across Europe in the early centuries of the Common Era, western philosophy was inseparable from theology, which is the study of the nature of a supreme being and religion. Christian thinkers filtered philosophical questions through a theological lens. Augustine of Hippo, for example, who lived in North Africa from 354 to 430, defined evil as a turning away from God. And the 13th-century Italian philosopher Thomas Aquinas said that to achieve happiness, people must follow God's laws.

At the time Christianity was beginning to dominate Europe, Islam was spreading rapidly throughout the Arabian peninsula and into parts of India and Africa. Like their Christian counterparts, Muslim scholars also linked philosophy and theology, relating ethical questions to religious principles.

One of the first to challenge the widely accepted linking of philosophy and theology was **Averroës**, a 12th-century Muslim philosopher from Andalusia, in present-day Spain. He said that theologians — those who study theology — are unfit to interpret divine law correctly because they are incapable of developing the highest forms of knowledge. Though Averroës's ideas had little effect on Islamic ethics, perhaps because he lived so far from the centres of Muslim scholarship, they did influence western thinkers and played a role in the early development of humanist ethics.

Humanist ethics took hold in Europe during the Renaissance, the 200-year period between 1350 and 1550. Thinkers such as Francesco Petrarch, Desiderius Erasmus, Niccoló Machiavelli, and Martin Luther fostered the early development of the humanist tradition in Europe by questioning traditional values.

Since that time, humanist and religion-based ethical theories have existed side by side in western philosophy. Some European thinkers, such as John Locke in 17th-century England and Søren Kierkegaard in 19th-century Denmark, searched for ways to reconcile humanist and religious ideas. Others, such as Immanuel Kant in 18th-century Germany and Friedrich Nietzsche in 19th-century Germany, rejected the notion of a link between the two.

In the 20th and 21st centuries, the debate continues over whether philosophy and religion can be linked. At the same time, many philosophers have continued to build on the humanist tradition. In the early 20th century, for example, the French philosopher Jean Paul Sartre suggested that ethics is a matter of individual responsibility. Later, in the United States, Ayn Rand advocated the virtue of selfishness, while Carol Gilligan and Nel Noddings focused on the ethics of care, which emphasizes people's relationships with others.

Figure 12.2

Extreme	Middle Path	Extreme
Stinginess	Generosity	Wastefulness

The Golden Mean is the middle path between two extremes of behaviour. Do you think that following the Golden Mean is leading a good life?

Web connection
http://www.mcgrawhill.ca/links/philosophy12
To find out more about Augustine of Hippo, follow the links on this Web site.

IDEAS IN CONTEXT

Over the centuries that the Romans dominated much of Europe, Northern Africa, and parts of the Middle East, the works of many ancient Greek philosophers were either ignored or lost. They might have remained so if not for Muslim philosophers such as Averroës. In the 12th century, Averroës studied the works of both Plato and Aristotle and wrote commentaries about their meaning. Among European thinkers, Averroës's work sparked renewed interest in the ancient philosophers and classical ideas.

Many 20th-century ethicists began to broaden their perspectives in searching for answers to the age-old ethical questions. Some, such as Gilligan, Noddings, and Virginia Held, began to investigate whether women and men approach ethical issues differently. In an article published in *Philosophy and Phenomenological Research*, Held wrote: "This history of philosophy, including the history of ethics, has been constructed from male points of view, and has been built on assumptions and concepts that are by no means gender-neutral." Held went on to give examples of these assumptions and concepts and to discuss the split between reason, which is often associated with men, and emotion, which is often associated with women.

Others began to study the ethics of societies and cultures that had previously been dismissed or ignored by western philosophers. Kwame Gyekye, for example, is an African philosopher who writes about the ethics of his own Akan people, who live in present-day Ghana. According to the community-focused ethic of the Akan people, the good of the community often takes precedence over the good of individuals.

Investigations such as these have shed new light on ethical issues and introduced new ideas to ethical debates.

How Philosophers Have Said It

Just as ethicists debate the answers to questions of good and bad, right and wrong, they often disagree over the precise meaning of the terms used in these debates. Still, some terms are used over and over in ethics and can be defined in a way that many ethicists find acceptable. Since ancient times, for example, philosophers have used the word "virtue" to refer to a character trait that is morally good. Trustworthiness and generosity are two qualities usually considered virtues.

Moral philosophers use the terms "good" and "bad" to describe desirable and undesirable people, actions, and consequences. At the same time, they use the terms "right" and "wrong" to describe morally acceptable and unacceptable people, actions, and consequences. Though these terms are used this way, ethicists often disagree about what is desirable and undesirable, as well as what is morally acceptable and unacceptable.

They also disagree over the relationship between good and right. Some ethicists say that good and right are the same thing; others say that they are not. Those who argue that the terms mean different things say that actions can be bad, but right — and good, but wrong. Imagine a shipwreck, for example. So many survivors have managed to climb into a lifeboat that it is overloaded, yet some people are still in the water. Preventing these survivors from climbing into the boat might be judged bad because it condemns them to drown. At the same time, this action might be judged right because taking more people into the boat would make it capsize, causing everyone to drown.

Many ethicists also use terms more carefully than people do in everyday speech. For example, people often use the terms "moral" and "ethical" as synonyms for "right," and "immoral" and "unethical" as synonyms for "wrong." Many ethicists prefer to use the term "moral" as a neutral adjective that means involving morals and the term "ethical" as a neutral adjective that means involving ethics.

When moral is used in this neutral sense, its antonym — or opposite — is "amoral." Unlike "immoral," which describes something that is not moral because it breaks the moral rules, "amoral" describes something that is not moral because moral rules do not apply to it. Amoral issues fall outside the realm of ethics.

Deciding whether to dry newly washed dishes with a tea towel or to let them air dry is an amoral issue, no matter what your parents might have said about the "right" way of doing this. In this context, the word "right" refers only to the effectiveness of the action, not to its moral rightness or wrongness.

> *There is only one good, knowledge, and one evil, ignorance.*
>
> – Socrates

Figure 12.3 OVERBOARD © 1999 UNIVERSAL PRESS SYNDICATE. Reprinted with permission. All rights reserved.

Clearly, Louie and his owner differ over their interpretation of the meaning of "good."

Deciding whether to cheat on a test is, by contrast, an ethical issue because it does involve moral right and wrong.

If morals are rules that guide people's behaviour, morality is a system of moral rules that guide all behaviour. Some ethicists insist that morality refers only to conduct toward other people because judgments about good and bad — and right and wrong — cannot be applied when other people are not affected. These ethicists argue, for example, that the actions of a castaway who is alone on a desert island affect no one but himself. As a result, judgments about right and wrong do not apply to anything he does. Other ethicists say that this view of morality is too broad because behaviour toward other people could be interpreted to include etiquette or manners.

The following chart summarizes some of the terms used in ethical debates.

Ethics is	the study of morality	
Morality is	a system of ethical beliefs about good and bad, right and wrong	
Issues can be	moral (i.e., involving right and wrong)	amoral (i.e., not involving right and wrong)
Actions can be	right (i.e., ethically or morally right)	wrong (i.e., ethically or morally wrong)
Actions can be	good (i.e., ethically or morally good)	bad (i.e., ethically or morally bad)
People can be	good (i.e., ethically or morally good)	bad (i.e., ethically or morally bad)

The words "value" and "values" often figure prominently in ethical debate. Values are different from facts. Saying "Nellie Furtado is a singer-songwriter" expresses a fact, but saying "Nellie Furtado is a talented singer-songwriter" expresses a value judgment. Making a value judgment involves assessing the worth of something, whether this is an action, a thought, an attitude, or even a person.

When speaking of values, ethicists often distinguish between intrinsic value and instrumental value. Knowledge, for example, has intrinsic value because it is desired for its own sake, independent of its consequences. Money, by contrast, has instrumental value because it provides a means for people to do or have something.

Other terms that often figure in ethical debates are **moral agent** and moral patient. A moral agent is someone who is capable of thinking about a moral problem, making a decision about how to act, and taking responsibility for this action.

Most adults are considered moral agents. Newborns and most non-human animals are not considered moral agents because they cannot understand the consequences of their actions and are seldom aware of their motivations. As a result, they are not considered morally responsible for their actions — and are called moral patients. Still, the interests and desires of moral patients are considered important and deserving of moral attention and treatment. Like moral agents, moral patients have moral standing in the moral community. For this reason, it is not considered morally right, for example, to abuse animals or newborns.

Why Ethics Matters

Every day, people make choices that involve moral issues. What are you going to tell a teacher about an unfinished assignment? Are you going to lie, tell the truth, or do a bit of both? Biologists may be required to decide whether it is right to use animals in experiments. Engineers may be required to decide whether it is right to develop certain natural resources. A hockey coach may be required to decide whether winning at all costs is an appropriate goal.

Other times, people must make extraordinary decisions. Should you risk your own life to help a stranger who is in danger? Should you report someone who is planning an assault or fraud? Should you join a boycott of companies that use child labour in their factories? Ethics helps people answer questions like these.

The enduring popularity of entertainment — whether this is literature, plays, films, or television — that deals with ethical issues may reflect people's continuing fascination with exploring solutions to the moral dilemmas they face in their own lives.

In the famous speech that begins "To be or not to be," for example, William Shakespeare's character Hamlet struggles with the issue of whether to commit suicide. Another Shakespearean play, *Romeo and Juliet*, is often read as a romance but has much to say about gang violence.

William Golding's novel *Lord of the Flies* explores why moral codes are necessary, and Margaret Atwood's *The Handmaid's Tale* portrays a world in which individual freedoms, especially those of women and the economically disadvantaged, are severely restricted.

Some of the most popular TV shows and movies also deal with ethical issues. Nearly every episode of *Star Trek: The Next Generation*, for example, deals with an ethical dilemma, as do medical dramas such as *ER*. And the movie *Gattaca*, which was released in the late 1990s but set in a not-too-distant future, dealt with the ethical implications of genetic engineering.

People's moral standards develop as a result of a variety of influences: parents, relatives, teachers, church, television, movies, books, newspapers, magazines, music, and friends. In *Dialogues*, Plato created a dialogue in which Socrates said that our values create our "self." In other words, we are what we are because of our moral values and because of the kind of life we choose to live. The way we think affects the way we act, and the way we act reflects the way we think. Think about your own moral standards. What standards do you use when making moral judgments? What influences have been most important in helping you develop your own ideas about right and wrong?

Suppose a friend is wrongly accused of spreading false rumours about someone. You know that your friend did not start the rumours but has no way of proving it. Your friend concocts a lie to prove her innocence and asks you to confirm the lie. Should you agree to your friend's request?

This dilemma raises several moral issues. Is honesty always the best policy? What makes lying wrong? Is it sometimes okay to lie? If so, when? Is lying okay, for example, if it helps get at the truth?

Studying ethics can help you

- recognize ethical issues
- resolve indecision or conflict and make decisions about ethical issues by clarifying your values; by considering, analyzing, and refining your arguments; and by making judgments about the worth of your values or principles.
- act in accordance with values you have chosen rather than with values you have inherited or been conditioned to accept
- communicate reasons for your decisions and actions

> **Recall...Reflect...Respond**
>
> 1. Create a three-column chart to show how three important ideas have affected the thinking of ethicists. At the top of each column, identify an idea, such as concern for others. Under each heading, write the names of two philosophers who have been influenced by the idea. Compare your chart with those of others.
> 2. A boy of six saw a friend being threatened with physical harm by a teenager. Asked later whether he saw the incident, the child answers no because he fears for his safety. Classify the child, his action, and the ethical issues raised by his action as good or bad, right or wrong. Be ready to explain your judgments.
> 3. In the film *First Knight*, King Arthur says, "There are laws that enslave man and laws that set them free … what we hold to be right, good and true must be right, good and true for all mankind under God.…" What do these words say about King Arthur's moral beliefs? What does it say about him as a ruler?

SOME METAETHICAL QUESTIONS

Though ethicists are certainly interested in answering specific questions about how people should act, they are also interested in examining the assumptions that underlie these specific questions. When they do this, they are "doing" metaethics. Consider, for example, the specific question, What is the right thing to do in this particular situation? Trying to answer it raises a number of metaethical questions about the underlying suppositions: Are moral choices possible? Why do the right thing? How should the rightness and wrongness of actions be determined? Are moral rules objective or subjective? Are legal and right the same thing?

ARE MORAL CHOICES POSSIBLE?

The metaethical question of whether moral choices are possible has sparked considerable debate because it really asks whether it makes sense to talk about morality at all. At various times in the history of western philosophy, some philosophers have insisted that making moral choices is impossible. And they argue that if making moral choices is impossible, there is no point in struggling to decide what is right and what is wrong.

Philosophers who have taken this stand have developed various arguments to support their beliefs. In the fourth century BCE, for example, the Sicilian philosopher **Gorgias** travelled to Greece to study philosophy and set out a view known as **nihilism**. Nihilism comes from the Latin word *nihil*, which means "nothing."

Nihilists believe that there can be no such thing as right and wrong because moral truths or facts do not exist. In fact, Gorgias argued that nothing exists. He also said that even if something does exist, it can never be known, and even if something does exist and can be known, it can never be communicated. He said that it can never be communicated because people use words to communicate, and words are nothing but symbols. No symbol can ever be the same thing as the thing it symbolizes. As a result, Gorgias said that knowledge — including knowledge of moral truths or facts — cannot be communicated.

Similar arguments were put forward by the skeptics, a school that originated in ancient Greece. The English word "skeptic" comes from the Greek *skeptikos*, which means a seeker or inquirer. Skeptics believe that nothing can be known for certain. They argue that if nothing can be known for certain, people can never know whether moral truths or facts exist. Ethical statements can be defended only with more ethical statements, say skeptics. They believe that people must doubt the truth of all these statements.

Other schools of thought have argued that making moral choices is impossible because forces that are beyond human control dictate people's actions. If people have no control over their moral decisions, they claim there is little point in talking about specific ethical questions or struggling with specific moral issues.

Determinists, for example, believe that everything that happens is determined by previous events or the laws of nature. Because these forces are beyond human control, determinists say that the idea of choice or free will is nothing but an illusion.

In the 17th century, the British scientist Isaac Newton, who is most famous for formulating the law of gravity, said that all matter functions according to universal laws of nature. Supporters of Newton's theory applied it to the functioning of the atoms that make up the human brain. They reasoned that if the atoms that make up the brain are governed by universal laws, then people cannot control their actions. If you decide to help a friend study, for example, determinists would argue that this action is not the result of free choice; rather, they would say that it is the result of the atoms that make up your brain moving in a way that is beyond your control.

The 19th-century British scientist Charles Darwin was also a determinist. He believed that people are incapable of choosing what to do — or be — because their behaviour is governed by their biological or genetic makeup. Darwin would say, for example, that criminals break the law not because they have freely chosen a life of crime but because they are biologically or genetically programmed to live criminal lives.

Determinist theories are controversial because they suggest that people cannot be held responsible for their actions. If criminals, for example, are biologically or genetically programmed, how can they be held responsible for their criminal acts?

Figure 12.4

CALVIN AND HOBBES © Watterson. Reprinted with permission of UNIVERSAL PRESS SYNDICATE. All rights reserved.

Calvin has clearly decided that taking the entire last piece of pie will give him more pleasure than sharing it with others. Is this a morally right decision?

The theory of determinism has been supported by one interpretation of a religious doctrine called predestination, which says that the fate of humans is predestined by God, who decides which people will be saved. Though most closely associated with Christian theologians such as Augustine of Hippo in the fourth and fifth centuries and Martin Luther and John Calvin in the 16th century, ideas similar to predestination also appear in other cultures. Like other doctrines that suggest that free will and choice play little role in people's lives, the idea of predestination also minimizes the ability of people to influence their fate.

In the 20th century, some philosophers used the theories of the psychologist Sigmund Freud to advance another argument against the idea that people are free to make moral choices. Building on Freud's assertion that human behaviour is governed by unconscious psychological desires, they developed a theory called psychological egoism. This theory says that humans are programmed to act only out of self-interest. As a result, people always make the choice that gives them the greatest pleasure, even when this choice seems to involve a sacrifice. Suppose, for example, that you and a friend have been hiking on a hot day. You brought along a bottle of water, but your friend brought nothing. Despite your own thirst, you share your water with your friend.

You claim that you did this out of concern for your friend. Those who subscribe to the theory of psychological egoism would say that this is not so. They would argue that you shared your water only because sharing gave you greater pleasure than drinking all the water yourself.

Another 20th-century psychologist, the American B.F. Skinner, also developed a theory that minimized the role of choice in human behaviour. Skinner said that the behaviour of animals, both human and non-human, is a conditioned response to stimuli. These conditioned responses govern the way people act, eliminating the possibility of choice.

THOUGHT EXPERIMENT: *The Magic Ring*

It's amazing what you can find at yard sales. While inline skating to your favourite hangout one summery Saturday morning, you check out a yard sale in front of a dilapidated old house. A wizened man with a long grey beard and a twinkle in his eye is selling strange things: shiny rocks, gothic jew-ellery, candles, astrology charts, broomsticks, potions in blue crystal bottles, good luck charms, and statues of goblins.

As you examine some of the items, the old man sidles up to you. "Interested in a special ring?" he asks. He holds out one with an emerald-green stone. It looks like a piece of junk from a cereal box. "It's only $10."

"Ten dollars? No, thanks," you snort.

"You'll sorely regret not buying it, Esmeralda. How about $5?"

You are stunned. How did this man know your name? You have never seen him before. Feeling a little creeped out, you hand him $5 and skate away.

Before joining your friends, you try on the ring. It isn't totally cool, but it's retro and matches your green hair. Maybe your friends will like it. Who knows?

As you approach the hangout, you see your friends and call out, "Hey, what's happening?"

They hear your voice and look in your direction, but don't see you. Terrified, they scatter. It turns out that you have bought a magic ring that makes you invisible. Put it on, and you fade from sight; take it off, and you reappear. You can walk anywhere — through crowds, stores, and classrooms — completely undetected. No one will see you. You can get away with anything.

Figure 12.5

How would you use your ability to make yourself invisible? Would you spy on your enemies, steal from banks, drag race stolen Ferraris through city streets, and reward your friends with diamonds or wads of stolen cash? Or would you try to do good things, like helping people and fighting injustice? Would you choose to be an invisible Robin Hood?

In *The Republic*, Plato asked his readers to imagine just such a situation. He called the magic ring the ring of Gyges, after the shepherd Gyges who discovered a magic ring and went on a rampage, killing the king of his country. Plato's story illustrates the theory of psychological egoism, the view that people are always motivated by self-interest. Glaucon, one of the characters in *The Republic*, said that everyone would act like Gyges if they knew that they could get away with it. The only reason people act justly is that they do not have the amazing powers bestowed by the ring. Without these powers, people are too weak and afraid of punishment to act unjustly. If they had the ring, said Glaucon, and knew that they would never be caught and punished, they would act unjustly.

Glaucon said that even a just person who got hold of the magical ring would be unable to resist its temptations. He said that self-interest and self-indulgence would take over. Possession of the ring would make the just and the unjust indistinguishable.

How would you act if you had such a ring? What if 10 percent of the population had such a ring? Or 30 percent? Would even good and honest people succumb to the temptations of the ring?

> *Generally speaking, the errors in religion are dangerous; those in philosophy only ridiculous.*
>
> – David Hume

Logical positivism, a theory supported by the 20th-century philosopher Alfred Jules Ayer, suggests that debating moral issues is impossible because ethical statements are meaningless. Logical positivists believe that the only statements that count are either those that are true by definition (e.g., 2 + 2 = 4) or that can be verified by evidence presented by the senses (e.g., It is raining). Because statements about morality (e.g., Presenting only one side of a news story is wrong) are neither true by definition nor verifiable by observation, logical positivists argue that they have no meaning. As a result, they say that there are no moral facts — and if there are no moral facts, it is impossible to make moral choices. At the same time, logical positivists argue that people should obey a law because it is a law. Their view on moral choices does not mean that they support lawlessness.

Various philosophers, such as the contemporary thinker Richard Rorty, have challenged the theory of logical positivism. Perhaps the most interesting challenge was mounted by those who used the logical positivists' own argument to refute their theory. These philosophers point out that the logical positivists' assertion that ethical statements are meaningless is neither true by definition nor verifiable by evidence presented by the senses. As a result, it must be meaningless.

Emotivism, or emotive theory, also disputes the idea of moral facts that exist. It says that moral claims are nothing but expressions of feeling or attitude. Originated in the 18th century by the Scottish philosopher David Hume, emotive theory was used by 20th-century philosophers such as Ayer to support logical positivism. Because ethical statements or moral claims are neither true by definition nor by observation, Ayer said that they are not factual. If these statements are not factual, they can express only approval or disapproval — and approval and disapproval express only feelings or attitudes.

Many of the same philosophers who challenged logical positivism also disputed emotive theory. They asked, for example, how emotive theory would view the suffering of an injured animal. Would this be bad only if someone knew of the suffering and disapproved of it? They said that this kind of thinking seems to play games with the fact of the animal's suffering.

Though various scientists, theologians, psychologists, and ethicists have argued that it is impossible to make moral choices, many others discount these theories. They believe that people have the freedom to make — and take responsibility for — choices about actions and that this freedom lies at the core of people's humanity. Indeed, they argue that people *must* make moral choices.

WHY DO THE RIGHT THING?

If people are free to make moral choices, why should they choose to do the right thing rather than the wrong thing? Since the earliest times, various philosophers have tried to answer this question. Gautama, for example, suggested that the goal of life is to end suffering and achieve nirvana or enlightenment, a state of harmony. He said that the way to do this is by living a simple life and following the Eightfold Path, which involves right understanding, right thought, right speech, right action, right livelihood, right effort, right mindfulness, and right concentration.

Kongfuzi also tried to answer this question, saying that harmony consists of the perfect individual living in a well-ordered society in which people recognize their proper role in relationships with others. These relationships may involve ruler and subject, father and son, husband and wife, friend and friend, and so on.

Web connection
http://www.mcgrawhill.ca/links/philosophy12
To find out more about Kongfuzi (Confucius), follow the links on this Web site.

PROFILE

Kongfuzi
The First Great Humanist Philosopher

Kongfuzi wanted to change the world. In the sixth century BCE, crime and violence were on the rise in China. Theft was common in the country, and murder was common both on the streets and in the courts of the nobility. The government was corrupt. Business was flourishing, but scholars were unemployed. The rich were becoming richer, the poor poorer.

Kongfuzi's ancestors may have been members of the nobility, but the family had fallen on hard times. By the time he was born in 551 BCE, his parents were poverty stricken. When Kongfuzi was three years old, his father died, making a bad situation even worse. Still, his mother tried to educate him, and by the time he was 15, he had developed a love of learning that would remain with him all his life.

As a young man, Kongfuzi spoke out against the corruption of those in power, something that may have prevented his getting a job with influence. As a result, he worked at various times as a shepherd, a cowherd, and a book clerk.

At the same time, he pursued learning, focusing on the classics of history, poetry, propriety, and especially the *Book of Changes* (the *Yi Jing* or *I Ching*). This was no mean feat as books at the time were made of bamboo strips tied by cords. Kongfuzi believed that if he could spend 50 years studying the *Book of Changes*, he might be free of great mistakes.

When he was 19, he married. Three years later, he established a school and is considered to be the first professional teacher in China. His goal was to make education available to all men, and to establish teaching as an honorable profession.

Kongfuzi and his students travelled from province to province, starting the tradition of wandering scholars. He believed that any situation could be a lesson and that education could bring about equality. As he and his students or disciples wandered the countryside, they spread his ideas of justice, personal conduct, ethics, government and morality and tried to influence the country's rulers to do the right thing. His focus on the secular, rather than the spiritual, realm and his emphasis on living a good life in a well-ordered society made him one of the first humanist philosophers.

Kongfuzi believed that without the love of learning, love of the six virtues — goodness, knowledge, faithfulness, uprightness, courage, and strong character — would degenerate.

"Love of goodness degenerates to simple-mindedness; love of knowledge to lack of principle; love of faithfulness to injurious disregard of consequences; love of uprightness to harshness; love of courage to insubordination; and love of strong character to mere recklessness," he wrote.

In addition to teaching, he edited the *Book of Odes* and the *Spring and Autumn Annals* and is thought to have written commentaries on the *Book of Changes*. He was also an avid fisher, but without a net, and a crack archer, though he never shot a bird at rest.

Kongfuzi died in 479 BCE. At the time of his death, he had about 3000 followers. Though he never became very powerful in his own time, his influence continued to grow after his death, and he is now one of the most revered philosophers in China.

Figure 12.6

Better known in western literature as Confucius, the Latin version of his Chinese name, Kongfuzi originated a philosophy that is now known as Confucianism. This picture of the Chinese philosopher was created in the 18th century, more than 2000 years after his death.

CAN PEOPLE BE GOOD WITHOUT GOD?

Over the millennia, many people have looked to a supreme being or beings for guidance about how to act. The ancient Greeks, for example, often consulted the gods about what to do. Jews and Christians look to the will of God, Muslims look to the will of Allah, and Hindus seek guidance from various deities. The idea that a supreme being — or beings — commands people to behave in specific ways is called divine command theory and is common to many societies and cultures.

What happens to people who do not believe in a supreme being or beings, however? How do atheists — those who do not believe in a supreme being — and agnostics — those who say that it is impossible to know whether a supreme being exists — make moral decisions? Can atheists and agnostics be morally good without adhering to the principles of a particular religion? Humanist ethicists would say yes, though their reasons for saying this vary.

Paul Kurtz, a contemporary humanist, points out that values based on religious principles do not necessarily differ from those based on humanistic principles. Kurtz wrote:

> Humanist ethics is so deeply ingrained in human culture that even religious conservatives accept many (if not all) of its ethical premises.... Humanist ethics is not some recent invention; it has deep roots in world civilization, and it can be found in the great thinkers, from Aristotle and Confucius to [Baruch] Spinoza, Adam Smith, [John Stuart] Mill, and [John] Dewey.... I submit that humanist ethical ideals, which emphasize the pursuit of happiness, moral freedom, tolerance, moral responsibility, and rational moral inquiry, are basic for social peace and ethical improvement, and that both religious and non-religious people can share these values.

One reason some humanist ethicists offer for doing the right thing is to avoid punishment and blame. The drawback of this reasoning is obvious: it applies only to wrongdoing that is likely to be discovered — and punished. What if, as Plato asked in *The Republic*, you could become invisible and act in any way you wanted with no fear of discovery or punishment? Would you still choose to be virtuous?

In answer, Plato said that choosing the right course leads to a state of inner peace and harmony. He argued that this inner harmony results from exercising self-control, which he said is a form of freedom because it means that people are not ruled by their desires.

Other ethicists have suggested other reasons for doing the right thing. If people know that you will do the right thing, they will respect and trust you — and they'll like you and enjoy being around you. Still other ethicists have argued that if people choose the morally right course — if they choose not to lie, steal, cheat, hurt, or kill — the world would be a better place for everyone. This doctrine, which is known as enlightened self-interest, echoes the Golden Rule of both Confucian teaching and Jewish and Christian theology. It suggests that the world would be safer and happier because everyone would experience security, peace, justice, freedom, and trust.

These answers to the question, Why do the right thing? assume that security, peace, justice, and so on are right and good. In a sense, this means that the answer to the question is circular: People should do the right thing because it is right. In fact, some have argued that the question itself — Why do the right thing? — makes no sense because it opens up the possibility that people should do something other than what is right; in other words, that we should do something other than what we should do. But what could this be? What should people do if not what we should do?

PHILOSOPHY IN ACTION

The Land of Certus

by Thomas D. Davis

Thomas D. Davis, the author of the following story, is an American philosopher turned mystery writer. The story is a fantasy, related by a wanderer who got lost in a treacherous forest. He stumbled across a farmer named Felanx, who led him to the town of Rechtsen in the land of Certus. When the wanderer asked about the strange green and red lights that glowed in people's faces, Felanx explained that the green light is the light of the good and the red light is the light of the bad. When people do something good, they glow green; when they do something bad, they glow red.

I marvelled at the words of my host. To have all good and bad deeds clearly marked so that everyone should know them for what they were: could anything be a greater boon to humanity? ... After some thought, I inquired about the origin of the lights.

"To that question," said Felanx, "there is no answer that seems to satisfy all. One answer is given in *The Book of the Beginning*. It says that the Creator made the skies and the earth and then, because He was lonely, He created human beings to be His companions. He put human beings in the most beautiful place on earth, the Valley of Peace, and He dwelt there with them."

Felanx then continued his tale, describing how the people decided to see what lay beyond the valley.

"[The Creator] said that He would give those who departed the lights of good and bad, so that they would know how to make themselves worthy to return to the valley. He said that one day He would walk the earth and lead those who glowed with the goodness of green back to the Valley of Peace.

"That, I say, is just one answer. It is the one that my wife accepts. Others have argued that there is no Creator, that the skies and earth have always been. They say that the lights of the good and bad are simply natural events that require no supernatural explanation. The light of the good, they say, is no more mysterious than the other colours of things whose significance is beauty. I, myself, am of this opinion."

I remarked that in my land there were also doubts about a Creator. But the disputes of the Certans were as nothing compared with ours. For in my land, each person interpreted good and bad "according to his or her own lights," and what each person saw was different. At least in Certus there were no doubts about goodness and badness: the lights were the same for everyone. And if there were doubts about a Creator, at least there could be no doubt how to please Him, should He exist.

The next day, Felanx showed the wanderer around town. The wanderer noticed that the green lights did indeed mark acts of goodness and the red lights acts of badness. He also noticed that the red lights allowed people to see their mistakes at once and to correct them.

At one home, we drank a delicious plum whiskey, and the green light over the gathering answered for me a question that divided those in my land, the question of whether it is evil to drink alcohol. The green light told me that drinking is good, though only in moderation. When one of the group became drunken, he glowed with a red light. He was led from the room, apologizing to us all.

As we emerged from another house, I noticed a ragged fellow stumbling as if inebriated, glowing the brightest of reds. The others with me jeered at him, but the fellow only smiled and made a sign with his hands, which I was given to understand was the vilest of profanities. I was surprised by the existence of this reprobate in Certus, and I asked Felanx about him.

"His name is Georges, and he is a difficult case," said Felanx. "At first, some thought that he might be blind to the lights of good and bad, as some are blind to colours and shapes. But he answers questions about the lights correctly. He just won't be guided by them. He knows the good but doesn't want to do it. His case is now before the town council. My guess is that there will be extreme punishment."

"But how can a man know good and not want to do it?" I exclaimed.

At once I saw the foolishness of my remark, remembering that in the sacred book of my land it says that many fall not through ignorance but through the wickedness of the heart. I told Felanx of this.

"And so it says in *The Book of the Beginning*. But Georges is especially dangerous. Not only does he say that he often prefers wickedness to goodness, but he suggests

CHAPTER 12 Introducing Ethics MHR **255**

that everyone should do so. He says that people should do what pleases them and should disregard the lights."

"But how can he be dangerous?" I asked. "Surely anyone can see that if all were to do as they pleased, with no thought of the good, with no thought of others, the result must be chaos, disastrous for all."

"Of course," said Felanx. "But Georges is subtle. He says that what all people should prefer is not only their own pleasures but also the pleasures of others. It is this that seems to absolve him of selfishness in the eyes of the young, and many are drawn to his words."

As the two continued walking, the wanderer asked about the cannons placed on the walls of the town. Felanx explained that the weapons were to defend the folk of Rechtsen against their enemies in the neighbouring town of Linksen. The people of the two towns were enemies because their interpretations of the lights were different.

"The Linksens ... have a religion that denies our own. They say that the lights of good and bad are not the work of the Creator, but the work of the Creator's enemy. They say that the lights of good and bad have been put in this land to confuse and lead astray the Creator's true friends. They say that we ... should instead follow the laws written in their book. These laws, they believe, express the Creator's true wishes.... Were you to compare [the Linksens'] rules of good and bad with the lights of the good and bad, you would find much agreement. It is this, they say, that shows the cleverness of the Creator's enemy. He makes the lights so that they seem to show the truth in every case. It is this that misleads so many. The Linksens say that women should be equal to men, that animals are not to be eaten, and that the Rechtsens are to be destroyed. That the red light shows on such deeds, they say, is the triumph of deception."

The next day, the wanderer awoke to yelling in the courtyard. Investigating, he discovered that Georges was being tortured before being burned at the stake.

I turned away in anger and horror, searching the faces in the crowd. All were watching the brutal spectacle with slight, solemn smiles. I saw Felanx near me and grabbed his arm.

"How can you do this?" I cried. "You who say you love the good."

"Georges is paying the price for his wickedness. The council decided last night. Georges ignores the good and incites others to do the same.... He has to be made an example. It is right that he be punished."

"Punished, yes," I said. "Perhaps even killed. But not like this. This is barbaric! This is horrible!"

Felanx pulled away from me, and his expression became fierce. He moved his hand, and for a moment I thought he was going to strike me. Instead he pointed toward Georges.

"Look again," he commanded.

"No. It is too terrible."

"Look at the men who are carrying out the sentence."

Reluctantly, I glanced toward the terrible scene. Then I saw what had escaped my attention before. The torturers of Georges were all glowing a faint green. This act that I had so readily condemned was, in fact, good, right. Suddenly my horror turned to shame.

"Forgive me," I said, bowing my head.

Felanx forgave the wanderer, then told him that he must leave the town for his own safety. The Linksens were planning to use George's punishment as an excuse to attack Rechtsen. A guide showed the wanderer the way home.

The land of Certus is often in my thoughts. For it seems to me that if there is any hope for humankind, it must lie with those brave people of Rechtsen who know the good, follow it, and will fight for it to the end. May the Creator help them in their struggle.

Source: From *Philosophy: An Introduction Through Original Fiction, Discussion and Readings*, 2nd ed., by Thomas Davis, McGraw-Hill, 1979.

---

1. This story raises questions relating to both normative ethics (theories of action, character, and value) and metaethics.

   a) List three questions relating to normative ethics raised by this story.

   b) List three metaethical questions raised by this story.

2. How does the story answer these questions? Do these answers reflect your own views on the ethical issues raised by the questions? Why?

3. In this story, a green light appears as Georges is being tortured. This persuades the narrator to change his mind about the moral rightness of torture. Would the green light have changed your mind in the same way? Why?

HOW SHOULD THE RIGHTNESS OR WRONGNESS OF ACTIONS BE DETERMINED?

The question of how to determine whether actions are right or wrong lies at the heart of most ethical debates because it underlies the choices people make about how to act. Some ethicists, called **ethical absolutists**, believe that one universally acceptable moral code determines the rightness and wrongness of actions. They think that everyone, regardless of consequences, circumstances, cultural background, and so on, should observe this moral code

Ethical universalists also believe that one universally acceptable moral code determines the rightness and wrongness of actions. They do not believe, however, that this code should be applied regardless of the consequences. They believe that moral rules can — and should — be broken in certain circumstances. Though ethical absolutists believe that moral rules are universal, ethical universalists do not necessarily believe that moral rules are absolute.

William Styron's novel *Sophie's Choice* includes a situation over which ethical absolutists and universalists might disagree. When Sophie Zawistowska, a young Polish mother, and her two children arrive at a Nazi concentration camp during World War II, a camp officer tells her she can take only one child into the camp. The other must go straight to the death chamber. The officer orders Sophie to choose which child will live and which will die. If she refuses to make a choice, he warns, he will send both children to the gas chamber. Distraught, Sophie decides to give up her daughter and keep her son because he is older and stronger — and is therefore more likely to survive in the camp.

> *There are two sides to every question.*
> – Protagoras

To give one of her children a chance at life, Sophie was forced to play an active role in the murder of her other child. Did she make the right choice? Ethical absolutists, who believe that there can be no exceptions to moral rules, might say that Sophie should have refused to make this choice, even though the consequence would be the death of both children. Ethical universalists, who believe that exceptions to moral rules are justified in some circumstances, might argue that Sophie's action was morally right in this situation.

If ethical absolutists and universalists sit at one end of the spectrum of thought about moral rules, **ethical relativists** sit at the other end. Relativists reject the idea of a universal moral code, claiming that all values are relative to time, place, persons, and situations. Relativists say that all moral rules are equally acceptable, because there is no way of judging between them. Ethical relativists, however, are neither nihilists nor skeptics: they do believe in moral right and wrong, but they do not believe that ideas about right and wrong are universal.

Protagoras in preSocratic times and Hume in the 18th century were relativists, arguing that morality depends on social customs. As relativists, they believed that ethical norms are relative to particular societies, and that if a society agrees that something is right, then it is right. In some American states, for example, capital punishment is considered morally acceptable. In other states — and in Canada — it is not. Ethical relativists would say that capital punishment is right in those American states where society says it is right — and wrong in those other states and in Canada, where society says it is wrong. Ethical relativists believe that morality involves conforming to the norms of the society in which a person lives.

Most ethicists are neither absolutists nor relativists. On a continuum that places absolutism at one end and relativism at the other, they would probably fall somewhere in the middle. They would agree that some moral standards, such as a prohibition against murder, should apply to everyone, while other standards, such as killing cows and pigs for food, are morally acceptable in societies where this is the norm. This means that they would move toward the absolutist end of the continuum in some ethical debates; in others, they might move toward the relativist end.

The idea that some moral rules are absolute while others are relative is especially important in a democratic and multicultural society like Canada's. Respecting diversity is an

Figure 12.7

```
Absolutists                                          Relativists
Some ethicists  ← Most ethicists →  Some ethicists
```

If beliefs about the universality of moral standards were pictured on a continuum like this, few ethicists would place themselves at one end or the other. Most would congregate toward the middle, though they might move toward one end or the other depending on the issue being debated.

important value of Canadian society. Most Canadians accept that people whose customs, traditions, beliefs, or values differ from those of the majority must not be subjected to the tyranny of the majority. At the same time, many people agree that some rules, such as the prohibition against theft, are absolute, even if these rules conflict with those of a different culture.

In her book *Heart and Mind*, **Mary Midgley** identified the risk involved in carrying ethical relativism to an extreme. Midgley said that it could lead to moral isolationism, the view that out of respect and tolerance people should not criticize the morality of other cultures. She wrote: "Moral isolationism would lay down a general ban on moral reasoning." Still, reconciling the moral rules observed by various cultures and deciding which are absolute and which are relative is often difficult. According to Midgley and other contemporary ethicists, however, this is no reason to shy away from making moral judgments.

> ### Recall...Reflect...Respond
>
> 1. Choose one theory that suggests that moral choices are impossible and explain how it leads to the conclusion that the moral struggle between right and wrong is futile.
> 2. Plato said, "We are what we are because of our moral values and because of the kind of life we choose to live." Reflecting on your position on the ethical continuum, list the moral values that you believe you possess.
> 3. Reproduce the ethical continuum shown in Figure 12.7. For each value you identified, locate your position on the continuum.

ARE RIGHT AND LEGAL THE SAME THING?

Many people make a direct link between ethics and the law. In some ways, this link is appropriate because laws often reflect a society's ethical beliefs. Canada's law against murder, for example, reflects Canadian society's belief that killing another person is morally wrong.

Many ethicists have pointed out, however, that relying only on the law to provide a guide to morality presents problems. One reason they say this is because laws change. And if a law changes, does this mean that morality also changes? In Canada, for example, performing an abortion was declared illegal in 1869 and remained so until 1969, when the law was relaxed somewhat. Then, in 1988, the Supreme Court of Canada declared the law governing abortion unconstitutional. Does this mean that abortions carried out between 1869 and 1969 were morally wrong while those performed since 1988 have been morally right?

Abortion is a divisive issue. Those who oppose a woman's right to choose to have an abortion maintain that this act is morally unacceptable no matter what the law now says. Others maintain that choosing to have an abortion was a morally acceptable decision even when the law declared it illegal. The division of opinion over this issue illustrates that most people distinguish between right and legal.

Furthermore, many moral questions are not addressed by laws. It is not illegal to break a promise to a friend, for example, but many people would argue that it is morally wrong.

To refer only to the law when making moral choices suggests that human behaviour is motivated only by the fear of punishment, an assumption that is not supported by most ethicists. Using the law as a guide also eliminates the possibility of civil disobedience, a form of protest made famous by the 20th-century Hindu political activist **Mohandas Gandhi**. The aim of civil disobedience is to use non-violent means to change a so-called bad law without rejecting the rule of law.

For these reasons, many ethicists argue that the law does not provide an appropriate moral guide. Some say that that the law should not determine morality; rather, they argue, morality should determine the law.

Web connection
http://www.mcgrawhill.ca/links/philosophy12
To find out more about Mohandas Gandhi's philosophy of non-violence, follow the links on this Web site.

ARE MORAL VALUES OBJECTIVE OR SUBJECTIVE?

The question of whether moral values are objective or subjective refers to the source of or justification for moral choices and has always divided ethicists. The word "objective" refers to knowledge that is supported by evidence. This kind of knowledge is independent of personal feelings, experience, or thought. The word "subjective" refers to opinions that *do* depend on personal feelings, experience, or thought.

Ethical or moral objectivists fall into three camps. One camp believes that moral values are objective because they are handed down by a supreme being or beings, such as God or Allah. A second camp believes that moral values are objective because they originate in nature. This camp includes determinists and those who believe that people are biologically or genetically programmed to act in certain ways. The third — and largest — camp believes that moral values result from the human ability to reason.

Ethical objectivism, however, does not necessarily suggest that moral values are either universal or absolute. An objectivist, for example, might believe that lying is morally acceptable at times. An absolutist would dispute this.

At the opposite end of the spectrum from objectivism is ethical subjectivism, which is sometimes called individual relativism. Subjectivists believe that morality is subjective. They believe that every person determines his or her own moral rules, and these rules are a matter only of opinion — with no recourse to a supreme being or beings, nature, or reason. Because all opinions are equally valid and because actions are not judged against objective or universal moral standards, subjectivists say that people can never be mistaken about what is morally right and wrong.

Like determinism and other theories that eliminate the idea of people's taking respon-sibility for their actions, subjectivism suggests that humans cannot be held accountable for their behaviour and that discussing moral issues is pointless. There is no reason to examine and assess the moral rightness or wrongness of actions — and no way that differences of opinion can be resolved.

Few philosophers agree that morality is either completely objective or completely subjective. As they do in other ethical debates, many ethicists prefer to chart a middle course between ethical objectivism and ethical subjectivism. Some philosophers lean more toward one end of the objective-subjective continuum than others, but most agree that both reason and opinion — especially well-supported opinions — have a role to play in making moral choices.

> ### IDEAS IN CONTEXT
>
> Many Canadians pride themselves on living in a multicultural society and believe that people should be encouraged to retain their customs, traditions, beliefs, and values. Yet doing this is sometimes difficult when customs conflict. Turbans and beards, for example, are important religious and moral symbols for Sikh men. For decades, however, many Canadian police forces banned beards and required the wearing of standard-issue hats. As a result, Sikhs could become police officers only if they gave up their turbans and beards. It took many years of struggle before regulations were changed to allow Sikh officers to wear turbans and beards. This change reflected Canadian society's belief in accommodating many of the moral values of minorities.

Chapter Review

Chapter Summary

This chapter has discussed
- some of the main questions asked by ethicists
- some of the responses of some major philosophers and some major schools of ethics to some of the main ethical questions
- how problems in ethics and the theories that address them may be illustrated in stories
- how moral problems and dilemmas that occur in everyday contexts can be analyzed using a variety of philosophical theories

Knowledge and Understanding

1. Identify and explain the significance to the study of ethics of each of the following key words and people.

Key Words	Key People
ethics	Gautama (the Buddha)
morals	Kongfuzi (Confucius)
theories of action	Plato
theories of character	Aristotle
theories of value	Averroës
virtue	Virginia Held
humanism	Kwame Gyekye
moral agent	Gorgias
nihilism	Paul Kurtz
ethical absolutists	Nancy Midgley
ethical universalists	Mohandas Gandhi
ethical relativists	

2. Recall five moral choices that you have made over the past year. Complete the following graphic organizer for each of these decisions.

Description of moral choice	Evidence to show that it was a moral choice	Values applied when making choice	What or who shaped values	Were values subjective or objective?

Thinking and Inquiry

3. Kongfuzi gave this advice to the leaders of society: "Lead the people by laws and regulate them by penalties, and the people will try to avoid offences and punishment, but will have no sense of shame; lead the people on moral principles and educate them with the rules of decorum, and the people will not only have a sense of shame, but also behave well."

260   MHR Unit 4 Ethics

How do you think Kongfuzi would have responded to this question: On what grounds should the rightness and wrongness of actions be determined? Based on his statement, where might Kongfuzi be placed on the ethical continuum? Explain why.

4. The Aboriginal writer N. Scott Momaday tells the story of a Navajo man who had lost his job and was having trouble making ends meet. He and his wife lived in a remote area and were expecting a child. One day a friend said, "You are a hunter. Why don't you kill a deer so that you and your family might have fresh meat to eat?" The man replied, "It is not appropriate that I should take life just now when I am expecting the gift of life."

What central issue of Aboriginal ethics does this story address? Do you share the value illustrated by Momaday's story? Why?

Communication

5. Write a short piece of fiction that clearly captures the essence of Buddhist ethics. To see how ethical theories can be illustrated in fiction, reread the story "The Land of Certus."

6. Create a collage of images that reflect your personal response to one of the main questions of ethics.

Application

7. Examine this cartoon (Figure 12.8), which comments on the issue of genetic engineering. Create a series of questions — and corresponding answers — that reflect your response to the issue of whether the traits of babies should be genetically engineered.

Figure 12.8

8. You recently attended a dinner party with some well-known ethicists. The lively conversation was dominated by a discussion of whether moral choice is possible. Write the dialogue that might have taken place between two philosophers with opposing points of view. With a partner, present your dialogue to a group or the class.

Chapter 13
Answering Questions That Matter

Chapter Expectations

By the end of this chapter, you will be able to
- evaluate the responses of some of the major philosophers and major schools of ethics to some of the main ethical questions, making reference to classic texts
- use critical and logical thinking skills to defend your own ideas about ethical issues and anticipate counter-arguments
- demonstrate how everyday moral problems and dilemmas can be effectively analyzed using a variety of philosophical theories
- describe how problems in ethics and the theories that address them may be illustrated in songs, religious stories, and parables
- compare the problems, principles, methods, and conclusions of various philosophers
- describe how the ideas of philosophers have influenced philosophers who have followed them

Key Words

Buddhism
Confucianism
hedonism
Stoicism
virtue ethics
Thomists
existentialism
divine command theory
utilitarianism
egoism
intuitionism
post-modernism

Key People

Socrates
Epicurus
Thomas Aquinas
Søren Kierkegaard
Friedrich Nietzsche
Jean Paul Sartre
Jeremy Bentham
John Stuart Mill
Immanuel Kant
Ayn Rand

A Philosopher's Voice

Do not do an immoral thing for moral reasons.

Thomas Hardy (1840–1928)

Questions Asked by Ethicists

Think back a few years. When you were a child, how might you have answered these questions?

- What is a good life?
- What is a good person?
- What is the right thing to do?

At the time, the answers might have seemed straightforward. You might have said that the good life is one full of fun; that a good person is someone who always listens to parents, guardians, or teachers; and that the right thing to do is whatever your parents, guardians, or teachers say is right.

Would you give the same answers today? Probably not. As you grew older and started to think for yourself, you may have come to realize that the answers to these three basic ethical questions are more complicated than they once seemed. You may, for example, have begun to realize that a good life involves more than having fun. You may also have started to question whether being a good person always means listening to your elders, and you may even have questioned things your elders told you about the right thing to do.

You may also have recognized that the answers to these three questions can overlap. You might say, for example, that leading a good life is the right thing to do or that being a good person is leading a good life. Despite the overlap, these questions do provide a helpful framework for considering answers developed by various philosophers. These answers may not be simple — and they are certainly not definitive — but knowing and thinking about how others have struggled to answer similar questions can be the first step toward developing your own ideas about morality.

What Is a Good Life?

In one way or another, philosophers have always contemplated questions about human life. What is the meaning of life? What is my reason for living? What is the justification for my life? What makes life worthwhile? What goals should I have? What is a good life?

Socrates, for example, taught Plato that the most basic philosophical question is, What is the life worth living? For Socrates and Plato, the life worth living — the good life — meant a life of ethical action within a community made up of family, friends, and the society around them. Other philosophers have offered different ideas. A person can live for pleasure, wisdom, harmony, virtue, happiness, satisfaction, fulfillment, joy, freedom, truth, love, art, an afterlife, and so on. If these things are considered good, ethics may provide a guide for living, a way to achieve the values that people consider good.

The 20th-century French writer Albert Camus, for example, said that what gives meaning to life is not what kind of life people lead; rather, it is the spirit in which the life is led. Camus believed that life is absurd and will never satisfy people's expectations of finding meaning and justice. Still, he rejected the conclusion that some might draw — that life is not worth living as a result. Rather, he said that people must make their lives worth living by rebelling against the absurdity. He maintained that people can do this by refusing to participate in the injustices of the world and by living life to the fullest.

THE BUDDHIST'S ANSWER

The four noble truths of **Buddhism**, a philosophy attributed to Gautama, the Buddha who lived in India during the sixth century BCE, are that life is suffering, that suffering arises from desire, that desire can be eliminated, and that this can be achieved by following the Eightfold Path. The Eightfold Path involves right understanding, right thought, right speech, right action, right livelihood, right effort, right mindfulness, and right concentration.

The goal of following the Eightfold Path is to reach nirvana, a state of enlightenment in which desires and ambitions are extinguished, enabling people to live in harmony with themselves and nature. For Buddhists, this is the good life. Buddhists believe that nirvana can be achieved by living a life of simplicity, which means abandoning possessions as well as pleasures. Someone who lives according to the Buddhist ethic would not try, for example, to dress in the latest fashion or to own the most up-to-date electronic gadgets.

Buddhists believe that people are reborn after death, though not always as human beings. Sometimes, they are reincarnated as other creatures. Depending on the life they have lived, each rebirth moves people either closer to or farther from nirvana. For this reason, Buddhists believe that all living creatures should be treated with compassion, kindness, and love. As a result, those who live according to the Buddhist ethic would probably not eat hamburgers, chicken wings, or any other meat.

Virtues play an important role in the Buddhist idea of the good life. In addition to the virtues already mentioned, Buddhists believe that cultivating virtues such as non-violence and patience enables people to move closer to nirvana.

The Buddhist ethic is inclusive and egalitarian, which means that everyone is considered equal and entitled to the same rights. Like western ethics, Buddhist ethics focus on the individual, who is considered ultimately responsible for his or her actions. At the same time, Buddhism emphasizes the importance of relationships with others, and these relationships are often considered more important than individual rights. Take a person's right to choose where to live. A Buddhist whose aging parents need care might choose not to exercise this right if moving would cause her parents distress. Only when her parents no longer need care would a Buddhist consider herself ethically justified in exercising her right to choose.

Like all philosophies, Buddhism has come in for its share of criticism. Some philosophers and theologians have pointed out that the idea that people are reborn cannot be proven and that much of life seems to contradict the claim that life is suffering. They have also argued that the definitions of right understanding, right effort, and so on are not clear. Still, many people agree that the Buddhist ideals of respecting life and living a simple life are admirable.

Figure 13.1

In 2001, these young Korean Buddhist monks took part in a festival celebrating the 2545th birthday of Gautama, the Buddha.

Web connection
http://www.mcgrawhill.ca/philosophy12
To find out more about the Eightfold Path, follow the links on this Web site.

THE CONFUCIANIST'S AND TAOIST'S ANSWER

Like Buddhists, Confucianists and Taoists believe that the good life involves searching for peace and enlightenment by achieving harmony. The harmony emphasized by **Confucianism** — the philosophy attributed to the sixth-century BCE Chinese philosopher Kongfuzi (Confucius) — is not the individual harmony so valued by Buddhists, however. Rather, Confucianism focuses on defining and cultivating the tao — or way — to a harmonious society. To Confucianists, the way to achieve a harmonious society is to follow traditional rituals and roles. As a result, they view morality as a social or cultural product.

Confucianists think of people not as individuals but as part of the whole. This whole is the community a person is born into and is raised and lives in. As a result, relationships and roles within the community are very important and duty to family and community is more important than individual desires. The career choice of someone who lives according to the Confucian ethic would, for example, be governed not by his own needs and desires but by those of his parents and the community.

Roger T. Ames described the role of the individual in Confucian society like this: "Self-realization [development of one's ability to reason] is fundamentally a social undertaking … [that] involves benefiting and being benefited by membership in a world of reciprocal loyalties and obligations which surround and stimulate a person and which define his or her own worth." Western notions of individual rights and equality are foreign to this traditional Chinese way of thinking.

Like Buddhism, Confucianism is a virtue ethic. It says that someone who lives a good life displays five main virtues: kindness, uprightness (or righteousness), decorum (or propriety), wisdom (or integrity), and faithfulness (to him- or herself and to others). Confucianists follow the Golden Rule set out by Kongfuzi: What you do not like when done to yourself, do not do to others.

Taoism, a philosophy attributed to the sixth-century BCE philosopher Laozi (Lao-tzu), also emphasizes harmony and a holistic concept of life. While Confucianism emphasizes living in harmony with one's community, Taoism emphasizes living in harmony with nature and the rhythms of the universe.

Though these ideas may be appealing, various philosophers have pointed out that neither Confucianism nor Taoism provides ready answers to all ethical questions. What happens, for example, if your elders expect you to act in a way that does not match your interpretation of community morality? And should you continue to respect elders who do not themselves live according to Confucian ideas of virtue?

What is more, Confucian ideas of community have been used to justify forcing people to conform. Mabel Lee pointed this out in her introduction to *Soul Mountain*, a book by Nobel Prize-winning author Gao Xingjian. Lee, who translated Gao's book into English from Chinese, wrote:

> [In 20th-century China,] self-sacrifice was promoted first in the name of patriotism and also in the name of the communist revolution which promised equality and social justice. Self-sacrifice became an entrenched habit that facilitated, aided and abetted the extremes of social conformity demanded by the Cultural Revolution which was engineered by sophisticated modern strategies for ideological control.

IDEAS IN CONTEXT

Ideas similar to the Confucian and Taoist concept of harmony are at the heart of the Aboriginal use of healing circles to help troubled people get their lives back in order. When people commit crimes, many Aboriginal people believe they do so because the spiritual, emotional, physical, or mental part of their being is out of harmony with nature. Rather than punishing wrongdoers, Aboriginal justice encourages them to learn what part of their being needs to be healed. Talking with elders and others in a healing circle is part of this learning process.

THOUGHT EXPERIMENT: The Experience Machine

In his book *Anarchy, State, and Utopia*, the Harvard University philosopher Robert Nozick concocts an ingenious thought experiment to cast light on some puzzles in ethics. Nozick asks you to imagine a wonderful machine — an experience machine — that can be programmed to give you any sort of experience that you want. All you have to do is sit in a chair, attach some electrodes to your head, and program the machine to call up the experience you desire.

The electrodes supply your brain and central nervous system with neuro-electrical stimulation that is identical to the stimulation it receives from the sensory perception ordinarily received though your five "doors of perception" — your eyes, nose, ears, tongue, and skin. This fools your brain into thinking that it is seeing, smelling, hearing, tasting, and feeling real things, but the experience is in your head.

The experience machine is versatile. You could program it to experience being a rock singer on stage before a sea of screaming fans. Or racing a Formula One car.

You could, for example, program the machine to give you the full Technicolor experience of bungee jumping off a high bridge into a deep chasm at 200 km an hour. Though you experience the stomach-churning free fall, the roaring rush of air, the blur of scenery, and the taste of your half-digested breakfast making its way back into your mouth, you are in fact sitting safely and motionless in a chair plugged into the machine. But it all seems real.

Nozick applies a few conditions, however. First, you can program the machine to run for an hour, a day, a week, a month, or a decade. You can even program it to run for your whole life. Second, you can choose from a library of hundreds of programs, mixing and matching some and cutting and pasting others. You could choose to run the famous explorer program for a week, followed by the car racer program and the rock singer program. Third, once you are plugged in, you forget your previous life — and even that you programmed the machine. In fact, you forget that you are attached to a machine at all. This guarantees that your experience will not be spoiled by the realization that it is artificial.

Would you choose to plug into the experience machine for the rest of your life? Is plugging in going to make you happy? Is it going to give you the good life?

Some people might be tempted to plug in for life. They could program the machine to ensure that they would always be happy, famous, attractive, or powerful, while avoiding the bad, boring, painful, or confusing parts of life. What could be better than having all the wonderful experiences that life has to offer without having to endure a down side? Would this not be an ideal way for people who are poor, sick, frail, or lonely to escape their condition and to experience things that they might otherwise never be able to?

Despite the appealing sound of this, Nozick argues that people should not choose to plug in for life.

Why? First, he says, people prefer to *do* things rather than merely experience them. We prefer to be real agents, affecting the real world, rather than imaginary agents engaged in playacting.

Second, people want to choose to be a certain way and to be a certain person. Being hooked up to the machine would make us nothing more than blobs, blank receptacles for the input of the machine. Nozick says that plugging in for life would be like committing suicide.

Third, the machine limits people to an artificial reality. We would be living in a kind of bubble, without any real contact with the outside world. There is no genuine novelty in this machine-controlled world.

Fourth, we prefer to be the authors of our own lives, whereas the machine lives our lives for us. It gives us the illusion of control, but no real control.

So, would you plug in to the experience machine for life? Would this be your idea of the good life?

Figure 13.2

THE HEDONIST'S ANSWER

Hedonists — those who adhere to an ethical philosophy called **hedonism**, which developed during the fifth century BCE — believe that the good life is one devoted to pleasure. In their view, only pleasure has intrinsic value that can lead to happiness.

Hedonists differ over what pleasure is, however. Some early hedonists believed that it meant the pleasures of the body. **Epicurus**, a Greek philosopher who lived during the fourth century BCE, disagreed. He believed that the pleasures of the mind — in particular, *ataraxia* or serenity — were more important. Epicurus claimed that serenity could be achieved by minimizing desires and overcoming fears, a view that is similar to Buddhist ideas.

Though hedonism does not constitute a complete morality, it has influenced the development of various ethical theories over the millennia.

THE STOIC'S ANSWER

Zeno of Citium, a fourth-century BCE Greek philosopher, is usually credited with founding **Stoicism**, a school of thought that was popular in both ancient Greece and Rome. Like hedonists, Stoics believe that the good life involves living happily. For Stoics, however, happiness is achieved through wisdom rather than pleasure.

According to the Stoics, the universe is a well-ordered place, guided by an underlying logos or reason, and people should strive to make their lives just as well-ordered. This can be done by living in harmony with the universe. The Stoics advocated exercising control over things that people can control, such as emotions and intent, while remaining indifferent to things, such as consequences, that cannot be controlled. They said that trying to control the uncontrollable leads to frustration and disappointment.

Like hedonism, Stoicism is not a complete morality, though a stoic attitude may certainly be helpful in some situations. Like a Buddhist, a Stoic seeking to live the good life would try to live wisely, controlling or eliminating desires and accepting things that cannot be controlled. Recognizing that genetics plays a role in defining people's appearance, for example, a Stoic who does not possess the currently fashionable body shape or size might refuse to be bothered.

> ### IDEAS IN CONTEXT
>
> For decades, members of Alcoholics Anonymous and other organizations dedicated to helping people recover from addictions have been drawing comfort from the serenity prayer. This prayer echoes ideas prominent in several philosophical traditions, including Stoicism.
>
> **The Serenity Prayer**
> God grant me the serenity to accept the things I cannot change, the courage to change the things I can, and the wisdom to know the difference.

Recall...Reflect...Respond

1. Create a chart summarizing philosophical responses to the question, What is a good life? Organize your chart under the following headings: School of Ethics, Response of School, Strengths of Response, and Weaknesses of Response.
2. The issue of animal rights raises many ethical questions. Should animals be used in medical testing or scientific research, for example? Which school of thought best represents your position on this issue? Explain why.
3. The thought experiment titled "The Experience Machine" offers one idea of a good life. Choose the philosophical response that best represents your idea of a good life. Would this philosophy support the use of an experience machine? Explain why.

What Is a Good Person?

You always try to do the right thing. Among other things, you take part in your school's annual Terry Fox run, return library books on time, and hand in assignments when they are due. Does this make you a good person? Perhaps. But what if your only motive for doing the right thing is to please God or your parents, to win praise from friends or teachers, or to elicit other positive consequences? Is someone who does the right thing for these reasons a good person? Philosophers disagree over the answer to this question.

THE VIRTUE ETHICIST'S ANSWER

Rather than focusing on the good life or the rightness or wrongness of actions, **virtue ethics** emphasizes the role of character. Virtue ethicists believe that a good person is a virtuous person, someone whose moral choices are guided by his or her good character rather than by simply weighing the consequences of specific actions.

Western ideas about virtue ethics originated with philosophers such as Socrates, Plato, and Aristotle, who developed remarkably similar interpretations of virtue. Their ideas were much broader than contemporary western ideas, which often suggest that virtue involves a kind of self-righteous moral uprightness or even chastity. To the ancient Greeks, virtue meant excellence and being virtuous meant doing things — no matter what these things were — in a way that reflected rational thought and involved making the best of one's skills, talents, and opportunities.

Though Socrates and Plato certainly talked and wrote about virtue, Aristotle is usually credited with developing the theory of virtue ethics. Like his predecessors, Aristotle believed that virtue is a matter of developing the unique human ability to reason. He wrote: "It is the life which accords with reason then that will be best and pleasantest for Man, as a man's reason is in his highest sense himself." By reasoning correctly, said Aristotle, people will understand that they can experience *eudaimonia*, an ancient Greek word that translates into English as happiness. To the ancient Greeks, however, *eudaimonia* meant happiness rooted in an overall sense of satisfaction with one's character and actions rather than happiness rooted only in pleasure.

To be a good person, according to Aristotle, is to act in accordance with right reason; in other words, the rational part of the soul must control the irrational parts by choosing to follow a middle path or mean between the extremes of excess and deficiency. This was Aristotle's theory of the Golden Mean, which he developed in a book titled *Nicomachean Ethics*. Named for Aristotle's son Nichomachus, this book identified a number of virtues, as well as the vices that resulted from failing to adhere to the mean.

IDEAS IN CONTEXT

Aristotle did not apply his idea of virtue to all people. He said that women are incapable of achieving *eudaimonia* because they do not have the capacity to reason. In fact, he called women "mutilated" males. For a long time in the history of western thought, statements like this went largely unchallenged and may explain in part why women's contributions to philosophical thought — and to other intellectual or scholarly disciplines, as well as to public life in general — were often minimized or dismissed.

Web connection

http://www.mcgrawhill.ca/philosophy12

To find out more about the ideas about virtue set out by Aristotle in *Nicomachean Ethics*, follow the links on this Web site.

A table of Aristotle's ideas about virtue and vice might look like this:

Vice of Deficiency	Virtuous Mean	Vice of Excess
cowardice	courage	foolhardiness
inhibition	temperance	overindulgence
self-deprecation	truthfulness	boastfulness
stinginess	generosity	extravagance
buffoonery (silliness or stupidity)	wittiness	boorishness (coarseness or rudeness)
listlessness (lack of spirit)	patience	impatience
shyness	modesty	shamelessness
callousness (insensitivity)	righteous indignation	spitefulness
humility	pride	vanity
unfriendliness	friendliness	obsequiousness (fawning)
unambitiousness	ambition	overambitiousness

Aristotle said that moral virtue is the result of habit and training. Because of this, he believed that people can be taught to be virtuous. He said that people must know — and then deliberately choose to do — what is good.

Since Aristotle's time, thinkers have revisited the idea of virtue ethics in various ways. **Thomas Aquinas**, for example, 13th-century Italian philosopher and Christian theologian, first combined the Christian idea of God with Aristotle's thinking about reason, happiness, and virtue. Aquinas, who was later made a saint by the Roman Catholic Church, said that people can achieve perfection only by using their reason to know God.

Like many theologians of other faiths, Aquinas and his followers, who were called **Thomists**, focused their idea of virtue on doing the right thing in obedience to God. As a result, the idea of virtue as right conduct became more important than the ancient Greek idea of virtue as good character, and Greek ideas about virtue ethics fell out of favour in the western tradition for many centuries.

In the 20th century, however, some western philosophers began to revive the notion of virtue as goodness of character. They did so to refute consequentialist ethical theories, which say that people make moral choices only to bring about good consequences or to avoid bad consequences. The English philosopher W.D. Ross, for example, listed the following virtues, from least to most important.

- fidelity — keeping promises and agreements
- reparation — making up for committing wrongful acts
- gratitude — repaying the favours of others
- justice — correcting injustices
- beneficence — improving the conditions of others
- self-improvement — improving one's own conditions
- non-maleficence — not hurting others

To Ross, the items on this list represented more than virtues. They were duties or obligations. He believed not only that people should be faithful, but also that they must be faithful. Unlike the ancient Greeks, who believed that people develop virtues as a result of rational thought, Ross maintained that people understand these duties intuitively because they are part of the fundamental nature of the universe.

If a friend, for example, asks whether you like her new shoes, Ross would say that your first duty is to be faithful by giving your friend a truthful answer. You think the shoes are ugly, but know that saying so would hurt your friend's feelings. According to Ross's list, however, the duty to be non-maleficent is more important than the duty to be faithful. As a result, your actual duty is to lie to your friend and tell her that you like her shoes.

Alasdair MacIntyre, a contemporary relativist who was born in Scotland but later moved to the United States, brings a different view to the idea of virtues. He says that qualities of character regarded as virtues depend on people's culture and their place and time in history. More specifically, he says that virtues depend on the practice involved: virtues are the traits needed to do with excellence whatever it is that one is doing. A virtuous soldier, for example, has the virtues of loyalty, physical courage, and physical resilience.

Aboriginal ethics is also a form of virtue ethics. Though various Aboriginal peoples may respond differently to specific ethical issues, a common virtue — respect and reverence for all living things — underlies their points of view.

Many philosophers have challenged the ideas of Aristotelian virtue ethics. Some, for example, question Aristotle's focus on reason and his assertion that reason is a uniquely human quality. To support their argument, they point to research showing that other animals, such as chimpanzees, are capable of reasoning.

These research findings have raised troubling ethical questions. Should animals that are capable of reason be granted legal rights? If so, which rights — and what responsibilities — should accompany these rights? What criteria should be used to answer questions like these?

Various philosophers have also pointed out the difficulty of coming up with precise definitions of the virtues identified by virtue ethicists. Consider the virtue of justice, for example. What does it mean?

Some have suggested that justice means egalitarianism, which means treating people the same. Others have argued that people should receive what they deserve, their just reward or punishment. And still others have said that a definition of justice must take people's needs into account. So far, these attempts at defining justice have succeeded only in raising more questions. Does egalitarianism mean treating everyone exactly the same, with no exceptions? What is a foolproof way of sorting out exactly what people deserve? Do "needs" refer to basic needs such as food, water, and shelter, or do they also include things like physical health, mental health, and so on?

Web connection
http://www.mcgrawhill.ca/philosophy12
To find out more about animal rights and ethics, follow the links on this Web site.

THE EXISTENTIALIST'S ANSWER

In the 20th century, some European philosophers developed a school of thought called *existentialism*, which emphasizes that a good person is one who makes individual moral choices and takes responsibility for those choices. Existentialists believe that absolute moral values such as those identified by virtue ethicists do not exist. Authenticity — the idea of being true to oneself when making moral choices — is the only virtue worth striving for in existentialist theory.

The roots of existentialism lie in the thought of Søren Kierkegaard, a 19th-century Danish philosopher. Raised in a devoutly Lutheran home, Kierkegaard embraced the Lutheran idea that each person has a direct relationship with and direct access to God. For Kierkegaard, this meant that people must make — and judge — their own moral choices. To do this, he thought that people must move beyond judging their actions according to reason or the standards of society and become accountable only to the judgments of God.

> *Philosophy is perfectly right in saying that life must be understood backward. But then one forgets the other clause — that it must be lived forward.*
>
> – Søren Kierkegaard

In Kierkegaard's view, authentic choices are very important. Authentic choices are those that involve consistency of perception, thought, and action. An inauthentic person, said Kierkegaard, runs away from the responsibility of creating her or himself. This person lives thoughtlessly and does not think or act independently. Attending school, for example, because this is what your friends, parents, and teachers tell you to do is inauthentic. Attending school because you have made the choice to be educated is, by contrast, authentic.

Kierkegaard's focus on the individual and individual *existenz*, the Danish word for "existence," was picked up in the 20th century by Gabriel Marcel, a French philosopher who used it to coin the term "existentialism."

Like Kierkegaard, the 19th-century German philosopher Friedrich Nietzsche urged people to make their own moral choices rather than to unthinkingly accept the values of the majority. Unlike Kierkegaard, however, Nietzsche rejected the view that people are ultimately accountable only to God. He said that faith in God was disappearing and, with it, the universal values provided by that faith. In the absence of universal values, he said, people must determine their own values.

Though thinkers such as Marcel and Camus carried Kierkegaard and Nietzsche's ideas into the 20th century, the French philosopher Jean-Paul Sartre became the best-known existentialist. Partly in reaction to the horrors of World War II, Sartre became an atheist who believed that human beings had no particular purpose in living. He said that no divine master plan governs human existence; all events are random; nothing makes sense; and life is absurd. As a result, Sartre declared that existence precedes essence. By this, he meant that people simply exist at first. Each person then creates her own essence — by defining her self, determining what she will be, and choosing what she values.

In the existentialist view, everything — actions, as well as beliefs, feelings, and attitudes — is a matter of choice. But no moral milestones exist to help guide these choices. Though this offers people great freedom, say existentialists, it also entails great responsibility. There can be no excuses and no blaming circumstances. Acknowledging this responsibility, according to existentialists, often inspires feelings of *angst*, a German word that means anxiety, as people weigh the consequences of their choices. Sartre recognized this paradox when he wrote that people are "condemned to be free."

Though existentialists offer no moral milestones for judging ethical decisions, they do place great importance on authenticity, an idea borrowed from Kierkegaard. In the existentialists' view, a good person is one who recognizes his or her freedom and responsibility — and makes authentic choices. In *Basic Moral Philosophy*, the contemporary philosopher Robert Holmes wrote: "For most, adolescence brings an unsettling awareness that the comforting framework of values taken for granted as children is not fixed and

> **IDEAS IN CONTEXT**
>
> Twentieth-century existentialists were not the only ones to borrow from Friedrich Nietzsche. After his death some of his ideas were seized by Nazi thinkers. Nietzsche said, for example, that everyone tries to dominate others and that a gifted man — someone he called an "overman" — has the right to step out of the mainstream and create his own moral values. The Nazis used this idea was to justify their own idea of an "overrace," an entire race that is superior to others. As a result, Nietzsche is often unfairly associated with Nazism, even though he would probably have been horrified by this use of his philosophy.

Figure 13.3

The political activism of Jean-Paul Sartre (second from left) and his lifelong companion Simone de Beauvoir, who was also a writer and philosopher, often made headlines. Here, reporters surround the two after they were arrested in 1970 for selling a newspaper that advocated the overthrow of the French government.

unchanging.... This moment is crucial. If, on realizing this, people refuse to accept their freedom in the face of the collapse of their childhood faith, they choose a life of self-deception. They choose to deny their freedom." Existentialists believe that responsibility for making choices cannot be evaded. Even refusing to choose involves a choice: the choice not to choose.

Though existentialism was very popular in the mid-20th century, philosophers have disputed its view that people have complete freedom to create their selves. Are other forces, such as genetic makeup, at work? The existentialist assertions that life is meaningless and that there are no criteria, beyond authenticity, for choosing moral values and deciding on a course of action have also been challenged by a variety of philosophers.

> ### Recall...Reflect...Respond
>
> 1. Create a chart summarizing philosophers' responses to the question, What is a good person? Organize your chart under the following headings: Key Characteristics of Philosopher's Theory, Virtue Guiding the Theory, Examples of Virtues Consistent with Theory, and Weakness of the Theory.
> 2. Consider the information summarized in this chart, then write a paragraph responding to this question: Can virtue be learned? Be sure to support your opinion.
> 3. Can existentialism be considered a consequentialist ethical theory? Include the views of at least three existentialists in your explanation.

WHAT IS THE RIGHT THING TO DO?

In many ways, questions about the right thing to do in a specific situation are inextricably linked to ideas about living the good life and being a good person. Faced with making a moral choice, Buddhists might refer to the Eightfold Path to guide their actions; Aristotelian virtue ethicists might try to determine the golden mean; Aboriginal people might choose the course that shows the greatest respect for living things; and existentialists might agonize over every possible course of action. Questions about the right thing to do fall into the realm of normative ethics because they ask how people should act. They are theories of action.

THE DIVINE COMMAND ETHICIST'S ANSWER

Throughout history, many societies have linked moral choices to religious beliefs. In these societies, people have looked for moral guidance to the will of a supreme being or beings. The idea that a supreme being defines right and wrong is called **divine command theory**. This theory has been embraced by a wide variety of religious thinkers, from the ancient Greeks and Romans to many contemporary Muslims, Jews, Christians, Hindus, and others.

At the heart of divine command theory is a belief in the existence of a supreme being or beings. The commands of this being are recorded in the sacred texts of the religion. For Christians, for example, the holy book is the Bible; for Muslims, it is the Qu'ran; for Jews, it is the Torah; and for Hindus, it is the Vedas and Upanishads.

For as long as people have embraced divine command theory, philosophers and theologians have argued over the answer to a question posed by Socrates: Is something right because it is favoured by the gods, or do the gods favour it because it is right? This question assumes a belief in supreme beings — or a single supreme being — and for much of history, this belief was a given in most societies.

John Duns Scotus, a 13th-century Christian theologian of Scottish origin, answered Socrates' question by saying that God's commands define what is right. This theme was picked up in the 19th century by Kierkegaard, who believed that people must look only to God to judge their actions. To illustrate, Kierkegaard used the Old Testament story of Abraham, who believed that God had commanded him to sacrifice his only son, Isaac. Though the idea of killing his son caused Abraham great suffering, he nevertheless took Isaac up a mountain and prepared to sacrifice him. At the last minute, Abraham heard God's voice telling him to stop, and Abraham was rewarded for his faith. Kierkegaard argued that Abraham was an example of someone who was willing to violate community ethics, which prohibit murder, and look only to God to judge his actions. In the end, he said that Abraham's faith in God proved to be justified.

Aquinas, who lived at roughly the same time as Duns Scotus, formulated a completely different response to Socrates' question. He tried to reconcile reason and religion by arguing that God commands people to do only things that are good and right, and that God knows what is good and right through the natural law of reason. Because God and humans share the ability to reason, people can use this ability to come to know God's commands.

If he had lived at the same time as Kierkegaard, Aquinas might have challenged the Danish philosopher's interpretation of the story of Abraham and Isaac. He might have said that the voice of God telling Abraham not to murder his son really represented the triumph of his own reason, which, by natural law, was in accord with God's command.

To engage in the continuing debate over the answer to Socrates' question requires a belief in a supreme being or beings. Many philosophers, however, would not participate in this debate because they deny the existence of a supreme being. Even many philosophers who believe in the existence of a supreme being do not necessarily embrace divine command theory. They argue, for example, that there is no way of knowing whether a particular holy book really represents the word of a supreme being. They also point out that many contemporary moral issues are not dealt with in holy books. Others, however, believe that holy books provide principles people can use to deal with issues today.

> ### IDEAS IN CONTEXT
>
> Throughout history, some religious extremists — people who embrace an extremely strict, and often selective, interpretation of the holy book of their religion — have used divine command theory to justify intolerance and even violence. This still happens. Extremists believe that only they are morally right because only their holy book reveals the true commands of a supreme being, whether this is God, Allah, Yahweh, or another divinity. Extremists often use their beliefs to justify violating the human rights of others. Sometimes, these "others" are women; other times, they are people who are different in some way. These different people might be atheists, agnostics, members of other religious groups, or even members of their own faith who do not share their extreme views.

THE UTILITARIAN'S ANSWER

The English philosopher **Jeremy Bentham**, who lived from 1748 to 1832, founded an ethical theory called **utilitarianism**. Utilitarianism is a consequentialist theory because it focuses on the consequences of moral acts.

The term "utilitarian" comes from the word "utility," which means usefulness. Utilitarians define utility — or usefulness — as the ability of an action to bring about benefit, advantage, pleasure, good, or happiness and to prevent mischief, pain, evil, or unhappiness. For utilitarians a morally good choice is the one that results in the greatest good for the greatest number of people.

Figure 13.4

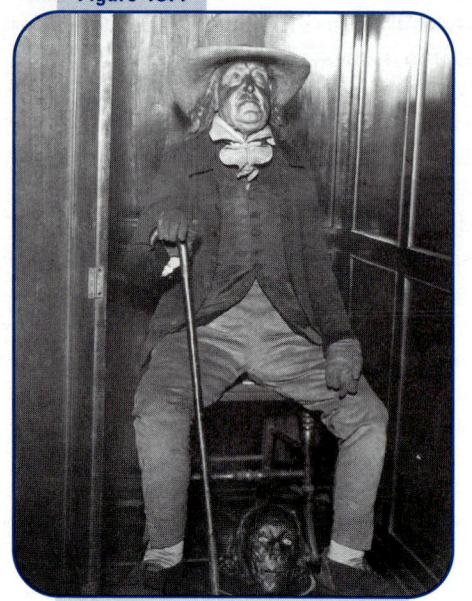

In his will, Jeremy Bentham donated his body to University College of London for medical research. He specified that when the research was complete, his body was to be displayed at the college's board meetings. Today, it sits in a glass case at the college. In this photograph, a wax head sits atop Bentham's mummified body. His real head, which is usually stored in a bag, is at his feet.

Because this definition of utility echoes some of the ideas of the hedonists of ancient Greece, utilitarianism is often called hedonistic utilitarianism. Utilitarianism also reflects ideas expressed by Moses Maimonides, a Spanish-born Jewish physician and philosopher who settled in Egypt in the 12th century. In the *Guide of the Perplexed*, Maimonides set out to show that reason and religion do not conflict. He argued that the commandments of God are justified by reason because they maximize the good.

Bentham also drew ideas from the work of other philosophers, such as Francis Hutcheson, who was born in Ireland in 1694. Hutcheson voiced the idea that later became the foundation of utilitarian ethics when he wrote: "That action is best which procures the greatest happiness for the greatest number." And the Scottish philosopher David Hume, who was born in 1711, actually coined the term "utilitarianism." Neither Hume nor Hutcheson developed their ideas into a moral theory, however.

Utilitarians believe that morally right choices are those whose consequences will bring about the greatest pleasure for the greatest number of people. To help people make these choices, Bentham created the hedonistic or hedonic calculus, which identified seven qualities of pleasure and pain.

Bentham instructed people to keep a kind of moral ledger by summing up "all the values of all the pleasures on the one side and those of all the pains on the other." He said that a balance on the side of pleasure will give the "general good tendency" of an act, while a balance on the side of pain will give the "general evil tendency."

Bentham's Hedonistic Calculus	
1. Intensity	How strong will the pain or pleasure be?
2. Duration	How long will the pleasure or pain last?
3. Certainty	How likely is it that the expected pain or pleasure will occur?
4. Propinquity (nearness)	How soon will the pleasure or pain be experienced?
5. Fecundity (productivity)	How likely is the pleasure or pain to generate or be followed by similar pleasure or pain?
6. Purity	How much pain is mixed with the pleasure and vice versa?
7. Extent	How many people will be affected?

In his work, Bentham often collaborated with his friend and fellow philosopher James Mill. In fact, when James Mill's son, John Stuart Mill, was born in 1806, Bentham became his godfather. At the time, no one knew that this baby's name would become even more closely linked with utilitarianism than Bentham's.

When Mill grew old enough to read his godfather's work, he was intrigued by the ideas but critical of Bentham's hedonistic calculus. Mill believed that determining the moral utility of an act required more than simply totting up the pros and cons. Like Epicurus, who spoke of long-term pleasure and emphasized the pleasures of the mind over those of the body, Mill said that aesthetic and intellectual pleasures are of "higher" or greater value than mere physical pleasures, something that the hedonistic calculus did not take into account. He also claimed that anyone who has experienced both kinds of pleasure knows which is more valuable. He set out his ideas in a book titled *Utilitariansim*.

> *It is better to be a human being dissatisfied than a pig satisfied; better to be Socrates dissatisfied than a fool satisfied.*
>
> – John Stuart Mill in *Utilitarianism*

The utilitarianism of Bentham and Mill is sometimes called act utilitarianism because it judges acts in isolation. What happens, though, if an act brings great misery to some people, but great happiness to many more? Is it morally right, for example, to force a few children in developing countries to work long hours in clothing factories so that many more people can enjoy wearing the clothes they produce? According to the principles of act utilitarianism, the answer seems to be yes.

In response to dilemmas like this, some 20th-century philosophers developed a theory called rule utilitarianism. Rather than judging individual acts, rule utilitarians look for general rules that apply to everyone. They maintain that no one should do something that they cannot imagine everyone else doing, because a rule that cannot be applied to everyone cannot have good consequences. In other words, someone who cannot imagine making his or her own child work long hours in a factory would also believe that it is morally wrong to make other people's children work in factories.

These contemporary ideas also echo the thoughts of Maimonides, who said that individual moral choices must be judged according to the rules set out in the Torah. These rules must be followed because they are justified by reason to maximize the good. In this respect, Maimonides was a rule utilitarian long before the term came into use.

The ethics of many Aboriginal groups can also be classified as a kind of rule utilitarianism. The Akan people of Ghana, for example, judge the right thing to do by asking whether it contributes to the good of the community. "What is morally good is generally that which promotes social welfare, solidarity, and harmony in human relationships. Moral value in the Akan system is determined in terms of its consequences for mankind and society," wrote Akan philosopher Kwame Gyekye.

As an ethical theory, utilitarianism has had a lasting influence on philosophy. One of its chief strengths is that it encourages people to consider alternatives. This contrasts with some ethical theories that focus only on making a choice between doing something and not doing it. Suppose, for example, that you are thinking of donating to a charity. A divine command theorist might consider only whether making a donation is the right thing to do. A utilitarian, by contrast, might consider the issue from many different angles to discover how to bring about the greatest good for the greatest number. Who should be responsible for supporting charities? Should incentives be in place to encourage donations? If so, what incentives? What strings, if any, should be attached to donations?

Despite its strengths, utilitarianism has many critics. Some have pointed to the failure of utilitarians to define terms like "good" and "pleasure" and have questioned the assumptions that pleasure is always good and that it is the only good. Suppose someone takes pleasure in torturing animals, for example. Is this good? And can things besides pleasure, such as knowledge and friendship, also be good?

Other critics argue that the emphasis of utilitarianism on the greatest good for the greatest number clears the way to establish a tyranny of the majority. What happens, they ask, to the rights of minorities?

Still others have pointed out the difficulty of accurately measuring pleasure, a process that is often completely subjective. Eating a chocolate bar, for example, might bring great pleasure to you but not to someone who does not like chocolate. Opponents of utilitarianism also claim that it is often difficult not only to determine the greatest good, but also to measure the greatest number. They ask how anyone can possibly anticipate all the consequences of an action.

PROFILE

Harriet Taylor
Thoughts and Speculations Completely in Common

As a young woman, Harriet Taylor seemed destined to live an unremarkable life. At the age of 18, she had married a wealthy businessman, John Taylor, and settled into a comfortable house in London. The couple soon started a family that quickly grew to include three children. Taylor's life was a model of decorum.

When Taylor was 23, however, a chance encounter changed all this. She met John Stuart Mill, a 25-year-old East India Company clerk who was publishing articles in magazines that advocated political reform. Almost immediately, the two became friends. For Taylor, the friendship proved irresistible. Mill was the first man to treat her as an intellectual equal, and she enjoyed stretching her intellect.

Taylor and Mill began spending more and more time together, deeply engrossed in conversation about ideas such as women's rights. When they were not together, they exchanged letters and articles.

The relationship strained Taylor's marriage, and she and her husband agreed that she would live most of the time in a country house while he remained in London. This arrangement was not unusual at a time when divorce was considered utterly scandalous.

Mill visited Taylor in the country on weekends, and the two sometimes travelled together. Their relationship set tongues wagging, and many former friends abandoned them. Still, Mill maintained that they were just friends. "Our relation to each other was one of strong affection and confidential intimacy only," he wrote in his autobiography. Consideration for Taylor's husband kept the relationship platonic, wrote Mill. "For though we did not consider the ordinances of society binding on a subject so entirely personal, we did feel bound that our conduct should be such as in no degree to bring discredit on her husband, nor therefore on herself." Only after Taylor's husband died in 1849 did she and Mill feel free to marry.

Throughout their relationship, Taylor wrote articles and collaborated with Mill in his work. Most of her articles were either published anonymously or under Mill's name. At the time, the only way most women could find a publisher was to write anonymously or use a man's name. In 1851, for example, Taylor wrote most of "The Enfranchisement of Women," which called for women to be granted the right to vote. The article was published under Mill's name.

In his autobiography, which was published 15 years after Taylor died in 1858, Mill tried to ensure that she received the credit she was due by penning these words:

> When two persons have their thoughts and speculations completely in common; when all subjects of intellectual and moral interest are discussed between them in daily life, and probed to much greater depths than are usually or conveniently sounded in writings intended for general readers; when they set out from the same principles, and arrive at their conclusions by processes pursued jointly, it is of little consequence in respect to the question of originality, which of them holds the pen; the one who contributes the least to the composition may contribute most to the thought; the writings which result are the joint product of both, and it must often be impossible to disentangle their respective parts and affirm that this belongs to one and that to the other. In this wide sense, not only during the years of our married life, but during many of the years of confidential friendship which preceded it, all my published writings were as much my wife's work as mine; her share in them constantly increasing as years advanced.

Despite this acknowledgment, Taylor's role as a philosopher in her own right is often underestimated. Even today, no one is sure how much of Mill's work was his own and how much was Taylor's.

Figure 13.5

In the 1800s, marriage laws in Britain and elsewhere made women dependent on men. Harriet Taylor campaigned to have the laws changed to ensure women's independence

By courtesy of the National Portrait Gallery, London.

THE KANTIAN ETHICIST'S ANSWER

At about the same time as Bentham was developing his theory of utilitarianism, the German philosopher **Immanuel Kant** was reaching very different conclusions about the right thing to do. Kant said that moral choices must be judged, not by their consequences, but by the good will of the moral agent. As a result, Kant's theory is a non-consequentialist theory.

Like Aristotle, Kant began his argument by examining what is intrinsically good. He concluded that the only thing that is good for its own sake is a good will. "Nothing can possibly be conceived in the world, or even out of it, which can be called good, without qualification, except a good will," he wrote.

But what is a good will? "That which accords with duty," Kant said. And what is duty? "That which is rational." These statements mean that to have a good will is to act on moral principles that are justified by reason. In expressing this belief in the importance of reason, Kant was following in the footsteps not only of Aristotle, but also of 17th-century European rationalists such as René Descartes.

What moral principles are justified by reason, then? Kant believed that there is only one, and that having a good will — acting on moral principles justified by reason — springs from this single principle.

Kant's called this principle the categorical imperative. An imperative is a command or rule, while "categorical" means absolute. The categorical imperative, then, is a rule that is absolute, one that must always be obeyed. Though there is only one categorical imperative, Kant stated — and restated it — in many different ways. This is the best-known version.

> Act only according to that maxim [principle or general rule] whereby you can at the same time will that it should become a universal law of nature.

This means that when faced with making a moral choice, people with a good will must choose the course of action that they would want everyone to choose all the time. Take telling the truth. Kant would say that to decide whether telling the truth is the right moral choice in a specific situation, you must ask whether telling the truth should become a universal law. In a different situation where telling a lie might seem to be the right choice, Kant would say that you must put lying to the same test. If you choose to lie, then you must agree that everyone can lie all the time.

Another of Kant's versions of the categorical imperative said this:

> Act in such a way that you treat humanity, whether in your own person or in the person of another, always as an end and never as a means.

This means that people must respect one another and not use others. When people respect one another, lying is morally wrong because it denies other people's autonomy — their ability to freely make rational decisions on the basis of a good will. Someone who has been lied to does not have accurate information on which to base moral choices. Lying also uses other people as a means of achieving the liar's end, or purpose, and ignores the purpose of the person who is being lied to.

Kant believed that people could make no exceptions to the categorical imperative. People have a moral duty to always tell the truth, for example, even if this leads to bad consequences. Because the categorical imperative ignores consequences and focuses on duty, it is often called a deontological theory. The word "deontological" comes from *deon*, the Greek word for duty, and *logos*, the Greek word for reason.

One strength of Kant's theory is its impartiality. Because the imperative must be applied without exception, there can be no playing favourites. Another strength is its emphasis on the intent or motive of the moral agent, regardless of the consequences. If someone means well

Figure 13.6

© Lynn Johnston Productions, Inc. Reproduced by permission.

Does Dawn's admission that she wants to meet Candace's older brother violate Kant's categorical imperative?

by acting in accordance with the categorical imperative, the action will be judged morally right, even it leads to injury or other bad consequences.

Despite these strengths, Kant's theory has been criticized by various philosophers. Not surprisingly, Mill disputed Kant's basic assertion that consequences are not important by arguing that the categorical imperative is based on considering consequences. Testing a moral choice by asking whether it should become universal law amounts to measuring the consequences, said Mill.

Like other rationalist theories, Kantian ethics have also been criticized by those who question its emphasis on reason and its insistence on applying moral rules without exception. Contemporary American philosophers such as Carol Gilligan and Nel Noddings, for example, focus on the ethics of care, which stresses the importance of taking responsibility for and empathizing with others when making moral choices. And the contemporary American philosopher Annette Baier argues that ethical theories that emphasize reason and principle ignore the importance of compromise and making connections with others.

Take a situation in which a friend is dying of a terrible illness. The illness can be cured, but neither you nor your friend has the money to pay for the medicine. Should you steal the medicine needed to save your friend's life? Kant would say no, because your action would say that everyone can steal all the time. If this happened, it would lead to the breakdown of society. Therefore, stealing is always wrong. Those who believe in the ethics of care might not agree. They might argue that stealing the medicine is morally right because saving your friend's life is the caring thing to do.

THE EGOIST'S ANSWER

The word "ego," which means "I" in Latin, refers to the self and, specifically, the conscious, thinking part of the human mind or self. From this use came the idea of **egoism**, which means acting in one's own interest.

Egoism is different from egotism, which refers to conceit and boastfulness. When used by philosophers, the term "egoism" does not mean the same thing as it does when used by psychologists. Psychological egoism is a psychological theory that says that people act in their own interest; in other words, it describes how people *do* act. Philosophical or ethical egoism is a philosophical or ethical theory that says that people *should* act in their own interest. Because it prescribes how people should act, it is a normative theory.

Faced with an ethical dilemma, an egoist would decide on a course of action by thinking about the consequences and deciding which consequences are in his best interest. Like utilitiarianism, egosim is a consequentialist school of ethical thought. Unlike utilitarianism, which focuses on the consequence that results in the greatest good for the greatest number, egosim focuses exclusively on the greatest good for the individual person.

Suppose that someone gives you a ticket to a Sunday afternoon ball game when you have promised to spend the afternoon helping a friend with a project. Is it morally acceptable to break your promise to your friend and go to the ball game? An ethical egoist would say yes — if you decide that attending the ball game will benefit you more than keeping the trust and respect of your friend.

One criticism levelled at egoism is that it seems to make a virtue of selfishness. This criticism was tackled by Ayn Rand, a 20th-century Russian-American philosopher who developed an ethical theory known as rational egoism or objectivist ethics. Like Aristotle, Rand believed that humans are rational beings. Unlike Aristotle, however, Rand focused on the individual rather than the community. "There is no such thing as 'society' … only individual men," she wrote in The Virtue of Selfishness: A New Concept of Egosim. As the title of her book suggests, Rand maintained that selfishness — considering one's own interests when deciding how to act — is a virtue. She maintained that acting in one's own interest does not rule out helping others. She said that rational people will help others if they get something in return and that this voluntary co-operation, which applies to dealings in trade and justice, should also apply to human relationships.

Figure 13.7

In this cartoon, Calvin relates his stuggle with a moral challenge.

Imagine that you had forgotten both your lunch and your wallet when you came to school. You notice that a classmate has left a five-dollar bill in his desk. Should you take the money and buy lunch? At first glance, the answer of a rational egoist might seem to be yes. Satisfying your hunger is in your interest. But is it really? If everyone stole things whenever it seemed to be in their interest, no one's possessions — including yours — would ever be safe. As a result, a rationalist egoist might decide that stealing is not in anyone's long-term best interest.

This conclusion makes Rand's theory of rational egoism similar to social contract theories, which say that ideas about what constitutes morally acceptable conduct are the result of agreement among members of a society. This view of society suggests that everyone agrees, either implicitly or explicitly, to certain social arrangements because these are in everyone's best interests. In this way, self-interest can be said to support a social morality.

In developing her theory, Rand criticized the ethics of altruism, which says that people should act out of unselfish concern for others. Why, she asked, should any other person count more than yourself?

The proper method of judging when or whether one should help another person is by reference to one's own rational self-interest and one's own hierarchy of values: the time, money or effort one gives or the risk one takes should be proportionate to the value of the person in relation to one's own happiness.

To illustrate this on the altruist's favourite example: the issue of saving a drowning person. If the person to be saved is a stranger, it is morally proper to save him only when the danger to one's own life is minimal; when the danger is great, it would be immoral to attempt it; only a lack of self-esteem could permit one to value one's life no higher than that of any random stranger....

If the person to be saved is not a stranger, then the risk one should be willing to take is greater in proportion to the greatness of that person's value to oneself. If it is the man or woman one loves, then one can be willing to give one's life to save him or her — for the selfish reason that life without the loved person could be unbearable.

Critics of egoism, such as the contemporary British philosopher Mary Midgley and the American philosopher Hazel Barnes, argue that it limits the development of the self. To be fully human, they argue, includes acknowledging one's responsibility to others. Indeed, those who define morality as conduct toward others often deny that egoism is a morality at all because it focuses exclusively on the self.

James Rachels, a contemporary American philosopher, also challenged egoism by presenting a different definition of selfishness. Rachels maintains that selfishness or unselfishness is not determined by the motives of the moral agent who carries out the act; rather, it is determined by the person who either benefits from or is damaged by the act. An act that helps another is therefore unselfish, no matter what the helper's motives. By the same token, says Rachels, an act that hurts another is selfish, even if causing hurt was not the intention of the person who carried out the act.

Other philosophers have argued against egoism on the grounds that it suggests that people are slaves to their own interests. These philosophers maintain that people do have the freedom to make choices and are not governed by forces beyond their control.

Figure 13.8

In expressing the principle that guides his life, has Calvin described ethical egoism in a nutshell?

THE INTUITIONIST'S ANSWER

For most of the history of western philosophy, ethicists have tried to answer questions about the right thing to do by appealing to reason. Thinkers as diverse as Aristotle, Kant, Mill, and Rand took this approach. Even philosopher-theologians such as Aquinas and Maimonides tried to incorporate reason into their religious theories.

Other ethicists, however, denied the importance of reason in making moral choices. This school, called **intuitionism**, suggests that some truths are understood by intuition, an experience that is independent of reasoning.

Some 20th-century philosophers took this idea a step farther. They said that all moral rules are intuitive or self-evident and cannot be justified by appealing to reason.

G.E. Moore, a 20th-century English philosopher, was one of these. He said that moral intuition is simply a gut feeling about right and wrong. An even more radical approach was taken by Richard Taylor, an American philosopher who advocated disregarding reason entirely. Taylor said that people should listen to their hearts and appeal to their compassion when making moral choices.

Intuition can be interpreted to mean, If it feels right, do it. This is why this theory is often dismissed by philosophers, who also point out that some people do not feel compassion. Does this mean that these people are incapable of making moral choices?

> ### Recall...Reflect...Respond
>
> 1. Consider three ethical theories that can be used to respond to the question What is the right thing to do? For each theory, write a sentence describing a characteristic of the theory that best differentiates it from the other theories.
> 2. Choose a personal ethical dilemma and consider how you might resolve it. Does an ethical theory support your resolution? Explain how.
> 3. Revisit the ethical theory that best supports your resolution of the ethical dilemma selected in Question 2. Consider the criticisms of this theory. How could you alter your decision-making process to take these criticisms into account?

THE POST-MODERNIST'S ANSWER

The term "modernism" is a catch-all phrase often associated with forms of expression that developed in the late 19th and early 20th centuries. They were evident in fields such as art, architecture, literature — and philosophy. In philosophy, the roots of modernism are found in the work of the 17th-century French philosopher René Descartes, whose focus on reason led to new ways of answering questions about the world.

If "modernism" was the watchword of the early 20th century, "**post-modernism**" was the word used in the late 20th century to describe reactions to modernism. Because the prefix "post" means after in Latin, the word "post-modernism" means after modernism. Like modernism, the term "post-modernism" is used to describe ideas in many different fields, including philosophy. Even today, however, there is little agreement about its precise meaning, except that it represents a turning away from the values and beliefs associated with modernism.

In philosophy, this turning away often means challenging the modernists' reliance on reason to formulate theories about issues. In ethics, for example, approaches that reject the idea that one moral code is better than another are often labelled post-modern. As a result, relativist or emotivist theories, such as those of the 20th-century ethicist A. J. Ayer, are often labelled post-modern.

The contemporary American philosopher Richard Rorty took post-modernists' criticisms of ethical theories a step farther. He said that judging moral choices according to objective values, even the relative values of a particular culture or community, is a waste of time. In Rorty's view, moral values are entirely subjective and most people make their own decisions about the right thing to do without seeking guidance from philosophers. Noting that people have always worked through their own moral dilemmas on their own terms, Rorty even suggested that philosophy is nothing but "a side-show" that has little to do with the reality of most people's lives.

Figure 13.9

Pablo Picasso, *Jaume Sabartes*, 1905. © Estate of Pablo Picasso (Paris)/SODRAC (Montréal) 2002

Pablo Picasso created this painting, titled *Portrait of Jaume Sabartes*, in 1905. Picasso's creation is considered an example of modernist art because it takes apart and rearranges images in different ways, causing viewers to reassess their perceptions of reality.

Chapter Review

Chapter Summary

This chapter has discussed
- the responses of some of the major philosophers and major schools of ethics to some of the main ethical questions, making reference to classic texts
- how everyday moral problems and dilemmas can be effectively analyzed using a variety of philosophical theories
- how problems in ethics and the theories that address them may be illustrated in songs, religious stories, and parables
- the problems, principles, methods, and conclusions of various philosophers
- how the ideas of philosophers have influenced philosophers who have followed

Knowledge and Understanding

1. Identify and explain the significance to the study of ethics of each of the following key words and people.

Key Words	Key People
Buddhism	Socrates
Confucianism	Epicurus
hedonism	Thomas Aquinas
Stoicism	Søren Kierkegaard
virtue ethics	Friedrich Nietzsche
Thomists	Jean Paul Sartre
existentialism	Jeremy Bentham
divine command theory	John Stuart Mill
utilitarianism	Immanuel Kant
egoism	Ayn Rand
intuitionism	
post-modernism	

2. Create a graphic organizer that shows the key criteria of a philosophy that is used to define a good life. Do the same for a philosophy used to define a good person.

Thinking and Inquiry

3. Select three of the following four quotations. Use knowledge gained from reading this chapter to identify and explain three strengths and three weaknesses of each argument. Write your own quotation to reflect your point of view on each issue.

    Immanuel Kant

    Power, riches, honour, even health, all comfort and contentment with one's condition which is called happiness frequently engender together with courage also an insolence, unless a good will is present which properly directs and thus fits to a general purpose their influence upon the mind and with it the entire principle of activity.

    John Stuart Mill in *Utilitarianism*

    Each person, so far as he believes it to be attainable, desires his own happiness. This, however, being a fact, we have not only all the proof which the case admits of, but all which it is possible to require, that happiness is a good, that each person's happiness is a good to that person, and the general happiness, therefore, a good to the aggregate of all persons. Happiness ... [is], consequently, one of the criteria of morality.

Aristotle in *Nichomachean Ethics*

The moral virtue is a mean ... between two vices, the one involving excess, the other deficiency ... Hence also it is no easy task to be good.

Kongfuzi in *Analects*

I do not worry about people not knowing me, I am worrying that I myself do not know others.

4. In the centre of a two-circle Venn diagram, list your own criteria for determining the right thing to do. Then list two philosophies that support these criteria in one circle, and list two philosophies that oppose them in the other. Predict what the criticisms of your criteria might be and list as many counter-arguments to these criticisms as you can.

Communication

5. Write a parable that delivers the commands of a supreme being to people through a sacred text of your choosing. The parable must describe how ethical dilemmas can be resolved by applying the supreme being's commands and must coincide with one of the main theories of ethics.

6. Create a flow chart that describes how the ideas of one ethicist have influenced the ideas of other ethicists.

Application

7. Here are the lyrics to the song "Adrian" by Jewel Kilcher.

Adrian came home again last summer
Things just haven't been the same around here
People talk
People stare
Oh, Adrian, come out and play
An unfortunate accident in a canoe
Dr. said, "I'm sorry not much I can do"...
Little Mary Epperson liked him
She vowed always to watch after him

Still he did not move...
She sat by his side, watched the years fly by
He looked so fragile, he looked so small
She wondered why he was still alive at all
Everyone in town had that "I'm sorry look"
They talked in a whispered hush, said
"I'd turn the machines off"
But still she sat by his side
Said, "Life he won't be denied"...

What moral dilemma does Mary Epperson face? If Adrian were your child, how would you respond to the suggestion that the machines be turned off? Can a severely handicapped person enjoy a good life?

After considering these questions, write a philosophical response to the lyrics of this song.

8. Write three questions that you could ask Aristotle about how effectively subsequent philosophers have applied his idea of the importance of reason in determining the good life, the good person, and good actions.

Provide a response Aristotle might give to each of your questions. Ensure that the reasoning is consistent with Aristotle's theory.

Chapter 14
Ethics in the World

Chapter Expectations

By the end of this chapter, you will be able to
- evaluate the responses of some major philosophers and main schools of ethics to some of the main ethical questions
- use critical- and logical-thinking skills to defend your own ideas about ethical issues and to anticipate counter-arguments to your ideas
- demonstrate how moral problems and dilemmas that occur in everyday contexts can be effectively analyzed using a variety of different philosophical theories
- describe how problems in ethics and the theories that address them may be illustrated in stories and parables

Key Words

moral choice
ethical dimensions
slippery-slope phenomenon
censorship
pacifist
militarist
just war theory
euthanasia
genethics
sustainable development
sentience

Key People

Sissela Bok
Harriet Taylor
Nadine Strossen
Hannah Arendt
Karen Warren
Peter Singer
Tom Regan
John Kenneth Galbraith

A Philosopher's Voice

It appears to me that in Ethics, as in all other philosophical studies, the difficulties and disagreements ... are mainly due to a very simple cause: namely to the attempt to answer questions, without first discovering precisely what question it is you desire to answer.

George Edward Moore (1873–1958)

A World of Moral Choices

Figure 14.1

These macaques live in a research centre where they are used in experiments to test AIDS vaccines. The use of animals for medical testing is just one of the controversial issues raised when animal rights are discussed.

Suppose that you treat your family pet — whether this is a dog, cat, guinea pig, bird, or some other non-human animal — with kindness and compassion. At first glance, this choice seems highly personal. After all, it affects only you and your pet. But does it really? Could you stand by and watch someone else mistreat a pet? What about the treatment of animals that are not considered pets? Wild animals, for example? Or animals that are farmed for food or clothing? Or animals that are used for breeding or scientific research?

Some philosophers would argue that your response to these questions involves a **moral choice** — a choice that involves right and wrong, good and bad. Whenever you make a moral choice, you are dealing with ethics in the world. Even choices that seem highly personal often have effects that touch family, friends, your school, your community, your country, and the wider world.

Canada is a pluralistic society in which people who come from many different backgrounds and who hold many different ethical and political views must co-operate. To co-operate effectively, people must be able to understand how others see the world, even if they do not agree with their views. When disagreements arise, people can hope to find common ground only if everyone takes the trouble to understand the views of others. Understanding points of view you don't share can be hard work.

When thinking about and discussing moral choices, it is often difficult to arrive at a single, right answer. This does not mean that thinking about the issues involved in moral decisions is a waste of time. Thoughtful people who wish to be confident that they are doing the right thing usually try to consider the **ethical dimensions** — the moral assumptions and implications — of various courses of action before deciding what they should do. A knowledge of influential and important ethical theories and principles is an important tool in helping to analyze the ethical dimensions of issues, explain how contrary views arise, and locate common ground. Recognizing and thinking about these assumptions and implications, then making moral judgments based on your own assessment of their worth helps you develop your own values. And developing these values helps you, as Socrates said, create your "self."

Ethics, the Self, and Society

Suppose Aiden has picked out a new CD in a crowded music store. He slips into place at the end of a long line of people waiting to pay for their purchases. Outside the store, Aiden's friends are becoming impatient. Because he is in a hurry and the checkout line is moving at a snail's pace, Aiden considers tucking the CD into his jacket and walking out without paying. Wouldn't this teach the store a lesson? he muses. After all, if it were really interested in the business, it would make it easier for customers to pay. Besides, he thinks, My $17 will never be missed. Anyone can see that the store is raking in the money.

Are these the only issues Aiden needs to consider? What other ethical issues would it be helpful for him to think about?

At first glance, Aiden seems to be facing a personal moral choice. In fact, his choice will affect many people, including everyone involved in creating, shipping, and selling the CD, as well as his waiting friends. This means that his choice is far from personal. It affects all of society.

LYING, CHEATING, AND STEALING

Moral choices like the one facing Aiden are among the most common ethical dilemmas. Every day, people decide whether to lie, cheat, or steal in all sorts of situations. These situations might involve deciding whether to tell someone that you like his new haircut when you do not, whether to pass off as your own an essay copied from the Internet, or whether to walk out of a store with a CD that you haven't paid for. But is lying, cheating, or stealing morally wrong in all — or any of — these circumstances?

> **IDEAS IN CONTEXT**
>
> Mention the word counsellor and people usually think of a teacher, therapist, psychologist, or psychiatrist. In the late 20th century, some philosophers also joined the counselling field. Philosophical counsellors are usually experts in both philosophy and counselling. Like traditional counsellors, they help people think through solutions to conflicts. Though some of these conflicts may involve psychological issues, many also involve ethical dilemmas. Philosophical counsellors often help people decide on the morally right thing to do.

According to Immanuel Kant's categorical imperative, lying, cheating, and stealing are always wrong. In Aiden's case, Kant would maintain that it would be morally right to steal the CD only if it is morally right for everyone to steal all the time. Kantian ethicists would expect Aiden to consider what would happen if everyone stole. If everyone felt free to steal from everyone else, would it mean the end of private possessions?

Kantian ethicists would also expect Aiden to consider whose purpose would be served by stealing the CD. Would the theft treat the store's owners — as well as their employees and everyone involved in creating the CD — as a means to Aiden's end, rather than as ends in themselves? Would the theft show respect for everyone involved in creating and selling the CD?

Many philosophers disagree with Kant's position that moral choices are categorical. Contemporary Swedish-born American philosopher **Sissela Bok**, for example, says that lying, cheating, and stealing are usually wrong and that people should always look for alternatives. Like the English philosopher W.D. Ross, however, Bok says that there may be cases in which the duty not to lie, cheat, or steal conflicts with a more important duty, such as protecting human life. When this happens, lying, cheating, or stealing may be morally right. Bok considers the consequences of various acts and ranks the importance of conflicting duties. Her ranking suggests that protecting a life is more important, for example, than telling the truth.

In addition, some ethicists argue that the intent of an act determines its moral rightness. Take lies, for example. They say that malicious lies, which are intended to hurt people, and self-serving lies, which are intended to benefit only the liar, are morally wrong. Lies that are intended to prevent harm, however, may be morally right. Though altruistic lies, which are uttered out of concern for other people, may violate the virtue of honesty, they do not necessarily violate the virtue of justice, assuming that it is unjust for people to suffer harm.

False words are not only evil in themselves, but they infect the soul with evil.

– Plato

The arguments of Bok and other ethicists suggest that it may be morally right to lie, cheat, or steal in certain circumstances. Among these circumstances, they say, are the following possibilities:

- to defend yourself (e.g., if the robber at your door asks if anyone else is at home)
- to gain advantage for yourself (e.g., to earn higher marks, get a better job, or win the admiration of friends)
- to avoid hurting or embarrassing people

- to achieve a greater good (e.g., lying on an income tax return and giving the money saved to a charity)
- to achieve justice (e.g., cheating to get the same marks as someone who doesn't work nearly as hard at school as you do)
- to respond in emergency situations (e.g., stealing a car in a medical emergency)
- to enjoy a thrill (e.g., stealing for the rush felt by getting away with it)

Among the reasons to consider lying, cheating, and stealing morally wrong, they suggest the following possibilities:

- People who are lied to feel betrayed, hurt, disappointed, resentful, angry, and upset.
- Lies diminish the autonomy of the person lied to because they force her or him to act without complete and accurate information.
- Lying, cheating, and stealing reduce people's trust in others.
- Lying, cheating, or stealing just once starts the slippery-slope phenomenon. This argument says that telling one lie, for example, makes it easier to tell the next and the next, so that lying soon becomes a habit.
- Lying, cheating, and stealing violate ideas about justice by giving the person committing the act an unfair advantage over those who do not lie, cheat, or steal.
- Lying, cheating, and stealing are self-destructive because other people do not trust liars, cheats, and thieves. And if you lie, cheat, or steal for personal gain, your self-esteem may suffer because you know that your achievements did not come honestly.

FREEDOM OF EXPRESSION AND CENSORSHIP

"Sticks and stones may break my bones, but names can never hurt me!" Is the claim in this familiar schoolyard chant true? Canadian courts have ruled that it is not. In 1984, for example, Alberta high school teacher James Keegstra was charged with unlawfully promoting hatred toward an identifiable group by making derogatory comments about Jews. Keegstra also told students that Jews fabricated the Holocaust in order to gain sympathy.

Keegstra fought the charges all the way to the Supreme Court of Canada. There, his lawyers argued that Canada's law against promoting hatred violated their client's right to freedom of thought and expression, a right guaranteed in the Canadian Charter of Rights and Freedoms.

In the end, the Supreme Court ruled that people do not have an unlimited right to express themselves freely. The first clause of the charter says that the rights and freedoms it guarantees are subject to reasonable limits that "can be demonstrably justified in a free and democratic society." The court ruled that, although the law against promoting hatred violates the charter, the limit imposed by the law is reasonable because the advantages outweigh the harmful effects.

In making this decision, the court echoed a principle that had been articulated by John Stuart Mill and Harriet Taylor. They said that limits on individual liberty are justified only to prevent harm to others. This harm is understood to include not only personal injury but also damage to society in general.

Philosophers and others have raised the possibility that censorship — the limiting of people's right to express themselves freely — may also be justifiably limited for other reasons. One of these is that expression should be censored if it offends others. However, a difficulty arises when trying to define offence. What is it? Shame? Embarrassment? Discomfort? Suppose the sight of snakes makes someone uncomfortable? Would this justify prohibiting pictures of snakes?

Another possible justification for censorship is to prevent behaviour that is morally wrong. Again, difficulties arise when trying to define morally wrong behaviour. Some say that the criteria used to measure this should be community standards, but others argue that these standards are difficult to define. Which "community" should set the standard, they ask. The religious community? The non-religious community? The business community? The sports community? The South Asian community? Another community? Even if community standards could be defined accurately, some argue that requiring everyone to conform to them amounts to imposing a tyranny of the majority.

A third possible reason is the utilitarian argument that censorship is justified, but only to prevent harm. Suppose, for example, that someone wants to publish instructions for manufacturing a certain drug. Some people argue that this should be illegal because people who use the instructions to make the drug could harm themselves. Others argue that mature adults are responsible for making their own decisions about what will harm them. It is unnecessary for the government to decide for them.

> *I may disapprove of what you say, but I will defend to the death your right to say it.*
> – Voltaire

Though many people support the idea of placing some limits on people's right to express themselves freely, many others believe that any form of censorship is morally wrong. They argue, for example, that the harm caused by allowing people like Keegstra to incite hatred of certain groups is outweighed by the greater good of upholding people's right to express themselves freely. This utilitarian argument is often challenged by those who say that it is unfair to expect members of minority groups to bear the burden of promoting a social good.

Some of those who oppose censorship argue that sound ideas will survive while those that are unsound will fall by the wayside. This conclusion is disputed by those who cite historical examples, such as the widespread acceptance of racist attitudes in pre-World War II Germany and their consequences during the war.

Opponents of censorship also argue that education is a more appropriate response to false or biased ideas than regulation. This argument assumes that educated and informed people will recognize lies and prejudice, a conclusion that others argue is not necessarily so.

Another argument maintains that any form of censorship starts society down a slippery slope. Censoring racist speech, for example, may be the first step toward censoring all unpopular ideas. Those who challenge this argument claim that people are able to draw a clear line between ideas that should be censored and those that should not.

In response to the arguments raised on both sides in the debate, many people try to chart a middle course, saying that an all-or-nothing approach is not the answer. **Nadine Strossen**, a lawyer who is president of the American Civil Liberties Union, argues that freedom of expression should be censored under the following conditions:

- when it is likely to cause immediate harm
- when it is part of violent behaviour
- when it is addressed to a captive audience that is unable to avoid its harmful effects

WAR

In 2001, American forces bombed Afghanistan after that country's Taliban government refused to hand over Osama bin Laden and other Al Quaeda leaders who were allegedly responsible for the September 11 terrorist attacks on New York and Washington. The American military campaign was supported by many other countries, including Canada.

This action renewed the centuries-old debate over the moral rightness of waging war to settle disputes. In the course of this debate, many questions have been raised. Is military aggression morally right or morally wrong? When? Is there a difference between offensive and defensive aggression? Does a person, group, or nation that provokes aggression bear any responsibility for the result? What, if anything, counts as legitimate provocation for resorting to war? Is it morally right to go to war to protect lives or property? Do people — or nations — have a moral obligation to prevent war or to intervene to stop war?

If the ethical debate over the moral rightness of war were pictured on a continuum, pacifists — people who believe that disputes between nations should be settled peacefully — might be at one end. Militarists — people who believe that using military force to settle disputes is morally right — might be at the other end. Most people would place themselves somewhere between these two extremes. Depending on the circumstances, however, they would probably move closer to one end of the continuum or the other.

Figure 14.2

Violence Continuum

Pacifists ———————————————————————— Militarists

In a debate over the use of military aggression to respond to the terrorist attacks of September 11, 2001, where would you position yourself on this continuum?

Hannah Arendt, a German-born 20th-century American political scientist and philosopher, was a pacifist who argued that human beings are morally obligated to use their unique capacity to settle disputes by non-violent means.

Philosophers have offered both consequentialist and non-consequentialist arguments to support pacifism. Consequentialists argue that non-violent methods work better than violent methods, that violence does more harm than good, and that violence leads only to more violence. Non-consequentialists argue that violence violates people's right to life or their right to live free of harm, as well as that it fails to respect people.

Some militarists support the just war theory, which has been articulated by various philosophers, including the ancient Roman thinker Cicero and the early Christian theologians Augustine of Hippo and Thomas Aquinas. In general, this theory requires that seven conditions be met before a war can be considered just. These conditions are

Figure 14.3

Trying to escape the bombing of their country, an Afghan family flees to a camp in Pakistan that is operated by the United Nations High Commissioner for Refugees.

- just cause: A war must be fought only for a just cause, such as self-defence. Revenge, rebellion, and gaining power are not considered just causes.
- right intention (related to the cause): In Augustine's view, the only right intention was to ensure peace.
- proper authority: War must be declared by a recognized political authority.
- proportionality: No more force than necessary must be used. If a war is a response to an aggressive act, the response must not exceed the harm caused by the act.
- reasonable hope of success: The war can be won.
- last resort: Alternatives to war have been tried.
- discrimination: Only combatants can be attacked; non-combatants and non-military targets must be protected from harm.

Other arguments in favour of war are also raised occasionally. One of these is that war is necessary to control the world's population. Another is that war is the "mother of invention" because technological advances developed for use in warfare have often been adapted or modified for peaceful uses. The development of nuclear power stations, which was

Web connection

http://www.mcgrawhill.ca/links/philosophy12

To find out how ethicist Sissela Bok responded to the September 2001 terrorist attacks on the United States, follow the links on this Web site.

speeded by research into nuclear bombs, is an example. Some people have also argued that war is good for national unity, that war changes the world in decisive ways, and that war develops hardiness and other virtues.

> ### Recall...Reflect...Respond
>
> 1. List three moral choices that you have made over the past week. For each, write a first- and second-order question that reflects the ethical dimensions of your dilemma.
> 2. Think about an ethical dilemma that you have recently faced. Create a flowchart showing everyone affected by your moral choice. Think about your choice. Can you claim that it was morally right? On what grounds? If you cannot claim that it was morally right, how could you alter your choice to make it morally right? Explain fully.
> 3. Create or find a newspaper headline that reflects one of the main ethical positions taken on the issue of censorship. Do the same thing for the issue of war.

ETHICS AND SCIENCE

In 1994, a doctor helped Sue Rodriguez of Saanich, British Columbia, end her life. Rodriguez had Lou Gehrig's disease and knew that she would suffer a slow, painful death. Earlier, she had asked the courts to grant her the right to choose when to die.

Though the courts upheld the law against doctor-assisted suicide and turned down her request, Rodriguez went ahead and orchestrated her own death with the help of a doctor.

Figure 14.4

The Rodriguez case highlighted just one of the ethical dilemmas facing scientists. Scientific advances mean that doctors are now capable of doing things barely dreamed of even 25 years ago. But just because doctors *can* perform certain procedures, *should* they perform them? Or should they perform them only in certain circumstances? If so, what are those circumstances?

Though these questions affect issues in many areas of science and medicine, two that are frequently in the public eye are euthanasia and genetic engineering.

When Sue Rodriguez, pictured here in 1993, ignored the law and ended her own life with a doctor's assistance, the identity of the doctor was never revealed and no charges were ever laid. Do you think that Rodriguez and the doctor were morally right?

EUTHANASIA

Euthanasia, which comes from a Greek word meaning good death, is sometimes called mercy killing or doctor-assisted suicide. The doctor who helped Sue Rodriguez end her life engaged in active euthanasia, which means taking an action, such as administering an injection, that hastens death. To many, this is morally different from passive euthanasia, which means withholding a treatment that might prolong life.

Some philosophers, such as James Rachels, argue that there is no moral difference between the two forms of euthanasia because both have the same intent and consequence: the death of a human being. Others disagree. Some theologians, for example, argue that active euthanasia is morally wrong because it amounts to "playing God." They say that decisions about life and death are God's alone. Still others distinguish between using ordinary and extraordinary measures to maintain life. They argue that refusing to take extraordinary measures, such as going to an extreme to resuscitate someone who seems to have died, is morally acceptable. At the same time, refusing to take ordinary measures, such as supplying food and water, is not morally acceptable.

An important issue in the debate over the moral rightness of euthanasia is the consent of the patient, because this helps society distinguish between euthanasia and murder. True consent must be competent, informed, and voluntary. Competent consent refers to the patient's ability to understand and judge the consequences of a decision. Determining competence is not always easy, however. Is it fair to expect people who are sick, injured, or heavily medicated for pain to make rational judgments? Informed consent means that the patient must possess the necessary knowledge — and understanding — of procedures, alternatives, positive and negative consequences, risk factors, and so on. But how informed is informed enough? Voluntary consent means just that. No coercion must be involved in obtaining the patient's permission.

To ensure that a patient's consent is competent, informed, and voluntary, medical professionals may require a written — and witnessed — request. They may also require that patients wait for a specified period, be given counselling, and seek more than one expert opinion about both their diagnosis and their prospects of recovery.

But what if the patient is a defective newborn or a comatose adult who is incapable of giving competent, informed, and voluntary consent? In these cases, proxy consent can be given. A proxy is someone authorized to act on behalf of someone else. Proxy consent for euthanasia must meet one of the following criteria:

- The decision must be what the person would have wanted if she or he had been able to speak for her- or himself. This assumes that the patient's feelings have been made known.
- The decision must be what a reasonable person would want.
- The decision is in the person's best interests.

The third criterion is often the justification cited in cases of euthanasia. When Saskatchewan farmer Robert Latimer killed his 12-year-old daughter, Tracy, in 1993, for example, she did not consent because she could not. An unusually severe form of cerebral palsy had left Tracy with the intellect of a three-month-old infant. Unable to walk, talk, or feed herself, she lived with constant excruciating pain. Her father decided that death, which would end her pain, was in his daughter's best interests and killed her by placing her in his truck and running a hose from the exhaust pipe into the cab of the truck. Tracy died of carbon monoxide poisoning.

Relieving suffering is one of the most frequently cited arguments in favour of euthanasia. Most people would not let animals suffer needlessly, say those who make this argument. Why should attitudes toward human suffering be different? Supporters of this position believe that active euthanasia is more humane than passive euthanasia because death is quick and painless.

Web connection
http://www.mcgrawhill.ca/links/philosophy12
To find out more about the issues raised in the Latimer case, follow the links on this Web site.

Another frequently cited argument appeals to the idea of autonomy. This was an important argument in the Rodriguez case. Rodriguez argued that her life was her own and that it was therefore her right to choose when to end it. She wanted to die with dignity rather than wasting away, losing her ability to do anything for herself, even her ability to communicate her wishes.

PROFILE

Peter Singer
The Most Dangerous Man in the World Today

When the appointment of bioethicist Peter Singer to a senior position at Princeton University in the United States was announced in 1999, placard-waving protesters took to the streets. One editorial writer called the Australian-born philosopher a crackpot and megalomaniac, and *The Wall Street Journal* compared him to Martin Bormann, Adolf Hitler's deputy who helped spearhead the persecution of Jews in Nazi Germany.

Others sprang to Singer's defence. "There's nothing scary or unique in what Peter's doing," bioethicist Catherine Mayser told Jeff Sharlet of *The Chronicle of Higher Education*. "It's mainstream Anglo-American philosophy."

What sparked the outcry? Singer takes strong positions that challenge people's ideas. A utilitarian, Singer is credited with inspiring the animal rights movement by challenging the assumption that humans are superior to animals. He coined the term "speciesism" to describe this assumption, which he called as outdated as racism. A vegetarian, he believes that raising animals in order to kill them for food is as morally wrong as slavery and set out these views in his best-selling 1975 book, *Animal Liberation: A New Ethics for Our Treatment of Animals*.

Singer also advocates an unusual form of charity. Most people would not hesitate to drive a valuable sports car into the path of a train if it meant saving the life of a child, he wrote in the *New York Times*. Why, then, do people balk at the idea of selling the same car and using the money to save the life of a starving child in another country? Putting his money where his mouth is, Singer donates 20 percent of his income to famine relief agencies.

Though ideas like these may be radical, they are not the primary focus of the controversy that swirls around Singer. What enrages some people is his stand in favour of euthanizing terminally ill adults and severely disabled newborns. Rather than letting nature run its course and waiting for newborns with extreme disabilities to die, he has proposed that parents and doctors be allowed to choose to kill them by lethal — but painless — injection. His reasoning? Newborns have no more right to life than other creatures, such as dogs or pigs, with similar abilities to reason and feel emotion.

Singer dismisses sanctity-of-life arguments and focuses on quality of life, which he says is based on rationality and self-awareness. He maintains that newborns, especially those with severe disabilities, are neither rational nor self-aware. "Infants are sentient beings (living creatures who can perceive things through their senses) who are neither rational nor self-conscious," he wrote. "So if we turn to consider the infants in themselves, independently of the attitudes of their parents, since their species is not relevant to their moral status, the principles that govern the wrongness of killing non-human animals who are sentient but not rational or self-conscious must apply here, too."

Though Singer favours active euthanasia, he believes that consent is critically important. He says, for example, that euthanizing a terminally ill adult who does not want to die is morally wrong, no matter what the circumstances. And in the case of infants and others who are unable to give consent, he says that the choice should be up to parents and doctors.

Ideas like these provoked one spokesperson for the disabled to call Singer the most dangerous man in the world today. At the same time, others have praised this philosopher's courage and thoughtfulness in raising difficult ethical issues and ensuring that they are thoroughly debated.

Figure 14.5

Though bioethicist Peter Singer is reviled in some circles for his views on the moral rightness of euthanasia, his many supporters believe that he is raising important ethical issues.

Both these arguments involve the idea of quality of life, a concept that assumes that extreme pain and suffering reduce people's quality of life so greatly that life is no longer worth living. The opposing view, which is often called the sanctity-of-life argument, maintains that all lives are worth living, regardless of their quality.

In her petition to the courts, Rodriguez also claimed that the law against doctor-assisted suicide violates the Charter of Rights and Freedoms because it discriminates against people with disabilities who need help to commit suicide. Though a majority of justices rejected this argument, it was supported by dissenting opinions.

Some advocates of euthanasia also raise financial arguments. Citing the high cost of keeping people alive on life-support systems, they say that euthanasia is justified when people are unlikely to recover from a coma or severe disability. Others counter that money should not matter where a human life is concerned.

As happens in many ethical debates, the slippery-slope argument is often raised by opponents of euthanasia. In the debate over the moral rightness of Robert Latimer's killing his daughter, for example, many people argued that allowing him to go unpunished would endanger everyone with a disability. If it was deemed morally right to euthanize someone with a severe disability, they argued, the next step would be to allow the killing of people with less severe disabilities.

Other arguments against euthanasia focus on the possibility that there might have been a misdiagnosis and that medical advances may find either a cure or new ways to manage pain if a patient is kept alive long enough. Opponents of euthanasia also cite the possibility of abuse. A patient's relatives, hoping to inherit his estate a little sooner, might pressure him into consenting to be euthanized, for example.

A final argument focuses on the dilemma of doctors, who are usually the ones asked to carry out a patient's request to be euthanized. Existentialists might argue that asking a doctor for help amounts to refusing to take responsibility for ending one's own life. Others argue that participating in acts of either passive or active euthanasia violates doctors' responsibility to preserve life.

> **IDEAS IN CONTEXT**
>
> More and more hospitals are establishing ethics committees made up of doctors, nurses, administrators, ethics experts, religious representatives, and community members. This broad membership reflects a desire to obtain a variety of opinions and to ensure that everyone likely to be affected by an ethical issue has a voice in making decisions. Ethics committees take on a variety of duties: screening research proposals, guiding hospital policy, developing and implementing a code of ethics, conducting education inside and outside the hospital, and acting as consultants when hospital staff and patients face ethical dilemmas.

GENETHICS

Recent advances in knowledge of the human genome, the genetic material that makes up the human organism, has led to the development of a new ethics specialty. Sometimes called **genethics** — a word coined by combining "genetics" and "ethics" — or bioethics, this field explores a variety of ethical issues stemming from scientists' increasing ability to manipulate the genetic makeup of living organisms, both human and non-human.

Mapping the human genome enables scientists to identify the genes responsible for various traits. This means that genetic engineering — manipulating genes to create a human being with particular traits — is quickly becoming a real possibility.

This possibility raises many ethical questions. Does the fact that scientists *can* do it mean that they *should* do it? Is genetic engineering morally right? If so, in what circumstances? Some ethicists say that the kind of procedure makes a difference. They distinguish between negative genetic engineering, which involves removing certain genes (e.g., those carrying inherited diseases), and positive genetic engineering, which involves enhancing certain genes (e.g., those that govern specific abilities, such as the ability to run fast). They consider negative genetic engineering morally acceptable, but do not accept positive genetic engineering.

No matter which form of genetic engineering is considered, who should take responsibility for making decisions about when manipulating genes is morally acceptable and which genes it is acceptable to manipulate? Parents? Private companies? Geneticists? Doctors? Governments? Society as a whole?

People have also raised utilitarian arguments about the consequences of genetic engineering. Do the good consequences outweigh the bad? Shirley Tilghman, for example, is a Canadian biochemist who is the president of Princeton University. She has mixed feelings about the answer to this question. "[Genetic research] has set in motion the possibility for both great benefit and some serious problems," she told Simon Houpt of *The Globe and Mail*.

Tilghman noted that genetic discrimination could become a reality if employers refuse to hire prospective employees who carry genes likely to cause cancer or other illnesses. In addition, she said that it may be possible for prospective parents to select the traits they want in their children. "From the point of view of the human race, this has profound implications for homogeneity (sameness). Do we really think it would be good if we had a regression to the mean, essentially, in the population, where the breadth of human diversity is essentially narrowed? I happen to think it would be a terrible thing."

And American ethicist Elizabeth Anderson has speculated that allowing parents to select their children's traits may have an unexpected negative effect. "A child who knew how anxious her parents were that she have the 'right' genetic makeup might fear that her parents' love was contingent upon her expression of these characteristics."

> **• IDEAS IN CONTEXT •**
>
> Every human being has about 100,000 genes, each providing a vital bit of information about everything from eye colour to inherited diseases. The Human Genome Project is an international initiative established to create a map of the human genetic code.
>
> Francis Collins, director of the National Human Genome Research Institute in the United States, has predicted that by 2010 scientists will have developed accurate tests — and preventive treatments — for many inherited illnesses. By 2020, doctors will be able to alter the genes inherited by children, and by 2030, advances in genetic research will mean most people in developed nations will live to the age of 90.

Other people warn of different consequences. Would people who carry genes that are considered undesirable be prohibited from reproducing these genes by having children? Would genetic screening become mandatory? Mandatory screening would certainly violate people's right to privacy, but could this right be overridden by the argument that babies have a right to be born healthy? And how would acceptance of mandatory screening affect people with illnesses or disabilities? Would society come to view their lives as less valuable? Would this affect their ability to get insurance or even a job

Web connection
http://www.mcgrawhill.ca/links/philosophy12
To find out more about the Human Genome Project, follow the links on this Web site.

Some scientists and ethicists also argue that the long-term effects of genetic engineering are unknown. Biochemical relationships are complex, they say, and ignorance of the long-term effects could have dire consequences for both individuals and society. As science expands the bounds of genetic research, the debate over genetic engineering is likely to raise some of the most pressing ethical concerns of the 21st century.

ETHICS AND THE ENVIRONMENT

In the 1940s, a synthetic insecticide called DDT (dichlorodiphenyltricholoroethane) came into widespread agricultural use. For nearly 30 years, DDT was used to kill mosquitoes and insects that destroy crops. Unfortunately, its effects were not limited to these insects. Traces of the highly toxic chemical began to appear in other insects and in rodents, fish, birds, and other insect-eating animals, as well as in people who ate crops or animals that had been contaminated with the pesticide. As a result, DDT was banned in Canada in 1969 and in the United States in 1972.

This experience with DDT illustrates a central principle of environmental ethics: everything is connected. As late as 1985, for example, traces of DDT were still being found in the flesh of polar bears whose habitat was far from areas where use of the pesticide had been common. As a result of these interconnections, environmental ethicists focus on the relationship between human beings and the natural environment, including the non-human animals that share it.

CONSERVATION AND PRESERVATION

When discussing issues related to the natural environment, ethicists often divide into two camps. One camp believes that the environment has instrumental value. This utilitarian approach says that the value of the environment lies in its usefulness to people. This view is taken by the conservationist movement, which was championed in the early 20th century by American Gifford Pinchot. The goal of conservationists is to conserve the natural environment for people's wise use and development.

The other camp argues that the environment has intrinsic value, independent of its usefulness to people. Even if human beings did not need to breathe clean air and drink clean water and even if no one found starry skies stunningly beautiful, the natural environment would still be valuable. This view is taken by the preservationist movement, which was championed by Sierra Club founder American John Muir. The goal of preservationists is to protect the natural environment against human development.

Like most ethical dilemmas, debates over environmental issues often involve weighing the pros and cons of various courses of action. Nearly everyone recognizes that if humankind is to survive, the environment must be developed to some extent. People require food to eat, for example, so land must be cleared to grow crops. The ethical debates arise over the extent of environmental destruction required to support human development — and this leads to tradeoffs based on value judgments. What kind of environmental destruction is morally acceptable? Is it morally right, for example, to cut down a forest to create agricultural land for growing food? To make room for houses? To create a golf course, a theme park, or a ski resort?

If tradeoffs must be made, who should be responsible for deciding which are morally acceptable? And how should value be measured? Is having bananas and fresh tomatoes to eat in winter, for example, worth the air pollution and noise created by the trains and trucks required to transport goods such as these to Canadian supermarkets? Or the energy that is used? If these goods were banned or if people refused to buy them, how would it affect the livelihood of those who produce them?

To answer questions like these, utilitarians would weigh the consequences of various courses of action. Those who take different philosophical positions might view the conflict as one of competing rights. Does one person's right to a certain quality of life outweigh someone else's?

Many ethicists believe that a concept called **sustainable development** reconciles the needs of human beings with environmental concerns. Sustainable development refers to conserving the ecological balance by minimizing the harmful effects on the environment.

A movement called ecofeminism, advocated by the Australian activist Val Plumwood and others, takes an even more holistic view by examining the implications of attitudes toward the environment. Contemporary American philosopher **Karen Warren**, for example, maintains that

> *Our ideals, laws, and customs should be based on the proposition that each generation in turn becomes the custodian rather than the absolute owner of our resources — and each generation has the obligation to pass this inheritance on to the future.*
>
> – Alden Whitman

ideas about the domination of nature are linked to the domination of women. Both ideas assume that some human beings are superior and therefore have a moral right to dominate everything else. This attitude contrasts sharply with Aboriginal and Taoist ethical beliefs that call for humans to live in harmony with nature.

> ### Recall...Reflect...Respond
> 1. Illustrate the difference between active and passive euthanasia by explaining how various moral arguments in favour of or against euthanasia apply to each.
> 2. Choose a moral position in favour of or against genetic engineering. Think of an argument that might be used to argue against your position. Devise a counter-argument to this.
> 3. Is the idea of sustainable development consistent with the goals of the conservationist movement, the preservationist movement, or both? Explain why.

TREATMENT OF NON-HUMAN ANIMALS

Suppose you are driving on a country road and hit a deer, injuring it severely. At the side of the road, the deer is thrashing about in pain. Do you have a moral obligation to this animal? If so, what is it? Are you obligated to try to save its life? To end its suffering by killing it? To do something else?

Does your treatment of the injured deer even qualify as a moral dilemma? Some philosophers maintain that it does not. They say that non-human animals have no moral standing because they are not members of the moral community made up of moral agents and moral patients. Others argue just as strongly that non-human animals are part of this community and do, therefore, have moral standing.

In western thought, the idea that non-human animals have no claim to membership in the moral community is rooted in the ideas of the ancient Greeks. Aristotle, for example, argued that animals have no moral standing because they have no soul. This argument was echoed by Aquinas in medieval times and, later, by the 17th-century French philosopher René Descartes. Descartes described animals as "thoughtless brutes," saying that they are mere automata, or machines, who feel no pain because they have no consciousness. As a result, said Descartes, they have no moral standing.

Kant agreed with Descartes, saying that only free, rational beings have moral standing — and non-human animals are neither free nor rational. "So far as animals are concerned," Kant wrote, "[human beings] have no direct duties. Animals are not self-conscious and are there merely as a means to an end. That end is man."

Figure 14.6

"We would like to be genetically modified to taste like Brussels sprouts."

Have these cattle come up with a reasonable rationale for supporting genetic modification?

PHILOSOPHY IN ACTION

Should the West Pay for China's Fridges?

by Thomas Hurka

Thomas Hurka is a Canadian philosopher who teaches at the University of Calgary. This essay, which was originally published in *The Globe and Mail*, illustrates how environmental concerns are linked to many other areas of ethical debate.

Right now, China's 1.2 billion people don't own refrigerators. But what if they get them, as China's government plans, and the country's per capita fridge ownership comes to equal that in the West? Who will pay for China's refrigerators?

If the refrigerators are of the traditional freon-cooled type, the whole world will pay. Freon is a chlorofluorocarbon, and CFCs damage the earth's ozone layer. They're also responsible for about 15 percent of the global warming trend known as the greenhouse effect. If China gets freon-cooled refrigerators, we'll all pay in increased cancers, dried out farming regions, and rising ocean levels.

Alerted to the dangers of CFCs, western governments have proposed international action to eliminate them. Forty countries agreed in Montreal in 1987 to halve CFC production by 1998; now they've agreed to a complete ban. The West want[ed] all countries to eliminate CFCs before the [end of the 20th century].

To the West's surprise, Third World countries, including China, have rejected these proposals as unfair. The developed world, they say, was able to industrialize using cheap materials such as CFCs. Now that the Third World stands poised for its own industrialization, it's not fair to ask it to use what are bound to be more expensive substitutes. It's not fair to delay even further its economic betterment.

Third World countries don't refuse to use substitutes for CFCs; they just want the developed world to pay them the difference between the cost of these substitutes and the CFCs they give up.

Should the West pay for China's refrigerators? There are many moral arguments why we should. Helping China would be kind, an act of generosity; it would also reduce international inequality. But these are not ideas to which our governments have traditionally given much credence, as their tiny foreign aid budgets attest. Are there reasons for paying that are more attuned to our governments' moral thinking?

Some say there are. Third World countries, they argue, wouldn't be in the position they're in now if the developed countries hadn't already damaged the ozone layer with their own CFCs. So, the developed countries owe the Third World compensation. They're responsible for the Third World's having to use more expensive materials and must therefore pay the extra cost of these materials.

This argument seems to have won a convert in former British prime minister Margaret Thatcher. At a conference about the ozone problem, she said it would be "intolerable" if the countries "which have already industrialized, and which have caused the greater part of the problems we face" expected others to pay to solve them.

Perhaps Mrs. Thatcher shouldn't have been so easily convinced. The harm to Third World countries wasn't done in the way normally required for compensation. Compensation is normally owed only for acts of negligence or carelessness. If, because of my careless driving, my car leaves the road and hits you on the sidewalk, I owe you compensation for your injuries. But if I drive as safely as possible and hit an unforeseeable patch of ice with the same result, I don't owe compensation. The patch of ice was bad luck; the bad luck ended up harming you; but since I wasn't at fault in what happened, I'm not liable for damages.

The developed world, it can be argued, is in the position of a driver who's skidded on unforeseeable ice.

When Kelvinator marketed the first refrigerator in 1918, it had no idea its product could damage the ozone layer. When Styrofoam was introduced, there was no evidence it would increase global temperatures. Although actions in the West have harmed the Third World, no one was at fault in most of those actions, and therefore no compensation is owed. The Third World's position is largely bad luck — unfortunate, but not something that calls for special aid.

Where does this leave us? Without the argument about compensation we face a moral choice. If our governments retain their old moral ideas, we'll ask China to buy costlier refrigerators and fall farther behind in economic development, all to protect our common environment. We may be unable to bring ourselves to this. But if we can't, as Mrs. Thatcher apparently couldn't, we'll have to change our moral thinking. We'll have to start caring more about international giving or equality for their own sake. And this will have far-reaching consequences.

Arguments about equality, for example, don't apply just to CFC substitutes; they support a general program of international redistribution. To accept them in one area is implicitly to accept a shift in all our dealings with poorer countries.

The issue of China's refrigerators foreshadows many the world will face in coming decades. We need to switch from damaging technologies to ones that are environmentally safer but also, inevitably, more expensive. This will repeatedly raise the question of who will pay the extra cost of these technologies in developing countries. And this question poses a moral challenge. Will we retain our old moral ideas, and ask the least well off countries to pay the most for environmental protection? Or will we find in the environment the beginnings of a new concern for global equality?

Source: *Principles: Short Essays on Ethics*. Thomas Hurka

1. What important ethical question is addressed in this article?

2. Select three arguments for or against the West's paying for China's fridges. Refer to Chapter 13 to determine the philosophical school of thought represented by each argument. Defend the argument that you think is most sound.

3. Knowledge of other subjects is required to respond effectively to the issues raised in this article. What are these subjects? Support your response with evidence from the article.

These arguments were supported by some divine command theorists who cite a passage in the biblical Book of Genesis that says that humans were created to "have dominion over the fish of the sea, over the birds of the air, and over the cattle, over all the earth and over every creeping thing that creeps on the earth." Even some people who do not subscribe to divine command theory argue that human interests should prevail over those of animals because people are more highly developed.

Arguments that animals have no consciousness were challenged by scientists and thinkers as diverse as the physicist Isaac Newton, the philosopher John Locke, the writer Voltaire, and the evolutionist Charles Darwin. It was only in the 20th century, however, that scientists began to conduct research proving that animals have feelings and emotions. This research gave fresh impetus to the longstanding philosophical debate over whether non-human animals have moral standing.

If non-human animals do have moral standing, many philosophers maintain that this raises a host of ethical questions about humans' attitudes toward and treatment of animals. If animals have moral standing, do they have rights? What are these rights? Is it morally right, for example, to disturb or destroy the habitat of wild animals? Is it morally right to eat animals? To use them for entertainment? To use them for experiments?

Some contemporary philosophers believe that non-human animals have instrumental value only. This means that their value lies in their usefulness to people. This usefulness may be scientific (e.g., they may be useful for research), commercial (e.g., they or their parts can be sold to generate income), life-supporting (e.g., they may be farmed or hunted for food), observational (e.g., they may be exhibits in zoos and sanctuaries), recreational (e.g., they are fun to play with), or ecological (e.g., a species may be important to the ecosystem).

Other philosophers maintain that non-human animals have intrinsic value. Some who take this position argue that animals' mere existence qualifies them for membership in the moral community. Others argue that the determining factor in deciding whether they have moral standing is consciousness, intelligence, interests, or moral autonomy.

The English utilitarian Jeremy Bentham, for example, argued that **sentience** — the ability to perceive things through the senses — is the factor that determines eligibility for membership in the moral community. In *Introduction to the Principles of Morals and Legislation*, he wrote:

> The day *may come*, when the rest of the animal creation may acquire those rights which never could have been withholden from them by the hand of tyranny.... Is it the faculty of reason, or perhaps the faculty of discourse? But a full-grown horse or dog is beyond comparison a more rational, as well as more conversable animal, than an infant of a day, or a week, or even a month old. But suppose they were otherwise, what would it avail? The question is not, Can they *reason*? nor Can they *talk*? but Can they *suffer*?

The contemporary American philosopher Joel Feinberg takes a different view, arguing that people have a moral duty toward animals because animals have "conscious wishes, desires, hopes; or urges or impulses; or unconscious drives, aims, or goals; or latent tendencies, direction of growth, and natural fulfilments."

The contemporary American bioethicist **Peter Singer** draws on the ideas of both Bentham and Feinberg when he says that sentience is a prerequisite for having interests. Singer maintains that all sentient animals, human and non-human, are morally equal. The interests of non-human animals, such as their interest in avoiding pain, mean that they should be subject to the moral consideration of humans.

In his book *Animal Liberation: A New Ethics for Our Treatment of Animals*, Singer wrote:

> Racists violate the principle of equality by giving greater weight to the interests of members of their own race when there is a clash between their interests and the interests of those of another race. Sexists violate the principle of equality by favouring the interests of their own sex. Similarly speciesists allow the interests of their own species to override the greater interests of members of other species.

He went on to claim that if using chimpanzees in experiments is morally right, then people should also be prepared to accept the idea of using brain-damaged humans with similar mental capacities.

Though Singer believes that non-human animals should be subject to humans' moral consideration, he stops short of claiming that they have rights. This view is challenged by **Tom Regan**, an American philosopher and animal rights activist. Regan argues that some animals do have rights on the grounds of their intrinsic value. In *The Case for Animal Rights*, Regan wrote that these animals are subjects-of-a-life.

> To be the subject-of-a-life ... involves more than merely being alive and more than merely being conscious. [It means to] have beliefs and desires; perception, memory, and a sense of the future, including their own future; an emotional life together with feelings of pleasure and pain; preference and welfare-interests; the ability to initiate action in pursuit of their desires and goals; a psychophysical identity over time; and an individual welfare in the sense that their experiential life fares well or ill for them, independently of their utility for others.

Philosophers such as Singer and Regan would argue that using animals for food, clothing, and entertainment is morally wrong. The issue of using animals in experiments raises even more questions. Is it right to conduct research using animals who are unable to give or refuse consent? Does the purpose of the research matter? Is there a moral difference, for example,

> *Our practice of rearing and killing animals in order to eat them is a clear instance of the sacrifice of the most important interests of other beings in order to satisfy trivial interests of our own.*
>
> – Peter Singer

between life-saving and life-enhancing research? Does the degree of harm to the animal matter? Are there moral differences between causing discomfort, pain, and death?

People's views on the use of animals for research vary widely. At one extreme are those who believe that animal research is morally acceptable. They argue that animals feel no pain, that humans have a right to use animals for any purpose, that scientists must be free to pursue their research by any means, that no suitable alternatives exist, or that making use of animals who will be killed anyway makes sense. At the other extreme are those who oppose all experimentation with animals. They argue that animals do feel both physical and emotional pain and that the experiments are unnecessary.

Many others take a stand between these two extremes. Regan, for example, believes that using animals for research may sometimes be morally acceptable — if there is very good reason to believe that it will prevent greater harm. And Donald VanDeVeer, another American philosopher, advocates distinguishing between basic human interests or needs, such as life, food, water, clothing, and freedom from intense pain, and non-basic interests or wants, such as indoor plumbing and cosmetics. When the interests of humans and non-humans conflict, VanDeVeer says that the basic interests of each are more important than the non-basic interests of the other.

Web connection
http://www.mcgrawhill.ca/links/philosophy12
To find out more about ethics and animal welfare, follow the links on this Web site.

ETHICS AND COMPUTERS

Some observers have identified the computer revolution of the late 20th century as one of the most significant developments in the history of humankind. Certainly, the personal computer has changed the way people live, work, and play. At the same time, the use of computers has raised myriad ethical issues that were undreamed of a few decades earlier. These issues range from the moral rightness of censoring ideas expressed on the Internet to questions about whether it is morally appropriate to continue developing artificial intelligence. One of the most pressing issues, however, is the effect of computers on the idea of intellectual property.

INTELLECTUAL PROPERTY

Suppose you are sitting at your computer listening to music that you have downloaded — free — from the Internet. Or you are playing a game that you borrowed from a friend and installed on your own computer. In both cases you are using someone else's intellectual property — without permission. Are these actions morally right?

Intellectual property is the product of a creative endeavour. These products include books, songs, plays, films, paintings, photographs, ideas for inventions, trademarks, and software programs that are owned by their creators. In Canada and most other countries, the creator's ownership is recognized by copyright, patent, or trademark laws. These laws ensure that creators receive payment for the talent, time, effort, and energy they have put into producing the product.

Take a song. The songwriter usually holds the copyright, which means that he or she owns the right to make copies. No one else is allowed to copy the song without permission, which is usually granted in return for a fee. A songwriter might grant a singer or musical group the right to include a song on a CD. By the time the song appears on the CD, however, the time and creative effort of many other people — singers, musicians, technicians, producers, artists, manufacturers, and salespeople — have also gone into producing and getting it to market. The value of these efforts is reflected in the selling price of the CD.

Is it morally right, then, to deprive creators of their reward by downloading music from the Internet free of charge? Or by borrowing and copying a CD?

Some ethicists might challenge the principle that underlies these laws, arguing that creators do not necessarily have the right to own the fruits of their labour. A Confucian, for example, might take a communal approach, arguing that everything should be free — offered and shared by all — for the benefit of everyone.

A Kantian ethicist would use the categorical imperative to decide. If it is morally acceptable for one person to download music free of charge, then it must be morally acceptable for everyone to do so. If this were the case, would singers, musicians, and so on stop recording CDs because there would be no reward for doing so? Would this limit musical creativity because everyone involved in producing a CD would need to find other ways of making a living? Furthermore, a Kantian ethicist might say that downloading music without compensating the creators serves the downloader's end but fails to respect the creator's end.

Some utilitarians might argue that the number of people who benefit from hearing recorded music free of charge far outweighs the number who are hurt by losing income. Other utilitarians might agree that this is true, but they might also conclude that this is a short-term benefit. In the long term, songwriters, singers, and musicians might stop producing recorded music — and then no one would benefit.

Even those in the music business hold diverse opinions. Some support the idea of free downloading. They argue that someone who enjoys listening to a downloaded song may later go out and buy the entire CD. Others say that all copying is morally wrong because the person making the free copy is enjoying the fruits of artists' labour without their permission.

Figure 14.7

When Napster shut down in 2001, these Winnipeg, Manitoba, students turned to other Web sites that allow them to download music free of charge.

Web connection

http://www.mcgrawhill.ca/links/philosophy12

To read cartoonist Gary Larson's thoughts about unauthorized copying of his work, follow the links on this Web site.

ETHICS AND BUSINESS

Many of the moral dilemmas that arise in workplaces are similar to those that confront people everywhere. Other issues are not, however. They are peculiar to the world of business.

Is it morally right, for example, to manufacture products, such as cigarettes or alcohol, that may harm people? Or to use child labour? Is it morally right for business owners to monitor employees' e-mail? Or to videotape employees as they work or take a break? Or to pay male employees higher wages than female employees? Or to discriminate when hiring employees?

Questions like these arise in workplaces every day. Like many hospitals, some large companies have hired ethics experts to help resolve ethical dilemmas, to audit the company's ethical practices, and to create and implement a code of ethics. One area of business that raises a host of ethical questions is advertising.

There are some jobs in which it is impossible for a man to be virtuous.

– Aristotle

Recall...Reflect...Respond

1. In E.B. White's children's story *Charlotte's Web*, a pig named Wilbur fears being slaughtered to provide food for people. Wilbur is befriended by a spider named Charlotte, who saves him from slaughter. Apply the concepts of instrumental and intrinsic value to this story. What value does Wilbur seem to believe he possesses? Why? What value does Charlotte seem to believe Wilbur possesses? Why?
2. Assume that a pet is an important member of your family. Which philosophical arguments about the rights of animals are you likely to find most appealing? Explain why your philosophical point of view might differ if you have never owned a pet.
3. Choose a moral issue relating to computer use or business decisions. Explain how a consequentialist ethical theorist might respond to this issue.

ADVERTISING

Suppose you arrive at school to find an advertisement for a particular product posted on a classroom wall. Your teacher explains that a manufacturer has paid the school for the right to display ads for its products. The school will use the revenue to help buy computers and fund school trips, dances, and sports. Is raising money this way morally right?

Advertising is a widely accepted part of life in the 21st century. Advertisements are so pervasive that most people do not think twice about them. Think about the advertising you saw on the way to school today. Can you even count the number of ads you saw on billboards, in newspapers, in or on buses, on bumper stickers, and even on people's clothing?

Yet not everyone accepts that advertising is a necessity. The Canadian-born American economist **John Kenneth Galbraith** has argued that advertising is morally wrong because it enables corporations to artificially create the desire to possess the goods or services it offers for sale. Galbraith maintains that this creates a "dependency effect," which leads to unhappiness and dissatisfaction.

The Lighter Side of Philosophy

For helping a client take care of some legal business, a lawyer charged a fee of $100. The client paid in cash, handing the lawyer a $100 bill. The client did not notice that a second $100 bill was stuck to the first.

The lawyer noticed the second bill immediately and realized that he faced an ethical dilemma. "Should I tell my partner about the extra $100?" he wondered.

Advertisers counter this argument by pointing out that advertising benefits the public by letting people know that certain products and services are available. They also argue that advertising is not only a form of freedom of expression, but also a right that enables companies to pursue profits. They suggest that creating demand for a product benefits society by supporting the economy. Increased demand for a product or service enables companies to grow, and this growth creates jobs, which is good for society.

Still, governments, advertisers, and the public acknowledge that advertisers must observe some limits. The ethical debate over advertising usually focuses on just what these limits ought to be.

In Canada, advertisers have developed a voluntary code to maintain standards of honesty, truth, accuracy, fairness, and propriety. The Canadian Code of Advertising Standards specifies, for example, that advertisements "must not contain inaccurate or deceptive claims, statements, illustration, or representations, either direct or implied, with regard to price, availability, or performance of a product or service."

Most advertisers probably agree that it is morally wrong to lie in advertisements. The situation is not as clear cut, however, when it comes to manipulation, persuasion, coercion, and control. Is it morally acceptable, for example, to create advertisements that manipulate consumers into believing that a product will enhance their life in some way? To persuade them that if they own a particular car or wear a particular brand of shoe they will be cool, popular, and happy?

A Kantian ethicist would say that manipulation of this kind is morally wrong because it fails to respect consumers' autonomy. Kantian ethicists would also assess the goal of the ads. If it is to increase sales and profits, this treats consumers as a means to the advertiser's end and ignores the consumer's end.

Ethicists also debate many other issues involved in advertising. Does the context in which the advertising is presented matter, for example? Are ads on buses more coercive than those in magazines or newspapers? Because people must ride buses to get to school, work, or other destinations, they are a captive audience. Magazines and newspapers, by contrast, can be easily set aside. And what about ads in schools? Are they coercive because students are a captive audience?

Does the technique used to present the advertiser's message matter? Is it morally acceptable to use rational argument to persuade consumers to buy a product or service, but morally unacceptable to appeal to emotion? If so, why? Are appeals to emotion harder to resist because they work on a subconscious level?

Does the target audience matter? Are some ads morally acceptable when presented to adults, but unacceptable when presented to children?

The Canadian Code of Advertising Standards seems to acknowledge this when it says that advertising directed to children "must not exploit their credulity, lack of experience, their sense of loyalty, and must not present information or illustrations which might result in their physical, emotional, or moral harm." In Quebec, advertising directed at children is prohibited by law. Are limits like these morally acceptable?

Finally, does the product matter? Are companies obligated to advertise some products? For example, are condom manufacturers obligated to advertise condoms because of their effectiveness in preventing the spread of AIDS and other sexually transmitted diseases? Are ads that promote harmful products, such as tobacco and alcohol, morally different from those that promote baby cribs, cars, books, and so on?

The Canadian government, as well as various organizations such as the Canadian Council for Tobacco Control, believes that they are. As a result, the federal government has placed strict limits on ads for tobacco and alcohol. Those who disagree with these restrictions argue that they fail to recognize people's autonomy and their right to make decisions for themselves.

The ethical issues involved in advertising are as difficult as those debated in other areas of business — and life. They do, however, indicate clearly how philosophical ideas affect the everyday moral choices people make.

Web connection

http://www.mcgrawhill.ca/links/philosophy12

To find out more about the Canadian Code of Advertising Standards, follow the links on this Web site.

Chapter Review

Chapter Summary

This chapter has discussed
- the responses of some major philosophers and main schools of ethics to some of the main ethical questions
- how moral problems and dilemmas that occur in everyday contexts can be effectively analyzed using a variety of different philosophical theories

Knowledge and Understanding

1. Identify and explain the significance to the study of ethics of each of the following key words and people.

Key Words	Key People
moral choice	Sissela Bok
ethical dimensions	Harriet Taylor
slippery-slope phenomenon	Nadine Strossen
censorship	Hannah Arendt
pacifist	Karen Warren
militarist	Peter Singer
just war theory	Tom Regan
euthanasia	John Kenneth Galbraith
genethics	
sustainable development	
sentience	

2. Select four moral issues discussed in this chapter. On a chart like the following, identify each issue. Under each of the questions, summarize the moral arguments that relate to each of the questions.

Moral Issue	What is right (or good) or wrong (or bad)?	What is the good life?	What is virtue?	Why be moral?	What obligations do people have to one another?

Thinking and Inquiry

3. In *On Liberty*, John Stuart Mill considered this question: What moral obligations do parents have to their children? He wrote: "To bring a child into existence without a fair prospect of being able, not only to provide food for its body, but instruction and training for its mind, is a moral crime, both against the unfortunate offspring and against society."

   Evaluate Mill's position from the point of view of at least two other schools of ethical thought.

4. Although thoughtful philosophers consider all the ethical dimensions of issues, it is often difficult to eliminate personal bias. Choose three important ethical issues. For each, list the factors that may have influenced the position taken by various philosophers and explain how these factors may have done so.

Communication

5. Imagine that you are a philosophical counsellor. Mary is a 19-year-old client who is trying to decide whether to start a sexual relationship with her boyfriend of six months. Write the dialogue that might occur between you and Mary. Be sure to

   • explain to Mary why her decision involves an ethical issue
   • talk about the ethical issues involved in her decision
   • talk about philosophical arguments that might help Mary reach a decision

6. In groups of three, create a co-operative wall display highlighting everyday moral dilemmas. Select a moral issue for your group to examine. Each group member should analyze one philosophical theory that addresses the issue. Create a series of visuals to support this analysis and post them on the classroom wall.

Application

7. In Dr. Seuss's children's story *The Lorax*, a Once-ler decides to use all the Truffula Trees in the forest to produce Thneeds, a Fine-Something-That-All-People-Need! By the end of the story, all the Truffula Trees, as well as the Lorax and other wildlife, have disappeared from the forest. As the story ends, the Once-ler lets a Truffula seed drop to the ground. He says

   It's the last one of all!
   You're in charge of the last of the Truffula Seeds.
   And Truffula Trees are what everyone needs.
   Plant a new Truffula. Treat it with care.
   Give it clean water. And feed it fresh air.
   Grow a forest. Protect it from axes that hack.
   Then the Lorax
   and all of his friends
   may come back.

   What moral dilemma does this story address? Respond personally to an important philosophical question that you believe is raised by this story.

8. Prepare five questions that you would like to ask an ethics expert who is helping you assess the advertising practices of a business. Answer these questions from the perspective of a particular philosophical school of thought. Use these answers to create a code of advertising for the business.

Write a feature article for a philosophical magazine.
CULMINATING ACTIVITY

EXPECTATIONS
By completing this activity, you will

- demonstrate an understanding of the main questions, concepts, and theories of ethics
- evaluate the strengths and weaknesses of the responses to ethical questions and moral problems defended by some major philosophers and schools of philosophy, and defend your own responses
- illustrate the relevance of philosophical theories of ethics to concrete moral problems in everyday life
- demonstrate an understanding of how philosophical theories of ethics are implicit in other subjects
- demonstrate an understanding of the character of philosophical questions
- effectively use a variety of print and electronic resources to conduct research
- effectively communicate the results of your inquiries

THE TASK
Everyone encounters ethical dilemmas every day. As they strive to define their role in society and their idea of a good life, people constantly make decisions about how to act and how to treat other people and living things.

People use a variety of tools to help them work out their ethical positions. Reading interesting feature articles in contemporary magazines often helps people deal with everyday moral issues. Though feature articles usually express the position of the author, effective articles take into account the views of others, including experts in the field, political or religious leaders, and members of the public.

By writing a well-researched feature article on an ethical issue of your choice, you will apply critical and analytical thinking skills to defend your own ideas and may persuade others to revise their own beliefs about the issue. The article should be 1500 to 2000 words long. When writing, remember that a useful, thought-provoking article not only promotes your philosophical position but also demonstrates your understanding of the ethical questions, concepts, and theories that you have learned.

At the end of this course, this feature article may be combined with the products of other unit-culminating activities to create a philosophy magazine.

THE SUBTASKS

Subtask 1: Annotated Bibliography
Before beginning your research on the ethical issue you have chosen, explore the resources that are available. Skim a variety of resources to evaluate them for content, usefulness, and bias.

Subtask 2: Research Notes
After identifying resources that provide a range of ethical viewpoints, create a detailed list of the information you intend to use from each source. Document your sources so that they are readily accessible. You may wish to consider creating a survey to obtain primary evidence of views held by members of the community.

Subtask 3: Statement and Defence of Your Philosophical Position
Your research will have helped you develop your own position on the ethical issue you have chosen to discuss. To help guide your thinking and ensure that you clearly connect your position to the philosophical debate on the issue, create three second-order ethical questions about the issue. Then state your ethical position in a sentence or two and write a paragraph showing how you intend to defend this position. You may also include graphic organizers or other illustrative material that will help you anticipate, analyze, and evaluate other responses to your second-order questions.

Subtask 4: Detailed Outline
Before writing a draft, consider how you will organize the article. Work out how you plan to develop both the article and the ideas in each paragraph. Decide how you will effectively link the ideas within paragraphs and from one paragraph to another.

Based on these plans, create a detailed outline of the article to ensure that you present your ideas in an effective structure. Check the assessment guidelines that follow to find out how your article will be assessed and to ensure that you have included everything required to meet the criteria.

Subtask 5: Draft
Prepare a draft of the article and ask an editor and other reviewers — your teacher, peers, parents, yourself, or others — to read it and make suggestions for improving it according to the assessment criteria.

Subtask 6: Revisions and Polished Copy
Use the feedback provided by the editor and other reviewers to reflect on how you can revise the article to improve its effectiveness. Assess your polished version to ensure that you have successfully met the assessment criteria.

ASSESSMENT CRITERIA

The following criteria will be used to assess your feature article.

Knowledge and Understanding
Does your article

- describe an ethical issue?
- integrate second-order ethical questions?
- outline various ethical positions?

Thinking and Inquiry
Does your article

- state your position on the issue?
- apply relevant research findings to defending your position?
- include second-order questions that are relevant to the issue?
- analyze and evaluate various theories of ethics?

Communication
Does your article

- present ideas in a planned and orderly fashion?
- structure the text to focus on the issue?
- use writing conventions?
- take into account your purpose and audience?

Application
Does your article

- illustrate in everyday contexts the relevance of ethical theories to the issue?
- connect the ethical issue with other subjects?

UNIT 5
AESTHETICS

CHAPTER

15 Introducing Aesthetics

16 Theories, Categories, and Types of Art

17 Beauty

Unit Expectations

By the end of this unit, you will be able to
- demonstrate an understanding of the main questions, concepts, and theories of aesthetics
- evaluate the strengths and weaknesses of responses to some of the main questions of aesthetics defended by some major philosophers and defend your own responses
- illustrate the relevance of aesthetics to other subjects

Think about the variety of art you encounter every day. A list might include the advertising images you see on TV or in magazines, a dance production you attend, a play or musical you help put on, photographs you look at, a book you read, and a song or other musical piece you listen to. Sometimes, artworks like these inform. Other times, they entertain. And still other times, they challenge people to think deeply about the beliefs they hold on issues such as race, gender, power, class, and sexuality. The impulse to create and appreciate art is an important part of being human.

But what is art? How should its meaning be judged? Must its meaning be judged at all? The study of aesthetics reveals how philosophers have answered these questions — and many more.

Chapter 15
Introducing Aesthetics

Chapter Expectations

By the end of this chapter, you will be able to
- demonstrate an understanding of philosophical questions of aesthetics
- evaluate the strengths and weaknesses of the responses of some of the major philosophers to some of the main questions of aesthetics, making reference to classic texts
- formulate and defend your own responses to some of the main questions of aesthetics
- explain how philosophical theories of aesthetics influence music, art, and fashion

Key Words

aesthetics
aesthetic triad
personal aesthetic
catharsis
taste
aesthetic experience
modernism
post-modernism
objectivity
subjectivity
descriptive
normative

Key People

Aristotle
Plato
René Descartes
Alexander Baumgarten
David Hume
Immanuel Kant
Georg W.F. Hegel
Friedrich Nietzsche
John Dewey
Arthur Danto
Benedetto Croce
Clive Bell

A Philosopher's Voice

There is nothing about an object — no special property or function — that makes something a work of art, except our attitude towards it and our willingness to accept it as art.

Suzi Gablik (1934–)

WHAT IS AESTHETICS?

Examine the three images on this page (Figures 15.1–15.3; see also p. I and II). Which of these images do you think is art? Or do you think that all are art?

Figure 15.1

In 1918, the French-born American artist Marcel Duchamp created this picture by altering a postcard of Leonardo da Vinci's famous *Mona Lisa*. Duchamp added a moustache, goatee, and the letters L.H.O.O.Q. The letters stand for a vulgar French pun. He called his action the ready-made principle, meaning that art can be anything.

Figure 15.2

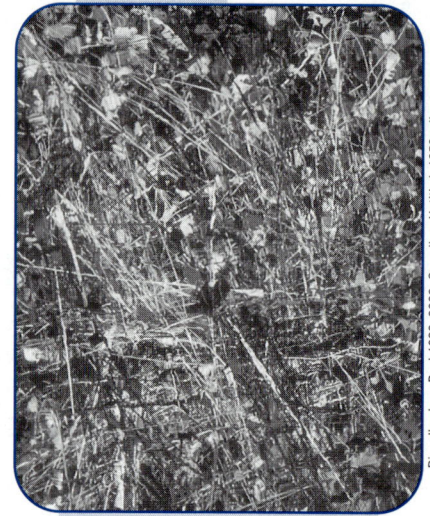

When he created this large painting, Canadian artist Jean-Paul Riopelle was interested in ideas about subject matter and spontaneity. The painting's rich textures are composed of layers of different-coloured paint that appears to be flung across the canvas.

Riopelle, Jean-Paul 1923–2002, Canadian, Untitled, 1952, oil on canvas, purchased 1964. © National Gallery of Canada, Ottawa. © Estate of Jean-Paul Riopelle/SODRAC (Montréal) 2002.

Figure 15.3

This small bronze figure is from the burial mound of a Chinese emperor. Figures like these were placed in the tombs of important families. With its outstretched tail, pounding hooves, and flaring nostrils, this horse demonstrates the maker's ability to represent both the power and likeness of a horse.

As you looked at the pictures, what went through your mind? How did you decide which are art? Did reading the caption that accompanies each image influence your answer? How do your selections reflect your definition of art?

Since ancient times, people have asked questions about art. Among them are, What is art? What makes it good or bad? Must art be beautiful? and What is beauty, anyway?

When people think about why something is — or is not — a work of art, ask why one work of art is more beautiful or moving than another, or question the value of a work of art, they are thinking aesthetically. The word "**aesthetics**" comes from the Greek *aisthetikos*, which means to perceive. Originally, aesthetics, which is sometimes spelled "esthetics," was restricted to the study of beauty. Today, its scope is considerably broader.

Aesthetics tries to explain how people perceive and assess the meaning, importance, and purpose of art. Indeed, some philosophers define aesthetics as the philosophy of art.

Traditional aesthetics focused on the nature of beauty and the relationship between the artist, the art object, and the perceiver, a relationship that is often called the **aesthetic triad**. Today, however, aesthetics explores the answers to many other questions, such as, When is something a work of art? What role do emotions play in appreciating art? What is taste? When is art beneficial? When is art destructive? Is censorship ever justified? Can ugly art be good art? and so on.

NATURE AND AIMS OF AESTHETICS

Have you ever been forced to defend a choice of music? Was it because the music was not appropriate for the time or place or because someone said the music was no good? Do you think some music is bad, or is all music good? Is some music good, but inappropriate on some occasions? These are aesthetic questions because they explore the meaning of art. They probe what art is, what makes it good, and what effect it has on others.

Asked to explain why you like a particular piece of music, you might say, "I like it because it's filled with images. It reminds me of what I see in the real world." In saying this, you would be supporting the idea that art should be realistic.

You might add that the music is good because it creates such perfect images. A friend might argue this point, saying, "No, it isn't that. It's good because it makes me feel connected with my world. I respond emotionally. That's why it's art. And that's why it's good art." Another friend might say, "This is the worst music I've ever heard. How can you even listen to it? It's definitely not art. All it does is make me want to fight someone."

All these responses pick at the edges of some of the broader questions about art: Can people know when something is a work of art? and Can people tell good art from bad art? By attempting to answer these questions, philosophers have made important contributions to the way people view and understand the world.

Since ancient times, philosophers have been interested in how poetry and sculptures, paintings and music influence people. They have sought to understand what is truly beautiful and to develop standards by which beauty can be judged. As they did so, the idea of art as it is known today gradually evolved, and philosophers' questions took on a broader focus.

THE PHILOSOPHER'S APPROACH TO AESTHETICS

In their quest to understand art, philosophers ask questions like, When is something a work of art? What is an aesthetic experience? What is good art — and why? What is the role of art in society? Questions like these examine the connection between people's senses, emotions, and reason. Aesthetics is important because it provides theories of the fine arts, which are usually defined as poetry, painting, acting, building, dancing, and music. People's **personal aesthetic** — their principles of taste and appreciation of beauty — affects the way they experience the world and the choices they make every day.

Philosophers approach aesthetic issues differently from others. Scientists, for example, are concerned with developing theories that describe, explain, or manipulate the world on the basis of logic and rational thought. They tend to focus on the physical qualities of objects, rather than on human responses to these objects. Asked to define music, for example, scientists might say that it is combinations of pitch, beat, rhythm, melody, and so on. The images and emotions it evokes in the minds of listeners are secondary.

Aestheticians do not attempt to find exact, permanent standards like those sought by scientists. They look for tendencies and correlations, understanding that issues of art and taste are complex and variable. They know that these issues change from person to person, context to context, and culture to culture. Philosophers might question scientists' insistence on trying to establish hard-and-fast standards of harmony and beauty, saying that works of art are important because of the varied responses they evoke.

This does not mean that philosophers never approach aesthetics from a scientific perspective, however. The ancient Greek philosopher **Aristotle**, who lived from about 384 to 322 BCE, maintained that art can be studied and analyzed in the same way as natural phenomena. In *Poetics*, for example, Aristotle analyzed Greek tragedy, a form of drama that emerged between the sixth and fourth centuries BCE. He took a scientific approach to identifying standards for this particular, narrowly defined, well-researched art form.

The search for a logical, scientific approach to art has been a recurring theme throughout the history of aesthetics. At various times, scientific ideas about predicting and controlling behaviour have been transferred to art, which is sometimes used to help manipulate what people think and do. Posters and music have been used to promote patriotism during times of war, for example. The art of great cathedrals has been used to inspire religious fervour, and contemporary advertising is designed to encourage people to buy products. Think about the number of advertisements you see in a day. Millions of dollars have been spent to create the 30-second pitch and the glossy ad layout. How many of your purchases are connected in some way to these advertisements? What compelled you to buy?

Because knowledge about art can be used for good purposes and bad, contemporary aesthetics includes questions about whether — and how — art and the knowledge of art can be used to achieve the best possible ends.

Figure 15.4

Posters like this inspired young Canadians to join the army during World War II. A collection of war posters was recently displayed at the Art Gallery of Ontario. Were these posters art before they were hung in the art gallery? Are they art now?

The role of the artist — the creator of art — is also important to aestheticians. According to Aristotle, the act of creating art brings about a sense of **catharsis**, an emotional purging that the artist experiences as an intuitive signal that a work is complete. Artists express themselves or their feelings in their works of art, and the physical form of the work conveys their message to an audience. The artist understands this message on an emotional and aesthetic level. At the same time, the audience must also be open to and capable of responding aesthetically to the message. As a result, attitude and ability play an important role in defining how art is perceived.

As artists create, they may work from one or more aesthetic stances or points of view. Some of these points of view suggest that

- art imitates reality and should be judged according to how well it does this
- art expresses feelings and should be judged according to how well it does this
- art is form and should be judged according to how effectively it is organized and put together
- art serves a useful social purpose and should be judged according to how much it benefits society
- art is anything that people in the art world — artists and art critics — say it is
- art is dead and no longer needs to adhere to outmoded ideas about what it should be

Despite their differences, most of these points of view share common elements. One of these is the idea that art represents a catharsis. Another is the need to make continuing judgments about the value of works of art, both during the creative process and when the works are complete.

Philosophers traditionally approach aesthetics from a theoretical point of view, providing detailed arguments and counter-arguments about the nature of art. In the western philosophical tradition, the focus of questions about aesthetics may be very broad (e.g., What is beauty?) or very narrow (e.g., What is the artist's message in this particular work?).

In general, however, philosophers attempt to discover overall answers to questions of aesthetics, rather than answers that apply only to a specific work or experience. A discussion that begins with a query about your choice of music, for example, might trigger a philosophical inquiry into a broader question such as, Should all music create perfect images?

> Recall...Reflect...Respond
> 1. How might knowledge of art improve your life?
> 2. Choose a piece of music that you like and list reasons it appeals to you. Which aesthetic point of view, or combination of points of view, does your list represent? Explain why.
> 3. Look around your classroom or school, in newspapers or magazines, or on the Internet to find a work of art that was created to serve a useful purpose. Explain what this purpose is and why you do — or do not — believe that this is an appropriate use of art.

WHAT PHILOSOPHERS HAVE SAID

What is beauty? This question, which was first asked by the ancient Greek philosopher **Plato** in the fourth century BCE, launched western aesthetic thought. Like Plato, philosophers have been trying to answer it ever since.

Paradoxically, Plato was hostile to the arts. He believed that works of art should mimic reality and that nature sets the standard of truth and beauty. "The artist can do no better than to try to accurately portray the universe in its infinite variety," he wrote. Art is merely a pale imitation of reality, he said, and can therefore never be as good or as meaningful as the real thing. Think about how much time you spend reading magazines or watching TV. Is this as interesting — or as important or entertaining — as being involved in real life? Plato said that in trusting art to teach about real life, people risk being misled by artists.

Plato believed that an intelligent person should strive to fully understand the eternal world of the soul. Because art appeals strongly to the senses and gives an impression of reality, he said that it keeps humans from achieving this goal.

> *All art is but imitation of nature.*
> – Lucius Annaeus Seneca

Though he favoured realistic art, Plato was also worried about the effect of art on people's emotions. He said that the more realistic a work of art, the greater its appeal. This appeal, he maintained, gives works of art greater power to mislead perceivers. He believed, for example, that unrestricted emotion in art encourages young people to become rebellious and difficult. Some people today might agree with Plato. How often have you heard people say that TV is bad for children and young people because it conveys a false impression of reality? Critics say that the violence, rudeness, or apathy portrayed on some programs sets a bad example by teaching impressionable children and young people to treat others badly.

Figure 15.5

Painted in the early 1500s, this detail from a famous painting by Raphael shows Plato (left) and Aristotle in conversation. Why do you think Raphael portrayed Plato pointing up, while Aristotle seems to gesture toward the ground? And why is Plato carrying *Timaeus*, a book about metaphysics, while Aristotle holds a book about ethics?

The power of art to influence social attitudes and behaviour sparked Plato to conclude that artists must be censored and controlled. He believed that good art ought to promote morally good behaviour and show people how to live harmoniously. These ideas laid the foundation of the longstanding tradition that maintains that what is beautiful is also morally good.

Aristotle, who was Plato's student at the School of Athens, disagreed with his teacher over many philosophical issues. Art was one of them. Though Aristotle agreed that art is artificial, he said that it can be classified and judged according to its physical attributes in much the same way as natural objects or species.

For this reason, Aristotle is often considered the first champion of the principle of art for art's sake. This principle involves taking a detached aesthetic interest in an art object, without considering its political or moral qualities. Whereas Plato considered art a tool that can be used to promote non-artistic purposes, Aristotle argued that it should be autonomous, or independent, and free of censorship.

At about the same time as philosophy was thriving in ancient Greece, a golden age of philosophy was also occurring in China and India. Kongfuzi, who lived from 551 to 479 BCE and is better known in the West as Confucius, introduced a view of philosophy and religion that dominated China for more than 2000 years. Kongfuzi believed that art — and especially poetry — stimulated the mind and taught important social rules. He said that beauty and harmony result from following the rules of propriety.

In the first century CE, a key aesthetic idea was expressed in a public-speaking manual titled *Peri Hupsous* (*On the Sublime*). Believed to have been penned by a Greek writer whose identity is unknown, this book introduced the idea that the sublime — something that inspires the highest degree of awe or reverence — has great emotional power, yet may be neither logical nor beautiful.

The author of *On the Sublime* was the first to ask — and answer — this question: Where does the sublime come from? He argued that the ability to appreciate the sublime is a unique characteristic of humans. He also asked whether artistic creativity can be taught, and if so, how. Debate over the answers to these questions and over the nature of the sublime has echoed through the ages. This debate became a key element of aesthetic discussions during the late 18th and early 19th centuries and sparked later ideas about artistic inspiration, genius, talent, and creativity.

The idea that artists have special talents emerged during the European Renaissance, the period between about 1350 and 1550. Before this time, which was marked by enormous intellectual and creative activity, makers of art were usually held in low esteem because they worked with their hands. They were considered to be on the same social level as slaves, serfs, and peasants.

Gradually, this attitude began to change, and artistic mastery came to be seen as an important element in judging the merit of works of art. The more difficult a work was to create, the more valuable it must be. Renaissance artists like Michelangelo and da Vinci came to be seen as geniuses. This change in attitude was signalled by a shift in the way people wrote about the arts. People began to call poetry, painting, acting, building, dancing, and music the fine arts.

In the 17th century, the thinking of the French philosopher **René Descartes** changed the direction of aesthetics. Descartes started with this statement: Beauty pleases. He then said that if this is true, then anything that pleases in a particular way must be beautiful. Descartes's logical, analytical approach gave birth to a new idea: that beauty is in the eye of the beholder. As a result, the emphasis of aesthetics shifted from investigating the beautiful object to investigating the mind that perceived it. Words such as "imagination," "taste," "sense of beauty," and "inner sense" entered the vocabulary of art criticism.

In the 18th century, aesthetics began to emerge as a separate area of philosophy. A German philosopher, **Alexander Baumgarten**, is credited with distinguishing aesthetics from other areas of philosophy — and giving it its name. In 1750, Baumgarten published a book titled *Aesthetica*. In it, he argued that there are two ways of knowing. One is cognitive (based on reason), analytical, and logical; the other is more intuitive, sensuous, and emotional. Baumgarten defined aesthetics as the science of sensitive knowing, maintaining that this way of knowing is completely autonomous and not in any way subordinate to logical ways. In Baumgarten's view, aesthetics does not deal with the nature or social effects of art; rather, it is a science that focuses on understanding people's intuitive, sensuous, and emotional ways of knowing.

During this period, two questions dominated debate about aesthetics: What is taste? and What is an aesthetic experience? These questions continue to be debated by philosophers and art critics today. Suppose that a good friend gives you a black-velvet painting of Elvis Presley. Your response may be mixed. Do you like it? Will you hang it on your wall? What do you think other people will think of it?

Taste refers to a person's ability to recognize the aesthetic features of an object. The challenge of taste often involves balancing what you like against what others consider good art. People fear that they might really like something that it is not correct — or cool — to like. As a result, the practical question of taste becomes, How can I like what I should like? And this leads directly to the question, How can people know what is truly beautiful?

At various times in the history of aesthetics, philosophers have decided that true beauty can be discovered empirically, through the five senses: seeing, hearing, tasting, smelling, and touching. The 18th-century Scottish philosopher **David Hume**, for example, argued that principles of taste are universal. Still, in an essay titled "Of the Standard of Taste," he wrote, "Though the principles of taste be universal, and nearly, if not entirely the same in all men; yet few are qualified to give judgment on any work of art, or establish their own sentiment as the standard of beauty."

Hume's contention raised this obvious question: If universal standards of taste exist, why are there differences of opinion over what constitutes good art? In Hume's view, differences can arise for

> ## IDEAS IN CONTEXT
>
> When Nicolaus Copernicus concluded in the 16h century that the sun — not the earth — is the centre of the universe, he set the stage for the scientific revolution that would change the way people viewed the world. People began looking to scientists, rather than religious or political leaders, to explain the natural world to them. This shift in thinking affected many areas of philosophy, including aesthetics. Philosophers began to try to analyze aesthetic issues in scientific terms. In this atmosphere, questions like, What evidence supports that idea? and What is the proof? became common responses to aesthetic statements.

Figure 15.6

Painting on velvet became popular in the mid-19th century, when it was considered a cultured hobby for young women. Today, companies in Mexico employ painters who produce up to 3000 velvet paintings of pop-culture images every week. Can this kind of mass-produced painting be called art?

many reasons. "A perfect serenity of mind, a recollection of thought, a due attention to the object; if any of these circumstances be wanting, our experiment will be fallacious, and we shall be unable to judge of the ... universal beauty," he wrote. Hume also said that people may lack the delicacy of imagination to make accurate judgments or they may be influenced by their own prejudices.

In *The Critique of Judgment*, the 18th-century German philosopher Immanuel Kant synthesized two important concepts: the theory of taste and the idea of aesthetic experience. Kant identified the pleasure felt when making a judgment of taste as an aesthetic experience. He said that this feeling comes from recognizing that the form of an object accommodates a kind of free play of understanding and imagination.

In Kant's view, art is autonomous, or independent. He maintained that aesthetic judgments should exclude the subject matter of the work, as well as its sense qualities. Art must not be judged in relation to anything other than itself and its own form. By form, he meant the formal properties that make an artwork a poem, novel, painting, building, or piece of music. These ideas laid the groundwork for the formalist movement that emerged in the early 20th century.

> **Web connection**
> www.mcgrawhill.ca/links/philosophy12
> To find out more about Immanuel Kant, follow the links on this Web site.

In the early 19th century, another German philosopher also made a lasting contribution to aesthetics. Georg W.F. Hegel theorized that everything in the world progresses through three stages — thesis, antithesis, and synthesis — that repeat constantly. A thesis might be an idea or a historical movement. An antithesis is a conflicting idea or movement that develops in reaction to the thesis. A synthesis resolves the conflict between thesis and antithesis by reconciling the truth found in both. This synthesis then becomes a new thesis, and the process continues toward the goal of achieving pure thought.

Because art expresses ideas in physical form, Hegel regarded art as the thesis, an early stage in the development of human thought. He said that the antithesis of art is religion, which expresses ideas as images or symbols. Philosophy is the synthesis that reconciles art and religion through pure thought.

Hegel believed that the messages expressed by art do not become clear until a work is complete, because only then can its message be expressed in words. He said that creating art is a two-stage process. The first involves creating an image of the work in the mind's eye of the artist; the second involves the artist's creation of the physical manifestation of this image.

The theories of Kant and Hegel greatly influenced the way subsequent thinkers approached questions of aesthetics. Supporters of Kant focused on form and how people experience it. Supporters of Hegel emphasized the meaning and interpretation of the ideas expressed in art.

The 19th-century German philosopher and critic Friedrich Nietzsche was a brilliant writer who often used vivid images to persuade others to look at things in a new way. In *Human, All Too Human*, for example, he wrote: "A strong and well-constituted man digests his experiences (deeds and misdeeds included) just as he digests his meats, even when he has some tough morsels to swallow." Because of his lively writing style, Nietzsche's books are considered works of art, and he is often described as an artist among philosophers.

Nietzsche believed that art is the real expression of truth. In his view, art does much more than merely imitate life.

> **IDEAS IN CONTEXT**
>
> During the 18th century, revolutionary ideas about democracy captured the imagination of people throughout the western world. These ideas led to a growing desire for self-rule and changed forever political and social structures. England experienced economic stability and emerged as a powerful maritime nation. London was the first modern city to reach a population of one million. France overthrew its monarchy and established a republic, and the United States battled for — and won — independence from Great Britain. In this social climate, it is not surprising that philosophers like Immanuel Kant began to question traditional ideas about taste, beauty, and art.

PROFILE

Immanuel Kant
Like a Fine Swiss Watch

Every day at precisely 3:30 p.m., Immanuel Kant would stroll along the Linden Allee — nicknamed the Philosopher's Walk — for one hour. Up and down, up and down he would walk, exactly eight times. The people of Königsberg, Germany, could set their clocks by the tap, tap, tap of his cane on the sidewalk. He was a tiny man, thin and slightly tilted, with twinkling blue eyes.

Kant regulated his life like a fine Swiss watch, never deviating from his strict routines. He was particularly conscious of his health. When he walked, for instance, he always went alone — to avoid conversation. He believed that this enabled him to breathe through his nose, filtering the air and keeping the "pneumonia winds" from entering his body through his mouth.

Kant's luncheons, to which he invited no fewer than three and no more than nine people, became famous. Every day at 12:45 p.m. sharp, Kant would drink a dram of wine, then wait for his guests. For two or more hours, he would lead the assembled company in lively conversation that was always spiced with humorous stories because Kant believed that laughter helped digestion.

Born in Königsberg in 1724, Kant was the fourth of 11 children. His parents were extremely poor, and the family often went hungry. What Kant's parents lacked in wealth, however, they made up for in religious fervour, instilling in their son a piety that lasted a lifetime. These humble beginnings did not prevent Kant's becoming one of the most important European philosophers of modern times.

During Kant's lifetime, Königsberg was a small city in East Prussia, part of northeast Germany. Renamed Kaliningrad, it is now part of Russia. Though Königsberg was isolated from cultural influences, the city boasted a population of about 55 000 and a small university with a library of 50 000 books. As a young man, Kant was able to attend the university with the help of an uncle.

Kant's education made it possible for him to work as a private tutor for nobles and clergy. As soon as he could, he began working to obtain a professorship at the university. When he was 31, he completed a doctorate in physics and metaphysics and was hired by the university as an unsalaried lecturer. Students paid him directly.

During this time, the man whose ideas have inspired and shaped modern philosophy, was twice rejected for the chair of philosophy. Finally, when he was 45, he was appointed professor of logic and metaphysics, a paid position that he held till he was 72.

Between the ages of 22 and 46, Kant published 22 books, pamphlets, and papers. But the works for which he is most famous were still to come. In 1781, when he was 57, *The Critique of Pure Reason* was published. This book was followed by *The Critique of Practical Reason* and *The Critique of Judgment*. These three volumes made Kant's reputation and changed the course of western thought.

In his final years, Kant suffered from severe migraines and memory loss. His poor health and failing eyesight made his life miserable until he died of senile dementia at the age of 80.

On the day of his funeral, thousands of people followed his coffin as the bells of every church in Königsberg tolled. Hundreds of candles lit the cathedral where his friends and admirers came to mourn his loss.

Figure 15.7

This silhouette of Kant was created in 1789, when his reputation was at its height.

> *It is my ambition to say in 10 sentences what everyone else says in a whole book — what everyone else does not say in a whole book.*
>
> – Friedrich Nietzsche

It transforms life by providing people with a powerful, life-affirming view of the world. He believed that rational philosophy and Christianity had combined to crush people's zest for life, and he supported Plato's idea that passion and reason, art and philosophy are always in conflict. Whereas Plato chose the side of reason and philosophy, Nietzsche chose passion and art.

The American philosopher **John Dewey**, who lived from 1859 to 1952, is best known for his influence on education. Dewey rejected the widely held belief that knowledge consists of impersonal, unquestionable, well-established facts.

He argued that people acquire knowledge by participating in its creation, a process he called learning by doing. In Dewey's view, art enables people to express their hopes, dreams, and other things that are important to them. Because this is an important function of art, he said that the arts should be an integral part of everyday life.

In contrast to philosophers like Kant, who believed that form is primary, Dewey argued that art becomes meaningful only when experienced by an audience. Before the audience becomes involved, a piece of art is simply an "art product." This art product does not become a work of art until an audience engages with it.

Web connection
www.mcgrawhill.ca/links/philosophy12
To find out more about John Dewey, follow the links on this Web site.

The period after World War II ushered in many changes in thinking about aesthetics. Ideas that had surfaced in the 18th, 19th, and early 20th centuries were distilled and expressed in a movement called **modernism**. Modernism is characterized by attempts to define the nature of the aesthetic experience. Two of its key tenets state that works of art are successful when they create a sense of unity and that works of art are autonomous and pure.

In the late 20th century, modernism gave way to **post-modernism**. Because the prefix "post" means after in Latin, it is not surprising that post-modernists reject most of what the modernists have to say.

Figure 15.8

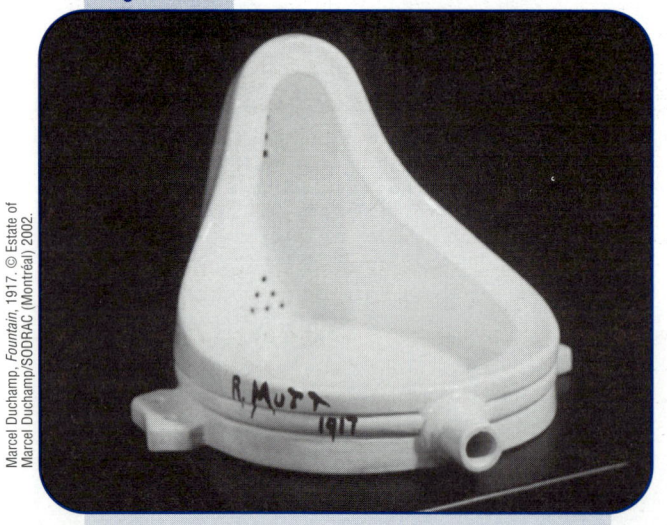

In 1917, Marcel Duchamp submitted a signed urinal titled *Fountain* for exhibition by the Society of Independent Artists. Though the work was rejected, this replica is now on display in Milan, Italy. Why do you suppose that a replica is now on display?

In *The Philosophical Disenfranchisement of Art*, published in 1986, the American post-modernist philosopher and art critic **Arthur Danto** argued that art is, in fact, dead. From the time of Plato until the invention of the camera in the 19th century, wrote Danto, artists created art that represented the world. Photographs, which could capture reality more perfectly than art, forced artists to experiment with new ways of creating art. As they did, styles of art came and went, and philosophers attempted to keep up with the trends by creating new definitions of art. As this process unfolded, Danto suggested, artists became philosophers, and art became nothing more than artists' attempts to understand themselves. As a result, he said, artists can create whatever they want without adhering to outmoded ideas of what art should be.

If art is dead, as Danto suggests, how does this affect popular art — films, television shows, rock music, novels, and so on? Are these things art? How can people know whether they are good? The questions continue.

How Philosophers Have Said It

Though ideas about what beauty is and whether art is good differ, philosophers can agree on the meaning of many of the terms that are used in discussions of aesthetics. Philosophers frequently talk about an aesthetic attitude, for example. By this, they usually mean a disinterested approach that enables someone to contemplate an object on its own terms, regardless of the use to which it may be put and the emotions it may arouse.

Note that "disinterested" is not a synonym for "uninterested." "Disinterested" means impartial, while "uninterested" means not interested. Kant, in particular, advocated taking a disinterested approach to judging art.

Asking questions about how art should be judged is part of the history of aesthetics. Discussions of value often involve two important terms.

- objectivity, which refers to judgments based on certain qualities or relations that are believed to be part of the object itself (e.g., rules of composition)
- subjectivity, which refers to judgments based on emotions — the amount of pleasure or displeasure the perceiver feels when experiencing the object

Morality and art are often connected in philosophical discussions. Kant, for instance, linked aesthetic experience with moral goodness. He believed that people cannot really understand aesthetic experience without connecting it to morality. This is because, for Kant, human nature had two sides: a sensuous side that he viewed as aesthetic and a rational side that he viewed as moral. In discussions about art, the word "morality" often refers to the ability to live according to widely accepted codes of virtuous behaviour.

Why Aesthetics Matters

Aesthetics is everywhere in everyday life. Think about how many people you know on diets, for example. Do they talk about what they trying to achieve? Are they dieting for health reasons or because they have decided that their current weight is not "beautiful"?

Decisions about weight, clothing, and a host of other things often come down to aesthetics. When you defend your favourite TV show or talk about whether you like a piece of music, you are engaging in a discussion of aesthetics. Have you ever attended a live concert? Was it awesome? Your feelings of awe and pleasure were aesthetic experiences. These experiences make life richer and more satisfying.

Figure 15.9

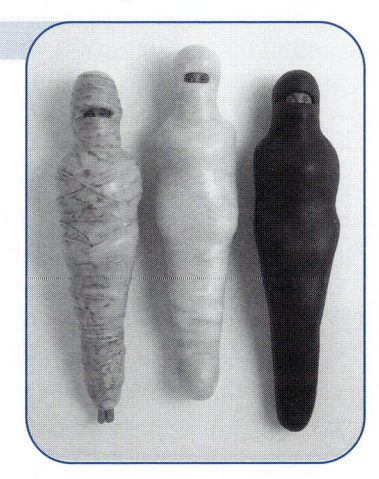

Aesthetic experiences are not the same for everyone, however. Aesthetic values and beliefs change across cultures, and aesthetic preferences are influenced by people's experiences, background, and culture. A work of art is often inextricably linked to the social, political, or historical context in which it was created. Considering this context often leads to a better understanding of a work's aesthetic significance.

In the West, many current works of art focus on issues related to the human body, for example. The sculptures in this photograph (Figure 15.9; see also p. III), titled *Mummified Barbies* were created by American artist E. V. Day by wrapping Barbie dolls in string or covering them with beeswax. Day's creations sparked debate over their meaning.

Though it is not always necessary to understand art to enjoy it, the aesthetic experience is richer when the subtleties of works of art are understood. Take this drawing by Saul Steinberg (Figure 15.10).

Figure 15.10

6. Saul Steinberg, *Giuseppe Verdi*, 1964. Ink on paper, 14 ¼ × 22 ⅜ in.
© 1964, 1992, The New Yorker Magazine, Inc.

To truly appreciate what Steinberg is portraying, it is essential to know that Giuseppe Verdi was a famous Italian composer. Knowing this enables viewers to "read" what is happening in the drawing. The meaning of artworks like this can remain nearly invisible to viewers who lack the background knowledge to interpret the pieces. Aesthetics challenges people to exercise their minds as they connect the social, historical, philosophical, and personal dimensions of art in order to understand what it is and what it means.

The ability to create and respond to art is unique to human beings. For at least 50 000 years, people have made objects to communicate ideas about things such as status and spirituality and to pass along traditions and history. Interestingly, humans have not been satisfied with simply creating objects that are useful. Since ancient times, artists and artisans have tried to make things that also please the eye. Think about things you own that have a use — and are also pleasant to look at. Does their appearance affect the way you feel about them? Did their appearance influence your decision to make the purchase?

An aesthetic attitude helps people become more aware of sensory experiences, and this leads to a heightened perception of life and opens the mind to learning. Social scientists, for example, use a knowledge of art to understand people's values, beliefs, and hopes. Historians glean enormous knowledge of other civilizations from studying their art. Throughout history, invading armies often tried to establish control over conquered peoples by destroying their art, an important symbol of their culture and traditions.

Mathematicians, too, use aesthetics to attempt to discover patterns and visualize concepts. The extraordinary images created by mathematical equations help them deepen their understanding of concepts. Similarly, scientists are often drawn to appreciate the beauty of nature as they study it in more detail. In fact, the ability to aesthetically experience the natural world balances a scientist's approach.

John Polanyi, Canadian co-winner of the 1986 Nobel Prize for chemistry, said, "The scientist whose eye has been educated through the arts has access to more subtle symmetries. Any individual who is required to think — and in a democracy one must pray that this is the majority — will do so more effectively if she or he has at some time experienced the creative process through the arts."

One of the great gifts of art is its ability to inspire wonder. As people reflect on their own aesthetic beliefs, they often begin to view alternative beliefs with fresh eyes. The study of aesthetics enriches everyone's experiences and reveals new possibilities.

The most beautiful thing we can experience is the mysterious. It is the source of all art and science.

– Albert Einstein

> **Recall...Reflect...Respond**
>
> 1. Choose one philosopher whose ideas support your response to this question: What is art? Write a paragraph explaining how the philosopher's ideas support your choice.
> 2. Imagine that you have just returned from a clothes-shopping spree with one of your parents or another adult. How might the choices made by the two of you have been similar? How might they have been different? List the non-monetary factors that might have influenced the buying decisions each of you made. What is the philosophical significance of these factors?
> 3. Re-examine E.V. Day's *Mummified Barbies* (Figure 15.9; see also p. III). Does the notion that many people in contemporary western societies are obsessed with body image affect the meaning you draw from this work? Explain your response to this question.

THE VALUE OF ART

In October 2001, British artist Damien Hirst assembled his latest installation in the window of a London, England, art gallery. The work, which was expected to sell for more than $100,000, included a painter's palette, an easel, a ladder, and paintbrushes. Strewn on the floor were candy wrappers, newspaper pages, half-empty coffee cups, cigarette butts, and empty beer bottles.

The next morning, everything was gone. The gallery's cleaning man had arrived at work the night before and cleaned up the "mess." Fortunately, Hirst was able to laugh about the mixup — after gallery staff retrieved the cleaning man's garbage bags and reassembled the work. A gallery spokesperson said that the event would encourage healthy debate about what is — and is not — art.

This incident illustrates the challenges involved in defining art. Definitions of art are closely connected to the way people view the world — and the things they value.

DESCRIPTIVE AND NORMATIVE DEFINITIONS OF ART

The terms "descriptive" and "normative" describe two different approaches to defining art. Descriptive definitions involve observations and experiences that explain what art is. Normative definitions define art according to specific standards, or norms.

When ancient Greek philosophers such as Plato described standards of human beauty, they were presenting a normative definition of art. Plato believed that art is representation, the accurate imitation of nature, and that harmonious proportions are essential. He said that art should be judged by its truthfulness: its accuracy in imitating nature, its psychological benefits, and its contribution to morality.

In the late 19th and early 20th century, many philosophers and critics such as **Benedetto Croce**, Leo Tolstoy, and John Dewey proposed descriptive definitions. Croce, an Italian philosopher and critic who lived from 1866 to 1952, explained his idea of art in *Theory of Aesthetics*, published in 1909:

> Intuitive activity possesses intuitions to the extent that it expresses them.... But be it pictorial, or verbal, or musical, or in whatever other form it appear, to no intuition

can expression in one of its forms be wanting; it is in fact an inseparable part of intuition.… Feelings or impressions, then, pass by means of words from the obscure region of the soul into the clarity of the contemplative spirit. It is impossible to distinguish intuition from expression in this cognitive process. The one appears with the other at the same instant, because they are not two, but one.

In *What Is Art?*, which was published in 1898, the Russian novelist and philosopher Tolstoy wrote: "Art is a human activity consisting in this, that one man consciously, by means of certain external signs, hands on to others feelings he has lived through, and that other people are infected by these feelings and also experience them."

And in *Art as Experience*, Dewey suggested a similar definition: "Language exists only when it is listened to as well as spoken.… The work of art is complete only as it works in the experience of others than the one who created it."

All three definitions suggest that art is something that evokes powerful feelings and that the ability of the art to transmit these feelings is what makes it good.

> *Art is a human activity whose purpose is the transmission of the highest and best feelings to which men have attained.*
>
> – Leo Tolstoy

Other philosophers and critics have proffered normative definitions. In "The Aesthetic Hypothesis," for example, the 20th-century English art critic **Clive Bell** wrote:

For either all works of visual art have some common quality, or when we speak of "works of art" we gibber.… What is the quality common and peculiar to all … [art]? There must be some one quality without which a work of art cannot exist; possessing which, in the least degree, no work is altogether worthless. What is this quality? What quality is shared by all objects that provoke our aesthetic emotions? What quality is common to St. Sophia [Hagia Sophia, an ancient basilica in Istanbul, Turkey] and the windows at Chartres, Mexican sculpture, a Persian bowl, Chinese carpets, Giotto's frescoes at Padua, and the masterpieces of Poussin, Piero della Francesca, and Cézanne? Only one answer seems possible — significant form. In each, lines and colours, these aesthetically moving forms, I call "Significant Form," and "Significant Form" is the one quality common to all works of visual art.… Let no one imagine that representation is bad in itself; realistic form may be as significant, in its place, as part of the design, as an abstract [form]. But if a representative form has value, it is as form, not as representation. The representative element in a work of art … is irrelevant.

Figure 15.11

"He knows all about art, but he doesn't know what he likes."

When talking about art, people often say, "I don't know anything about art, but I know what I like." In this cartoon, James Thurber turns this saying upside down. Given the variety of conflicting definitions of art, is it up to everyone to define art for her- or himself?

In Bell's view, art is simply the effective organization of art elements and principles. It is autonomous, having nothing to do with religion, morality, or social politics. The standard of good art is based on the effective organization of the formal elements.

The 20th-century American philosopher George Dickie defined art differently. Dickie argued that art is identified and defined by the artworld. He defined the

Other philosophers, especially in the 20th century, have denied that art and morality are linked. The American philosopher Monroe Beardsley, for example, said that art objects and aesthetic experiences are completely autonomous. They may generate certain moral effects, but this is not a necessary component of the work. For philosophers like Beardsley, aesthetic experience is pleasurable in and of itself.

Tolstoy, by contrast, rejected the idea that art is an enjoyable experience for its own sake. In his view, art must help bring people together into one universal brotherhood. He agreed with Plato's assertion that moral criteria should be used to judge aesthetic experiences and works of art.

Recall...Reflect...Respond

1. Think about the action of the man who "cleaned up" Damien Hirst's installation at a London gallery. Would his definition of art be descriptive or normative? Why? Would Hirst's definition of art be descriptive or normative? Why?
2. Some people say that anything that is viewed might be art. Debate this theory with a partner, drawing on the ideas of Clive Bell, Arthur Danto, and other philosophers. Report the results of your debate to the class.
3. Suppose that you have been asked to list the criteria that will be used to judge the works in an exhibition of visual art. What criteria would you include?

FORGERIES AND ARTISTIC VALUE

Forgeries are works of art that have been created to deliberately mislead perceivers. What bothers most people about forgery is that a breach of trust has been committed. This is a moral concern.

Philosophers are more interested in questions of the artistic value of forgeries. They might ask, Does a forgery have artistic value? and Is a forgery of less value than the original? Both questions have sparked great debate.

Some philosophers, such as Beardsley, believe that the value of the forgery is the same as that of the original — if it is impossible to distinguish the forgery from the original work. This belief accords with the view that art should be judged by its formal qualities alone.

Unlike Beardsley, however, most contemporary philosophers believe that aesthetic value is based, at least in part, on the perceiver's belief that a work is authentic. The psychological effect of knowing that an artwork is a forgery leads people to view it differently — and reduces its aesthetic value. This is as it should be, say these philosophers, because forgeries do not include any of the qualities that confer value on a work of art or aesthetic experience.

Chapter Review

Chapter Summary

This chapter has discussed
- some of the philosophical questions of aesthetics
- the strengths and weaknesses of the responses of some of the major philosophers to some of the main questions of aesthetics, making reference to classic texts

Knowledge and Understanding

1. Identify and explain the significance to the study of aesthetics of each of the following key words and people.

Key Words	Key People
aesthetics	Aristotle
aesthetic triad	Plato
personal aesthetic	René Descartes
catharsis	Alexander Baumgarten
taste	David Hume
aesthetic experience	Immanuel Kant
modernism	Georg W.F. Hegel
post-modernism	Friedrich Nietzsche
objectivity	John Dewey
subjectivity	Arthur Danto
descriptive	Benedetto Croce
normative	Clive Bell

2. Create a chart that includes the following headings: Defining Beauty, Role of Art, Value of Art, Defining Art, Judging Art. Place each of the questions of aesthetics introduced in this chapter under the appropriate heading. Examine the questions grouped under each heading, then write one question that represents the main idea of all the questions in the group.

Defining Beauty	Role of Art	Value of Art	Defining Art	Judging Art

Thinking and Inquiry

3. Summarize the definitions of art offered by Leo Tolstoy, Clive Bell, John Dewey, and George Dickie. Choose a piece of visual art illustrated in this chapter to represent each definition. Explain how the work of art represents the definition.

4. Listen to your favourite piece of music. While listening, think about why you believe the piece is art and why the musicians are artists. List the criteria you used to make these judgments. Write a personal response defending your judgment.

Communication

5. Create a timeline that illustrates how ideas about the meaning, importance, and purpose of art have changed over time. Use pictures or titles of works of art to support your description. Include a description of historical events that have influenced the changes.

6. Scan a magazine or newspaper and select an advertisement that you find appealing. What does this ad lead you to believe? Plato argued that in trusting art to teach about real life, people risk being misled by artists. With Plato's words in mind, re-examine the advertisement. On the basis of this ad, would you agree with him? Write an assessment of how well this advertisement reflects reality and provides consumers with useful, accurate information.

Application

7. Work with a group to create survey questions that can be used to find out whether people view understanding art as an objective or subjective exercise. As a group, survey at least 30 people. Summarize your findings on a chart. Include this chart in a report of your conclusions.

8. Re-examine Marcel Duchamp's postcard of the Mona Lisa (Figure 15.2; see pp. 308 and I).

   How do you perceive this piece of art?

   What does it mean to you?

   What if Duchamp had done this to the original of the Mona Lisa? Would this be art?

   Compare your reactions with those of a classmate. How do your reactions reflect your beliefs about art?

Chapter 16
Theories, Categories, and Types of Art

Chapter Expectations

By the end of this chapter, you will be able to
- demonstrate an understanding of some of the philosophical questions of aesthetics
- evaluate the strengths and weaknesses of the responses of some of the world's major philosophers to some of the main questions of aesthetics, making reference to classic texts
- formulate and defend your own responses to some of the main questions of aesthetics
- explain how philosophical theories of aesthetics influence music, art, and fashion
- apply logical- and critical-thinking skills to problems that arise in jobs and occupations
- compare the problems, principles, methods, and conclusions of various philosophers

Key Words

rationalist
empiricist
mimesis
formalism
expressionist
phenomenology
representational
abstract
non-representational
eclecticism
genre
censorship

Key People

Leo Tolstoy
R.G. Collingwood
Edmund Husserl
Søren Kierkegaard
Martin Heidegger
Jean-Paul Sartre
Joanna Frueh
Suzi Gablik
Friedrich von Schelling
Arthur Schopenhauer

A Philosopher's Voice

We are accustomed to understand art to be only what we hear and see in theatres, concerts, and exhibitions, together with buildings, statues, poems, novels.

Leo Tolstoy (1828–1910)

ORIGINS OF THE WESTERN TRADITION

In the West, the quest for wisdom was shaped by two remarkable ancient Greek thinkers: Plato and his student, Aristotle. Their differing beliefs about knowledge and perception laid the foundation of two distinct approaches to philosophy — and to aesthetics.

Plato believed that knowledge is innate in human beings. A **rationalist**, he distrusted sense experience. Have you ever, for example, looked down a long stretch of highway on a hot, sunny day and seen, shimmering in the distance, what looks like water? When you reach the spot, however, the water turns out to have been an illusion. Your senses have played a trick on you. For reasons like this, Plato believed that the senses deceive.

According to Plato, the human soul exists in an unchanging world that is similar to the external world. He called this unchanging world, which exists outside time and space, the world of forms. Forms are the essence of all the things people eventually learn in their mortal lives. The form of "horse," for example, has nothing to do with the size, texture, or sensory qualities of horse. It refers only to properties that are absolutely essential to something's being a horse.

Figure 16.1

In this painted quilt, artist Faith Ringgold recalled a childhood picnic on the roof of the family's apartment building in New York City's Harlem district. Ringgold's memories of childhood helped shape her understanding of the world.

Plato maintained that the soul knows all the forms but seems to forget them at birth. He also said that these ideas are not really forgotten, however. They re-emerge in the right circumstances. Rationalists like Plato believe that sensory experiences may trigger the emergence of ideas, though these experiences are not the source of ideas.

Aristotle, by contrast, was an **empiricist**. Empiricists like Aristotle believe that the human mind is a *tabula rasa* — a blank slate — at birth. In each person, this slate is waiting to have information "impressed" on it.

According to Aristotle, sensory experiences are transformed into knowledge by the human ability to reason. Have you ever stuck something into a blob of soft wax? As the wax cooled, an impression of the object that you pressed into it remains. Something similar happens, said Aristotle, when an object impresses the senses. Sense experiences become concepts by impressing themselves on the intellect and creating an idea.

The thoughts of Plato and Aristotle influenced the development of every area of western philosophy, including aesthetics. Even contemporary views of art can trace their roots to both Plato's and Aristotle's ideas about knowledge and perception.

Traditional Theories of Art

Since ancient times, philosophers have tried to explain what art is and why it has value and meaning. Their explanations focus on identifying the essential nature or essence of artworks and have traditionally fallen into three broad categories: mimesis, formalism, and expressionism.

These categories are often identified as theories of art, though the use of the term "theory" presents problems in discussions of aesthetics. The word "theory" is often used loosely in a variety of contexts. People may talk about literary theory or film theory, for example. Despite the lack of consensus on the meaning of the word "theory," there is little doubt that most people's opinions of art are shaped by one of these three traditional theories that attempt to identify the central features of artworks.

MIMESIS

Plato's statement that art imitates reality lies at the heart of the theory of **mimesis**, which is also known as imitationalism. Derived from a Greek word that means to mimic or imitate, mimesis refers to the idea that art represents, mirrors, or creates an illusion of reality.

Though Plato's remark about imitation was intended to be disparaging, other philosophers have praised realistic art for helping people see things that might otherwise have been missed. Mimesis theories focus on the objective properties of works of art and judge a work successful if it reflects the real world. This usually means that it portrays the subject matter realistically.

Mimesis is not necessarily limited to judging art according to standards of realism, however. Art that shows spirituality, for example, can be judged according to mimetic theory if the real world is viewed as a spiritual place.

FORMALISM

In art, the term "form" refers to the formal properties or organization of a work. Traditional sonnets, for example, display a common form — the same elements and principles. They are 14-line poems on a single theme, are usually written in iambic pentameter, and follow one of several specified rhyme schemes.

> *Books are well written or badly written. That's all.*
> — Oscar Wilde

Twentieth-century art critics like Great Britain's Clive Bell and the American Clement Greenberg argued that the most important thing about a work of art is its formal qualities. Unlike mimetic theories, which usually judge art by how well it represents the natural world, **formalism** judges only how well the work conforms to its form. It is not necessary for a work of art to represent anything.

Formalist theory maintains that the form of art and the aesthetic experiences prompted by art are universal. In other words, art is autonomous, independent of religion, politics, history, and any other human endeavours. According to formalists, a work of art is successful if the elements are organized according to the principles associated with its particular form.

EXPRESSIONISM

Philosophers who have advocated an **expressionist** theory of art include Benedetto Croce, **Leo Tolstoy**, and **R.G. Collingwood**. Tolstoy believed that artists communicate their feelings through their art and that the perceiver experiences what the artist felt while creating the work.

In contrast to formalist theory, which ignores both the subject matter and feelings evoked by works of art, expressionist theory focuses on the emotional qualities of artworks. This does not mean that expressionists consider form unimportant, however. Many expressionists maintain that formal elements and subject matter can help works of art evoke strong feelings. For expressionists, however, the emotional impact of an artwork is the measure of its success.

> *Painting is self-discovery.*
> – Jackson Pollock

Recall...Reflect...Respond

1. Examine Faith Ringgold's *Tar Beach* (Figure 16.1: pp. 329 and III). Explain this work of art from Plato's rationalist point of view. Explain it from Aristotle's empiricist point of view. What characteristics do their points of view share?
2. On a chart, list the three traditional theories of aesthetics. Summarize how each defines the nature and purpose of art.
3. Select a magazine advertisement that captures your attention. Is this ad a work of art? Explain how your answer to this question reflects your beliefs about what constitutes art. Which traditional theory of aesthetics best supports your position? Why?

PHILOSOPHICAL PERSPECTIVES ON AESTHETICS

Though the thought of philosophers such as Plato, Aristotle, Immanuel Kant, Georg W.F. Hegel, and Friedrich Nietzsche influenced — and was influenced by — ideas about the arts, these are far from the only philosophers who have left a lasting imprint on aesthetic debate. Idealists, phenomenologists, existentialists, feminists, modernists, and post-modernists have also tried to answer questions raised by aesthetics.

IDEALISM

One of the most frequently asked questions of philosophy is, If a tree falls in the forest, does it make a sound? Idealists believe that if no one is present to hear the sound, the answer to this question is no. This, they maintain, is because reality is created in the mind.

Consider this book, for example. You can feel its texture, read its words, and turn its pages. You know that the book exists because it is right here, in your hands. Idealists would say, however, that this book exists only because you believe in your mind that this collection of ink-covered pages is a book. All your judgments about this book — its size, its weight, its colour, and so on — are made in your mind. Therefore, the reality of the book is in your mind, not in the material world.

Because of his belief that true reality exists in the world of forms, Plato is often called the first idealist. Idealist theory is important to aesthetics because it places judgments about beauty in the mind of the beholder. In doing this, it lays the groundwork for various theories that maintain that judgments about art are subjective.

Web connection
www.mcgrawhill.ca/links/philosophy12
To find out more about idealism, follow the links on this Web site.

PHILOSOPHY IN ACTION

What Is Art?

by Leo Tolstoy

The Russian author Leo Tolstoy is best known for his novels *War and Peace*, which was published in 1869, and *Anna Karenina*, which was published in 1877. Tolstoy also wrote non-fiction, much of it focusing on philosophical and social issues. In 1898, he published *What Is Art?* In this book, Tolstoy argued that art is successful when it arouses emotion, brings people together, and enriches the human spirit.

What is art — if we put aside the conception of beauty, which confuses the whole matter? The latest and most comprehensible definitions of art, apart from conception of beauty, are the following: (1) Art is an activity arising even in the animal kingdom, *a*, springing from sexual desire and the propensity to play (Schiller, Darwin, Spencer), and *b*, accompanied by a pleasurable excitement of the nervous system (Grant Allen). This is the physiological-evolutionary definition. (2) Art is the external manifestation by means of lines, colours, movements, sounds, or words, of emotions felt by man (Véron). This is the experimental definition. According to the very latest definition, (3) Art is the "production of some permanent object or passing action, which is fitted, not only to supply an active enjoyment to the producer, but to convey a pleasurable impression to a number of spectators or listeners, quite apart from any personal advantage to be derived from it" (Sully).

Notwithstanding the superiority of these definitions to the metaphysical definitions which depended on the conception of beauty, they are yet far from exact. The first, the physiological-evolutionary definition (1*a*), is inexact because, instead of speaking about the artistic activity itself, which is the real matter in hand, it treats of the derivation of art. The modification of it (1*b*), based on the physiological effects on the human organism, is inexact because within the limits of such definition many other human activities can be included, as has occurred in the neo-aesthetic theories, which reckon as art the preparation of handsome clothes, pleasant scents, and even victuals [food].

The experimental definition (2), which makes art consist in the expression of emotions, is inexact because a man may express emotions by means of lines, colours, sounds, or words, and yet may not act on others by such expression, and then the manifestation of his emotions is not art.

The third definition (that of Sully) is inexact because in the production of objects or actions affording pleasure to the producer and a pleasant emotion to the spectators or hearers, apart from personal advantage, may be included the showing of conjuring tricks or gymnastic exercises and other activities which are not art. And further, many things, the production of which does not afford pleasure to the producer and the sensation received from which is unpleasant, such as gloomy, heartrending scenes in a poetic description or a play, may nevertheless be un-doubted works of art.

The inaccuracy of all these definitions arises from the fact that in them all (as also in the metaphysical definitions) the object considered is the pleasure art may give, and not the purpose it may serve in the life of a man and of humanity.

In order correctly to define art, it is necessary, first of all, to cease to consider it as a means to pleasure and to consider it as one of the conditions of human life. Viewing it in this way we cannot fail to observe that art is one of the means of intercourse between man and man.

Every work of art causes the receiver to enter into a certain kind of relationship both with him who produced, or is producing, the art, and with all those who, simultaneously, previously, or subsequently, receive the same artistic impression.

Speech, transmitting the thoughts and experiences of men, serves as a means of union among them, and art acts in a similar manner. The peculiarity of this latter means of intercourse, distinguishing it from intercourse by means of words, consists in this, that whereas by words a man transmits his thoughts to another, by means of art he transmits his feelings.

The activity of art is based on the fact that a man, receiving through his sense of hearing or sight another man's expression of feeling, is capable of experiencing the emotion which moved the man who expressed it. To take the simplest example: one man laughs, and another who hears becomes merry; or a man weeps, and another who hears feels sorrow. A man is excited or irritated, and another man seeing him comes to a similar state of mind.

By his movements or by the sounds of his voice, a man expresses courage and determination or sadness and calmness, and this state of mind passes on to others. A man suffers, expressing his sufferings by groans and spasms, and this suffering transmits itself to other people; a man expresses his feelings of admiration, devotion, fear, respect, or love to certain objects, persons, or phenomena, and others are infected by the same feelings of admiration, devotion, fear, respect, or love to the same objects, persons, and phenomena.

And it is upon this capacity of man to receive another man's expression of feeling and experience those feelings himself, that the activity of art is based.

If a man infects another or others directly, immediately, by his appearance or by the sounds he gives vent to at the very time he experiences the feeling; if he causes another man to yawn when he himself cannot help yawning, or to laugh or cry when he himself is obliged to laugh or cry, or to suffer when he himself is suffering — that does not amount to art.

Art begins when one person, with the object of joining another or others to himself in one and the same feeling, expresses that feeling by certain external indications. To take the simplest example: a boy, having experienced, let us say, fear on encountering a wolf, relates that encounter; and, in order to evoke in others the feeling he has experienced, describes himself, his condition before the encounter, the surroundings, the wood, his own lightheartedness, and then the wolf's appearance, its movements, the distance between himself and the wolf, etc. All this, if only the boy, when telling the story, again experiences the feelings he lived through and infects the hearers and compels them to feel what the narrator had experienced, is art. If even the boy had not seen a wolf but had frequently been afraid of one, and if, wishing to evoke in others the fear he had felt, he invented an encounter with a wolf and recounted it so as to make his hearers share the feelings he experienced when he feared the wolf, that also would be art. And just in the same way it is art if a man, having experienced either the fear of suffering or the attraction of enjoyment (whether in reality or in imagination), expresses these feelings on canvas or in marble so that others are infected by them. And it is also art if a man feels or imagines to himself feelings of delight, gladness, sorrow, despair, courage, or despondency and the transition from one to another of these feelings, and expresses these feelings by sounds so that the hearers are infected by them and experience them as they were experienced by the composer.

Source: From *What Is Art?* Leo Tolstoy.

1. In Leo Tolstoy's view, what makes something a work of art?
2. Tolstoy begins this excerpt by providing three widely accepted definitions of art. What elements of Tolstoy's definition coincide with these three definitions?
3. Jot down three questions that you would like to ask Tolstoy about art as a result of reading this excerpt. Share your questions with a group or the whole class and try to answer one another's questions as Tolstoy might have.

PHENOMENOLOGY

The **phenomenology** movement, which evolved into a form of idealism, was founded at the beginning of the 20th century by the German philosopher **Edmund Husserl**, who lived from 1859 to 1938. Husserl advocated setting aside the longstanding debate over whether true reality exists only in the mind. His approach assigned equal importance to the role of reason and sense experience.

Phenomenologists believe that it is impossible to separate the act of observing from the thing being observed. Because the thinking process may be different for each observer, however, they say that subjectivity plays an important role in investigations. In their view, understanding the world depends as much on human intuition and insight as on empirical data. In other words, people's gut reactions to things are as significant as data derived from the senses.

Web connection
www.mcgrawhill.ca/links/philosophy12
To find out more about Edmund Husserl, follow the links on this Web site.

Figure 16.2

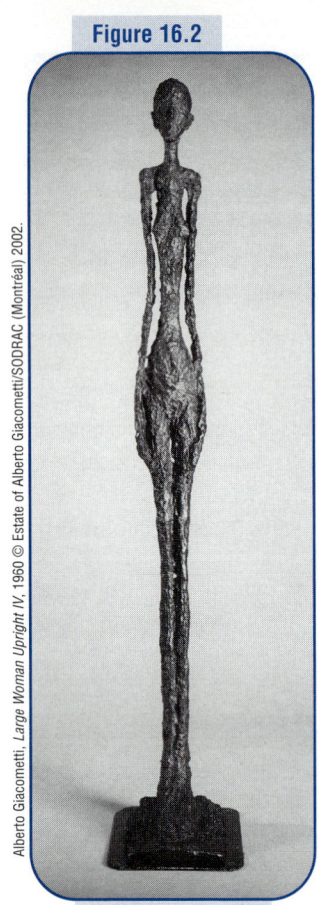

Alberto Giacometti, Large Woman Upright IV, 1960 © Estate of Alberto Giacometti/SODRAC (Montréal) 2002.

Created in 1960, this sculpture by Alberto Giacometti reflects the existentialist *angst* and isolation felt when people are free to make their own choices and create themselves.

Husserl's phenomenological approach focused on a systematic analysis of experience. As a result, aestheticians often came to talk about the phenomenology of art. By this, they mean the analysis of art as a conscious activity.

EXISTENTIALISM

Although the Danish philosopher **Søren Kierkegaard** laid the groundwork for existentialism in the 19th century, this philosophical school of thought did not become popular until after World War II. Existentialists believe that it is impossible to really know anything in the world. As a result, the only thing people can do is make authentic choices. In existentialist philosophy, authenticity means being true to oneself.

A devout Christian, Kierkegaard believed that people must move beyond judging their actions according to reason or the standards of society and become responsible only to the judgments of God. It is through the choices people make, he argued, that people come to know who they are and what they value. What are you planning to do once you graduate from high school, for example? Will you go to university or college? How will you choose your course of study? Will you find a job instead of continuing your education? Will you travel? Kierkegard believed that your decisions about what to do should be based on what you believe is important, not on what your parents, teachers, or friends urge you to do.

Kierkegaard tried to understand aesthetics through the lens of nihilism. Nihilism comes from the Latin word *nihil*, which means "nothing." Nihilists believe that life has no meaning and that existence is senseless. Works of art are not real, said Kierkegaard. They are meaningless and lack purpose. Despite this, he believed that artistic activity is a way of demonstrating personal authenticity, which is embodied in the work of art.

In the 20th century, other philosophers built on Kierkegaard's ideas, but rejected his religious focus. The German philosopher **Martin Heidegger**, who lived from 1889 to 1976, and the French philosopher **Jean-Paul Sartre**, who lived from 1903 to 1980, were the chief advocates of a humanist, or secular, form of existentialism. They believed that people can never be certain that they have made the right choices. This induces *angst*, a German word that means anxiety. Despite this, existentialists celebrate the idea that authentic people make their own rules and discover what is important through personal experiences.

Heidegger believed that poetry and art open up the world and provide a unique way of presenting the truth. Sartre argued that aesthetic contemplation is a self-generated dream. For him, beauty and art are imaginary. When people experience an aesthetic response, he said, they are engaged in denying the world as they know it. As a result, they may become more open to seeing the world with fresh eyes.

Web connection
www.mcgrawhill.ca/links/philosophy12
To find out more about existentialism, follow the links on this Web site.

FEMINISM

Just as western history often discouraged, dismissed, or ignored women's contributions to fields like science, politics, and philosophy, women's creative role in the arts was often played down. Works created by women were often identified as crafts, for example, while those created by men were elevated to the status of fine art. In the 20th century, some philosophers

IDEAS IN CONTEXT

One of the issues in debates about women's contribution to art focuses on how — and where — works by women should be exhibited. In 1987, the National Museum of Women opened in Washington, the capital of the United States. Although the purpose of this museum is to showcase women's art and address women's issues, many people fear that its existence will further marginalize art created by women. They continue to lobby for a more balanced representation of men's and women's art in so-called mainstream galleries and museums.

and artists began to lobby to change this situation. They urged people to look at women's "crafts," such as quilting or embroidery, and recognize that these works can be fine art in the same way as paintings, sculptures, literature, and music. Their efforts have renewed debate over the difference between arts and crafts.

Feminist ideas about new definitions of art gathered force in the 1970s, spurred by the work of artists such as Joyce Wieland (see Figure 16.8; pp. 342 and V)) and Judy Chicago. The contemporary American art historian Joanna Frueh has identified three phases in the history of feminist art theory. The first focused on finding and reviving interest in lost or ignored women artists. The second argued that there is a distinctively female imagination and suggests that art created by women displays certain characteristics. The third phase is more theoretical, focusing on analyzing art created by both men and women.

MODERNISM AND POST-MODERNISM

The modernist movement, which began in the late 19th century and reached its final phase after World War II, exalts the ability of artworks to stand on their own as pure form. Modernists believe that the more a work of art stands on its own without borrowing imagery or technique from other art, the more pure it is. For modernists, purity and unity — the ability of a work to bring together various elements in a unified whole — are the standards of good art.

Disdainful of public acceptance, modernists dismissed all forms of popular art. Styles of the past and imitations of reality were also rejected, eliminating traditional ways of understanding art. This opened the doors to the idea, proposed by George Dickie, that art can be identified and defined only by those involved in the art world. Sometimes gallery patrons wondered whether the art they were looking at was simply a hoax.

By the early 1970s, modernism was beginning to give way to post-modernism, as people looked for new ways of making sense of the world. Post-modernist aesthetics rejects the modernist emphasis on autonomy and the doctrine of purity and unity, saying that these are restrictive. Instead, post-modernists embrace mixed meanings, the appropriation or borrowing of ideas, and impurity. They also emphasize the way art is interpreted.

Because viewers and artists engage in art from many diverse perspectives, say post-modernists, deconstruction — breaking down the meaning of an image, often by placing it in a new context — is an essential part of the aesthetic experience. The expectation that a work of art will have many different

Figure 16.3

This 1986 photograph shows American post-modernist artist Keith Haring painting the infamous Berlin Wall in East Germany — at the invitation of the West German government. Haring, who started his career painting blank advertising space in New York subways, embodied the post-modernist idea of taking art to the street.

CHAPTER 16 Theories, Categories, and Types of Art MHR **335**

meanings for many different people is a key characteristic of post-modernist aesthetics. This departs from modernism's reliance on the authority of art critics to understand and explain art.

The contemporary American art critic and philosopher Suzi Gablik is one of those who challenges the modernist idea that art is separate from life. Gablik argues in favour of what she calls a connective aesthetic, one that embraces a participatory world view of relationships and responsibility. According to Gablik, this shift is necessary if art is to be meaningful.

Contemporary western culture and technological advances have strongly influenced post-modernist ideas. Post-modernists believe that all ideas in art owe their existence to previous concepts. Because of this, nothing is original. Because they attach no importance to producing authentic, original art, they embrace technology that allows art to be easily and quickly reproduced. They also welcome non-western influences and often view the process of creating art as a collective, rather than a solitary, experience. As a result, post-modernism has taken art out of museums and placed it firmly in the street.

CATEGORIES AND TYPES OF ART

Humans have learned to understand art on the basis of conventions that apply to various categories and types of art. When you look at a work of art, for example, how do you know that it is a painting and not a poem? You probably make this distinction without even thinking about it consciously. The conventions that differentiate paintings from poems are so deeply ingrained that you are able to distinguish between the two as easily as you tell the difference between a table and a chair.

Humans have created art since the beginning of time. When examining the artworks of early civilizations, however, archaeologists and historians have concluded that it was usually created for utilitarian — or useful — purposes. Indeed, the languages of many early cultures included no word for art, a situation that continues to exist in some contemporary traditional cultures. For these societies, art was — and is — part of everyday life. It is not something separate.

Even in western cultures, the idea of fine arts did not emerge till the 18th century. Once this idea emerged, however, the arts came to be broken down into various categories, usually based on their form. Within these broad categories are various types of art. Each type often has its own form, which sets it apart from other types within each category.

Figure 16.4

Newman, Barnett, 1905–1970, American, *Voice of Fire*, 1967, acrylic on canvas, purchased 1989. © National Gallery of Canada, Ottawa. © Estate of Barnett Newman/SODRAC (Montréal) 2002.

When American artist Barnett Newman exhibited this large abstract, titled *Voice of Fire*, at Expo 67 in Montreal, many people reacted with disbelief. They asked how something that looks so easy to create could be art. What do you think?

VISUAL ARTS

Visual arts present visual interpretations of an artist's ideas, experiences, or feelings. Drawings, paintings, sculptures, and prints are traditionally considered visual arts. Contemporary art forms such as videos, photography, films, and collages also fall into this category. Visual artists may choose to show what they see in the physical world in a way that is immediately recognizable. They may also alter it in some way, or they may invent entirely new forms.

PROFILE
Suzi Gablik
Challenging Accepted Ideas

Suzi Gablik listened intently as Robert Motherwell, her teacher at Hunter College, immersed his students in a modernist approach to aesthetics. A famous American painter, Motherwell believed strongly in the concept of art for art's sake. He trained his students to accept that art had no purpose and should be value-free.

Motherwell's teachings had a profound effect on Gablik. Under his tutelage, she spent an entire semester studying one essay: "The Dehumanization of Art" by the Spanish philosopher Ortega y Gasset. Abstract expressionism dominated western painting through the 1950s, and abstract expressionists revered this essay. In it, Gasset emphasized that art's only function is to have no function at all.

Gablik was born in New York in 1934 and grew up surrounded by art and artists. As a teenager, she embraced the modernist spirit that gripped post-war New York. She attended concerts by John Cage, who composed pieces that were not supposed to be played the same way twice, as well as performances by the Living Theatre, an unconventional alternative to commercial theatre.

After graduating from Hunter College, Gablik applied for a scholarship to write a book about the surrealist painter René Magritte. Although Magritte is well-known today, few people had heard of him at the time. Gablik's application was turned down, but this did not stop her. She decided to travel to Brussels, where Magritte lived. Through a surprising twist of fate, she ended up living with him and his wife for eight months in 1959. For the next 10 years, Gablik studied Magritte and his work, and in 1970, her first book, titled *Magritte*, was finally published.

Throughout this time, Gablik had enthusiastically continued to support the idea of art for art's sake. As she started work on a new book, however, she found herself questioning the doctrine of value-free, purposeless art. By the time she had finished writing out her ideas, she realized that she was no longer satisfied with the aesthetics of her youth. What had once seemed significant suddenly seemed ridiculous.

In *Has Modernism Failed?*, published in 1984, Gablik challenged the idea of art for art's sake, a position that immediately thrust her into the public eye. Her thoughts struck a chord with artists who were also becoming disenchanted with the status quo. Suddenly, Gablik was being invited to teach and lecture throughout North America.

As an art critic and philosopher, Gablik was subsequently drawn to explore the relationship between the artist and society. In questioning the modernist idea of artists as gifted geniuses and rugged individualists, she began to form a new understanding of their relationship with society.

In the 1980s, people were beginning to talk about the need to live life in a more interconnected way. When Gablik discovered Marilyn Ferguson's book *The Aquarian Conspiracy: Personal and Social Transformation in the 1980s*, she was struck by the absence of artists among those Ferguson identified as envisioning social change. This provoked Gablik to call for radical change in the way artists think about themselves and their work. Her book, *The Re-Enchantment of Art*, which was published in 1991, asked this question: What does it mean to be a "successful" artist working in the world today?

Gablik strongly disagrees with the idea that art is nothing but a commodity. She argues that art and the work of artists are essential to society. Her idea of connective aesthetics rejects power and promotes relationships. As a result, she has become known as one of the most thought-provoking contemporary aestheticians and continues to be in great demand as a teacher and lecturer.

Figure 16.5
Art critic and philosopher Suzi Gablik challenges the idea of art for art's sake.

IDEAS IN CONTEXT

When the National Gallery of Canada paid $1.76 million for a large abstract painting in 1990, the purchase sparked a public outcry. The work, by American artist Barnett Newman, was titled *Voice of Fire* (see Figure 16.4; pp. 336 and IV) and consisted of a vertical red stripe between two dark blue stripes. People wrote outraged letters to newspapers, and Manitoba MP Felix Holtmann, who chaired the House of Commons committee on communications and culture at the time, told a Winnipeg radio audience: "It looks like two cans of paint and two rollers and about 10 minutes would do the trick." Others defended the work, calling it a modern masterpiece.

Representational visual art portrays the world as it is. Depending on the artist's philosophy, this kind of art can range from extreme realism to more expressionistic representations. Expressionistic representations are often identified as **abstract**, a catch-all term that may be used to describe everything from a work that represents an altered form of reality to a work that bears no resemblance whatsoever to reality.

When visual art is so abstract that it bears no resemblance to reality, it is often described as **non-representational**, non-objective, or non-figurative. Non-representational art is pure form. In the case of a painting, for example, this pure form is expressed by applying paint to a surface. The painting has no recognizable subject matter and makes no reference to recognizable objects. Some philosophers and critics have argued that non-representational art is not art at all. Formalists such as Immanuel Kant would disagree, saying that judgments about art should exclude both the subject matter of the work and its sense qualities.

ARCHITECTURE

Architecture is the art and science of creating buildings. As an art, architecture is similar to sculpture in its use of three-dimensional space. As a science, architecture must deal with the laws of physics. To meet the demands of both art and science, architects must design structures that are both utilitarian and aesthetically pleasing.

Architecture ... [is] the adaptation of form to resist force.
— John Ruskin

When designing a building, architects must address three key areas.

- function: the building's use
- structure: the building's stability
- form: the building's appearance

A lasting record of the society in which it was created, architecture developed in concert with the materials available and the changing expectations of society. During the Middle Ages, for example, giant cathedrals were built in Europe to glorify God. Made of stone and often taking decades or even centuries to build, these churches were the tallest, most beautiful buildings in towns and cities.

In today's capitalist western societies, the tallest buildings are the business towers made of concrete, steel, and glass. From the late 18th century to the mid-20th century, many architects borrowed freely from historic styles. This practice, which involves combining diverse styles, is called **eclecticism**. Other architects rebelled against this practice, preferring to build simple, unadorned steel and glass structures in a modernist style.

Post-modernist architects reject this style and are returning to the idea of eclecticism, which

Figure 16.6

The new city hall in Mississauga, Ontario, was designed by Edward Jones and Michael Kirkland. Because the design reflects a variety of influences, this building is considered an example of post-modernist architecture

Figure 5.8

Figure 6.9

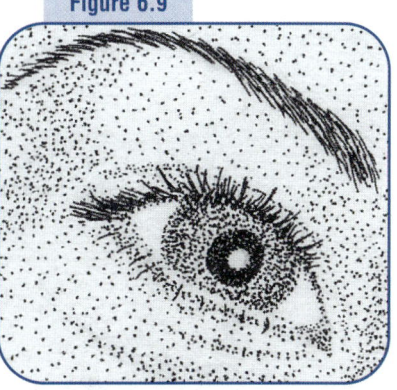

Figure 15.1

In 1918, the French-born American artist Marcel Duchamp created this picture by altering a postcard of Leonardo da Vinci's famous *Mona Lisa*. Duchamp added a moustache, goatee, and the letters L.H.O.O.Q. The letters stand for a vulgar French pun. He called his action the ready-made principle, meaning that art can be anything.

Figure 15.2

When he created this large painting, Canadian artist Jean-Paul Riopelle was interested in ideas about subject matter and spontaneity. The painting's rich textures are composed of layers of different-coloured paint that appears to be flung across the canvas.

Riopelle, Jean-Paul 1923–2002, Canadian, Untitled, 1952, oil on canvas, purchased 1964. © National Gallery of Canada, Ottawa. © Estate of Jean-Paul Riopelle/SODRAC (Montréal) 2002.

MHR

Figure 15.3

This small bronze figure is from the burial mound of a Chinese emperor. Figures like these were placed in the tombs of important families. With its out-stretched tail, pounding hooves, and flaring nostrils, this horse demonstrates the maker's ability to represent both the power and likeness of a horse.

Figure 15.4

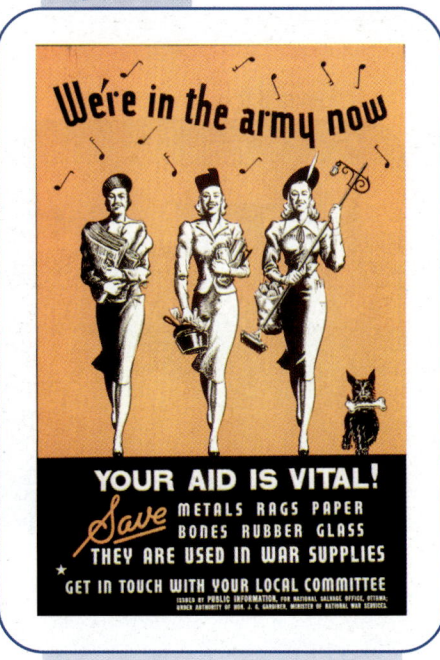

Posters like this inspired young Canadians to join the army during World War II. A collection of war posters was recently displayed at the Art Gallery of Ontario. Were these posters art before they were hung in the art gallery? Are they art now?

Figure 15.5

Painted in the early 1500s, this detail from a famous painting by Raphael shows Plato (left) and Aristotle in conversation. Why do you think Raphael portrayed Plato pointing up, while Aristotle seems to gesture toward the ground? And why is Plato carrying *Timaeus*, a book about metaphysics, while Aristotle holds a book about ethics?

Figure 15.6

Painting on velvet became popular in the mid-19th century, when it was considered a cultured hobby for young women. Today, companies in Mexico employ painters who produce up to 3000 velvet paintings of pop-culture images every week. Can this kind of mass-produced painting be called art?

Figure 15.8

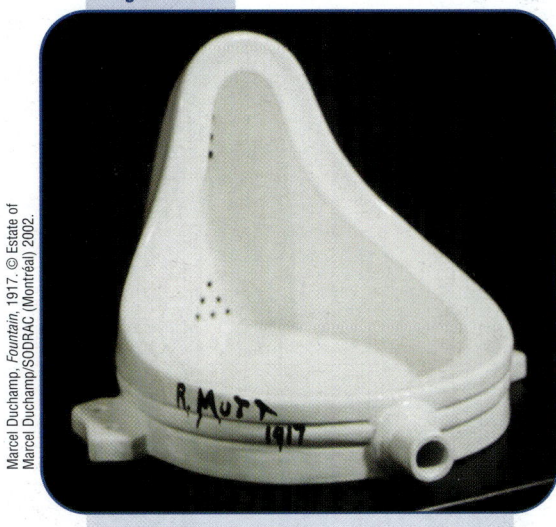

Marcel Duchamp, *Fountain*, 1917. © Estate of Marcel Duchamp/SODRAC (Montréal) 2002.

In 1917, Marcel Duchamp submitted a signed urinal titled *Fountain* for exhibition by the Society of Independent Artists. Though the work was rejected, this replica is now on display in Milan, Italy. Why do you suppose that a replica is now on display?

Figure 15.9

Figure 16.1

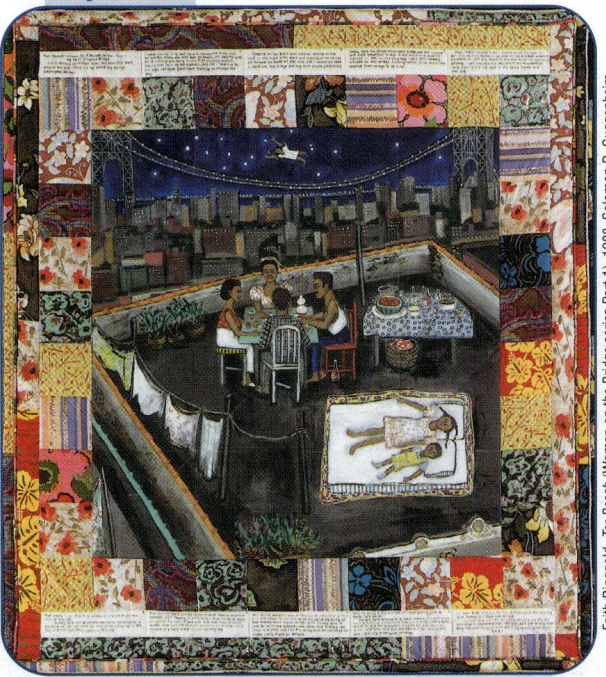

Faith Ringgold, *Tar Beach* (Woman on the Bridge series Part 1), 1988, Solomon R. Guggenheim Museum, New York, Gift, Mr. and Mrs. Gus and Judith Lieber 1988, 88.3620, photograph by David Heald, © The Solomon R. Guggenheim Foundation, New York, © Faith Ringgold 1988.

In this painted quilt, artist Faith Ringgold recalled a childhood picnic on the roof of the family's apartment building in New York City's Harlem district. Ringgold's memories of childhood helped shape her understanding of the world.

MHR **III**

Figure 16.2

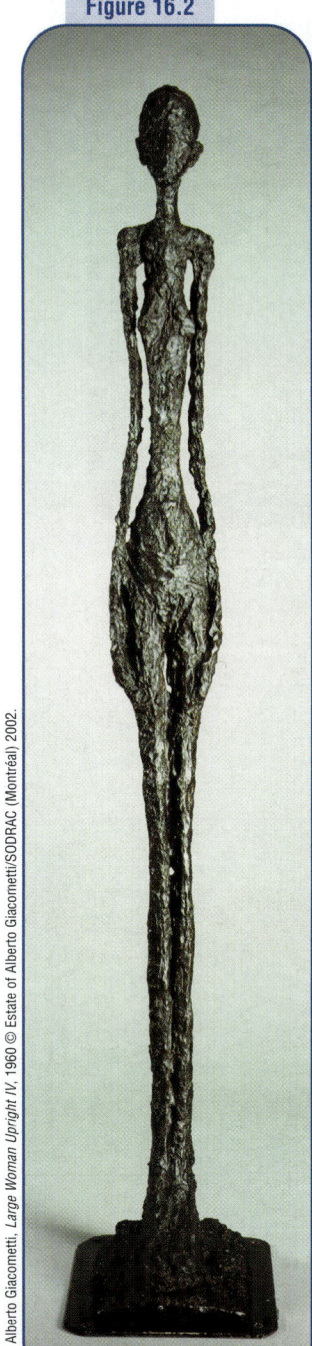

Alberto Giacometti, *Large Woman Upright IV*, 1960 © Estate of Alberto Giacometti/SODRAC (Montréal) 2002.

Created in 1960, this sculpture by Alberto Giacometti reflects the existentialist *angst* and isolation felt when people are free to make their own choices and create themselves.

Figure 16.4

Newman, Barnett, 1905–1970, American, *Voice of Fire*, 1967, acrylic on canvas, purchased 1989. © National Gallery of Canada, Ottawa. © Estate of Barnett Newman/SODRAC (Montréal) 2002.

When American artist Barnett Newman exhibited this large abstract, titled *Voice of Fire*, at Expo 67 in Montreal, many people reacted with disbelief. They asked how something that looks so easy to create could be art. What do you think?

Figure 16.7

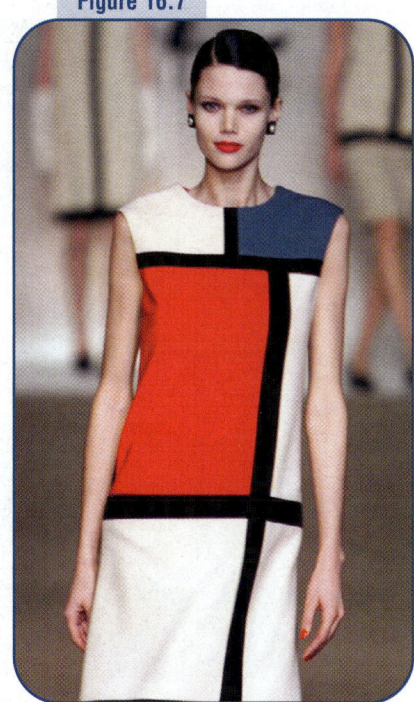

In 1965, designer Yves Saint Laurent presented this dress, inspired by artist Piet Mondrian's paintings, at a Paris fashion show. Is this dress art?

Figure 16.6

The new city hall in Mississauga, Ontario, was designed by Edward Jones and Michael Kirkland. Because the design reflects a variety of influences, this building is considered an example of post-modernist architecture.

Figure 16.8

In 1968, Canadian artist Joyce Wieland used the traditional women's craft of quilting to give new meaning to the personal motto of Pierre Trudeau, who had just been elected prime minister. Wieland's quilt now hangs in the National Gallery of Canada.

Figure 16.9

Figure 16.10

Figure 17.1

This 17th-century painting by Jian Zhu illustrates the Chinese idea that beautiful art is understated, subtle, and evocative. Artists achieve ex-cellence by refining their skills, mastering the principles of their form, and seeking har-mony. How is this different from the western aesthetic?

Figure 17.2

Figures like these surround the pillars of the Kandariya Mahadeva Temple in Khajuraho, India. The female figure represents a standard of female beauty that prevailed when the temple was built in the early 11th century.

Figure 17.3

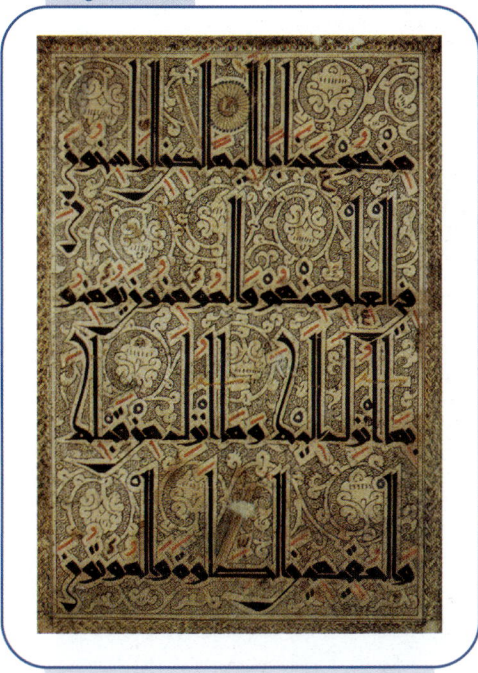

This leaf from an 11th-century Qu'ran shows the ornate calligraphy that is an important feature of Islamic art.

Figure 17.5

American artist Mark Tansey used a 19th-century style to show Aboriginal people pondering *Spiral Jetty*, a work created by Robert Smithson in the Great Salt Lake. Smithson's work was based on prehistoric earthworks of Aboriginal Americans.

Figure 17.7

This photograph presents natural beauty as a picture within a picture. Why do you think people are drawn to wilderness areas such as this?

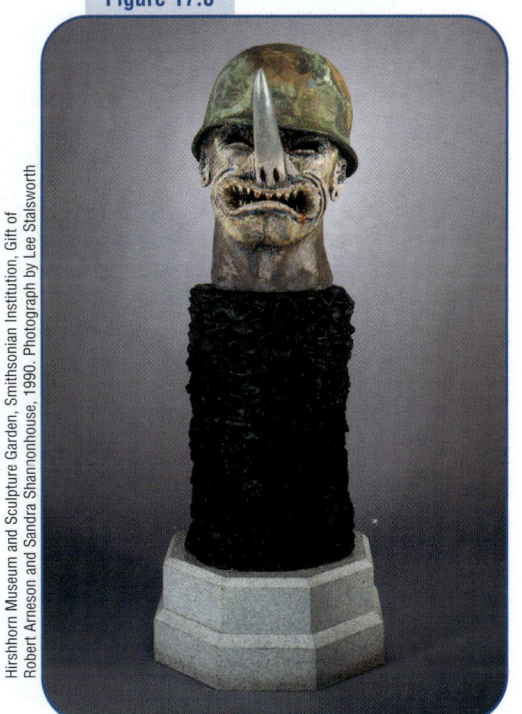

Figure 17.8

This powerful work by American artist Robert Arneson deals with concerns about nuclear war. For many people, this is a frightening work. Would you call it art?

MHR VII

Figure 17.9

Award-winning Canadian designer Karim Rashid designed the pieces of this chess set to look like small sculptures.

Figure 17.11

This sculpture by Inuit artist Sakkiassee Anaija is an example of a culture-specific art form. Would an understanding of Inuit culture contribute to your appreciation of this work?

Figure 17.12

assigns equal value to modern and traditional styles. Post-modern architects introduce the elements of excitement and surprise into their designs as an antidote to what they view as the severity of the glass boxes of modernism.

LITERARY ARTS

The literary arts use language to express ideas, experiences, and emotions through poetry, prose, and drama. Poetry, which is sometimes written in verse and metre, concentrates language to express emotions and ideas. To do this, poets use techniques such as sound, rhythm, and ambiguity, which means that words and phrases may have more than one meaning.

> *Painting is silent poetry, and poetry painting that speaks.*
> – Simonides

Prose sounds more like everyday language. Its patterns are more irregular than poetry's, and its rhythms are closer to speech. Prose is often identified by genre, a word borrowed from French. It means "kind" and refers to a category of literary composition that has a particular style, content, or form. At one time, genres were strictly defined as epic, tragedy, lyric, comedy, and satire. Today, the word is used more loosely to include fiction and non-fiction, essays, epic novels, and short stories. In France, the anti-novel is a genre that attempts to reveal what happens in the recesses of the main character's mind rather than what appears to happen on the surface.

The two main forms of drama, comedy and tragedy, may be written in either poetry or prose. Drama usually involves conflict and emotions developed through dialogue and action. Most dramatic works are designed for theatrical performance.

In the same way as other arts, literature has reflected the ideas and philosophies of its times. Sartre, for example, was a playwright whose works, such as *Nausea*, *The Flies*, and *The Devil and the Good Lord*, reflected existentialist themes that focused on people's freedom to influence their destiny through the choices they make.

MUSICAL ARTS

> *Music is a language without a dictionary whose symbols are interpreted by the listener according to some unwritten Esperanto of the emotions.*
> – Aaron Copeland

The musical arts use the language of sound — high and low, loud and soft, long and short, quick and slow — to express feelings and ideas. Music is a mixture of harmony, melody, and rhythm and can be sung or played on an instrument. Types of music include classical, jazz, folk, pop, rock, opera, and rap.

Like all the arts, music reflects the time and place in which it is created. During the European Renaissance from about 1350 to 1550, for example, people focused on ideas and forms drawn from ancient Greece and Rome. As a result, poets, actors, artists, and musicians drew on Aristotle's careful analysis of Greek tragedy and his ideas about the autonomy of art to create opera, a new musical style that mimicked Greek tragedy. Opera's scripts, or *libretti*, were specifically written to be set to music, and Greek legends inspired the stories.

THEATRICAL ARTS

Actors, artists, architects, costumiers, composers, musicians, dancers, and choreographers interact as a group to present drama to an audience. This collaborative experience is called theatrical arts. All theatre creates illusions, and it is the team's job to persuade the audience that the illusion is real.

Because theatre often reflects the social beliefs and concerns of its time, it is a powerful force in shaping and reflecting the opinions of societies. Political and religious authorities have often feared that ideas raised in dramatic works will persuade audiences to ask questions about controversial issues. As a result, theatre has suffered the greatest censorship of all the arts. Theatre was banned in Christian Europe for four centuries after the fall of Rome, for example. It was also banned in India for eight centuries after the Islamic conquest of the 10th century.

Today, some critics and philosophers might argue that rock concerts and events such as World Wrestling Entertainment extravaganzas are theatrical events because they include many elements of traditional theatre. Have you ever attended a rock concert or a WWE event? Have adults ever discouraged you from doing so? What were they worried about? The debate over what should — and should not — be considered theatre continues.

DANCE

Dance is an art form that expresses ideas, emotions, and stories through stylized, rhythmic movements of the body. Dance differs from other physical activities because of its aesthetic function, intentional rhythm, patterned sequences, and non-verbal movement.

Types of dance include ballet, modern dance, folk, and classical forms that are part of the cultural expression in countries such as India and China.

No matter what type of dance is involved, dancers create illusions and generate aesthetic experiences in audiences by manipulating time, space, weight, and flow.

FASHION ARTS

As an art, fashion — the way people clothe and decorate their bodies — is a relatively new phenomenon. Until the late 19th century, dress was a purely functional matter for most people in the West. Indeed, from the Middle Ages to the 18th century, laws in some parts of Europe dictated which fabrics, colours, and styles people of various social classes were allowed to wear. Fashion began to develop as an art form at about the same time as the middle class emerged as an important social force during the Industrial Revolution of the last half of the 18th century and the first part of the 19th.

Fashion decides what is stylish and often influences — or is influenced by — social trends. Today, popular fashion is shaped as much by consumers who combine clothing and accessories in their own way, as it is by professional designers. In fashion, the single constant is that it is always changing.

Figure 16.7

In 1965, designer Yves Saint Laurent presented this dress, inspired by artist Piet Mondrian's paintings, at a Paris fashion show. Is this dress art?

Recall...Reflect...Respond

1. Think about rock videos you have seen recently. In which category of art would you place them? Why?
2. Buildings are sometimes described as art forms that people live, work, and play in. Think about the design of your school. How effectively did the architect fuse form and function in its design?
3. Fashion is a relatively new — and not universally accepted — addition to the list of the arts. Should fashion be included when the arts are mentioned? Why?

MAKING CONNECTIONS

Artifacts decorated with paintings that are at least 15 000 years old tell archaeologists and historians that art has been an integral part of human existence since before the beginning of recorded history. The desire to create seems to be an innate, driving force in human beings. Philosophers talk about art, and artists talk about philosophy. But how does aesthetics connect with real life?

ART AND NATURE

For many people, the easiest way to understand art is to judge its success at representing things in the natural world. Plato and Aristotle agreed that the arts imitate nature, and until the invention of the camera in the 19th century, most western artists and philosophers assumed that representing nature in a realistic way was a primary purpose of the visual arts.

One of the chief advocates of this approach was the German idealist philosopher Friedrich von Schelling, who lived from 1775 to 1854. Schelling argued that all life, including human, is a creation of nature and that nature and humankind are part of the same unity. He believed that humans are nature's greatest creation and are themselves creative.

Although there are many ways to be creative, Schelling said that the most advanced are through the arts, which enable people to explore themselves and gain a deeper understanding of reality. In fact, said Schelling, this is the purpose of nature: to reach this deeper understanding.

In Schelling's view, the arts provide the reason for existence, and artists have reached the pinnacle of human existence. Schelling's ideas about the importance and unity of nature, the importance of art, and the elevated status of artists, are reflected in the romantic movement that became popular at the time. This movement emphasized imagination and emotion over reason and intellect.

ART AND TECHNIQUE

Until the European Renaissance, what people today think of as the fine arts were considered crafts, little different from weaving, metalworking, potting and quilting. During the Renaissance, this attitude began to change. Painting and sculpture, for example, came to be separated from the practical crafts and viewed as branches of higher learning.

In the West, craftspeople continued to fashion individual utilitarian objects until mass production was introduced by the Industrial Revolution of the late 18th and early 19th centuries. At that time, factory-made goods, which could be sold at cheaper prices, began flooding the marketplace, and many craftspeople were put out of work.

At the same time, people began to look at handmade crafts with different eyes. They began to ask questions like, Why is a picture painted on canvas classified as art when a picture painted on a teapot is classified as craft? and Why is someone who chisels a piece of marble into a human form considered an artist while someone who moulds a piece of clay into a bowl is considered a craftsperson? Questions like these sparked debate over the difference between the fine arts and crafts.

In *The Principles of Art*, the British philosopher and critic R.G. Collingwood, who lived from 1889 to 1943, tried to distinguish between art and craft. He argued that a craft is predominantly about process and materials, such as clay, glass, metal, and fibre, while art focuses on form and content.

The debate over arts and crafts continues today. Craft-based artists often argue that an artist's intention is more important in defining art than the material used. As a result, they argue that the use of clay, a traditional craft material, to create a sculpture may be called art rather than craft if the artist intended it to be art.

Figure 16.8

In 1968, Canadian artist Joyce Wieland used the traditional women's craft of quilting to give new meaning to the personal motto of Pierre Trudeau, who had just been elected prime minister. Wieland's quilt now hangs in the National Gallery of Canada.

Technique and tools are linked to expression in ways that people may not always notice. The tools and techniques used by artists can extend or limit their ability to express ideas and feelings in a particular way.

When using watercolours, for example, an artist must work quickly, letting the colours flow together to create subtle gradations and atmospheric effects. Oil paint, by contrast, dries slowly and can be applied thickly (impasto) or thinly (glaze). Using oil paint enables an artist to work on a painting for a longer time, carefully modelling the form. This means that an artist can blend colours in layers, add thin, coloured glazes over built-up areas, and create rich surface effects by applying the paint with a palette knife rather than a brush.

The astonishing new colour effects that painters began to create at the end of the 19th century became possible because synthetic pigments were invented. New materials cause artists to develop new techniques. Combined with artistic genius and philosophies such as art for art's sake, these new techniques set the stage for continuous exploration of what art can be.

ART AND FREEDOM

Questions about artistic freedom and **censorship** have been raised for as long as art has existed. Plato, for example, believed that the arts should be censored. In its broadest sense, censorship refers to any restraint imposed by a public authority on the content of creative expression. In the 20th century, democratic societies oppose censoring most forms of creative expression, including art. Even democracies, however, do not allow complete artistic freedom. In Canada, for example, distributing child pornography and hatred of identifiable groups is illegal.

Proponents of artistic freedom argue that more is lost than gained by suppressing the expression of ideas, even ideas that are repugnant to most people. Those who oppose any censorship at all believe that the dialogue that results when ideas and attitudes conflict is important in a free society. Art, they say, is on the cutting edge of freedom, leading the way to new ideas and values.

The most severe form of censorship is prior restraint. This means that a work cannot be shown to the public until the offending parts have been removed or altered in some way. Prior restraint is most often used by governments to protect public security. Totalitarian regimes, for example, use prior restraint to control their citizens.

Sometimes censorship occurs without prior restraint. If a work of art is judged to be indecent, evil, subversive, or harmful to society as a whole, it may be banned even after it has been shown. This kind of censorship seeks to limit public exposure to the work. Both James Joyce's novel *Ulysses* and D.H.

> *The sooner we all learn to make a distinction between disapproval and censorship, the better off society will be ... Censorship cannot get at the real evil, and it is an evil in itself.*
>
> – Granville Hicks

Lawrence's *Lady Chatterley's Lover*, for example, were banned in various countries at various times. The bans were lifted only after the courts ruled that these books had serious aesthetic value.

The question of artistic merit as a defence against censorship raises important philosophical questions about what art is and how art should be judged. To support claims of artistic merit, expert testimony must be presented to the courts. The problem is that the merit of many innovative, experimental artworks may not be evident at the time.

During the Renaissance, for example, Michelangelo painted the *Last Judgment* on the wall of the Vatican's Sistine Chapel. This work was widely criticized. People said that Michelangelo had indulged in too much artistic licence because he had not followed the description set out in the Bible. His angels did not have wings, and the angels blowing trumpets were shown in a group rather than at the four corners of the world. What outraged most people, however, was the nudity of many of the figures. To protect the painting from vandals, subsequent popes ordered clothing to be painted over the nude figures.

In the 1940s, the Nazis confiscated more than 16 000 works of modern art from German museums and burned most of them in a huge fire. They selected some for particular public ridicule, exhibiting them in a show titled Degenerate Art.

In 1990, obscenity charges were laid against the Contemporary Art Centre in Cincinnati, Ohio, when the gallery exhibited sexually explicit pictures by the American photographer Robert Maplethorpe. Although the jurors did not like the pictures and had no art appreciation background, they acquitted the gallery's director on the basis of the testimony of experts, who said that the pictures displayed artistic merit.

> **Web connection**
> www.mcgrawhill.ca/links/philosophy12
> To find out more about freedom of expression and censorship, follow the links on this Web site.

ART AND TRUTH

One of the most important questions of aesthetics focuses on the issue of truth. Can art reveal what is true and what is false? This question is often linked to another question: Does the way to truth lie in art or in science?

The German philosopher **Arthur Schopenhauer**, who lived from 1788 to 1860, claimed that art and poetry, not science or cognitive philosophy, are the way to truth. This idea was supported in the 20th century by Heidegger, who used a phenomenological approach to describe the world as humans see it, rather than as scientists do.

It is not truth that makes man great, but man who makes truth great.

— Kongfuzi

As you hold this book, for example, do you see it as a collection of atoms that have taken the form of a book? If so, you would be viewing it as a scientist. Perhaps you see the book differently, however. Perhaps you see it as something to be read so that you can understand the information it contains. This view focuses on the book's function in your world. You want to understand the information to improve your chances of getting a good mark on this course. And you want a good mark to improve your chances of being accepted at the university of your choice, and so on.

Heidegger argued that humans do one thing for the sake of another and that connecting things for a purpose is the way people make their world meaningful and discover the truth. For Heidegger, the being of this book — its essential character — is our sense of what it is.

According to Heidegger, an object can tell a complete story of a human world and so help people understand what is true. To show how, he used a painting (Figure 16.9; see also p. V) by the 19th-century Dutch artist Vincent van Gogh.

Titled *A Pair of Boots*, the painting shows a pair of well-worn, heavy work boots. Their laces are untied and one of the boots is lying on its side. According to Heidegger, these boots bring to light the world inhabited by peasants who work in the fields. It tells about their poverty and their exhausting way of life. As a result, he believed that this painting tells people what is true.

Heidegger meant that art shows the truth by portraying objects as things that have meaning in the human world. Art encourages people to stop and think about ordinary things in life. In this way, people come to understand the truth and being of objects.

Figure 16.9

ART AND CULTURE

Because North America was largely settled by people of European background, attitudes toward art were shaped nearly exclusively by European points of view, and for a long time, most artists attempted to create art in styles that reflected European perspectives. In this milieu, the art of Aboriginal peoples, as well as that created in non-European cultures, was sometimes dismissed as primitive, crude, or inferior.

> *"Colonialism reduces the culture of the colonized person to the level of folklore and propaganda."*
>
> – André d'Allemagne

Starting in the late 19th century, these attitudes began to change, partly as a result of the work of cultural anthropologists, people who study societies. They found that the culture of many so-called primitive societies was, in reality, very complex. As a result, many cultural anthropologists began to use the term "small scale," rather than "primitive," to describe cultures with few members and simple technologies. As people came to understand the cultural complexity of small-scale societies, they began to view their art differently.

At the same time as this was happening, the nature of North American immigration was changing. More and more people from non-European countries were settling in Canada and the United States. To ensure that people of all cultural backgrounds feel welcome in Canada, the government officially adopted a policy of multiculturalism. This policy encourages all Canadians to take pride in their cultural heritage.

These developments profoundly affected aesthetics. Rather than trying to imitate European styles, artists began to celebrate their cultural differences.

Recall...Reflect...Respond

1. Examine Joyce Wieland's quilt (Figure 16.8; pp. 342 and V). Is this quilt art or craft? Explain why you think so, referring to R.G. Collingwood's definition of art and craft, as well as the definitions of others.
2. What purposes are served by censoring art?
3. Martin Heidegger used Vincent van Gogh's painting of a pair of boots (Figure 16.9; pp. 344 and V), to show that art can show truth. Choose another illustration from this chapter and explain why it supports your belief that art does — or does not — tell people what is true.

ART AND HAPPINESS

Many philosophers believe that aesthetic experiences provide pleasure, or moments of happiness. Schopenhauer, for example, said that aesthetic experience provides an escape from the unhappiness of life. He argued that life is unhappy because the ultimate reality is will or the will to live. In willing, people constantly seek to change the way they are. Achieving this change does not make people any happier, said Schopenhauer, because they then want to change to something else. In Schopenhauer's view, this is human nature.

This pessimistic philosophy views humans as perpetually frustrated and unhappy with their current circumstances. Schopenhauer did offer some hope, however. He said that aesthetic experiences enable people to suspend their will by contemplating beauty in a disinterested way. Because people have no desire to own — or change — the work of art, the experience gives pleasure.

> *To have read the greatest works of any poet, to have beheld or heard the greatest works of any great painter or musician, is a possession added to the best things in life.*
>
> – Algernon Charles Swinburne

Schopenhauer combined Aristotle's and Kant's ideas about art for art's sake, claiming that the content of art becomes universal when it is contemplated in this way. In the presence of art, said Schopenhauer, people experience happiness because they are briefly released from the urge to act.

Many philosophers have disagreed with Schopenhauer's analysis of aesthetic experience. Nietzsche, for example, believed that Schopenhauer had it wrong. Art does not suspend the will to act, he said. Rather, it celebrates the will to power. Schopenhauer viewed art as a way of escaping the pessimism of life, while Nietzsche saw art as a celebration of human courage in facing the difficulties of life.

Others offered different ideas about the source of happiness provided by art. Clive Bell argued that people experience aesthetic pleasure when they contemplate an object's purely formal aspects, while Monroe Beardsley said that the pleasure comes from contemplating both its formal aspects and expressive qualities.

Despite their disagreements over how — and why — art provides pleasure or happiness, most philosophers do connect art and pleasure. They maintain that the altered state people feel in the presence of great art — in other words, the aesthetic experience — has delighted humans throughout the ages.

Chapter Review

Chapter Summary

This chapter has discussed
- some of the philosophical questions of aesthetics
- the strengths and weaknesses of the responses of some of the world's major philosophers to some of the main questions of aesthetics, making reference to classic texts
- how philosophical theories of aesthetics influence music, art, and fashion
- the problems, principles, methods, and conclusions of various philosophers

Knowledge and Understanding

1. Identify and explain the significance to the study of aesthetics of each of the following key words and people.

Key Words	Key People
rationalist	Leo Tolstoy
empiricist	R.G. Collingwood
mimesis	Edmund Husserl
formalism	Søren Kierkegaard
expressionist	Martin Heidegger
phenomenolgy	Jean-Paul Sartre
representational	Joanna Frueh
abstract	Suzi Gablik
non-representational	Friedrich von Schelling
eclecticism	Arthur Schopenhauer
genre	
censorship	

2. Create a graphic organizer like the one shown here. In the "Question" column, fill in four key aesthetical questions discussed in this chapter (e.g., What is art?). Then complete the chart.

Question	Theory That Addresses Question	How Theory Addresses Question

Thinking and Inquiry

3. Read the following quotation by the Buddhist Zen master Seung Sahn in an article titled "The Three Treasure Structure of Buddhism."

   Beauty does not come from the outside appearance of things. In the treasure of Buddha, "beauty" means that when your mind is not moving, everything is beautiful. I was teaching in Paris several years ago, and saw an exhibition of paintings. An important picture was hanging alone on a large wall…. As I walked up to it, this picture became clear — two old and worn-out socks, with holes in them, hanging from a frame! All dirty! …What do these socks mean? What is their inside-meaning? …
   The inside-meaning of this picture is that some human being did a lot of walking in these socks, putting a great deal of energy into them….

So this picture of old socks is making an important point: this picture teaches us something about a human life's being. So though the socks are very dirty, the meaning is very beautiful.

What is Seung Sahn saying about the nature and purpose of art? Write a short response explaining why you do — or do not — agree with Seung Sahn's point of view. Cite the beliefs of at least one philosopher to support your opinion.

4. Select a work of art that you find particularly appealing. Respond to this work from the perspective of a philosopher of aesthetics whose theory you disagree with.

Communication

5. You are a candidate for a university scholarship in one of the fine arts. To assess your strengths and weaknesses, the school has asked you to choose a work of art and answer the following questions about it:

 • What category or type of art does the work you chose reflect?
 • Why did you choose this particular work?
 • What purposes does the work serve?
 • What is the personal and social value of the work?
 • Does the work reveal what is true and false about you?

Write the report you would submit in response to these questions.

6. Create an abstract self-portrait to include with the report submitted in Question 5. Explain how the self-portrait represents your strengths and weaknesses.

Application

7. Examine this advertisement (Figure 16.10; see also p. VI), then answer these questions:

 • What feelings does this ad evoke?
 • How does this ad connect to real life?
 • Do you consider this ad a work of art? Why?

After considering your answers to these questions, write a reflection on the importance of the study of philosophy in understanding the role of art in everyday life.

Figure 16.10

8. Write two series of statements to be used in an advertisement promoting a product of your choosing. One series should be designed to persuade Plato to buy the product; the other should be designed to persuade Aristotle to do the same.

Chapter 17
Beauty

Chapter Expectations

By the end of this chapter, you will be able to
- demonstrate an understanding of some of the philosophical questions of aesthetics
- evaluate the strengths and weaknesses of the responses of some of the world's major philosophers to some of the main questions of aesthetics, making reference to the classic texts
- formulate and defend your own responses to some of the main questions of aesthetics
- explain how philosophical theories of aesthetics influence music, art, and fashion
- compare some of the problems, principles, methods, and conclusions of various philosophers
- summarize main philosophical concepts and theories from information gathered from encyclopedias or surveys

Key Words

Confucianist
Taoism
arabesque
pluralistic
iconology
popular art

Key People

Jean-François Lyotard

[Handwritten note:]
David Hume
→ taste = person's ability to recognize the aesthetic features of an object
→ "Standard of Taste"
↳ argued that judgements about beauty based on feeling — not fact
↳ Beauty is in the eye of the beholder

A Philosop...

The beautiful thing is that...

Aristotle (38...

WHAT IS BEAUTY?

Many people are naturally drawn to attractive clothing, people, places, and things. In western societies today, advertisers spend billions of dollars appealing to people's desire for beauty. And according to Statistics Canada, consumers spend about $2 billion a year on cosmetics and fragrances. This statistic alone reflects people's desire to make themselves beautiful.

But what, exactly, is beauty? The first to try to answer this question were the ancient Greek philosophers — and the debate has raged ever since.

PLATO: THE TRANSCENDENCE OF BEAUTY

As one of the first philosophers to equate beauty and goodness, Plato blazed the way for those who believe that art must have social value. In *The Republic*, this ancient Greek philosopher described the need for gifted artists to create truly beautiful and graceful art. Doing so, he believed, was an important way to inspire goodness and reason in citizens, especially young people.

To Plato, the ideas of beauty and moral goodness were inseparable. His theory of forms — the idea that a concept of pure beauty is innate in people — set the standard for all things and provided a way for him to conclude that people can know pure beauty. In *The Symposium*, Plato asserted that beauty, which is eternal, awakens in the soul a desire to pursue goodness. He believed that a noble soul results from the pursuit of beauty because beauty is a force that transforms attitudes and behaviour.

ARISTOTLE: THE BEAUTY OF THIS WORLD

Aristotle was the first philosopher to claim that aesthetic experiences and activities have a character of their own. Because all disciplined arts are orderly and purposeful, he argued, they are the same as the workings of nature. As a result, he said that artworks can be explained.

> *A thing of beauty is a joy forever.*
> – John Keats

Aristotle maintained that the imagined world of works of art must connect directly to the real world experienced by their audiences and at the same time provide a sense of wholeness, or unity. When art does this, he said, it causes the audience to experience a deeper, more profound understanding. To him, works of art were beautiful because of their unity.

HISTORICAL PERSPECTIVES ON BEAUTY

In the western tradition, the idea that beauty and taste are linked began to emerge in the 16th century. This notion suggests that people can agree on what is beautiful and, therefore, on what is in good taste. But how does anyone know what good taste is? Various philosophers have tried to explain this elusive concept.

DAVID HUME: A QUESTION OF TASTE

In aesthetics, taste usually refers to a person's ability to recognize the aesthetic features of an object. In "Of the Standard of Taste," the 18th-century Scottish philosopher David Hume examined characteristics of beauty. He argued that judgments about beauty are based not on facts but on feelings. In other words, beauty is in the eye of the beholder.

Have you ever bought a beautiful article of clothing, only to have someone, such as your grandmother, say that it was ugly? This is the kind of situation Hume was referring to when he said that beauty, or taste, is a matter of feeling. According to Hume, the true critic of beauty is someone who has good sense, an open mind, and a discriminating imagination. Unfortunately, this theory offers no help in identifying whose judgment — yours or that of your grandmother — was correct in assessing the beauty of the disputed article of clothing.

IMMANUEL KANT: A DISSENTING PERSPECTIVE

The German philosopher Immanuel Kant disagreed with Hume, though Kant applied his idea of beauty mainly to natural objects and only secondarily to works of art. According to Kant, people have a natural aptitude for making aesthetic judgments. In *The Critique of Judgment*, he explained that for people to have aesthetic experiences, they must contemplate an object in a disinterested manner, disregarding its use, moral significance, and possible personal connections.

Kant claimed that the formal features of an object — in particular, its harmony, unity, and balance — are most likely to trigger an aesthetic response. He believed that subject matter, emotions, and social issues are external to the artwork and have no aesthetic importance. As a result, he said that it is impossible to settle arguments about taste.

GEORG W.F. HEGEL: THE PHILOSOPHY OF FINE ART

Georg W.F. Hegel claimed that aesthetics is about the beauty of art rather than, as others argued, about natural beauty. He said that art is more than a representation of the natural world. It expresses a human idea of the world. The beauty of art, claimed Hegel, lies in presenting ideas in sensuous form.

Hegel's chief contribution to understanding beauty is his proposal that true beauty is a construct of the human mind and can therefore be found only in humans and their artworks. As a result, he believed that nature cannot be aesthetically beautiful. Works of art that show the many forms of human consciousness and represent the subjective act of perception and human vision were, for Hegel, the most beautiful.

CONTEMPORARY PERSPECTIVES ON BEAUTY

Ideas of beauty and taste have taken on new meanings in today's world. In the West, the influence of people whose voices were not previously heard has changed the way many people view works of art.

Many contemporary philosophers question the idea of a fixed concept of beauty. In *The Postmodern Condition*, which was published in 1979, the 20th-century French philosopher Jean-François Lyotard argued that the grand narratives that have formed the foundation of western societies since the 18th century are no longer viable.

Lyotard proposed that thinking about art has shifted from an aesthetic to a societal model. In this societal model, people's differing interests, desires, and concerns mean that, among other things, they have differing ideas of beauty.

> *Skill without imagination is craftsmanship and gives us many useful objects, such as wickerwork picnic baskets. Imagination without skill gives us modern art.*
> – Character in Tom Stoppard play

PHILOSOPHY IN ACTION

The Critique of Judgment

by Immanuel Kant

Published in 1790, Immanuel Kant's *The Critique of Judgment* introduced the idea of "aesthetic purposiveness" in judgments that ascribe beauty to things. These judgments are based on feelings rather than reason, wrote Kant. Despite this, he said that judgments can lay claim to general validity because they spring from the free play of a person's understanding and imagination. This excerpt from *The Critique of Judgment* traces Kant's argument that taste is not governed by rules.

If we estimate objects merely by conceptions, all idea of beauty is lost. So there can be no rule by which anybody can be compelled to recognize anything as beautiful. No one allows his judgment on the beauty of a coat, a house, a flower, to be coerced by reasons or principles. He wants to have the thing before him, just as if his satisfaction were sensuous; yet, if he then calls it beautiful, he claims to have the universal voice on his side, whereas sensation is private and decides nothing beyond the satisfaction of the man who has it....

If the pleasure in a given object came first and only the universal communicability of the pleasure were to be attributed to the idea of the object by the judgment of taste, we should have a contradiction. For such a pleasure would be nothing but mere pleasantness of sensation, and so could naturally only have private validity, as depending immediately on our perception of the object.

Consequently it is the universal communicability of our state of mind, in having the idea, which must occasion in our minds the judgment of taste and be a condition of it; and the pleasure in the thing must be the result of this. But nothing can be universally communicated except knowledge, and ideas so far as they belong to knowledge. For only so far as ideas are objective, and only so have they a common point of reference in which the ideas of all men are bound to agree. Now when we have to think that what makes us judge our idea to be universally communicable is merely subjective — is in fact no conception of the object — it can be nothing but the state of mind consisting in the mutual relation of our faculties for forming ideas, so far as these faculties employ a perception for purposes of knowledge in general.

The faculties of knowledge brought into play by the idea are in such a case in free play, because no definite conception of the object's nature confines them to any particular principle of knowledge. So the state of mind in having such an idea must be a feeling of the free play of our faculties for ideas in using perception for purposes of knowledge in general. Now for any idea of an *object*, and so for knowledge in general, there are required *Imagination* to combine the manifold apprehended and *Understanding* to afford a conception which can unify the ideas. This state of the free play of our faculties of knowledge in the idea of an object must be one that can be shared universally; for knowledge (being distinction of an object, with which all perceptions, to whomever they belong, must agree) is the only kind of idea that is valid for every man....

The following contradiction arises about the principle of taste:

(1) *Thesis.* The judgments of taste cannot depend on conceptions, for otherwise we could argue about them, that is to say, give conclusive proofs.
(2) *Antithesis.* The judgments of taste must depend on conceptions, for otherwise, however much they differed, we could not even quarrel about them, that is to say, demand that other people should necessarily agree with us. [We do not make this demand about mere sensations.] ...

All contradiction disappears if we say that the judgment of taste does depend on a conception, but only on a general conception of some reason for the seeming adaptation of nature to our powers of judgment. From such a conception nothing could be learned or proved about the nature of an object, since no particular object can be *known* to exemplify conception....

[On an empirical or sensationalist theory of taste] the object of aesthetic satisfaction would be merely pleasant, but on a rationalist theory (if the judgment depended on definite conceptions) it would be merely good. So beauty would be shuffled out of the world, and all that would be left would be a particular name given perhaps to a certain mixture of these two kinds of satisfaction. But we have shown that there are grounds of satisfaction other than empirical, and therefore consistent with the rationalist principle, although they cannot be grasped as definite conceptions.

Such rationalist principles of taste must further be distinguished according as they take the apparent adaptation [of art and nature to our faculties] to be really designed or only accidental....

One fact positively proves that, as the ground of our aesthetic judgments, we assume only an apparent adaptation of beautiful nature, to the exclusion of any explanation which asserts its real adaptation to our perceptive faculties. I mean the fact that, wherever we estimate beauty, we do not seek any criterion from experience, but judge for ourselves aesthetically whether the thing is beautiful. This could not be if we assumed a designed adaptation of nature, for then we should have to learn from nature what we had to find beautiful, and the judgment of taste would have to bow to experience. But such an estimation does not depend on what nature is or even on how it is in fact adapted to us, but on how we look at it. If nature had produced its forms for our satisfaction, that would in the end be an objective design in nature, not a merely apparent suitability to us resting on the free play of our imagination; it would be a grace done to us by nature, whereas in fact we confer one upon her. In beautiful art it is even easier to recognize that the adaptation can only be known as apparently designed.... The fact that the beauties of art by their nature must be considered as products not of scientific understanding, but of genius, plainly shows that, even on a rationalistic theory, it is only apparent and not necessarily real design which accounts for our satisfaction. ...

Now I say that the beautiful is the symbol of the morally good; and only from this point of view (which every man naturally takes and thinks it the duty of others to take) do we claim that all men should agree about the pleasure it gives.... In the faculty of taste the judgment does not find itself, as in judging by experience, constrained by empirical laws; it legislates for itself on the objects of so pure a satisfaction, just as reason legislates autonomously on the faculty of desire in morality. And owing to this capacity in ourselves and to the capacity in external nature to harmonize therewith, the judgment finds in itself a reference to something in us and also outside us, which is neither physical necessity nor moral freedom but is allied to the supersensible [though intelligible] conditions of freedom. In this supersensuous reality, the theoretical faculty [of judgment] and the practical faculty [of moral reason] are mutually and mysteriously interwoven.

Source: From *The Critique of Judgment*. Immanuel Kant.

1. How does Immanuel Kant use contradiction to prove his argument that no rules govern what makes an object beautiful?
2. According to Kant, how does nature help people make aesthetic judgments?
3. How does Kant's theory of aesthetics draw on elements of Plato's and Aristotle's theories?

FEMINIST AESTHETICS

Why have there been no great women artists? Philosopher Linda Nochlin asked this vexing question in her 1971 book *Women, Art, and Power and Other Essays*. Nochlin's question presented one of the first feminist challenges to established traditions of art history, which had focused nearly exclusively on art created by men. Nochlin argued that the lack of women's names in the history of art contrasted sharply with a reality in which women were actively creating art. Maintaining that women had been systemically excluded by the artworld, Nochlin raised awareness of feminist issues in art and aesthetics.

Web connection
www.mcgrawhill.ca/links/philosophy12
To find out more about women in the arts, follow the links on this Web site.

The American author **Marilyn French** is an example of a feminist artist who continuously raises issues of women's experiences. When her novel *The Women's Room* was published in 1977, it became an international best-seller. In this book, she presented a world in which there is no co-existence between the sexes. In *The War against Women*, an extended essay published in 1992, French argued that women "have been increasingly disempowered, degraded, and subjugated" and that violence against women has become more threatening in response to the feminist movement. French maintained that physical, economic, and political attacks on women are a deep-rooted part of today's male-dominated global society.

The common thread in contemporary feminist aesthetics is the constant probing of prevailing thoughts about gender, race, power, class, and sexuality. Feminism provides insights into women as subjects and objects of artmaking and allows for a new model in which artists are more attentive to issues of gender.

> ### IDEAS IN CONTEXT
>
> In the mid-1980s, a group of New York feminist artists dubbed themselves the Guerilla Girls and joined forces to confront what they perceived as the male-dominated art world. They plastered neighbourhoods near art galleries with lists identifying galleries that rarely showed works by women. The posters were signed with this message: "A public service message from the Guerrilla Girls — conscience of the art world." Over the years, this group has produced a steady stream of posters and appearances that have drawn attention to the exclusion of women from mainstream public art institutions.

> ### Recall...Reflect...Respond
>
> 1. How does Georg W.F. Hegel define beauty? Do you agree — or disagree — with his definition? Why?
> 2. Choose a work of art, such as a book, a piece of music, or a painting, that addresses gender equity issues. Explain how the work does this.
> 3. Compare David Hume's and Immanuel Kant's explanations of how beauty is judged. What elements, if any, do their explanations share?

GLOBAL PERSPECTIVES ON BEAUTY

Throughout history, humans have been compelled to create things of beauty. Ideals of beauty vary among cultures, however. To fully appreciate the beauty of some objects, it is often necessary to understand the cultural context in which they were created.

CHINESE AESTHETICS

The earliest records of a Chinese philosophy of art appeared in the third century BCE, though these ancient writings focused mainly on music and ritual. From at least the time of **Kongfuzi** (Confucius), a philosopher who lived from about 551 to 479 BCE, Chinese aesthetic thought has linked art, moral goodness, and enjoyment. This link is evident even in Chinese writing, which uses logograms instead of letters. The character that represents music, for example, is the same as the character that represents joy.

Early **Confucianists** — followers of Kongfuzi — were musicians and dancers as well as teachers. As advocates of a philosophy that emphasizes living in harmony with one's community and taking a holistic approach to life, they believed that moral goodness shaped art: the greater the virtue of the artist, the greater the art. In their view, for example, the integrity of a composer influenced the greatness of the music produced.

Confucianists connected the arts with moral conduct, self-improvement, and public virtue. In later centuries, as the moral elements of Confucianism grew even stronger, the idea that art must teach moral lessons led to a focus on literature. Historical writing, prose, and poetry gained in stature, while the importance of dance and music declined. Engaging in painting and calligraphy, a form of stylized or beautiful handwriting, came to be considered ways of cleansing and harmonizing the emotions.

Like Confucianism, Taoism, a philosophy attributed to the sixth-century BCE philosopher Laozi (Lao-tzu), also emphasizes harmony and a holistic concept of life. While Confucianism emphasizes living in harmony with one's community, Taoism emphasizes living in harmony with nature and the rhythms of the universe. As a result, Taoists link aesthetics with nature and the laws of the universe.

Both Confucianists and Taoists were intensely interested in the character of representation and systems that link the many phenomena of life into one energetic whole. In the third century, Lu Ji (Lu Chi) wrote a book titled *Wen fu* (*On Literature*). He argued that creating art was related to the way of Taoists. To Taoists, the way represents the idea of essence. All things depend for life on the way.

In art, this idea of the way is embodied in works that appear to be created with an apparent artless spontaneity that produces a direct, intuitive, perfectly appropriate expression of beauty and emotion. This concept is an integral part of art and art criticism in traditional China.

The *Wenxin diaolong*, written by Liu Xie, who lived from 465 to 523, is often considered the greatest Chinese work on aesthetics. In it, Liu Xie deals with questions of imagination, emotion, content, ornamentation, beauty, defects, cultivation, timeliness, objectivity, and audience response. Most writings related to art make some reference to this work.

Figure 17.1

This 17th-century painting by Jian Zhu illustrates the Chinese idea that beautiful art is understated, subtle, and evocative. Artists achieve excellence by refining their skills, mastering the principles of their form, and seeking harmony. How is this different from the western aesthetic?

INDIAN AESTHETICS

In India, where the Hindu religion dominates, artworks were traditionally created to glorify the divine nature of the gods. Artists followed rules of harmony and proportion in the creation of beautiful, abstract representations of the human form. Whereas ancient Greek artists attempted to show divinity by creating an idealized, perfect human body, Indian artists presented their deities as superhumans, often with many heads and arms. These are metaphors for the divinities' many powers.

According to the Hindu theory of aesthetic experience, a work of art is created with a particular *rasa*, or flavour. There are nine flavours: humorous, erotic, heroic, despicable, furious, frightful, wondrous, pathetic, and peaceful. The elements of an artwork that evoke an aesthetic response are theme, deliberate actions, moods, and the nine *rasas*. Many Indian philosophers believe that tasting *rasa* is an aesthetic experience that depends largely on both the innate and learned perceptiveness of the observer.

Indian thinking about aesthetics and art has focused on the issue of *pratibha*, which means creative or internal disposition. *Prathiba* applies to all forms of creative activity including visual arts and music. Without *pratibha*, Hindus believe that there can be no meaningful or beautiful art.

Figure 17.2

Figures like these surround the pillars of the Kandariya Mahadeva Temple in Khajuraho, India. The female figure represents a standard of female beauty that prevailed when the temple was built in the early 11th century.

Is *pratibha* spontaneous and innate or the result of hard work? Just as the question of the origin of creativity has been debated by western philosophers, it has also been debated in India. Most Indian philosophers agree that some people are born with an innate creative ability.

But is *prathiba* the only thing required to create beautiful art? Or is something more necessary? The ninth-century philosopher Anandavardhana believed that practice is also necessary, and the 10th-century poet Rudrata believed that training plays a role. Mammata, another 10th-century figure, said that training, knowledge, and practice are required in addition to innate creative ability.

Many Indian philosophers believe that creating something beautiful involves combining form and content. In this way, the artwork conveys deeper meaning and provides a better understanding of the world. They also believe that *pratibha* should be accompanied by *abhyasa*, or serious effort, as well as *vyutpatti*, or strength, and *cittaikagryamavadhanam*, or concentration. Beauty in the form of a poem or other work of art can be created only when all these elements are in place.

Jiddu Krishnamurti, who lived from 1895 to 1986, was a non-traditional Indian philosopher who believed that analytic theory cannot help people discover truth and beauty. He said that these things can be found only through observation and by understanding what is in our own minds. He encouraged an approach that he called "choiceless awareness," which involves critical *looking* rather than the western idea of critical thinking.

ISLAMIC AESTHETICS

By 751, Islam, a term that means surrender (to Allah, the name of the Muslim supreme being), was the established religion in an area that stretched from central Asia to Spain.

Figure 17.3

This leaf from an 11th-century Qu'ran shows the ornate calligraphy that is an important feature of Islamic art.

Because of the scarcity of water in much of this area, many Muslims lived as nomads, or wandering herders. Islamic teachings combined with this nomadic lifestyle to influence Muslim attitudes toward aesthetics.

In general, Muslims take a practical approach to the arts and consider aesthetics a normal part of everyday life. Because aesthetics is linked so closely to the everyday, it was not studied separately and philosophers developed no definitions or theories of aesthetics. This does not suggest, however, that Muslims are not aware of the relationship between art and beauty. The arts are meant to inspire the imagination, not to give a realistic accounting of objects or events.

In the eighth and ninth centuries, when the Muslim world was ruled by the Abbasids, Baghdad — the capital of present-day Iraq — was the centre of Islamic learning and culture. During this period, the criteria that became the foundation of Arab-Islamic art were developed. These were calligraphy, geometry, and a style known as **arabesque**. This style uses interlacing lines to create an intricate pattern that often depicts flowers, fruit, or foliage.

PROFILE

Jiddu Krishnamurti
Drinking at the Fountain of Eternal Joy and Beauty

In the early summer of 1909, Charles Leadbeater, a former Church of England priest who had joined the Theosophical Society, was in Madras, India. There, he met a thin, scruffy teenage boy. A special aura seemed to surround the boy, whose name was Jiddu Krishnamurti. Leadbeater was sure that he was in the presence of someone destined to become a great spiritual leader.

Like all theosophists, whose religion drew on Hindu and Buddhist teachings, Leadbeater had been on the lookout for a child who was the human form of the *maitreya*, or world teacher. Theosophists had predicted the coming of this teacher, whom they believe appears in human form from time to time to bring salvation to the world.

After conducting a series of tests, the theosophists decided that Krishnamurti was the one. He and his brother Nitya were taken into the fold and sent to England to be educated and trained. There, Krishnamurti became the ward of Annie Besant, the society's president.

Born on May 11, 1895, in Madanapalle, India, Krishnamurti was the eighth of eleven children. His parents were poor and had moved to Madras so that his father could take a job in a factory. Nothing in Krishnamurti's childhood had prepared him for the mission thrust on him by the theosophists.

Still, he tried to fulfil their expectations of him, becoming head of a theosophical organization called the Order of the Star in the East. Then, while living in California in 1922, Krishnamurti began meditating every day. One day, he had a vision that changed his life. In later writings, he described what he had seen.

> There was a man mending the road; that man was myself; the pickaxe he held was myself; the very stone which he was breaking up was a part of me; the tender blade of grass was my very being, and the tree beside the man was myself.

The next day, he had another vision.

> I was supremely happy, for I had seen. Nothing could ever be the same.... I had touched compassion which heals all sorrow and suffering; it is not for myself, but for the world. I have stood on the mountain top and gazed at the mighty Beings. Never can I be in utter darkness; I have seen the glorious and healing Light. The fountain of truth has been revealed to me and the darkness has been dispersed. Love in all its glory has intoxicated my heart; my heart can never be closed. I have drunk at the fountain of Joy and eternal Beauty.

As a result of these visions, Krishnamurti began to develop his own way of thinking and to distance himself from the teachings of theosophy. Because he came to believe that truth cannot be found by following any religion, sect, or any path whatsoever, he formally dissolved the Order of the Star in the East in 1929. He encouraged people to look at themselves and their relationships and to think for themselves. He said that to follow authority is to deny intelligence.

After this, Krishnamurti dedicated his life to travelling and teaching and continued to do so for more than 55 years until his death, at the age of 90, in 1986. During this time, he emphasized that he spoke and wrote not as a guru, but as a lover of truth. He stayed nowhere for more than a few months because he did not consider himself part of any country or any religion.

Figure 17.4
A young Jiddu Krishnamurti arrives in New York City, the starting point of a lecture tour of the United States.

Because of the reverence accorded to the writing of Allah's word, Muslims granted elevated status to the book arts. Calligraphy follows strict and precise rules and is judged aesthetically. Beautiful calligraphy is viewed as the manifestation of a clear mind.

> **IDEAS IN CONTEXT**
>
> The ninth-century scholar Al-Bukhari told a story of what happened when Muhammad, the prophet who founded Islam, discovered that his wife Aisha had hung a curtain decorated with figures of animals. When Muhammad told her that those who imitate Allah's creative acts would be severely punished on Judgment Day, Aisha cut up the curtain and made it into cushion covers. Although this anecdote is often cited to show that Muhammad forbade representations that might lead to the worship of idols, it also shows that he accepted these representations in some forms.

According to the Muslim teachings, Allah's absolute power does not allow humans to act as creators. During various periods, this principle was interpreted very strictly, and Muslim artists were forbidden to depict living beings. As a result, Muslim art often focused on elaboration or decoration. In Arabic, *zina* is the word for beauty, including moral beauty. *Zina* also means ornament, and ornamentation is an essential element of beauty in Arabic culture, in which the beauty of a work is judged by the amount of pleasure it evokes in the perceiver.

Many Muslims believe that art is based on learning and skill, not artistic genius. Beautiful works must be skilfully crafted, elaborate, and ornate. Avicenna, a Muslim scholar who lived from 981 to 1037, argued that the human imagination, not divine vision, provides images. For him the highest degree of abstraction can be reached only by using the active intellect, which he viewed as a kind of intermediary between the human and the divine.

POST-MODERN PERSPECTIVES ON BEAUTY

The French philosopher and social critic **Michel Foucault**, who lived from 1926 to 1984, argued that when people rely on a system of thinking or a set of principles, they effectively stop thinking. Foucault said that once people have the framework for their thought, every new piece of learning is placed within this framework — so that people know only what they already know.

Figure 17.5

American artist Mark Tansey used a 19th-century style to show Aboriginal people pondering *Spiral Jetty*, a work created by Robert Smithson in the Great Salt Lake. Smithson's work was based on prehistoric earthworks of Aboriginal Americans.

Much of the framework of modern western thinking about aesthetics was established in the 18th century, a time that was also known as the Age of Enlightenment. Post-modernism is an approach that attempts to move away from this aesthetic framework.

Post-modernists such as Lyotard point out that social forces shape what people become. They question the idea of the existence of absolutes, such as truth and beauty; examine social, political, and historical issues; and embrace diversity.

According to the contemporary American literary critic and philosopher Fredric Jameson, the passage from modernist aesthetics to post-modernist aesthetics can be seen as the movement away from a "deep" aesthetic of unique personal style to a "flat" aesthetic of pastiche, a style that imitates other styles, as well as the multiplication of styles.

THOUGHT EXPERIMENT: *A Beautiful Life*

Many years ago, at the tender age of 16, you died in an accident. At the time, you were a dynamic teenager living a more or less ordinary life: ordinary parents, ordinary siblings, ordinary neighbourhood, ordinary school. Nothing about your life was extraordinary. In fact, a lot of it seemed boring.

You took much for granted, including your life. You felt that it was all ahead of you. You gave no thought to death. Indeed, you felt as if you were indestructible — and that there would always be a tomorrow. Often, you felt as if you were living a dress rehearsal for a more real life, which was just around the corner, when you grew up and got real about things.

Then it was all taken away. In a split second. You didn't have time to say good bye to anyone. There was no suffering, no prolonged illness. You existed one minute — and the next you didn't.

You have now been dead for many years. But what if you were handed a once-in-a-lifetime — oops! deathtime — opportunity and allowed to choose one day of your life to live over again? What would it be like? How would you feel? What would your experience be like? Which day would you choose?

Figure 17.6

The American playwright Thornton Wilder imagined a situation like this in his play *Our Town*. Emily, who died when she was a young woman, is given an opportunity to live one day of her life all over again. She chooses her 12th birthday.

As Emily lives this day, she finds that nothing about the life that she had once taken for granted is ordinary. Every second of her existence counts. Every detail is filled with intense meaning. She is acutely aware of the *specialness* of the ordinary. She can treat nothing nonchalantly, as if it did not matter or as if there will always be a tomorrow. Things that she had never noticed while she was alive suddenly overflow with a marvellous and poignant beauty. When she is with her mother again, for example, it's as if Emily sees her — really sees her for who she is — for the first time.

Sadly, Emily cannot finish the day. Her feelings of loss are too intense. She returns to the graveyard, crying out, "Oh earth, you're much too wonderful for anybody to realize you."

If you were in Emily's shoes, would everything be overwhelmingly beautiful? If so, why don't you experience that beauty now, while you are alive and well?

QUESTIONS THAT MATTER

Questions that are at the foundation of human activity call out for answers. In addition to wondering about things such as knowledge, beliefs, wrongdoing, and virtue, philosophers also ask questions about beauty and taste because the answers affect the decisions people make. Which person will I date? Which concert will I attend? and Which sweater will I buy? The answers to questions like these are based in part on people's notion of beauty and art.

Since antiquity, people have debated the answers to questions like, What is beauty? Does beauty lie in the eye of the beholder? Is it even possible to define beauty? and Is it necessary to define beauty in order to discuss it?

In *Poetics*, Aristotle analyzed what constitutes beauty in Greek tragedy and maintained that works of art can be judged only when they have reached their highest, fullest levels. In other words, people must know the whole before they can judge its parts. Aristotle also said that it is possible to describe the formal qualities that make a work of art beautiful.

Unlike Aristotle, John Dewey believed that beauty cannot be analyzed. He said that the sensory qualities of a work and its perceived meaning are intrinsically linked in an aesthetic experience. This link arouses admiration and a sense of beauty. Dewey argued that artists select and organize the features that will create this aesthetic experience in viewers. For Dewey, art and beauty are experiences that result from reflective thought.

Web connection
www.mcgrawhill.ca/links/philosophy12
To find out more about John Dewey, follow the links on this Web site.

WHY DO PEOPLE FIND BEAUTY IN NATURE?

Have you ever watched the setting sun, heard a flock of geese flying overhead, or walked beside a trickling stream in a spring forest? If so, did you pause to contemplate the beauty in what you saw? Was your experience of these things — or other natural phenomonena — special because nature is beautiful? Why do people find beauty in nature?

Figure 17.7

N.E. THING CO. Canadian 1936 • *Reflected Landscape* (Detail: Unit B only. - 1 of 2 parts) • Cibachrome transparency in light box • 54.3 x 64.3 x 21.5 cm • ART GALLERY OF ONTARIO, Toronto

This photograph presents natural beauty as a picture within a picture. Why do you think people are drawn to wilderness areas such as this?

According to Dewey, human experience is a process in nature. He believed that art comes from people's ability to transform ordinary experiences into fulfilling events, and he said that people find beauty in nature because they are constantly involved with the world. Through nature, he said, people connect with the underlying rhythms of life and the world as a whole.

In his book *Landscape, Natural Beauty and the Arts*, the contemporary American scholar Arnold Berleant said that it is through total engagement in nature, not disinterested contemplation, that people are able to find beauty in nature. Supporting Immanuel Kant's theory of aesthetic experience, he argued that nature stimulates the free play of thought and imagination. He also said, however, that this is not enough. Nature also sparks aesthetic experience by stimulating a variety of sensory responses.

HOW ARE AESTHETICS, ART, AND BEAUTY RELATED?

Large cities today are not considered sophisticated without at least one public art gallery. Some cities boast several, and many are filled with both historical and contemporary art. Private collectors and public galleries often compete to spend millions of dollars to buy a single painting. Few people today would challenge the notion that works of art have significant cultural value.

In the West, this elevated status has been granted to the arts only since the European Renaissance. During this 200-year period from about 1350 to 1550, the Neoplatonists revived Plato's idea that beauty in art is a reflection of moral goodness. In keeping with

Figure 17.8

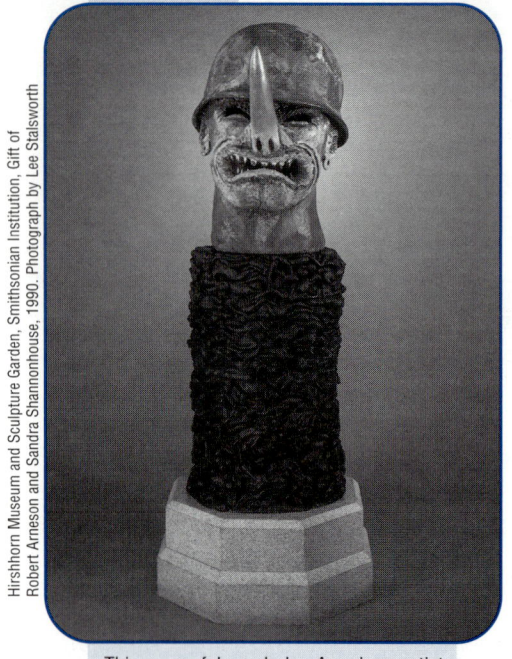

This powerful work by American artist Robert Arneson deals with concerns about nuclear war. For many people, this is a frightening work. Would you call it art?

Hirshhorn Museum and Sculpture Garden, Smithsonian Institution, Gift of Robert Arneson and Sandra Shannonhouse, 1990. Photograph by Lee Stalsworth

Figure 17.9

Award-winning Canadian designer Karim Rashid designed the pieces of this chess set to look like small sculptures.

Plato's ideas, representational works were, for a long time, considered to be the most beautiful and, therefore, the most morally good. Beauty in art was believed to have transcendental, or visionary, powers.

Over time, philosophers like Kant and Friedrich Nietzsche proposed new ways of thinking about art in response to the new kinds of art that were being created. This began to change the way people think about aesthetics, art, and beauty. Today, the words "art" and "beauty" are not necessarily considered synonyms. People accept that "good" art may evoke profound reactions and may even be ugly. As a result, aesthetics — which began as the study of beauty, then progressed to the study of beauty *and* art — has in large part disowned beauty and become primarily the study of art.

ARE UTILITY AND BEAUTY COMPATIBLE?

Though philosophers have never agreed on a definition of beauty, the general belief is that a beautiful, or aesthetic, object, possesses a quality that seems to make it complete within itself. The parts combine to create a sense of harmonious unity. Objects with this quality provide an aesthetic experience for the perceiver.

Dewey claimed that the person who crafts utilitarian objects does not necessarily have beauty in mind. He said that objects such as chairs are often made to be "satisfactory" — to serve the functional need of providing a place to sit, while sacrificing beauty for profit.

This does not mean that something that is beautiful cannot be useful or vice versa. Beauty can be achieved even in mass-produced objects. Many contemporary designers are trying to do just this. Think about the excitement that greeted iMac computers when they first appeared. The idea that computers could be produced in vivid colours appealed to the aesthetic tastes of millions of consumers.

Recall...Reflect...Respond

1. Create a chart to summarize how Chinese, Indian, and Islamic aesthetic traditions deal with definitions of beauty and the purposes of art.
2. Compare ideas of beauty that prevailed during the European Renaissance with post-modernist views.
3. Take an imaginary stroll through your home and identify a functional object that you consider beautiful. List the characteristics that make this object beautiful. Then explain why you agree — or disagree — with philosophies that claim that something that is both beautiful and useful can be called art.

Art, the Individual, and Society

Art is everywhere. Images, music, poetry, and dance show up on T-shirts, in museums, on CD and book covers, and on radio and TV. This abundance of art raises interesting questions about the way people view art.

WHAT IS A WORK OF ART?

As many 20th-century philosophers came to believe that art and beauty are not necessarily synonymous, they were left with this question: If art is not beauty, what is it?

In the early part of the century, art was defined as either formalist or expressionist. After this, however, definitions became broader. According to Leo Tolstoy, three conditions are necessary to determine what is, or is not, art: individuality, clarity, and sincerity. Dewey took a different approach, saying that artworks are the highest form of human achievement. They are experiences. And the 20th-century American philosopher Susanne Langer maintained that artworks are symbols of the various forms of feeling.

By the 1950s, however, many philosophers were arguing that defining art is impossible. Although no single theory may explain what an artwork is, the form itself and the feelings it evokes are clearly part of the mystery of a work. People must decide for themselves whether something is a work of art — and this is exactly what they do.

> *Art is the community's medicine for the worst disease of the mind, the corruption of consciousness.*
>
> – R.G. Collingwood

SHOULD ART HAVE SOCIAL VALUE?

No matter how art is defined, it is important in society. Though philosophers, artists, and the general public cannot agree on a single definition of art, there is general consensus in western societies that art performs a unique function in human life. Since the time of Plato and Aristotle, however, debate has raged over whether art should serve a social purpose or whether its value is intrinsic — for itself alone.

In 19th-century Europe and North America, for example social reformers believed that art should be used to promote the common good. This position was supported in the 20th century by philosophers such as Tolstoy, who believed that it should be used to promote social harmony and moral goodness. Others, like Dewey and Langer, disagreed. They said that art should be valued for its own sake.

The debate over whether art has social value has continued for 2500 years — and it is not likely to be settled in the 21st century.

Figure 17.10 The Canadian *AIDS Memorial Quilt* is displayed to raise awareness of AIDS. Is this an appropriate use of art?

CONTEMPORARY ART: IS IT ART?

Ideas about what is — and is not — art have often coincided with the view of the world held by most people of a particular culture at a particular time. In Canada, views of art were shaped for a long time by European ideas because most people were from European backgrounds.

Today, this has changed. Canada is a multicultural society. As a result, what people identify as art reflects many different world views. Canadian society has also undergone profound change as a result of technological advances. Things like rock videos, movies, and advertisements have become accepted parts of everyday life.

As a result of these changes, people have begun to recognize that art can be many different things and that aesthetic theories of art provide no final correct or true definition of art. These theories show only how others have tried to define it. In a **pluralistic** society, in which cultural groups are encouraged to celebrate their heritage, contemporary art can be judged according to a range of different theories. *Understanding* an artwork is considered more important than trying to identify one *true* meaning in it. Deciding whether a contemporary work is art depends on which theory of art is applied.

Web connection
www.mcgrawhill.ca/links/philosophy12
To find out more about art in Canada, follow the links on this Web site.

THE ROLE OF ART IN CONTEMPORARY LIFE

In contemporary western societies, technology has made art almost universally available. Want to hear a particular piece of music? Go to a music store and buy a CD. Want to see a great acting performance? Go to a movie theatre or rent a video or DVD. Want to read a great book? Borrow it from the library or order your own copy over the Internet. Art is everywhere.

Today, art is often used as a product, to sell products, and to entertain. As entertainment, its role is to provide people with a momentary escape from the realities of life. Not all art plays this role, however.

Some art is more challenging. It is designed to provoke people to think deeply about their own experiences and beliefs and to inspire new ideas. People are changed because of their encounter with the work. This kind of art often functions as a social critic, encouraging people to see what they have learned to ignore. It leads perceivers to dream dreams and consider what might be.

WHAT KNOWLEDGE IS REQUIRED TO APPRECIATE ART?

Have you ever looked at a work of art and wondered what it was supposed to represent? Or felt nervous about expressing your opinion of a work? People are often confused by art, a situation that has led some to wonder whether only experts can correctly interpret and appreciate art.

Though it is possible to appreciate art on the basis of form alone, greater understanding of the context in which a work was created and its expressive content may lead to a richer aesthetic experience. Art historians connect artworks to the time in which they were created by tracking historical styles. Similar characteristics are often found in works created at the same time and within the same culture. As a result, a knowledge of styles helps people place works in a historical milieu.

Iconology is the study of the meaning of the subject matter relative to the culture in which an artwork was produced. The word "iconology" comes from the Greek *eikon*, which means image.

To appreciate a work of art, then, it is helpful to know about formal analysis, historical styles, iconology, function, and the political, economic, philosophical, or religious values that prevailed when it was created. This knowledge leads to the discovery of greater meaning in works — and this often leads to a deeper appreciation.

WHO CAN BE AN ARTIST?

The ability to create art is often identified as one of the characteristics of human beings. In some small-scale, traditional societies, everyone is an artist and there is no separate word for art. In these societies, everyone sings, dances, carves, and creates images to the best of his or her ability. Artistic sensitivity seems to be universal, and the function of objects is inseparable from their aesthetics.

By contrast, large, highly developed, multicultural western societies have such a range of customs that it is difficult to define a traditional art form. As a result, most people have learned to think of art as something that can be created only by an artist, someone who was born with a *gift* for making art.

Figure 17.11

This sculpture by Inuit artist Sakkiassee Anaija is an example of a culture-specific art form. Would an understanding of Inuit culture contribute to your appreciation of this work?

The idea of the artist as a gifted genius makes many people hesitant to create or explore ideas in art. For most people, artistic sensitivity and the ability to create meaningful art require specific instruction in the arts. They believe that only with this instruction can they learn — or perhaps relearn — what is an innate human ability.

IS ART CULTURE SPECIFIC?

Art inspires, transforms, entertains, and serves a useful purpose. Sometimes, it does one of these things; other times, it does more than one. In the formalist view expressed by philosophers such as Kant, art is pure form and the culture in which it was created is irrelevant. To properly appreciate art, formalists believe that the cultural context must be ignored.

In contrast to this view, post-modernists insist that understanding the cultural context in which a work was created is essential if people are to truly appreciate art. Some cultures use art to connect with the spiritual forces of nature. The formal characteristics of the artworks of these societies are readily identifiable, and the work can be described as culture specific.

Recall...Reflect...Respond

1. Summarize the responses of various philosophers to this important question of aesthetics: Should art have social value?
2. What role does art play in your life? Write a brief reflective response to this question.
3. Choose a work of art presented in this chapter and analyze your ability to truly appreciate this particular work. What knowledge and skills do you think you need to develop to become a connoisseur of art?

WHAT IS POPULAR ART?

Most people today are familiar with art in the form of television programs, movies, radio shows, rock videos, and pop music. This **popular art** — or pop art — is produced primarily to make money. Because popular art must make a profit, it focuses on providing entertainment at the same time as it reinforces the values and beliefs of the public it serves. But is it art?

Though philosophers such as Kant and Hegel might argue that most popular art is not art at all, some of these popular commercial art forms will no doubt take their place in history as artistic classics, much as opera has. Many 19th-century operas were considered vulgar when they were first produced. Now, they are viewed as "high art," which can be appreciated only by sophisticated audiences.

Will some of today's popular art forms end up being revered as classics? Already, some works that were dismissed as crass or exploitive at the time of their release are being viewed from a different perspective. Jazz by artists like Duke Ellington, Charlie Parker, and Louis Armstrong, for example, is already viewed as serious art, even though it was originally produced for commercial consumption. And some so-called spaghetti westerns — low-budget western movies produced in Italy or other European countries — are being reassessed as movie-making classics with important artistic value.

For these reasons, philosophers do not dismiss popular art. It is a product of its time, and history may decide that some popular works are among the most interesting and important art produced in the 20th and 21st centuries.

Chapter Review

Chapter Summary

This chapter has discussed
- some of the philosophical questions of aesthetics
- the strengths and weaknesses of the responses of some of the world's major philosophers to some of the main questions of aesthetics, making reference to the classic texts
- how philosophical theories of aesthetics influence music, art, and fashion
- some of the problems, principles, methods, and conclusions of various philosophers

Knowledge and Understanding

1. Identify and explain the significance to the study of aesthetics of each of the following key words and people.

Key Words	Key People
Confucianist	Jean-François Lyotard
Taoism	Linda Nochlin
arabesque	Marilyn French
pluralistic	Kongfuzi (Confucius)
iconology	Laozi (Lao-tzu)
popular art	Jiddu Krishnamurti
	Michel Foucault
	Susanne Langer

2. Create a graphic organizer that summarizes the characteristics of six of the main aesthetic theories that respond to the question, What is beauty? Highlight the characteristics that support generally accepted beliefs about beauty. Draw on the information in this summary to write your own working definition of beauty. Place this at the top of the organizer.

Thinking and Inquiry

3. In an interview published in *Philosophy Now*, Emmanuel Eze, an authority on African philosophy, said the following in response to criticisms of ethnophilosophy. Ethnophilosophers believe that some philosophical traditions were not devised by individuals. Rather, these traditions evolved collectively and were conveyed orally rather than in writing.

   > In non-literate African societies it is almost impossible to maintain faithfully and over time attributions of origin of ideas, including philosophical ideas. African proverbs, by design it seems, are notorious for this sort of fluidity in exchange and ambiguity of attributions of authorship. Ethnophilosophy, when critically and nicely done, is often an effort to extract ideas and knowledge embedded in media such as proverbs or everyday language.

   What do Eze's words imply about the importance of culture-specific art forms?

4. Close your eyes and reflect on one of your experiences with nature. This experience might have been as simple as waking to the sound of chirping birds or staring at a starry night sky. What do you remember as you revisit this experience? What do you feel and see? Do you consider the natural phenomenon you contemplated a work of art? Or would it become art only after it had been expressed as a piece of music, a dance, a photograph, a painting, a play, or a poem? Drawing on various aesthetic approaches to art, explain your position.

Communication

5. You are writing an illustrated story for Grade 1 students. The story's underlying theme focuses on whether judgments of beauty and ugliness are subjective or objective. Draw on various theories of aesthetics to create a story outline that illustrates this theme.

6. You have recently started your own interior design business. As a marketing strategy, you have decided to redesign a room in your home to show that interior design is about creating art and beauty. Drawing on a philosophical belief about beauty or the definition that you devised earlier, create before-and-after pictures of the room. Use these pictures to create an advertisement for your service.

Application

7. Examine this photograph (Figure 17.12; see also p. VIII) by William Wegman, an American artist whose pictures of his Weimaraners have become famous. Create a series of questions that draw on various aesthetic theories to help guide your response to the photograph. Write a response based on your questions.

Figure 17.12

8. With a group, prepare a series of questions to use in a survey of opinions about whether cultural influences affect people's interpretation of art. Survey at least 10 people of various cultural backgrounds. Summarize your findings and use them to identify the cultural factors that might be considered when marketing a product or service.

Create an advertisement.
CULMINATING ACTIVITY

EXPECTATIONS

By completing this activity, you will
- demonstrate an understanding of main questions, concepts, and theories of aesthetics
- evaluate the strengths and weaknesses of responses to some of the main questions of aesthetics defended by some major philosophers and defend your own responses
- illustrate the relevance of aesthetics to other subjects
- correctly use the terminology of aesthetics
- demonstrate an understanding of the unique character of aesthetic questions
- effectively use a variety of print and electronic sources and telecommunications tools in research
- effectively communicate the results of your inquires

THE TASK

On television and radio, on billboards, in magazines and newspapers, and at movie theatres, people are bombarded with advertising that tries to sell things. Advertising is an accepted fact of life in Canadian society. Art is often used in advertisements to capture the attention of potential buyers by entertaining them and providing information about a product or service. In other words, art is used to promote consumerism. Whether you believe this to be good or bad, morally right or morally wrong, it is an important role of art in contemporary life.

This culminating activity provides you with an opportunity to explore how art can be integrated into an advertisement to serve a purpose beyond merely selling a product or service. This purpose might be to provide consumers with accurate information, to challenge people to think more deeply about their own experiences and needs and the needs of others, to inspire new ideas, to generate happiness or pleasure, or to promote accepted social values. Doing this effectively requires an understanding of the questions, concepts, and theories of aesthetics. Aestheticians often say that what is beautiful and what is art depends on which theory of art is applied. This is an opportunity to explore and apply various approaches to aesthetics as you create an advertisement for a product or service of your choice.

At the end of this course, this advertisement may be combined with the products of other unit-culminating activities to create a philosophy magazine.

THE SUBTASKS

Subtask 1: Summarize Thinking
Explore existing philosophical thought about the questions, What is beauty? What makes something a work of art? What is the role of art? and Can art tell people what is true and false? Create a graphic organizer that summarizes various responses to these questions.

Subtask 2: Identify Common Elements
Group the characteristics of the aesthetic approaches identified on your organizer according to their common elements. Once you have done this, assign a name to each grouping. The name should sum up the common elements of the characteristics in the group.

Subtask 3: Write a Supported Opinion Paper
Focusing on the characteristics of one of the groupings you created in Subtask 2, write a 500-word paper that explains whether art can be used in advertising to do more than simply promote the sale of a service or product. Support your opinion by citing the thinking of at least one philosopher.

Subtask 4: Research, Evaluate, and Select a Work of Art
Before creating your advertisement, consider which category and type of art you will use. Once you have researched artworks, evaluate how well each might promote values that go beyond the sale of a product or service. Choose the one that seems to do this best and, on a graphic organizer, show how you reached this decision.

Subtask 5: Create the Advertisement
Create the advertisement by incorporating the work of art you selected. Remember that your challenge is to create an advertisement that tries to do more than simply sell a product or service, though selling is also one of your objectives.

ASSESSMENT CRITERIA

The following criteria will be used to assess your advertisement.

Knowledge and Understanding
Does you advertisement

- include with it a graphic organizer that groups common elements that summarize the characteristics of various approaches to the questions identified in Subtask 1?
- include with it a second graphic organizer showing how you chose a work of art for your advertisement?

Thinking and Inquiry
Does your advertisement

- include with it a graphic organizer that identifies, groups, and names common elements of various approaches to aesthetics?
- include with it a supported opinion paper that explains whether art can be used in advertising to serve a purpose other than simply promoting the sale of a service or product?

Communication
Does your advertisement

- include with it a supported opinion paper that correctly uses the terms of aesthetics?
- include with it graphic organizers that are appropriate to the purposes of the tasks?
- use symbols and visuals that effectively advertise the product or service?

Application
Does your advertisement

- illustrate the relevance of aesthetics to marketing and media by effectively incorporating art for marketing and purposes beyond marketing?

UNIT 6
SOCIAL AND POLITICAL PHILOSOPHY

CHAPTER

18 Introducing Social and Political Philosophy

19 Theories of Social and Political Philosophy

20 The Individual, the Law, and Justice

Unit Expectations

By the end of this unit, you will be able to
- demonstrate an understanding of the main questions, concepts, and theories of social and political philosophy
- evaluate the strengths and weaknesses of the responses to the main questions of social and political philosophy defended by some major philosophers and schools of philosophy, and defend your own responses
- demonstrate the relevance of social and political philosophy to other subjects and everyday life
- correctly use the terminology of social and political philosophy

Everyone lives within a complex social web governed by written and unwritten rules. To survive and thrive in this web, people must weigh their individual rights and responsibilities against the good of both informal social groups and formal social organizations, including the state. This is can be a delicate balancing act that may involve giving up certain rights and taking on certain responsibilities.

But what rights — if any — should people be prepared to relinquish in return for the security of living in an organized state? What are people's responsibilities? What are the just limits of state authority? What is justice — and do people have a right to expect it?

The study of social and political philosophy helps people think about answers to these questions. The answers offered by thinkers in the past affect the lives of people today — and the answers developed today will play an active role in influencing the political and social practices of the future.

Chapter 18
Introducing Social and Political Philosophy

Chapter Expectations

By the end of this chapter, you will be able to
- demonstrate an understanding of some of the main questions of social and political philosophy
- evaluate the responses of major philosophers and major schools of social and political philosophy to some of the main questions of social and political philosophy, making reference to classic texts
- use critical- and logical-thinking skills to develop and defend your own ideas about some of major questions of social and political philosophy, and to anticipate counter-arguments to them
- analyze how theories of social and political philosophy are adopted and realized in contemporary political policy making and how the adoption of a particular theory makes a difference to political and social practices
- demonstrate an understanding of how particular philosophical theories have influenced the development of subjects such as political science, economics, and law

Key Words

social and political philosophy
utopianism
social contract
ideologies
negative freedom
positive freedom
legitimate
egalitarians
liberal individualism
communitarians
categorical imperative
utilitarianism

Key People

Plato
Aristotle
Thomas More
Niccolò Machiavelli
Martin Luther King Jr.
Thomas Hobbes
John Locke
Karl Marx
Charles Taylor
Jean-Jacques Rousseau
John Stuart Mill
Isaiah Berlin

A Philosopher's Voice

The only government that I recognize, is that power that establishes justice, never that which establishes injustice.

Henry David Thoreau (1817–1862)

What Is Social and Political Philosophy?

Why do governments exist? And why must people obey the laws that governments make? What is the best form of government? What makes a good political leader? Why should people care about politics at all? If you have ever asked these questions, you are in excellent company. These are the kinds of questions asked by social and political philosophers.

Both social philosophers and political philosophers are concerned with defining and interpreting concepts like freedom, justice, authority, and democracy, and both apply their ideas to historical and contemporary social and political institutions. Some have focused on justifying the systems that prevailed during their time, while others have depicted imaginary, ideal societies that are quite different from anything that has ever existed.

In fact, **social philosophy and political philosophy** overlap so thoroughly that it is difficult to distinguish between the two and they are often treated as a single area. Both ask questions about how society should be organized to meet people's needs. If there is a difference between the two, it is that political philosophers are interested in probing the nature of the ideal society, while social thinkers pay more attention to the effects on people of various forms of social and political organization.

NATURE AND AIMS OF SOCIAL AND POLITICAL PHILOSOPHY

Just as the interests of social philosophers and political philosophers overlap, so their interests spill over into other areas of philosophy and other disciplines. Some social and political thinkers consider themselves ethicists, for example, because this area of philosophy deals with questions of right and wrong, justice and injustice, and good and bad. In fact, social and political philosophy is sometimes called applied ethics.

Other social and political philosophers deal with topics of concern to political scientists, sociologists, anthropologists, historians, and economists. Like social scientists, who study human behaviour, they are interested in examining and evaluating how human beings have organized themselves into societies and political units. Social and political philosophy is also related to the law, because it deals with issues of justice and the rights and responsibilities of people in society. Because one of the main roles of government is to design laws for citizens, social and political philosophers are concerned with the way laws are made, who has the power to enact and enforce them, what punishments are appropriate for those who violate laws, and whether laws embody fundamental ideals such as justice, fairness, and equity.

Human societies have taken radically different forms over the course of recorded history. Even today, many different social and political systems exist. Social and political philosophers examine and evaluate these systems, analyzing how they function, comparing their strengths and weaknesses, and speculating on the kind of social and political order that would help humans achieve their potential.

Figure 18.1

Many western concepts of social and political philosophy originated in the ancient Greek city of Athens. The word "politics" comes from the Greek word *polis,* which means city and state. To the ancient Greeks, politics meant matters of public concern.

The Philosopher's Approach to Social and Political Philosophy

When social and political philosophers investigate the forms that societies and governments take and have taken, they ask questions like, What are the just limits of state authority? Do people have the right to equal treatment in society? Should citizens be free to do whatever they choose? What are the rights and responsibilities of the citizens of a society? What people make the best leaders, and how should they be selected? What is justice? and What are the proper boundaries between public and private concerns and between public and private morality?

Ever since the ancient Greek philosopher **Plato** struggled in *The Republic* to define the nature of justice, social and political thinkers have sought answers to questions like these. Their answers were often shaped by the times in which they lived. Their theories were — and are — the product of specific historical contexts. Though the answers of these thinkers have sometimes changed radically since the time of the ancient Greeks, many of the questions asked more than 2000 years ago remain relevant today.

What Philosophers Have Said

In the western philosophical tradition, social and political philosophy originated in the thought of Plato and his student **Aristotle**. Both teacher and student were interested in the origins and organization of political societies, the differences between forms of government, the nature of justice, the qualifications of a good ruler, the obligations of citizens to their rulers and to one another, and the ideal form of government.

Plato's ideas, expressed in *The Republic*, were highly speculative and imaginative, while Aristotle's investigations, summarized in *Politics*, were more practical and down-to-earth. Despite the difference in their approaches, the ideas of these two philosophers have had a lasting influence on social and political thought.

In medieval Europe, an important concern of social and political thinkers was the relationship between church and state. They asked whether the pope, the leader of the Roman Catholic Church that dominated Europe at the time, should be the primary authority in people's lives or whether this honour should be accorded to one of the secular, or non-religious, rulers who were emerging as powerful forces. This debate sparked many controversies, as religious and secular leaders struggled to control people's hearts and minds.

In the 15th and 16th centuries, Europe and the rest of the world began undergoing changes that marked the transition to the modern period. The writings of the English philosopher **Thomas More** and the Italian political thinker **Niccolò Machiavelli** demonstrate the conflicting views that prevailed at the beginning of this period. In *Utopia*, published in 1516, More portrayed an imaginary ideal society in which money does not exist. As a result, this society includes no division between rich and poor, and everyone shares equally in its resources.

Along with Plato's much earlier *The Republic*, *Utopia* established a tradition known as **utopianism**. This view sets out people's vision of the ideal state. In the 20th century, writers and philosophers such as Aldous Huxley, Edward Bellamy, and William Morris continued this tradition.

• IDEAS IN CONTEXT •

In 15th- and 16th-century Europe, the ideas of the Renaissance and new scientific ideas challenged traditional ways of thinking. Monarchs began to consolidate their power, establishing centralized systems of government in the countries they ruled. The Protestant Reformation split the religious unity of Europe, triggering a prolonged period of conflict. Voyages of exploration opened up new continents — Africa, Asia, and the Americas — to European traders, merchants, missionaries, and colonists. Feudalism gave way to a dynamic, new mercantile economy, in which towns and cities became important centres of social and commercial life.

Unlike More, Machiavelli had no time for imagining ideal societies. He was far more concerned with the here-and-now political reality of 16th-century Florence, the city that was his home. In *The Prince*, written in 1513, Machiavelli described the unscrupulous political strategies that rulers should follow to gain and hold power over their subjects. He completely rejected traditional religious notions of a good ruler. Instead, he described a world of power politics in which the end justifies the means and rulers are guided by whatever enhances their power to govern firmly and effectively.

Since Machiavelli's time, political realists have adopted his approach to analyzing governments and leaders on the basis of what *is* rather than what *should be*, as well as his cynical view of human nature. Indeed, his approach gave rise to words like "Machiavellian," which describes schemers, or those who use unscrupulous methods to achieve their ends.

Web connection
www.mcgrawhill.ca/links/philosophy12
To find out more about Niccolò Machiavelli, follow the links on this Web site.

Both More and Machiavelli were influenced by the intellectual changes that were occurring during the European Renaissance. Still, their approach to politics and government could hardly have been more different. From More comes the prescriptive tradition of social and political philosophy. Followers of this tradition focus on envisioning an ideal form of government and discussing what should be. Machiavelli, by contrast, is an important founder of the school of political realism, which focuses on what the world is like rather than on what it could be like.

Combined with the changes that were occurring in the 15th and 16th centuries, books like *Utopia* and *The Prince* triggered new approaches to western social and political thought. For the first time since the ancient Greeks, thinkers started to examine governmental institutions from a secular point of view. At the same time, travellers were returning from voyages of exploration with tales that stimulated interest in the forms of government they had encountered in Asia, Africa, and the Americas.

In the 17th and 18th centuries, a new wave of social and political thinkers became interested in explaining the origins of political societies and communities, and in specifying the rights and responsibilities of both rulers and those who were ruled. These thinkers became interested in the idea of a **social contract**. They believed that this unwritten contract, which binds rulers and subjects, explained what happened when human beings departed from their original, or natural, state and gathered in societies. Although these thinkers differed over what this social contract entailed and the kind of government system that best preserved order and fulfilled human needs, their ideas laid the groundwork for modern social and political thought and remain influential today.

By the 19th century, Europe and other parts of the world were undergoing an economic transformation called the Industrial Revolution. As workers demanded greater social, economic, and political rights, governments were forced to address social issues that they had previously ignored. The **ideologies** — beliefs about important economic, social, and political issues — that emerged during this period continue to influence thinkers today.

During the 20th century, these ideologies shaped beliefs about political rights, equality, and the power of the state, and generated mass political movements that sought to act on them. Women, workers, and non-Europeans living under European rule began to demand a

> **IDEAS IN CONTEXT**
>
> The Industrial Revolution, which began in England in the late 18th century, sparked the growth of cities, the expansion of factories, and the creation of two powerful new social classes in Europe: a middle class of businesspeople and professionals and a working class of factory employees. In addition, events like the French Revolution of 1789 sparked new ways of thinking about economic, social, and political issues. Ideas that emerged at this time continue to influence political thought.

greater voice in society. In many countries, oppressed minorities began to demand equal opportunity and equal treatment. In the United States, for example, Martin Luther King Jr. led a campaign of non-violent civil disobedience that sparked changes in laws that had entrenched racial segregation.

Web connection
www.mcgrawhill.ca/links/philosophy12
To find out more about Martin Luther King Jr., follow the links on this Web site.

At the same time, revolutions upset traditional regimes in many countries and served as examples for others to follow. New ideologies, such as communism and fascism, emerged and found influential advocates in countries around the world. Because of this, the 20th century is sometimes called the age of political ideology.

Much of the social and political thought of the last half of the 20th century was influenced by the Cold War. This ideological conflict pitted democratic capitalist governments led by the United States against communist governments led by the Union of Soviet Socialist Republics. During this time, many newly independent states sought a path that combined elements of both democratic capitalism and communism.

When communism collapsed in many parts of the world in the 1990s, however, it marked the beginning of a new era. Unchallenged economically, politically, and militarily, the United States emerged as the world's only superpower. As a result, the American political thinker Francis Fukuyama, a supporter of the democratic capitalist system, claimed that the post-Cold War period represented the "end of history," the final defeat of alternatives to this dominant ideology.

At the same time, however, nationalism was reasserting itself, sometimes violently, in various parts of the world as rival ethnic groups struggled for power. Various forms of religious fundamentalism also took on a political shape, with extremely violent consequences. In addition, new political and social movements like feminism, environmentalism, postmodernism, neo-conservatism, communitarianism, and anti-globalization began to emerge and engage the attention of a new generation of social and political thinkers and activists.

The rapid changes of the late 20th and early 21st centuries have had important effects on social and political philosophy around the world. Some ideologies have been either abandoned or transformed radically, while new ways of thinking about society and politics have appeared.

Recall...Reflect...Respond

1. What common concerns unite social and political philosophers? How do their approaches differ?
2. Sketch a timeline showing the evolution of western social and political thought.
3. Next to each era on your timeline, fill in a question that dominated social and political thought during the period. Justify your choice with a logical explanation.

How Philosophers Have Said It

Social and political thinkers have always tried to define key concepts like freedom, equality, justice, the state, rights, and democracy. They have also tried to assess specific social and political arrangements in light of these concepts.

In *The Republic*, the first question Plato asked was, What is justice? To this ancient Greek philosopher and many political thinkers since his time, this is a fundamental question because justice is the foundation of a society's value system. People expect to be treated fairly, with rewards and punishments allotted to those who deserve them. Every form of government

PROFILE
Martin Luther King Jr.
A Moral Responsibility to Disobey Unjust Laws

When Martin Luther King Jr. was born in Atlanta, Georgia, in 1929, racial segregation was enshrined in the laws of many American states. Black people were prevented from doing many things that are taken for granted today. They could not attend certain schools, for example, and were either barred from entering certain restaurants and theatres or were forced to sit in designated areas.

Both King's father and grandfather had been preachers, and King's family was able to afford to send him to university. He earned degrees in theology and philosophy before carrying on the family tradition and becoming a Baptist minister himself.

While at university, King pored over the works of the 19th-century American philosopher Henry David Thoreau and the 20th-century Indian leader Mohandas Gandhi, absorbing their messages about civil disobedience and non-violence as methods of political protest. The young man became convinced that black Americans should adopt these methods to challenge the laws that promoted racial segregation.

One of King's first political campaigns was a bus boycott in Montgomery, Alabama, where he was the minister of a local congregation. The bus company's regulations required black passengers to sit at the back of buses and to give up their seats to white people who requested this. King led black residents of Montgomery — and their white supporters — in a mass boycott of the buses and eventually succeeded in forcing the local government to change its discriminatory public transit policies.

Inspired by this success, King engaged in a number of campaigns in various southern states to bring segregation to an end and quickly became the leader of the national black civil rights movement. In April 1963, he was arrested and jailed in Birmingham, Alabama, for staging an illegal parade after local authorities had refused to grant him a permit. While in prison, he wrote his famous "Letter from Birmingham Jail," a response to a group of white religious leaders who had criticized his non-violent civil disobedience campaign. In this letter, he distinguished between just and unjust laws:

> One may well ask: "How can you advocate breaking some laws and obeying others?" The answer lies in the fact that there are ... two types of laws: just and unjust. I would be the first to advocate obeying just laws. One has not only a legal but also a moral responsibility to obey just laws. Conversely, one has a moral responsibility to disobey unjust laws. I would agree with St. Augustine, who wrote, "An unjust law is no law at all."

King's letter quickly became a rallying cry for the civil rights movement, and it is often quoted by those who believe that non-violent civil disobedience is an effective means of promoting social and political change.

A few months after the Birmingham Jail incident, King led the famous 1963 March on Washington. There, he delivered his most famous speech — "I Have A Dream" — to half a million people. In 1964, he was awarded the Nobel Peace Prize for his efforts to promote equality. He became an internationally renowned campaigner for human rights. The civil rights movement prompted U.S. President Lyndon Johnson to enact the Civil Rights and Voting Rights Acts in 1964 and 1965. These measures effectively ended racial segregation in the southern states, but did little to alleviate other forms of racial oppression endured by blacks.

By the late 1960s, King had become disheartened by the slow pace of social change, especially in the northern states, where many blacks lived in poverty-stricken, violent ghettos. He came to believe that the movement for black civil rights must be broadened to include a multi-racial assault on economic, social, and political inequality.

While leading a campaign in support of striking public sanitation workers in Memphis, Tennessee, in April 1968, King was assassinated by a white extremist. The killing triggered a wave of racial upheavals across the United States. Enraged by the murder of their greatest champion, blacks expressed their fury and frustration at a system that continued to deny them equal opportunity and equal treatment.

Figure 18.2

Martin Luther King Jr. delivers his famous "I Have a Dream" speech in Washington, D.C. King was dedicated to non-violent actions as a means of promoting social and political change.

establishes a system of laws that impose punishment on those who violate them. But many thinkers also maintain that justice should be more than a system of laws. They view it as a way of apportioning the benefits of social co-operation, such as material well-being, among the members of a society. Social and political thinkers investigate how laws and other institutions can enhance ideals of social co-operation.

Freedom and equality are two important terms in social and political philosophy. Freedom, or liberty, refers to the condition of being an autonomous individual, someone who has the right to make choices without being constrained by others. It also means being able to act on these choices. Social and political thinkers frequently distinguish between two kinds of freedom: negative and positive. Negative freedom refers to freedom from physical or emotional coercion, or force. No person, institution, or government can pressure someone to act in a certain way. Positive freedom refers to people's power to control their own lives and to make their own decisions.

> *Justice to me is a warm spirit, born of tolerance and wisdom, present everywhere, ready to serve the highest purposes of rational man. To seek to create the just society must be amongst the highest of these human purposes.*
>
> – Pierre Elliott Trudeau

Equality is a term that has meant different things to political thinkers at various times. In many obvious respects, of course, people are not equal. Some are physically stronger, while some may be more intelligent than others. Still, contemporary democratic societies tend to agree that people should be treated equally. This usually involves legal, political, social, and economic equality. In democratic states like Canada, equality before the law is guaranteed, and people's legal and political rights are set out in the Canadian Charter of Rights and Freedoms.

Though the term "state" usually refers to people who live in an organized political community within certain geographic boundaries, many social and political thinkers consider states fictitious entities that have no separate existence of their own.

Still, most of the world is now divided into nation states that claim sovereignty over the people living within their borders. Sovereignty is the absolute right of a state to rule over those who live in it. A sovereign state has the right to tax, make and enforce laws, punish wrongdoers, defend the country from attack, protect the freedom of its citizens, and promote their well-being by implementing social and economic policies.

A state's power is considered legitimate, or worthy of respect and obedience, when its leaders have gained power by the consent of the people, when leaders exercise their power fairly and with restraint, and when they can remain in power only as long as a majority of citizens wish them to. When these conditions are met, the state is considered a democracy, a word that comes from Greek and means rule by the people.

Why Social and Political Philosophy Matters

The questions that social and political philosophers investigate are related to other areas of philosophy, including ethics and the philosophy of science. They are also linked to other disciplines such as history, ethics, the law, political science, and sociology. All these fields are concerned with human societies and the people and groups that compose them.

Social and political thinkers often provide general theoretical interpretations and perspectives that help provide a broader context for the specific issues dealt with by other disciplines. In recent years, for example, forms of religious and ethnic nationalism have emerged as strong and sometimes violent political forces, touching off serious international crises. Social and political philosophers who have studied nationalism and its links to religion and ethnicity are in a position to offer important insights that can help policy makers and others understand the cultural contexts and issues that explain upheavals like these.

Why Do States Exist?

Since the time of the ancient Greeks, social and political thinkers have grappled with questions about why states exist as political entities, how their authority can be justified, and what limits, if any, should be placed on their power.

STATE JUSTIFICATION

What gives any government the authority to make decisions for its citizens? This question underlies all others about the power of states. And like most philosophical questions, it is the subject of fierce debate.

Plato was one of the first to explore this question. In his view, the authority of the state can best be justified if those who rule are chosen from among the "best" people in society. From this principle, he developed his theory of philosopher kings, a group of specially trained people who would be the guardians of the state.

Aristotle, by contrast, believed that the state can be justified according to how effectively it incorporates the best features of the three kinds of government he analyzed:

- monarchy (a state governed by a monarch)
- aristocracy (a state governed by a small group of people)
- democracy (a state governed by the people).

In the 17th century, the English thinkers **Thomas Hobbes** and **John Locke** also developed theories that explored the justification for state authority. In Hobbes' view, the state provided the only protection against the innate tendencies of human beings to resort to violence in their social arrangements. He believed that the state's authority must be absolute to ensure peace and order in a society.

Locke took a different view. He believed that the state could justify its authority over its subjects only if it respected and defended their natural rights. In Locke's view, people had natural rights to life, liberty, and property. If rulers infringed these rights, he said, the state lost its legitimacy, and the people were justified in rebelling against it.

In contemporary western democracies, many social and political philosophers believe that the state's claim to legitimacy should also have an ethical dimension. In their view, a state cannot demand obedience from its citizens only because its authority is based on historical tradition, a written constitution, or a legal system. They say that a state must work toward achieving goals that involve the good of all members of society, demonstrating that its actions are worthy of respect as well as obedience.

JUST LIMITS OF STATE AUTHORITY

If a state can claim that its authority is legitimate and that it therefore deserves the respect and obedience of its citizens, what limits — if any — should be placed on its power? Hobbes said that the answer was none, while Locke argued that the state must respect the natural rights of its citizens.

Most contemporary democratic states are governed according to rules set out in written constitutions or by unwritten understandings and agreements that have developed over time. These written and unwritten agreements impose what are usually considered just and reasonable limits on the power of the state.

Though the powers of democratic states such as Canada are limited, most governments have the power to suspend citizens' rights in specific exceptional circumstances, such as war or a national emergency. Some social and political philosophers argue that the state is justified in assuming these sweeping powers in the interests of protecting national security. Others have criticized these powers, saying that they violate the spirit of democracy by giving the state too much power — power that it might be tempted to abuse.

> ### Recall...Reflect...Respond
> 1. What is the difference between positive and negative freedoms? Provide examples from your own life to support your explanations.
> 2. How well do you think the Canadian state promotes justice, freedom, and equality? Explain your views in a short personal reflection.
> 3. Which theory or theories justifying state authority might the Canadian government cite to claim legitimacy? Explain your response.

THE INDIVIDUAL AND THE STATE

Underlying the debate over justification for state authority is the issue of individual rights and responsibilities and whether the state or the individual is more important. This debate often focuses on four areas: equality and the distribution of goods; equal opportunity and equal treatment; freedom, individualism, and just limits on behaviour; and crime and punishment.

EQUALITY AND THE DISTRIBUTION OF GOODS

Since ancient times, some thinkers have dreamed of a society of complete equality. In *The Republic*, Plato imagined rulers who possessed no personal property and could not, therefore, be corrupted by the desire to acquire material possessions. He believed that if leaders could not be corrupted, they would use their political power to promote the well-being of citizens rather than for their own enrichment.

More's *Utopia* envisaged an ideal society in which private property would be unknown. And more recently, socialist and communist thinkers such as **Karl Marx** have championed the ideal of social and economic equality for the poor, the exploited, and the dispossessed. Philosophers such as Marx accused the rich of gaining their wealth by oppressing working people.

> *Wherever there is great property, there is great inequality. For one very rich man, there must be at least 500 poor.*
> – Adam Smith

People who support the idea of the state's stepping in to correct the inequalities of society and promote economic and social justice are called **egalitarians**. Though egalitarians do not claim that everyone is completely equal in every respect, they do insist that people should be treated equally when it comes to legal, political, social, and economic rights. In practice, this means that egalitarians support giving everyone roughly equal access to basic social benefits like money, education, housing, health care, employment, and political influence.

Even the most extreme egalitarians have never proposed a society in which there is absolutely no difference in the income or wealth of its members. Still, many of those who promote social and political equality advocate government intervention to redistribute wealth and reduce extreme differences between rich and poor. They believe that this can be achieved if governments exercise their power to tax. They say that those with high incomes should be taxed at a much higher rate than those with lower incomes and that tax revenues should be used to benefit the poor. Critics call this the "Robin Hood" version of egalitarianism, describing it as stealing from the rich to give to the poor.

Some egalitarians also advocate a guaranteed annual income, or at least the provision of generous social programs like health care, education, pensions, employment insurance, and welfare. They believe that measures like these would ensure that no one falls below a minimum economic level, known as the poverty line.

Supporters of egalitarianism include traditional socialists like Marx and contemporary social democratic thinkers like Charles Taylor and G.E. Cohen. They believe the egalitarian approach is morally right because it would reduce social inequities by enabling the poor to participate more fully in social life. It would also enable the poor to more fully realize their existing legal and political rights.

Egalitarians believe that greater economic equality will benefit everyone, not just the poor. If poverty is reduced, they say, there will be less violence, crime, homelessness, and social tension. They attribute these ills to the division of society into two groups — the haves (those who have wealth) and the have-nots (those who do not have wealth) — and the hostility that this division creates. If economic inequality is reduced and everyone has roughly equal access to society's resources, egalitarians say that this will improve social solidarity and opportunities for people to reach their potential, no matter what their socio-economic background.

Critics of egalitarianism, such as the Austrian philosopher Friedrich Hayek and the American economist Milton Friedman, argue that it will not work because human nature will prevent it. Even if a government enacted measures to guarantee basic economic and social equality, they maintain that the arrangement would not last. Though some people might use their money for productive purposes such as getting an education or starting a business, they say that others would squander it on material things, drugs, or alcohol.

Critics argue that the only way of maintaining an egalitarian system is to grant the state sweeping powers to regulate nearly every aspect of social, political, and economic life. They charge that this amounts to a form of communism. The collapse of the Soviet Union and other communist states at the end of the Cold War in the late 1980s and early 1990s fuelled their arguments. Anti-egalitarians view the fall of these states as conclusive proof that social engineering in the name of promoting equality cannot work.

Anti-egalitarians also maintain that capitalism, a system in which the means of production is privately owned and people have an opportunity to get ahead through hard work and investment, is the most efficient and practical way of structuring a nation's economy. Friedman, for example, maintains that freedom is inseparable from capitalism, even if its consequences are social inequality and great differences in people's personal wealth.

Opponents of egalitarianism also believe that the private ownership of property is a basic right, which the state has a duty to defend. Locke argued that the right to property is one of the three key natural rights that human beings possessed even before they began developing organized forms of government. In Locke's view, a government that tries to infringe the property rights of its subjects is acting unjustly, and this frees citizens of their obligation to obey the government's laws.

Locke's idea of property rights has been challenged by various thinkers who have suggested that this right was an early form of expropriation or theft. The 18th-century French political philosopher Jean-Jacques Rousseau, for example, claimed that the origins of all forms of inequality and injustice in society can be traced to the establishment of the idea of private property.

> *Property is theft.*
> – Pierre Joseph Proudhon

EQUAL OPPORTUNITY AND EQUAL TREATMENT

Egalitarian political philosophers also promote equal opportunity and equal treatment for all members of society, regardless of their race, religion, cultural background, age, sex, or sexual orientation. In the egalitarian view, equality of opportunity and equal treatment do not mean that everyone can expect to do whatever she or he wants, regardless of qualifications, training, knowledge, and experience. Rather, it means that anyone with the appropriate qualifications to, for example, perform a job or gain entrance to an educational institution should receive equal consideration.

Though support for the ideas of equal opportunity and equal treatment is widespread today, this has not always been the case. For most of recorded western history, for example, women were considered inferior to men and were barred from playing a significant role in public life. Contemporary feminists have drawn attention to this historical inequity and have been strong advocates of greater opportunities for women, especially in the areas of education and employment.

Women were not the only oppressed group in ancient and medieval times. Slavery was a widespread, sanctioned institution. Slaves had no political, social, or economic rights and were considered property. They were compelled to perform the most basic kinds of work for the benefit of the social elite. In ancient times, political thinkers like Aristotle justified slavery by maintaining that some people were superior to others. And when European states began establishing colonies in other parts of the world in the 16th and 17th centuries, they did not hesitate to treat non-Europeans as inferiors. Non-Europeans were often enslaved, dispossessed, massacred, and subjected to harsh colonial rule.

For most of history, the idea that people should be able to rise to the limit of their abilities was seen as absurd and impractical, if not dangerous and subversive. This situation began to change during the 17th and 18th centuries, when enlightened thinkers such as Locke, Rousseau, Thomas Paine, and others began to advocate greater equality. Their ideas sparked violent revolutions in countries such as the United States and France and quieter revolutions in places such as England. At first, the call for equal rights was meant to apply only to adult white males, however. Not until the 19th and 20th centuries was this idea expanded to include women, non-whites, and other previously marginalized or exploited groups in society.

> **IDEAS IN CONTEXT**
>
> Though Plato favoured a ruling elite, this ancient Greek philosopher also challenged prevailing notions about the inferiority of women. He believed that membership in the elite should not be restricted to men. In *The Republic*, he argued that it was wrong for society to deny young women the educational opportunities granted as a matter of course to young men. Doing so, he said, deprived society of the potential abilities of half the human race. In his view, philosopher kings, the wise rulers of society, could just as easily be philosopher queens. This view was not popular during Plato's time — or for more than 2000 years afterward.

One of the ways greater equality of opportunity has been realized today is through systems of free public education, at least to the end of high school. This has made it possible for people of all socio-economic backgrounds to gain the necessary training, skills, and knowledge to assume a wide variety of positions in society.

Still, in most western countries, a university education remains costly, and many young people are unable to afford the education required to enter highly skilled professions. Until well into the 20th century, women and other groups were either barred completely or actively discouraged from entering fields such as law, medicine, and engineering. Although women have made much progress in recent years, members of visible minority groups in Canada and elsewhere are often underrepresented in important areas of economic, social, and political life.

Figure 18.3

Even today, slavery has not been abolished everywhere. In 2000, a photographer took this picture of women scraping salt from the floor of an ancient lake in Mauritania. Though Mauritania officially abolished slavery in the 20th century, many of these women labourers are slaves.

PHILOSOPHY IN ACTION

The Politics of Recognition

by Charles Taylor

Charles Taylor is a Canadian political philosopher who teaches at McGill University in Montreal. Dedicated to finding a balance between individual and collective rights, Taylor maintains that understanding philosophical arguments requires people to be aware of the origins of these arguments, the contexts in which they were interpreted, and the way their meanings have been transformed over time. To help readers appreciate the forces that have shaped the ideas of political thinkers, Taylor often reconstructs history. This excerpt is from an essay titled "The Politics of Recognition," which appeared in *Multiculturalism: Examining the Politics of Recognition*. It explores the significance of multiculturalism in societies like Canada's.

A number of strands in contemporary politics turn on the need, sometimes the demand, for *recognition*. The need, it can be argued, is one of the driving forces behind nationalist movements in politics. And the demand comes to the fore in a number of ways in today's politics, on behalf of minority ... groups, in some forms of feminism, and in what is today called the politics of "multi-culturalism."

The demand for recognition in these latter cases is given urgency by the supposed links between recognition and identity, where the latter term designates something like a person's understanding of who they are, of their fundamental defining characteristics as a human being. The thesis is that our identity is partly shaped by recognition or its absence, often by the misrecognition of others, and so a person or group of people can suffer real damage, real distortion, if the people or society around them mirror back to them a confining or demeaning or contemptible picture of themselves. Nonrecognition or misrecognition can inflict harm, can be a form of oppression, imprisoning someone in a false, distorted, and reduced mode of being.

Thus, some feminists have argued that women in patriarchal societies have been induced to adopt a depreciatory image of themselves. They have internalized a picture of their own inferiority, so that even when some of the objective obstacles to their advancement fall away, they may be incapable of taking advantage of the new opportunities. And beyond this, they are condemned to suffer the pain of low self-esteem. An analogous point has been made in relation to blacks: that white society has for generations projected a demeaning image of them, which some of them have been unable to resist adopting. Their own self-depreciation, on this view, becomes one of the most potent instruments of their own oppression. Their first task ought to be to purge themselves of this imposed and destructive identity. Recently, a similar point has been made in relation to indigenous and colonized people in general. It is held that since 1492 Europeans have projected an image of such people as somehow inferior, "uncivilized," and through the force of conquest have often been able to impose this image on the conquered....

Within these perspectives, misrecognition shows not just a lack of due respect. It can inflict a grievous wound, saddling its victims with a crippling self-hatred. Due recognition is not just a courtesy we owe people. It is a vital human need....

But the importance of recognition has been modified and intensified by the new understanding of individual identity that emerges at the end of the 18th century. We might speak of an *individualized* identity, one that is particular to me, and that I discover in myself. This notion arises along with an ideal, that of being true to myself and my own particular way of being....

This new idea of authenticity was, like the idea of dignity, also in part an offshoot of the decline of hierarchical society. In those earlier societies, what we would now call identity was largely fixed by one's social position. That is, the background that explained what people recognized as important to themselves was to a great extent determined by their place in society, and whatever roles or activities attached to this position. The birth of democratic society doesn't by itself do away with this phenomenon, because people can still define themselves by their social roles. What does decisively undermine this socially derived identification, however, is the ideal of authenticity itself. As this emerges ... it calls on me to discover my own original way of being. By definition, this way of being cannot be socially derived, but must be inwardly generated....

The importance of recognition is now universally acknowledged in one form or another; on an intimate plane, we are all aware of how identity can be formed or malformed through the course of our contact with significant others. On the social plane, we have a continuing politics of equal recognition. Both planes have been shaped by the growing ideal of authenticity, and recognition plays an essential role in the culture that has arisen around this ideal.

On the intimate level, we can see how much an original identity needs and is vulnerable to the recognition given or withheld by significant others. It is not surprising that in the culture of authenticity, relationships are seen as the key loci of self-discovery and self-affirmation. Love relationships are not just important because of the general emphasis in modern culture on the fulfillments of ordinary needs. They are also crucial because they are the crucibles of inwardly generated identity.

On the social plane, the understanding that identities are formed in open dialogue, unshaped by a predefined social script, has made the politics of equal recognition more central and stressful. It has, in fact, considerably raised the stakes. Equal recognition is not just the appropriate mode for a healthy democratic society. Its refusal can inflict damage on those who are denied it, according to a widespread modern view.… The projection of an inferior or demeaning image on another can actually distort and oppress, to the extent that the image is internalized. Not only contemporary feminism but also race relations and discussions of multiculturalism are undergirded by the premise that the withholding of recognition can be a form of oppression. We may debate whether this factor has been exaggerated, but it is clear that the understanding of identity and authenticity has introduced a new dimension into the politics of equal recognition, which now operates with something like its own notion of authenticity, at least so far as the denunciation of other-induced distortions is concerned.…

This brings us to the issue of multiculturalism as it is often debated today, which has a lot to do with the imposition of some cultures on others, and with the assumed superiority that powers this imposition. Western liberal societies are thought to be supremely guilty in this regard, partly because of their colonial past, and partly because of their marginalization of segments of their populations that stem from other cultures. It is in this context that the reply "this is how we do things here" can seem crude and insensitive. Even if, in the nature of things, compromise is close to impossible here — one either forbids murder or allows it — the attitude presumed by the reply is seen as one of contempt. Often, in fact, this presumption is correct. Thus we arrive again at the issue of recognition.…

[The demand] we are looking at here is that we all recognize the equal value of different cultures; that we not only let them survive, but acknowledge their worth.

What sense can be made of this demand? In a way, it has been operative in an unformulated state for some time. The politics of nationalism has been powered for well over a century in part by the sense that people have had of being despised or respected by others around them. Multinational societies can break up, in large part because of a lack of (perceived) recognition of equal worth of one group by another. That is at present, I believe, the case in Canada — though my diagnosis will certainly be challenged by some. On the international scene, the tremendous sensitivity of certain supposedly closed societies to world opinion … attests to the importance of external recognition.…

There is perhaps after all a moral issue here. We only need a sense of our own limited part in the whole human story to accept the presumption. It is only arrogance, or some analogous moral failing, that can deprive us of this. But what the presumption requires of us is not peremptory and inauthentic judgments of equal value, but a willingness to be open to comparative cultural study of the kind that must displace our horizons in the resulting fusions. What it requires above all is an admission that we are very far away from that ultimate horizon from which the relative worth of different cultures might be evident.

Source: Taylor, Charles, *Multiculturalism: Examining the Politics of Recognition*. Copyright © 1992, expanded 1994 by Princeton University Press. Reprinted by permission of Princeton University Press.

1. What does Charles Taylor mean when he uses the term "misrecognition"?
2. How do your relationships with others affect your self-recognition and your understanding of your own identity?
3. What conclusion does Taylor draw about the future of Canada's multicultural society? Do you agree or disagree? Why?

FREEDOM, INDIVIDUALISM, AND JUST LIMITS ON BEHAVIOUR

The 19th-century English political thinker **John Stuart Mill** was a strong advocate of individual freedom. In *On Liberty*, he argued that the state has no right to involve itself in the private affairs of citizens. As long as people's actions do not harm others, said Mill, the government has no business restricting what people do. Mill illustrated his point by using illegal drugs as an example. He acknowledged that a state might have the right to ban the production of illegal drugs because of their negative effects on society. At the same time, he said that a government does not have the right to prevent individuals from using them because the negative consequences affect only the user.

Mill's distinction between the public good and an individual's freedom to make his or her own choices sometimes leads to difficulties and contradictions. In Mill's view, the government's duty is to prevent people from becoming drug addicts. If people have already chosen this path, however, he said the state has no right to interfere, as long as this choice is causing no direct harm to others.

Mill was an influential advocate of **liberal individualism**. This ideology, which he championed and which gained considerable support in western democracies during Mill's time and in the 20th century, championed the rights of the individual as one of the most important values in society. Liberalism's favouring of individual rights over the rights of the group has been challenged by communitarians such as Charles Taylor. **Communitarians** argue that the rights of collectivities, or larger social groups, should sometimes prevail over those of individual members of society.

Thinkers like the African political philosopher Kwame Gyekye and others who come from a non-western philosophical tradition, tend to emphasize group rights over individual freedom. Communitarians would respond to Mill's defence of the right of drug addicts to pursue their addiction by arguing that their lifestyle choice does harm society as a whole and should therefore be prevented. This is because addicts might turn to crime to gain the money needed to support their habit or pose a health hazard to others as a result of it.

In addition, communitarians might claim that society has the right to limit the self-destructive behaviour of certain individuals for the good of both the individual and the group. In this way, communitarians transform negative freedom into positive freedom and uphold the principle that the state has the right — and even the responsibility — to promote particular forms of desirable behaviour among its citizens, while preventing them from carrying out actions that are harmful to themselves and others.

In the 20th century, the Latvian-born English political philosopher **Isaiah Berlin** took a different view. He argued that it is important for governments to extend the scope of citizens' negative freedom while refraining from instituting policies that encourage positive freedom. In Berlin's view, a government's promotion of positive freedom could develop into a form of social coercion in which people are pressured to behave in certain ways — for their own good and that of society as a whole.

A strong critic of totalitarian regimes such as Nazi Germany and the Soviet Union under Stalin, Berlin said that these governments abused their power by promoting their ideas of desirable behaviour. To Berlin and others who support his position, even state policies like

Figure 18.4

In 1997, protesters gathered in Toronto city council chambers to oppose plans to ban smoking in restaurants. Where do you think these protesters would stand on issues of negative and positive freedom?

encouraging physical fitness or discouraging smoking are suspect. If policies like these are promoted zealously, they could threaten people's ability to exercise freedom of choice.

When the hippies of the 1960s demanded the right to do their own thing, they probably had some combination of negative and positive freedom in mind. At that time, many governments in North America and Europe began increasing the scope of citizens' freedoms by relaxing or even abolishing laws that had restricted the use of soft drugs, banned abortion, and limited certain forms of expression and sexual behaviour.

During this period, a new prosperity combined with a relaxing of traditional religious and cultural taboos against some kinds of unconventional behaviour to enhance people's positive freedom. More people came to feel empowered and entitled to openly pursue the lifestyle of their choice. This was particularly true of homosexuals, who had once suffered considerable harassment and social rejection. They began to feel greater acceptance in society. Despite these changes, liberal individualists and communitarians continue to debate whether negative or positive freedom is more beneficial for people.

Recall...Reflect...Respond

1. How well do your school's policies embody the ideas of equality, equal opportunity, and individual freedom? Explain, using examples for support.
2. With a partner, choose a current social or political issue. Decide how a liberal individualist and a communitarian would approach the issue. Debate the issue from these two points of view.
3. Draw a continuum with negative freedom at one end and positive freedom at the other. Consider four social issues: recycling, smoking, using illegal drugs, and eating meat. Decide whether each issue is better handled by promoting negative or positive freedom and locate your position on each issue on the continuum. Over all, would you say that you favour handling issues by promoting negative or positive freedom?

CRIME AND PUNISHMENT

One of the state's most important powers is to impose punishment on those who have been convicted of committing crimes. Since ancient times, social and political thinkers have argued that laws are necessary to preserve social order and to prevent society from reverting to violence and chaos. Every society has recognized the need for laws, which everyone is expected to obey, and every society has established punishments that can be administered to those who fail to obey them. The right of the state to impose penalties on those who commit crimes is widely accepted.

Still, actions that are defined as crimes, as well as the punishments meted out, have varied considerably throughout history. Even today, considerable variation exists from country to country and culture to culture.

Many social and political thinkers have struggled with questions relating to crime and punishment. One of the most fundamental is, On what basis is the state's power to punish wrongdoers justified?

Though various thinkers have offered answers to this difficult question, most have been influenced by one of the two major schools of ethical philosophy: Immanuel Kant's categorical imperative and utilitarianism.

Kant proposed the **categorical imperative** as an ideal of personal ethical conduct to which everyone should aspire. An imperative is a command or rule, while categorical means absolute. The categorical imperative, then, is a rule that is absolute. It must always be obeyed. In Kant's view, this meant that when making a moral choice, people must choose the course of action that they would want everyone to choose all the time. Take stealing, for example. Kant would say that to decide whether stealing is the morally right choice, you must test your choice by asking whether stealing should become a universal law. Is it something that everyone should always do? If your answer is yes, then you must agree that everyone can steal all the time. If the answer is no, then stealing is always wrong. In Kant's view, actions that are wrong deserve punishment.

This view was challenged in the late 18th and 19th centuries by **utilitarianism**, an ethical theory advocated by philosophers such as Jeremy Bentham and Mill. The word "utilitarian" refers to usefulness, and utilitarians say that people should act in a way that produces the greatest good for the greatest number. As a result, they believe that punishing criminals is justified only if the punishment benefits society as a whole.

RETRIBUTION

Retributionists — those who believe that actions lead to retribution, which may be either an appropriate reward or punishment — endorse the Kantian idea that those who violate the law should be punished. To support their position, retributionists often cite the Old Testament verse that says, "An eye for an eye, and a tooth for a tooth." In other words, they believe that the punishment should fit the crime. Jewish, Christian, and Islamic religious leaders have tended to support this position, which was originally set out in the Babylonian Code of Hammurabi, which dates to the second millennium BCE.

In general, retributionists support imposing a punishment that reflects the crime committed. They often favour capital punishment for murderers, for example, because they believe that someone who has knowingly taken the life of another deserves to forfeit his or her own.

Historically, the principle of retribution was the foundation of many penal systems, and it is still a component of many contemporary systems. Many people support the retributionist view that lawbreakers should pay for their crimes by suffering harsh punishment, regardless of the benefit to society.

The retributionist view, which prevailed for at least 2000 years, was challenged in the 18th century by legal reformers such as the Italian thinker Cesare Beccaria, who advocated a more humane penal system. Since then, critics of retributionism have argued that it appeals to one of the basest human motives: revenge. Supporting the idea that vengeance is appropriate, say critics, brutalizes the state, reducing it to the same level as the criminal. They say that retribution imposed by the state is little different from the primitive blood feud, in which members of a crime victim's family took revenge on the offender's family.

Distrust all men in whom the impulse to punish is powerful.

– Friedrich Nietzsche

Critics also argue that retribution fails to deal with the consequences of crime. They say that if retribution, or revenge, is the sole motive for punishment, this does little to address important questions such as, Will the punishment deter the criminal from committing another offence? Will it deter others from committing similar offences? and Will it benefit society? Because many thinkers now recognize that these are complex questions that cannot be answered with a simple yes or no, most contemporary states have developed different approaches to structuring their legal systems. Still, elements of retributionism remain in practice today.

DETERRENCE

Those who believe that the goal of punishment should be to deter criminals and discourage crime often use utilitarian arguments. They maintain that society benefits when a criminal who is punished severely reconsiders before committing another crime and risking the same — or worse — punishment. This principle is sometimes offered to support capital punishment, the most serious penalty imposed by some states. If a convicted killer is executed, say advocates of the death penalty, society can be certain that he or she will never again take a life. They also maintain that severe punishment can act as an example to other criminals who might be tempted to commit similar offences.

Those who take this position believe that deterrence helps protect society from criminals. Whether the offender receives a punishment appropriate to the crime is not an important issue for advocates of deterrence. But does deterrence work? Statistics produced in the United States, where many states continue to impose the death penalty, have been cited to prove that capital punishment does little or nothing to reduce the murder rate in these jurisdictions. And since Canada abolished the death penalty in 1976, the homicide rate in this country has declined. In 2000, for example, 542 homicides were committed in Canada. This is 159 fewer than were committed in 1975, the year before capital punishment was abolished. The United States also has the highest rate of imprisonment in the western world, yet that country also has the highest rate of violent offences. Critics of deterrence cite statistics like these to support their belief that this theory of justice does not work.

REHABILITATION AND REFORM

The idea of using punishment to encourage wrongdoers to reform their criminal ways is a relatively late development in legal theory. Until quite recently, criminals were viewed as morally incorrigible, unlikely to change their ways. For this reason, capital punishment, long prison sentences, and harsh prison conditions were considered suitable penalties.

Influenced by the research of psychologists, sociologists, and others, however, many contemporary thinkers take a more optimistic view of the possibility of rehabilitating wrongdoers. They believe that the prison sentences imposed as a form of punishment should also be viewed as an opportunity to encourage criminals to reform.

Figure 18.5

"You were hungry? Case dismissed."

Which theory of crime and punishment does the judge in this case support?

In the view of those who support this approach, it serves two worthwhile purposes. First, it benefits individual criminals, who will stop engaging in anti-social and self-destructive behaviour and will become functioning, productive members of society. Second, it protects society by reducing the likelihood that these offenders will commit more crimes when they are released from prison. Supporters say that consistent efforts to rehabilitate criminals, combined with social policies that address the causes of crime, such as poverty and social injustice, will make society not only safer, but also more humane and civilized.

The reformist position has been challenged by those who question what they believe is its optimistic view of human nature. Though it may be possible to reform some criminals, especially first offenders or young people, they say, others are incorrigible, unable to be corrected. They argue that criminals like this should be imprisoned for life and that the resources of the state should not be wasted in futile attempts to rehabilitate them. In response, reformists argue that the number of criminals who might be considered incorrigible is quite small when compared to the large number of offenders who are candidates for rehabilitation. They also say that new discoveries in brain chemistry and the treatment of mental disorders raise the possibility of finding treatments for even the most violent and anti-social criminals.

Web connection
www.mcgrawhill.ca/links/philosophy12
To find out more about the myths and realities of crime and punishment in Canada today, follow the links on this Web site.

Chapter Review

Chapter Summary

This chapter has discussed
- some of the main questions of social and political philosophy
- the responses of major philosophers and major schools of social and political philosophy to some of the main questions of social and political philosophy, making reference to classic texts
- how theories of social and political philosophy are adopted and realized in contemporary political policy making and how the adoption of a particular theory makes a difference to political and social practices
- how particular philosophical theories have influenced the development of subjects such as political science, economics, and law

Knowledge and Understanding

1. Identify and explain the significance to the study of social and political philosophy of each of the following key words and people.

Key Words	Key People
social and political philosophy	Plato
utopianism	Aristotle
social contract	Thomas More
ideologies	Niccolò Machiavelli
negative freedom	Martin Luther King Jr.
positive freedom	Thomas Hobbes
legitimate	John Locke
egalitarians	Karl Marx
liberal individualism	Charles Taylor
communitarians	Jean-Jacques Rousseau
categorical imperative	John Stuart Mill
utilitarianism	Isaiah Berlin

2. On a chart like the following, summarize the theories that address the philosophical questions raised in this chapter.

Main Philosophical Questions	Main Philosophical Theories	Philosophers

Thinking and Inquiry

3. Some non-western philosophers believe that destiny — a predetermined fate — plays a role in dictating the course of people's lives. Read the following statements by the 20th-century Indian philosopher Sarvepalli Radhakrishnan and the contemporary African philosopher Kwame Gyekye.

    Sarvepalli Radhakrishnan
    > The principle of Karma [destiny] reckons with the material or the context in which each individual is born. While it regards the past as predetermined, it allows that the future is only conditioned. The spiritual elements in man allow him freedom within the limits of his nature.

Kwame Gyekye
> The concept of destiny held by most of the traditional wise persons with whom I had discussions makes the destiny of man a *general* destiny. That is, the message (*nkra*) borne by the soul is said to be comprehensive; it determines only the broad outlines of an individual's mundane life, not the specific details. It follows that not every action a person performs or every event that occurs in one's life comes within the ambit of his destiny.

Explain how these beliefs might challenge western concepts of individual freedom, equality, and just limits on individual behaviour.

4. Write a philosophical reflection defending your position on capital punishment. Drawing on the philosophical arguments set out in this chapter, confront the counter-arguments that might be raised to challenge your position.

Communication

5. Create a poster that summarizes possible Kantian and utilitarian responses to an important question of social and political philosophy.

6. On a graphic organizer, show how events in various periods of history affected the development of social and political thought. For each period, use a symbol or phrase to represent how one philosophical school of thought influenced the development of a subsequent ideas.

Application

7. Read this excerpt from "Marcelle," a short story published in 1942 by Simone de Beauvoir, a 20th-century French feminist writer and philosopher.

> Marcelle leaned her forehead against the cool window-pane: in rejecting commonplace pleasures, playthings, finery, social success and easy flirtation she had always saved herself for some splendid happiness. Yet it was not happiness that had been granted to her: it was suffering. But perhaps it was only suffering that could satisfy her heart at last. "Higher than happiness," she whispered. This great bitter thing was her lot on earth and she would know how to receive it; she would know how to transform it into beauty; and one day strangers, brothers, would understand her disincarnate soul, and they would cherish it. Higher than happiness. Tears came into her eyes; she could already feel the dawn of sublime poems quivering within her.
>
> For the second time she had the wonderful revelation of her fate. "I am a woman of genius," she decided.

In this excerpt, de Beauvoir suggests that a woman must suffer to claim her freedom. If this theory is true, how might it affect women's roles in politics and society? What might be done to change this?

After considering responses to these questions, write a letter to de Beauvoir outlining how policies might be altered to ensure that women need not suffer.

8. Imagine that you are hosting a radio discussion between Thomas Hobbes and John Locke on the topic of the social contract that links citizens and their governments. List five questions that you would ask each philosopher to draw out the similarities and differences in their ideas. Make notes that summarize how each is likely to answer the questions.

Chapter 19
Theories of Social and Political Philosophy

Chapter Expectations

By the end of this chapter, you will be able to
- demonstrate an understanding of the main questions of social and political philosophy
- evaluate the responses of major philosophers and major schools of social and political philosophy to some of the main questions of social and political philosophy
- use critical- and logical-thinking skills to develop and defend your own ideas about some of the major questions of social and political philosophy, and to anticipate counter-arguments to them
- analyze how theories of social and political philosophy are realized in contemporary policy making, and how this affects political and social practices
- demonstrate an understanding of how particular philosophical theories have influenced the development of other subjects
- describe how the ideas of philosophers have influenced subsequent philosophers

Key Words

philosopher kings
totalitarianism
democracy
natural law
satyagraha
general will
capitalism
socialism
libertarianism

Key People

Thomas Aquinas
Kongfuzi (Confucius)
Mohandas Gandhi
Dalai Lama
Olympe de Gouges
Mary Wollstonecraft
Edmund Burke
Thomas Paine
Karl Marx
Robert Nozick
Herbert Marcuse

A Philosopher's Voice

I came to the conclusion that all existing states were badly governed, and that their constitutions were incapable of reform without drastic treatment and a great deal of good luck. I was forced, in fact, to the belief that the only hope of finding justice in society or for the individual lay in true philosophy, and that mankind will have no respite from trouble until either real philosophers gain political power or politicians become by some miracle true philosophers.

Plato (c. 428–347 BCE)

The Western Tradition

Until the 17th century, the ideas of Plato and Aristotle were the chief influences on western political theory. Both were fascinated by political communities and how they make decisions, various forms of government, and the kind of government that works best. These ancient Greek philosophers were also interested in the nature of justice and the obligations of citizens to one another and to their leaders. Plato presented his vision of an ideal society in *The Republic*, and Aristotle examined the political systems of his day and tried to figure out which worked best.

PLATO: THE ANTI-DEMOCRATIC REPUBLIC

The Republic represents a highly developed vision of an anti-democratic state. Plato believed that governing a state requires great skill and wisdom. When he looked around his own Athenian society, however, he became convinced that the average person did not possess the skill to exercise political rights responsibly or wisely. As an alternative, he proposed a society organized into three groups: workers, soldiers, and guardians, or rulers. The workers would produce goods and provide the services necessary for society to survive; the soldiers would defend the state from foreign aggression; and the guardians would perform the most important task — making laws and serving as political rulers.

This three-part division of roles sprang from Plato's tripartite theory of the soul, which said that the human soul includes three elements: reason, spirit, and appetite. Of these, Plato believed that reason is the most important. As a result, he maintained that members of the guardian class, whom he sometimes called **philosopher kings**, would base their decisions on rational thought. Their upbringing and education, along with their innate abilities and intelligence, would equip them to play this leadership role. In Plato's view, soldiers were people who were dominated by spirit, which often expressed itself as courage. They would not hesitate to risk their lives in defence of the state. As for the workers, he believed that they were ruled by their appetites. For this reason, they would be allowed to work but would play no part in governing the state.

In Plato's ideal state, the family would not exist as an institution. All children would be raised communally and would never know their biological parents. Everyone in this society would belong to a colour-coded group: gold for guardians, silver for soldiers, and bronze for workers. Still, there was room for some social mobility, and people could move up to the next level if they demonstrated certain abilities. In addition, people would usually marry within their group, though they could marry outside their group if the union was likely to result in the birth of gifted children who could benefit the state.

Though Plato's vision of the ideal social organization was hierarchical, it included something that was unheard of in the ancient world. He believed that women should have the same rights as men to be educated and participate in public life.

> *Wealth is the parent of luxury and indolence, and poverty of meanness and viciousness, and both of discontent.*
>
> – Plato

In some respects, Plato's ideal society resembled a communist state. Everyone would own property in common, and money would not exist. Plato strongly believed that abolishing wealth and private ownership of property would eliminate the differences between rich and poor. This would mean that people would be distinguished only by their intelligence and character, not by family background or personal wealth. The ban on private ownership would extend to the philosopher kings, who would be forbidden to possess material objects that might corrupt them. They would be distinguished, however, by their unique education in mathematics, music, gymnastics, and philosophy.

Plato's city state was intended to be serene and organized, run by a group of wise, incorruptible governors. Everyone would know and accept his or her position in society, and everyone would have enough material comforts and education to function in her or his designated role. Because people's social class would correspond to their innate characteristics, Plato believed that the citizens of his imaginary city state would know true happiness. For the guardian class, the reward was particularly lofty — an opportunity to study philosophy while experiencing the satisfaction of serving the public. This would truly be a state where philosophers ruled for the good of all.

Despite some of its enlightened aspects, such as equality for women, Plato's ideal society has been condemned as a model for **totalitarianism**, a dictatorial form of government that requires absolute obedience to the state. The abolition of the family, the censorship of art and literature, the rigid class divisions, and the granting of absolute, unchecked power to the guardian class have all been questioned. Could such a system ever work?

Plato presented the following argument in defence of his ideal state.

- Ruling a society requires special skills and knowledge.
- Not everyone possesses these skills and knowledge.
- Those who appear to have these skills and knowledge should be made rulers.
- Rulers should have power over all other citizens for the good of the state.

How sound is Plato's argument? The idea that ruling requires special skills and knowledge is not unreasonable. Most people today expect their political leaders and judges to display both. Still, many would argue that the most effective rulers are those who understand and respond to the wishes of the people rather than those who simply impose their views on others.

Even if Plato's first three arguments are accepted, however, does it follow that rulers should be granted complete authority over those they rule? Many people would say no. The main criticism of totalitarian states and dictatorships is the absolute power of political leaders. Though Plato suggested safeguards to prevent guardians from taking advantage of their absolute power, he could offer no guarantee that they would not act in an irresponsible or arbitrary manner. He did not imagine their being required to answer to the people, as political leaders are in democratic states where elections and other procedures guarantee accountability.

Figure 19.1

Cartoonist Jack Ziegler pokes fun at Plato's vision of society.

Another criticism of Plato's ideal society is that it impedes progress. For the most part, people would remain in their designated roles, and the ruling group could become a self-perpetuating elite. Critics have said that this could cut off the elite from the needs and desires of the people they are supposed to rule, something that happened in 17th- and 18th-century European monarchies.

Though *The Republic* was written more than 2000 years ago, Plato's vision of an ideal society continues to spark controversy. Some philosophers charge that he laid the groundwork for contemporary totalitarian ideologies, such as fascism and communism, because of his championing of eugenics, the science of improving human characteristics by controlling breeding, and the abolition of private property. The contemporary Canadian political scientist Thomas Pangle, by contrast, views *The Republic* as a satire, or an attempt to prove that an ideal state could never exist. At the same time, some contemporary feminist thinkers such as Martha Nussbaum have applauded Plato's commitment to sexual equality, saying that he was ahead of his time.

> **Web connection**
> www.mcgrawhill.ca/links/philosophy12
> To read Plato's *Republic*, follow the links on this Web site.

ARISTOTLE: THE BEST STATE FOR EACH SOCIETY

Unlike Plato, Aristotle was not interested in promoting a vision of an ideal state. His main work of social and political philosophy was *Politics*, a volume compiled from notes that he had prepared for lectures at his school in Athens. His approach was very different from Plato's.

Aristotle examined the political systems that existed at the time, comparing their strengths and weaknesses. This meant that his approach to political theory was less prescriptive and more descriptive than Plato's. Because of this contribution, he is viewed as the founder of political science. He believed that "man is a political animal" and that the best chance for human happiness and security lies in an organized political state governed by just laws and wise rulers.

Throughout his life, Aristotle observed phenomena closely so that he could understand the nature of things. He also believed that everything in nature moved toward a predetermined goal. If the goal of human beings is happiness, he believed that this could be achieved best in a society that encourages people to move toward this goal. For Aristotle, this was a society in which reason rules, people act moderately and control their emotions, and the state guarantees the security and well-being of its citizens. In his view, human beings can achieve a superior level of civilization if they live in a well-governed city state. At the same time, the existence of a well-ordered state depends on citizens' ability to achieve their goals.

Aristotle viewed the family unit as the foundation of larger political entities. When human societies are goal-oriented, he said, they evolve from families to clans and then to larger communities because these units of government are large enough to meet the needs of those living in them. At the same time, they never become so big that they are ungovernable, unlike some of the empires that existed in Aristotle's time.

Aristotle grouped the governments of his day into three categories: monarchies, aristocracies, and democracies, or polities. He said that each has advantages, but he also warned that all could fail, especially if they fostered extreme behaviour. He said that monarchies can succeed if the rulers are as wise as Plato's philosopher kings, but they can fail if the rulers are tyrants who oppress the people. Aristocracies can also succeed, provided the small group of people who hold power do not enslave the people they rule. Aristotle's third form of government was called a **democracy** or polity, a word derived from *polis*, which is Greek for city and state. In a democracy, all citizens have some say in governing.

> *Democracy ... arises out of the notion that those who are equal in any respect are equal in all respects; because men are equally free, they claim to be absolutely equal.*
>
> – Aristotle

Aristotle believed that it might be possible to combine the best of each category of government while avoiding the worst excesses. Yet he also acknowledged that no one system of government suited every society. Much depended on the aims of the state and whether the rulers could be trusted to act for the benefit of all citizens.

Aristotle believed that a democracy can function well if its citizens are informed and serious about their civic duties. A state can administer its affairs more effectively if more people are involved in the process. He wrote: "If liberty and equality ... are chiefly to be found in a democracy, they will be best attained when all persons alike share in the government to the utmost." At the same time, he maintained that there could be too much democracy, especially if most people are ignorant or easily swayed. This could lead to chaos. Like Plato, Aristotle feared that democracy might lead to the rule of the ignorant many over the educated few.

Unlike Plato, Aristotle believed firmly that the rule of law is the foundation of political order. In his view, the law can guarantee that reason prevails, and it can balance the forces that contend for power in society. In this respect, he championed the rights of individual citizens over the power of a single ruler. He also believed, however, that women should be excluded from political life and defended slavery as a necessary institution that benefits the state.

Above all, Aristotle stressed the need for moderation and stability in the political life of the state. He said that the ideal state is one that each society must determine for itself. Still, he did warn against societies that are sharply polarized between haves and have-nots. "Where some people are very wealthy and others have nothing, the result will be either extreme democracy or absolute oligarchy, or despotism will come from either of those excesses," he wrote.

THOMAS AQUINAS: NATURAL LAW

Aristotle believed in **natural law**, which he described as a force of nature that is reasonable and purposeful. In his view, natural law governs both the natural and social orders, an idea that influenced later thinkers in both Roman and medieval times. Roman philosophers such as Cicero and Seneca believed that natural law was universal and eternal. They said that it applied to all people in all times and places. In the Middle Ages, Christian thinkers such as Augustine of Hippo and **Thomas Aquinas** adopted Aristotle's view of natural law to justify the authority of the Roman Catholic Church in political as well as religious matters.

A 13th-century Dominican monk and philosopher, Aquinas believed that God's natural law is designed to benefit humanity. He was interested in how God's laws could apply in the secular world, and what kind of relationship should exist between the dominant Roman Catholic Church and the state. Aquinas concluded that earthly laws should reflect the divine ideal of justice. If earthly laws are unjust, however, he said that they violate natural law — and this releases people from their duty to obey them. To Aquinas, the role of the state is to promote the common good, while the main duty of the Church is to attend to people's spiritual needs. Still, he argued that the state is subordinate to the Church, because natural law, which the Church symbolizes, is superior to laws created by humans.

Aquinas described natural law as the eternal law that governs people's actions. It is the basis of morality, ethics, and political behaviour, and it directs people toward their natural goal of happiness. He said that natural law can also be understood through reason and conscience. In his view, anyone who knows the difference between right and wrong, and acts accordingly, is following the dictates of natural law.

Web connection
www.mcgrawhill.ca/links/philosophy12
To read more about Thomas Aquinas' theory of natural law, follow the links on this Web site.

He believed that human law — laws made by people — should do more than reflect the whims and desires of those in power. They should correspond to natural law. He viewed the church as the ultimate authority in determining whether this was the case. Aquinas upheld the biblical injunction that people ought to "obey God rather than men." In other words, when human law conflicts with natural law, natural law prevails.

Aquinas' views on human and natural law had a lasting effect on political thought and government. His belief that people are not required to obey human laws that do not conform to natural law sent a clear message to the powerful monarchs of Europe. To Aquinas, a ruler who does not govern in accordance with natural law is a tyrant, unworthy of respect or obedience. In cases of severe tyranny, he said that the Church could release people from their duty to obey secular leaders and even encourage people to rebel against injustice, provided they sought guidance from the Church. In keeping with Aquinas' teachings, medieval popes sometimes excommunicated (expelled from the Church) rulers who were acting tyrannically. In the view of the Church, this removed these rulers' claim to authority over their subjects, who were no longer required to obey laws they had passed.

> ### Recall...Reflect...Respond
> 1. Both Plato and Aristotle proposed social and political systems. What was the common goal of these systems? How does this goal reflect one or more of the main themes of social and political philosophy?
> 2. Both Plato and Aristotle divided societies into three groups. Create an organizer to display each system. Which do you find more appealing? Explain why.
> 3. Briefly summarize how Plato, Aristotle, and Thomas Aquinas defined justice and how it is determined. Draw a continuum with public policy at one end and private morality at the other. Locate each of their definitions on the continuum and be prepared to defend your placement.

THE EASTERN TRADITION

One of the most important social and political thinkers in the eastern tradition is **Kongfuzi**, who is better known in the West as Confucius. The theories of this Chinese philosopher, who lived from 551 to 479 BCE, emphasize the importance of the community. His theories about human beings and their relationship to the state continue to influence ideas about government and society in China and many other Asian countries — and stand in sharp contrast to the western tradition.

KONGFUZI: A GOOD STATE FOR THE PEOPLE

Two centuries before Plato, Kongfuzi was teaching a generation of China's future leaders. His curriculum of study included poetry, music, history, and literature, as well as politics and government. These teachings, which were passed down in *The Analects*, became a philosophy that embraced many aspects of human life and thought. Kongfuzi's philosophy can be summed up in his idea of the *tao*, which means the right road or the way.

Ethics are at the core of Confucian social and political thought. Kongfuzi maintained that a combination of personal moral goodness and good government enables people to reach their potential. Virtue, or *de*, was the goal of human existence, and he stressed the qualities of *ren* (generosity), *li* (respect for tradition), and *yi* (right conduct). He said that those who attained these desirable qualities — and received suitable instruction — could be fit to govern the state. Kongfuzi also advocated honesty; loyalty to family, friends, and rulers; and respect for elders and those with a superior education. Like Plato, Kongfuzi saw similarities between individual people and the political order, and his code of conduct applied not only to individuals, but also to the state.

Kongfuzi believed that the state is responsible for the well-being of the people. As a result, he said that rulers should strive for *ren* at all times and make it a hallmark of government.

This will bring both rulers and states closer to the goals of goodness and justice. *Yi* is important because it encourages both citizens and rulers to do the right thing and satisfy their moral obligations. *Li* emphasizes propriety and good manners based on tradition. It helps establish the boundaries of conduct — how people should treat one another in certain situations. In Kongfuzi's view, rulers who do not take their subjects' interests to heart will not hold power for long. "No state can exist without the confidence of the people," he wrote.

Kongfuzi's views of politics and government were grounded in an appreciation of tradition and custom. As a result, Confucian social and political philosophy seems impervious to change or improvements in its basic principles. Nevertheless, Confucian principles do give rulers the option of changing policies, provided the changes can be justified in light of the other principles, especially *yi*.

Kongfuzi had strong ideas about the qualities of leaders. He believed that they should study the classics and the lives of rulers who exemplified wise political leadership. In fact, he said that studying history is all-important for students and rulers alike. He believed that a prudent course of action can be determined by learning and applying the lessons of the past. "A man who reviews the old so as to find out the new is qualified to teach others," he wrote.

For centuries after Kongfuzi's death, Chinese mandarins — important civil servants — immersed themselves in his teachings. Later, as his ideas were carried to other parts of Asia, they laid the foundation for much Japanese, Korean, Vietnamese, and other political thought. To this day, Confucianism dominates Asian philosophy and provides a world view and a basic understanding of politics and government for millions of people. This is evident in their emphasis on education, respect for authority and tradition, and the importance of the rights of the group over those of the individual.

MOHANDAS GANDHI: NON-VIOLENT CIVIL DISOBEDIENCE

Known as Mahatma, or great soul, **Mohandas Gandhi** was born in British-ruled India in 1869. When he travelled to Natal, a British colony that is now part of South Africa, to practise law, he experienced racism, injustice, and oppression — and became convinced that change was necessary. He was also convinced that the best way to achieve this change was through a strategy of non-violence.

When Gandhi returned to India, he threw himself into the independence movement that was seeking to free his country from British rule. Through the force of his intellect and personality, he was able to convince a reluctant leadership that non-violent civil disobedience could achieve political results. Gandhi called this method *satyagraha*, or holding to the truth, and he adhered to this principle for the rest of his life.

In developing this philosophy, Gandhi drew on a number of religious ideas, including his own Hindu tradition, as well as Jainism, Islam, and Christianity. To Gandhi, *satyagraha* was both a philosophy and a tool of political action. It inspired a mass movement among millions of Indians opposed to British rule over their country and resulted in their winning of independence in 1947.

Gandhi was one of the first modern, non-western philosophers to develop a practical theory of political change and social justice based on the traditions of his people. His concept

• IDEAS IN CONTEXT •

In the 1950s and '60s, the American civil rights leader Martin Luther King Jr. modelled his campaign against racial segregation in the southern United States on Gandhi's non-violent principles. The African National Congress, which Gandhi helped found in the early 1900s, also tried to use non-violent tactics to end European oppression of the black majority in South Africa — until unrelenting government opposition forced the ANC to rethink its methods. Despite this, ANC leader Nelson Mandela borrowed from Gandhi's approach to wage his own campaign to win social and political change.

of communal, co-operative social and political life at the community level was based on the example of small, rural Indian communities. Gandhi believed that this model of development presented an alternative to the way Britain and other European states wanted to modernize and industrialize the non-western world. He was also deeply suspicious of western political and social philosophy, which he believed placed far too much emphasis on the rights of the individual.

Gandhi believed that the philosophy of non-violence was ethically superior to the rule of force. He also maintained that it represented the first step in people's liberating themselves from tyranny. He said, "The moment the slave resolves that he will no longer be a slave, his fetters fall. He frees himself and shows the way to others. Freedom and slavery are mental states."

THE DALAI LAMA: BUDDHIST NON-VIOLENCE

The Tibetan version of Buddhism emphasizes the leadership of *lamas*, or priests. Over the centuries, the *lamas* have emerged as the political and spiritual leaders of the Tibetan people. The 14th Dalai Lama, or head of the Tibetan Buddhist religion, is an important political figure and thinker who helped make non-western philosophy popular in the West. When China invaded Tibet in 1959, he left his country and has remained in exile ever since. At the same time, he has conducted a non-violent campaign to free his people from Chinese rule and re-establish the traditional Buddhist religion and culture in Tibet.

> *What difference does it make to the dead, the orphans, and the homeless, whether the mad destruction is wrought under the name of totalitarianism or the holy name of liberty and democracy?*
>
> – Mohandas Gandhi

The Dalai Lama's non-violent approach is a natural outgrowth of his Buddhist faith. Despite the urging of many Tibetan exile groups frustrated by the lack of progress in freeing their country from Chinese rule, the Dalai Lama has steadfastly refused to promote armed uprisings against the occupying forces. Instead, he has repeatedly asked the Chinese government to open a dialogue that could lead to his return to Tibet and the establishment of peaceful relations between the two peoples.

In recognition of his devotion to the cause of peace and the promotion of non-violence as a method of achieving social and political change, the Dalai Lama was awarded the Nobel Peace Prize in 1989. In his acceptance speech, he credited the teachings of Buddha with inspiring his non-violent struggle. He also acknowledged the influence of other champions of non-violence, especially Gandhi. He stated, "No matter what part of the world we come from, we are all basically the same human beings. We all seek happiness and try to avoid suffering. We have the same human needs and concerns. All of us human beings want freedom and the right to determine our own destiny as individuals and as peoples. That is human nature."

Recall...Reflect...Respond

1. Compare the social and political theories of Plato and Kongfuzi. Consider their ideas about the goals of society, the qualities of an ideal ruler, and so on.
3. Choose an example of a current conflict and decide whether Gandhi's philosophy of political change and social justice might be applied to it. Explain your thinking.
2. Why do you think the ideas of non-western philosophers such as the Dalai Lama are becoming more popular in western culture?

THE SOCIAL CONTRACT

By the last half of the 17th century, the power of the Roman Catholic Church in Europe had declined, and its role in granting legitimacy to political leaders was no longer as important as it had been during the Middle Ages. European thinkers began to break new ground in their thinking about the evolution of the relationship between rulers and those who are ruled. As a result, this period of European history is often called the Enlightenment.

Social and political theorists such as Thomas Hobbes, John Locke, and Jean-Jacques Rousseau led the way in developing new social and political theories. They explored how states justify their authority and whether citizens are always bound to obey their leaders. Much of their thinking focused on the idea of a social contract. Though each of these thinkers developed his own definition of the social contract and his own ideas about society and government, their thought triggered a debate that continues today.

THOMAS HOBBES: LAW AND ORDER

During his long life, the English philosopher Thomas Hobbes witnessed many unsettling changes in his country. One of these was the growing hostility between the king and Parliament. Their disagreements led to a civil war in the 1640s and the beheading of the king. Perhaps as a result of this experience, Hobbes' view of the importance of state power was extreme.

Hobbes made no appeal to tradition or to natural law to justify the power of the state. Unlike some medieval Christian philosophers, such as Thomas Aquinas, he believed that nothing justified rebellion against the state. He said that unjust rule is preferable to the chaos that follows when central authority breaks down, a stance that may have been influenced by the disorder he had witnessed during England's civil war. He came to believe that the power of the state must be absolute if it is to effectively preserve peace, order, and stability.

Hobbes set out these ideas in a book titled *Leviathan*, which was published in 1651. This book described the life of the earliest humans — those who had lived in a natural state without the benefit of government institutions — as "poor, nasty, brutish, and short." In this state, Hobbes wrote, people were motivated by self-preservation and the instinct to avoid pain or violent death. In his view, people are by nature self-seeking, egoistic, aggressive, pleasure-seeking animals who have no respect for the interests of others. He expressed little faith in the ability of humans to make appropriate choices, and believed that governments exist to ensure that people do not give in to their instincts.

To avoid the chaos of their natural state, Hobbes wrote, human beings created civil societies. When they did this, they entered into a social contract with their rulers. Under the terms of this contract, people surrendered their natural rights and their freedom to conduct their affairs free of the influence of others. In return, they received the protection offered by a superior power. In exchange for complete obedience, rulers guaranteed security, law, and order.

Though Hobbes maintained that rulers should have absolute power over their subjects, he also believed that rulers should use this power

Figure 19.2

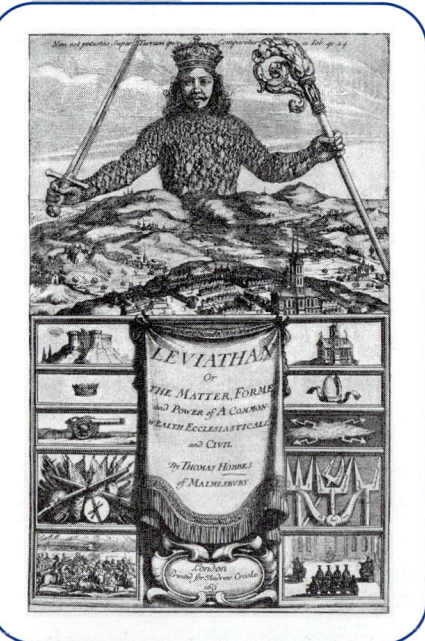

Hobbes titled his book *Leviathan* after a biblical sea monster who is "king over all the children of pride." How does the title page of the book, shown here, reflect Hobbes' view of the role of rulers?

wisely. He maintained that no sensible monarch would enforce policies that harmed his or her subjects, because the consequences would undermine the power of the nation.

In Hobbes' view, subjects have no right to resist the state's power, no matter how harsh or unjust it is. By rejecting an ethics-based theory of the way governments should work, his ideas represented a turning away from the idea of the common good, which had driven political philosophy in ancient and medieval times. He ushered in an age of secular social and political thought in Europe. Like Niccolò Machiavelli, Hobbes based his view of the state on a new kind of political realism, as well as his own negative view of human nature. Even today, those who believe that law and order are preferable to the disorder of rebellion and civil disobedience find Hobbes' theory appealing.

JOHN LOCKE: THE WILL OF THE PEOPLE

Like Hobbes, John Locke was shaped by the events that occurred in England during his lifetime. Born in 1632, he was a boy at the time of the civil war that horrified Hobbes. Years later, he also witnessed the Glorious Revolution of 1688. This event resulted in the peaceful overthrow of the English monarch, James II, by a group of nobles and members of Parliament who feared that the despotic Roman Catholic king would try to force Catholicism on the largely Protestant country. As a result of this struggle, James' daughter Mary and her husband, the Protestant Dutch ruler William of Orange, were invited to take over the throne.

Locke wrote his most influential political work, *Two Treatises of Government,* during this period. In this book, he set out his views on the state of nature, the rights of rulers and the ruled, and the social contract. Like Hobbes, Locke believed that human beings had originally lived in a state of nature, in which they had been completely free to enjoy their natural rights to life, liberty, and property. In Locke's view, the main drawback of this existence was not that it was nasty, brutish, and short, as Hobbes had maintained, but that people could fully enjoy their rights only when other people were required to respect them. No force guaranteed this respect, however. As a result, said Locke, human beings had agreed to enter civil society under a social contract that stipulated how they would be governed.

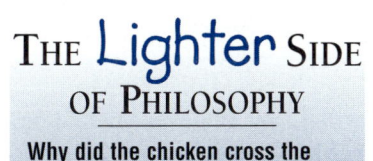

The Lighter Side of Philosophy

Why did the chicken cross the road?

John Locke: Because he was exercising his natural right to liberty.

Unlike Hobbes, Locke supported Aquinas' idea of natural law and believed in the natural goodness of people. He said that entering into a social contract that created a civil society did not mean that people surrendered their natural rights. In fact, Locke maintained that the duty of civil society is to enhance and protect these rights. Whereas Hobbes had argued that any state, no matter how unjust, is preferable to the anarchy of the state of nature, Locke denied that the state of nature is worse than the worst government. For this reason, he opposed handing unlimited power to monarchs and said that rulers are obligated to respect the natural rights of their subjects.

Locke also insisted that political power originated in the will of the people, who had freely formed the government and passed laws to protect their natural rights. "The only way by which anyone divests himself of his natural liberty and puts on the bonds of civil society is by agreeing with other men to join and unite into a community," he wrote.

As a result, said Locke, rulers are not exempt from the terms of the social contract. Rather, they must respect and preserve the natural rights of their subjects. Should they fail to do this, their subjects have the right to rebel.

Locke's views found a large and enthusiastic audience among American colonists who were unhappy with British rule during the late 18th century. The leaders of the American Revolution, which began in 1776, were steeped in Locke's political philosophy and incorporated large sections of it into their own political writings, which were designed to justify their rebellion. In France, where an emerging middle class of urban businesspeople and professionals resented the arbitrary rule of the king, Church, and hereditary nobility, Locke's support of religious freedom, a propertied middle class, constitutional government, and limitations on a monarch's power also held great appeal and was influential in shaping the ideas that sparked the French Revolution in 1789.

> *The only government that I recognize, is that power that establishes justice, never that which establishes injustice.*
>
> — Henry David Thoreau

Despite his ideas about natural rights, Locke was no democrat. Though his philosophy would inspire the founding of many democracies, he did not believe that the "people" meant everyone. Like most thinkers of his day, he believed that only male property owners possessed rights. Women, slaves, wage earners, landless peasants, and servants were excluded from discussions of rights.

The contemporary Canadian political thinker C.B. MacPherson once called Locke's political philosophy possessive individualism because it stressed property owning as the basis for entitlement to political rights. In Locke's view, only those with a material stake in society should have a say in the way they are governed. Though his philosophy stressed political liberty, it also sanctioned considerable social and economic inequality.

Web connection
www.mcgrawhill.ca/links/philosophy12
To find out more about John Locke's *Two Treatises of Government*, follow the links on this Web site.

JEAN-JACQUES ROUSSEAU: THE GENERAL WILL

The tension between political freedom and social and economic inequality was an issue that intrigued Jean-Jacques Rousseau. Born in Switzerland in 1712, Rousseau moved to France as a young man to pursue his intellectual ambitions in the salons of Paris, where the *philosophes* — a group of thinkers who had been inspired by René Descartes's emphasis on reason — held court. Although Rousseau wrote on many topics, including education, the arts, and science, he is best known as a political thinker.

Rousseau tried to show that states justified their power through an idea he called the **general will**, an expression of what is best for the community as a whole. Like his predecessors, Hobbes and Locke, Rousseau believed that human beings originally existed in a state of nature, free of governmental or legal authority. Rousseau's view of humanity's natural state was completely positive, however. He believed that humanity had enjoyed true happiness in this original state and that every form of constituted government was a departure from this ideal. In the introduction to his book *General Will*, he wrote: "Man is born free but is every-where in chains."

Rousseau envisaged a radically new form of government, one that rested not on a few rich and powerful individuals, but on the will of all. Unlike Locke, who believed that political rights should be restricted to property owners, Rousseau argued for a democracy that embraced all male citizens living in the country. They would enter into a voluntary social contract, and the state would respect and guarantee everyone's freedoms. This was the embodiment of the general will. Leaders would understand the general will and how to apply it for the good of everyone. Individuals or groups who disagreed with the general will would not be allowed to act on their disagreement because this would harm the social contract — and themselves.

Figure 19.3

Jean-Jacques Rousseau tried careers in law, engraving, and teaching before becoming a philosopher.

Rousseau believed that those who had society's interests at heart best understood the general will and were fit to be rulers. He also said that rulers had the right to coerce people into adhering to the general will — to "force them to be free." Rousseau envisioned a perfect political society, in which happy citizens would join together willingly to create a new order based on harmony, mutual aid, and complete equality. There was a darker side to his vision, however. Those who did not share these ideas would be labelled anti-social and would be corrected. Not surprisingly, some critics of Rousseau see the dangers of totalitarianism lurking in his theories.

Rousseau's ideas were especially attractive to the leaders of the French Revolution. Based on his writings, they tried to establish what they called a Republic of Virtue in post-revolutionary France during the 1790s. This involved promoting the rights of citizens and championing liberty, equality, and fraternity. At the same time, however, it gave the leaders of the revolution the right to hunt down, persecute, and even execute those who refused to conform to the new political order. For this reason, Rousseau is viewed as something of a paradox. Though his views on the rights of citizens laid the groundwork for much modern democratic thought, they also helped justify the tyrannies that would later emerge in Europe and elsewhere. On the one hand, he is hailed as the first philosopher of modern democracy; on the other, he is criticized as a thinker who helped pave the way for contemporary totalitarian governments and dictatorships.

> *Men who use terrorism as a means to power, rule by terror once they are in power.*
>
> — Helen MacInnes

THE FRENCH REVOLUTION

The French Revolution of 1789 raised social and political issues that are debated to this day. When, if ever, is violence justified as a means of achieving social and political goals? When, if ever, are people entitled to overthrow their government by force of arms? What kind of regime should replace one that has been toppled as a result of a popular revolution? On what basis can new leaders claim legitimacy? Can society be reshaped to become more just and humane?

In addition to these questions, the French Revolution also sparked questions about the role of women in society. No longer willing to play a secondary role, some women began pointing out that their rights had been ignored in various revolutionary declarations. In France, for example, **Olympe de Gouges** supported the revolution but challenged the language of the revolutionary Declaration of the Rights of Man and the Citizen, which asserted only the natural rights of men. Calling for the inclusion of women, she published her own tract called *The Declaration of the Rights of Women*. When she pressed her ideas, however, she was arrested, found guilty of treason, and executed.

De Gouges was not alone in her campaign to win recognition for the rights of women, however. Other women, such as the English thinker **Mary Wollstonecraft**, were also beginning to question the emphasis on men's rights and assert that women were entitled to the same consideration.

Figure 19.4

This woodcut shows women who supported the ideals of the French Revolution entering the National Assembly to demand the execution of aristocrats. Despite the important role played by women, their rights were ignored when the male revolutionary leaders established the new republic.

EDMUND BURKE: THE CONSERVATIVE TRADITION

When the French Revolution broke out, many hailed it as a progressive step toward enlightenment and liberation for humanity. But as events took an increasingly violent turn, culminating in the execution of King Louis XVI and the notorious reign of terror, opinion in Europe began to shift. In 1790, the Irish-born British politician and thinker Edmund Burke wrote a book titled *Reflections on the Revolution in France*. Many consider this work to be the founding text of political conservatism.

Burke had not always opposed political alterations in society and government. He had supported the American colonists during their revolution against British rule, for example, and he had condemned British colonial rule in Ireland and India. But when the French rose against their king and challenged the authority of both the church and the nobility, Burke reacted with horror. He rejected Rousseau's belief in the inherent rights of humanity and viewed democracy as a system that would lead to the tyranny of the ignorant many over the educated few.

Burke also disputed the notion that radical political change could reshape society and transform human nature. He believed that traditional institutions, such as the monarchy, the aristocracy, and an established religion, hold society together and foster a natural class of leaders. Emphasizing the rights of the community over those of the individual, he insisted that most people are guided by irrational prejudices and traditional beliefs rather than by abstract political notions such as liberty, equality, and fraternity.

> *People will not look forward to posterity who never look backward to their ancestors.*
>
> — Edmund Burke

Above all, Burke maintained that society is built upon the traditions and customs handed down by previous generations. He wrote: "Society is indeed a contract. It becomes a partnership not only between those who are living, but between those who are living, those who are dead, and those who are to be born."

Burke is considered the founder of modern conservatism, which is critical of radical change but does not resist all reform. He acknowledged that social and political institutions must sometimes be re-examined, but he also believed that this was best accomplished slowly. "A state without the means of some change is without the means of its conservation," he once noted. Burke held up England's own government as a model for France and other European states to follow. In his view, the various elements that made up Britain's unwritten constitution, including a hereditary monarchy, a Parliament composed of elected and non-elected representatives, an established church, and a landed nobility, were essential building blocks for preserving tradition in society and guaranteeing social peace and stability.

Web connection
www.mcgrawhill.ca/links/philosophy12
To read Edmund Burke's *Reflections on the Revolution in France*, follow the links on this Web site.

THOMAS PAINE: THE RADICAL DEMOCRATIC TRADITION

The English democrat Thomas Paine opposed Burke's views. A writer who had spent many years living in Britain's American colonies, Paine had sided with the colonial revolutionaries. When revolution erupted in France, Paine hailed the event as another example of liberation from the forces of monarchy, organized religion, and aristocracy. He believed that these institutions were holding back society and preventing progress.

The publication of Burke's *Reflections* inspired Paine to publish *The Rights of Man* in 1791. This became the most widely read political tract of its day. It inspired a radical movement in England and elsewhere as ordinary people rose to defend the principles of liberty, equality, and fraternity.

PROFILE

Mary Wollstonecraft
Advocating a New Social Order

When Mary Wollstonecraft was born in 1759, the idea that women were intellectually inferior to men and therefore unfit to play a role in public affairs was firmly entrenched in European society. Though ideas about natural rights were gaining ground, few people dared suggest that the concept should be extended to include women. Even political radicals such as Jean-Jacques Rousseau, Thomas Paine, and the leaders of the French Revolution did not take the issue of women's rights very seriously.

In this milieu, it is not surprising that Wollstonecraft was denounced as a "hyena in petticoats" when she published *A Vindication of the Rights of Woman* in 1792. Written in response to Thomas Paine's *Rights of Man,* this book attacked attitudes that encouraged women to be "docile and attentive to their looks to the exclusion of all else." It also condemned marriage as "legalized prostitution."

Critics reacted immediately, attacking Wollstonecraft as a hysterical and dangerous woman whose ideas about political and social equality were preposterous. The book's championing of the cause of equal rights for women was considered outrageous, though not as outrageous as a woman's daring to advance the claim.

Wollstonecraft's father had been a farmer who struggled to support his family, which included six children. As a child, she saw how her mother and other women suffered because of social inequities. She struggled to educate herself and later founded a school for girls. In 1786, she published *Thoughts on the Education of Girls,* a book that attacked traditional teaching methods and suggested new topics that girls should study. When the school failed, she worked as a governess and a translator. In her spare time, she associated with the liberals and radicals of London society, soaking up ideas about social and political reform.

Wollstonecraft was convinced that education was the key to social and political equality for women. Denying the charge that she wanted to replace a male-dominated society with one where women ruled — an accusation that continues to dog contemporary feminists — she responded, "I do not wish women to have power over men, but over themselves." She also believed that women had allowed themselves to be diverted from the important issues: "Taught from infancy that beauty is a woman's sceptre, the mind shapes itself to the body, and roaming round its gilt cage, only seeks to adorn its prison."

When the French Revolution broke out in 1789, Wollstonecraft hailed it as a great leap forward for both men and women. Because the revolution was dedicated to principles of liberty, equality, and fraternity, she believed it could mark the beginning of a new social order, one in which women could enjoy equality with men and could contribute meaningfully to society. But the leaders of the revolution had no such ideas. When Wollstonecraft visited France in 1793, she was horrified by the violence and disorder she witnessed and became disillusioned with the leaders' lack of commitment to equal rights for women.

In 1797, she married the British radical thinker William Godwin, who is considered to be the founder of anarchism, a philosophy that advocates the abolition of government. Later that year, she gave birth to a daughter, but died of complications 11 days later. Her daughter, also named Mary, would later marry the English poet Percy Bysshe Shelley and achieve fame as the author of the Gothic horror novel *Frankenstein.*

Reviled by many in her own time, Wollstonecraft is hailed today as one of the first modern feminists. Her demands that women be granted full political rights, opportunity for education, and legal equality with men are widely accepted in modern democratic states.

Figure 19.5

Mary Wollstonecraft agreed with many 18th-century thinkers who believed that people would not be equal until the hereditary monarchy as well as Church and military hierarchies were abolished.

To Burke's claim that society should be governed by tradition, Paine responded that generations of the dead should not dictate government policy to the living. "I am contending for the rights of the living and against their being willed away by the manuscript-assumed authority of the dead," he wrote. He strongly believed that human beings, endowed with reason, can change society for the better and institute a more humane, rational, and just form of government once the barriers of tradition and ignorance are swept away.

As a result, Paine supported French revolutionaries who wanted to abolish the monarchy and grant sovereignty to the people. He hailed the end of aristocratic privilege as a step toward greater social equality and delighted in the reduction in the power of the Church. He believed that any social or political position based on the principle of heredity was utter folly. "The idea of hereditary legislators is as inconsistent as that of hereditary judges, or hereditary juries, and as absurd as hereditary mathematicians, or as hereditary wise men, and as ridiculous as hereditary poets laureate!" he wrote.

> ### • IDEAS IN CONTEXT •
>
> The political terms "left" and "right" were first used during the French Revolution. When the new National Assembly was convened in 1789 to draw up a constitution for France, members who wanted to abolish the monarchy and adopt a republican form of government sat to the left of the speaker. More conservative members, who hoped to preserve a form of limited monarchy, sat to the right. To this day, the words "left" and "right" are used as political shorthand to define people's basic beliefs and principles.

Paine spent his last years in the United States, where he continued to rail against organized religion and support liberal ideals. By then, however, he was a forgotten man, largely ignored by the very government his writings had helped bring to power. Still, he never abandoned his optimism and continued to believe that people could achieve a better form of government if only they united in the name of liberty and equality. Near the end of his life, he wrote: "My country is the world, and my religion is to do good."

If Burke was the founder of modern conservatism, Paine was the first champion of radical liberal democracy. He believed that society could be transformed in a positive way if people were only granted their natural rights and provided with education, employment, and a government that attended to their interests. His views helped to define democracy as it developed in Europe, the Americas, and elsewhere. Much of what Paine advocated — legal equality, universal public education, the right to vote, and representative democratic institutions — has now become commonplace in modern democracies like Canada.

> ### Recall...Reflect...Respond
>
> 1. The differing views of Thomas Hobbes, John Locke, and Jean-Jacques Rousseau on the natural state of humanity shaped their theories on the proper relationship between a government and the people. Describe each thinker's view and show how it affected his political beliefs.
> 2. Consider the Canadian Charter of Rights and Freedoms (go to www.mcgrawhill.ca/links/philosophy12). How does this document reflect the ideas of Olympe de Gouges and Mary Wollstonecraft? How does it extend their ideas?
> 3. Create a short role-play of the dialogue that might have occurred if Olympe de Gouges and Thomas Paine had collaborated in writing *The Rights of Man*.

THE STRUGGLE BETWEEN CLASSES

Though the 19th-century thinker **Karl Marx** was not a professional philosopher, his background in philosophy shaped his view of the world. Though he did not live to see it, his condemnation of the capitalist system, which had emerged in Europe during the Industrial

Revolution of the 18th and 19th centuries, inspired 20th-century communist revolutions in Russia, China, and other countries.

Born in Germany, Marx moved to England, where he completed most of his writing. He set out to develop what he called a "philosophy of action" that would serve as a guide for the infant socialist movement of his day. "The philosophers have only interpreted the world in various ways; the point, however, is to change it," he once noted. Marx spent much of his life pursuing this goal.

By analyzing the weaknesses of industrial capitalism, he hoped to inspire the workers of Europe to recognize their strength. When they did, Marx was convinced, they would replace capitalism, a commodity-producing system that uses capital, or money, to hire workers for wages, with socialism, an economic and social system that tries to correct the flaws of capitalism by putting workers' interests first.

With his wealthy colleague and benefactor, Friedrich Engels, Marx wrote the famous *Communist Manifesto* in 1848. In this document, Marx and Engels analyzed human history as a succession of struggles between various social classes. They believed that each struggle had led to better conditions for most people. Capitalism, they wrote, was the result of the struggle between the old aristocracy and the rising middle class of factory owners, professionals, and businesspeople. In this conflict, they said, the middle class had triumphed.

Marx and Engels were convinced, however, that capitalism, like all the systems that had preceded it, was destined to be overthrown and replaced by an even more advanced system. In their view, this was socialism, which they believed would dominate after an epic class struggle between the bourgeoisie, or capitalists, and the proletariat, or industrial working class.

Marx believed that forces of production — the tools and technology necessary for productive labour — exist in every society. He maintained that the way these tools are organized gives rise to certain relationships between various social classes. In a capitalist society, the industries that produce manufactured goods are the most important productive force. The two classes are the middle-class capitalists, who own the factories, and the workers, who labour in them. Marx said that the relationship between the two is loaded with conflict because factory owners want to obtain the greatest amount of labour for the lowest possible cost, while the workers try to improve their lot through the very system that is exploiting them.

In Marx's view, the continuing struggle between opposing social forces guaranteed progress. In other words, a new and better society would always emerge from conflict between classes. He believed that the process that drove historical change would end only when this class struggle ceased — and this would happen only when the working class had rebelled, overthrown capitalism, and replaced it with communism. Only then, said Marx, would there be a classless society.

> ## THE Lighter SIDE OF PHILOSOPHY
>
> **Why did the chicken cross the road?**
>
> Karl Marx: Because it was a historical inevitability.

Marx was convinced that capitalism would fall because it would generate a series of economic crises, each worse than the one before. This would increase the exploitation of the workers, whose numbers, organization, and revolutionary consciousness would grow. Marx was certain that the workers would rebel and transform society.

Since Marx's death more than a hundred years ago, communist states have tried to organize their economies and societies along Marxist lines. No one knows whether Marx would have approved of these social experiments performed in his name, however. Marx's major concern was analyzing capitalism. He was not very interested in envisioning the society that would replace the capitalist system.

> **Web connection**
> www.mcgrawhill.ca/links/philosophy12
> To read Friedrich Engels' biography of Karl Marx, follow the links on this Web site.

When the communist regimes in the Soviet Union and Eastern Europe collapsed at the end of the Cold War, many anti-communist political thinkers and writers believed that these events disproved Marx's theories. Other thinkers have pointed to the growing gap between haves and have-nots in Canada and abroad, as well as the growth of global capitalism, as evidence that at least some of Marx's forecasts about the future of capitalism may be accurate.

LIBERALISM VERSUS MARXISM: THE GREAT 20TH-CENTURY DEBATE

As political parties and governments inspired by Marx gained support and power during the 20th century, democratic liberalism and its economic counterpart, capitalism, faced a serious challenge. Not surprisingly, the clash between liberalism and Marxism dominated social and political debate. Two 20th-century social and political thinkers, the American liberal-libertarian Robert Nozick and the German-born Marxist philosopher Herbert Marcuse, represent the extremes of thinking in this debate.

ROBERT NOZICK: THE VIRTUE OF PRIVATE PROPERTY AND FREE ENTERPRISE

Robert Nozick's *Anarchy, State, and Utopia,* published in 1974, described an extreme version of political liberalism known as **libertarianism**. Like liberals, libertarians believe that the purpose of political society is to defend the lives, liberties, and possessions of its citizens. But unlike most liberals, who support the idea of governments' providing basic necessities to less prosperous members of society, libertarians argue that the state should not be involved in redistributing wealth.

Nozick said that a democratic government that promotes social or economic equality at the expense of liberty is taking a first, dangerous step down the slippery slope toward totalitarianism. Appealing to Locke's idea that the state must defend and promote citizens' life, liberty, and property, Nozick regarded any government-sponsored plan to redistribute society's economic resources as a betrayal of purpose.

Nozick argued, for example, that the state has no right to require people to pay taxes, which are used to fund public services. He said that compulsory taxation threatens people's right to acquire, possess, enhance, and enjoy their personal wealth. If individuals wish to contribute voluntarily to charities or help the less fortunate in other ways, said Nozick, they should be able to do this. At the same time, however, he maintained that people have a basic right to retain every penny of the wealth they have legally acquired, whether this was through hard work, enterprise, luck, or family inheritance. Critics of libertarianism point out that most wealthy people in contemporary western societies acquired their money through family inheritances and connections and warn that allowing them to keep all this money could lead to the establishment of a new kind of aristocracy.

> *When there is an income tax, the just man will pay more and the unjust man less on the same amount of income.*
>
> — Plato

Nozick's theories have inspired libertarian political movements in North America and elsewhere. These political parties urge governments to reduce their involvement in people's economic, social, and political lives. Though they rarely gain much support from the electorate, their ideas have been adapted by mainstream parties since the 1970s. Political leaders such as former United States president Ronald Reagan, former British prime minister Margaret Thatcher, and former Canadian prime minister Brian Mulroney, for example, believed that governments should limit their involvement in their countries' economies and do more to promote private enterprise and personal prosperity. This ideology, sometimes called neo-liberalism or neo-conservatism, has inspired governments to reduce taxes, cut back on social spending, and privatize formerly state-owned businesses.

HERBERT MARCUSE: THE ILLUSION OF SUCCESS

Herbert Marcuse was one of several Marxist social and political thinkers who emerged in Germany before the rise of Nazism in 1933. Because most members of this group were Jewish and anti-Nazi, they were forced into exile after Hitler came to power. Marcuse immigrated to the United States, where he spent the rest of his life teaching and writing. During the 1960s, his theories became popular among members of the so-called new left. This movement included many young people, who were beginning to challenge the ideas and methods of the political and economic establishment.

Marcuse wondered why the working classes of Europe and North America had not rebelled against capitalism, as Marx had predicted they would. To answer his own question, he theorized that workers were being sold an "illusion of success." He said that rising economic prosperity and security masked the fact that the capitalist system continued to exploit people and deny them true fulfillment.

In *One-Dimensional Man,* published in 1964, Marcuse argued that people were oppressed without being aware of it. Their oppression was masked by the rise in the standard of living, a measure of material comfort. Marcuse said that this material comfort — the ability to buy things that made their lives more comfortable — gave people the illusion of success. In his view, society assigned too much importance to acquiring material possessions, and most people were forced to work long hours to buy everything that was advertised. He believed that this was capitalism's fundamental flaw.

Marcuse acknowledged that most North American workers and their families enjoyed a standard of living well beyond the imagination of their ancestors. But he also believed that their lives were often empty of meaning. They were "one-dimensional," because they were driven by the need to acquire more money and material goods. He theorized that most people worked at jobs that held no enjoyment or meaning and that they viewed only their leisure time as their own. Drawing on psychological theories, Marcuse argued that capitalism's worship of individualism and private property undercut people's human instincts to seek happiness, play, freedom, and social solidarity.

Marcuse also maintained that capitalism has a dark side. Poverty had not disappeared, the environment was damaged, social conflict and crime had increased, and more people were turning to drugs, alcohol, and other forms of escape from their meaningless lives.

Figure 19.6

"TRY IT COMRADE... IT'S CALLED A 'HAPPY MEAL.'"

How does this cartoon comment on Herbert Marcuse's theory?

Marcuse imagined a new society, one in which the economic goals of industrial states would no longer be to make a profit. Instead, the goal would be to provide basic social goods for all. He believed that it was possible for a modern economy to meet the needs of its citizens without requiring them to work more than a small number of hours a week at jobs that were both meaningful and enjoyable. He said that technology could be used to abolish poverty, preserve the natural environment, and promote social engagement.

How could a society like this be achieved? Because most workers accepted the material rewards of capitalism, Marcuse considered it unlikely that the working class would lead the revolution. Instead, he said, marginalized and exploited groups, such as students, non-whites, and women, were likely to lead the way.

Though Marcuse's writings are a product of their times, his ideas contain a serious critique of liberal democracy and capitalism. Whether a system like the one he envisioned can benefit average citizens is still the subject of debate.

Chapter Review

Chapter Summary

This chapter has discussed
- some of the main questions of social and political philosophy
- the responses of major philosophers and major schools of social and political philosophy to some of the main questions of social and political philosophy
- how theories of social and political philosophy are realized in contemporary policy making, and how this affects political and social practices
- how particular philosophical theories have influenced the development of other subjects
- how the ideas of philosophers have influenced subsequent philosophers

Knowledge and Understanding

1. Identify and explain the significance to the study of social and political philosophy of each of the following key words and people.

Key Words	Key People
philosopher kings	Thomas Aquinas
totalitarianism	Kongfuzi (Confucius)
democracy	Mohandas Gandhi
natural law	Dalai Lama
satyagraha	Olympe de Gouges
general will	Mary Wollstonecraft
capitalism	Edmund Burke
socialism	Thomas Paine
libertarianism	Karl Marx
	Robert Nozick
	Herbert Marcuse

2. Create a graphic organizer that illustrates the social and political philosophy of the western tradition, the eastern tradition, and the modern era. Display the origin of the main ideas, the impact of these ideas on later philosophers, and the important issues at each stage of development.

Thinking and Inquiry

3. Read this excerpt from Simone de Beauvoir's *The Second Sex*, which was published in 1949.

    > The advantage man enjoys, which makes itself felt from his childhood, is that his vocation as a human being in no way runs counter to his destiny as a male.... [H]is social and spiritual successes endow him with a virile prestige. He is not divided. Whereas it is required of woman that in order to realize her femininity she must make herself object and prey, which is to say that she must renounce her claims as a sovereign subject. It is this conflict that especially marks the situation of the emancipated woman....

   In your own words, explain what de Beauvoir means. Compare this statement to Mary Wollstonecraft's views, which were set out more than 150 years earlier. Do you think that women face the same problem today? Use logical- and critical-thinking skills to defend your ideas and anticipate counter-arguments.

4. Events such as the French Revolution have sparked debate over the most appropriate way of bringing about social and political change. Are revolutions, even radical and violent ones, sometimes more effective than more moderate approaches? Consider examples of change in your own personal experience, as well as responses from a variety of philosophers, to answer this question. Which approach to social and political change would you recommend? Formulate and defend your position in the form of a personal reflection that incorporates first- and second-order questions.

Communication

5. Select three philosophers with differing views on the formation of social and political institutions. For each, prepare a social contract that includes three guiding principles for society. The guiding principles should show the differences between their theories.

6. Form a group and create a video montage that explores how films reflect various social and political philosophies. In your montage, include four or five short clips (less than a minute each) that show the relationship between social and political philosophy and subjects such as political science, economics, or law. Prepare questions to stimulate discussion of your clips after you present your montage to the class.

Application

7. Examine this cartoon by Jay N. "Ding" Darling (Figure 19.7). Its title is *The Russian Excursion into Utopia*. List three images used in this work and explain how each relates to a central question of social and political philosophy. What message do you think Darling was trying to portray?

8. Imagine that Socrates is meeting Karl Marx, Robert Nozick, or Herbert Marcuse in a philosophy café. Choose a social or political issue and write a Socratic dialogue to illustrate the conversation that might occur as Socrates probes Marx's, Nozick's, or Marcuse's ideas.

Figure 19.7

Chapter 20
The Individual, the Law, and Justice

Chapter Expectations

By the end of this chapter, you will be able to
- demonstrate an understanding of the main questions of social and political philosophy
- evaluate the responses of major philosophers and major schools of social and political philosophy to some of the main questions of social and political philosophy
- use critical- and logical-thinking skills to develop and defend your own ideas about some of the major questions of social and political philosophy and to anticipate counter-arguments
- analyze how theories of social and political philosophy are adopted and realized in contemporary policy making and how this affects political and social practices
- demonstrate an understanding of how particular philosophical theories have influenced the development of other subjects
- describe how the ideas of philosophers have influenced subsequent philosophers
- clearly explain your own views and display your use of philosophical reasoning skills in philosophical discussions in class, in exchanges with peers, and in written papers

Key Words

classical liberalism
individualism
positive law
natural law
naturalists
legal positivists
retributive justice
distributive justice
economic laissez-faire
contractarian
entitlement

Key People

Hugo Grotius
Charles L. Black Jr.
Pierre Elliott Trudeau
Jeremy Bentham
John Rawls

A Philosopher's Voice

I think the first duty of society is justice.

– Alexander Hamilton (1757–1804)

The Individual and Society

The main character in Darby Conley's *Get Fuzzy* comic strip, Bucky the Cat, is a rugged individualist who lives by his philosophical convictions. In this particular strip (Figure 20.1), Bucky expresses the tensions felt by many people.

Figure 20.1

There is a bit of Bucky in everyone. Most people want the good things that living at home, going to school, and being a part of a community provide. At the same time, most people also want to carve out personal space for themselves. Like Bucky, they cherish personal freedom and insist that they have the right to do their own thing. This is part of striving for a good life. But balancing the conflicting demands of the individual and society can create tensions — and Bucky expresses these in this cartoon.

When people talk about striving for a good life, what do they have in mind? This question is as old as philosophy itself. Some philosophers, like the Stoics of ancient Greece, claimed that society is not important. They said that people can find peace and harmony by looking inward. Other thinkers, such as Plato, Aristotle, John Locke, Jean-Jacques Rousseau, and Karl Marx, disagreed over many issues but agreed that a truly good and just life can be found only in a truly good and just society. These thinkers did not agree, however, on what this society ought to be like.

In discussions of the nature of a good and just society, questions about the relationship between the individual and society, or citizens and the state, are inevitable. One of the most basic is, What is the proper balance between the rights of the individual and the rights of the state and how can this balance be achieved? This question raises many others: What role should the state play in its citizens' lives? What is an appropriate dividing line between too much and too little state involvement in issues that pit individual rights against the security and well-being of the country? How should the state dispense justice and safeguard the economic, social, and political rights of individuals? What is justice, and does it mean the same thing for everyone? What is a just balance between individual freedom and human rights?

In western philosophical thought, the relative importance of the individual in society has increased greatly over the years. In *The Republic*, for example, Plato emphasized the primacy of the state over the individual, a view that prevailed for more than 2000 years.

This thinking began to shift at the beginning of the modern age. In the 17th century, John Locke became one of the first advocates of an approach called **classical liberalism**, a political and social philosophy that advocates freedom from excessive government interference and maintains that the function of the state is to protect the rights and liberties of individual people. Locke argued that the rights and liberties of individuals stem from natural law and that the foundation of natural law is God. In Locke's view, the individual takes precedence over the state.

Some philosophers say that classical liberalism and **individualism**, a view that emphasizes the importance of the individual, are the same thing. Though others disagree, it can certainly be said that individualism is the cornerstone of classical liberalism.

Since Locke's time, individualism has gained ground as a political and social principle. Still, some thinkers have raised concerns about its possible negative consequences. They have argued that it fosters shallowness, an aloofness from society, and selfishness.

Charles Taylor, for example, is a communitarian who expresses serious reservations about the effects of individualism on modern society. In *The Malaise of Modernity*, he writes that "the dark side of individualism is a centring on the self, which both flattens and narrows our lives, makes them poorer in meaning, and less concerned with others or society."

JUSTICE AND LAW

Although few people give it much thought, most live their lives within an intricate web of social groups. Most people also accept the need for governing bodies with the authority to create and enforce laws for these groups. In Canada, for example, the federal and provincial governments make general rules that ensure that groups and organizations operate within the law. These rules apply to all kinds of groups, from environmental associations with international connections to national charitable organizations, large corporations, and your school hockey, volleyball, or basketball team.

In some senses, the operation of a school sports team can be compared with that of a state. Both establish laws or rules and ways of enforcing them. On a team, players who don't abide by the rules suffer the consequences. They may be assessed a penalty, ejected from the game, or thrown off the team.

In both sports and life, the more serious the offence, the more severe the penalty usually is. If you steal a large amount of money, for example, you are likely to go to jail. Many factors determine whether the laws and rules of a given organization or state are fair and whether the justice dispensed is swift. In the case of a state, some of these factors are its history, its current values, and its form of government.

To be accepted by its members, a governing body — whether of a country, a professional association, an amateur hockey league, a fan club, or a volunteer group — must be legitimate. Something must give this body the authority to make and enforce decisions on behalf of the group.

People also expect decision-making bodies to act in the best interests of the organization's members. No one wants a bully for a team captain, a tyrant for a coach, or a national leader who believes that he or she is above the law. Nor do people want any organization, governmental or otherwise, to invade their privacy or control their lives.

Figure 20.2

A linesman guides Tie Domi of the Toronto Maple Leafs to the penalty box during an NHL game. Few people question the idea that penalties are an appropriate form of justice in sport.

As a student, you might protest if your school adopts a new dress code that requires you to wear a uniform. In the same way, citizens who are not consulted might protest restrictions on their liberties or the imposition of new taxes. In most democracies, citizens expect rules and laws to conform to their notion of justice. When this is not the case, they feel justified in organizing protests and working to bring about change.

PHILOSOPHY IN ACTION

Virtual Communities and Virtuous Reality

by George D. Randels Jr.

George D. Randels Jr. is an assistant professor of social ethics at the University of the Pacific in California. This article, which assesses the pros and cons of individualism and communitarianism, was printed in *A Publication on Information Technology at Emory University.*

All across the political spectrum, we hear calls for community. Although some notion of community has always been important, philosophical and political communitarianism developed in the 1980s and into the '90s, ostensibly as a challenge to liberalism. Among other things, it voices concern for individualism run amok without regard for the common good.

Communitarian critiques often begin with examples — sometimes theoretical, sometimes concrete, sometimes both — of the ills of liberal modernity. Although I will defend a moderate liberal-communitarian position that recognizes the strengths of liberalism and communitarianism, it nevertheless seems appropriate to list a few such examples here at the outset.

A communitarian critique of cyberspace would focus on how it magnifies the real world problems of liberal individualism. On the theoretical side, while the term "Internet" suggests an interconnected network of persons, the popular metaphor "information superhighway" connotes an express route for individuals to get where and what they want as quickly as possible. A superhighway allows us to minimize intersections with other roads, and so avoid connections with others. We remain isolated in our vehicles as we travel. The metaphor encourages viewing the Net strictly as an infrastructure for achieving individual needs, a narrow focus back on self. Similarly, surfing is an activity done by a lone individual. These metaphors give rise to the image of a solitary computer hacker, clicking away at a keyboard in a remote apartment or office. The philosopher Charles Taylor would use the term atomistic individualism to describe this situation.

This image of the solitary user becomes more insidious when it moves beyond using the Net strictly as a research and information-gathering tool, to how this condition affects others encountered along the road. Probably all of us have experienced belligerent computer users with an exaggerated sense of self-importance, any one of whom could provide an illustrative negative benchmark. At the University of Virginia, for example, one user calling himself Dr. Rocket, terrorized the local newsgroups, pontificating and flaming at will....

There have been several recent events in cyberspace that have gained national prominence, illustrating the excesses of individualism and providing ample seed for a virtual-communitarian critique. Much attention has gone to the presence of pornographic images on the Net, with federal legislation promoted to curb it, and a proposal for global action at an international religious conference against pornography. The problem of pornography is magnified on the Net for at least two reasons. First, there is easier access to it, especially for children, and so we cannot even achieve the benefits of zoning and age restrictions. Second, there is an exponentially increased scale of distribution for such already problematic things as child pornography or revenge publication of private pictures....

If nothing else, these cases show that cyberspace is rife with ethical problems, some of which can be connected to the most radical individualism. Communitarianism can provide a useful way to think about these problems, emphasizing the common good, although it brings difficulties of its own. These difficulties include finding a good balance between the benefits of community and the benefits of liberal individualism, and the applicability of communitarianism to the Net.

Community and Individual

I have a lot of sympathy with communitarian thought, but I think that we need to be careful in our use of the term community. One of the most crucial questions we need to ask is what we mean by it. Ferdinand Toennies' influential ideal types of *gemeinschaft* and *gesellschaft* remain useful starting points. *Gemeinschaft* connotes kinship and unified moral vision, whereas *gesellschaft* indicates separation "in spite of all uniting factors." Toennies' typology clearly influences the famous liberal philosopher John Rawls. He essentially accepts *gemeinschaft* as a proper definition of community, contending that community involves a "shared, comprehensive religious, philosophical, or moral doctrine." Rawls then rightly rejects this conception of community as inappropriate for a liberal, democratic society.

One of the virtues of liberal individualism is that it protects us from the tyranny involved in enforcing such comprehensive doctrines and other infringements of personal liberty. While the term "community" carries positive connotations of important shared values, a sense of membership, and the benevolent bonds of social existence, negatively it can mean a tyranny of the majority, and not just for radical individualists.... One [interesting and troubling example] concerns neighbourhood associations, some of which are notorious for enforcing community in cases that many of us would find objectionable. I know of an instance in Reston, Virginia, a few years ago, where neighbourhood association members tore down a tree house that a boy had built in his family's backyard. Tree houses violated the Association's code — the rules for that community — which strictly governed the maintenance of property. Similarly, the St. Louis suburb Ladue applied its strict sign ordinance to a notebook-size piece of paper taped to a bedroom window. The wealthy community forbids nearly all signs on the basis of "aesthetics, safety, and property values."

Gemeinschaft may still be appropriate, of course, for smaller communities within a more liberal society, such as the Amish and other religious or quasi-religious groups. It is, however, only one type of community, and one that is nearly extinct, especially in the U.S. We live in a post-modern world, where cultural and communal boundaries increasingly collapse or overlap — remote African villagers drink Coca-Cola; Amazon peasants buy Avon.... Cultural pluralism has made most of us multicultural individuals, with diverse influences and allegiances.

If this is the case in the real world, then it is so much more so for virtual reality, which cannot provide one's entire identity, because one cannot live completely within it. Virtual reality also can increase our exposure to other ideas and cultures, and allow us to experiment with alternative identities. By defining community narrowly as *gemeinschaft*, virtual community is an oxymoron [a figure of speech that includes contradictory terms], except potentially for small groups whose relationships extend very far into the real world. It also would unnecessarily force us to choose between individual liberty and community. We must, then, expand this overly restrictive definition.

Liberty and Community

In a liberal society, many of us want to obtain the positive aspects of community, while avoiding the dangers of tyranny. We want liberty and community. If communitarianism is at base a rejection of nihilism and radical focus on individual rights, then most of us are, and always have been, communitarians. We desire a sense of us, of having shared values, a feeling of membership and fellowship. In many ways communitarianism provides nothing new, but reminds us of something important. I am inclined to agree with Amy Gutman, that while communitarianism can help us find something better than atomistic individualism, liberalism contains many virtues worth retaining. So, merely juxtaposing individualism and communitarianism as opposites is overly simplistic. It would also be a mistake to speak of communitarianism as a monolithic movement. There is wide divergence, for example, between moderate communitarians like William Galston, Michael Walzer, and Amitai Etzioni, and their more radical counterparts Alasdair MacIntyre, Michael Sandel, and Charles Taylor. Communitarianism is better characterized as a genre that rejects a radical focus on individual rights and liberties, but with different positive visions.

It is also worth noting that the term community can be either descriptive or prescriptive. Descriptively, it often means that we cannot speak of individuals apart from their communities. If we do not insist upon *gemeinschaft*, then this descriptive use is accurate. To paraphrase John Donne [an English poet], no one is an island. Humans are social creatures, not atomistic individuals. Even that rugged individualist, the cowboy, exists within a larger social structure and is shaped by it.

Communitarians often use the term prescriptively, however, arguing that individualist conceptions of persons are not only descriptively inadequate,... [but also] destructive of social order, and hence, of any ethics other than egoism. Communitarians often point to various problems in liberal societies as moral indictments of liberal individualism. If they extended their critiques to cyberspace, they might cite the cases that I noted at the beginning of this article. Community as a normative concept requires us to shape our societies, our personal outlooks, characters, and behaviour to reflect shared values and ideals.

Although we must reject *gemeinschaft* as an inadequate definition in both the descriptive and prescriptive senses, community remains a worthy moral ideal when it seeks a balance between communal goods and individual liberty....

I hold community as a normative concept, meaning that all societies should progress toward that middle ground. Size, adversity, and other contingencies, however, will determine the degree to which a particular society can approximate community. For example, the larger the society, the less responsibility it can take for its members and the more diversity it must tolerate; the less extensive participation it can have, and the more diminished the prospect for membership. Smaller communities within the society must fill the gaps, if they are filled at all.

Source: "Virtual Communities and Virtuous Reality." George D. Randels Jr. In *A Publication on Information Technology at Emory University.* November-December 1996.

1. In the view of George Randels, what are the shortcomings of extreme individualism and extreme communitarianism? Do you agree with him?

2. Do you agree with Randels' assertion that societies should find a middle ground between extreme individualism and extreme communitarianism? Why? Present a counter-argument to Randels' position from the point of view of either an individualist or a communitarian.

3. How does the title of Randels' article express the essence of the ideas he presents?

THE LAW

The law is a set of rules that tell people what they can and cannot do. In Canada, you must pay GST and obey traffic signs, for example, and you must not hit people or ignore parking tickets. Failure to abide by these rules usually entails consequences or punishments. This is fine with most people, who obey laws that they consider reasonable and just. The situation is not as clear cut, however, when people consider laws unreasonable or unjust.

How do people distinguish between reasonable and unreasonable, or just and unjust, laws? Do fixed principles help them make this judgment? How does the law differ from and relate to moral right and wrong? In an attempt to answer some of these questions, social and political philosophers have traditionally distinguished between two kinds of law: positive law and natural law.

The more laws, the less justice.

– Cicero

Though Plato and Aristotle were the first to suggest the existence of two kinds of law, the terms "positive law" and "natural law" did not appear in philosophical discussions of legal theory until the 12th century.

POSITIVE LAW

Positive law is created by humans. It refers to written rules — against theft, murder, and so on — that are enforced by the courts of the land. Judges render verdicts of innocence or guilt and give reasons for their decisions.

If you are fined for littering, receive an inheritance from a rich aunt, or lose your Porsche to the finance company, laws make or allow these things to happen. Matters like these are covered by a jurisdiction's written laws.

NATURAL LAW

Unlike positive law, natural law is unwritten. It does not appear in rule books or statutes, yet many believe that it compels people to seek a higher, objective standard that can be used to judge positive laws. Supporters of the idea of natural law are often called naturalists. They consider natural law to be the law as it would be in its ideal form and regard it as the conscience of a state's legal system.

Natural law theory emphasizes the role of moral right and wrong, saying that a universal moral command exists for making laws. For example, one theory of the origin of natural law says that it is the supreme being's eternal laws applied to humans. Those who support this theory believe that natural law underlies moral principles and that people can learn what it is by reasoning and heeding their consciences. Some thinkers believe that human law that does not conform to natural law is invalid; others view natural law only as a standard that can be used to assess positive law.

THE DEBATE BETWEEN LEGAL POSITIVISTS AND NATURALISTS

Most **legal positivists** oppose natural law theory and reject the idea that there is a relationship between the law and moral right and wrong. Indeed, some legal positivists claim that moral truth cannot be known. They say that rules that have been enacted by governments or courts are the only sources of law. They maintain that, as a result, the law is identified only by reference to factual information such as legal precedents and legislation. Legal positivists also argue that any law passed by a legitimate authority must be obeyed by everyone, even those who consider the law morally wrong or unjust.

The Dutch thinker **Hugo Grotius**, who lived from 1583 to 1645, defended the idea of natural law. "The law of nature is a dictate of right reason, which points out that an act, according as it is or is not in conformity with rational nature, has in it a quality of moral … necessity, and that, in consequence, such an act is either forbidden or enjoined by the author of nature, God," he wrote.

> **Web connection**
> www.mcgrawhill.ca/links/philosophy12
> To find out more about Hugo Grotius, follow the links on this Web site.

Taking his cue from Plato and Aristotle, who emphasized that human beings are essentially rational by nature, Grotius concluded that people can arrive at just laws by using their ability to reason. In other words, he said, natural law can be inferred from human nature.

Some people have made natural law a central, guiding feature of their social and political philosophy. The social contract theorist John Locke, for example, said that natural law justifies people's obedience to rulers in return for guarantees that their rights will be protected. Others have gone farther, maintaining that rules that conflict with natural law cannot be positive laws. Though natural law is not binding or obligatory in the same way as positive law, naturalists believe that it provides a moral guide — and maintain that this is its value.

Also central to the notion of natural law is the concept of natural or human rights. The right to life and liberty figure prominently among these. Naturalists claim that rules that diminish a person's sense of dignity and equality violate natural law.

In the 20th century, natural law theory fell out of favour. The widespread recognition of conflicting moral beliefs undermined its reliance on a universal or absolute system of beliefs about moral right and wrong.

> *Law is twofold — natural and written. The natural law is in the heart, the written law on tables. All men are under the natural law.*
>
> — Ambrose

Some critics simply ignore the concept of natural law; others dismiss it as speculation and unsound reasoning, with no foundation in objective reality. According to these critics, natural law is nothing more than the expression of subjective moral beliefs that change according to time and place. They point out, for example, that various societies at various times have accepted infanticide as natural. If acts like this are natural, they say, it diminishes the appeal of natural law.

Despite the criticisms, the notion of natural law has played an important role in western society. Although few believe that natural law provides absolute standards of law and justice, many philosophers agree with the 20th-century American constitutional law expert **Charles L. Black Jr.**, who wrote: "There remains a value in the concept which the term 'natural law' seeks to suggest." Most people, maintained Black, strive for the betterment of law and the perfection of justice.

According to Black, the fact that someone cannot be punished for an action committed before the passage of a law governing the action is an example of natural justice at work. Similarly, he said, the fact that a person cannot be imprisoned for debt recognizes natural rights. Black also claims that judges are often required to fill the gaps in positive law by resorting to natural law.

In *Political Philosophy*, Anthony Quinton offered this assessment of natural and positive law:

> There is a minimum interpretation in which only those who take the service of the state to be the highest conceivable duty for man could possibly reject [natural law]. It can be taken to say simply that there are moral considerations by which the state's claim to authority must be judged. Unless one holds with [Georg W.F.] Hegel that private morality is a crude, primitive anticipation of the higher morality of positive law or, attaching no meaning to moral discourse, abstain from it altogether, one cannot consistently oppose this position....
>
> In practice there is a good deal of correspondence between the content of positive law and natural law, if this is understood as the broad moral consensus of the citizens. Unless the state in question is very effectively tyrannous, indeed, there must be, since if a state's positive law is morally repugnant to most of its citizens they will have a reason for disobeying it.... But there is always some divergence between positive law and the generally accepted hard core of morality.

Recall...Reflect...Respond

1. Does the philosophy of individualism suggest that social responsibility is unimportant? Explain your response.
2. On a continuum with naturalism at one end and legal positivism at the other, where would you place yourself? Explain why.
3. What conditions make decision-making bodies legitimate? Does this support the position of legal positivists or naturalists? Explain why.

WHAT IS JUSTICE?

Justice is one of the most important ideas in social and political philosophy. If you have ever objected to something like your school's rules governing where students can and cannot eat, a curfew imposed by a parent or guardian, or the law stipulating the age at which you can get a driver's licence, you may have asked, Where's the justice in this?

In asking this question, you were probably less concerned about the legal status of the rule than its fairness or justice. But what do people mean when they talk about fairness and justice? Can a rule or law be considered fair and just by anyone if it is not accepted by everyone affected? These are some of the questions that social and political philosophers focus on when they discuss justice.

Laws are conceived, enacted, and sometimes repealed according to the needs and wishes of a society. Some laws come and go in a relatively short time, while others seem to last forever, unaffected by social, political, or economic change. In democratic societies, at least, the catalyst for changing any system of law is the notion of justice.

But what does this notion entail? Over the millennia, social and political philosophers have struggled to answer this question. Dictionaries are little help. One dictionary might define justice as conformity to the law. But are there not unjust laws? Another dictionary might say that justice is the quality, or fact, of being just. The shortcomings of this definition are obvious. It launches a vicious circle.

It is not surprising that dictionary definitions of justice end up raising as many questions as they answer. Over the past 2500 years, some of the most brilliant minds in western philosophy have tried to come up with a universally acceptable definition of justice — and failed. One of the reasons for this failure is that individuals, groups, and societies often propose radically different conceptions of justice.

Despite this, states are often called upon to find justice in conflicts between the claims of individuals or groups on the one hand and society on the other. In other words, the state is often called upon to spell out the correct relationship between the individual and society.

In courts of law, for example, judges and juries are called upon every day to decide how justice might best be served in the rendering of verdicts. When verdicts are handed down in widely publicized criminal cases, however, individual citizens often respond positively or negatively to the rulings. These reactions often have little to do with the technicalities of the law; rather, they are based on people's perceptions — well informed or not — of whether justice has been done. Indeed, for many people, justice means a punishment that fits the crime.

> *There is one thing, and one thing only, which defies all mutation; that which existed before the world, and will survive the fabric of the world itself: I mean justice.*
>
> – Edmund Burke

RETRIBUTION AND JUSTICE

Crime and retribution, or punishment, have been central to humanity's understanding of justice for a long time. In the Judeo-Christian tradition, for example, the idea of retribution is set out in the biblical phrase, "An eye for an eye and a tooth for a tooth." Even today, many people are attracted by the concept of **retributive justice**, the idea that people ought to get what they deserve or that the punishment should match the crime. In its simplest terms, retributive justice means that if you deliberately break someone's arm, your arm would be broken in return. And if you kill someone, you would be put to death.

Many people argue, however, that the notion of retribution, especially in its simplest eye-for-an-eye version, is fundamentally flawed. What is the appropriate response to crimes such as fraud and blackmail, for example? What punishment does the poor, starving person who steals groceries deserve? In some past societies, this person's hand might have been cut off.

Depending on the time and place, one person's justice is another's barbarism. Few would deny that the notion of retribution is closely linked to the desire for revenge, a human emotion that many find unappealing. Critics of retribution also insist that punishment has no demonstrable beneficial effects for either the criminal or society.

> *Probably all laws are useless; for good men do not want laws at all, and bad men are made no better by them.*
>
> – Demonax

DISTRIBUTION AND JUSTICE

In democratic societies such as Canada's, many people believe that a retributive definition of justice is too narrow. They say that justice involves more than getting even for criminal acts. In societies like these, the principle of distributive justice, which suggests that people ought to share equally in the distribution of a society's resources, is an important underlying concept. Just how this principle should be applied, however, is a source of controversy.

How should a country's wealth and finite resources be distributed? If some people should receive more than others, how should this be decided? Should the most needy get a larger share than others? Should the person who contributes more to society get a proportionately larger share? If so, how much more? Does someone who prefers to lounge around all day deserve the same monetary reward as the person who works hard at a tough, boring, low-paying job? Should a single mother who, for various reasons, must stay home to care for a child receive the same reward as a single mother who can — and does — work outside the home?

Who should decide the best way of distributing society's resources? Should groups whose members have been subjected to unjust discrimination on the basis of sex, age, religion, race, and so on receive special consideration? Is implementing reverse discrimination an appropriate way of redressing past grievances?

In addition to answering questions about how wealth and resources should be distributed, the principles of distributive justice can also be applied to issues such as health, education, power, privilege, and recognition. In Canada for example, the question of two-tier health care — a government-funded component for those who cannot afford to pay for medical care and a private component for those who can afford it — is a contentious issue. Supporters of two-tier care argue that those who are willing and able to pay extra deserve to receive the best medical care that money can buy. They also say that enabling people to do this would reduce the financial strain on the system. Critics contend that this would drain the health-care system so that the poor would end up waiting in long lines for no-frills medical care while the rich would leap to the front of the line and receive top-flight service.

Consider a situation in which two people need a heart transplant. One is wealthy and prepared to make a substantial donation to the hospital if she gets the next available heart. The new equipment that the hospital could buy with her donation would help save many lives. The other person has no money to offer. Which candidate would you choose?

Would the choice become easier to make if you knew that one of the prospective heart recipients is a derelict who has never contributed to society while the other is a famous brain surgeon who would unquestionably save many lives if she receives a new heart and is able to continue her career?

This example makes it clear that the dividing line between issues of morality and justice is very thin — and helps explain why philosophers often discuss ethical issues

Figure 20.3

Where do you think this protester stands on the issue of two-tier health care?

in the same context as social and political issues. Both justice and morality require people to think very carefully about what is right before deciding on a course of action.

Web connection
www.mcgrawhill.ca/links/philosophy12
To find out more about distributive justice, follow the links on this Web site.

Power is another area in which principles of distributive justice are often applied. Consider how families, schools, business organizations, and large government bureaucracies are organized. The many layers, or levels, of power are readily apparent.

Think of the vote, which is considered a basic right in the individual's exercise of power. Who should be allowed to vote and at what age? Should the vote of someone who pays higher taxes carry more weight? In democratic countries like Canada, the principle of one person, one vote is widely endorsed because it ensures that each person's vote has the same power — or does it?

John Courtney, a political scientist at the University of Saskatchewan, has highlighted a longstanding distribution issue in the Canadian electoral system. The 2001 census showed that the populations of Alberta, British Columbia, and Ontario are growing faster than those of the other provinces. As a result, Courtney found, some provinces are over-represented in Parliament.

Prince Edward Island is an example. The population of this province is shrinking, yet the people of Prince Edward Island are constitutionally guaranteed four elected representatives in the House of Commons. If the principle of representation by population were strictly applied, they would have only one. And Saskatchewan elects 14 members of Parliament, even though its population would entitle it to only nine.

According to Courtney, this situation skews the idea of representation by population and the principle of one person, one vote. It makes the votes of Canadians who live in slow-growth provinces worth more than the votes of those who live in the fast-growing provinces of British Columbia, Alberta, and Ontario. According to Courtney, this situation highlights an injustice in the Canadian electoral system. He says that seats in the House of Commons should be allotted in accordance with each province's share of the total Canadian population.

IDEAS IN CONTEXT

One percent of the world's water is drinkable, and 10 percent of the world's fresh water is in Canada. To many people, the question is not if — but when — Canada's water will become a prized resource, as oil is today. At present rates of global consumption and population growth, some experts have predicted that many regions of the world will face critical water shortages by 2025. This situation will raise the stakes in the distributive justice debate. How will water-rich countries like Canada react to requests for water from poor nations? How *should* they react? How will governments deal with issues involving a life-and-death resource like water?

For social and political philosophers, the problem Courtney highlights raises philosophical issues. What are the rights of the individual in this particular case? What are the rights of the provinces? Does might make right? In other words, should the largest and fastest-growing provinces be able to flex their political muscle to gain more seats in the House of Commons? A utilitarian might suggest that changing the distribution of federal ridings would produce the greatest happiness for the greatest number. But would it really? Applying a utilitarian formula could also tear the country apart, as several provinces might question the value of remaining in Confederation.

In attempting to answer questions like those raised by the issue of parliamentary representation, social and political philosophers have proposed several criteria and a variety of theories of distributive justice. Merit, need, fairness, and benefit to society are among the most-often discussed.

Recall...Reflect...Respond

1. Is justice best defined narrowly as retributive or more broadly as distributive? Explain why you think so.
2. Do you believe that marks are a just entrance requirement for post-secondary educational institutions? Include references to distributive justice in a philosophical argument for or against making post-secondary education accessible to everyone.
3. Suppose that you have been asked to make the Canadian electoral system more equitable. What solution would you propose? Think about possible counter-arguments to your solution and develop arguments to refute them.

MERIT AS JUSTICE

An important plank of Plato's social and political philosophy was the state, which he considered more important than the individual. Plato believed that people must be part of society to be fully human. What makes people human — language and values, for example — are the benefits of living in a society. In his view, it therefore followed that the individual is subservient to society, or the state.

In *The Republic*, Plato wrote that people are naturally unequal, that class distinctions are normal and proper, and that some people are better suited to certain jobs than others. He said that human beings should behave and be treated according to their abilities, training, and knowledge. In Plato's view, this meant that everyone should do the kind of work that nature decrees. The state's rulers, having acquired true knowledge of justice, would naturally rule the state justly. When this happens, he said, justice would prevail and people would get what they deserve. Some philosophers have called this Plato's merit theory of justice.

To Plato, justice within the individual was the same as justice within the state. Just as an individual would achieve harmony and justice when reason, spirit, and appetite play their proper roles, he said, so the state would achieve harmony and justice if all groups attend to the jobs for which they are best suited.

From a 21st-century perspective, it is difficult to take seriously Plato's contention that, if justice is to prevail, the individual must always be subordinate to the state. Many philosophers dispute Plato's argument that what is good for the state is also good for the individual. They charge that on some issues, such as individual liberty and self-determination, Plato was unable to look beyond the belief structures of his time and place.

Canadian prime minister **Pierre Elliott Trudeau**, who led the Canadian government from 1968 to 1979 and again from 1980 to 1984, admired Plato but rejected his ideas of justice as merit. In Trudeau's view, the people are sovereign and deserve to be free of discrimination. He supported this principle so strongly that he engineered the adoption of the Canadian Charter of Rights and Freedoms, which enshrines individual equality rights in the Canadian Constitution.

IDEAS IN CONTEXT

Aristotle shared most of Plato's views on class distinctions, natural inequality among people, and the nature of justice. Aristotle argued, for example, that slaves would be unhappy if they were freed. His argument was based on the assumption that slaves derived their happiness from doing what they were naturally suited for.

Like Plato, Aristotle associated justice with the idea that each person should receive what is due to him or her on the basis of natural ability or merit. He said, "Justice is treating equals equally, and unequals unequally, according to the differences between them."

PROFILE

Pierre Elliott Trudeau
Translating Philosophy into Action

Canadian Prime Minister Pierre Elliott Trudeau articulated a social and political vision of a just society that balanced the concepts of the individual, the law, and justice. In doing so, he showed that philosophy can be translated into action.

Born in 1919 in Montreal, Trudeau was the son of a millionaire French-speaking father and an English-speaking mother. At home, the family spoke both English and French. During his youth, he backpacked through Europe, the Middle East, and Asia — and gained a wealth of experience. He was flamboyant in every respect. Colourful clothes, fast cars, a brown belt in judo, and skin diving were just a few of his many interests.

Trudeau also had a serious, scholarly side. One of his teachers recalled that ideas of justice and liberty were important to him. This may explain why his first degree was in law. Later, he earned a degree in political economy from Harvard and undertook further studies in England at the London School of Economics and Political Science.

Trudeau also published several books and many articles expressing his ideas about justice, the state, the individual, federalism, and nationalism. Trudeau joined the Liberal party and entered federal politics in November 1965, when he defeated the now internationally famous Canadian philosopher Charles Taylor in the Montreal riding of Mount Royal. Trudeau went on to win the leadership of his party and became prime minister in 1968.

As prime minister, Trudeau introduced laws and policies that changed the Canadian social and political landscape. He supported divorce and abortion reform and the Official Languages Act, and engineered the patriation of the Constitution, making sure that it included the Charter of Rights and Freedoms. All were key elements of his idea of a just society.

Because of this, Trudeau is sometimes called the philosopher king. In a 1982 interview, he said, "I like my job but I also like philosophy."

Like Plato, Trudeau was a committed rationalist for whom justice was paramount. In *Federalism and the French Canadians,* he wrote:

> Thus the great moment of truth arrives when it is realized that in the last resort the mainspring of federalism cannot be emotion but must be reason.... The title of the state to govern and the extent of its authority will be conditional upon rational justification; a people's consensus based on reason will supply the cohesive force that societies require.... The rise of reason in politics is an advance of law; for is not law an attempt to regulate the conduct of men in society rationally rather than emotionally.

Plato's rationalism led him to believe that the state was more important than the individual. Trudeau's rationalism led him to a completely different conclusion. He placed the individual above the state. And whereas Plato exalted the state, Trudeau mistrusted excessive state power. He conceived the Charter of Rights as a counterbalance to the power of the state. For him, this provided justice.

Trudeau did, however, perceive a central role for the state in one area: to counter market forces in a free market system. In this area, he believed that state intervention was necessary to help the weaker segments of the world's population.

Easily the most controversial prime minister of the 20th century, Trudeau was not without contradictions. A staunch supporter of individualism, he nevertheless invoked the War Measures Act during the 1970 October Crisis in Quebec. This action severely restricted individual liberties. He later remarked that the decision was necessary, even though it was repugnant.

When he died in 2001, people lined the streets of Montreal to view the funeral procession. Many millions more watched the service on television. Though many people admired him, others despised him. Still, few were indifferent, and none would question his commitment to reason over passion.

Figure 20.4
Pierre Trudeau slides down a hotel banister during the 1968 Liberal party leadership convention. Hi-jinks like this endeared him to many voters — and launched a phenomenon known as Trudeaumania.

UTILITY AS JUSTICE

Although Plato's ideas often provide a starting point for discussions of justice, a number of competing theories have been proposed, especially in the modern age. One of the most influential is utilitarianism, a philosophy with ethical, social, and political dimensions.

Utilitarianism gained prominence in the late 18th and early 19th centuries as the result of the efforts of several British philosophers. In contrast to Plato's conception of justice as merit, utilitarians associate justice with social utility.

The roots of utilitarianism are detectable in some of the social contract ideas proposed by Thomas Hobbes and John Locke. Both believed that peace and security are necessary if justice is to be achieved. In their view, whatever advances the welfare of the greatest number of people or whatever is socially useful is just. And though early contract theorists certainly talked about a limited kind of equality, they maintained that individuals would find justice only in the context of the common good.

These ideas probably inspired the English philosopher **Jeremy Bentham**, who lived from 1748 to 1832 and helped found utilitarianism. Bentham was intent on reforming laws and institutions based on privilege and tradition because he believed that they benefited only the upper classes. In his view, Britain's existing legal and social systems perpetuated gross inequalities and injustice.

Bentham advocated the adoption of the principle of utility as the best way of reforming society and the law. Bentham's formula for deciding utility was simple: if something is pleasurable, it is good; if it is painful, it is bad. Because each individual must judge what is pleasurable and painful, Bentham believed that his philosophy created an equal playing field for everyone. Because the only relevant criterion for deciding the appropriateness of a course of action was the amount of pleasure or pain involved, Bentham believed that the principle of utility made expertise and social position irrelevant. By applying the same principle to social and political reform, he said that greater equality and justice for the greatest number could become a reality.

Bentham also believed, however, that justice was unlikely to prevail as long as people were held back by false beliefs, superstitions, and ignorance. In his view, the solution was to institute an education program to free people's minds. He believed that educated people would have the know-how to support the best policies — those aimed at promoting the greatest happiness for the greatest number.

> **Web connection**
> www.mcgrawhill.ca/links/philosophy12
> To find out more about Jeremy Bentham, follow the links on this Web site.

Inspired by the work of the 18th-century Scottish thinker Adam Smith, many utilitarians also integrated **economic laissez-faire** into their philosophy. Laissez-faire is a French phrase that means let act. Laissez-faire economics calls for minimum government intervention in the marketplace.

Utilitarians reasoned that in trying to maximize their profits — or units of pleasure — capitalists would aim to make the best and most efficient use of resources, something that would benefit society. In other words, they believed that selfishness would promote the greatest happiness of the greatest number in a way that altruism could not.

Utilitarianism acquired much greater depth and sophistication in the 19th-century writings of John Stuart Mill, who rejected Bentham's arguments that any pleasure is as good as any other and that pleasure is a simple matter of quantification. Instead, he sided with Plato and others who had insisted that quality is more important than quantity and that some pleasures are superior to others.

Although Mill believed that individual rights are a component of justice, his theory that not all pleasures are equal suggested that some opinions are better than others. Whereas

Bentham's approach suggested a democratic one-person–one-vote scenario, Mill's qualitative correction suggested a less egalitarian view.

Mill was a product of his times. He believed that the educated minority should have a greater say in determining social policies. And though Mill believed that equality is one aspect of justice, he did not believe that it lies at the core of concepts of justice. In his view, utility determines what is just and unjust.

Think about the earlier example of the two candidates — a derelict and a brain surgeon — for a heart transplant. Mill would probably support the notion of treating the two candidates unequally. In his view, the principle of utility would dictate that the surgeon should get the transplant because her life is of greater social benefit.

> ### Recall...Reflect...Respond
> 1. With a partner, choose a contemporary economic, political, or legal issue such as Aboriginal land claims. Explain how the concept of justice as merit or justice as utility might apply to debate over the issue.
> 2. Consider a rule imposed by the administration of your school. Draw on various philosophical concepts of justice to argue for or against retaining this rule.
> 3. Consider the concepts of justice discussed so far in this chapter. Which most closely reflects your own definition? Explain how.

CONTEMPORARY IDEAS OF JUSTICE

In the late 20th century, various philosophers drew on earlier concepts of justice to propose new ways of looking at the relationship between the individual and the state. As these ideas evolved, the positions taken by the contemporary American philosophers John Rawls and Robert Nozick came to represent the two extremes of the debate over justice. Rawls supported state intervention for the good of society, while Nozick opposed it. Their differing views have become the touchstone of contemporary debate, which has focused on fairness and entitlement as the criteria for deciding justice.

FAIRNESS AS JUSTICE

In the 1970s, John Rawls combined the principles of personal liberty and social equality to arrive at a new concept of justice based on fairness. He set out his ideas in two books, *Justice as Fairness* and *A Theory of Justice*.

Like utilitarianism, Rawls' theory is rooted in the ideas of 17th- and 18th-century social contract theorists such as Thomas Hobbes, John Locke, and Jean-Jacques Rousseau. In his case, however, the connection is much stronger. As a result, he is often identified as a contractarian.

> *The oppressed are always morally in the right.*
> – Robert Briffault

Just as Locke used human beings' existence in the state of nature as the starting point for his contract theory, Rawls used a starting point that he called the original position. When drawing up an imaginary social contract, Rawls said, the interests of a wealthy factory owner would be different from those of someone who worked in the factory. How can a social contract take into account the interests of both? Rawls' goal was to find a way of balancing everyone's interests.

To achieve this, Rawls said that people must try to devise a principle of justice under a "veil of ignorance." By this, he meant that people must be ignorant of their position in the society they create. They must imagine that they do not know whether they will be rich or poor, male or female, brilliant or ignorant, and so on. Only when they emerge from under this veil of ignorance into the society that they have created will they have knowledge of their own interests. If a society were developed in this fashion, Rawls said, fairness would be the guiding principle.

In Rawls' view, justice would then be based on equality of both means and needs. He maintains that a liberal society can retain its commitment to individualism while helping the disadvantaged gain more equitable access to the state's resources. The state can engineer this by imposing taxation and other programs that redistribute wealth and provide the disadvantaged with choices and power.

According to Rawls, justice is the first virtue of social institutions, as truth is of systems of thought. Just as a theory must be rejected or revised if it is untrue, so laws and institutions — no matter how efficient and well arranged — must be abolished or reformed if they are unjust.

Figure 20.5

If you thought you might emerge from the veil of ignorance to become a homeless person, like this resident of a shantytown in Toronto, what kind of society would you devise?

In Rawls' view, justice is based on two principles.

- The principle of equal basic liberty for all: Each person is to have an equal right to the most extensive basic liberty compatible with a similar liberty for others.
- The difference principle: Social and economic inequalities are to be arranged so that they are reasonably expected to be to everyone's advantage and attached to positions and offices open to all.

According to Rawls, these two principles are particular expressions of a more general concept — that all social values are to be distributed equally unless an unequal distribution of any, or all, of these values is to everyone's advantage.

Web connection
www.mcgrawhill.ca/links/philosophy12
To read more about John Rawls, follow the links on this Web site.

ENTITLEMENT AS JUSTICE

Rawls' theory of justice has generated much debate and criticism. One of his fiercest critics was the libertarian philosopher Robert Nozick, who proposed a very different theory of justice.

In his groundbreaking book, *Anarchy, State and Utopia*, Nozick maintained that libertarianism is a "framework for utopia." He also advocated a "night watchman" state, in which the role of government is restricted to enforcing contracts and protecting citizens from theft and violence.

In Nozick's minimalist state, there would be no central bank, no welfare programs, no departments of education, and so on. If institutions like these existed at all, they would be operated by private individuals or corporations on a for-profit basis or out of public interest.

THOUGHT EXPERIMENT: *The Veil of Ignorance*

What if you were given the chance to design a society from scratch? You would be the supreme architect of an entire government and social system. Your blueprint would influence the lives of millions of people, determining how leaders would be chosen and how resources like health care, education, welfare, job opportunities, and environmental resources, for example, would be distributed among people.

The task is huge. You can design any kind of society that you want. There is one catch, however. In designing this society, you do not know anything about your eventual place in it. You are completely in the dark about who you will be. You do not know which social class you will belong to, what social status you will enjoy, which natural talents you will have, which psychological traits you will have, what your concepts of good and bad will be, what your values will be, what age you will be, what your cultural heritage will be, what good or bad fortune will befall you, or whether you will be male or female.

From this position of ignorance, try to design the basic rules and principles of a society.

Be careful, however. Remember that you must be prepared to live with the consequences of the rules and principles you design. You must be prepared to end up being anyone. As the saying goes, you must lie in the bed that you make.

So, what kind of society would you design?

Figure 20.6

John Rawls, who presented this thought experiment in his book *A Theory of Justice,* maintained that behind this "veil of ignorance," people would play it safe. They would design a society with fair principles — in case they ended up among the disadvantaged. They would take into account the interests of everyone in society, ensuring a minimum degree of fairness for all.

Rawls claimed that people's uncertainty about their future would result in a design based on "maximin rule." This is a cost-benefit analysis that measures the expected benefit of an action (determined by the probability that it will occur, as well as the benefit that comes from it) against the expected cost of an action (the probability that it will not occur, as well as the cost if it does not occur). In Rawls' view, designing a society according to this principle would ensure that the least fortunate individuals are placed in the least *un*fortunate situations.

To understand what Rawls meant, imagine that you and your best friend are hungry. In front of you is one piece of cake. You both want the entire piece but realize that you must share it. But how do you share it?

In the interest of fairness, you might decide to apply the maximin principle. You agree that one of you will cut the cake, and the other will choose one of the two pieces. This guarantees that the cake will be cut and shared fairly.

In the same way, said Rawls, people would design a society using the maximin principle.

The idea of **entitlement** lies at the heart of Nozick's theory. The complete antithesis of Rawls' notion of the state's responsibility to engineer a form of distributive justice, entitlement theory says that individual people are entitled to retain the fruits of their labour without government interference.

Nozick's critics have argued that a minimalist state would be — at least from the perspective of the old, the sick, and the disadvantaged members of society — a nightmare rather than a utopia. A few have even suggested that some people would starve while others could legally allow their foodstuffs to rot.

Nozick assumed that kind, wealthy people would help those in need. He also said, however, that the rich would not be obligated to do this, though he acknowledged that choosing not to help others might be considered morally wrong. Those in need would have no right, however, to expect assistance.

In the final analysis, Nozick believes that the debate over whether a welfare state or a libertarian state would be better at getting rid of poverty is irrelevant. From a libertarian perspective, a welfare state is, by definition, morally wrong. What is morally right is that all people have the liberty to dispose of their possessions as they wish.

Nozick's assessment of the moral rightness of the entitlement theory of justice has been disputed by a variety of critics. The contemporary American philosopher Samuel Scheffler, for example, wrote: "It is an extraordinary but apparent consequence of this view that for a government to tax each of its able-bodied citizens five dollars a year to support cripples and orphans would violate the right of the able bodied, and would be morally impermissible, whereas to refrain from taxation even if it meant allowing the cripples and orphans to starve to death would be morally required government policy."

The British philosopher Jonathan Wolff points out that Nozick does not advocate a dog-eat-dog society. Nevertheless, Wolff predicts that this would be the result if Nozick's vision were implemented. "If the rich can flee with their property at any time, it is hard to see how we will avoid ending up with something like a barely regulated free market economy with rather haphazard voluntary philanthropy: 19th-century capitalism," Wolff wrote. "And this, of course is just the result that Nozick's critics warned us of. It is not that Nozick is a direct advocate of such a system, but that it is to this that the system he advocates is likely to lead."

Despite the criticism, Nozick's concept of justice presents a strong counterpoint to Rawls' theory. In some ways, the choice between the ideas presented by these two philosophers symbolizes the debate over one of philosophy's most important questions: What does it mean to be human? In more than 2500 years, many philosophers have offered answers to this question — and their answers have often shaped the attitudes of societies. Still, for every answer, there has been a dissenting theory. As the world moves farther into the 21st century, there is every likelihood that this debate will continue.

IDEAS IN CONTEXT

The influence of philosophers such as Robert Nozick is most visible in highly industrialized nations, where contemporary conservatives advocate laissez-faire economics and support cutting social welfare programs. Though receptive to moderate change, they favour the maintenance of order on social issues and actively support deregulation and privatization in the economic sphere. Entitlement theories of justice shaped the policies of former United States president Ronald Reagan and former British prime minister Margaret Thatcher, and continue to influence the thinking of the governments of some Canadian provinces.

Web connection

www.mcgrawhill.ca/links/philosophy12

To read more of Jonathan Wolff's critique of Robert Nozick's theory, follow the links on this Web site.

Chapter Review

Chapter Summary

This chapter has discussed
- some of the main questions of social and political philosophy
- the responses of major philosophers and major schools of social and political philosophy to some of the main questions of social and political philosophy
- how theories of social and political philosophy are adopted and realized in contemporary policy making and how this affects political and social practices
- how particular philosophical theories have influenced the development of other subjects
- how the ideas of philosophers have influenced subsequent philosophers

Knowledge and Understanding

1. Identify and explain the significance to the study of social and political philosophy of each of the following key words and people.

Key Words	Key People
classical liberalism	Hugo Grotius
individualism	Charles L. Black Jr.
positive law	Pierre Elliott Trudeau
natural law	Jeremy Bentham
naturalists	John Rawls
legal positivists	
retributive justice	
distributive justice	
economic laissez-faire	
contractarian	
entitlement	

2. Create a graphic organizer that shows how contemporary philosophers' ideas of justice have drawn on the ideas on earlier philosophers.

Thinking and Inquiry

3. In *The Islamic Law and Constitution,* the 20th-century Muslim philosopher Abu'l A'la Mawdudi described the first principle of Islamic political theory.

   The belief in the Unity and the sovereignty of Allah is the foundation of the social and moral system propounded by the Prophets. It is the very starting-point of the Islamic political philosophy. The basic principle of Islam is that human beings must, individually and collectively, surrender all rights of overlordship, legislation and exercising of authority over others.... None is entitled to make laws on his own authority and none is obliged to abide by them. This right vests in Allah alone.... He alone is the law-giver. No man, even if he be a Prophet, has the right to do or not to do certain things.

Choose two western philosophers and compare this principle with their thoughts about justice. Write a 500-word evaluation of the similarities and differences.

4. Imagine that you have worked for a large corporation for 15 years. During this time, you have studied hard to upgrade your education and skills. You recently applied for a promotion to an executive position but were rejected because of your age. To fill the spot, the company is planning to hire a younger woman who now works for another firm. You believe that this is discrimination. You decide to appeal the decision in a letter to your bosses. Write the letter, drawing on various theories and concepts of justice to explain why the company's decision is unjust.

Communication

5. Imagine that you have been asked to make a five-minute presentation at a conference of government officials from around the world. The topic is, How philosophical theories of law and justice have been applied in Canada in the 20th and 21st centuries. Work with three or four classmates to create a presentation. Make it as visually appealing and concise as possible.

6. Create a concept map that shows how Plato's theories about the relationship between the individual and society influenced the ideas of subsequent philosophers. Use visuals and symbols to help communicate the concepts that are central to Plato's theory and to show his influence on the ideas of others.

Application

7. According to Mohandas Gandhi, the following are the seven deadly social sins:

   1. Politics without principle
   2. Wealth without work
   3. Commerce without morality
   4. Pleasure without conscience
   5. Education without character
   6. Science without humanity
   7. Worship without sacrifice

   Why do you suppose Gandhi described these as "deadly social sins"? What do these statements imply about justice and its role in society? Which statements correspond to ideas about justice presented in this chapter? How do they do this?

8. Is there a relationship between social justice and the rights and responsibilities of individuals in society? Imagine that you are one of the philosophers in this chapter. Choose a partner who will play the role of a philosopher with a differing point of view. Each of you should prepare a list of five questions to ask the other — and make notes on the responses you expect. Prepare counter-arguments to these responses. Present your questions in an informal debate with your partner.

Challenge the power of "They."
CULMINATING ACTIVITY

EXPECTATIONS

By completing this activity, you will
- demonstrate an understanding of the main questions, concepts, and theories of social and political philosophy
- evaluate the strengths and weaknesses of the responses to the main questions of social and political philosophy defended by some major philosophers and schools of philosophy, and defend your own responses
- identify instances of theories of social and political philosophy that are presuppositions in everyday life
- demonstrate the relevance of social and political philosophy to other subjects
- correctly use the terminology of social and political philosophy
- demonstrate an understanding of the unique character of philosophical questions
- effectively use a variety of print and electronic sources and telecommunications tools in research
- effectively communicate the results of your inquires

THE TASK

Think about how often people use the phrase "They say …" to make a point. It is as if "they" are a group of authoritative beings who know the truth — and whose opinions are beyond challenge. But just who are "they"? And how reliable are their opinions?

Your task in this culminating activity is to work in a small group to challenge the power of "they." First, your group will act as Council of They to prepare a series of statements that begin with the phrase, "They say …." Your group will then challenge the "they say" statements of another Council of They by preparing philosophical arguments that counter the statements.

Each group member will conclude this activity by writing a 500-word critique of the group's challenge. At the end of this course, your written critique may be combined with the products of other unit-culminating activities to create a philosophy magazine.

THE SUBTASKS

Subtask 1: A Council of They
Form small groups. For now, each group will be called a Council of They. Choose a contemporary issue related to one of the main questions of social and political philosophy. The issue may be local, provincial, national, or international (e.g., on a local level, some municipalities have banned ownership of certain dog breeds that are considered aggressive, an issue that relates to the conflict between individual rights and the common good). Brainstorm to create a list of at least five arguments on both sides of the issue. Transform these arguments into "they say" statements (e.g., They say that banning ownership of certain dog breeds infringes individual rights).

Subtask 2: A Graphic Organizer
Continuing to act as a Council of They, take a position on one side of the issue (e.g., in favour of or against banning certain dog breeds). On a graphic organizer, record both the issue selected, your council's position on the issue, and the "they say" statements that support your council's position.

Subtask 3: A Philosophical Position
Exchange graphic organizers with another Council of They. Then switch roles and prepare to challenge the position set out on the other council's organizer. As a group, discuss the issue identified on the organizer and the "they say" statements presented in support of the other council's position. Review various philosophical arguments that might be used to refute the other council's "they say" statements.

Working individually, choose one or more of the "they say" statements on the organizer and research arguments that might be used to challenge it. Make notes on your research and be sure that your notes include references to specific philosophers or philosophical schools of thought (e.g., Communitarian argument: the good of the community takes precedence over the right of individual dog fanciers to own a certain breed), as well as an annotated bibliography of your research sources.

When you have finished, meet as a group to review individual members' arguments. Make suggestions for strengthening one another's arguments and for dealing with likely counter-arguments.

Subtask 4: A Challenge
Meet the Council of They with whom your group exchanged graphic organizers. First one council, then the other, should reassume the role of a Council of They and engage in an informal debate on the "they say" statements set out on its graphic organizer.

Subtask 5: A Critique
Working individually, prepare a 500-word written critique of the strength of the arguments presented by your group in challenging the "they say" statements of the Council of They. Which arguments did you find most compelling? Least compelling? Why? Did the arguments persuade you to rethink your personal position on the issue? Why? Include an annotated bibliography with your critique.

ASSESSMENT CRITERIA

The following criteria will be used to assess your critique.

Knowledge and Understanding
Does your critique

- identify an issue and explain how it reflects one of the main questions of social and political philosophy?
- demonstrate an understanding of the theories of a particular philosopher or school of philosophical thought in evaluating the "they say" statements?

Thinking and Inquiry
Does your critique

- evaluate philosophical theories or schools of social and political thought and reach a conclusion?
- include an annotated bibliography?

Communication
Does your critique

- use the terminology of social and political philosophy?
- communicate the arguments presented in the informal debate?
- demonstrate an understanding of what is required in a critique that will be published in a philosophy magazine?

Application
Does your critique

- transfer the ideas presented in the informal debate to the critique format?
- make connections between the ideas presented in the informal debate and your own conclusions?

Timeline

BCE	Philosophers	World Events
600 – 501	Thales of Miletus Laozi	Mayan civilization thrives in Mexico First Olympic games Athens develops a democracy Soldering of iron invented
500 – 401	Gautama, the Buddha Kongfuzi Gorgias	Rome declared a republic Cyrus II consolidates Persian Empire Indian vina (two hollow gourds connected by strings and bamboo reeds) becomes first stringed instrument
400 – 301	Socrates Pyrrho of Elis	Peloponnesian War ends as Sparta defeats Athens Old Testament Pentateuch completed Wineries begin in Italy and Gaul (France)
300 – 201	Plato Aristotle Mengzi Xun-zi	Plato founds Academy in Athens China unified and construction of Great Wall starts Alexander the Great's armies reach India Catapults used as weapons of war
200 – 101		Eratosthenes suggests that the earth is round and moves around sun Hsü Shen produces a Chinese dictionary Rome controls much of Europe, North Africa, and Asia Minor
100 – 1		Julius Caesar born Chinese ships reach east coast of India

CE	Philosophers	World Events
1 – 100		Jesus crucified; Christianity founded Nero rules Rome Mount Vesuvius erupts London founded
101 to 200		Ptolemy develops earth-centred theory of the universe
201 to 300	Nagarjuna	Magnetic compass invented in China
301 – 400	Augustine of Hippo	Chinese astronomers discover moons of Jupiter Buddhism introduced to Korea Christianity becomes official religion of Roman Empire
401 to 500		Fall of Rome
501 – 600		Indian mathematics introduce zero (0) and start using decimal system
601 – 700	Muhammad	Islam founded by Muhammad
701 – 800		Arabic numerals in use in Europe
801 – 900		Charlemagne crowned emperor in Rome Buddhism banned in China
901 – 1000		Paper money introduced in China Viking explorer Eric the Red established colony in Greenland
1001 – 1100	Anselm of Canterbury Averroës	First crusade launched
1101 – 1200	Peter Abelard Moses Maimonides	University established in Paris

CE	Philosophers	World Events
1201 – 1300	Roger Bacon John Duns Scotus Thomas Aquinas	King John signs Magna Carta in England Genghis Khan invades Russia Marco Polo arrives in China Empire of Mali established in Africa
1301 – 1400		Aztecs found Tenochtitlan (Mexico City) Black Death rages across Europe
1401 – 1500	Niccolò Machiavelli	Johannes Gutenberg uses movable type Works of Plato and Aristotle printed in Latin Christopher Columbus finds way to Americas Inca Empire thriving in South America
1501 – 1600	Nicolaus Copernicus Francis Bacon Thomas More	Leonardo da Vinci paints *Mona Lisa* King Henry VIII of England breaks with Rome Martin Luther prints Bible in German William Shakespeare born Nicolaus Copernicus offers sun-centred theory of the universe Spanish defeat Aztecs in Mexico
1601 – 1700	Hugo Grotius Thomas Hobbes René Descartes Baruch Spinoza Blaise Pascal John Locke Isaac Newton Gottfried Wilhelm Leibniz	Quebec founded by French settlers King James Bible published Civil War and Glorious Revolution take place in England

CE	Philosophers	World Events
1701 – 1800	Joseph Butler David Hume George Berkeley Jean-Jacques Rousseau Immanuel Kant Edmund Burke Thomas Paine Jeremy Bentham Voltaire Mary Wollstonecraft Olympe de Gouges	British forces capture Quebec United States founded after American Revolution French Revolution overthrows monarchy in France Industrial Revolution begins in England Napoleon takes power in France First electric battery in operation Detroit founded by Antoine de Cadillac
1801 – 1900	Georg W.F. Hegel Charles Darwin Arthur Schopenhauer Friedrich von Schelling John Stuart Mill Harriet Taylor Søren Kierkegaard Alexander Baumgarten Karl Marx Friedrich Nietzsche George Boole Charles Peirce William James Leo Tolstoy	Napoleon defeated at Waterloo American Civil War ends with defeat of South British colonies in Canada start to enter Confederation Wireless telegraphy in use The electron discovered Canadian Pacific Railway opens up Canadian West

CE	Philosophers		World Events
1901 – Present	Daisetsu Teitaro Suzuki Benedetto Croce Gottlob Frege Kurt Gödel Edmund Husserl John Dewey Bertrand Russell Ludwig Wittgenstein Albert Einstein Martin Heidegger Jiddu Krishnamurti Clive Bell Mohandas Gandhi R.G. Collingwood Jean-Paul Sartre Simone de Beauvoir Karl Popper A. J. Ayer Albert Camus Edmund Gettier Herbert Marcuse Hannah Arendt John Rawls Thomas Kuhn Robert Pirsig Brenda Almond Jacques Derrida Ayn Rand Susanne Langer Karl Jaspers Paul Feyerabend Willard Van Orman Quine	Michel Foucault Kwame Gyekye Noam Chomsky Roderick M. Chisholm Sissela Bok Linda Nochlin Annette Baier Derek Parfit Daniel Dennett Charles Taylor Thomas Nagel Alan Turing Jean-François Lyotard Nancy Midgley John Searle Stuart Hampshire Robert Nozick Richard Rorty Peter Singer Tom Regan Suzi Gablik Virginia Held Mary Ann Warren Nadine Strossen Karen Warren Joanna Frueh Arthur Danto Felipe Fernández-Armesto John McGuire Steven Pinker	First airplane flies Communist Revolution overthrows monarchy in Russia World suffers through Great Depression World War I and World War II result in death of millions Atom bomb used Israel becomes independent state Communist government under Mao Zedong established in China Cold War dominates international politics for much of second half of 20th century Apollo 11 lands on moon Microcomputers come into widespread use Space station construction begins, including installation of Canadarm Cold War ends with collapse of communist governments in Union of Soviet Socialist Republics and Eastern Europe Terrorist attack on sites in United States

Glossary

abduction (abductive reasoning) A kind of inductive reasoning used to explain a specific case based on the best guess or best explanation for something that has been observed.

abstract In aesthetics, a term used to describe a broad range of art, including works that represent an altered form of reality and works that bear no resemblance to reality.

aesthetic experience In aesthetics, the pleasure felt when making a judgment of taste.

aesthetics (philosophy of art) The area of philosophy that studies how people perceive and assess the meaning, importance, and purpose of art.

aesthetic triad In aesthetics, the relationship between the artist, the art object, and the perceiver.

altruism Unselfishness.

anarchistic epistemology An approach that denies the existence of a body of rules that can be used to decide what counts as knowledge.

anti-foundationalism A theory that denies traditional ideas saying that knowledge must rest on a foundation of reality.

a posteriori knowledge Knowledge that comes after sense experience. This kind of knowledge depends on evidence presented by the senses.

a priori knowledge Knowledge that is gained before sense experience. This kind of knowledge comes from the human ability to reason.

arabesque A style of art, often associated with Arab-Islamic art, that uses interlacing lines to create an intricate pattern that often depicts flowers, fruit, or foliage.

areas of philosophy Areas of philosophical inquiry: logic and the philosophy of science, metaphysics, epistemology, ethics, aesthetics, and social and political philosophy.

argument In logic, a group of statements consisting of a premise or premises designed to justify a conclusion.

argument from design (teleological argument) An argument that says that the order that characterizes the universe must have been designed and set in motion by a supreme being.

atheism A theory that rejects the idea of the existence of a supreme being.

autonomy The ability to freely make rational decisions.

behaviourism A theory that says that people's behaviour is controlled by their environment.

Buddhism A school of ethical, metaphysical, and epistemological thought that emphasizes individual harmony. It was developed by Siddhartha Gautama, the Buddha.

capitalism A commodity-producing economic and social system that uses capital to hire workers for wages.

categorical imperative In ethics and social and political philosophy, a moral rule that is absolute. The term was developed by Immanuel Kant.

catharsis In aesthetics, an emotional purging experienced by artists as an intuitive signal that a work is complete.

causality A cause-and-effect relationship in which one event causes another.

censorship The limiting of the right to express oneself freely.

Chinese room A thought experiment, devised by John Searle, to show that computers lack intentionality.

classical liberalism A social and political philosophy that advocates freedom from excessive government interference and maintains that the purpose of the state is to uphold and protect individual rights.

coherence theory A theory that says that beliefs are true when they cohere, or are consistent, with an existing belief or body of knowledge.

common-sense realism (naïve realism) A theory that says that people perceive the world exactly as it is: what you see is what you get.

communitarianism An ideology that says that the rights of communities and societies are sometimes more important than individual rights.

competence knowledge (knowledge-as-ability) Know-how, or knowledge that is acquired by doing or seeing something demonstrated rather than by hearing or reading about it.

conclusion In logic, a statement that follows from a premise or premises.

Confucianism A philosophy, attributed to Kongfuzi (Confucius), that emphasizes living in harmony with society.

contractarian A term that describes thinkers whose philosophies are rooted in social contract theory.

correspondence theory A theory that says that beliefs are true when they correspond, or agree, with reality.

cosmological argument An argument that says that a supreme being must exist because the chain of causes must have a beginning, and this beginning was a supreme being.

deconstructionism An anti-foundationalist approach, developed by Jacques Derrida, that involves deconstructing, or taking apart, language to show that its meaning is unstable.

deduction (deductive reasoning) A reasoning process that involves drawing a specific conclusion from a general statement or premise.

deism A theory that says that a supreme being created the universe but does not intervene in its workings.

democracy (polity) A form of government in which all citizens have some say in the decisions made by leaders.

descriptive In aesthetics, a term that refers to an approach to defining art. A descriptive definition involves observations and experiences that explain what art is.

determinism A theory that says that every event, including one's own choices and actions, is determined by a chain of causes extending back in time.

direct knowledge (simple knowledge, perceptual knowledge) Knowledge that is acquired directly through experience.

distributive justice A principle of justice that says that a society's resources should be distributed equally among all people.

divine command theory A theory that says that right and wrong are defined by the commands of a supreme being.

doctrine of impermanence The belief, often associated with Buddhism, that all things, including human beings, are constantly changing and moving.

dualism A theory that says that reality consists of two fundamentally different kinds of things: mind and matter.

eclecticism An artistic practice that involves borrowing from and combining diverse styles.

economic laissez-faire An economic theory that calls for minimizing government intervention in the marketplace.

edifying An anti-foundationalist approach, developed by Richard Rorty, that involves redefining the world over and over in order to make it work better.

egalitarianism A social and political philosophy that supports correcting inequalities in society and promoting economic and social justice.

egoism An ethical theory that says that people should act in their own interest.

eliminative materialism A theory that says that neuroscientific brain-state terms will eventually replace everyday psychological terms to describe desires, beliefs, and attitudes.

empiricism A theory that says that knowledge is a posteriori. It comes from experience, or evidence presented by the senses.

entitlement A social and political theory, advocated by Robert Nozick, that says that individuals are entitled to retain the fruits of their labour without government interference.

epistemology The area of philosophy that deals with the study of knowledge.

essence The fundamental nature of a thing — what makes the thing what it is.

essentialism A theory that says that the ability to reason is the distinguishing feature of human beings.

ethical absolutism The belief that one universally acceptable moral code determines the rightness and wrongness of all actions in all circumstances.

ethical dimensions The moral assumptions and implications involved in various courses of action.

ethical relativism The belief that no moral code is absolute or universal. Relativists believe that moral values are relative to time, place, persons, and situations.

ethical universalism The belief that one universally acceptable moral code determines the rightness and wrongness of actions, though this code is not necessarily absolute. Exceptions may be made in certain circumstances.

ethics The area of philosophy that deals with the study of theories of morals and morality.

euthanasia (mercy killing, doctor-assisted suicide) The act of killing — or allowing to die — a person or animal suffering from an incurable illness or condition.

existentialism A philosophical movement that focuses on individual autonomy and the necessity of making reasoned decisions for oneself.

expressionism A theory that measures the success of a work of art by its impact on the emotions.

fallacy In logic, a flaw or fault in an argument.

falsificationism A theory that suggests that science is a process of making guesses, then setting out to prove them false.

feminism A movement that views the historical relationship between the sexes as unequal and attempts to correct this.

first-order language A specific statement or question about an observation or event.

form A concept, developed by Plato, that refers to the timeless, unchanging, immaterial, and perfect essence of particular things.

formal fallacy In logic, a structural error in deductive reasoning.

formalism A theory that says that the most important thing about a work of art is its formal qualities. As a result, art should be judged according to how well it conforms to its form.

free will The idea that the will is uncaused.

functionalism A materialist theory that says that mental states can be realized in various ways, such as through brain tissue or computer chips.

general will A concept, developed by Jean Jacques Rousseau, that expresses what is best for the community.

genethics (bioethics) A word coined by combining "genetics" and "ethics." Genethicists explore ethical issues that stem from scientists' ability to manipulate the genetic makeup of living organisms.

genre A literary term used to identify kinds of prose. Traditional literary genres were defined as epic, tragedy, lyric, comedy, and satire. Today, genres include fiction, non-fiction, essays, epic novels, and short stories.

hard determinism A theory that denies the existence of free will and says that all thoughts, actions, desires, and physical events are caused by previous events.

hedonism A philosophy that emphasizes that the good life is one devoted to pleasure.

humanism An ethical approach that emphasizes the human or secular (non-religious) realm over the religious or spiritual realm.

human nature Characteristics or qualities that make human beings different from anything else.

iconology The study of the meaning of the subject matter of art in the context of the culture in which the work was produced.

idealism A metaphysical theory that says that reality consists of ideas and the minds that house them. In aesthetics, idealists maintain that judgments about art are subjective.

identity theory A metaphysical theory that says that mental states are identical to brain states.

ideology A system of beliefs about important economic, social, and political issues.

indirect knowledge (complex knowledge, inferential knowledge) Knowledge that is acquired indirectly by using reason to connect pieces of direct knowledge.

individualism A social and political philosophy, similar to classical liberalism, that emphasizes the importance of individual rights.

induction (inductive reasoning) A reasoning process that involves drawing a general conclusion from specific observations.

informal fallacy In logic, a kind of argument that persuades by means other than reason.

instrumentalism An approach that regards theories as useful instruments, or tools. In the philosophy of science, for example, instrumentalists say that scientific theories are merely useful instruments that enable scientists to impose a sense of order on random natural phenomena.

intentionality In metaphysics, the idea that mental states are about or represent something.

intuitionism In ethics, a theory that denies the importance of reason in making moral choices. Intuitionists say that some truths are understood by intuition, an experience that is independent of reasoning.

justified true belief A definition of knowledge that says that three conditions are necessary to claim knowledge: a statement must be true; a person must believe that the statement is true; and a person must be justified in believing that the statement is true.

just war theory A theory, supported by Cicero, Augustine of Hippo, and Thomas Aquinas, that says that certain conditions (e.g., a just cause) must be met before a war is considered just.

knowledge by acquaintance Direct knowledge that is acquired through the senses. It is the same as sense perception.

knowledge by description Indirect knowledge that is acquired by using reason to connect pieces of knowledge by acquaintance.

legal positivism In social and political philosophy, a view that denies the existence of natural law and says that governments and the courts are the only sources of law.

legitimate In social and political philosophy, a term that refers to state power that is considered worthy of respect and obedience.

li A Chinese word that refers to ritual principles or people's obligations based on their social position.

liberal individualism An ideology that champions the rights of the individual as one of the most important values of a society.

libertarianism An extreme version of liberal individualism. Libertarians believe that the purpose of the state is to defend the lives, liberties, and property of citizens, and argue that the state should not be involved in redistributing wealth.

linguistics The study of the structure of human language.

logic The area of philosophy that studies correct reasoning and sound judgment. Sometimes called the science of the laws of thought.

logical consistency In logic, refers to statements that do not contradict each other.

logical contradiction In logic, refers to statements that contradict each other or violate Aristotle's law of non-contradiction.

logical positivism In science and ethics, an approach that says that something must be true by definition or through verification by evidence presented by the senses.

materialism (physicalism) A metaphysical theory, developed by the PreSocratic philosophers, that says that everything, including a person's thoughts, consciousness, and personality, is composed of matter.

MHR **439**

media literacy The ability to communicate in various media, as well as the ability to understand and evaluate the messages of contemporary mass media.

metaphysics The area of philosophy that deals with the study of the basic structures of reality: being and nothingness, time and eternity, freedom and determinism, mind and body, thinghood and personhood, space and time, and a supreme being and nature.

militarism The belief that using military force to settle disputes is morally right.

mimesis (imitationalism) A theory of art that says that art represents, mirrors, or creates an illusion of reality.

mind-brain problem The metaphysical debate over the nature of the connection between thoughts and the physical events that occur in the human brain.

modernism In aesthetics, a 20th-century movement characterized by attempts to define the nature of the aesthetic experience. Modernists consider works of art successful if they create a sense of unity and are autonomous and pure.

monism A metaphysical theory that says that reality consists of one all-encompassing thing and that all particular things are expressions of this one thing.

monotheism A theory that says that the universe is the creation of a single, perfect, all-powerful supreme being.

moral agent Someone who is capable of thinking about a moral problem, making a decision about how to act, and taking responsibility for this action.

moral choice A choice that involves right and wrong, good and bad.

morals (morality) Customary beliefs about how people should be and act.

naturalism A theory, developed by Aristotle, that says that everything, including human behaviour, belongs in nature and can therefore be studied in the same way as natural phenomena.

naturalists Supporters of naturalism and natural law theory.

natural law An unwritten law code that governs both the natural and social orders and represents the law as it might be in its ideal form. Developed by Aristotle, the concept was adopted by medieval European thinkers such as Thomas Aquinas, who used it to refer to the law of God.

negative freedom Refers to freedom from physical and emotional coercion, or force.

nihilism A theory that says that life is meaningless and that human striving is pointless because nothing matters. In ethics, nihilists believe that there is no such thing as right or wrong because moral truths do not exist.

normative In aesthetics, a term that refers to an approach to defining art. A normative definition involves defining art according to specific standards, or norms.

NOMA (non-overlapping magisteria) principle Refers to the idea that the magisteria, or areas of authority and teaching, of science and religion are separate. Religion and philosophy lie outside the realm of science, and science lies outside the realm of religion and philosophy.

non-representational (non-objective, non-figurative) In aesthetics, a term used to describe abstract art that bears no resemblance to reality.

objectivism In aesthetics, a theory that says that aesthetic judgments are based on how well the objective qualities of a work of art adhere to the rules of composition.

ontological argument An argument, developed by Anselm of Canterbury, that says that God must exist because God is perfect and existence is a feature of perfection.

ontology The area of metaphysics that deals with the nature of being and reality.

pacifism The belief that disputes between nations should be settled peacefully.

pantheism A theory that says that a supreme being is everywhere and that everything in the universe contains the spirit of this being.

paradigm shift Phrase coined by Thomas Kuhn and used to describe the change that occurs when one way of thinking about the world is discredited and replaced by another.

personal aesthetic An individual person's principles of taste and appreciation of beauty.

personal identity The characteristics, or qualities, that make one the same person over time.

personhood What it means to be a person.

phenomenalism An epistemological theory that says that people can never know objects in the world as they really are. The best people can do is to know objects as they appear.

phenomenology A theory that says that things in the real world and people's consciousness of things in the real world are the same thing.

philosopher kings In Plato's ideal state, a guardian class of people whose innate abilities, intelligence, upbringing, education, and training equip them to lead society.

philosophical argument A debate between two or more people who present reasoned ideas for the purpose of discovering the truth.

philosophical system builder Someone who tries to construct a complete system of knowledge.

philosophy Thinking about thinking, or the love of wisdom.

pluralistic A term used to describe a society in which members of various cultural groups are encouraged to celebrate their heritage.

polytheism A theory that says that many gods govern the universe.

positive freedom Refers to people's power to control their own lives and to make their own decisions.

positive law Written rules, created by human beings, that are enforced by the state.

post-modernism A catch-all term used to describe various cultural and philosophical movements that question the stability of ideas and language. In ethics, the term "post-modernism" is often used to define views that reject the idea of the existence of a single moral code that governs all actions. In aesthetics, the term often refers to the idea that artists can create works of art without adhering to traditional ideas of what art should be.

pragmatic theory A theory that says that truth is neither fixed nor absolute. Pragmatists say that people create their own truths on the basis of whether something works, is useful, or is successful.

pragmatism An anti-foundationalist approach to epistemology. Pragmatists say that people should believe only things that are useful to them.

premise In logic, a factual statement or proposition.

propositional knowledge Knowledge that can be conveyed in words as information.

pseudo-science False science.

rationalism A theory that says that knowledge is a priori. It comes from exercising the human ability to reason.

realism A metaphysical theory, developed by Plato, that says that reality consists of ideal forms, or ideas, that are timeless, unchanging, immaterial, and more perfect than things in the material world of sense perception.

representational In aesthetics, a term that refers to art that portrays the world as it is.

representative theory of perception (epistemological dualism) An epistemological theory, developed by John Locke, that says that ideas in the mind are merely representations of objects in the real world. The object and the idea in the mind are separate and distinct.

retributive justice A principle of justice based on retribution, or punishment. Retributionists say that lawbreakers should get the punishment they deserve or that the punishment should match the crime.

satyagraha A philosophy and a tool of political action, developed by Mohandas Gandhi, that means holding to the truth, and refers to non-violent civil disobedience.

second-order language (higher-order language, metalanguage) A term used to describe language that is used to discuss and clarify first-order language.

sentience The ability to perceive things through the senses.

skepticism A philosophical tool that leads philosophers to question assumptions. Extreme skepticism denies that any knowledge is possible.

slippery-slope phenomenon An expression that means that doing something once, such as lying, starts a person or society down a slippery slope toward disaster.

social and political philosophy The area of philosophy that studies how society should be organized to meet people's needs.

social contract In social and political philosophy, an unwritten contract that sets out the relationship between rulers and those who are ruled. It explains what happened when human beings departed from their natural state and gathered in societies.

socialism An economic and social system that tries to correct the flaws of capitalism by focusing on workers' interests.

Socratic method A question-and-answer process named after Socrates. It is used to zero in on knowledge by challenging commonly held assumptions.

soft determinism A theory that says that free will and determinism are compatible. Though desires are determined by a chain of causes extending back in time, people can be self-determined if they are free of coercion.

solipsism An extreme form of subjective idealism. A solipsist believes that only he or she exists to perceive things.

sound In logic, refers to arguments in which the premises are true and the form is valid.

state Refers to people who live in an organized political community within specified geographic boundaries.

Stoicism A school of thought that focuses on achieving happiness by living wisely and striving to live a well-ordered life.

strong artificial intelligence thesis A functionalist theory that says that computers can be programmed to think.

subjective idealism An epistemological theory, developed by George Berkeley, that says that what is perceived as real or true exists only in the mind.

subjectivism In aesthetics, a theory that says that aesthetic judgments are based on the amount of pleasure a work of art arouses in the perceiver.

substance In metaphysics, something that has an independent existence.

survival A person's continued existence over time.

sustainable development A concept that refers to people's efforts to reconcile the needs of human beings and the environmental concerns associated with human development.

syllogism A form of formal deductive argument, developed by Aristotle, that consists of premises that lead to a conclusion.

tao In Taoist and Confucian thought, a concept that means the way, or the right path.

Taoism A philosophy, attributed to Laozi (Lao-tzu), that emphasizes living in harmony with nature and the rhythms of the universe.

taste In aesthetics, a term that refers to the ability to recognize the aesthetic features of an object.

theism A theory that says that the universe was created by a perfect, all-powerful supreme being who continues to be interested in its well-being and can intervene to perform miracles or make revelations.

theories of action In ethics, theories that deal with how people should act.

theories of character (virtue theories) In ethics, theories that deal with questions about character traits that are morally good and morally bad.

theories of value In ethics, theories that deal with questions about the things people value.

Thomism A school of thought developed by Thomas Aquinas. Thomists focus on the idea of virtue as right conduct or doing the right thing in obedience to God.

thought experiment A tool used by philosophers to encourage people to re-examine common-sense beliefs. Often begins with or includes the question, What if…?

three laws of thought Developed by Aristotle, they are the law of non-contradiction (something cannot be said both to be and not to be at the same time), the law of the excluded middle (something must either be or not be), and the law of identity (something is what it is).

totalitarianism A dictatorial form of government that requires absolute obedience to the state.

tripartite theory of the soul A theory, developed by Plato, that said that a person's soul, or personality, psyche, mind, or inner self, is made up of reason, spirit, and appetite.

truth The quality or state of being true, though philosophers do not agree on what makes something true.

Turing test A test, developed by Arthur Turing, to discover whether a computer can converse in a way that would fool a human being.

utilitarianism In ethics and social and political philosophy, a theory, developed by Jeremy Bentham and John Stuart Mill, that says that morally good choices are those that result in the greatest good for the greatest number of people.

utopianism A term that refers to a vision of an ideal state.

validity In logic, refers to the correctness of the reasoning in deductive arguments.

virtue A character trait, such as courage and wisdom, that is considered morally good.

virtue ethics An ethical school that emphasizes the role of character in guiding moral choices.

Index

A
Abductive reasoning, 73, 75
Abelard, Peter, 52
Aboriginal ethics, 270, 275
Aboriginal healing circles, 265
Abortion, 135, 258
Abraham, 273
Absolutism, ethical, 257
Abstract art, 338
Accident, fallacy of, 78
Act utilitarianism, 275
Adventures of Huckleberry Finn (Twain), 155, 160, 161
Advertising
 aesthetics, 312
 creating an advertisement (culminating activity), 366-367
 ethics, 302-303
Aenesidemus, 200
Aesthetic attitude, 319, 320
Aesthetic experience, 316, 319
Aesthetics *see also* Art; Beauty
 Aristotle, 312, 314, 329, 341, 349, 359
 art and truth, 343-344
 censorship, 342-343
 Chinese philosophy, 353-354
 connective aesthetics, 336, 337
 Descartes, 315
 Dewey, 318, 322, 359, 360, 361
 existentialism, 334
 feminism, 334-335, 352-353
 forgeries, 325
 Hegel, 317, 350
 Hume, 323-324, 349-350
 idealism, 331
 importance of, 319-320
 Indian philosophy, 354-355

 Islam, 355, 357
 Kant, 317, 319, 323, 324, 338, 350, 351-352
 Nietzsche, 316, 318, 345
 objectivism and subjectivism, 319, 323-324, 331
 and other studies, 320
 phenomenology, 333-334
 philosophical schools, 311-313, 331-336
 Plato, 329, 331, 341, 342, 349
 points of view, 312-313, 349-360
 relationship to art and beauty, 359-360
 and science, 315, 320
 scope of study, 310-311
 taste, 315, 317
Aesthetic triad, 311
African National Congress (ANC), 394
Agnosticism, moral values, 254
Alcoff, Linda Martín, 219
Algren, Nelson, 41
"Allegory of the Cave" (Plato), 8-9, 10, 16, 114-117, 204, 224
Almond, Brenda, 5
Altruism or egoism, 28-31, 38-39
 Rand's views, 279-280
American Revolution, 397-398
Ames, Roger T., 265
Amoral issues, 246
Amphiboly, a fallacy of ambiguity, 79
Analects, The (Kongfuzi), 393
Anarchistic epistemology, 102
Anderson, Elizabeth, 294
Angier, Natalie, 38
Angst, 40, 271, 334

Animals
 animal research, 299-300
 consciousness, 133, 134, 151, 296, 298-299
 intelligence in, 19, 38, 150-151, 270, 299
 rights, 133, 270, 296, 298-300
Anselm of Canterbury, 159-160
Anthropic principle, 105
Anti-foundationalism, 193, 214-215
Apes, communication by, 150-151
A posteriori knowledge, 185, 193, 213
Appeal to authority as logical fallacy, 77
Appeal to emotion as logical fallacy, 77
Appeal to force as logical fallacy, 76
Appeal to ignorance as logical fallacy, 78
Appeal to pity as logical fallacy, 76-77
Appearance and reality *see* Cave, allegory of
A priori knowledge, 185, 193, 213
Aquinas, Thomas, 91, 245, 269, 273
 empiricism, 209
 on natural law, 392-393
 profile, 210
Arabesque, 355
Architecture, 338-339
Areas of philosophy, 17-20
Arendt, Hannah, 289
Argument *see also* Logic
 form of logical arguments, 60-62
 limits of, 59

meaning in philosophy, 15, 17, 54, 58
recasting arguments as syllogisms, 83-84
sound or unsound, 62
strong or weak, 56
syllogisms, 60-61
valid or invalid, 56, 62
Argument from design, 161
Aristotle
aesthetics, 312, 314, 329, 341, 349, 359
on animals, 296
on being, 121
empiricism, 184, 208, 221
epistemology, 181-182, 184, 192, 208, 211
focus on reason, 35, 270
golden mean, 244, 245, 268, 269
on human nature, 26, 35
logic, 51-52
a philosophical system builder, 7
philosophy of science, 90-91, 93
political philosophy, 371, 389, 391-392
prejudices, 21, 39, 268, 419
profile, 53
three laws of thought, 52, 63
virtue ethics, 268
Art *see also* Aesthetics; Beauty
architecture, 338-339
"art for art's sake," 314, 337, 345
artistic freedom and censorship, 342-343
artistic merit, 343
arts and crafts, 341-342
contemporary art, 361-362
and culture, 319-320, 344, 362, 363
dance, 340
descriptive definitions, 321-322
fashion arts, 340
and happiness, 345
influence on behaviour, 312, 313-314
literature, 339
and morality, 319, 324-325
music, 19, 339
and nature, 341
normative definitions, 321, 322
philosophers' ideas, 313-319
and reality, 313-314, 362
Renaissance in Europe, 314, 339
and society, 338-340, 342-343, 361-363
techniques and tools, 342
theatre, 339-340
traditional theories, 330-331
and truth, 343-344
value of, 319, 321-325, 362
visual arts, 336, 338
women artists, 334-335
Artificial intelligence, 17, 57, 96
photo of dog robot, 38
strong artificial intelligence, 148, 149
Assessing information, 84-85
Assumptions, old and new, 204
Astrology, 104
Atheism, 162-164
moral values, 254, 271
Sartre, 40, 42, 162, 171
Atomism, 90
Attack on the person as logical fallacy, 77-78
Augustine of Hippo, 5, 35, 245, 250, 289
Authenticity, 122, 270, 271, 334, 380
Autonomy, 6
consumers and advertising, 303
and euthanasia, 291
Auxiliary hypothesis, 100, 101
Averroës, 105, 245
Avicenna, 357

Ayer, Alfred Jules, 252, 281

B
Bacon, Francis, 52, 93
Baier, Annette, 135, 278
Barnes, Hazel, 280
Baumgarten, Alexander, 315
Beardsley, Monroe, 325, 345
Beauty, 19, 313
contemporary views, 350, 352-353, 357
global perspectives, 353-357
historical perspectives, 349-350
Kant, 350, 351-352
in nature, 359
Plato and Aristotle, 349
questions on beauty and art, 349, 358-363
a thought experiment, 358
and utility, 360
Beccaria, Cesare, 384
Begging the question, fallacy, 79
Behaviourism, 39, 251
Being, various explanations, 120-122
Being and Time (Heidegger), 121
Beliefs
justified true belief, 189-191
opinions, beliefs, and knowledge, 187-188
sources of untrue beliefs, 224
true belief, 188-189
Bell, Clive, 322, 330, 345
Bentham, Jeremy, 26, 273, 299, 384, 421
hedonistic calculus, 274
Berkeley, George, 113, 221
subjective idealism, 227
Berleant, Arnold, 359
Berlin, Isaiah, 382-383
Bias, 21
Bible, 298
Billiard balls and causality, 212
Bioethics, 293-294

Black, Charles L., Jr., 415
Bok, Sissela, 286
Book of Changes, 253
Boolean logic (Boolean algebra), 52, 57
Boole, George, 52, 57
Brain in a vat, 201-202
Briffault, Robert, 91
Browne, Sir Thomas, 59
Bruno, Giordano, 5
Buddha *see* Gautama, Siddhartha (the Buddha)
Buddhism
    challenge to essentialist ideas, 37
    Eightfold Path, 252, 264
Bundle theory of the self, 122, 125
Burke, Edmund, political conservatism, 400
Business ethics, 301-303
Butler, Joseph, 28, 29, 31, 33

C
Calligraphy, 354, 355, 357
Calvin, John, 250
Camus, Albert, 40, 168, 169, 263
Canadian Charter of Rights and Freedoms, 375, 419, 420
Canadian Code of Advertising Standards, 302, 303
Capitalism, 373, 378, 403
Categorical imperative, 277-278, 286, 383-384
    decision on downloading music, 301
Categorical syllogisms, 67-70
    testing validity of, 69-70
Catharsis, 312
Causality, 95, 165
    Hume's denial, 95, 212-213
    Kant's view, 213
Cave, allegory of, 8-9, 10, 16, 114-117, 204, 224
Censorship, 287-288, 314, 340, 342-343
Charter of Rights *see* Canadian Charter of Rights and Freedoms

Chimpanzees, 19, 38, 270, 299
Chinese philosophy, 7, 63 *see also* Kongfuzi (Confucius)
    aesthetics, 353-354
    Confucianism, 32, 244, 252, 253
    Taoism, 265
Chinese room, 149
Chisholm, Roderick M., 222
Choice *see* Moral choice
Chomsky, Noam, 105, 206, 207
Christianity *see also* God (Christian view)
    Golden Rule, 244, 254
    humanity's fallen state, 31
    and philosophy, 7, 245
    predestination, 250
Christina, Queen of Sweden, 183
Churchland, Patricia and Paul, 113, 142
Church and state relationship, 371
Civil disobedience, 259, 374, 394-395
Classical liberalism, 409
Clothing, 340
Coercion by governments, 382-383
Cogito ergo sum, 182
Coherence theory of truth, 230-232
Cold War, 373
Collingwood, R.G., 330, 341
Common-sense realism, 113, 186, 226
Communism
    in China, 265
    Marx, 402-404
    partial collapse in 1990s, 373
    and Plato's ideal society, 389
Communist Manifesto (Marx and Engels), 403
Communitarianism, 382, 410, 411-413
Community, 246
    and Confucianism, 265
    and individual, 411-413
Competence knowledge, 192

Complex question, fallacy, 79
Composition, fallacies of, 80
Computers *see also* Artificial intelligence
    and ethics, 300-301
    and logic, 52, 54, 57
    and minds, 147-149
Comte, Auguste, 102-103
Conclusion of argument, 54, 60, 61
Conditioned responses, 251
Conformity, 265
Confucianism
    aesthetics, 353-354
    community and the good life, 265
    Golden Rule, 244, 254, 265
Confucius *see* Kongfuzi (Confucius)
Connective aesthetics, 336, 337
Conscience (Butler's ideas), 29
Consciousness *see also* Self
    animals, 133, 134, 151, 296, 298-299
    Kant's theory, 184
    Locke's ideas, 136, 137-138
    Nagel's thoughts, 144, 145
Consequentialist theories, 269, 273, 278-279
    arguments against war, 289
Conservationist movement, 295
Conservatism, 400
Contractarian, 422
Contradiction in logic, 55
Control, Stoics, 267
Converse accident, fallacy of, 78
Co-operation, 38
    ideas of Hobbes, 29
Copernicus, Nicolaus, 91, 180, 205, 315
Correspondence theory of truth, 229-230
Cosmological argument for supreme being, 160-161
Courtney, John, 418
Crafts, 341-342
Creativity, 16
Crime and punishment, 383-385, 416

Critical thinking, 11, 13-14
Critique of Judgment (Kant), 350, 351-352
Croce, Benedetto, 321-322, 330
Culture and knowledge, 204

D
Dalai Lama, 395
Dance, 340
Danto, Arthur, 318
Darwin, Charles, 94, 105
    a determinist, 250
Davis, Thomas D., 255-256
Dawkins, Richard, 97
Death, 36
de Beauvoir, Simone, 40, 126
    profile, 41
Decisions, ethical *see* Moral choice
Declaration of the Rights of Women (de Gouges), 399
Deconstructionism, 214-215, 335
Deduction (deductive logic), 50, 51, 52, 56
    deductive reasoning, 205-206
    syllogisms, 61
Deep structure of language, 206
Definitions in philosophy, 10-11, 13
de Gouges, Olympe, 399
Deism, 156
Democracy
    Aristotle's view, 391-392
    Paine's ideas, 400, 402
Dennett, Daniel, 134
    concept of a person, 134, 135
Deontological theories, 277
Derrida, Jacques, 214-215
Descartes, René
    aesthetics, 315
    on animals, 150, 296
    deductive reasoning, 205-206
    epistemology, 182, 184, 194, 200, 281
    on mind-brain problem, 122, 123-124, 143-144, 145, 150
    profile, 183
    rationalism, 9, 170, 182, 183, 194, 205-206, 222, 281
    skepticism, 223
Descartes's method, 182
Descriptive approach to human behaviour, 243
Designing a society, 424
Determinism, 114, 164-168, 250
    hard determinism, 165, 166-167
    and responsibility, 167, 250
    soft determinism, 168
Deterrence of crime, 384-385
Deutsch, David, 95, 101
Dewey, John, 214, 232
    aesthetics, 318, 322, 359, 360, 361
Dharmakirti, 208
Dickie, George, 322-323, 335
Direct knowledge, 191
Disinterested approach to art, 319
Disjunctive syllogisms, 70-71
Distributive justice, 417-418
Divine command theory, 254, 272-273
    beliefs about animals, 298
Division, fallacies of, 80
Doctrine of impermanence, 37
Dostoyevsky, Fyodor, 114
Doubt, 199-201 *see also* Skepticism
    Descartes, 9, 205
    ten arguments, 200
Dualism, 114, 143-144
    and mind-brain problem, 143-144
    substance dualism, 143-144
Duns Scotus, John, 273
Duties, ethical, 269-270 *see also* Responsibility
    Kant's ideas *see* Categorical imperative

E
Earle, William James, 231
Eclecticism, 338-339
Ecofeminism, 295-296
Economic laissez-faire, 421
Edifying (Rorty), 215
Education
    against lies and prejudice, 288
    and equal opportunity, 379
    and goodness, 32-33
Egalitarianism, 270, 377-378
Egoism, 28, 278-280 *see also* Self-interest
    altruism or egoism, 28-31
    psychological egoism, 250-251
Eightfold Path, 252, 264
Einstein, Albert, 13, 94, 180, 185
Electoral system, Canadian, 418
Eliminative materialism, 142
Emotive theory, 252, 281
Empiricism, 93, 185, 208-209, 211-213, 221, 329
    Aquinas, 209, 210
    Aristotle, 184, 208-209, 221
    Hume, 209, 212-213
    Locke, 182, 184, 209, 211-212
Engels, Friedrich, 403
Enlightened self-interest, 254
Enlightenment, 357, 396
Entitlement theories of justice, 423, 425
Environmental ethics, 294-295
    and Third World countries, 297-298
Environmental problems, 96, 98
Epicurus, 267, 274
Epistemology *see also* Knowledge; Skepticism
    anti-foundationalism, 214-215
    Aristotle, 181-182, 184, 208, 211
    contemporary ideas, 214-215

Descartes, 182, 183, 184, 194, 200, 205-206, 281
empiricism *see* Empiricism
Hume, 95, 212-213
Kant, 184, 202, 213, 228
Locke, 182, 184, 211-212
Plato, 181, 202-205
rationalism *see* Rationalism
statements and propositions, 193
study or theory of knowledge, 18, 179-180
Equality
among social groups, 204, 374, 375, 419
in distribution of resources, 377-378, 417-418
Equal opportunity and equal treatment, 378-379
Charles Taylor on, 380-381
education, 379
Equivocation fallacy, 79
Essence, 114
and existence, 35-36, 37, 40, 42
Essentialist views of human nature, 33-35
challenges to, 37-42
Ethical absolutists, 257
Ethical dimensions of actions, 285
Ethical issues, 19, 243, 248, 278, 285-290 *see also* Moral choice
advertising, 302-303
computers and intellectual property, 300-301
crime and punishment, 383-385
environmental concerns, 294-295, 297-298
euthanasia, 290-291, 292, 293
freedom of expression, censorship, 287-288
genethics, 293-294
lying, cheating, and stealing, 285-287
treatment of animals, 296, 298-300
war, 288-290
Ethical objectivism, 259
Ethical relativists, 257-258, 281
Ethical subjectivism, 259
Ethical universalists, 257
Ethics
altruism, 28-30, 279-280
amoral issues, 246
applied ethics *see* Ethical issues
area of philosophy, 7, 18-19
and business, 301-303
choice *see* Moral choice
codes *see* Moral standards
distinction from morals, 242
egoism, 28-31, 278-280
emotive theory, 252
good and evil, 25, 29, 31-33
humanism, 245
intuitionism, 280-281
logical positivism, 252
metaethics, 243, 249-259
normative approach, 242-247, 272, 278
post-modernism, 281
reasons to study, 248
right and wrong, 246, 247
and science, 290-294
terms, 247
theories of action, 242-243
theories of character, 243, 268-270
theories of value, 243
utilitarianism, 273-275, 288, 301
Ethics of care, 245, 278
Eudaimonia (Greek word for happiness), 268
Eugenics, 390
Euthanasia, 290-291, 292, 293
Evil, 31-33, 38, 162-163
Ewing, A.C., 230, 231-232
Excluded middle, law of, 52

Existentialism
aesthetics, 334
challenge to essentialism, 40, 42
de Beauvoir, 41
idea of being, 122
Kierkegaard, 40, 270-271
in literature, 339
on responsibility, 42, 171, 271-272
Sartre, 40, 42, 245, 271, 334
view of a good person, 270-272
Experience machine, 266
Expressionism, 330-331, 337, 338
External world, Plato and Descartes on, 206

F
Fairness as justice, 422-423
Fallacies *see* Logical fallacies
Fallacies of ambiguity, 79-80
Fallacies of presumption, 78-79
Fallacies of relevance, 76-78
Fallen state (Christian belief), 31
False cause, fallacy, 78
Falsificationism, 98
Family
Aristotle's view, 391
Plato's ideas, 389
Fashion arts, 340
Feinberg, Joel, 299
Feminism, 98
Feminist philosophers, 9
aesthetics, 334-335, 352-353
challenge to essentialism, 39-40
epistemology, 194-195
Mary Wollstonecraft, 401
Simone de Beauvoir, 41
Fernández-Armesto, Felipe, 219, 220-221, 222, 234-235
Feyerabend, Paul, 102
Fielding, Henry, 59

Fine arts, difference from crafts, 341
First-order language, 10
Foreign aid, ethics of, 297-298
Forgeries and artistic value, 325
Formal fallacies, 75-76
Formalism, 317, 330, 338, 363
Forms, Plato's theory, 113, 118-119, 181, 185, 202-205, 208, 226, 329
Foucault, Michel, 357
Foundationalism, 193, 214
Freedom *see also* Moral choice
  behaviourist views, 39
  de Beauvoir, 41
  just limits on behaviour, 382-383
  negative freedom, 375, 382-383
  positive freedom, 375, 382, 383
  Sartre, 40, 42, 167-168
Freedom of expression, 287-288, 314, 340, 342-343
Free will, 25, 165, 166, 167, 250
Frege, Gottlob, 54
French, Marilyn, 353
French Revolution, 399-400, 402
Freud, Sigmund, 35, 39, 250
  on religion, 163
Friedman, Milton, 378
Frueh, Johanna, 335
Fukuyama, Francis, 373
Functionalism, 142-143, 148

G
Gablik, Suzi, 336
  profile, 337
Gaia hypothesis, 105
Galbraith, John Kenneth, 302
Galilei, Galileo, 93, 205
Gandhi, Mohandas, 259, 394-395
Gautama, Siddhartha (the Buddha), 37, 244
  Eightfold Path, 252, 264
  on knowledge, 187, 192
Generalization, 208

General will (Rousseau), 398-399
Genethics, 293-294
Genetic engineering, 17, 96, 293-294
Genre of literature, 339
Geocentric theory of the universe, 91
Gettier, Edmund, 190
Gilligan, Carol, 245, 246, 278
God (Christian view) *see also* Supreme Being
  Aquinas, 209, 210, 245, 269, 273, 392-393
  Augustine, 35, 245
  Kierkegaard, 270
  moral codes, 244, 245, 259
  Nietzsche, 271
Gödel, Kurt, 54
Gods of ancient Greeks, 19
Godwin, William, 401
Golden Mean (Aristotle), 244, 245, 268, 269
Golden Rule
  of Christian teaching, 244, 254
  of Confucianism, 244, 254, 265
Good
  in behaviour towards others, 246, 247
  goodness of character, 269-270
  goodness as right conduct, 268-269, 270
  relationship to right, 246
  and religion, 254
  a working definition, 31
"Good Brahman, The" (Voltaire), 27-28
Good and evil, 31-33
  in human beings, 25, 29, 38-39, 42
Good life, 263-267
  Buddhism, 264
  Chinese philosophy, 265
  experience machine, 266
  hedonism, 267

  Socrates and Plato, 263
  Stoicism, 267
Good person, 268-272
  existentialism, 270-272
  virtue ethics, 268-270
Gorgias, 249
Gould, Stephen Jay, 105
Government *see* State
Greenberg, Clement, 330
Grotius, Hugo, 414
Gyekye, Kwame, 246, 275, 382

H
Hampshire, Stuart, on self-knowledge, 128
Happiness
  to the ancient Greeks, 268
  and art, 345
  Buddhist view, 37
  and knowledge, 26
  for Stoics, 267
  views of Aquinas, 245
Hard determinism, 165, 166-167
Harmony, 265
Hawking, Stephen, 90
Heath, Joseph, 19-20
Hedonism, 267
Hedonistic calculus (Bentham), 274
Hegel, Georg W.F., 21
  aesthetics, 316, 350
  coherence theory, 230
Heidegger, Martin
  aesthetics, 334, 343-344
  metaphysics, 121-122
Heisenberg, Werner, 180
Held, Virginia, 246
Hinduism, 27, 354-355
Hirst, Damien, 321
Hobbes, Thomas
  materialism, 113
  negative view of human nature, 28-29, 30, 33
  political philosophy, 376, 396-397
  supporter of "scientific" answers, 9, 28, 37
Hoekema, David A., 16

Hollis, Martin, 25
Holmes, Robert, 271-272
Hospital ethics committees, 293
Humanism
    ethical ideals, 245, 254
    Kongfuzi (Confucius), 244, 253
Human nature
    altruism or egoism, 28-31
    challenges to essentialist views, 37-42
    and choice, 20
    continuing discussion, 42-43
    desire for knowledge, 26-28
    essentialist beliefs, 33-36
    existentialist views, 40-42
    good or evil, 25, 29, 31-33, 38-39, 42
    will to live, 345
Human needs classified, 15, 16, 26
Hume, David, 21, 161, 185, 274
    aesthetics, 315-316, 317, 323-324, 349-350
    bundle theory of the self, 122, 125
    denial of causality, 95, 212-213
    development of Locke's empiricism, 212
    emotive theory, 252
    a relativist, 257
Hurka, Thomas, 297-298
Husserl, Edmund, 103-104, 333-334
Hutcheson, Francis, 274
Hypatia, 5
Hypothetical syllogisms, 71

I
Iconology, 362
Idealism, 113, 331
Ideal world *see* Forms, Plato's theory
Identity, law of, 52
Identity theorists, and mind-brain problem, 141-142

Ideologies, 372, 373
Illusion
    overcoming illusion, 223-224
    Plato's cave, 8-9, 10, 16, 114-117, 204, 224
Imitationalism, 330
Imitation game, 147
Immortality of the soul, 35, 36
Impermanence, doctrine of, 37
Indian philosophy, 7, 63
    Buddhism, 37, 264
    Hindu theory of aesthetics, 354-355
Indirect knowledge, 191
Individualism, 382-383, 410, 412
Individual relativism, 259
Individual and state, 377-385, 409-410, 419
Induction (inductive logic)
    applying inductive reasoning, 72-73
    Aristotle, 208
    foundation of scientific method, 52, 95
    reasoning process in, 50-51
    reliable or unreliable, 62-63
Industrial Revolution, and art, 340, 341
Inferences, 57
Informal fallacies, 76-80
    fallacies of relevance, 76-78
Innate ideas, 181, 185, 202-203, 206
Instrumentalism, 102, 232
Intellectual property, 300-301
Intentionality, 149
Internet, 57
Intrinsic and instrumental values, 247
    non-human animals, 298
Intuitionism, 280-281
Irrelevant conclusion as logical fallacy, 77
Islamic philosophy, 91, 245
    aesthetics, 355, 357
    Averroës, 105, 245

J
Jameson, Fredric, 357
James, William, 214, 232
Jaspers, Karl, 7
Jesus Christ, 245
Justice, 270, 373, 375, 415-423, 425
    based on fairness, 422-423
    and distribution, 417-418
    entitlement theories, 423, 425
    and law, 410
    merit as, 419
    and retribution, 416
    utility as, 421-422
Justified true belief, 189-191, 193
Just war theory, 289

K
Kant, Immanuel, 21, 245
    aesthetics, 316, 319, 323, 324, 338, 350, 351-352
    on animals, 296
    categorical imperative, 277-278, 383-384
    epistemology, 184, 202, 213, 228
    profile, 317
Kanzi (a bonobo ape), 150-151
Keegstra, James, 287, 288
Kierkegaard, Søren, 245, 273
    aesthetics, 334
    existentialism, 40, 270-271
King, Martin Luther, Jr., 373, 394
    profile, 374
Knowledge *see also* Beliefs; Epistemology; Opinions
    by acquaintance or by description, 192
    analyzing and rating information, 15
    Aristotle, 181-182, 184, 208, 211
    competence knowledge, 192

Descartes, 9, 182, 183, 184, 194, 205-206
direct and indirect, 191
doubt, 199-201, 205
empiricism, 93, 185, 209, 211-213, 329
epistemology as study of, 18, 179-180
foundationalism and anti-foundationalism, 193, 214
and happiness, 26, 27-28
Hume, 212-213
Kant, 227-228, 184, 202, 213
Locke, 210-212, 184, 185
objective and subjective, 194, 195
opinions, beliefs, and knowledge, 187-188
Plato, 202-205, 181, 185, 188-189, 206, 208, 225, 226
a priori or a posteriori, 185, 193, 213
propositional knowledge, 193
and reason *see* Rationalism; Reason
science as a source, 18
Socratic method, 11, 13
truth and belief necessary, 188-191
Kohn, Alfie, 43
Kongfuzi (Confucius), 32
aesthetics, 314, 353-354
epistemology, 181
ethics, 244, 252, 265
political philosophy, 393-394
profile, 253
Krishnamurti, Jiddu, 355
profile, 356
Kuhn, Thomas, 91, 97
profile, 92
Kurtz, Paul, 254

L
"Land of Certus, The" (Davis), 255-256
Langer, Susanne, 361
Language
Chomsky's ideas, 206, 207
of different groups, 215
first- and second-order language, 10
illogical language and comedy, 61
precision in, 10-11
words as symbols, 249
Laozi (Lao-tzu), 120, 121, 265, 354
Latimer, Robert, 291, 293
Lavine, T.Z., 35
Law
civil disobedience, 259, 374, 394-395
and justice, 410
legal positivism, 252, 414
and moral choices, 258-259
natural law, 392-393, 413-415
positive law, 413, 414, 415
Law of the excluded middle, 52
Law of identity, 52
Law of non-contradiction, 52
Laws of nature, 96
Leaders
Kongfuzi's ideas, 394
Plato's philosopher kings, 389-390
Rousseau's ideas, 399
views of Aquinas, 393
Lee, Mabel, 265
Legal positivism, 414, 415
Legitimacy of state power, 375, 376
Leibniz, Gottfried Wilhelm, 163
Leviathan (Hobbes), 28-29, 396
Li, 32, 33
Liberal individualism, 382-383, 412
Liberalism versus Marxism, 404-405

Libertarianism, 404, 423, 425
Life after death, 36
Life, meaning of, 97, 168-171
Limits, to state power, 376-377
Linguistics, 206
Literary arts, 339
Liu Xie, 354
Locke, John
on consciousness, 136, 137-138
definition of a person, 134, 135, 136
epistemology, 182, 184, 209, 211-212
on natural human rights, 376, 378
on natural law, 409, 414
philosophy and religion, 245
political philosophy, 376, 397-398, 409, 414
representative theory of perception, 227
Logic *see also* Argument
applications of, 62
area of philosophy, 17-18
Aristotle, 51-52
Boolean logic (symbolic logic), 52
and computers, 52, 54
deduction *see* Deduction (deductive logic)
defined, 50
form of logical arguments, 60-62
importance of, 56-57
induction *see* Induction (inductive logic)
and mathematics, 54
Logical consistency, 54, 55
Logical contradiction, 55
Logical fallacies, 75-80
formal fallacies, 75-76
informal fallacies, 75, 76-80
Logical positivism, 102-103, 252
"Love is a Fallacy," 81-83

Lu Ji (Lu Chi), 354
Luther, Martin, 205, 250
Lying, cheating, and stealing, 285-287
Lyotard, Jean-François, 350

M
Machiavelli, Niccolò, 371, 372
MacIntyre, Alasdair, 270
MacPherson, C.B., 398
Maimonides, Moses, 274, 275
Maintenance needs, 15
Male dominance, 21, 296
Mandela, Nelson, 394
Marcel, Gabriel, 271
Marcuse, Herbert, 405
Marginalized groups, 20-21
Marx, Karl, 162, 163, 377, 402-404
Maslow, Abraham, 15, 26
Materialism, 7, 37-38, 113
    and mind-brain problem, 141, 145
    and teletransporters, 140
Mathematics
    and aesthetics, 320
    ideas as a priori knowledge, 185
    theory of incompleteness, 54
Maximin rule, 424
Mazzarese, Michael, 63
McGuire, John, 220, 223-224
Meaning of life, 18, 168-171
    nihilist approach, 169
    non-theistic approach, 170-171
    theistic approach, 170
Media literacy, 84-85
Mengzi (Mencius), 32, 33
Merit as justice, 419
Metaethics, 243, 249-252, 254, 257-259
    possibility of moral choices, 249-252, 257
Metalanguage, 10

Metaphysics *see also* Mind-brain problem; Reality; Supreme being
    being, 120-122
    Berkeley, 113, 221, 227
    defined, 18, 112
    Descartes, 114, 143-144, 145, 182
    Heidegger, 121-122
    Hobbes, 9, 28, 37, 113
    Plato's cave, 8-9, 10, 16, 114-117, 204, 224
    Plato's ideal world, 113, 118-119, 181, 185, 202-205, 208, 226, 329
    self, theories about, 122-125
    Spinoza, 113, 145
    Wittgenstein, 146
Michelangelo, 343
Midgley, Mary, 258, 280
Militarists, 289
Mill, John Stuart, 26, 274-275, 276
    on individual freedom, 287, 382, 384
    on justice, 421-422
Mimesis, 330
Mind-brain problem
    dualism of Descartes, 9, 122, 123-124, 143-144, 145, 150
    functionalism, 142-143
    identity theory, 141-142
    materialistic views, 37-38, 141, 142
    monism, 145
    subjectivist ideas, 144-145
    Turing test, 147-148
Minimalist state, 423, 425
Modernism, 281, 318, 335
Monism, 113, 214
    and mind-brain problem, 145
Monkeys, 38

Monotheism, 157
Moore, George Edward, 31, 280
Moral agent, 247
Moral choice *see also* Ethical issues; Moral standards
    absolutism or relativism, 257-258
    different views, 285
    existentialism, 40, 42, 270-272, 334
    and human nature, 20
    issues *see* Ethical issues
    possibility of, 249-252, 257
    reason in, 280-281
    responsibility *see* Responsibility
    utilitarianism, 273-275, 288, 301
Moral isolationism, 258
Morality
    and art, 319, 324-325
    terms: "ethics", "morality", "morals," 242, 247
Moral patient, 247
Moral philosophy *see* Ethics
Moral standards *see also* Moral choice
    absolute, relative, or universal, 257-258
    categorical imperative, 277-278, 286, 301, 383-384
    developing, 248
    divine command theory, 254, 272-273, 298
    God's laws, 244, 245
    Golden Mean (Aristotle), 244, 245
    Golden Rule, 244, 254, 265
    and law, 258-259
Moral values
    of minorities, 259
    objective or subjective, 259
    and religion, 254
More, Thomas, 371
Morris, Tom, 58-59
Moses, 244

Motherwell, Robert, 337
Muhammad, 357
Multiculturalism
    Charles Taylor on, 380-381
    in contemporary art, 361-362
    moral values of minorities, 259, 285
Music, 19, 339
Muslims *see* Islamic philosophy
Myths, 19

N
Nagel, Thomas, 144, 145, 199
Nagarjuna, 200
Narrative theory of the self, 125
Nationalism, 373
Nation states, 375
Natural beauty, 359
Naturalists, 103, 413
Natural law, 392-393, 409, 413-415
Natural selection, 94, 105
Near-death experiences, 36
Needs, 270
    Maslow's classification, 15, 16, 26
Negative freedom, 375, 382-383
Neo-liberalism or neo-conservatism, 404
Neoplatonists, 359
Newton, Isaac, 16-17, 93, 94
    a determinist, 250
Nicomachean Ethics (Aristotle), 268
Nietzsche, Friedrich, 245
    aesthetics, 316, 318, 345
    on moral choices, 271
    on supreme being, 162, 163
Nihilism, 94, 169, 249, 334
Nirvana (in Buddhism), 252, 264
Nishitani, Keiji, 94
Nochlin, Linda, 353
Noddings, Nel, 245, 246, 278
NOMA principle, 105
Non-consequentialist theories, 277
    arguments against war, 289
Non-contradiction, law of, 52
Non-representational art, 338
Non-theistic approach to life, 170-171
Non-violence, 394, 395
Normative definitions of art, 321, 322
Normative ethics, 242-247, 272, 278
Nozick, Robert, 266, 404, 422, 423, 425
Nussbaum, Martha, 391

O
Objectivism and subjectivism
    aesthetics, 319, 323-324, 331
    ethics, 259, 279
    knowledge, 194-195
Objectivity
    in judgment of art, 319, 323
    scientific, 97-98
One-Dimensional Man (Marcuse), 405
On Liberty (Mill), 382
Ontological argument for supreme being, 159-160
Ontology, 114
Opinions
    inferior to knowledge, 11, 187
    not based on critical thinking, 6
    should be well-supported, 187, 243
Opposites, theory of, 200

P
Pacifists, 289
Paine, Thomas, 400, 402
Panentheism, 157, 159
Pangle, Thomas, 391
Panpsychism, 145
Pantheism, 157
Paradigm shifts, 91, 92
Paradox of bisection, 55
Parallel universes, 95
Parfit, Derek, 138-139, 140
Pascal, Blaise, "Pascal's wager" for God's existence, 161-162
Peirce, Charles Sanders, 73, 75, 214, 232
    profile, 74
Perception and truth, 225-228
Personal identity, 136-140 *see also* Mind-brain problem
    Locke's ideas, 137-138
Personality, Freud's tripartite theory, 35
Person, concept of (personhood), 114, 133-135
Phenomenalism, 228
Phenomenology, 103-104, 333-334
Philosopher kings, 389
Philosophical argument *see* Argument
Philosophical counsellors, 286
Philosophical system builders, 7, 9
Philosophy
    in the 17th century, 9
    in the 20th century, 9
    areas of philosophy, 17-20
    connecting philosophical areas, 20
    definition, 5
    eastern and western, 7, 20-21
    philosophical questions, 4, 17
    reading philosophy, 14
    reasons to study philosophy, 15-17
    and religion, 20-21, 245
    and science, 6, 17-18
    social and political philosophy, 19-20
    why philosophy matters, 14-15
Pinker, Steven, 151

Pirsig, Robert, 51
Plato
    aesthetics, 313, 314, 324, 325, 329, 331, 341, 342, 349
    allegory of the cave, 8-9, 10, 16, 114-117, 204, 224
    and Aristotle, 53
    attitude toward women, 21, 39
    on being, 120-121
    on class distinctions, 419
    ethics, 119, 244, 248, 254, 263
    idea of forms, 113, 118-119, 181, 185, 202-205, 208, 226, 329
    on knowledge, 181, 185, 188-189, 202-205, 206, 208, 225, 226
    a philosophical system builder, 7
    on reason, 34-35, 181, 204, 329
    Republic, The, 371, 373, 389-391, 419
    Ring of Gyges, 251, 254
    theory of the soul, 34-36, 329
    on truth, 220, 225, 226
Platonic realism, 113
Pluralism, 214, 285, 362
Polanyi, John, 320
Political philosophy
    Aristotle's *Politics*, 391-392
    Burke and political conservatism, 400
    class struggle (Marx and Engels), 402-404
    eastern tradition, 393-395
    general will (Rousseau), 398-399
    liberalism versus Marxism, 404-405
    Paine and radical liberal democracy, 400, 402
    Plato's *Republic*, 389-391
    power, 390, 396-397
    social contract ideas, 396-399
    utilitarianism, 421-422
    will of the people (Locke), 397-398
Political realism, 372, 397
Polkinghorne, John, 105
Polls and surveys, analyzing, 85
Polytheism, 157
Popper, Karl, 98, 99-100
Popular art, 363
Positive freedom, 375, 382-383
Positive law, 413, 414, 415
Post-modernism, 97, 281
    aesthetics, 318, 335-336, 337, 357, 363
    in architecture, 338-339
Power of political leaders, 390, 396-397
Pragmatism, 75, 214
    pragmatic theory of truth, 232, 234
Pratibha, 354-355
Predestination, 250
Prejudice
    among philosophers, 21, 419
    opposed by education, 288
Premise of argument, 54, 60
Preservationist movement, 295
Pre-Socratic philosophers, 6-7, 12, 105, 113
Primary and secondary qualities, 211-212
Prince, The (Machiavelli), 372
Prior restraint, 342
Prisoner's dilemma, 30-31
Project theory of the self, 125
Property rights, 378
Propositional knowledge, 193
Protagoras, 59, 221, 225, 226, 257
Pseudo-science, 103, 104
Psychological egoism, 250-251
Ptolemy, Claudius, 91
Public interest in philosophical questions, 17
Putnam, Hilary, 201-202
Pyrrho of Elis, 199-200
Pythagoras, 195

Q
Quality of life, 293
Quantum physics, 52, 112-113
Quesada, Francisco Miró, 43
Quine, Willard Van Orman, 100, 101, 103
Quinton, Anthony, 5, 415

R
Rachels, James, 280, 290
Radical democratic movement, 400, 402
Rand, Ayn, 245, 279-280
Randels, George D., Jr., 411-413
Rational egoism, 279
Rationalism, 93, 184-185, 202-206, 221, 222
    Chomsky, 206, 207
    Descartes, 9, 182, 183, 194, 205-206, 222, 281
    Plato, 202-205, 226, 329
Rawls, John, 422-423, 424
Realism, 113
    political realists, 372
    scientific realists, 98
Reality, 112-113, 199 *see also* Metaphysics
    and appearance *see* Cave, allegory of
    Descartes, 9, 143, 145, 182
    ideal forms *see* Forms, Plato's theory
    materialists *see* Materialism
    Taoism, 120
Reason
    Aristotle's theories, 182
    essentialist views, 33-35, 270
    Kant's beliefs, 277
    in moral choice, 280-281
    Plato's ideas, 34-35, 39, 181, 202-205

source of knowledge *see* Rationalism
superiority to emotions disputed, 39-40
using reason to know God, 269
Reasoning *see* Logic
Recasting arguments as syllogisms, 83-84
Regan, Tom, 299, 300
Rehabilitation and reform, 385
Reincarnation, 264
Relationships
   in aesthetics, 337
   Buddhism, 264
   ethics of care, 245
   Kongfuzi (Confucius), 252, 265
Relativism, ethical, 257-258, 281
Relativity, 94
Reliability of inductive argument, 62-63
Religion
   and art, 338, 339-340
   beginnings, 7
   and moral values, 254
   and philosophy, 20-21, 245
   and science, 93, 104-105
   theology, 245
   Tolstoy, 170
Religious extremists, 273
Renaissance in Europe
   and art, 314, 339
   social and political thought, 371, 372
Representational art, 338
Representation by population, 418
Representative theory of perception, 227
Republic, The (Plato), 371, 373, 389-391, 419
Responsibility
   Buddhism, 264
   and determinism, 167, 250
   to disobey unjust laws, 259, 374, 394-395
   in euthanasia, 293

existentialist view, 42, 171, 270-272
individual responsibilities and the state, 382, 383-385
legal and moral systems, 167
and subjectivism, 259
Retributionists, 384
Retributive justice, 416
Right *see also* Ethical issues
   in behaviour towards others, 246, 247
   deciding right actions, 257-259, 272-281
   divine command theory, 272-273
   Kant's theory *see* Categorical imperative
   reasons for doing right, 252, 254
   relationship to good, 246
   study of ethics, 18-19
   utilitarianism, 273-275
Rights
   Canadian Charter of Rights, 375, 419, 420
   natural rights, 376, 378, 397, 402
   property rights, 378, 398
Rights of Man, The (Paine), 400
Ring of Gyges, 251, 254
Rock concerts, 340
Rodriguez, Sue, 290, 291, 293
Rogers, Carl, 16, 39
Roman Catholic Church, 105, 396
Romantic movement, 341
Rorty, Richard, 215, 232, 252, 281
   on self-knowledge, 128-129
Ross, W.D., 269-270, 286
Rousseau, Jean-Jacques, 378, 398-399
Rule utilitarianism, 275
Russell, Bertrand, 189, 192, 229
Ryle, Gilbert, 37

S
Sartre, Jean-Paul
   atheism, 40, 42, 162, 171
   existentialism, 40, 42, 171, 245, 271, 334
   profile, 126
   project theory of the self, 125
Satyagraha, 394
Scheffler, Samuel, 425
Schelling, Friedrich von, 341
Schiller, Friedrich von, 324
Scholastic movement, 52
Schopenhauer, Arthur
   aesthetics, 343, 345
   nihilism, 169
Science
   influence on Hobbes, 9, 28
   natural laws, 96
   objectivity in, 97-98
   and philosophy, 6, 9, 180
   philosophy of science, 18
   and religion, 93, 104-105
   scientific realists, 98
   views of human nature, 37-39
Science wars, 96, 103
Scientific hylozoism, 105
Scientific method
   causality questioned by Hume, 95, 212-213
   challenges in the 20th century, 101-103
   Francis Bacon, 52, 93
   inductive reasoning, 52, 95
   Isaac Newton, 93
Scotus, John Duns, 273
Scruton, Roger, 200
Searle, John, 149
Second-order language, 10
Seinfeld, Jerry, 61
Self *see also* Consciousness
   Buddhist ideas, 37
   created by values, 248
   Descartes's views, 122, 123-124, 143-144, 145, 150
   different theories, 122-125

Plato's theory of the soul, 34-36, 329
Self-actualization, 15-16
Self-control (Plato's ideas), 254
Self-deception, 125, 127
Self-interest *see also* Egoism
    Freud's ideas, 38
    psychological egoism, 250-251
    Rand's ideas, 245, 279-280
    views of Hobbes, 28-29
Selfishness, 279-280
Self-knowledge, 128-129
Self-realization in Confucianism, 265
Sellars, Wilfrid, 112
Semantic Web, 57
Sense experiences, 93, 191, 192, 329 *see also* Empiricism
    aesthetics, 320
    Aristotle's ideas, 182
    can be deceptive, 178, 202
    Locke and Hume, 209, 211-213
    Plato's ideas, 181
Sentience among animals (Bentham), 299
Serenity, 267
Ship of Theseus, 14
Singer, Peter, 292, 299
Skepticism, 97, 199-200, 204, 205, 223, 249-250
Skinner, B.F., 39, 251
Slippery-slope phenomenon, 287, 293
Smith, Adam, 421
Smuts, Barbara, 38
Social constructionism, 97
Social contract ideas, 279, 372, 396-399, 422-423
Socialism, 403
Social and political philosophy *see also* Political philosophy
    as area of philosophy, 19-20
    relationship to other subjects, 370, 375
    "social" and "political," 370

Society and art, 338-340, 342-343, 361-363
Sociology, 103
Socrates, 31, 34, 188, 225
    critical thinking, 10, 11, 13
    on good and evil, 31
    the good life, 263
    on logical argument, 59
    trial, 4
    views on ethics, 7
Socratic method, 11, 13
Soft determinism, 168
Solipsism, 227
Sophie's Choice (Styron), 257
Sophisticated objectivism, 323
Sophisticated subjectivism, 323
Sophists, 221, 226
Soul, Plato's theories, 34-36, 329
Soundness of arguments, 62
Sovereignty, 375
Spinoza, Baruch
    monism, 113, 145
    profile, 158
    on God, 157, 159
Star Trek, 143
State
    and individual, 377-385, 409-410, 419
    legitimate authority, 375, 376
    limits to authority, 376-377
    reduced involvement in economy, 404
    relationship with church, 371
Statements and propositions, 193
Stich, Stephen, 232
Stoicism, 267
Strong artificial intelligence, 148, 149
Strossen, Nadine, 288
Subjective idealism, 227
Subjective knowledge, 194, 195
Subjectivism, mind-brain problem, 144-145
Subjectivity in judgment of art, 319, 323-324
Sublime, 314

Substance, 114
    theory of the self, 122
Substance dualism, 143-144
Supreme being
    Christian God *see* God (Christian view)
    concepts of, 155-157, 159
    divine command theory, 254, 272
    existence of, 114, 159-164, 272
    objective moral values, 259
    Sartre's views, 40, 42
    study of theology, 245
Surveys, analyzing, 85
Survival, 138-139
Sustainable development, 295
Suzuki, Daisetsu Teitaro, 220, 233
Syllogisms, 56, 60-61, 67-71
    categorical, 67-70
    disjunctive, 70-71
    hypothetical, 71
    recasting arguments as syllogisms, 83-84
Symbolic logic, 52, 54

T

Tabula rasa (blank slate), 184, 329
Taoism, 120, 265
    aesthetics, 354
Taste, 315, 317
Taylor, Charles, 378
    a communitarian, 382, 410
    on multiculturalism, 380-381
Taylor, Harriet, 276, 287
Taylor, Richard, 281
Television as a source of illusion, 223-224
Ten Commandments, 244
Teresa, Mother, 29
Thagard, Paul, 104
Thales of Miletus (profile), 12
Thatcher, Margaret, 297
Theatre, 339-340

Theism
- approach to meaning of life, 170
- concept of supreme being, 156

Theology, 245
Theories of action, 242-243
Theories of character, 243, 268-270
Theories of value, 243
"Theory," meanings of term, 95-96
Theory of opposites, 200
Theosophists, 356
Thesis, antithesis, and synthesis, 317
Third World countries, and environmental concerns, 297-298
Thomists (followers of Aquinas), 269
Thought experiments, 13-14
- a beautiful life, 358
- brain in the vat, 201-202
- Chinese room, 149
- conscious stone, 166
- experience machine, 266
- explained, 13, 14
- magic ring, 251
- ship of Theseus, 14
- something about Mary, 116
- stuck in school forever, 55
- teletransporters, 140
- thick as a brick, 93
- veil of ignorance (designing a society), 424

Three laws of thought (Aristotle), 52, 63
Three-part theory of the soul (Plato), 34
Tilghman, Shirley, 98, 294
Time, 5-6
Tolstoy, Leo
- on art, 322, 325, 330, 332-333, 361
- on religion, 170

Totalitarianism, 390, 399

Trompe l'oeil, 178
Trudeau, Pierre Elliott, 419
- profile, 420

Truman Show, The (film), 223-224
Truth
- Aristotle's three laws of thought, 52
- and art, 343-344
- and belief, conditions of knowledge, 188-191
- categorical imperative, 277-278
- distinguished from validity, 56
- lying, cheating, or stealing, 286-287
- overcoming illusion, 223-224
- and perception, 225-228
- philosophy's search for, 5, 15

Turing, Alan, 147-148
Turing test, 147-148, 149

U
Umen, Samuel, 25
Unrau, Norman J., 11
Utilitarianism, 273-275, 384
- on ethical issues, 288, 295, 301
- justice and social policy, 421-422

Utilitarianism (Mill), 26, 275
Utility as justice, 421-422
Utopia (More), 371, 372
Utopianism, 371

V
Validity
- of arguments, 62
- distinguished from truth, 56

Values
- of art, 319, 321-325, 362
- of humanism and of religion, 254
- intrinsic and instrumental, 247
- and "self," 248

VanDeVeer, Donald, 300
Van Gogh, Vincent, 343-344
Vienna Circle, 103
Virtue ethics, 243, 268-270
Virtues, 5, 243, 268-270
- Buddhism, 264
- character traits, 246, 269-270
- existentialism, 270-272
- Kongfuzi (Confucius), 253, 265
- as mean between extremes, 244
- right conduct, 269, 270
- Ross, 269-270

Voltaire, 26
- "The Good Brahman," 27-28

W
Wang Chong, 208
War, an ethical issue, 288-290
Warren, Karen, 295-296
Warren, Mary Ann, 135
Watson, Lyall, 32, 38
What Is Art? (Tolstoy), 332-333
White, Andrew Dickson, 105
Wieland, Joyce, 335, 342
Wilder, Thornton, 358
Will to live (Schopenhauer), 345
Wittgenstein, Ludwig, profile, 146
Wolff, Jonathan, 425
Wollstonecraft, Mary, 399
- profile, 401

Women
- artists, 334-335
- Ayn Rand, 245, 279-280
- cultural assumptions about, 204
- feminist philosophers, 9, 39-40, 41, 194-195
- Harriet Taylor, 276
- male views, 21, 39, 268, 334
- Mary Wollstonecraft, 401

    Plato's views on women's rights, 389
    Simone de Beauvoir, 41
Wrangham, Richard, 38
Writing a feature article, 306-307
Writing a philosophical reflection, 108-109
Wrong
    in behaviour towards others, 246, 247
    deciding rightness or wrongness, 257-259
Wrong *see also* Ethical issues

X
Xun-Zi (Hsün-tzu), 32, 33

Y
Yin and yang, 32, 63, 120

Z
Zarathustra, 7
Zen Buddhism, 220, 233
Zeno of Citium, 267
Zeno of Elea, 55
Zhuangzi, 178

Credits

COVER CREDIT

Lawren S. Harris 1885-1970, *Winter Comes from the Arctic to the Temperate Zone* (detail) c. 1935, oil on canvas, 74.1x 91.2 cm, purchase 1994, McMichael Canadian Art Collection, 1994.13. Reprinted by permission of the family of Lawren S. Harris.

PHOTO CREDITS

Page xi © King Features Syndicate. Reprinted with permission – The Toronto Star Syndicate; **page 4** Bettmann/CORBIS/MAGMA; **page 12** © Bettmann/CORBIS/MAGMA; **page 17** CP/Maclean's/Craig Shivers; **page xiii, xiv, 29** Bettmann/CORBIS/MAGMA; **page 31** CP/AP/Camay Sungu; **page 32** Archivo Iconografico, S.A./CORBIS/MAGMA; **page 38** CP/AP/Koji Sasahara; **page 39** CP/AP/Lawrence Jackson; **page xii, 41** Hulton-Deutsch Collection/CORBIS/MAGMA; **page 53** Bettmann/CORBIS/MAGMA; **page 61 bottom** CP/AP/Richard Drew; **page 72, 74** Bettmann/CORBIS/MAGMA; **page 85** CP/AP/Byron Rollins; **page 89, 91** Bettmann/CORBIS/MAGMA; **page 92** CP/AP/MIT Museum; **page 94** Stapleton Collection, UK/Bridgeman Art Library; **page 95** Private Collection/Bridgeman Art Library; **page 102** NASA; **page 107** Bettmann/CORBIS/MAGMA; **page 117** The Warburg Institute; **page 121** Bettmann/CORBIS/MAGMA; **page 126** Hulton-Deutsch Collection/CORBIS/MAGMA; **page 131** From drawing titled *A Portrait of Kristin Sine* by Melissa Schatzmann; **page 133** CP/AP/Hans Edinger; **page 146** Wittgenstein Archive, Cambridge; **page 148** MGM/Courtesy of Getty Images; **page 151** T. Brakefield/firstlight.ca; **page 155** Kaj A. Strand; **page 158** Bettmann/CORBIS/MAGMA; **page 161** World Films Enterprise/CORBIS/MAGMA; **page 165** CP/AP/Hans Deryk; **page 178** Bill Williams; **page 183, 210** Bettmann/CORBIS/MAGMA; **page 226** Phototheque R. Magritte-ADAGP/Art Resource, New York; **page 231** Bettmann/CORBIS/MAGMA; **page 233** Robert Linssen's Archives by permission of Samir Coussa; **page 237** O. Lewis Mazzatenta/National Geographic Society; **page 242** CP/Tom Hanson; **page 253** Archivo Iconografico, S.A./CORBIS/MAGMA; **page 264** CP/AP/Ahn Young-joon; **page 271** Bettmann/CORBIS/MAGMA; **page 274** Hulton-Deutsch Collection/CORBIS/MAGMA; **page 281** Archivo Iconografico, S.A./CORBIS/MAGMA; **page 285** CP/AP/Gregory Smith; **page 289** CP/AP/Jerome Delay; **page 290** CP/Chuck Stoody; **page 292** CP/AP/Jim Cole; **page 301** CP/Ruth Bonneville; **page 310 bottom** Erich Lessing/Art Resource, New York; **page 310 top left** Cameraphoto/Art Resource, New York; **page 312** National Archives of Canada/C-033442; **page 314** Bettmann/CORBIS/MAGMA; **page 317** Bibliotheque

Nationale, Paris, France/Lauros-Giraudon/Bridgeman Art Library; **page 319** Courtesy Henry Urbach Architecture; **page 318** Burstein Collection/CORBIS/MAGMA; **page 334** Christie's Images/CORBIS/MAGMA; **page 335** Reuters NewMedia Inc./CORBIS/MAGMA; **page 337** Suzi Gablik; **page 338** CP/Edmonton Journal/Rob Draper; **page 340** Reuters NewMedia Inc./CORBIS/MAGMA; **page 344** Art Resource, New York; **page 347** Benetton Group; **page 354** Sakamoto Photo Research Laboratory/CORBIS/MAGMA; **page 355 top** David Cumming/Eye Ubiquitous/CORBIS/MAGMA, **bottom** Burstein Collection/CORBIS/MAGMA; **page 356** Bettmann/CORBIS/MAGMA; **page 357** Mark Tansey, *Purity Test*, 1982, oil on canvas, 6 x 8 in., Collection of the Chase Manhattan Bank, NA, © Mark Tansey; **360 bottom** Bozart/Lien/Nibauer; **page 361** CP/Jim Young; **page 365** *Puppet*, 1995, WI# 5175, Color Polaroid, 24 x 20 in., © William Wegman; **page 370** Roger Wood/CORBIS/MAGMA; **page 374** CP/AP; **page 379** CP/AP/Clement Ntaye; **page 382** CP/Toronto Star/John Mahler; **page 396, 398, 399** Bettmann/CORBIS/MAGMA; **page 401** CORBIS/MAGMA; **page 410** CP/Frank Gunn; **page 417** CP/The Whig-Standard/Michael Lea; **page 420** CP/Ted Grant; **page 423** CP/Kevin Frayer

COLOUR INSERT PHOTO CREDITS

Page I top left Bettmann/CORBIS/MAGMA, **top right** From a drawing titled "A Portrait of Kristin Sine" by Melissa Schatzmann, **bottom left**, Cameraphoto/Art Resource, NY; **page II top left** Erich Lessing, Art Resource, NY; **top right** National Archives of Canada/C-033442, **bottom** Bettmann/CORBIS/MAGMA; **page III top right** Marcel Duchamp, *Fountain*, 1917. © Estate of Marcel Duchamp/SODRAC (Montréal) 2002, **bottom left** Courtesy of Henry Urbach Architecture; **page IV left** Alberto Giacometti, *Large Woman Upright IV*, 1960 © Estate of Alberto Giacometti/SODRAC (Montréal) 2002, **top right** Reuters NewMedia Inc./CORBIS/MAGMA, **bottom** CP/Edmonton Journal/Rob Draper; **page V bottom** Art Resource, NY; **page VI top** Benetton Group; **bottom left** Sakamoto Photo Research Laboratory/CORBIS/MAGMA, **bottom right** David Cumming/Eye Ubiquitous/CORBIS/MAGMA; **page VII top left** Burstein Collection/CORBIS/MAGMA, **top right** Mark Tansey, *Purity Test*, 1982, oil on canvas, 6 x 8 in., Collection of the Chase Manhattan Bank, NA, © Mark Tansey; **page VIII top** Bozart/Antoine Bootz, **bottom right** *Puppet*, 1995, WI# 5175, Color Polaroid, 24 x 20 in., © William Wegman

TEXT CREDITS

Page 7 From Karl Jaspers, *Basic Philosophical Writings: Selections* edited, translated and with introductions by Edith Ehrlich, Leonard H. Ehrlich, and George B. Pepper (Athens, OH: Ohio University Press), pp. 382-387. Reprinted by permission of Dr. Hans Saner; **pages 11, 13** From *Philosophy: A Text with Readings*, 5th ed., by Manuel Velasquez, Wadsworth, Inc., 1994, pp. 19-20; **page 25 top** From *Invitation to Philosophy* by Martin Hollis, Basil Blackwell, 1985, **bottom** From *Images of Man* by Samuel Umen, *Philosophical Library*, 1984, pp. 7-8; **page 32** From Wing-Tsit

Chan, *A Source Book in Chinese Philosophy*. Copyright © 1963, renewed 1991, by Princeton University Press. Reprinted by permission of Princeton University Press; **page 35** From From *Socrates to Sartre: The Philosophic Quest* by T. Z. Lavine, Bantam Books, 1984, p. 53; **page 38 top** From *Dark Nature: A Natural History of Evil* by Lyall Watson, Hodder & Stoughton, 1995, pp. x, xi, 49, **centre** From "Of Altruism, Heroism and Nature's Gifts in the Face of Terror" by Natalie Angier. Copyright © 2001 by The New York Times Co. Reprinted by permission; **page 40, 42** From *Existentialism and Human Emotions* by Jean-Paul Sartre, The Wisdom Library, a division of Philosophical Library, 1957, p. 15; **page 43** From *The Brighter Side of Human Nature: Altruism and Empathy in Everyday Life* by Alfie Kohn, Basic Books, 1990; **page 51** From *Zen and the Art of Motorcycle Maintenance* by Robert M. Pirsig, © 1974, 1984 Robert Pirsig, William Morrow & Company, pp. 92-93; **page 61-62** From *Seinlanguage* by Jerry Seinfeld, William Morris, 1993; **page 63** From "Where Do Leaders Come From?" by Michael Mazzarese. Reprinted by permission of Michael L. Mazzarese, PhD, Mazzarese & Associates, Westfield, New Jersey; **page 172** From *A Brief History of Time: From the Big Bang to Black Holes* by Stephen W. Hawking, Bantam Books, 1998, pp. 173-174; **pages 188-189 top** From *Theaetetus* by Plato, translated by Robin A. H. Waterfield (Penguin Classics, 1987), pp. 114-115, translation copyright © Robin A. H. Waterfield, 1987. Reproduced by permission of Penguin Books Ltd. and Robin A. H. Waterfield; **page 189 centre** From *The Problems of Philosophy* by Bertrand Russell, Oxford University Press, 1967, 1980, 1983, p. 76; **pages 216-217** Daisetz T. Suzuki, "Zen Knowledge" from Daisetz T. Suzuki, "The Meaning of Satori," in *Philosophical Explorations*, edited by Peter A. French (Morristown, NJ; General Learning Press, 1975), pp. 633-639. Originally from Daisetz T. Suzuki, "The Meaning of Satori," *The Middle Way*, The Journal of the Buddhist Society, 1969, London; **page 217 bottom** Reprinted by permission of Shelley Smith; **page 219** From *Epistemology: The Big Questions* edited by Linda Martín Alcoff, Blackwell Publishers, 1998; **page 231** From *The Fundamental Questions of Philosophy* by A. C. Ewing, Routledge & Kegan Paul Ltd., 1951, pp. 55-56; **page 234** From *Truth: A History* by Felipe Fernández-Armesto, Black Swan, 1998, pp. 165-166; **page 236** From *The Seven Spiritual Laws for Parents: Guiding Your Children to Success and Fulfillment* by Deepak Chopra, 1997, pp. 38; **page 279** From *The Virtue of Selfishness* by Ayn Rand, Penguin Books, 1964, pp. 49-52; **page 283** song titled "Adrian" by Jewel Kilcher and Steve Poltz from the album *Jewel: Pieces of You,* Warner/Chappell Music Inc.; **page 305** From *The Lorax* by Dr. Seuss, ® and copyright © by Dr. Seuss Enterprises, L. P. 1971, renewed 1999. Used by permission of Random House Children's Books, a division of Random House, Inc.; **pages 297-298** From *Principles: Short Essays on Ethics*, 2nd edition, by Thomas Hurka © 1999. Reprinted with permission of Nelson Thomson Learning, a division of Thomson Learning; **pages 346-347** © The Kwan Um School of Zen; **page 364** From an interview with Professor Emmanuel Eze in the Spring 1999, Issue 23, of *Philosophy Now*. Reprinted by permission; **page 387** From "Marcelle" by Simone de Beauvoir, first published in *Quand prime le spirituel*, 1979, copyright © 1979 Editions Gallimard, English translation copyright © 1982 by Patrick O'Brian; **page 415** From *Political Philosophy* edited by Anthony Quinton, Oxford University Press, 1967, pp. 7-8;